HUMAN GEOGRAPHY
Places and Regions in Global Context

Paul L. Knox
Virginia Tech

Sallie A. Marston
University of Arizona

Michael Imort
Wilfrid Laurier University

HUMAN GEOGRAPHY
Places and Regions in Global Context

FIFTH CANADIAN EDITION

PEARSON

Toronto

Executive Acquisitions Editor: Cathleen Sullivan
Marketing Manager: Kim Teska
Program Manager: Darryl Kamo
Project Manager: Richard di Santo
Developmental Editor: Johanna Schlaepfer
Production Services: Hardik Popli and Harleen Chopra, Cenveo® Publisher Services
Copy Editor: Audrey Dorsch
Proofreader: Söğüt Y. Güleç
Permissions Project Manager: Kathryn O'Handley
Photo Permissions Researcher: Abdul Khader, Lumina Datamatics Ltd.
Literary Permissions Researcher: Elaine Kosta, Lumina Datamatics Ltd.
Interior Designer: Tani Hasegawa
Cover Designer: Anthony Leung
Cover Image: Reuters/Nicky Loh
Cover Photo Credit: Nicky Loh/REUTERS

Credits and acknowledgments for material borrowed from other sources and reproduced, with permission, in this textbook appear on the appropriate page within the text.

Statistics Canada information is used with the permission of Statistics Canada. Users are forbidden to copy the data and redisseminate them, in an original or modified form, for commercial purposes, without permission from Statistics Canada. Information on the availability of the wide range of data from Statistics Canada can be obtained from Statistics Canada's Regional Offices, its World Wide Web site at www.statcan.gc.ca, and its toll-free access number 1-800-263-1136.

Environmental Statement

This book is carefully crafted to minimize environmental impact. Pearson Canada is proud to report that the materials used to manufacture this book originated from sources committed to sustainable forestry practices, tree harvesting, and associated land management. The binding, cover, and paper come from facilities that minimize waste, energy usage, and the use of harmful chemicals. Equally important, Pearson Canada closes the loop by recycling every out-of-date text returned to our warehouse. We pulp the books, and the pulp is used to produce other items such as paper coffee cups or shopping bags.

The future holds great promise for reducing our impact on Earth's environment, and Pearson Canada is proud to be leading the way in this initiative. From production of the book to putting a copy in your hands, we strive to publish the best books with the most up-to-date and accurate content, and to do so in ways that minimize our impact on Earth.

5   17

Library and Archives Canada Cataloguing in Publication

Imort, Michael, 1962–, author
       Human geography : places and regions in global context / Michael
Imort.—5th Canadian edition.

Includes index.
Revision of: Human geography : Toronto : Pearson Canada, 2012.
ISBN 978-0-321-92016-4 (pbk.)

       1. Human geography—Textbooks. I. Title.

GF41.I46 2015   304.2   C2014-907861-7

ISBN 978-0-321-92016-4

Brief Contents

Contents

Chapter 10 URBANIZATION 362

Chapter 11 CITY SPACES: URBAN STRUCTURE 394

List of Maps

List of Boxes

Geography Matters

Visualizing Geography

Window on the World

Virtual Geographies

Preface

Welcome to the fifth Canadian edition of *Human Geography: Places and Regions in Global Context*! What can this book do for you? Well, as the authors, we hope that it will guide you in some small way as you look for your own place in this world—after all, that is what university *really* is about. We hope that it will help you answer some of the questions that every generation has been facing to some degree but that have become even more pressing as your generation gets ready to work and live in an increasingly globalized world. How will your future job be affected by globalization? What role will your country play in the global competition for power, wealth, and security? Will we have enough resources for a growing global population? Are we living in the "Chinese Century"? To answer these and similar questions and find out what the answers mean for your life, you can do no better than to start with a solid understanding of the tools and concepts geographers use to discuss, research, and ultimately affect the world.

This book introduces you to human geography: the study of how people and places interact. The idea for this book evolved from conversations among the authors and colleagues about how to teach human geography at the university level. Our intent is to find a way not only to capture the exciting and troubling changes that are rewriting the world's landscapes and reorganizing the spatial relationships between people, but also to convincingly demonstrate why the study of geography matters. Our aim is to show why a geographical imagination is important, how it can lead to an understanding of the world and its constituent places and regions, and how it has practical relevance in many realms of life.

Places and Regions in Global Context also insists on interpreting these aims from an inherently *Canadian* perspective. Since European contact, the country that we now call Canada has been developing according to a very different geographical set of principles than our neighbour to the south, whether we are talking about economic, demographic, or cultural development. For example, because Canada's population is made up of a far greater proportion of recent immigrants from a wider range of countries than is the population of the United States, it can be argued that Canada's interest in world affairs is of a far different nature. Many Canadians, for example, view the geographic processes of globalization through the prism of their local connections with other parts of the world—and not, as in an American case, from the geopolitical perspective of a superpower.

NEW TO THE FIFTH CANADIAN EDITION

The fifth Canadian edition of *Places and Regions in Global Context* represents a thorough revision. Every part of the book was examined carefully with the dual goals of keeping topics and data current and improving the clarity of the text and the graphics. We have also sought to enhance the utility of the book for both instructors and students.

- Chapter-opening vignettes introduce students to the subject matter with interesting and varied topics.

- A list of Learning Outcomes in each chapter opener offers students a structured learning path that guides them through the main learning goals for the chapter. These Learning Outcomes are revisited and expanded upon at the end of each chapter, with summaries of chapter content correlated to the Learning Outcomes.

- Throughout every chapter, conceptual Apply Your Knowledge questions are integrated within the text, giving students a chance to pause and apply their understanding for a more active learning approach.

- We have increased the focus on basic introductory human geography content in Chapter 1, allowing the text to be more accessible to a wide range of introductory courses and students.

- Material from the final chapter of the fourth Canadian edition, on Future Geographies, has been updated and integrated into each chapter, thus placing the "futures" content in thematic context.

- The boxed feature essays on Visualizing Geography have been fundamentally redesigned to incorporate edgy, modern applications and visualizations of geography data.

- A new boxed feature called Virtual Geographies highlights the many effects of the new information and communications technologies on geography at all scales.

- The fifth Canadian edition also incorporates a comprehensive updating of all of the data, maps, photographs, and illustrative examples.

- We have added or expanded upon quite a few topics, including the global financial crisis; the credit crunch and mortgage foreclosures; climate change and issues of sustainability; the effect of the retiring baby boomer cohort on Canada; global interdependence and food supplies; the restructuring of Canadian agriculture; water supply problems; oil and energy; geopolitics; political ecology; religion; biotechnology and agricultural systems; fast food and slow food; virtual social networks; current events like the Arab Spring, the Japanese earthquake and tsunami, and typhoon Haiyan in the Philippines; global film and music; big-box retailing and global commodity chains; the "experience economy"; and the landscapes of the polycentric metropolis. These changes are designed to ensure that we offer the most up-to-date coverage in the field of human geography.

- The new MasteringGeography™ platform is linked to the Learning Outcomes and contains a wide range of resources and activities designed to reinforce basic concepts in human geography, including MapMaster™ interactive maps, Google Earth™ activities, geography videos, and more.

OBJECTIVE AND APPROACH

The objective of the book is to introduce the study of human geography by presenting not only a body of knowledge about the creation of places and regions but also fostering an understanding of the interdependence of places and regions in a globalizing world. More precisely, we hope that you recognize the daily interconnections between your own life and the lives of people in other parts of the world.

The book takes a fresh approach to human geography, reflecting the major changes that have recently been impressed on global, regional, and local landscapes. These changes include the globalization of industry, the rise of China and India, the upwelling of ethnic regionalisms on the heels of decolonization and the formation of new states, the rapid urbanization of the periphery and the physical restructuring of cities, the transformation of traditional agricultural practices, the trend toward transnational political and economic organizations, and the dramatic advances in information and communication technologies. *Human Geography: Places and Regions in Global Context* introduces the many new ideas, concepts, and theories that address these changes while also teaching the fundamentals of human geography: the principles, concepts, theoretical frameworks, and basic knowledge that are necessary to more specialized studies.

The most distinctive feature of this approach is that it emphasizes the interdependence of places and processes at different geographical scales. In overall terms, this approach is designed to provide an understanding of relationships between the global and the local and the outcomes of these relationships. It follows that one of the chief organizing principles is how globalization frames the social and cultural construction of particular places and regions at various scales.

This approach has several advantages:

- It captures aspects of human geography that are among the most compelling in the contemporary world—the geographical bases of cultural diversity and their impacts on everyday life, for example.
- It encompasses the salient aspects of new emphases in academic human geography—geography's new focus on the social construction of spaces and places, for example.
- It makes for an easier connection between topical and regional material by emphasizing how processes link them—technological innovation and the varying ways in which technology is adopted and modified by people in particular places, for example.
- It facilitates meaningful comparisons between places in different parts of the world—how the core-generated industrialization of agriculture shapes gender relations in households both in the core and the periphery, for example.

In short, this textbook is designed to focus on geographical processes and to provide an understanding of the interdependence

among places and regions without losing sight of their individuality and uniqueness.

Several important themes are woven into each chapter, integrating them into the overall approach:

- the relationships between global processes and their local manifestations
- the interdependence of people and places, especially the interactive relationships between core regions and peripheral regions
- the continuing transformation of the political economy of the world-system, and of nations, regions, cities, and localities
- the social and cultural differences that are embedded in human geographies (especially the differences that relate to ethnicity, gender, age, and class)

CHAPTER ORGANIZATION

The organization of the book is innovative in several ways. First, the chapters are organized in such a way that the conceptual framework—why geography matters in a globalizing world—is laid out in Chapters 1 and 2 and then deployed in thematic chapters (Chapters 3 through 11). Second, the conceptual framework of the book builds on two introductory chapters rather than the usual one. The first describes the basics of a geographic perspective; the second explains the value of the globalization approach.

Third, the distinctive chapter ordering within the book follows the logic of moving from less complex to more complex systems of human social and economic organization, always highlighting the interaction between people and the world around them. The first thematic chapter (Chapter 3) focuses on human population. Its early placement in the book reflects the central importance of people in understanding geography. Chapter 4 deals with the relationship between people and the environment as it is mediated by technology. This chapter capitalizes on the growing interest in environmental problems and develops a central theme: all human geographical issues are about how people negotiate their environment—whether the natural or the built environment.

The chapter on nature, society, and technology is followed by Chapter 5 on cultural geographies. The intention in positioning the cultural chapter here is to signal that culture is the primary medium through which people operate and understand their place in the world. In Chapter 6 the impact of cultural processes on the landscape is explored, together with the ways in which landscape shapes cultural processes.

In Chapter 7, the book begins to move toward more complex concepts and systems of human organization by concentrating on economic development. The focus of Chapter 8 is agriculture. The placement of agriculture after economic development reflects the overall emphasis on globalization. This chapter shows how processes of globalization and economic development have led to the industrialization of agriculture at the expense of more traditional agricultural systems and practices.

The final three thematic chapters cover political geographies (Chapter 9), urbanization (Chapter 10), and urban structure (Chapter 11). Devoting two chapters to urban geography, rather than a more conventional single chapter, is an important indication of how globalization increasingly leads to the rapid urbanization of the world's people and places.

At the end of each chapter, a new section called Future Geographies projects globalization processes and trends into the future and speculates how future geographies may unfold.

FEATURES

The book employs four different boxed features, as well as more familiar pedagogical devices such as chapter overviews and end-of-chapter exercises:

Geography Matters boxes examine a key concept of the chapter, providing an extended example of its meaning and implications through both visual illustration and text. The Geography Matters features demonstrate that the focus of human geography is on real-world problems.

Visualizing Geography boxes highlight key concepts of the chapter with a photographic essay. This feature helps students recognize that the visual landscape contains readily accessible evidence about the impact of globalization on people and places.

The new **Virtual Geographies** boxes are brief vignettes that highlight how the new information and communications technologies are changing geography at all scales.

New **Window on the World** boxes take a key concept and explore its application in a particular location. This feature allows students to appreciate the relevance of geographic concepts to world events and brings far-flung places closer to their comprehension.

SUPPLEMENTS

The book includes a complete supplement program for both students and instructors.

For the Student

MasteringGeography™ for *Human Geography: Places and Regions in Global Context* is the most effective and widely used tutorial, homework, and assessment system for the sciences. The Mastering system empowers students to take charge of their learning through activities aimed at different learning styles, and engages them in learning science through practice and step-by-step guidance—at their convenience, 24/7. MasteringGeography offers

- assignable activities that include MapMaster™ interactive maps, *Encounter Human Geography* Google Earth Explorations, geography videos, Thinking Spatially and Data Analysis activities, end-of-chapter questions, reading quizzes, and more
- student study area with MapMaster™ interactive maps, geography videos, Glossary, "In the News" RSS feeds, reference maps, self-quizzing, an optional Pearson eText, and more. www.masteringgeography.com

We also offer prebuilt assignments for instructors to make it easy to assign this powerful tutorial and homework system.

The Mastering platform is the only online tutorial/homework system with research showing that it improves student learning. A wide variety of published papers based on NSF-sponsored research and tests illustrate the benefits of the Mastering program. Results documented in scientifically valid efficacy papers are available at www.masteringgeography.com/site/results.

For the Instructor

The following instructor supplements are available for downloading from a password-protected section of Pearson Canada's online catalogue (www.pearsoned.ca/highered). Navigate to the book's catalogue page to view a list of supplements that are available. See the local sales representative for details and access.

Instructor's Resource Manual: The Instructor's Resource Manual, intended as a resource for both new and experienced instructors, includes a variety of lecture outlines, additional source materials, teaching tips, advice on how to integrate visual supplements, answers to the end-of-chapter exercises, and various other ideas for the classroom.

Activities Manual: This manual contains 20 different activities, tailored to the needs of individual chapters. Each activity identifies concepts to be learned and includes instructor's notes and assessment options.

Computerized Test Bank: Pearson's computerized test banks allow instructors to filter and select questions to create quizzes, tests, or homework. Instructors can revise questions or add their own, and may be able to choose print or online options. These questions are also available in Microsoft Word format.

PowerPoint® Lecture Slides: The PowerPoint lecture slides include selected illustrations, maps, figures, and tables from the text.

Image Library: The Image Library includes many of the illustrations, maps, figures, and tables from the text.

COURSESMART

CourseSmart goes beyond traditional expectations—providing instant, online access to the textbooks and course materials you need at a lower cost for students. And even as students save money, you can save time and hassle with a digital eTextbook that allows you to search for the most relevant content at the very moment you need it. Whether it's evaluating textbooks or creating lecture notes to help students with difficult concepts, CourseSmart can make life a little easier. For more information, visit www.coursesmart.com.

LEARNING SOLUTIONS MANAGERS

Pearson's Learning Solutions Managers work with faculty and campus course designers to ensure that Pearson technology products, assessment tools, and online course materials are tailored to meet your specific needs. This highly qualified team is dedicated to helping educators take full advantage of a wide range of educational resources by assisting in the integration of a variety of instructional materials and media formats. Your local Pearson Canada sales representative can provide you with more details on this service program.

PEARSON CUSTOM LIBRARY

For enrollments of at least 25 students, you can create your own textbook by choosing the chapters that best suit your own course needs. To begin building your custom text, visit www.pearsoncustomlibrary.com. You may also work with a dedicated Pearson Custom editor to create your ideal text—publishing your own original content or mixing and matching Pearson content. Contact your local Pearson representative to get started.

ACKNOWLEDGMENTS

I want to thank Alan Nash for the solid foundation he built with the first three Canadian editions. It was a pleasure to assist with developing them, and it is an honour to carry the spirit of his work into future editions.

I am indebted to the following professors for their assistance, advice, and constructive criticism in the course of preparing this edition:

Jorge Virchez
Laurentian University
Colin Mills
Langara College
Heather Nicol
Trent University
Walter Peace
McMaster University
Joshua Evans
Athabasca University
Godwin Arku
Western University

Similarly, I am grateful to the thousands of undergraduate students who unknowingly tested ideas and the materials included in this fifth Canadian edition.

I would like to thank Pearson Canada for its continuing commitment to this project, and especially Cathleen Sullivan (Executive Acquisitions Editor), Darryl Kamo (Program Manager), Johanna Schlaepfer (Developmental Editor), Richard di Santo (Project Manager), Audrey Dorsch (Copy Editor), and Harry Popli and Harleen Chopra (Production Editors) for all their help and support. A special thank you goes to Paul McInnis, who was the first to see the potential, and to Kathleen McGill (Sponsoring Editor), who trusted me to realize it.

It is a privilege to record here my indebtedness to the many people who have helped me with advice, information, understanding, and support. In particular, I thank my colleagues in the Department of Geography and Environmental Studies at Wilfrid Laurier University: Mary-Louise Byrne, Doreen Dassen, Jim Hamilton, Jo-Anne Horton, Cherie Mongeon, Bob Sharpe, and Lindsay Woodside. The team in the Dean of Arts Office, especially the indomitable Julie Pong, made sure that every day was filled with camaraderie and laughter—they did not know it, but in their own way they were writing this book, too.

Many able minds have tried to polish the rough diamond of my own geographical imagination. It all started in high school with Werner Wallert, who made me realize that everything is geography, and that geography is everything. At Brock University, the late Alun Hughes introduced me to the joys of methodical learning by doing. At Queen's University, I found magnificent role models that sustain me to this day: Peter Goheen, Brian Osborne, and most of all Anne Godlewska. Thank you for your trust, your patience, and your challenges. If I am a geographer at all, you have made me one.

This fifth Canadian edition is dedicated to Maggie, who keeps me smiling; my mother, who keeps dancing; and Cathie, who keeps me in her heart. It is from her that I stole many of the hours it took to conceive and produce what you are now holding in your hands. Thank you.

Michael Imort

About the Authors

Paul L. Knox

Paul Knox received his Ph.D. in geography from the University of Sheffield, England. In 1985, after teaching in the United Kingdom for several years, he moved to the United States to take up a position as professor of urban affairs and planning at Virginia Tech. His teaching centres on urban and regional development, with an emphasis on comparative study. In 1989, he received a university award for teaching excellence. He has written several books on aspects of economic geography, social geography, and urbanization. He serves on the editorial board of several scientific journals and is co-editor on a series of books on world cities. In 1996, he was appointed to the position of University Distinguished Professor at Virginia Tech, where he currently serves as dean of the College of Architecture and Urban Studies.

Sallie A. Marston

Sallie Marston received her Ph.D. in geography from the University of Colorado, Boulder. She has been a faculty member at the University of Arizona since 1986. Her teaching focuses on the historical, social, and cultural aspects of American urbanization, with particular emphasis on race, class, gender, and ethnicity issues. She received the College of Social and Behavioral Sciences Outstanding Teaching Award in 1989. She is the author of numerous journal articles and book chapters and serves on the editorial board of several scientific journals. In 1994 and 1995, she served as Interim Director of Women's Studies and the Southwest Institute for Research on Women. She is currently a professor in, and serves as head of, the Department of Geography and Regional Development.

Michael Imort

Michael Imort received his Ph.D. from Queen's University in Kingston, Ontario. Ever the geographer, he took the long way to get there, studying at Brock, York, Waterloo, and Freiburg, Germany, with stints in the Arctic, Hawaii, Mali, and Zaire (now DRC), and taking a teaching appointment in an English castle—not to mention the days when he worked as a lumberjack or ran a bookstore. When the time came to get serious, he joined the Department of Geography and Environmental Studies at Wilfrid Laurier University, where he currently is the Associate Dean of Arts. Originally trained as a forest scientist with an interest in fire ecology, he soon became interested in the human side of environmental problems. Today his research interests include environmental thought and the many ways in which representations of landscape are used and abused for political purposes.

HUMAN GEOGRAPHY
Places and Regions in Global Context

1

GEOGRAPHY MATTERS

In early 2011, an unprecedented wave of popular uprisings washed across the Arab world. Organized through social networks and text messaging, the protests drew more and more people into the streets to demand political reforms and improvements to their daily lives. Quickly, governments found themselves under increasing pressure. In Tunisia, Egypt, and Libya, regimes fell. In Jordan, Morocco, and other countries, governments held on to power by making concessions. Meanwhile, in Syria the protests morphed into a civil war that rages to this day, creating the greatest humanitarian crisis since the end of World War II. In each country, a different mix of political, religious, and ethnic tensions had been simmering below the surface, but it was the spiking food prices, particularly for bread, that caused open revolts to erupt in so many countries at once. With bread being the staple of poor people's nutrition across the entire region, steep increases in its price were the proverbial straw that broke the camel's back.

The problem of rising bread prices in the Arab countries and in many other places is a reflection of the increasing geographic interdependence of the world. The situation is partly the result of increasing food consumption in other parts of the world, especially in booming China and India, where many have stopped growing their own food and now have the cash to buy a lot more of it. Increasing meat consumption helped drive up demand for feed grain, and this in turn drove up the price of bread everywhere. Sensing an opportunity for easy

A protester brandishes a baguette as a sign of discontent while facing Tunisian riot police in January 2011. (*Source: Martin Bureau/Staff/Getty Images*)

profit, speculators in international commodity markets hoarded grain, further accelerating price hikes.

Energy prices are another key link: the increase in oil prices (itself the result of China's ballooning hunger for energy and fears over diminishing global oil reserves) pushed up fertilizer prices and shipping costs. Meanwhile, in an attempt to reduce their dependence on oil and become more environmentally friendly, many industrialized countries started to pay subsidies for the production of biofuels from grain, corn, and soybeans. As these subsidies lured farmers away from growing crops for food, the food supply was further strained: the grain needed to fill the tank of a car once could feed a person for an entire year! In short, we begin to see that food shortages are not just local events, but the result of the interaction of environmental, economic, and political factors in far-flung parts of the world.

Then there is climate change. In 2007–2008, harvests were severely disrupted by prolonged droughts in Australia and southern Africa, floods in West Africa, and frost in China. 2009–2010 brought another season of extreme weather: floods in Australia and drought in Russia caused wheat prices to double, leaving poor people worldwide struggling to pay for bread. As the bread revolts of the Arab Spring pushed up the oil price, food became even more expensive—starting yet another feedback loop.

Human geography can help us make sense of all of this. As we learn about the world by finding out *where* things are, *why* they are there, and *how* they affect things elsewhere, we begin to recognize and understand the interdependence among places and regions. In this book, we will explore the tools and methods geographers use to study this interdependence and ultimately understand and explain the world. By the time you read this book, the events described above will be history already, but with the help of these tools and methods, you will be able to make sense of *your* world and the events and processes that are shaping it right now. ∎

WHY GEOGRAPHY MATTERS

The importance of geography as a subject of study is becoming more widely recognized as people everywhere struggle to understand a world that is increasingly characterized by instant global communications, rapidly changing international relationships, unexpected local changes, and growing evidence of environmental degradation. Geographers learn by finding out where things are and why they are there. Human geography is about recognizing and understanding the interdependence among places and regions, without losing sight of the uniqueness of each specific place. **Places** are specific geographic settings with distinctive physical, social, and cultural attributes. **Regions** are territories that encompass many places, all or most of which share attributes different from the attributes of places elsewhere. Through an appreciation of the diversity and variety of the world's peoples and places, geography provides real opportunities not only to contribute to local, national, and global development but also to understand and promote multicultural, international, and feminist perspectives on the world.

VIRTUAL GEOGRAPHIES

Geographical knowledge and technology are present (if not always visibly so) in almost every aspect of your life. To learn how omnipresent geography is, watch the trailer for the Geospatial Revolution Project launched by Penn State University: http://geospatialrevolution.psu.edu/trailer.php

Most people want to understand the intrinsic nature of the world in which we live. Geography enables us to understand where we are both literally and figuratively. Geography provides knowledge of Earth's physical and human systems and of the interdependency of living things and physical environments. That knowledge, in turn, provides a basis for people to co-operate in the best interests of our planet. Geography also captures the imagination: it stimulates curiosity about the world and the world's diverse inhabitants and places. By obtaining a better understanding of the world, people can overcome closed-mindedness, prejudice, and discrimination.

APPLY YOUR KNOWLEDGE List three reasons why a corporate employer would feel it is important for prospective employees to have some knowledge of geography. ∎

WHY PLACES MATTER

An appreciation of the diversity and variety of peoples and places is a theme that runs through all of **human geography**, the study of the spatial organization of human activity and of people's relationships with their environments. This theme is inherently interesting to nearly all of us. *Canadian Geographic* is a popular magazine that literally illustrates the wonder and endless fascination that Canadians have for this country (**Figure 1.1**). Similarly, the *National Geographic* magazine shows us the seemingly unlimited variety of people and places around the world. More than 5 million households in North America, representing more than 20 million regular readers, subscribe to these magazines, and millions more read them occasionally in waiting rooms, offices, lobbies, or online.

Yet, at the same time, many surveys show how little we really know about Canada or the world in general (**Figure 1.2**). In fact, a 2005 survey conducted by the Royal Canadian Geographic Society found that "about one-third of Canadian adults can be considered geographically illiterate"—and that the rate is even higher among Canadians aged 18 to 24.[1] How does this compare internationally? In a nine-country survey conducted by the National Geographic Society in 2002, Canada had the third-lowest level of geographic literacy, with only the United States and Mexico faring worse.[2]

So although most people are fascinated by different places, relatively few have a systematic knowledge of them. Fewer still understand how different places came to be the way they are or

FIGURE 1.1 Geography's popularity *Canadian Geographic* magazine is available on newsstands across this country and is sent across the world to many subscribers. Focusing on Canada, it deals with many geographical issues that affect Canada. Its popularity reflects Canadians' interest in the variety of landscapes and communities across this country.

(*Source:* Canadian Geographic)

[1] See the results at www.ccge.org/programs/geoliteracy/docs/geoliteracy_survey_presentation.ppt. You can take the 20-question survey yourself at www.ccge.org/programs/geoliteracy/survey/q1.asp.

[2] www.nationalgeographic.com/geosurvey2002/index.html

FIGURE 1.2 Earthquake damage in Christchurch, New Zealand Although much of the international news Canadians hear in the mainstream media is about disasters, only a minority of Canadians are able to "place" these events on a world map, much less understand them in a geographical context. Where is Christchurch and what triggered the earthquake? How badly are its inhabitants affected by the damage? What effects, if any, did these events have on globalized resource markets, supply chains, or food production? (*Source:* M. Imort. Photo on the top has been used by permission of Christchurch City Council.)

why places matter in the broader scheme of things. This lack of understanding is problematic because geographic knowledge is more than a glimpse of the inherently interesting variety of peoples and places—it is quickly becoming an indispensable qualification for success in a globalizing world. As we negotiate our increasingly globalized lives, we thus face the task of learning about the world and interpreting it for ourselves: each of us needs to be a geographer. The first step on this journey is to understand the basic geographic concept of "places."

The Influence of Places

Places are dynamic, with changing properties and fluid boundaries that are the product of the interplay of a wide variety of environmental and human factors. This dynamism and complexity is what makes places so fascinating—it is also what makes places so important in shaping people's lives and in influencing the pace and direction of change. Places provide the settings for people's daily lives and their social relations (patterns of interaction among family members and between genders, at work, in social life, in leisure activities, or in political activity). It is in these settings that people learn who and what they are, how they are expected to think and behave, and what life is likely to hold for them. Moreover, because different places can foster rather different values, attitudes, and behaviours, they can also make it difficult for people raised in different settings to understand and appreciate one another.

Places thus exert a strong influence, for better or worse, on people's physical well-being, opportunities, and lifestyle choices. For example, living in a small seaside town makes for an unhurried pace of life, but it also means a limited range of job opportunities and lifestyle options, dependence on seasonal tourism, and a lack of amenities such as theatres, specialized stores and restaurants, and recreational facilities (**Figure 1.3**). Living in a central neighbourhood of a large metropolitan area, on the other hand, usually means having a wider range of job opportunities, lifestyle options,

FIGURE 1.3 Smalltown life in Atlantic Canada Life in small Canadian towns often unfolds at a slower pace, offers more opportunities for informal meetings with neighbours throughout the day, and is less focused on material wealth. (*Source:* M. Imort)

and amenities accessible within a short distance (**Figure 1.4**). But it also means generally living a more hectic, louder, and relatively anonymous life.

The Meaning of Places

Places also contribute to people's collective memory and become powerful emotional and cultural symbols that can evoke patriotic feelings, for example (**Figure 1.5**). On the other hand, seemingly ordinary places (a childhood neighbourhood, a hockey arena, or a family vacation spot) can have very special meaning for some people. Such places exist, and are constructed by their inhabitants, from a *subjective* point of view. We are also influenced in these assessments by our wider social and cultural frames of reference. This layering of meanings reflects the way that places are *socially constructed*—given different meanings by different groups for different purposes.

At times, the meanings given to a place may be so strong that they become a central part of the identity of the people experiencing them. Your **identity** is the sense that you make of yourself through your subjective feelings based on your everyday experiences and social relations. Your own neighbourhood, for example, centred on yourself and your home, is probably heavily laden with personal meaning and sentiment. However, your neighbourhood may well be viewed very differently, and perhaps unsympathetically, from an outsider's perspective (including geographers).

It is in specific locales that important events happen, and it is from them that significant changes spread around the world

FIGURE 1.4 **Downtown life in Toronto** Compared to small-town life, Canada's large cities offer more diverse opportunities for employment, entertainment, and the pursuit of non-conformist lifestyles. On the other hand, large cities are often perceived as anonymous. (*Source:* Bert Hoferichter/Alamy)

FIGURE 1.5 **The power of place** Some places acquire a strong symbolic value because of the buildings, events, people, histories or myths, and images with which they are associated. For example, for many Canadians, the Peace Tower on Parliament Hill in Ottawa is a place that draws its meaning from its associations with important events in this country's political life, whether they be patriotic commemorations or political protests. Other places in Canada evoke more general, but no less powerful, symbolic associations. For example, this picture of a canoe trip (on the Bloodvein River in Manitoba) has a much wider symbolic meaning because of its connotations with our images of a vast northern landscape and all the cultural values we associate with such a landscape. Indeed, for many people, especially those outside this country, such pictures are iconic of Canada and serve as a shorthand for "everything Canadian" in tourist and other promotional literature. (*Source:* Photography by Rolf and Debra Kraiker [left]. Library of Parliament/Bibliothèque du Parlement-Tom Littlemore [right])

FIGURE 1.6 Argentine dance spreads to China Popular trends are easily spread around the world. Here, tango dancers practise on a public square in Beijing. Tango originated in Argentina at the end of the nineteenth century as a mixture of Argentine, Cuban, and African music played on European folk instruments. (*Source:* Paul Chesley/The Image Bank/Getty Images)

FIGURE 1.7 Tahrir Square, Cairo, Egypt Egyptian anti-government demonstrators flood Cairo's landmark Tahrir Square on February 11, 2011, the 18th day of protests against President Hosni Mubarak, who subsequently resigned. In 2013, the army staged a counter-revolution. Knowing that control of this iconic place would be crucial to the success of their *coup d'etat,* the generals were quick to restrict access to Tahrir square. (*Source:* STR/UPI/Newscom)

(**Figure 1.6**). For instance, the unique characteristics of specific places can provide the preconditions for new modes of economic organization (such as the digital revolution that spread from Silicon Valley near San Francisco) or for new cultural practices (the hipster lifestyle that emerged in Brooklyn). Finally, places are sites not only of innovation and change, but also of resistance and conflict: controlling an iconic place such as a central square can be crucial for maintaining or challenging political power over an entire region (**Figure 1.7**).

Nevertheless, the influence of places is by no means limited to the occasional change or innovation. Because of their distinctive characteristics, places always modify and sometimes resist the imprint of even the broadest economic, cultural, and political trends. Consider, for example, the way that a global cultural trend—rock 'n' roll—was modified in Jamaica to produce reggae. And how in Iran and North Korea rock 'n' roll has been resisted by the authorities, with the result that it has acquired an altogether different kind of value and meaning for the citizens of those countries.

To consider a different illustration, think of the ways some communities have declared themselves "nuclear-free" zones: places where nuclear weapons and nuclear reactors are unwelcome or even banned by local laws. By establishing such zones, individual communities are seeking to challenge trends toward using nuclear energy and maintaining nuclear arms. They are, to borrow a phrase, "thinking globally and acting locally." Similarly, some communities have established "GM-free" zones, taking a stance against genetically modified crops and food. In adopting such strategies, they hope to influence thinking in other communities so that eventually their challenge could result in a reversal of established trends (**Figure 1.8**).

FIGURE 1.8 Acting locally The town of Überlingen, Germany, has established itself as a "GM-free" zone. Shown here is Cornelia Wiethaler, who initiated the movement to ban genetically modified crops and food from the town. The photo on the delivery truck encourages customers to buy "meat from here." The example shows how individual action in one place can cause local change and, through the very fact that you are reading this, foster global awareness. (*Source:* Paul L. Knox. Photo on the left has been used by permission of Farber.)

In summary, places are settings for social interaction that, among other things,

- structure the daily routines of people's economic and social life.
- provide both opportunities and constraints in terms of people's long-term social well-being.
- provide a context in which everyday, common-sense knowledge and experience are gathered.
- provide a setting for processes of socialization.
- provide an arena for contesting social norms.

APPLY YOUR KNOWLEDGE Explain how and why a particular place has mattered to you. How might others' experience or perception of that same place differ from yours? How does your place influence your health or job prospects? ■

STUDYING HUMAN GEOGRAPHY

The study of geography involves the study of Earth as created by natural forces and modified by human action. This, of course, covers an enormous amount of subject matter. There are two main branches of geography: physical and human. **Physical geography** deals with Earth's natural processes and their outcomes. It is concerned, for example, with climate, weather patterns, landforms, soil formation, and plant and animal ecology. As we said earlier, human geography deals with the spatial organization of human activities and with people's relationships to their environments. This involves looking at natural physical environments insofar as they influence, and are influenced by, human activity. To that end, the study of human geography must cover a wide variety of phenomena. These include, for example, agricultural production and food security, population change, the ecology of human diseases, resource management, environmental pollution, regional planning, and the symbolism of places and landscapes.

Regional geography combines elements of both physical and human geography. **Regional geography** is concerned with the way that unique combinations of environmental and human factors produce territories with distinctive landscapes and cultural attributes. The concept of region is applied by geographers to larger-sized territories that encompass many places, all or most of which have similar attributes distinct from the attributes of other places.

What is distinctive about the study of human geography is not so much the phenomena that are studied as the way they are approached. The contribution of human geography is to reveal *how and why geographical relationships are important*, in relation to a wide spectrum of natural, social, economic, political, and cultural phenomena. Thus, for example, human geographers are interested not only in patterns of agricultural production but also in the geographical relationships and interdependencies that are both causes and effects of such patterns. To put it in concrete terms, geographers are interested not only in what a specialized agricultural subregion is like (for example, how the dairy farming area of

Quebec produces its agricultural output, what makes its landscapes and culture distinctive, and so on) but also in its role in national and international agro-food systems (e.g., its interdependence with producers, distributors, consumers, taxes, tariffs, and subsidies in other places and regions—see Chapter 8).

Geography is thus very much an applied discipline as well as a means of understanding the world. Geographers are trained to use geographic theories and techniques to understand and solve a variety of specific problems in the real world. Employers in business, industry, and government value this broad expertise. (See Box 1.1, "Geography Matters: Geographers at Work").

THE BASIC TOOLS AND METHODS OF HUMAN GEOGRAPHERS

In general terms, the basic tools employed in geography are similar to those in other disciplines. Like other social scientists, human geographers usually begin with observation. Information must be collected and data recorded. This can involve many different methods and tools. Fieldwork (surveying, asking questions, using scientific instruments to measure and record things), laboratory experiments, and archival searches all are used by human geographers to gather information about geographical relationships. Geographers also use **remote sensing**, the collection of information about parts of Earth's surface by means of aerial photography or satellite imagery designed to record data on visible, infrared, and microwave sensor systems (**Figure 1.9** on page 10). For example, agricultural productivity can be monitored by remotely sensed images of crops, and energy efficiency can be monitored by remotely sensed levels of heat loss from buildings.

Once data have been obtained through some form of observation, the next important step is to portray and describe them through *visualization* or *representation*. This can involve a variety of tools, including written descriptions, charts, diagrams, tables, mathematical formulas, and maps. Visualization and representation are important activities because they allow large amounts of information to be explored, summarized, and presented to others. They are nearly always a first step in the analysis of geographical relationships, and they are important in conveying the findings and conclusions of geographic research.

At the heart of geographic research, as with other kinds of research, is the *analysis* of data. The objective of analysis, whether of quantitative or qualitative data, is to better understand reality. And to that goal geographers often use models (abstractions of reality) that help explain the real world. Once again, we find that geographers are like other social scientists in that they use a wide range of analytical tools, including conceptual and linguistic devices, maps, charts, and mathematical equations.

In many ways, therefore, the tools and methods of human geographers are parallel to those used in other sciences, especially the social sciences. In addition, geographers increasingly use some of the tools and methods of the humanities—interpretive analysis and inductive reasoning, for example—together with ethnographic research (the systematic recording of human cultures) and textual analysis. There are, however, two distinctive tools in the geographer's kit bag that we will look at in more detail: maps and geographic information systems (GIS).

Career options for geography majors are diverse, challenging, and exciting. Most geography graduates enter careers in which they have the opportunity to make a positive contribution to the world through their analytical skills. These careers include **cartography** (the art and science of making maps), geographic information systems (GIS), laboratory analysis, private consulting, urban and regional planning, international development, teaching, and management in private industry. Because of the broad nature of the field, these careers engage every aspect of human activity on every scale from the local to the global. The following examples reflect this diversity:

- **International Affairs.** Geographers' knowledge and understanding of regional histories and geographies, along with their ability to analyze the interdependence of places and regions, enables them to effectively contribute to discussions of international policy. Geographers' work within governmental agencies, corporations, and nonprofit organizations in shaping international strategies is especially important in view of the accelerating process of globalization.

- **Location of Public Facilities.** Geographers use specialized techniques to analyze the location patterns of particular population groups, to analyze transportation networks, and to analyze patterns of geographic accessibility to alternative sites. Such analysis enables geographers to determine the most effective locations for new public facilities, such as transit terminals, public libraries, or emergency shelters.

- **Marketing and Location of Industry.** Similar techniques are used in determining the most efficient, or most profitable, location for new factories, stores, and offices. Geographical research is also used to analyze the changing geography of supply and demand, allowing industry to determine whether, and where, to relocate. Techniques of geographic analysis are also widely used in marketing research.

- **Geography and the Law.** Geographical analysis can help resolve complex social and environmental issues. One important example is the issue of property development and the implications of environmental hazards such as flooding, coastal erosion, toxic waste dumps, and earthquake fault zones for policies, codes, and regulations affecting development. Another example is the task of maintaining geographical boundaries for electoral ridings to ensure equal representation as the population distribution changes. Finally, geographic techniques have been successfully used in law enforcement, for example, in identifying, tracing, and predicting the mobility patterns of criminal offenders.

- **Disease Ecology.** By analyzing social and environmental aspects of diseases, geographers are able to shed light on the causes of disease, to predict the spread of particular outbreaks, and to suggest ways in which the incidence of disease might be controlled.

- **Urban and Regional Planning.** Urban and regional planning adopts a systematic, creative approach to address and resolve physical, social, and economic problems of neighbourhoods, cities, suburbs, metropolitan areas, and larger regions **(Figure 1.A)**. Planners work directly on preserving and enhancing the quality of life in communities, protecting the environment, promoting equitable economic opportunity, and managing growth and change of all kinds. Planning has roots in engineering, law, architecture, social welfare, and government, but it is geography that offers the best preparation for specialized professional training in urban and regional planning, because of its focus on the interdependence of peoples and places.

- **Economic Development.** Geographers' ability to understand the interdependence of places and to analyze the unique economic, environmental, cultural, and political attributes of specific regions enables them to contribute effectively to strategies and policies aimed at economic development. Geographers are involved in applied research and policy formulation concerning economic development all over the world, addressing the problems not only of individual places and regions but also of the entire world economy.

- **Security.** Geographers' knowledge and understanding of geopolitics, political geography, demographics, medical geography, and cultural geography, together with an appreciation of the interdependent relationships among local, regional, and global systems, provide a sound basis for work in many areas of security. Knowing how places and regions "work" also means knowing about their vulnerability to potential security risks. Together with a regional or language specialization, this knowledge qualifies geographers for work as intelligence analysts.

FIGURE 1.A Urban and Regional Planning Planning professionals examine a model of Scharnhauser Park, a new town near Stuttgart, Germany. (*Source:* Paul L. Knox)

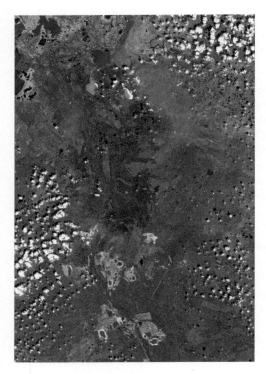

Landsat satellite images are digital images captured from spectral bands both visible and invisible to the human eye. In the processed image, different kinds of vegetation cover, soils, water surfaces, and built environments can be rendered in different colours. For example, in this image of a forest fire in southeastern Alberta, healthy vegetation appears green; recently burnt ground appears brown; smoke from ongoing fires appears light blue; water surfaces appear dark blue; clouds appear white; and the open pit mines of the Alberta tar sands appear in shades of grey. (*Source:* Courtesy NASA)

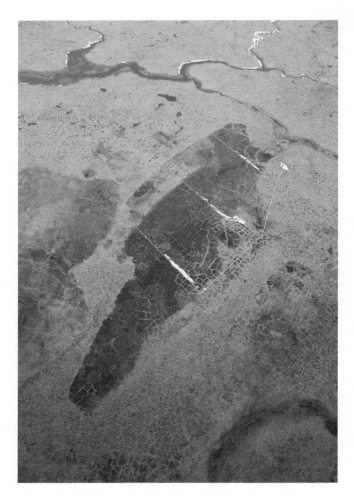

Aerial photographs can be helpful in mapping and explaining what would otherwise require expensive ground surveys. They are especially useful in remote locations such as the Canadian Arctic where access is difficult during the summer season, when the ground is no longer frozen. (*Source:* George Burba/Shutterstock)

Using a collection of satellite-based observations, scientists and visualizers stitched together months of observations of the land surface, oceans, sea ice, and clouds into a seamless, true-colour mosaic of every square kilometre of the planet. Much of the information contained in this image came from a single remote-sensing device—NASA's Moderate Resolution Imaging Spectroradiometer, or MODIS—flying more than 700 km above the Earth on board the Terra satellite. (*Source:* Courtesy Reto Stöckli)

FIGURE 1.9 Remotely sensed images Remotely sensed images can provide new ways of seeing the world, as well as unique sources of data on all sorts of environmental conditions. Such images can help explain problems and processes. Examples of such applications include studies of the deforestation of the Amazon rain forest, urban encroachment onto farmland, water pollution, and bottlenecks in highway systems.

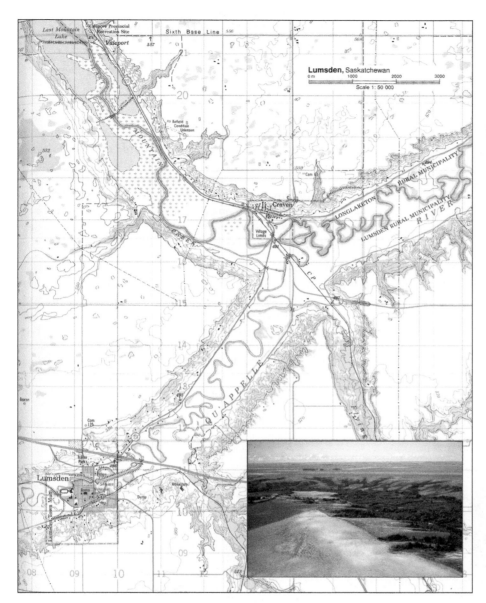

FIGURE 1.10 Topographic maps
Topographic maps represent the Earth's surface in both horizontal and vertical dimensions. This excerpt is from a map of the Qu'Appelle Valley, near Lumsden, Saskatchewan. The height of landforms is represented by contours (lines that connect points of equal elevation above sea level), which on this map are drawn every 10 metres. Note how the contours are more closely spaced in the green areas representing the wooded slopes of the river valley. Features such as roads, power lines, built-up areas, and so on are shown by stylized symbols.

Maps

Maps are representations of the world. They are usually two-dimensional graphic representations that use lines and symbols to convey information or ideas about spatial relationships. Maps express particular interpretations of the world, and they affect how we understand the world and how we see ourselves in relation to others. As such, all maps are "social products." In general, maps reflect the power of the people who draw them up. Just including things on a map—literally "putting something on the map"—can be empowering. The design of maps—what they include, what they omit, and how their content is portrayed—inevitably reflects the experiences, priorities, interpretations, and intentions of their authors. The most widely understood and accepted maps—"normal" maps—reflect the view of the world that is dominant in universities and government agencies.

Maps that are designed to represent the *form* of Earth's surface and to show permanent (or at least long-standing) features such as buildings, highways, field boundaries, and political boundaries are called *topographic maps* (**Figure 1.10**). The usual device for representing the form of Earth's surface is the *contour*, a line that connects points of equal elevation above sea level.

Maps that are designed to represent the spatial dimensions of particular conditions, processes, or events are called *thematic maps*. These can be based on any one of a number of devices that allow cartographers or map makers to portray spatial variations or spatial relationships. One of these is the *isoline*, a line (similar to a contour) that connects places of equal data value (for example precipitation, as in **Figure 1.11**). Maps based on isolines are known as *isopleth maps*. Another common device used in thematic maps is the *proportional symbol*. Circles, squares, spheres, cubes, or some other shape can be drawn in proportion to the frequency of occurrence of some particular phenomenon or event at a given location. **Figure 1.12** shows an example of a map featuring proportional circles. Symbols such as arrows or lines can also be drawn proportionally in order to portray flows of things between particular places.

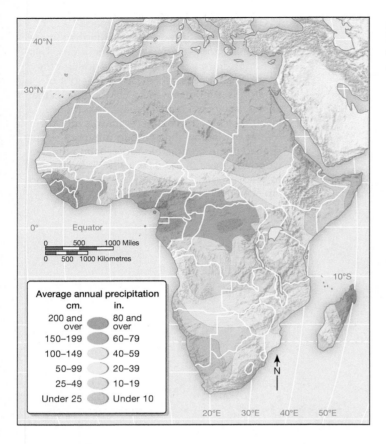

FIGURE 1.11 Isoline maps Isoline maps portray spatial information by connecting points of equal data value. This map shows average annual precipitation for the continent of Africa.

(*Source*: Reprinted with permission of Pearson, from D. Hess and D. Tasa, *McKnight's Physical Geography: A Landscape Appreciation*, 10th edition, 2011, p. 36.)

Dot maps, in which a single dot or other symbol represents a specified number of occurrences of some particular phenomenon or event, can effectively portray simple distributions (for an example, see **Figure 4.26** on p. 140). Another device is the *choropleth map*, in which tonal shadings are graduated to reflect variations in numbers, frequencies, or densities. (For examples, see **Figures 3.10** to **3.13** on pp. 85–89.) Finally, thematic maps can be based on *located charts*, in which graphs or charts are located by place or region (**Figure 1.13**).

Map Scales

A *map scale* is the ratio between linear distance on a map and linear distance on Earth's surface. It is usually expressed in terms of corresponding lengths, as in "one centimetre equals one kilometre," or as a *representative fraction* (in this case, 1/100 000) or ratio (1:100 000). *Small-scale* maps are maps based on small representative fractions (for example, 1/1 000 000 or 1/10 000 000). A map drawn on this page to the scale of 1:10 000 000 would cover less than half of Canada; a map drawn to the scale of 1:16 000 000 would easily cover the whole of North America. *Large-scale* maps are maps based on larger representative fractions (e.g., 1/25 000 or 1/10 000).

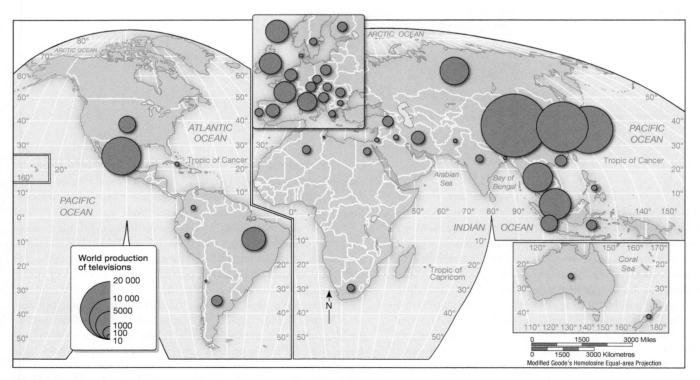

FIGURE 1.12 An example of proportional symbols in thematic mapping Proportional circles showing worldwide television receiver production. East Asia has become the leading area in the manufacture of this commodity. (*Source*: Adapted from F. P. Stutz and B. Warf, *The World Economy: Geography, Business, Development*, 6th edition, Pearson, 2012, p. 204.)

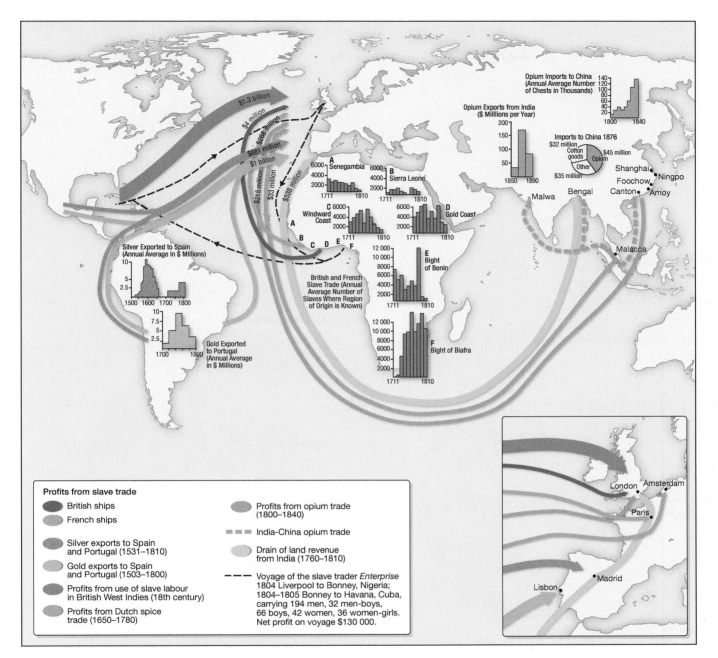

FIGURE 1.13 A map combining located charts with proportional symbols By combining graphs, charts, or symbols with base maps, a great deal of information can be conveyed in a single figure. This example illustrates the profits generated through European plunder of global minerals, spices, and human beings over a 300-year period. (*Source:* Adapted from B. Crow and A. Thomas, *Third World Atlas*. Milton Keynes: Open University Press, 1982, p. 27.)

A map drawn on this page to the scale 1:10 000 would cover a typical suburban subdivision; a map drawn to the scale of 1:1000 would cover just a block or two of it.

Map Projections

Maps not only describe data but also serve as important sources of data and tools for analysis. Because of their central importance to geographers, they can also be objects of study in their own right, as in the case of map projections. A **map projection** is a systematic rendering on a flat surface of the geographic coordinates of the features found on Earth's surface. Because Earth's surface is curved and it is not a perfect sphere, it is impossible to represent on a flat sheet of paper or monitor screen without some distortion. Cartographers have devised a number of different techniques for projecting latitude and longitude (see **Figure 1.19** on p. 19) onto a flat surface, and the resulting representations of Earth each have advantages and disadvantages. None of them can represent distance correctly in all directions, though many can represent compass bearings or area without distortion. The choice of map projection depends largely on the purpose of the map.

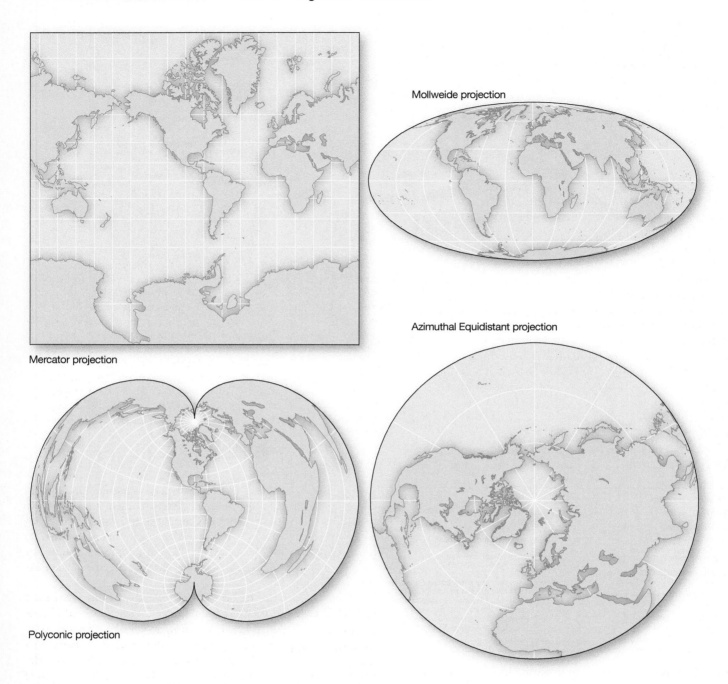

FIGURE 1.14 Comparison of map projections Different map projections have different properties. The polyconic projection is true to scale along each east–west parallel and along the central north–south meridian. It is neither conformal nor equal-area, and it is free of distortion only along the central meridian. On the Mercator projection, compass directions between any two points are true, and the shapes of landmasses are true, but their relative size is distorted. On the Azimuthal Equidistant projection, distances measured from the centre of the map are true, but direction, area, and shape are increasingly distorted as the distance from the centre point increases. On the Mollweide projection, relative sizes are true, but shapes are distorted.

Projections that allow distance to be represented as accurately as possible are **equidistant projections**. These projections can represent distance accurately in only one direction (usually north–south), although they usually provide accurate scale in the perpendicular direction (which in most cases is the equator). Equidistant projections are often used for representing large portions of Earth.

An example is the depiction of the Americas in the polyconic projection in **Figure 1.14**.

Projections that render compass directions accurately are known as **conformal projections**. On the Mercator projection (**Figure 1.14**), for example, a compass bearing between any two points can be plotted as a straight line. As a result, the

Mercator projection has been widely used in navigation for hundreds of years.

Some projections are designed such that compass directions are correct only from one central point. These are known as *azimuthal projections*. They can be equidistant, as in the Azimuthal Equidistant projection (**Figure 1.14**), which is sometimes used to show air-route distances from a specific location, or equal-area, as in the Lambert Azimuthal Equal-Area projection.

Projections that portray areas on Earth's surface in their true proportions are known as **equal-area** or **equivalent projections**. Such projections are used where the cartographer wishes to compare and contrast distributions on the Earth's surface: the relative area of different types of land use, for example. Equal-area projections, such as the Mollweide projection, are especially useful for thematic maps showing economic, demographic, or cultural data (**Figure 1.14**). Unfortunately, preserving accuracy in terms of area in world maps tends to result in many areas to appear squashed and have unsatisfactory outlines.

For some applications, aesthetic appearance is more important than conformality, equivalence, or equidistance, so cartographers have devised a number of other projections. Examples include the Times projection, which is used in many world atlases, and the Robinson projection, which is used by the National Geographic Society in many of its publications. The Robinson projection (**Figure 1.15**) is a compromise projection that distorts both area and directional relationships but provides a general-purpose world map.

There are also political considerations to take into account when considering different projections. Countries may appear larger and so more "important" on one projection rather than another. The Mercator projection (see **Figure 1.14**) has been widely used as the standard map of the world in classrooms and television news for many years, and its image of the world is deeply ingrained into general consciousness. As a result, many Europeans and North Americans have an exaggerated sense of the size of the northern continents and are unaware of the true size of Africa. The Peters projection, in contrast (**Figure 1.16**), is a deliberate attempt to correct this misperception

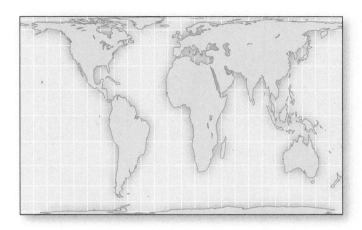

FIGURE 1.16 The Peters projection This equal-area projection was an attempt to offer an alternative to traditional projections, which, filmmaker and historian Arno Peters argued, exaggerated the size and apparent importance of the higher latitudes—that is, the world's developed, rich countries—and so promoted the "Europeanization" of Earth. While it has been adopted by the World Council of Churches and various agencies of the United Nations and other international institutions, it has been criticized by cartographers on the grounds of aesthetics: one of the consequences of equal-area projections is that they distort the shape of landmasses. (*Source:* Adapted from E. F. Bergman, *Human Geography: Cultures, Connections, and Landscapes,* © 1995 by Pearson, p. 13.)

and give equal prominence to the developing countries of the equatorial regions and the Southern Hemisphere. As such, it was officially adopted by the World Council of Churches and by numerous agencies of the United Nations and other international institutions. Its unusual shapes give it a shock value that gets people's attention. For some, however, its unusual shapes are unattractive; it has been likened to laundry hung out to dry.

One particular kind of map projection that is sometimes used in small-scale thematic maps is the *cartogram*. In this kind of projection, space is transformed according to statistical factors, with the largest mapping units representing the greatest statistical values. **Figure 1.17** shows a cartogram of the world in which the relative size of countries is based not on area but on the proportion of people with extremely low incomes. The deliberate distortion of the shapes of the continents in this sort of projection dramatically emphasizes spatial variations. The precondition for understanding a cartogram, however, is that the map reader knows what the undistorted map would look like in the first place.

APPLY YOUR KNOWLEDGE Describe four different scenarios that illustrate situations in which the use of (a) equidistant, (b) conformal, (c) azimuthal, and (d) equal-area projections would be appropriate. ■

Geographic Information Systems (GIS)

The combination of high-performance computing and digital record keeping has led to an unprecedented increase in the

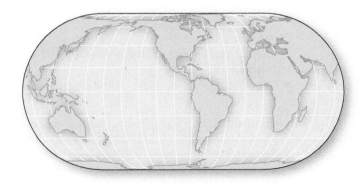

FIGURE 1.15 The Robinson projection On the Robinson projection, distance, direction, area, and shape are all distorted in an attempt to balance the properties of the map. It is designed purely for appearance and is best used for thematic and reference maps at the world scale. (*Source:* After E. F. Bergman, *Human Geography: Cultures, Connections, and Landscapes,* © 1995 by Pearson, p. 12.)

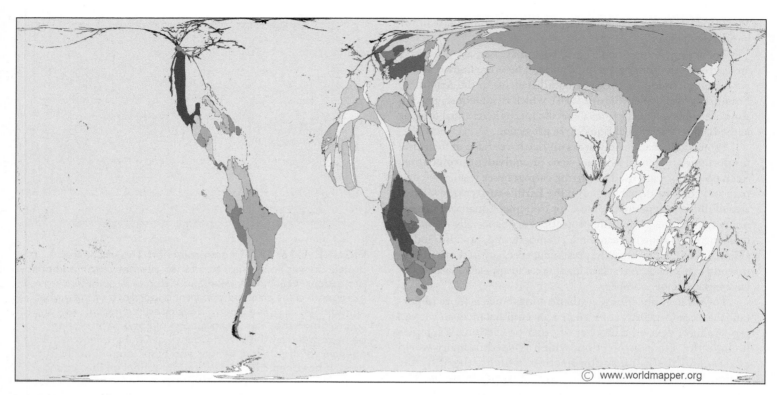

FIGURE 1.17 Example of a cartogram In a cartogram, space is distorted to emphasize a particular attribute of places or regions. This example shows the relative size of countries based on the proportion of all people living on US$10 or less a day; the cartographers have maintained the shape of each country as closely as possible to make the map easier to read. As you can see, population-based cartograms are very effective in demonstrating spatial inequality. *(Source:* © Copyright SASI Group [University of Sheffield] and Mark Newman [University of Michigan].)

volume and availability of geographic data. Geographic information systems (GIS) enable geographers to handle that data and produce maps more quickly than ever before. Consequently, they have rapidly grown to become one of the most important methods of geographic analysis, particularly in planning, commercial, and military applications. **Geographic information systems (GIS)** involve an organized set of computer hardware, software, and spatially coded data that is designed to capture, store, update, manipulate, and display geographically referenced information.

The primary requirement for data to be used in GIS is that the locations for the variables—the characteristics under consideration—are known. Location may be annotated by x, y, and z coordinates of longitude, latitude, and elevation, or by such systems as postal codes or highway kilometre markers. Any variable that can be located spatially can be fed into a GIS. Data capture—putting the information into the system—is the most time-consuming component of GIS work. Different sources of data, using different systems of measurement, scales, and systems of representation, must be integrated with one another; changes must be tracked and updated. Many GIS operations in the United States, Europe, Japan, and Australia have begun to contract out such work to firms in countries where labour is cheaper. India has emerged as a major data-conversion centre for GIS.

VIRTUAL GEOGRAPHIES

Notwithstanding the global outsourcing, GIS is one of the ten "hottest" fields in terms of job creation for Canadian geography graduates. Penn State University has produced a four-minute video showing the astounding technological development and capabilities of GIS technology. You can watch it here: **http://geospatialrevolution.psu.edu/episode1/chapter3**

The most important aspect of GIS, from an analytical point of view, is that they allow data from several different sources, on different topics, and at different scales, to be merged. This allows analysts to emphasize the spatial relationships among the objects being mapped. A geographic information system makes it possible to link, or integrate, information that is difficult to associate through any other means. For example, using GIS technology and water billing information, it is possible to simulate the discharge of materials into the septic systems in a neighbourhood upstream from a wetland.

GIS technology can render visible many aspects of geography that were previously unseen. GIS can, for example, produce

FIGURE 1.18 Map of land cover This extract is from a map of land cover in the United States that was compiled from several data sets using GIS technology. These include 1-kilometre resolution, Advanced Very High Resolution Radiometer (AVHRR) satellite imagery, and digital data sets on elevation, climate, water bodies, and political boundaries. Each of the 159 colours on the U.S. map represents a specific vegetation region. The purples and blues represent various subregions of western coniferous forests, the yellows are grasslands, and the reds are shrublands. The grey-brown region is the barren area of the Mojave Desert. (*Source:* United States Geological Survey, Map of Seasonal Land Cover Regions, 1993; see T. Loveland, J.W. Merchant, J.F. Brown, D.O. Ohlen, B.C. Reed, P. Olson, and J. Hutchinson, "Seasonal Land Cover Regions of the United States," Annals, Association of American Geographers, 85, 1995, 339–355.)

Some of the most influential applications of GIS have resulted from geodemographic research. (See Box 1.2, "Visualizing Geography: Geodemographic Research.") **Geodemographic research** uses census data and commercial data (such as sales data and property records) about the populations of small districts in creating profiles of those populations for market research. The digital media used by GIS make such applications very flexible. With GIS it is possible to zoom in and out, evaluating spatial relationships at different spatial scales. Similarly, it is possible to vary the appearance and presentation of maps, using different colours and rendering techniques.

Within the past five years, applications of GIS have resulted in the creation of more maps than were created in all previous human history. One result is that as maps have become more commonplace, more people and more businesses have become more spatially aware. Nevertheless, some critics have argued that GIS has been exploited by those who already possess power and control to increase the level of surveillance of the population. The fear is that GIS may be helping to create a world in which people are not treated and judged by who they are and what they do, but more by where they live. People's credit ratings, ability to buy insurance, and ability to secure a mortgage, for example, are all routinely judged in part by GIS-based analyses that take into account the attributes and characteristics of their neighbours.

APPLY YOUR KNOWLEDGE Choose the geographic representations and tools that you would use to illustrate alternative views of a local issue that is currently the subject of public discussion in your community. Explain your choice. ∎

incredibly detailed maps based on millions of pieces of information—maps that could never have been drawn by human hands. One example of such a map is the satellite image reconstruction of the land cover of a part of the western United States, shown in **Figure 1.18**. At the other extreme of spatial scale, GIS can put places under the microscope, creating detailed new insights using huge databases and effortlessly browsable media.

GIS technology allows an enormous range of problems to be addressed. For instance, it can be used to decide how to manage farmland, to monitor the spread of infectious diseases, to monitor tree cover in metropolitan areas, to assess changes in ecosystems, to analyze the impact of proposed changes in the boundaries of legislative districts, to identify the location of potential business customers, and to provide a basis for urban and regional planning.

VIRTUAL GEOGRAPHIES

For a very candid peek at how UPS uses GIS to optimize their operations and keep tabs on every single one of their delivery truck drivers, you can watch this five-minute video at **http://geospatialrevolution.psu.edu/episode2/chapter2**

SPATIAL ANALYSIS

The study of many geographic phenomena can be approached in terms of their arrangement as points, lines, areas, or surfaces on a map. This is known as **spatial analysis**. *Location*, *distance*, *space*, *accessibility*, and *spatial interaction* are five concepts that are key to spatial analysis. Although these concepts may be familiar from everyday language, they require some elaboration.

Location

In everyday speech, location is often *nominal*, or expressed solely in terms of the names given to regions and places. We speak, for example, of Vancouver, or of Stanley Park, a location within Vancouver. Location can also be used as an *absolute* concept, whereby locations are fixed mathematically through coordinates of latitude and longitude (**Figure 1.19**). **Latitude** refers to the angular distance of a point on Earth's surface, measured in degrees, minutes, and seconds north or south of the equator, which is assigned a value of 0°. Lines of latitude around the globe run parallel to the equator, which is why they are sometimes referred to as *parallels*. **Longitude** refers to the angular distance of a point on Earth's surface, measured in degrees, minutes, and

Market research consultants, using statistical methods similar to those used by urban social geographers, are able to identify the geographical distribution of different types of Canadian households. They classify households according to their distinctive consumption patterns and preferences as well as their socioeconomic and demographic attributes and their typical residential settings. The best-known and most comprehensive classification of households in Canada is the PRIZM C2® segmentation system by Environics Analytics, a polling and research firm based in Toronto.

The PRIZM C2® segmentation system merges census data with household demographic and lifestyle data from marketing surveys and databases, along with other measures of consumer buying behaviour and lifestyle descriptors. The combined data are crunched into fourteen major socio-geographic groups such as the Urban Young, Suburban Elite, or Rural Downscales. Each of these is further subdivided, giving a total of 66 distinctive lifestyle types or segments based on characteristics such as income, education, occupation, and home value that are cross-referenced with social attitudes, consumer preferences, and cultural backgrounds. Examples include Park Bench Seniors, Solo Scramble, Crafting & Curling, Newcomers Rising, Tools & Trucks, as well as Francophone segments such as Le Québec Rustique, and immigrant segments such as Asian Up-and-Comers.

All sorts of marketers and market researchers use this geodemographic classification, not only to identify and find potential consumers of houses and apartments, cars, consumer goods, and magazines but also to help make location decisions about stores, restaurants, gas stations, and supermarkets. Increasingly, political campaigners and fundraisers use the segmentation system to focus their efforts on the most promising neighbourhoods.

The following examples illustrate the kind of detailed market segmentation that is possible. In downtown Ottawa, the prevalent segment is Grads & Pads, a young, diverse, progressive mix of well-educated singles who are either in or just out of university (**Figure 1.B**). With an average household income of $64 588 in 2010, they are not wealthy, but they spend their paycheques freely on themselves for personal experiences such as adventure tours, audio equipment, and premium ice cream. On the other hand, they spend less than $10 000 on their car and hunt for vintage clothing. Being single, they frequent a variety of entertainment venues and restaurants that are located within walking distance from their rented apartments. In terms of social and political attitudes, they are among the most liberal Canadians.

More toward the edges of central Ottawa, we find the Young Digerati, another segment in the Urban Young social group. Like the Grads & Pads, they are university-educated, tech-savvy, and ethnically mixed, but their profile is remarkably different in financial

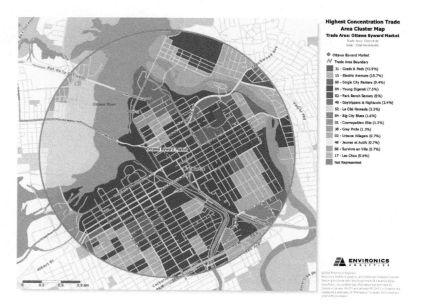

FIGURE 1.B **The geography of consumer groups in Ottawa** This map of Ottawa shows the relative concentrations of consumer groups with certain income and lifestyle characteristics. Businesses can use such maps to increase the accuracy and efficiency of their marketing campaigns. (*Source:* Environics Analytics 2014.Prizm C2.Used with Permission.environicsanalytics.ca.© 2014.Environics Analytics.)

terms: their household income is twice as high and their assets tend to be several times more valuable. They also tend to own trendy condos surrounded by swanky fitness clubs, boutiques, restaurants, and all types of bars—from juice or coffee to craft beer. They are socially conscious consumers whose distinctive preferences include Pilates classes, midsize SUVs, organic foods, and art gallery visits.

To a casual observer walking the streets of Ottawa, then, the neighbourhoods in which these two segments live may resemble each other. Below the similar lifestyle surface, however, the two segments differ considerably in the degree to which they have succeeded in turning their education into economic standing. Knowing about the respective financial backgrounds, in combination with detailed information about the demographic composition, social attitudes, and political views is extremely valuable to marketers and political campaigners. Not only are they able to narrow their campaigns down to the most promising city blocks, but they can also avoid offending their audience with culturally insensitive messages or excessive donation requests. For instance, by taking into account the probable income of households, campaigners can customize the solicited donation amount so it falls within an acceptable range.

Source: Environics Analytics, www.environicsanalytics.ca/.

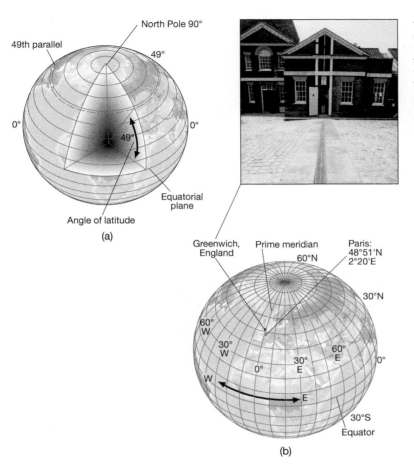

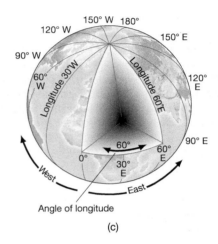

The prime meridian at the Royal Observatory in Greenwich, England: the observatory was founded by Charles II in 1675 with the task of setting standards for time, distance, latitude, and longitude—the key components of navigation. (*Source:* Paul L. Knox)

FIGURE 1.19 Latitude and longitude Lines of latitude and longitude provide a grid that covers Earth, allowing any point on Earth's surface to be accurately referenced. Latitude is measured in angular distance (i.e., degrees and minutes) north or south of the equator, as shown in (a). Longitude is measured in the same way, but east and west from the prime meridian, a line around Earth's surface that passes through both poles (North and South) and the Royal Observatory in Greenwich, just to the east of central London, in England. Locations are always stated with latitudinal measurements first. The location of Paris, France, for example, is 48°51'N and 2°20'E, as shown in (b). (*Source:* [a] and [c] adapted from R. W. Christopherson, *Geosystems: An Introduction to Physical Geography*, 2nd ed., © 1994, pp. 13 and 15. [b] adapted from E. F. Bergman, *Human Geography: Cultures, Connections, and Landscapes*, © 1995, Figs. 1–10 and 1–13.)

seconds east or west from the *prime meridian* (the line that passes through both poles and through Greenwich, England, which is assigned a value of 0°). Lines of longitude, called *meridians*, always run from the North Pole (latitude 90° north) to the South Pole (latitude 90° south). Vancouver's coordinates are precisely 49°20'N, 123°10'W.

Thanks to the **Global Positioning System (GPS)**, it is now very easy to determine the latitude, longitude, and elevation of any given point. The GPS consists of approximately 30 satellites that orbit Earth on precisely predictable paths, broadcasting highly accurate time and locational information. Using those signals, GPS receivers in cars, smartphones, and even wrist watches can calculate their precise position day or night, in all weather conditions, in any part of the world. The GPS has drastically increased the accuracy and efficiency of collecting spatial data. In combination with GIS technology and remote sensing, the GPS has revolutionized map-making and spatial analysis.

VIRTUAL GEOGRAPHIES

The Geospatial Revolution Project at Penn State features a two-minute video describing how GPS works: **http:// geospatialrevolution.psu.edu/episode1/chapter2**

The GPS capabilities of smartphones make it possible to locate the positions of their users—for better or for worse: GPS locators have helped find people buried under rubble or washed out to sea by the 2011 earthquake and tsunami in Japan; but they can also be used to track the movements of people without their knowledge and so reveal whether homes are unattended or where victims of abusive spouses have sought refuge. To learn why you should be aware of the locator settings on *your* smartphone, go to **http:// geospatialrevolution.psu.edu/episode3/chapter4**.

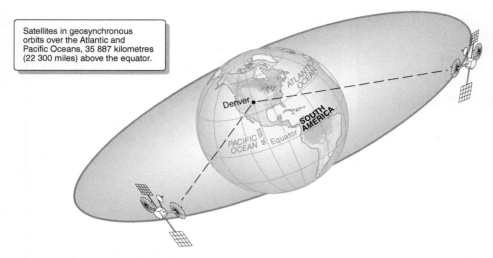

Satellites in geosynchronous orbits over the Atlantic and Pacific Oceans, 35 887 kilometres (22 300 miles) above the equator.

FIGURE 1.20 **The importance of site and situation** The location of telecommunications activities in Denver, Colorado, provides a good example of the significance of the geographic concepts of site (the physical attributes of a location) and situation (the location of a place relative to other places and human activities). Denver houses the headquarters of large U.S. cable companies, an industry-wide research lab, and a cluster of specialized support companies that employ thousands of people. Denver's high elevation *site* (1600 metres above sea level) is important because it gives transmitter and receiver dishes a better "view" of communications satellites. Its *situation*, on the 105th meridian and equidistant between the telecommunications satellites that are in geostationary orbit over the Pacific and Atlantic Oceans, allows it to send cable programming directly, not just to the whole of the Americas, but to every continent except Antarctica. This is important because it avoids "double-hop" transmission (in which a signal goes up to a satellite, then down, then up and down again), which increases costs and decreases picture quality. Before the construction of telecommunications facilities in Denver, places east or west of the 105th meridian had to double-hop some of their transmissions because satellite dishes would not have a clear "view" of both the Pacific and Atlantic telecommunications satellites.

Location can also be *relative*, fixed in terms of site or situation (**Figure 1.20**). **Site** refers to the physical attributes of a location: its terrain, soil, vegetation, and water sources, for example. **Situation** refers to the location of a place relative to other places and human activities: its accessibility to routes, for example, or its nearness to population centres. For example, Stanley Park has a coastal site and is situated northwest of downtown Vancouver.

Finally, location also has a *cognitive* dimension, in that people have cognitive images of places and regions, compiled from their own knowledge, experiences, and impressions. **Cognitive images** (sometimes referred to as *mental maps*) are psychological representations of locations that spring from people's individual ideas and impressions of these locations. These representations can be based on direct experiences, written or visual representations of actual locations, hearsay, imaginations, or any combination of these sources. Location in these cognitive images is fluid, depending on a given individual's changing information and perceptions of the principal landmarks in their environment.

Figure 1.21 shows one person's cognitive image of Montreal. As the drawing shows, many places may not appear in a person's cognitive image at all. Canadian architectural scholar Witold Rybczynski observes of his own years as a student at McGill

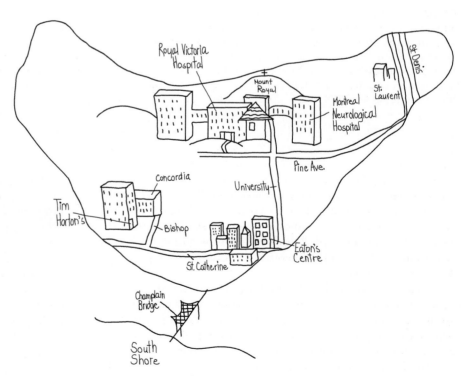

FIGURE 1.21 **One person's cognitive image of Montreal** This mental map was drawn by a geography student at Concordia University in Montreal as part of a class exercise. The student has included some (but not all) of Montreal's prominent landmarks, particularly "the mountain" in the city's centre. In addition, the shape of Montreal's island is distorted, emphasizing areas most familiar to the student.

University in Montreal that "the gym marked the northernmost edge of my campus world, just as Joe's Steak House circumscribed it to the south. The latter does not appear on the official map of the university, but each of us carries mental place maps within us—maps that often bear little resemblance to reality." Yet, for us, he concludes, "they are truer depictions than those of cartographers." (*Source:* Witold Rybczynski, *Looking Around: A Journey through Architecture.* Toronto: HarperCollins, 1992, p. 116.)

Distance

Like location, distance can be expressed in absolute, relative, and cognitive terms. *Absolute* distance is a physical measure that we may count in kilometres, for example. By contrast, *relative* distance is measured in terms of time, effort, or cost. For instance, it can take more time to travel 10 kilometres from point A to point B than it does to travel 10 kilometres from point A to point C. Similarly, it can cost more (or less).

Geographers also have to recognize that distance can sometimes be in the eye of the beholder: it can *seem* longer or more pleasant to go from A to B than from A to C. This is **cognitive distance**, the distance that people *perceive* to exist in a given situation. Cognitive distance is based on people's personal judgments about the degree of spatial separation between points. It is precisely this cognitive distance that is reflected in mental maps.

Distance is a fundamental factor in determining real-world relationships, and this is a central theme in geography. It was once described as the "first law" of geography: "Everything is related to everything else, but near things are more related than distant things." Waldo Tobler, the geographer who put it this way, is one of many who have investigated the friction of distance, the deterrent or inhibiting effect of distance on human activity. The **friction of distance** is a reflection of the time and cost of overcoming distance.

What these geographers have established is that these effects are not uniform—that is, they are not directly proportional to distance itself. This is true whether distance is measured in absolute terms (i.e., kilometres) or in relative terms (i.e., time or cost). The deterrent effects of extra distance tend to lessen as greater distances are involved. Thus, for example, while there is a big deterrent effect in having to travel 2 kilometres instead of 1 to get to a grocery store, the deterrent effect of the same extra distance (1 kilometre) after already travelling 10 kilometres is relatively small.

This sort of relationship creates what geographers call a distance-decay function. A **distance-decay function** describes the rate at which a particular activity or phenomenon diminishes with increasing distance. Typically, the farther people have to travel, the less likely they are to do so. Distance-decay functions reflect people's behavioural response to opportunities and constraints in time and space. As such, they reflect the utility of particular locations. The **utility** of a specific place or location is its usefulness to a particular person or group. In practice, utility is thought of in different ways by different people in different situations. The emphasis may be on cost, profitability, prestige, security, or ease of mobility, for example, or more likely on some combination of attributes. The business manager of a supermarket chain, for example, will decide on the utility of potential new store locations by weighing the projected costs and revenues for each potential location. When deciding where to retire, however, that same manager will be weighing a wide range of quality-of-life aspects such as climate, prestige, convenience, or feelings of personal safety that may well modify or override financial aspects as the dominant measure of utility.

However place utility is determined, people in most circumstances tend to *seek to maximize the net utility of location*. The supermarket chain's business manager, for example, will seek the new store location that is most likely to yield the greatest profit. Seeking to maximize the net utility of location means that a great deal of human activity is influenced by what University of Washington geographer Richard Morrill once called the "nearness principle." According to this principle—a more explicit version of Tobler's first law—people will seek to

- maximize the overall utility of places at minimum effort.
- maximize connections between places at minimum cost.
- locate related activities as close together as possible.

The result is that patterns of behaviour between people and places come to take on fairly predictable, organized patterns. One of the tasks of geographers is to identify, describe, map, and analyze these patterns, thus making them intelligible to non-geographers.

APPLY YOUR KNOWLEDGE From your own life, provide three examples of the inhibiting effect distance has on human activity. ■

Space

Similar to location and distance, space can be measured in absolute, relative, and cognitive terms. Absolute space is a mathematical space, described through points, lines, areas, and planes whose relationships can be fixed precisely through mathematical reasoning. The conventional way is to view space as a container, defined by rectangular coordinates and measured in absolute units of distance (kilometres, for example). Geographers also use other mathematical conceptions of space, however. One example is **topological space,** defined as the connections between, or connectivity of, particular points in space (**Figure 1.22**). Topological space is measured not in conventional measures of distance but rather by the nature and degree of connectivity between locations.

Relative measurements of space can take the form of, among others, *socioeconomic space.* When we divide the world into economic blocks, or according to gross domestic product (GDP), we employ relative measures of socioeconomic space such as cost, profit, and productivity. Finally, **cognitive space** is defined and measured in terms of people's values, feelings, beliefs, and perceptions about places and regions.

When we begin to think about space in these relative terms, we can understand that space is much more than an objective "container" in which activity occurs; in many ways, space is itself *produced* by our activity. Consider the history of European settlement of the Prairies, and imagine being one of the first immigrants to establish a farm there. In the first phase of settlement, distance has little meaning to us because we are isolated and self-sufficient. But once a town is established in that landscape, a "centre" is created and the location of our farm is now redefined in terms of its distance from that centre with its amenities, railroad station, and grain elevator. In other words, *distance* and all of the effects of the friction of distance are *produced* by our activities.

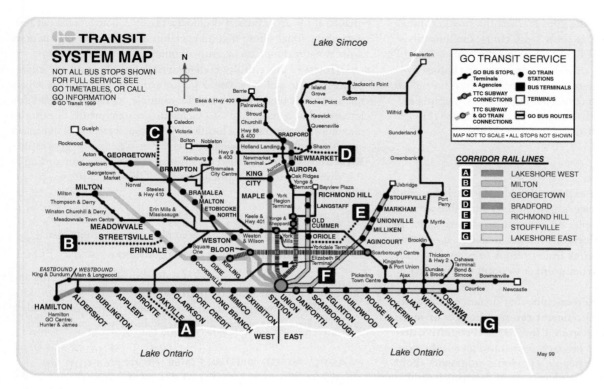

FIGURE 1.22 Topological space Some dimensions of space and aspects of spatial organization do not lend themselves to description simply in terms of distance. The connectivity of people and places is often important: whether they are linked, how they are linked, and so on. These attributes of connectivity define topological space. This map of the GO Transit system in Toronto is a topological map, showing how specific points are joined within a particular network. The most important aspects of networks of any kind, from the geographer's viewpoint, are their connectivity attributes. These attributes determine the flow of people and things (goods, information) and the centrality of places. For example, the GO system gives Brampton a very high degree of connectivity because several lines intersect there. Brampton is therefore relatively central within the "space of flows" of passenger traffic in the Greater Toronto Area. Bramalea—nearby in absolute terms—is much less central, however, and much less of a nexus of passenger flows. Note that, in a topological map, distances are not necessarily drawn to scale. (*Source:* Transit Toronto, http://transit.toronto.on.ca/archives/maps/go99.gif)

Accessibility

Because it is a fundamental influence on the utility of locations, distance is an important influence on people's behaviour. **Accessibility** is generally defined by geographers in terms of relative location: the opportunity for contact or interaction from a given point or location in relation to other locations. It implies proximity, or nearness, to something. Distance is one aspect of accessibility, but it is by no means the only important aspect.

Connectivity is also an important aspect of accessibility because contact and interaction are dependent on channels of communication and transportation: streets, highways, telephone lines, and wave bands, for example. Effective accessibility is a function not only of distance but also of the configuration of networks of communication and transportation. Commercial airline networks provide many striking examples of this. Cities that operate as airline hubs are much more accessible than cities that are served by fewer flights and fewer airlines.

Accessibility is often a function of economic, cultural, and social factors. In other words, relative concepts and measures of distance are often as important as absolute distance in determining

accessibility. A nearby facility, such as a health care clinic, is accessible to us only if we can actually afford the cost of getting there, if we can afford to use the facility, if we feel that it is socially and culturally acceptable for us to use it, and so on. To take another example, a day care centre may be located just a few blocks from a single-parent family, but the centre is not truly accessible if it opens after the parent has to be at work, if the cost of care is too high, or if the parent feels that the staff, children, or other parents at the centre are from an incompatible social or cultural group.

Spatial Interaction

Interdependence between places and regions can be sustained only through movement and flows. Geographers use the term **spatial interaction** as shorthand for all kinds of movement and flows involving human activity. Freight shipments, commuting, shopping trips, telecommunications, electronic cash transfers, migration, and vacation travel are all examples of spatial interaction. The fundamental principles of spatial interaction can be reduced to four basic concepts: complementarity, transferability, intervening opportunities, and spatial diffusion.

Complementarity

For any kind of spatial interaction to occur between two places, there must be a demand in one place and a supply that matches, or complements, it in the other. This complementarity can be the result of several factors. One important factor is the variation in physical environments and resource endowments from place to place. For example, the flow of sun-starved Canadian vacationers to the Caribbean during the winter is the result of climatic complementarity. To take another example, the flow of crude oil from Saudi Arabia (with vast oil reserves) to Japan (with none) is a function of complementarity in natural resource endowments.

A second factor contributing to complementarity is the international division of labour that derives from the evolution of the world's economic systems. The more developed countries of the world have sought to establish overseas suppliers for their food, raw materials, and exotic produce, allowing these more developed countries to specialize in more profitable manufacturing and knowledge-based industries. (See Chapter 2.) Through a combination of colonialism, imperialism, and sheer economic dominance on the part of the more developed countries, less powerful countries have found themselves with economies that directly complement the needs of the more developed countries. Among the many flows resulting from this complementarity are shipments of sugar from Barbados to the United Kingdom, bananas from Costa Rica and Honduras to Canada, palm oil from Cameroon to France, automobiles from France to Algeria, school textbooks from the United Kingdom to Kenya, and investment capital from Canada to mining projects in Peru.

A third contributory factor to complementarity is specialization and economies of scale. Places, regions, and countries can derive economic advantages from the efficiencies created through specialization, which allows for larger-scale operations. **Economies of scale** are cost advantages to manufacturers in high-volume production; the average cost of production falls with increasing output. Among other things, fixed costs (for example, the cost of renting or buying factory space, which is the same—fixed—whatever the level of output from the factory) can be spread over higher levels of output so that the average cost per unit of production falls. Economic specialization results in complementarities, which in turn contribute to patterns of spatial interaction. For example, Israeli farmers specialize in high-value fruit and vegetable crops for export to the European Union, which in return exports grains and root crops to Israel.

Transferability

Another precondition for interdependence between places is *transferability*, which depends on the frictional (or deterrent) effects of distance. Transferability is a function of two things: the cost of moving a particular item, measured in money and/or time, and the ability of the item to bear these costs. If, for example, the costs of moving a product from one place to another make it too expensive to sell successfully at its destination, then that product does not have transferability between those places.

Transferability varies between places, between kinds of items, and between modes of transportation and communication. The transferability of coal, for example, is much greater between places that are connected by rail or by navigable waterways than between places connected only by highways. This is because it is much cheaper to move heavy, bulky materials by rail, barge, or ship. The transferability of fruit and salad crops, on the other hand, depends more on the speed of transportation and the availability of specialized refrigerated vehicles so the fruits and vegetables stay fresh. While the transferability of money capital is much greater by telecommunications than it is by surface transportation, it is also higher between places where banks are equipped to deal routinely with electronic transfers. Computer microchips have high transferability because they are easy to handle, and transport costs are a small proportion of their value. Computer monitors have lower transferability because of their fragility and their relatively lower value by weight and volume.

Transferability also varies over time, with successive innovations in transport and communications technologies and successive waves of **infrastructure** development (canals, railways, harbour installations, roads, bridges, and so on). New technologies and new or extended infrastructures alter the geography of transport costs and the transferability of particular things between particular places. As a result, the spatial organization of many different activities is continually changing and readjusting. The consequent tendency toward a shrinking world gives rise to **time–space convergence**, the rate at which places move closer together in travel or communication time or costs. Time–space convergence results from a decrease in the friction of distance as space-adjusting technologies have, in general, brought places closer together over time.

Overland travel time between Montreal and Toronto, for example, has been reduced from one week (when regular stagecoach service began in 1817) to 10 hours (on the first train in 1856) to six hours by car today. Other important space-adjusting innovations include air travel and air cargo; telegraphic, telephonic, and satellite communications systems; national postal services and package delivery services; and fax machines, cell phones, fibre-optic networks, and email.

VIRTUAL GEOGRAPHIES

The latest developments in communication infrastructure in particular have had significant effects on time–space convergence in the sense that they are not only global in scope but also penetrate to local scales. As this penetration occurs, some places that are distant in kilometres are "moving" closer together, whereas some that are close in terms of absolute space are becoming more distant in terms of their ability to reach one another electronically. Much depends on the extent to which people in different places have access to new communication technologies. For instance, cell phones are the new standard for person-to-person communication, but they are limited to populated areas with a transmission tower grid. Similarly, fibre-optic cable networks can offer fast broadband Internet connections only in areas of high-population density. In principle, telecommunications satellites can fill this gap and offer comparable access to people in remote areas, but only at significant cost. We can see that, while the new communication technologies may contribute to the shrinking of space, they do so in very uneven ways: the degree to which people are "plugged in" still very much depends on local and personal factors.

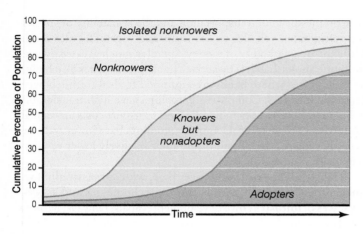

FIGURE 1.23 Spatial diffusion The spatial diffusion of many phenomena tends to follow an S-curve of slow buildup, rapid spread, and levelling off. In the case of the diffusion of an innovation, for example, it usually takes a while for enough potential adopters to find out about the innovation, and even longer for a critical mass of them to adopt it. After that the innovation spreads quite rapidly, until most of the potential adopters have been exposed. (*Source:* Adapted from D. J. Walmsley and G. J. Lewis, *Human Geography: Behavioural Approaches.* London: Longman, 1984, Fig. 5.3, p. 52.)

Intervening Opportunity

While complementarity and transferability are preconditions for spatial interaction, intervening opportunities are more important in determining the *volume* and *pattern* of movements and flows. Intervening opportunities are alternative origins and/or destinations. Such opportunities are not necessarily situated directly between two points or even along a route between them. Thus, to take one of our previous examples, for Canadians considering a Caribbean winter vacation, Florida or Mexico are likely to be intervening opportunities if they can be reached more quickly and cheaply than Caribbean destinations.

Spatial Diffusion

Disease outbreaks, technological innovations, political movements, and new musical fads all originate in specific places and subsequently spread to other places and regions. The way that things spread through space and over time—**spatial diffusion**—is one of the most important aspects of spatial interaction and is crucial to an understanding of geographic change.

Diffusion seldom occurs in an apparently random way, jumping unpredictably all over the map. Rather, it occurs as a function of statistical probability, which is often based on fundamental geographic principles of distance and movement. The diffusion of a contagious disease, for example, is a function of the probability of physical contact, modified by variations in individual resistance to the disease. The result is typically a "wave" of diffusion that describes an S-curve, with a slow buildup, rapid spread, and final levelling off. The same principle also applies to the diffusion of a new idea, fashion, or innovation (**Figure 1.23**).

It is possible to recognize several different spatial tendencies in patterns of diffusion. In *expansion diffusion* (also called *contagious diffusion*—**Figure 1.24a**), a phenomenon spreads because of the proximity of carriers, or agents of change, who are fixed in their location. A good example is the spread of a contagious disease across a region. With *hierarchical diffusion* (also called *cascade diffusion*), a phenomenon can be diffused from one location to another without necessarily spreading to places in between (**Figure 1.24b**). Fashion trends, for example, often spread first *between* major world cities, before spreading *down* the urban hierarchy to city to town to village. A third type of diffusion that involves the actual movement of people is called *relocation*

diffusion (not shown in Figure 1.24). The spread of European religions and languages to the new world we will discuss in Chapter 5 are examples of relocation diffusion.

One example of hierarchical diffusion would be the initial spread of the HIV-1 virus from a hearth area in Central Africa to other parts of the world. The virus initially appeared almost simultaneously in the major metropolitan areas of North and South America, the Caribbean, and Europe. From these areas it then cascaded down to major metropolitan areas in Asia and Oceania and to larger provincial cities in North and South America, the Caribbean, and Europe. Next in this cascading pattern of diffusion were provincial cities in Asia and Oceania and small towns in North and South America, the Caribbean, and Europe.

Hierarchical diffusion has two important consequences. First, it can spread phenomena much more quickly around the world than expansion diffusion, and the opportunities for hierarchical diffusion are greatly enhanced by the processes of globalization. Second, although hierarchical diffusion can be faster than expansion diffusion, it is not always as thorough in reaching everywhere quickly, illustrating our earlier observation that phenomena close together in one type of space may be far apart in another type of space.

Actual diffusion processes often occur in mixed forms as different aspects of human interaction come into play at different times in different geographic settings (**Figure 1.24c**). The diffusion of communicable diseases, for example, usually involves a combination of hierarchical and expansion diffusion that largely reflects the existing networks of transportation.

> **APPLY YOUR KNOWLEDGE** Referring to spatial analysis concepts, discuss a national or international environmental issue. Provide examples of how complementarity, transferability, intervening opportunities, and diffusion each relate to the issue you have chosen. ∎

REGIONAL ANALYSIS

Not all geographic phenomena are most effectively understood through spatial analysis. Geographers also seek to understand the complex relationships between peoples and places in terms of the

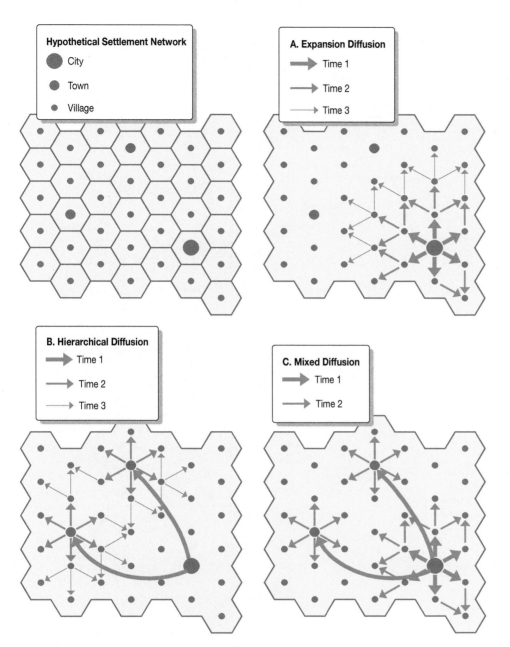

FIGURE 1.24 Patterns of spatial diffusion (a) Expansion diffusion (for example, the spread of an innovative agricultural practice, such as the use of hybrid seed stock, across a rural region); (b) hierarchical diffusion (the spread of a fashion trend from large metropolitan areas to smaller cities and towns); (c) mixed diffusion. (*Source:* E.K. Cromley and S. L. McLafferty, *GIS and Public Health* 2nd edition, New York; Guilford Press, p. 239.)

similarities and differences among and between them and the identities and qualities associated with them. Here the key concepts are regionalization, landscape, and sense of place.

Regionalization

The geographer's equivalent of *scientific classification* is **regionalization**, with individual places or areal units being the objects of classification. Geographers are especially interested in **functional regions** (sometimes referred to as nodal regions)—regions that, while they may exhibit some variability in certain attributes, share an overall coherence in structure and economic, political, and social organization. The coherence and distinctive characteristics of a region are often stronger in some places than in others. This point is illustrated by geographer Donald Meinig's *core-domain-sphere* model, which he set out in his classic essay on the Mormon region of the United States (**Figure 1.25**). In the core of a region, the distinctive attributes are very clear; in the domain, they are dominant but not to the point of exclusivity; in the sphere, they are present but not dominant.

People's own conceptions of place, region, and identity may generate strong feelings of regionalism and sectionalism that feed back into the processes of place-making and regional

FIGURE 1.25 The Mormon culture region Cultural attributes often gradually shade from one region to another, rather than having a single, clear-cut boundary. Geographer Donald Meinig's work on the Mormon culture region of the United States identified a "core" region, which exhibits all the attributes of Mormon culture; a "domain," where not all these attributes may be present (or may be less intense); and a "sphere," where some attributes of Mormon culture are present but often as a minority. (*Source:* Adapted from D. Meinig, "The Mormon Culture Region: Strategies and Patterns in the Geography of the American West," *Annals, Association of American Geographers*, 55, 1965, pp. 191–220.)

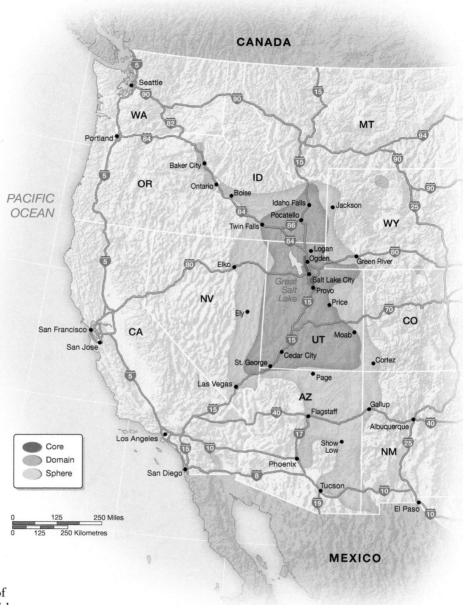

differentiation. **Regionalism** is a term used to describe situations in which different religious or ethnic groups with distinctive identities coexist within the same state boundaries, often concentrated within a particular region and sharing strong feelings of collective identity. If such feelings develop into an extreme devotion to regional interests and customs, the condition is known as **sectionalism**. Regionalism often involves ethnic groups whose aims include autonomy from a national state and the development of their own political power. (See Chapter 9.) In certain cases, enclaves of ethnic minorities are claimed by the government of a country other than the one in which they reside. Such was the case, for example, of Serbian enclaves in Croatia, claimed by nationalist Serbs. **Irredentism** is the assertion by the government of a country that a minority living outside its formal borders belongs to it historically and culturally. In some circumstances, as with Serbia's claims on Serbian enclaves in Croatia in the early 1990s, irredentism can lead to war.

Landscape

Geographers think of **landscape** as a comprehensive product of human action such that every landscape is a complex repository of society. It is a collection of evidence about our character and experience, our struggles and triumphs as humans. To understand better the meaning of landscape, geographers have developed different categories of landscape types based on the elements contained within them.

Ordinary landscapes (or vernacular landscapes, as they are sometimes called) are the everyday landscapes that people create in the course of their lives together. From crowded city centres to leafy suburbs and quiet rural villages, landscapes are lived in and changed and influence and change the perceptions, values, and behaviours of the people who live and work in them.

Symbolic landscapes, by contrast, represent particular values or aspirations that builders and financiers want to impart to a larger public. Parliament Hill in Ottawa, for example, with

FIGURE 1.26 The power of place In some countries, particular landscapes have become powerfully symbolic of national identity. In Italy it is the classical landscape of Tuscany, with its scattered farms and villas, elegant cypress trees, silvery-green olive trees, and rolling fields with a rich mixture of cereals, vegetables, fruit trees, and vines, as in this photograph. (*Source: LianeM/Shutterstock.*)

its neo-gothic style of architecture, is intentionally designed to invoke the British tradition of parliamentary democracy. (See Figure 1.5 on p. 6.)

Some landscapes become powerfully symbolic of national identity. Nation building depends heavily on stories of golden ages, enduring traditions, heroic deeds, shared hardships, and dramatic destinies, all located in traditional (or promised) homelands with hallowed sites and scenery. Landscapes thus become a way of picturing a nation. With the creation of modern Italy during the *Risorgimento* ("revival through unification"—1815–1861), for example, the classical Tuscan landscape (**Figure 1.26**) became emblematic of Italy itself and has attracted landscape painters, romantic poets, and novelists ever since. Similarly, the West of Ireland (**Figure 1.27**) came to symbolize the whole of Ireland to

Irish nationalists in the early twentieth century—partly because it was seen as the region least affected by British colonization, but also because its bare and rugged landscape seemed to contrast so strikingly with the more bucolic rural landscapes (**Figure 1.28**) by which England was popularly imagined.

Geographers now recognize that there are many layers of meaning embedded in the landscape. Landscapes reflect people's dreams and ideas as well as their material lives. The messages embedded in landscapes can be read as signs about values, beliefs, and practices, though not every reader will take the same message from a particular landscape (just as people may differ in their interpretation of a passage from a book). In short, landscapes both produce and communicate meaning, and one of our tasks as geographers is to interpret those meanings.

FIGURE 1.27 The national landscape of Ireland The rugged landscapes of the West of Ireland have come to symbolize the whole country to many people, both within Ireland and beyond. This photograph shows part of rural County Kerry. (*Source: xamnesiacx/Shutterstock.*)

FIGURE 1.28 Rural England The well-ordered and picturesque landscape of the southern parts of rural England has long been taken to be emblematic of England as a whole and of the values and ideals of its people—even though urban and industrial development, together with modern agricultural practices, have brought about significant changes to both landscapes and society. (*Source:* M. Imort)

Sense of Place

Everyday routines experienced in familiar settings allow people to derive a pool of shared meanings. Often this carries over into people's attitudes and feelings about themselves and their locality. When this happens, the result is a self-conscious sense of place. A **sense of place** refers to the feelings evoked among people as a result of the experiences and memories they associate with a place and to the symbolism they attach to that place. It can also refer to the character of a place as seen by outsiders: its distinctive physical characteristics and/or its inhabitants.

For *insiders,* this sense of place develops through shared dress codes, speech patterns, public comportment, and so on. A crucial concept here is that of the **lifeworld**, the taken-for-granted pattern and context for everyday living through which people conduct their day-to-day lives without conscious attention. People become familiar with one another's vocabulary, speech patterns, dress codes, gestures, and humour as a result

of routine encounters and shared experiences in bars and pubs, cafés and restaurants, shops and street markets, and parks. This is known as **intersubjectivity**: shared meanings that are derived from everyday practice. Elements of daily rhythms (such as mid-morning grocery shopping with a stop for coffee, the *aperitivo* en route from work to home, and the after-dinner stroll) are all critical to the intersubjectivity that is the basis for a sense of place within a community (**Figure 1.29**). The same is true of weekly rhythms, such as street markets and farmers' markets, and of seasonal rhythms, such as festivals.

These rhythms, in turn, depend on certain kinds of spaces and places: not only streets, squares, and public open spaces but also "third places" (after home, first, and workplace, second): the sidewalk cafés, pubs, post offices, drugstores, corner stores, and family-run *trattoria* that are the loci of routine activities and sociocultural transactions. Third places accommodate "characters," "regulars," and newcomers, as well as routine patrons and,

FIGURE 1.29 Intersubjectivity Routine encounters such as this, in Chiavenna, Italy, help develop a sense of community and a sense of place among residents. (*Source:* Paul L. Knox)

FIGURE 1.30 Community art Community art can provide an important element in the creation of a sense of place and identity for members of local communities. This example is from the village of St. Jacobs, a focal point of Mennonite settlement in Ontario. (*Source: M. Imort*)

like public spaces, facilitate casual encounters as well as settings for sustained conversations. The nature and frequency of routine encounters and shared experiences depend a great deal on the attributes of these spaces and places.

A sense of place also develops through familiarity with the history and symbolism of particular elements of the physical environment—a mountain or lake, the birthplace of someone notable, the site of some particularly well-known event, or the expression of community identity through art (**Figure 1.30**). Sometimes it is deliberately fostered by the construction of symbolic structures such as monuments and statues. Often it is a natural outcome of people's familiarity with one another and their surroundings. Because of this consequent sense of place, insiders feel at home and "in place."

For *outsiders*, a sense of place can be evoked only if local landmarks, ways of life, and so on are distinctive enough to evoke a significant common meaning for people who have no direct experience of them. Central Paris, for example, is a setting that carries a strong sense of place to outsiders who have a sense of familiarity with the riverside panoramas, busy streets, and distinctive monuments and historic buildings.

APPLY YOUR KNOWLEDGE What are the most distinctive characteristics of the region in which you live? How would you describe its landscapes? What, from your perspective, gives your community a sense of place? ■

DEVELOPING A GEOGRAPHICAL IMAGINATION

A **geographical imagination** allows us to understand changing patterns, processes, and relationships among people, places, and regions. Developing this capacity is increasingly important as the pace of change around the world increases to unprecedented levels.

It is often useful to think of places and regions as representing the cumulative legacy of successive periods of change. Following this approach, we can look for superimposed layers of development, or evidence of the imprint of different phases of local development. (See Box 1.3, "Window on the World: South Beach, Miami Beach"). We can show how some patterns and relationships last, while others are modified or obliterated. We can show how different places bear the imprint of different kinds of change, perhaps in different sequences and with different outcomes. To do so, we must be able to identify the kinds of changes that are most significant.

We can prepare our geographical imagination to deal with an important aspect of spatial change by making a distinction between the *general* and the *unique*. This distinction helps account for geographical diversity and variety because it provides a way of understanding how and why one kind of change can result in a variety of spatial outcomes. Because the *general effects* of a particular change always involve some degree of modification as they are played out in different environments, *unique outcomes* result.

Although we can usually identify some general outcomes of major episodes of change, there are almost always some unique outcomes, too. Let us take two related examples. The Industrial Revolution of 19th-century Europe provides a good example of a major period of change. A few of the general spatial outcomes were increased urbanization, regional specialization in production, and increased interregional and international trade. At one level, places could be said to have become increasingly alike: generic coalfield regions, industrial towns, ports, downtowns, worker housing, and suburbs.

It is clear, however, that these general outcomes were mediated by the different physical, economic, cultural, and social attributes of different places. Beneath the dramatic overall changes in the geography of Europe, new layers of diversity and variety also existed. Industrial towns developed their own distinctive character as a result of their manufacturing specialties, their politics,

South Beach provides a vibrant illustration of a place that embodies the layered legacy of successive waves of development and change. In just over 100 years, South Beach has gone from a coconut plantation to a speculative development of modest single-family residences, a booming resort and retirement district, a run-down district infiltrated by crime and vice, and a renovated district on the U.S. National Register of Historic Places. Its latest incarnation is as an exclusive residential enclave—an international destination district and celebrity haunt. In the process, it has changed from a segregated Anglo-American community to a predominantly Jewish community and then to a multiethnic, cosmopolitan population, the setting for an unabashedly vulgar hedonism. Elements of all of these changes are visible in the landscapes of the district today.

Construction of a small oceanfront residential district began in 1913. A year later, Carl G. Fisher, a successful entrepreneur who made millions selling a business to Union Carbide, began to invest in property development and infrastructure improvements (including a vital road bridge to the mainland). South Beach steadily filled up in the 1920s in a real estate boom supercharged by the palatial homes built by several prominent millionaires. The boom coincided with the blossoming of stylish Modern architecture inspired by the Paris Exhibition of 1925. The new styles reflected a fascination with the streamlined design and comfort features of mass transportation of the era, especially transatlantic ocean liners, luxury automobiles, and passenger trains. Property development and redevelopment continued even during the Great Depression of the 1930s, creating a distinctive district of hotels and residences—about 800 buildings in approximately 2.5 square kilometres (1 square mile)—in what later became known as Art Deco styles (**Figure 1.C**).

After World War II, South Beach became a glamorous destination district, a seasonal haven for wealthy northerners. The arrival of retirees from the American Northeast and Midwest brought a new dimension of ethnic diversity to the city. Jewish retirees were drawn to Miami Beach but had to contend with segregation ordinances that restricted them to the area south of Fifth Street, the southern tip of South Beach. Civil rights activism, combined with the sheer weight of increasing numbers, overcame segregation by the 1960s, and within a few years Jews had come to dominate the entire city of Miami Beach. In South Beach, synagogues, Yiddish theatres, kosher restaurants, and delicatessens proliferated. While there were some upscale hotels and residences, the district was dominated by modest, deteriorating, low-rise buildings populated by retirees on small, fixed incomes.

Meanwhile, as metropolitan Miami absorbed increasing numbers of immigrants from Cuba and Latin America, South Beach was infiltrated by drug dealers and the associated crime and vice. Wealthy households moved out, leaving behind less

FIGURE 1.C South Beach Architecture Characteristic elements of buildings in the Art Deco district of South Beach include building forms based on geometric shapes, with sharp angles and/or curved corners; "eyebrows" above windows; jutting towers, ziggurat rooflines, glass-block windows, porthole windows, deck railings, racing stripes, and chevron decorations; the use of the modern materials like chrome, plastic, and aluminum; distinctive signage and lettering with exaggerated or multiline details; and neon lighting. (*Source:* Paul L. Knox)

affluent households, such as the retirees on fixed incomes. For a while, South Beach acquired the nickname of "God's Waiting Room." By the mid-1970s, South Beach was down-at-heel, no longer attracting many new retirees and on the cusp of irretrievable deterioration. It was saved by the activism of conservationists, who secured a 2.5-square kilometre portion of South Beach as the Miami Beach Art Deco District on the U.S. National Register of Historic Places. Conservationists promoted the idea of renovating the buildings by applying a palette of pastel

FIGURE 1.D **South Beach Lifestyle** Luxury condominiums at the southern tip of South Beach. (*Source: Richard Cavalleri/Shutterstock.*)

hues—flamingo and bubblegum pink, peach, periwinkle, purple, aqua, and lavender blue—on what had previously been white-washed surfaces. Hotels and restaurants also began to invest in classic Art Deco neon lighting that provides an exotic night-scape. The makeover was enough to attract new investment, new visitors, and new residents. The combination of distinctive archi-tecture and wide stretches of soft, almost-white sandy beaches, together with the subtropical light, made South Beach an attrac-tive location for photo shoots. Many of the large New York–based modelling agencies moved in, bringing an influx of fashion indus-try professionals. Sidewalk cafés, boutiques, nightclubs, and chic restaurants followed, along with more models, celebrities, and international tourists.

South Beach became a hedonistic setting, a 24-hour play-ground dominated by the young and affluent. Restored Art Deco and Mediterranean Revival buildings were joined by new contem-porary architecture and ultraluxurious condominiums. The south-ern tip of the district was redeveloped with exclusive, resort-like condominium towers (**Figure 1.D**). Inevitably, the district's demog-raphy changed again. Jewish households had represented almost two-thirds of the total population of Miami Beach in 1980. By 2010, the figure was less than 15 percent. Similarly, whereas elderly households had long dominated South Beach, less than 15 per-cent of its population was aged 50 or more by 2010. The majority

were aged between 20 and 40. The traditional flow of Jewish retir-ees on modest incomes had been priced out of the district, while the more affluent gravitated to Broward and Palm Beach coun-ties. Today, South Beach has developed a unique cultural mix, which is in many ways like the Mediterranean European coast or parts of Latin America. Spanish is the first language of more than half of the population, while English is the first language of only about a third.

Colombian discos, European club scenes, traditional American bars, Cuban cafés, and restaurants specializing in "Eurasian," "New World," and "Nuevo Latino" cuisine have dis-placed the kosher delis and seafood shacks. Bikini shows and wet T-shirt contests have replaced the mahjong and canasta games of retirees. Lounge music from the 1950s has been displaced by Europop, samba from Brazil, salsa from Colombia, tango from Argentina, reggae from the English-speaking Caribbean, flamenco from Spain, and merengue and bachata from the Dominican Republic. The influence of sun, sea, and the warm weather has fostered a distinctive body-consciousness and stan-dard of public exposure that would be censured in many other American cities.

Source: Based on "South Beach" in Paul Knox, *Palimpsests: Biographies of 50 City Districts*, Basel: Actar/Birkhauser, 2012.

FIGURE 1.31 Hersbrück, Germany Hersbrück was once a prosperous regional centre on an overland trade route—the "Golden Road"—between Nuremberg and Prague. After 1806, when Napoleon redrew the political map of Europe, the reorganization of the European economy, together with the onset of the Industrial Revolution, left Hersbrück somewhat isolated and economically disadvantaged. Hersbrück was never drawn into the industrial development of Germany and is not well connected to the transportation infrastructure of canals, railways, or major highways. (*Source:* Paul L. Knox)

characteristics making them unsuited to the new economic and spatial order (**Figure 1.31**).

The second example of general and unique outcomes of change is the introduction of the railroad, one of the specific changes involved in the Industrial Revolution. In general terms, the railroad contributed to time–space convergence, to the reorganization of industry into larger market areas, to an increase in interregional and international trade, and to the interconnectedness of urban systems. Other unique outcomes, however, have also contributed to distinctive regional geographies. In Britain, the railroad was introduced to an environment that was partially industrialized and densely settled. The increased efficiencies provided by the railroad helped turn Britain's economy into a highly integrated and intensively urbanized national economy. In Spain, however, the railroad was introduced to an environment that was less urbanized and industrialized and less able to afford the costs of railroad construction. The result was that the relatively few Spanish towns connected by the railroads gained a massive comparative advantage. This situation laid the foundation for a modern Spanish space-economy that was much less integrated than Britain's, with an urban system that to this day is dominated by just a few towns and cities.

APPLY YOUR KNOWLEDGE Describe the region in which you live, emphasizing the imprint of different periods of development. Which features of the region can be said to be the result of general spatial effects, and which are unique? ■

the personalities and objectives of their leaders, and the reactions and responses of their residents. Downtowns were differentiated from one another as the general forces of commerce and land economics played out across different physical sites and within different patterns of land ownership. Various local socioeconomic and political factors gave rise to different expressions of urban design. Meanwhile, some places came to be distinctive because they were almost entirely bypassed by this period of change, their

Future Geographies

Places and regions are constantly in a state of change. This raises the question of what we may expect to see in the future. An understanding of geographic processes and principles, together with a knowledge of past and present spatial patterns, allows us to make informed judgments about future geographies: an important dimension of applying our geographical imagination.

Whereas much of the world had remained virtually unchanged for decades, even centuries, the Industrial Revolution and long-distance, high-speed transportation and communications brought a rapid series of rearrangements to the countryside and to towns

and cities in many parts of the world. Today, with a globalized economy and global telecommunications and transportation networks, places have become much more interdependent, and still more of the world is exposed to increasingly urgent imperatives to change.

Will social networking sites bring about new patterns of human interaction? Will we be able to cope with the environmental stresses of increasing industrialization and rapid population growth? Will the United States retain its position as the world's most powerful and influential nation? What kind of problems will the future bring for local, regional, and international development? What new technologies are likely to have the most impact in reshaping human geographies? Will globalization undermine regional cultures? These are just a few of the many questions that spring from the key themes in human geography.

As we begin to look to the future, we can appreciate that some dimensions of human geography are more certain than others (**Figure 1.32**). We can only guess, of course, at some aspects of the future. Two of the most speculative realms are those of politics and technology, which are both likely to spring surprises at any time. On the other hand, in some ways the future is already here, embedded in the world's institutional structures and in the dynamics of its populations. We know, for example, a good deal about the demographic trends of the next quarter century, given present populations, birth and death rates, and so on. We also know a good deal about the distribution of environmental resources and constraints, about the characteristics of local and regional economies, and about the legal and political frameworks within which geographic change will probably take place. The tools and concepts of human geography allow us to understand change in terms of local place-making processes that are subject to certain broader principles of spatial organization as well as the overall framework of the global economy. In subsequent chapters, as we look more closely at specific aspects of human geography, we shall be able to see how geographic process and principles can suggest future patterns and pathways of change.

APPLY YOUR KNOWLEDGE Make a list of likely future changes to the geography of the region in which you live. ∎

FIGURE 1.32 Affluent China Some aspects of future geographies are relatively certain. The unprecedented shift in relative wealth and economic power from West to East now under way will continue, though it will inevitably increase social and spatial inequalities within the East, the consequences of which are highly uncertain. The image shows part of the Grandview luxury mall in Guangzhou, China. It is bigger than any mega mall in North America. (*Source:* Francesca Lo Cascio/Fotolia.)

CONCLUSION

Human geography is the systematic study of the location of peoples and human activities across Earth's surface and of their relationships to one another. An understanding of human geography is important both from an intellectual point of view (that is, understanding the world around us) and a practical point of view (for example, contributing to environmental quality, human rights, social justice, business efficiency, political analysis, and government policymaking).

Human geography reveals how and why geographical relationships matter in terms of cause and effect in relation to economic, social, cultural, and political phenomena. Human geographers strive to recognize these wider processes and broad geographical patterns without losing sight of the uniqueness of specific places.

Geography matters because it is in specific places that people learn who and what they are and how they are expected to think and behave.

Places are also a strong influence, for better or worse, on people's physical well-being, their opportunities, and their lifestyle choices. Places also contribute to people's collective memory and become powerful emotional and cultural symbols. Places are the sites of innovation and change, of resistance and conflict.

To investigate specific places, we must be able to frame our studies of them within the compass of the entire globe. This is important for two reasons. First, the world consists of a complex mosaic of places and regions that are interrelated and interdependent in many ways. Second, place-making forces—especially economic, cultural, and political forces that influence the distribution of human activities and the character of places—are increasingly operating at global and international scales. In the next chapter, we describe the changing global context that has shaped places and regions around the world.

Learning Outcomes Revisited

■ Explain how the study of geography has become essential for understanding a world that is more complex, interdependent, and changing faster than ever before.

Geography matters because it enables us to understand where we are both literally and figuratively. Geography provides an understanding of the interdependency of people and places and an appreciation of how and why certain places are distinctive or unique. From this knowledge, we can begin to understand the implications of future spatial patterns and political power.

■ Identify four examples of how places influence inhabitants' lives.

Specific places provide the settings for people's daily lives. Places are settings for social interaction that, among other things, structure the daily routines of people's economic and social lives; provide both opportunities for—and constraints on—people's long-term social well-being; establish a context in which everyday common-sense knowledge and experience are gathered; provide a setting for processes of socialization; and provide an arena for contesting social norms and political power.

■ Distinguish the differences among major map projections and describe their relative strengths and weaknesses.

The choice of map projection depends largely on the purpose of the map. Equidistant projections allow distance to be represented as accurately as possible but in only one direction (usually north–south). Conformal projections render compass directions accurately but tend to exaggerate the size of northern continents. Equivalent projections in world maps portray areas on Earth's surface in their true proportions but result in many areas to appear squashed and have unsatisfactory outlines.

■ Explain how geographers use geographic information systems (GIS) to merge and analyze data.

New technologies combine high-performance computing, global positioning systems (GPS), and digital record keeping. The most important aspect of these technologies, from an analytical point of view, is that they allow data from several different sources, on different topics and at different scales, to be merged and visualized.

■ Summarize the five concepts that are key to spatial analysis and describe how they help geographers analyze relationships between peoples and places.

The study of many geographic phenomena can be approached in terms of their arrangement as points, lines, areas, or surfaces on a map. This is known as spatial analysis. Location, distance, space, accessibility, and spatial interaction are five concepts that are key to spatial analysis. Each of these concepts is multi-faceted and can be applied to different spatial scales. Together, they provide a powerful set of tools for describing and analyzing places and regions.

■ Describe the importance of distance in shaping human activity.

The first law of geography is that "Everything is related to everything else, but near things are more related than are distant things." Human activity is influenced by the "nearness principle," according to which people tend to seek to maximize the overall utility of places at minimum effort, to maximize connections between places at minimum cost, and to locate related activities as close together as possible.

■ Summarize the three concepts that are key to regional analysis and explain how they help geographers analyze relationships between peoples and places.

The key concepts of regional analysis are regionalization, landscape, and sense of place. Regionalization is the geographer's equivalent of scientific classification; landscapes embody many layers of meaning and reflect the influence of past processes of change, while sense of place derives from everyday routines experienced in familiar settings. Geographers also seek to understand the complex relationships between peoples and places in terms of the similarities and differences among and between them and the identities and qualities associated with them.

KEY TERMS

REVIEW AND DISCUSSION

1. Consider the term *symbolic landscapes*. Identify and list five examples of symbolic landscapes in your town. (See **Figures 1.26–1.28**.) For each of the landscapes, interpret the values, beliefs, and aspirations that it embodies. If necessary, find a picture of the specific landscape to aid with your observations.

2. Decide on a location that all members of your group are familiar with, such as your downtown, city hall, or student union. As individuals, take 10 minutes to make a cognitive sketch or mental map of the agreed-upon location. (See **Figure 1.21** for an example of a cognitive sketch.) Come back together as a group and compare your drawings. How did the cognitive sketches in your group differ? How were they similar? List five things that are most striking about your sketches.

3. Consider the features that give your specific location a sense of place by creating a list of at least ten items. Make sure your list is specific; take into consideration things like vocabulary, speech patterns, clothing, and "in jokes," as well as physical geography. Once this is complete, consider how an "outsider" would interact with and understand your place.

4. Consider spatial interaction from the point of view of your own life. Take an inventory of the food you consume in a day, noting, where possible, the location where each item of food was produced, bought, and consumed. Was the store where you bought the food part of a regional, national, or international chain? Where was the food processed? How far did it travel from point of production to the grocery store to your plate? How would you go about representing the journey your food travelled on a thematic map?

5. Describe, as exactly and concisely as possible, the site of your campus. Then describe its situation. Think of three reasons why the campus is sited and situated where it is. Would there be a better location in your community or further afield? If so, why?

6. Explain how map projections can influence our perception of the world. What sort of real-life consequences might a distorted perception produce?

7. **Figures 1.26–1.28** show examples of landscapes that have acquired a strong symbolic value because of the buildings, events, people, or histories with which they are associated. Find five photographs of landscapes that have strong symbolic value to a large number of citizens of your own region or country, and state in 25 words or less why each setting has acquired such value.

Log in to www.masteringgeography.com for MapMaster™ interactive maps, geography videos, RSS feeds, flashcards, weblinks, an eText version of *Human Geography: Places and Regions in Global Context,* and self-study quizzes to enhance your study of geography matters.

MapMaster™ presents 13 Place Name and 13 Layered Thematic interactive maps to help students practise and master their geographic literacy, spatial reasoning, and critical thinking skills.

2

THE CHANGING GLOBAL CONTEXT

Throughout April and May 2010, after lying dormant for nearly 200 years, Iceland's Eyjafjallajökull volcano erupted. The massive ash cloud from the eruption reached into the jet stream and quickly spread as far as Newfoundland in the west and China in the east. Because volcanic ash can damage jet engines, the cloud halted air traffic to, from, and within Europe and showed just how interdependent places and regions around the world have become. Over 100 000 flights were cancelled, stranding millions of passengers in airports from North America to Asia. Suddenly, the vulnerability of the highly interconnected world was exposed. Top military and political leaders were not exempt from the travel disruptions. General Stanley McChrystal, the commander of NATO forces in Afghanistan, had to take a 17-hour bus trip from Paris to Berlin to get to an important briefing. Angela Merkel, the German chancellor, was visiting San Francisco; to get back to her office in Berlin she had to fly to Rome via Portugal and then take a bulletproof limousine from Italy to Germany.

The disruptions went far deeper than travel inconveniences, though. Travel companies collapsed, time-sensitive pharmaceutical shipments were delayed or spoiled in airport warehouses, and car makers and electronics manufacturers that relied on just-in-time delivery of components had to halt assembly lines. Meanwhile, with most European airports closed, specialized fruit and vegetable farmers and flower growers in Africa, the Middle East, and the Caribbean were cut off from their markets. Kenya, for example, more than 8000 kilometres away from the Icelandic ash plume, normally ships about 850 tonnes of fresh produce to

Passengers wait for a flight inside El Prat de Llobregat Airport in Barcelona, Spain, after flights between Europe and North America were either delayed or cancelled due to a spreading cloud of volcanic ash stretching across much of the northern Atlantic. (*Source: Emilio Morenatti/AP Images*)

Europe every night. As soon as air traffic to Europe was halted, the flower farms that employ thousands of people began to lay off workers, and roses, lilies, and carnations wilted. Of no use to locals, most flowers were thrown into compost pits. Vegetables, such as baby corn, zucchini, broccoli, green beans, and carrots were also left to rot. Hundreds of thousands of labourers were laid off and the effects of the stalled horticultural industry—Kenya's leading hard currency earner—were felt throughout the country. On the other hand, New Zealand's salmon exporters enjoyed a boom as their northern European competitors could not supply the international markets.

Things quickly returned to normal when Eyjafjallajökull's activity subsided at the end of May. But the disruption that it had caused was a sharp reminder of the complexity of the world's geographies and the fact that, despite our increasing integration into a virtual world of information flows, geography still matters—and that it may well become more important than ever. In this chapter we take a long-term, big-picture look at changing human geographies, emphasizing the evolving interdependence among places and regions. We show how geographical divisions of labour have evolved with the growth of a worldwide system of trade and politics and with the changing opportunities provided by successive technology systems. As a result of this evolution, the world is now structured around a series of core regions, semiperipheral regions, and peripheral regions; and globalization seems to be intensifying, rather than diminishing, many of the differences among places and regions. ■

THE PREMODERN WORLD

The essential foundation for human geography is an ability to understand places and regions as components of a constantly changing global system. In this sense, all geography is historical geography. Built into every place and each region is the legacy of major changes in world geography. The world is an evolving, competitive, political–economic system that has developed through successive stages of geographic expansion and integration. This evolution has affected the roles of individual places in different ways. It has also affected the nature of the interdependence among places. This explains why places and regions have come to be distinctive and how this distinctiveness has formed the basis of geographic variability. To understand the sequence of major changes in world geography, we need to begin with the hearth areas of the first agricultural revolution.

Hearth Areas

The first agricultural revolution involved a transition from hunter-gatherer groups to agricultural-based minisystems that were both more extensive and more stable. A **minisystem** is a society with a *reciprocal* social economy. That is, each individual specializes in particular tasks (tending animals, cooking, or making pottery, for example) and shares any excess product with others. The recipients reciprocate in turn by giving up the surplus product of their own specialization. Such societies are found only in subsistence-based economies. Because they do not have (or need) an extensive physical infrastructure, minisystems are limited in geographic scale.

The transition to minisystems began in the Proto-Neolithic (or early Stone Age) period, between 9000 and 7000 B.C.E., and was based on a series of technological preconditions: the use of fire to process food, the use of grindstones to mill grains, and the development of improved tools to prepare and store food. Another important breakthrough was the domestication of cattle and sheep, a technique that had become established in a few regions by Neolithic times.

These agricultural breakthroughs could take place only in certain geographic settings: where natural food supplies were plentiful; where the terrain was diversified (thus offering a variety of habitats and species); where soils were rich and relatively easy to till; and where there was no need for large-scale irrigation or drainage. Archaeological evidence suggests that the breakthroughs took place independently in several agricultural hearth areas and that agricultural practices diffused slowly outward from each (**Figures 2.1** and **2.2**). **Hearth areas** are geographic settings where new practices have developed and from which they have spread. The main agricultural hearth areas were situated in four broad regions:

- *In the Middle East:* in the so-called Fertile Crescent between Anatolia and the Red Sea.
- *In South Asia:* along the floodplains of the Ganges, Brahmaputra, Indus, and Irawaddy rivers.
- *In China:* along the floodplain of the Huang He (Yellow) River.
- *In the Americas:* in Mesoamerica and along the western slopes of the Andes in South America.

The transition to food-producing minisystems had several important implications for the long-term evolution of the world's geographies:

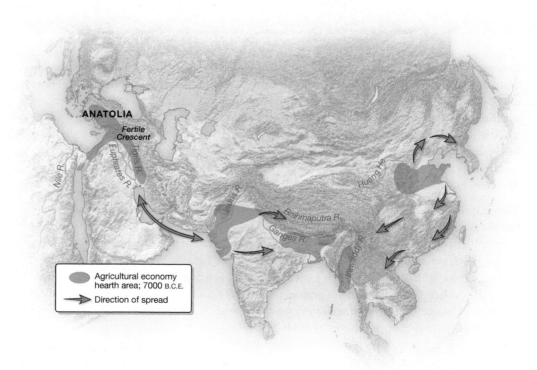

FIGURE 2.1 Old World hearth areas The first agricultural revolution took place independently in several hearth areas where hunter-gatherer communities began to experiment with locally available plants and animals in ways that eventually led to their domestication. From these hearth areas, improved strains of crops, domesticated animals, and new farming techniques diffused slowly outward. Farming supported larger populations than were possible with hunting and gathering, and the extra labour allowed the development of other specializations, such as pottery making and jewellery.

ANATOLIA
Fertile Crescent
Nile R.
Euphrates R.
Tigris R.
Indus R.
Ganges R.
Brahmaputra R.
Irawaddy R.
Huang He

Agricultural economy hearth area; 7000 B.C.E.
Direction of spread

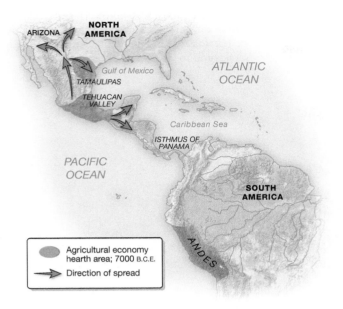

FIGURE 2.2 New World hearth areas The agricultural hearth areas in Central America eventually gave rise to the Aztec and Mayan world-empires; the hearth area of the Andes in South America developed into the Inca world-empire.

FIGURE 2.3 A remnant minisystem An Amazon tribal group, photographed in May 2008. Minisystems are rooted in subsistence-based social economies, organized around reciprocity. Each person specializes in certain tasks and freely gives any surplus to others, who in turn pass on their surplus. Today, few of the world's remnant minisystems are "pure," unaffected by contact with the rest of the world. This group is believed to be related to the Tano and Aruak tribes of the Peru–Brazil border region. Brazil's National Indian Foundation believes there may be as many as 68 "uncontacted" groups around Brazil, although only 24 have been officially confirmed. Anthropologists say almost all of these tribes know about Western civilization and have sporadic contact with prospectors, rubber tappers, and loggers but choose to turn their backs on civilization, usually because they have been attacked. *(Source: Ho Hew/Reuters)*

1. It allowed much higher population densities and encouraged the proliferation of settled villages.

2. It brought about a change in social organization, from loose communal systems to systems that were more highly organized on the basis of kinship. Kin groups provided a natural way of assigning rights over land and resources and of organizing patterns of land use.

3. It allowed some specialization in nonagricultural crafts, such as pottery, woven textiles, jewellery, and weaponry.

4. Specialization led to a fourth development: the beginnings of barter and trade between communities, sometimes over substantial distances.

Most minisystems vanished a long time ago, although some remnants have survived to provide a stark counterpoint to the landscapes and practices of the rest of the contemporary world. Examples of these residual and fast-disappearing minisystems are the bush people of the Kalahari, the hill tribes of Papua New Guinea, and the tribes of the Amazon rain forest (**Figure 2.3**).

APPLY YOUR KNOWLEDGE What makes it so difficult for the remaining minisystems to survive in the contemporary world? ∎

The Growth of Early Empires

The higher population densities, changes in social organization, craft production, and trade brought about by the first agricultural revolution provided the preconditions for the emergence of several world-empires. A **world-empire** is a group of minisystems that have been absorbed into a common political system while retaining their cultural differences. In world-empires, wealth flows from producer classes to more powerful elite classes in the form of tribute or taxes. This redistribution of wealth is most often achieved through military coercion, religious persuasion, or a combination of the two. The best-known world-empires are the largest and longest lasting of the ancient civilizations—Egypt, Greece, China, Byzantium, and Rome. These world-empires brought two important new elements to the evolution of the world's geographies: urbanization and colonization.

Urbanization emerged when towns and cities became essential centres of administration and tax collection, military garrisons, transportation hubs, and theological centres that helped the ruling classes hold their empires together. The most successful world-empires, such as the Greek and Roman, established quite extensive urban systems. In general, the settlements in these urban systems were not very large—typically ranging from a few thousand inhabitants to about 20 000. The seats of empire, however, could grow as large as 100 000 inhabitants (Athens) and even up to one million (Rome). The most impressive thing about these cities, though, was not so much their size as their degree of sophistication: elaborately laid out, with paved streets, piped water, sewage systems, massive monuments, grand public buildings, and impressive city walls.

The second important contribution of world-empires to evolving world geographies was **colonization**, the physical settlement in a new territory of people from a colonizing state. In part, colonization was an indirect consequence of the **law of diminishing returns.**

FIGURE 2.4 Terraced rice fields This photo shows rice cultivation on terraced fields in Guangxi province, China. The carefully maintained landscape is the legacy of a hydraulic empire. (*Source:* air/Fotolia)

This law refers to the tendency for productivity to decline with the continued application of capital and/or labour to a given resource base. In other words, for each additional person working the land, the gain in output per worker becomes smaller. Because of the law of diminishing returns, world-empires could support growing populations only by colonizing nearby land and thus enlarging their resource base. Such colonization immediately established uneven power relationships between dominant original areas of settlement and subordinate colonies. Other spatial consequences were the creation of settlement hierarchies and improved transportation networks. The military underpinnings of colonization also meant that new towns and cities became carefully sited for strategic and defensive reasons.

The legacy of these important changes is still apparent in many of today's landscapes. The clearest examples are in Europe, where the Roman world-empire colonized an extensive territory that was controlled through a highly developed system of towns and connecting roads. Most of today's important Western European cities had their origin as Roman settlements, and in quite a few we can trace the original Roman street layouts. In some it is still possible to glimpse remnants of Roman defensive city walls, paved streets, aqueducts, viaducts, arenas, sewage systems, baths, and public buildings. In the modern European countryside we can still read the legacy of the Roman world-empire in arrow-straight roads built by Roman engineers and maintained by successive generations. (See Box 2.1, "Visualizing Geography: The Legacy of World-Empires.")

These early world-empires were also significant in developing a lasting foundation of geographic knowledge. Greek scholars, for example, developed the idea that places embody fundamental relationships between people and the natural environment and that the study of geography provides the best way of understanding the interdependencies between places and between people and nature. The Greeks were also among the first to appreciate the practical importance and utility of geographic knowledge, not least in colonization, business, and trade. The word *geography* is in fact derived from the Greek language, the literal translation meaning "earth-writing" or "earth-describing." As Greek civilization developed,

descriptive geographical writing came to be an essential tool for recording information about sea and land routes and for preparing colonists and merchants for the challenges and opportunities of faraway places.

Several world-empires, for example Ancient Egypt, Sri Lanka, and the Maya and Inca empires were so-called **hydraulic empires**—states in which despotic rulers organized labour-intensive irrigation and drainage schemes that allowed for significant increases in agricultural productivity. Today, their legacy can still be seen in the landscapes of terraced fields that have been maintained for generations in such places as Sikkim, India; East Java, Indonesia; and Guangxi, China (**Figure 2.4**).

The Geography of the Premodern World

Figure 2.5 shows the generalized framework of human geographies in the Old World as they existed around 1400 C.E. The following characteristics of this period are important. First, harsher environments in continental interiors were still sparsely peopled by isolated, subsistence-level, kin-ordered hunting and gathering minisystems. Second, the dry belt of steppes and desert margins stretching across the Old World from the western Sahara to Mongolia was a continuous zone of kin-ordered pastoral minisystems. Third, areas with various forms of sedentary agricultural production formed a discontinuous arc from Morocco to China, with two main outliers: in the central Andes and in Mesoamerica. The dominant centres of global civilization were China, northern India (both of them hydraulic empires), and the Ottoman Empire of the eastern Mediterranean. They were all linked by the Silk Road, a series of overland trade routes between China and Mediterranean Europe (**Figure 2.6**). Other important world-empires were based in Southeast Asia, in Muslim city-states of coastal North Africa, in the grasslands of West Africa, around the gold and copper mines of East Africa, and in the feudal kingdoms and merchant towns of Europe.

Over time, all of these more developed realms were interconnected through trade, which meant that several emerging centres of capitalism came into existence. **Capitalism** is a form of economic

The Legacy of World-Empires

Long after imperial systems have collapsed, their physical remains survive in today's landscape. Ancient roads, along with ruined defensive systems, cities, walls, and aqueducts provide some of the tangible signs that these places were once part of a previous economic and political system.

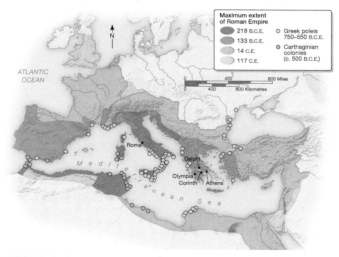

(c) This spectacular aqueduct was built in the time of Augustus (63 B.C.E. to 14 C.E.) to supply the city of Nîmes, a thriving Roman provincial capital in southern France, with water from Uzès, 50 kilometres away. The water dropped only 17 metres over the whole distance. (*Source:* Elena Elisseeva/Shutterstock)

FIGURE 2.A **The premodern world** (a) Greek colonies and the extent of the Roman empire. This map shows the distribution of the Greek poleis (city-states) and Carthaginian colonies and the spread of the Roman empire from 218 B.C.E. to 117 C.E. (*Source:* Adapted from R. King et al., *The Mediterranean*. London: Arnold, 1977, pp. 59 and 64.)

(d) Hadrian's Wall, a Roman defensive barrier built during the reign of emperor Hadrian to guard the northern frontier of the province of Britain. Completed in 136 C.E., it extended almost 120 kilometres from the eastern coast to the western coast of northern England with an original height of 6 metres, a thickness of 2.5 metres, and a parallel ditch. The wall was protected by a series of small forts, but it was abandoned in 383 C.E. after several incursions by northern tribes. (*Source:* Martyn Unsworth/Getty Images)

(b) The Roman world-empire relied on a highly developed infrastructure of roads, settlements, and utilities. Many of the roads that were built by Romans became established as major routes throughout Europe. Wherever they could, Roman surveyors laid out roads in straight lines. This photo shows part of a Roman road that crosses the moorlands across Blackstone Edge in Northern England. (*Source:* Robert Estall photo agency/Alamy)

(e) Known as the "abandoned city of the Mughals," Fatephur Sikri was built in the 1540s to serve a Muslim kingdom after the invasion of Central India. It was abandoned after only 14 years because of a lack of nearby water. (*Source:* Alan Nash)

and social organization characterized by the profit motive and the control of the means of production, distribution, and exchange of goods by private ownership. Port cities were particularly important to the development of capitalism. Among the leading centres were the city-state of Venice, the Hanseatic League of independent city-states in northwestern Europe (including Antwerp, Hamburg, and Stockholm), as well as Cairo, Calicut, Canton, and Malacca in North Africa and Asia. Traders in these port cities began to organize the production of agricultural specialties, textiles, and craft products in their respective hinterlands. The **hinterland** of a town

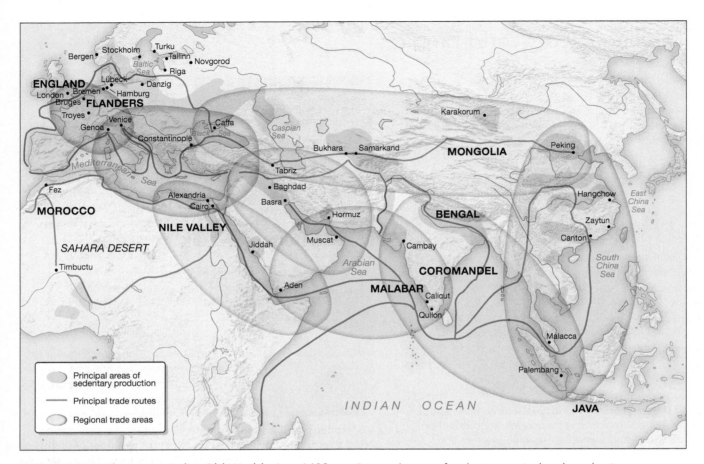

FIGURE 2.5 The precapitalist Old World, circa 1400 C.E. Principal areas of sedentary agricultural production are shaded. Some long-distance trade took place from one region to another, but for the most part it was limited to a series of overlapping regional circuits of trade. (*Source:* Adapted from R. Peet, *Global Capitalism: Theories of Societal Development.* New York: Routledge, 1991; J. Abu-Lughod, *Before European Hegemony: The World-System A.D. 1200–1350.* New York: Oxford University Press, 1989; and E. R. Wolf, *Europe and the People Without History.* Berkeley: University of California Press, 1983.)

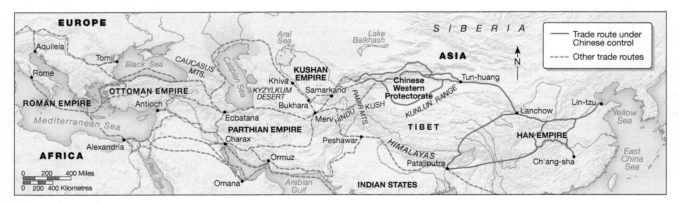

FIGURE 2.6 The Silk Road This map shows the trade routes of the Silk Road as they existed between 112 B.C.E. and 100 C.E. From Roman times until Portuguese navigators found their way around Africa and established seaborne trade routes, the Silk Road provided the main East–West trade route between Europe and China. This shifting trail of caravan tracks facilitated the exchange of silk, spices, and porcelain from the East and gold, precious stones, and Venetian glass from the West. The ancient cities of Samarkand, Bukhara, and Khiva stood along the Silk Road, places of glory and wealth that astonished Western travellers, such as Marco Polo in the thirteenth century. These cities were East–West meeting places for philosophy, knowledge, and religion, and in their prime they were known for producing scholars in mathematics, music, architecture, and astronomy. The cities' prosperity was marked by impressive feats of Islamic architecture.

or city is its sphere of economic influence—the tributary area from which it collects products for export and throughout which it distributes imports.

> **APPLY YOUR KNOWLEDGE** Explain how the "law of diminishing returns" contributed to the colonization of new territories by the Roman empire. Describe how such colonization was linked to urbanization. ■

AN INTERDEPENDENT WORLD GEOGRAPHY

When exploration beyond European shores began to open up new opportunities for trade and economic expansion, a modern world-system emerged. A **world-system** is an *interdependent* system of countries linked by political and economic competition. The hyphenation in the term *world-system,* which was coined by historian Immanuel Wallerstein in the 1970s, is meant to emphasize the interdependence of places and regions around the world: they are all part of a system in which every place or region reacts to changes occurring in another.

By the sixteenth century, new techniques of shipbuilding and navigation had begun to bind more and more places and regions together through trade and political competition. Their different resources, social structures, and cultural systems resulted in quite different pathways of development, however. Some societies were incorporated into the new, European-based international economic system faster than others; some resisted incorporation; and some sought alternative systems of economic and political organization. Australia and New Zealand, for example, were discovered by Europeans only in the late eighteenth century and were barely penetrated, if at all, by the European world-system until the mid-nineteenth century. Regions not yet absorbed into the world-system are called **external arenas**.

With the emergence of this modern world-system at the beginning of the sixteenth century, a whole new geography began to emerge. Although several regions of budding capitalist production existed, and although imperial China could boast of sophisticated achievements in science, technology, and navigation, it was European merchant capitalism that reshaped the world. Several factors motivated European overseas expansion. A relatively high-density population and a limited amount of cultivable land meant that it was a continuous struggle to provide enough food. Meanwhile, the desire for overseas expansion was intensified both by competition among a large number of small monarchies and by inheritance laws that produced large numbers of impoverished aristocrats with little or no land of their own. Many of these landless nobles were eager to set out for adventure and profit.

Added to these motivating factors were the enabling factors of innovations in shipbuilding, navigation, and gunnery. In the mid-1400s, for example, the Portuguese developed a cannon-armed ship—the caravel—that could sail anywhere, defend itself against pirates, pose a threat to those who were initially unwilling to trade, and carry enough goods to be profitable. Naval power enabled the Portuguese and the Spanish to enrich their economies with gold and

FIGURE 2.7 **Champlain's astrolabe** This astrolabe allowed French explorers to determine their latitude by measuring the noon altitude of the sun. Lost by Champlain soon after he set out through the Ottawa Valley, it was recovered in the nineteenth century and is now on exhibit in the Canadian Museum of Civilization in Gatineau, Quebec. (*Source:* Canadian Museum of Civilization, 989.56.1, photo Harry Foster, S94-37062)

silver capital plundered from the Americas. The quadrant (1450) and the astrolabe (1480) enabled accurate navigation and mapping of ocean currents, prevailing winds, and trade routes (**Figure 2.7**). With their new technology, Europeans embarked on a succession of voyages of discovery, seeking out new products and new markets. (See Box 2.2, "Geography Matters: Geography and Exploration.")

Equipped with better maps and navigation techniques, Europeans were able not only to send adventurers overseas for gold and silver, but also to commandeer land and exploit coerced labour to produce high-value crops (such as sugar, cocoa, tobacco, cotton, and indigo) on **plantations**, large landholdings that specialized in the production of one particular crop for markets back in Europe (**Figure 2.8**). Only those regions whose populations were resistant to European disease and which also had high population densities, a good resource base, and strong governments were able to keep Europeans at arm's length. For the most part, these regions were in South and East Asia. Their dealings with Europeans were conducted through a series of coastal trading stations. Textiles were an important commodity in this exchange; to this day, the English language preserves how geographically extensive the textile trade was:

> The word *satin* comes from the name of an unknown city in China that Arab traders called Zaitun. *Khaki* is the Hindi word for dusty. The word *calico* comes from India's southwestern coastal city of Calicut; *chintz*, from the Hindi name for a printed calico; *cashmere*, from the region of Kashmir. *Percale* comes from the Farsi word *pargalah*. Another Farsi derivative is *seersucker*, whose bands of alternating smooth and puckered fabric prompted a name that literally means milk and sugar. Still another Farsi borrowing is *taffeta*, which comes from the Farsi for "spun." The coarse cloth we call *muslin* is named for Mosul—the town in Iraq—whereas *damask* is a short form of Damascus. Finally, cotton takes its name from *qutun*, the Arabic name of the fiber.[1]

[1]B. Wallach, *Understanding the Cultural Landscape.* New York: Guilford Press, 2005, p. 148.

Geography and Exploration

In the early fifteenth century, the Portuguese began to explore the Atlantic and the coast of Africa, at the same time improving methods of navigation and cartography. **Figure 2.B** shows the key European voyages of discovery. Portuguese explorer Bartholomeu Dias reached the Cape of Good Hope (the southern tip of Africa) in 1488. Ten years later, Vasco da Gama reached India; two years after that, Pedro Cabral crossed the Atlantic from Portugal to Brazil. A small fleet of Portuguese ships reached China in 1513, and the first circumnavigation of the globe was completed in 1522 by Juan Sebastián del Cano, a survivor of the expedition originally led by Portuguese navigator Fernando de Magellan in 1519 (**Figure 2.C**). Portuguese successes inspired other countries to attempt their own voyages of discovery. For instance, in 1492, Christopher Columbus sailed to Hispaniola (the island that is now Haiti and the Dominican Republic) under the sponsorship of the Spanish monarchy. These explorations led to an invaluable body of knowledge about ocean currents, wind patterns, coastlines, peoples, and resources, which in turn helped Europeans establish dominance

FIGURE 2.C Departure from Lisbon for Brazil, the East Indies, and America (*Source:* Illustration from *Americae Tertia Pars...*', 1592 (engraving), Bry, Theodore de (1528-98)/Service Historique de la Marine, Vincennes, France Giraudon/The Bridgeman Art Library)

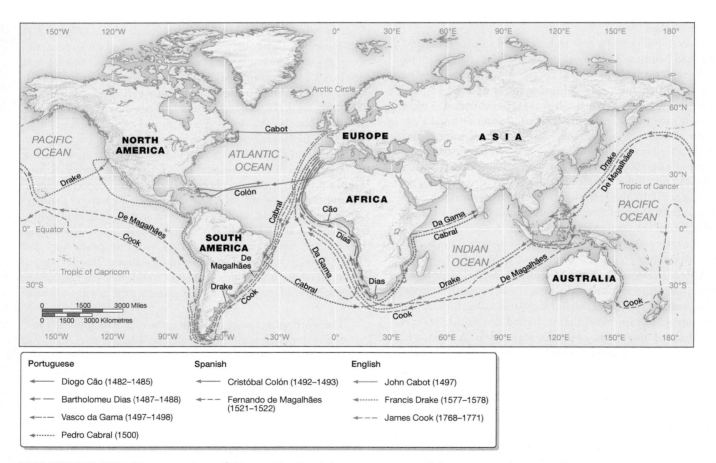

Portuguese
- ⟵ Diogo Cão (1482–1485)
- ⟵-- Bartholomeu Dias (1487–1488)
- ⟵--- Vasco da Gama (1497–1498)
- ⟵······ Pedro Cabral (1500)

Spanish
- ⟵ Cristóbal Colón (1492–1493)
- ⟵--- Fernando de Magalhães (1521–1522)

English
- ⟵ John Cabot (1497)
- ⟵········ Francis Drake (1577–1578)
- ⟵--- James Cook (1768–1771)

FIGURE 2.B The European Age of Discovery The European voyages of discovery can be traced to Portugal's Prince Henry the Navigator (1394–1460), who set up a school of navigation and financed numerous expeditions with the objective of circumnavigating Africa in order to establish a profitable sea route for spices from India. The knowledge of winds, ocean currents, natural harbours, and watering places built up by Henry's captains was an essential foundation for the subsequent voyages of Columbus, da Gama, de Magellan, and others. The end of the European Age of Discovery was marked by Captain James Cook's voyages to the Pacific in the 1770s.

over the newly "discovered" parts of the world. Barred from access to more southerly parts of America by prior Portuguese and Spanish claims, French and British explorations focused instead on the land that became known as Canada and based their initial routes on earlier information about the rich fishing grounds known to lie off its shores. (See Chapter 4.)

Geographical knowledge acquired during this Age of Discovery was crucial to the expansion of European political and economic power in the sixteenth century. In European societies that were becoming more commercially oriented and profit conscious, geographical knowledge became a valuable commodity in itself. Information about regions and places was a first step toward controlling and influencing them, and this in turn was an important step toward amassing wealth and power. As the New World was being affected by European colonists, missionaries, and adventurers, the countries of the Old World found themselves pitched into competition with one another for overseas resources. Meanwhile, new crops, such as corn and potatoes, introduced to Europe from the New World, profoundly affected local economies and ways of life.

The growth of a commercial world economy meant that cartography and geographical writing became essential for knowing about other places. Navigation, political boundaries, property rights, and rights of movement all hinged on accurate, impartial, and reliable record keeping. Success in commerce depended on how clearly and reliably geographical writings described the opportunities and dangers presented by one region or another. International rivalries required sophisticated understandings of the relationships among nations, regions, and places. In short, geographical information became a key area of knowledge and a foundation of power. The historical period in Europe known as the Renaissance (from the mid-fourteenth to the mid-seventeenth centuries) saw an explosion of systematic mapmaking and the development of new map projections (see Chapter 1) and geographical descriptions. Throughout the seventeenth and eighteenth centuries, the body of geographic knowledge increased steadily as Europeans explored and mapped more and more of the world, using increasingly sophisticated techniques of survey and measurement.

Within Europe, meanwhile, innovations in business and finance (banking, loan systems, credit transfers, commercial insurance, and courier services, for example) helped increase savings, investment, and commercial activity. European merchants and manufacturers also became adept at **import substitution**—copying and making goods previously available only by trading. The result was the emergence of Western Europe as the core region of a world-system that was penetrating and incorporating significant portions of the rest of the world.

In Europe itself, this overseas expansion stimulated further improvements in marine technology, including nautical mapmaking, naval artillery, and shipbuilding. The whole experience of overseas expansion also provided a great practical school for commercial entrepreneurship, investment, and long-distance trade. In this way, the self-propelling growth of European merchant capitalism was further intensified and consolidated.

For the periphery, European overseas expansion meant dependency (as it has ever since for many of the world's peripheral

FIGURE 2.8 Cotton plantation
Plantation agriculture dominated the many territories acquired by European settlers. This lithograph, dated 1884, shows a cotton plantation on the Mississippi River. Most of the slave-cotton grown on American plantations was destined for the cloth industry in Manchester and other British cities. (*Source: Archive Images/Alamy Limited*)

FIGURE 2.9 Merchant vessels of the Dutch and English East India Companies The English East India Company was established in 1600 as a monopolistic trading company and agent of British imperialism in India. In response, the Dutch East India Company was founded in 1602 to protect Dutch trading interests in the Far East. It was granted a trade monopoly in the waters of the Indian and Pacific Oceans, together with the rights to conclude treaties with local rulers, to build forts and maintain armed forces, and to carry on administrative functions through officials who were required to take an oath of loyalty to the Dutch government. The company was almost a branch of the government and thus illustrates how interwoven political imperialism and economic expansionism were. For the next two centuries, the Dutch East India Company remained the world's largest company.
(*Source:* Harper Collins Publishers/The Art Archive at Art Resource, NY)

regions). At worst, territory was forcibly occupied and labour systematically exploited. At best, local traders were displaced by Europeans, who imposed their own terms of economic exchange (**Figure 2.9**). Europeans soon destroyed most of the Muslim shipping trade in the Indian Ocean, for example, and went on to capture

a large share of the oceangoing trade *within* Asia, selling Japanese copper to China and India, Persian carpets to India, Indian cotton textiles to Japan, and so on.

As revolutionary as these changes were, however, they ultimately were constrained by a technology that rested on wind and water power, on wooden ships and structures, and on wood for fuel. Mills, for example, were built of wood and powered by water or wind. They could generate only modest amounts of power and only at sites determined by physical geography, not human choice. Within the relatively small European landmass, wood for construction and fuel competed with food, animal feed, and textile fibres for the available acreage. More critical, however, was the size and strength of timber, which imposed structural limits on the size of buildings, the diameter of waterwheels, the span of bridges, and so on. In particular, it imposed limits on the size and design of ships (especially their masts), which in turn imposed limits on the volume and velocity of overseas trade. Overland transportation was similarly limited by the expense and relative inefficiency of horse- or ox-drawn wagons and particularly by the absence of a road network. This meant that for a long time the European world-system could penetrate into continental interiors only along waterways.

The Early Integration of Canada into the World-System

Canada provides a good illustration of this importance of waterways for early European access to peripheral regions. Basque whalers from northeastern Spain were probably the first Europeans to exploit this country's natural resources on a regular basis. In their whaling stations on the lower St. Lawrence (such as the one at Red Bay in Labrador, established in the 1540s and recreated in the Canadian Museum of Civilization in Gatineau, Quebec), whales were rendered into lamp oil and candle wax for the European market (**Figure 2.10**). From the early sixteenth century onward, French, Portuguese, and Basque fishing ships took increasingly large quantities of cod from the Grand Banks off Newfoundland and Labrador. Initially only a summer undertaking from Europe, by the 1680s French and British fishing crews overwintered on the

FIGURE 2.10 Red Bay, Labrador Archaeologists have found that this camp provided shelter for the production of whale oil and summer accommodation for the small Basque crews engaged in whaling in the 1540s.
(*Source:* Courtesy of Alan E. Nash)

FIGURE 2.11 Moose Factory From its bases, such as this one at Moose Factory, the Hudson's Bay Company tapped the wealth of Rupert's Land and shipped furs out through northern waters to England.

(*Source:* Courtesy of Alan E. Nash)

coasts of Newfoundland and Labrador. Occasional exchanges of goods between sailors and Aboriginal groups led to the beginnings of the fur trade. By the eighteenth century, Canada had thus become a peripheral region in the modern world-system.

The subsequent development of an almost insatiable European market for Canadian furs lured itinerant French traders farther up the St. Lawrence and into the Great Lakes by the late seventeenth century to exploit the animal resources of those vast watersheds. An alternative method of fur trading was practised by the British. Using permanent bases (or "factories," such as Moose Factory), the Hudson's Bay Company established a fur trade network in the huge territory of Rupert's Land (encompassing the Hudson's Bay drainage basin), which it had been granted by the Crown in 1670 (**Figure 2.11**).

In both cases, the real profits from the fur trade were realized in Europe, where furs were made into hats and garments. The Hudson's Bay Company was headquartered in London, where political and financial control over its Canadian resources was exercised. Only in the case of Montreal, where individual French traders based themselves and where the rival North West Company had its centre of operations from the 1780s to the 1820s, do we find any substantial profits from the fur trade being retained in Canada. Such merchant capital enabled the growth of Montreal's early business elite, which expressed itself in the mansions and built form of the city. That elite then invested in the early development of railroads in the Montreal region to profit from the encouragement of local trade and agriculture.

After 300 years of evolution, roughly between 1450 and 1750, the world-system had thus incorporated mainly those parts of the world that were relatively accessible by water: Mediterranean North Africa, Portuguese and Spanish colonies in the Americas, Indian ports and trading colonies (**Figure 2.12**), the East Indies, African

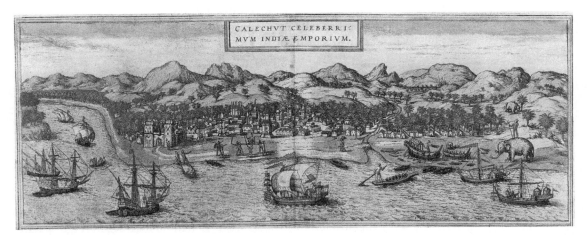

FIGURE 2.12 British, Portuguese, French, and Dutch ships in the harbour at Kolkata (Calcutta), India, around 1600 The expansion of European trade and the protection of trade routes required strong navies and a willingness to use them. English explorer Sir Walter Raleigh expressed the sentiment succinctly in 1608: "Whoever commands the sea, commands the trade of the world; whosoever commands the trade of the world, commands the riches of the world." (*Source:* The New York Public Library)

and Chinese ports, the Greater Caribbean, and eastern North America. The rest of the world functioned more or less as before, with slow-changing geographies based around modified minisystems and world-empires that were only partially and intermittently penetrated by market trading. This changed dramatically with the advent of industrialization in Europe and its associated technological advances, which gave Europe (and later the entire core) the power to rise to global dominance in both economic and political terms.

> **APPLY YOUR KNOWLEDGE** Search the Internet to find a map of Canada in the 1700s as well as a current map of Canada. How would you interpret the historical map in terms of the world-system of the time? How has it changed over time? ∎

Core and Periphery in the Modern World-System

With the new production and transportation technologies of the Industrial Revolution (from the late 1700s), capitalism truly became a global system that reached into virtually every part of the inhabited world and into virtually every aspect of people's lives. It is important to recognize that the Industrial Revolution was really an extended transition to new forms of organization and new technologies and that its effects were uneven, reflecting the influence of principles of spatial organization. In Europe, the cradle of the Industrial Revolution, it took the best part of a century for industrialization to work its way across European landscapes, with very different outcomes for different regions. (See Box 2.3, "Geography Matters: The Diffusion of Industrialization in Europe.")

Human geographies were recast again, this time with a more interdependent dynamic. New production technologies, based on more efficient energy sources, helped raise levels of productivity and create new and better products that stimulated demand, increased profits, and created a pool of capital for further investment. New transportation technologies triggered successive phases of geographic expansion, allowing for internal development as well as for external colonization and **imperialism** (the deliberate exercise of military power and economic influence by powerful states in order to advance and secure their national interests—see Chapter 9).

Since the seventeenth century, the world-system has been consolidated, with stronger economic ties among countries. It has also been extended, with all the world's countries eventually becoming involved to some extent in the interdependence of the capitalist system. Although there have been some instances of resistance and adaptation, the overall result is that a highly structured relationship between places and regions has emerged. This relationship is organized around three tiers: *core, semiperipheral,* and *peripheral* regions. These broad geographic divisions have evolved—and are still evolving—through a combination of processes of private economic competition and competition among states.

The **core regions** of the world-system at any given time are those that dominate trade, control the most advanced technologies, and have high levels of productivity within diversified economies. As a result, they enjoy relatively high per capita incomes. The first core regions of the world-system were the trading hubs of Holland and England,

joined soon afterward by France. But the continuing success of core regions depends on their dominance and exploitation of other regions. This dominance in turn depends on the participation of these other regions within the world-system. Initially, such participation was achieved by military enforcement, then by European colonialism.

Colonialism involves the establishment and maintenance of political and legal domination by a state over a separate and alien society. This domination usually involves some colonization (that is, the physical settlement of people from the colonizing state) and always results in economic exploitation by the colonizing state. After World War II, the sheer economic and political influence of the core regions was sufficient to maintain their dominance without direct political and legal control, and colonialism was gradually phased out.

Weaker regions that have remained economically and politically unsuccessful throughout this process of incorporation into the world-system are called peripheral. **Peripheral regions** are characterized by dependent and disadvantageous trading relationships, obsolete technologies, and undeveloped or narrowly specialized economies with low levels of productivity. As a result, their per capita incomes are low.

Transitional between core regions and peripheral regions are semiperipheral regions. **Semiperipheral regions** are able to exploit peripheral regions but are themselves exploited and dominated by core regions. They consist mostly of countries that were once peripheral. The existence of this semiperipheral category underlines the dynamic nature of the world-system: neither peripheral status nor core status is necessarily permanent. Canada, the United States, and Japan all achieved core status after having been peripheral. Spain and Portugal, both part of the original core in the sixteenth century, became semiperipheral in the nineteenth century but are now once more part of the core. Quite a few countries, including Brazil, India, Mexico, South Korea, and Taiwan, have become semiperipheral after first having been incorporated into the periphery of the world-system and then developing a successful manufacturing sector that moved them into semiperipheral status.

An important determinant of these changes in status is the effectiveness of states in ensuring the international competitiveness of their domestic producers. They can do this in several ways: by manipulating markets (protecting domestic manufacturers by charging taxes on imports, for example); by regulating their economies (enacting laws that help establish stable labour markets, for example); and by creating physical and social infrastructures (spending public funds on road systems, ports, educational systems, and so on). Because some states are more successful than others in pursuing these strategies, the hierarchy of three geographical tiers is not rigid. Rather, it is fluid, providing a continually changing framework for geographical transformation within individual places and regions.

So far, we have talked about core, peripheral, and semiperipheral regions mainly by looking at entire countries, and we have treated them as uniform, homogeneous areas. However, they are not. The same types of economic, political, social, and cultural processes that have created and that sustain core regions at a global level also operate at regional and local scales (**Figure 2.13**). The "global core," if we look at it more closely, is itself made up of a number of *regional cores, semiperipheries,* and *peripheries.* For example, Canada, a rich industrialized country, is undoubtedly part of the global core. However, we know that not all of Canada's provinces and territories share uniformly in this prosperity. In fact, this

The Industrial Revolution began in England toward the end of the eighteenth century and eventually resulted not only in the complete reorganization of the geography of the original European core of the world-system but also in an extension of the world-system core to the United States and Japan.

In Europe, three distinctive waves of industrialization occurred. The first, between about 1790 and 1850, was based on the initial cluster of industrial technologies (steam engines, cotton textiles, and ironworking) and was very localized (**Figure 2.D**). It was limited to a few regions in Britain where industrial entrepreneurs and workforces had first exploited key innovations and the availability of key resources (coal, iron ore, water). Although these regions shared the common impetus of certain key innovations, each of them retained its own technological traditions and industrial style. From the start, then, industrialization was a regional-scale phenomenon.

The second wave of industrialization, between about 1850 and 1870, involved the diffusion of industrialization to most of the rest of Britain and to parts of northwest Europe, particularly the coalfields of northern France, Belgium, and Germany (Figure 2.D). This second wave also brought a certain amount of reorganization to the first-wave industrial regions as new technologies (steel, machine tools, railroads, steamships) brought new opportunities, new locational requirements, new business structures, and new forms of societal organization. Railroads and steamships made more places accessible, bringing their resources and their markets into the sphere of industrialization. These new activities brought some significant changes to the logic of industrial location.

The importance of railway networks, for example, attracted industry away from smaller towns on the canal systems toward larger towns with good rail connections. The importance of steamships for coastal and international trade attracted industry to larger ports. At the same time, the importance of steel produced concentrations of heavy industry in places that had nearby supplies of coal, iron ore, and limestone. The scale of industry increased as improved technologies and transportation made larger markets accessible to firms. Local, family firms became small companies that were regional in scope. Small companies grew to become powerful firms serving national markets. Specialized business, legal, and financial services emerged within larger cities. The growth of new occupations transformed the structure of social classes, and this transformation in turn was reflected in the politics and landscapes of industrial regions.

The third wave of industrialization, between 1870 and 1914, saw a further reorganization of the geography of Europe as new technologies such as electricity and telecommunications imposed different needs and created new opportunities. During this period,

FIGURE 2.D The spread of industrialization in Europe
European industrialization began with the emergence of small industrial regions in several parts of Britain, where early industrialization drew on local mineral resources, water power, and nascent industrial technologies. As new rounds of technologies emerged, industrialization spread to other regions with the right locational attributes: access to raw materials and energy sources, good communications, and large labour markets.

industrialization spread for the first time to more southern, eastern, and northern parts of Europe, as Figure 2.D illustrates. Up to the end of World War I, however, the core of European (and indeed global) prosperity remained centred on the "Golden Triangle" stretching between London, Paris, and Berlin.

FIGURE 2.13 A simplified model of the world-system The arrows indicate the various economic, political, military, and cultural means used by cores to dominate their peripheries. The diagram illustrates how the world-system is made up of a nested set of cores and peripheries.

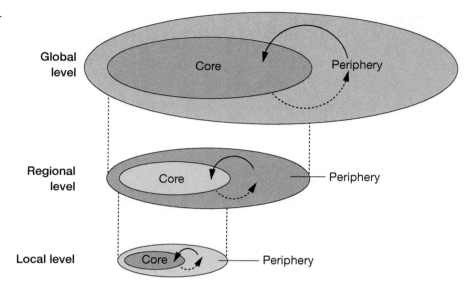

country could be divided into at least one heartland and several hinterlands, as many Canadian geographers have come to call the regional cores and peripheries within this country.

Similarly, regional cores are made up of *local cores* and *peripheries,* the result of more local processes of development. The city of Toronto, for example, as a whole represents a highly developed region within the "heartland" of southern Ontario, but there are relatively wealthier and poorer sections, including those with widespread homelessness: in 2013, shelter statistics showed that on average almost 4000 Torontonians stayed in homeless shelters every night. We will be considering these regional and local levels in greater detail in later chapters (especially in Chapters 7 and 10). The important point to understand here is that the world-system is not made up of a few homogeneous regions. It is much more geographically varied than that. In fact, it is made up of a nested set of cores, semiperipheries, and peripheries at different scales of analysis.

We also need to understand that in certain cases—and Canada is one of them—a region can be simultaneously part of the global core and semiperiphery. Canada has a GDP and standard of living that places it in the global core. Canadian-owned businesses and banks make substantial profits from investments overseas, especially in the Caribbean periphery. Yet, at the same time, we recognize characteristics of the semiperiphery: large parts of the Canadian economy are American-owned, and Canada's political and economic influence over the behemoth to its south is negligible. Canada's dual position helps us understand the difficulties a middle power faces on the world scene.

Because the world-system model is so useful in understanding the human geography of the world, it is well worth summarizing its most important features here.

- The world-system model states that the world can be divided into a series of cores, semiperipheries, and peripheries.

- In dividing the world in this way, we are using a relative concept of space, based on a socioeconomic measure of distance. (See Chapter 1.)

- The global core maintains its dominance through the exercise of the economic, political, military, and cultural forces at its disposal.

- The core also maintains its dominance through environmental and ecological means. For example, the introduction of European crops and animals overseas itself became an instrument of imperialism, and genetic modification is increasingly enabling Western agribusiness corporations to control the seed supply of cash crops grown in the periphery.

- The global periphery is kept in a dependent position by the global core. Some experts have even suggested that the core actively "undevelops" the periphery; others point out how space is, in at least an economic or social sense, *created* in the first place by these interplays between the core and the periphery.

- The global core and periphery have changed their locations over time.

- The world-system is made up of a nested series of cores and peripheries. In this, we see another of the concepts that we examined in Chapter 1, the concept of scale. In this way, local developments are transmitted to the regional and global levels, and the forces of globalization manifest themselves at the local level.

VIRTUAL GEOGRAPHIES

Recently, the acronym BRICS has been used to denote a grouping of countries that is similar to the semiperipheral category we use in this book. The letters stand for Brazil, Russia, India, China, and (since 2010) South Africa, some of the largest emerging economies, which are expected to surpass the economies of the current core countries by 2050. Its leaders now meet at annual summits to discuss common strategies for economic development that foster their own interests, rather than those of the core countries. The BRICS category shows the power of the written word to *create* reality, rather than merely describe it: the term BRIC was first used as a theoretical construct in a paper written by an economist in 2001, years before the group actually constituted itself in 2009.

The colonization and imperialism that accompanied the expansion of the world-system was closely tied to the evolution of world leadership cycles. **Leadership cycles** are periods of international power established by individual states through economic, political, and military competition. In the long term, success in the world-system depends on economic strength and competitiveness, which brings political influence and pays for military strength. With a combination of economic, political, and military power, individual states can dominate the world-system, setting the terms for many economic and cultural practices and imposing their particular ideology by virtue of their pre-eminence. The modern world-system has so far experienced several distinct leadership cycles. In much simplified terms, they have involved dominance by Portugal and Spain (for most of the sixteenth century), the Netherlands (for the first three-quarters of the seventeenth century), Great Britain (from the early eighteenth century through the early twentieth century), and the United States (from the 1950s). (See Chapter 9.)

This kind of dominance is known as hegemony. **Hegemony** refers to domination over the world economy, exercised—through a combination of economic, military, financial, and cultural means—by one national state in a particular historical epoch. Over the long run, the costs of maintaining this kind of power and influence tend to weaken the hegemon. This phase of the cycle, when the dominant nation is weakened, is known as *imperial overstretch*. It is followed by another period of competitive struggle, which brings the possibility of a new dominant world power.

For instance, since 2000, China has been mounting an increasingly serious challenge to American financial and economic dominance, just when America's decade-long military engagement in Iraq and Afghanistan was causing what many analysts see as a prime example of imperial overstretch. Since 2013, China has been aggressively extending this challenge to the political and military arenas as well, exemplified by the dispute over the Senkaku/Diaoyu islands. Most analysts now predict that China will become the next hegemon by mid-century.

> **APPLY YOUR KNOWLEDGE** Can a country "leave" the world-system and pursue its own path? What sort of obstacles and difficulties would this country face? ■

Canada: from Periphery to Semiperiphery

By the end of the nineteenth century, the core of the world-system had expanded to include parts of North America. Its vast natural resources of land and minerals provided the raw materials for a wide range of industries that could grow and organize without being hemmed in and fragmented too much by political boundaries. Its population, growing quickly through immigration, provided a large and expanding market and a cheap and flexible labour force. Its cultural and trading links with Europe provided business contacts, technological know-how, and access to capital for investment in a basic infrastructure of canals, railways, docks, warehouses, and factories.

As in Europe, industrialization developed around pre-existing centres of industrialization and population and was shaped by the resource needs and market opportunities of successive technology systems. North American industrial strength was established at the beginning of the twentieth century with the development of a new technology system that included the internal combustion engine, oil and plastics, electrical engineering, and radio and telecommunications. (See Chapter 7.) The outcome was a distinctive economic core south of the Great Lakes with an extensive periphery surrounding it (**Figure 2.14**).

By 1900, Canada had moved from peripheral to semiperipheral status on a world scale. Since Confederation in 1867, Canada was, nominally at least, in charge of its own affairs, but the increasing involvement of U.S. financial interests in Canada's economy was causing another change: Canada was shifting from being dependent on Britain to being dependent on the U.S. regional core. In 1900, for example, U.S. capital represented 15 percent of all foreign investment in Canada; by 1920, it totalled more than 50 percent.

Nineteenth-century developments were greatly aided by British and American investments in Canada's rail system and by the implementation of Canada's *National Policy* of 1879. This policy promoted the completion of a transcontinental rail link to tie the country together, encouraged immigration to the Prairies, and introduced tariffs to protect Canadian industry from cheaper American manufacturers. As a result, industrialization (which had begun by the 1850s) gathered pace, and by 1900 small manufacturing belts lay between Niagara (where hydropower was already in use) and Toronto, in the Montreal region, and around the Cape Breton coalfields of Nova Scotia.

To the existing Canadian exports of fish and furs, the nineteenth century added the development of a significant timber trade in Quebec and Ontario, the export of wheat from the Prairies to European markets, and, by the 1920s, the beginnings of pulp and paper production in British Columbia for American markets. After 1945, the development of northern mining sites and Alberta's substantial reserves of oil and gas meant that Canada's post-war economy continued to depend on the exploitation of its natural resources, or *staples*, for sale abroad.

One danger of this was the **staples trap**, an over reliance on the export of staples (such as fur, fish, timber, grain, and oil) that leaves an economy (national or regional) vulnerable to fluctuations in world prices and without alternatives when resource depletion occurs. Another problem was the paradox of how such high levels of staples exports could result in such low levels of economic growth in Canada itself. This question prompted scholars, such as Harold Innis (1894–1952), to develop the staples thesis—50 years before Immanuel Wallerstein advanced his more general world-system model. The **staples thesis** argues that the export of Canada's natural resources, or staples, to more advanced economies has delayed the development of this country's economic, political, and social systems: the value added in the subsequent manufacture of products derived from those staples (and the profits realized) accrued not to this country but to the manufacturers in Britain and the United States.

In this view, Canadian industry was stultified because it was cheaper and easier to export raw materials and to use that income to import manufactured items from Britain and the United States. Escape from this over reliance on the export of basic commodities would have required the establishment of locally owned factories

FIGURE 2.14 The North American core and periphery, 1911

(*Source:* Based on L. McCann and A. Gunn, *Heartland and Hinterland: A Regional Geography of Canada.* Scarborough: Prentice-Hall, 1998.)

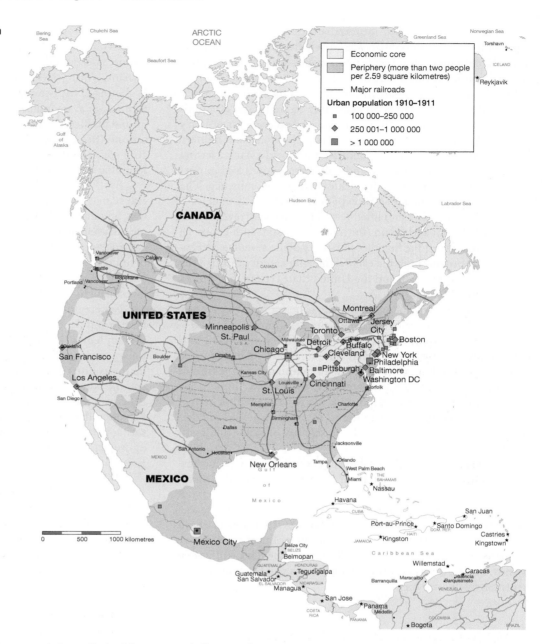

and a widely diversified industry. But finance capital was limited in Canada (because profits accrued elsewhere), and domestically produced products would be more expensive than British or American imports (because of the small production runs). According to the staples thesis, Canadian economic growth could thus be achieved only by the continual discovery of new forms of staples to export. The staples thesis enables us to explain why many resource-producing activities in Canada (such as, for example, coal mining in Kimberley, British Columbia, or fishing along the shores of Newfoundland and Labrador) have not produced sustained growth in other sectors of the local economy.

Organizing the Periphery

The growth and internal development of the core regions simply could not have taken place without the foodstuffs, raw materials, and markets provided by the colonization of the periphery and the incorporation of more and more territory into the sphere of industrial capitalism. Early in the nineteenth century, the industrial core nations embarked on the penetration of the world's inland midcontinental grassland zones in order to exploit them for grain or livestock production. This led to the settlement, through the immigration of European peoples, of the temperate prairies and pampas of the Americas, the veld in southern Africa, the Murray-Darling Plain in Australia, and the Canterbury Plain in New Zealand. At the same time, as the demand for tropical plantation products (sugar, cotton, coffee, cocoa, tea, tobacco, and rubber, for example) increased, most of the tropical world came under the political and economic control—direct or indirect—of one or another of the industrial core nations. In the second half of the nineteenth century, and especially after 1870, there was a vast increase in the number of colonies and the number of people under colonial rule.

The International Division of Labour

The fundamental logic behind all this colonization was economic: the need for an extended arena for trade, an arena that could supply foodstuffs and raw materials in return for the industrial goods

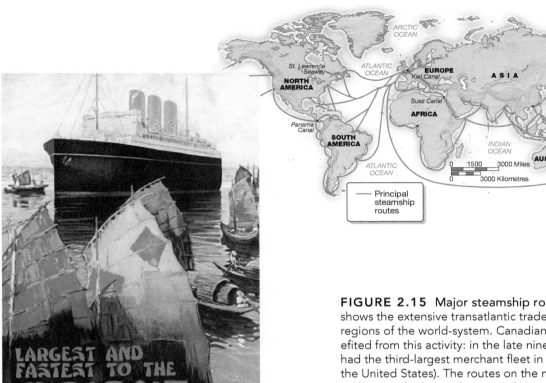

FIGURE 2.15 Major steamship routes in 1920 This map shows the extensive transatlantic trade between the bipolar core regions of the world-system. Canadian interests in particular benefited from this activity: in the late nineteenth century, Canada had the third-largest merchant fleet in the world (after Britain and the United States). The routes on the map also reflect the colonial and imperial relations between the world's core economies and the periphery. These uneven relations are also expressed by the symbolism contained in the poster dating from 1924: note how the gleaming white and angular modernity of the ocean liner is literally towering over the outdated technology of ragged sails rendered in smudgy, earthy colours. (*Photo source:* akg-images/Newscom)

of the core. The outcome was an international division of labour, driven by the needs of the core and imposed through its economic and military strength. This **division of labour** involved the specialization of different people, regions, and countries in certain kinds of economic activities. In particular, colonies began to specialize in the production of commodities meeting certain criteria:

- where an established demand existed in the industrial core (for foodstuffs and industrial raw materials, for example)

- where colonies held a **comparative advantage** in specializations that did not duplicate or compete with the domestic suppliers within core countries (Tropical agricultural products like cocoa and bananas, for example, simply could not be grown in core countries.)

The result was that colonial economies were founded on narrow specializations that were oriented to and dependent upon the needs of core countries. Examples of these specializations were many: bananas in Central America; cotton in India; coffee in Brazil, Java, and Kenya; copper in Chile; cocoa in Ghana; jute in East Pakistan (now Bangladesh); palm oil in West Africa; rubber in Malaya (now Malaysia) and Sumatra; sugar in the Caribbean islands; tea in Ceylon (now Sri Lanka); tin in Bolivia; and bauxite in Guyana and Surinam. Most of these specializations persist today. For example, 45 of the 55 countries in sub-Saharan Africa still depend on just three products—tea, cocoa, and coffee—for more than half of their export earnings.

This new global economic geography took some time to establish, and the details of its pattern and timing were heavily influenced by technological innovations. The incorporation of the temperate grasslands into the commercial orbit of the core countries, for example, involved changes in regional landscapes resulting from critical innovations—such as barbed wire, the railroad, and refrigeration.

The single most important innovation stimulating the international division of labour, however, was the development of metal-hulled, oceangoing steamships. This development was cumulative, with improvements in engines, boilers, transmission systems, fuel systems, and construction materials adding up to produce dramatic improvements in carrying capacity, speed, range, and reliability. The Suez Canal (opened in 1869) and the Panama Canal (opened in 1914) were also critical, providing shorter and less hazardous routes between core countries and colonial ports of call. By the eve of World War I, the world economy was effectively integrated by a system of regularly scheduled steamship trading routes (**Figure 2.15**). This integration, in turn, was supported by the second most important innovation stimulating the international division of labour: a network of telegraph communications (**Figure 2.16**) that enabled businesses to monitor and coordinate supply and demand across vast distances on an hourly basis. Together, these improvements in transportation and communications technology both integrated and "shrank" the world.

The international division of labour brought about a substantial increase in trade and a huge surge in the overall size of the

FIGURE 2.16 The international telegraph network in 1900 For Britain, submarine telegraph cables were the nervous system of its empire. Of the global network of 246 000 kilometres of submarine cable, Britain had laid 169 000 kilometres.

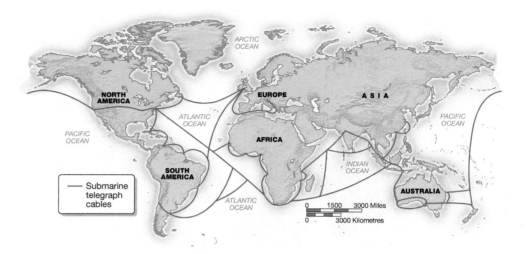

capitalist world economy. By the end of the nineteenth century, the core of the world-system had extended to include the United States and Japan. The peripheral regions of the world contributed a great deal to this growth. By 1913, Africa and Asia provided more *exports* to the world economy than either North America or the British Isles. Asia alone was *importing* almost as much, by value, as North America. The industrializing countries of the core bought increasing amounts of foodstuffs and raw materials from the periphery, financed by profits from the export of machinery and manufactured goods to the periphery. We should remember that companies that produced these foodstuffs and raw materials in the periphery usually were owned by entrepreneurs in the core. In this sense, the core actually traded with itself but in the process used the resources and labour of the periphery.

Patterns of international trade and interdependence became increasingly complex. Britain, the hegemonic power of the nineteenth century, controlled a trading empire that was truly global (**Figure 2.17**), using its capital to invest not just in peripheral regions but also in profitable industries in newly emerging core countries, especially the United States and Canada. At the same time, these

emerging core countries were able to export cheap manufactured goods to Britain. Britain financed the purchase of these goods, together with imports of food from its dominion states (Canada, South Africa, Australia, and New Zealand) and colonies, through the export of its own manufactured goods to peripheral countries. India and China, with large domestic markets, were especially important. Thus, a widening circle of exchange and dependence developed, with constantly switching patterns of trade and investment.

APPLY YOUR KNOWLEDGE Look at some of the clothes and products that you possess and see where they were made. List the materials that go into making your clothing. Can you speculate about where the cotton was grown? Who drove it to the factory? Who produced the cloth? Who sewed the clothing together? How do these questions relate to the principles of division of labour and comparative advantage? ■

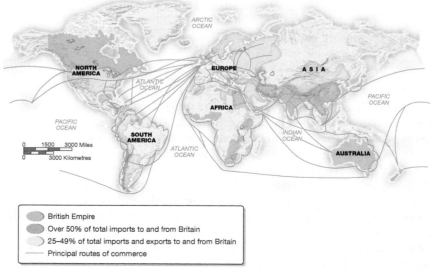

FIGURE 2.17 The British Empire in the late 1800s Protected by the all-powerful Royal Navy, the British merchant navy established a web of commerce that collected food for British industrial workers and raw materials for its industries, much of it from colonies and dependencies appropriated by imperial might and developed by British capital. So successful was the trading empire that Britain also became the hub of trade for other states. (*Source:* Adapted from P. Hugill, *World Trade Since 1431.* Baltimore: Johns Hopkins University Press, 1993, p. 136.)

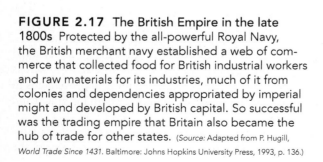

Imperialism: Imposing New Geographies on the World

The incorporation of the periphery was by no means motivated only by the basic logic of free trade and investment: the expansion of European influence was also seen as a question of power and even national pride. Although Britain was the hegemonic power in the late nineteenth century, several other European countries (notably Germany, France, and the Netherlands) together with the United States—and later Japan—were competing for global influence. The core countries engaged in pre-emptive geographical expansionism to protect their established interests and to limit the opportunities of others. Through a combination of military coercion, administrative control, and economic regulations, they tried to ensure stable and profitable environments for their traders and investors. This competition escalated into a veritable scramble for territorial and commercial domination: between 1870 and 1900, European countries added more than 25 million square kilometres and 150 million people to their spheres of control—20 percent of Earth's land surface and 10 percent of its population.

Africa, more than any other peripheral region, was given an entirely new political geography. At the 1884 Berlin Conference, 14 core countries simply carved up the African continent into a patchwork of European colonies and protectorates—without any African representation and with little regard for physical geography, ethnic groups, or the pre-existing human geographies of minisystems. This "arrangement" essentially continued until decolonization began in the 1950s. The only change was that, after losing World War I, Germany had to give control over its four colonies to the League of Nations—which promptly placed them under the mandate of other colonizing core states. Even after finally gaining their independence, many African nations retained the curiously straight and regular borders that the European powers had imposed on the map of Africa. They did so in an effort to avoid bloody border conflicts, but the price was that they continue to live with a political geography that was established to serve the interests of the core nations, rather than reflecting traditional affiliations. As a result, many African states are a patchwork of often quite disparate ethnicities and religions and thus are prone to civil unrest.

At the same time that the whole of Africa became incorporated into the modern world-system, the major powers jostled and squabbled over small Pacific islands that suddenly became valuable as strategic coaling stations for their roaming navies and merchant fleets. Resistance from indigenous peoples was quickly brushed aside by imperial navies with ironclad steamers and troops with rifles and cannons. European weaponry was so superior that Otto von Bismarck, the first chancellor (1871–1890) of the German empire, referred to these conflicts as "sporting wars." Quickly, all but one island (Tonga) came under the control of colonial powers.

As these examples show, the imprint of imperialism and colonization on the peoples and geographies of the newly incorporated peripheries of the world-system was immediate, profound, and lasting—often to this day. The periphery quickly became almost entirely dependent on European and North American capital, shipping, managerial expertise, financial services, and news and communications. Consequently, it also became dependent on European cultural products: language, education, science, religion, architecture, and planning. All of these influences were etched into the landscapes of the periphery in a variety of ways as new places were created, old places were remade, and regions were reorganized—including all the human suffering that came with such reorganization.

The discipline of geography played an important role in providing a "scientific" rationale for the domination of peripheral countries by Europeans and North Americans. Prominent geographers argued that civilization and successful economic development are largely the result of "invigorating" temperate climates with marked seasonal variations and varied weather but without prolonged extremes of heat, humidity, or cold. Conversely, tropical climates, they asserted, limit people's vitality and made them "lazy." This racist reasoning reflects an underlying ethnocentrism and environmental determinism. **Ethnocentrism** is the attitude that one's own race and culture are superior to those of others. **Environmental determinism** is a doctrine holding that human activities are shaped and constrained by the environment. Most of the geographic writing in the nineteenth and early twentieth centuries was strongly influenced by this assumption that the physical attributes of geographical settings are the root not only of people's physical differences but also of differences in people's economic vitality, cultural activities, and social structures.

The Third World and Neo-colonialism

The imperial world order began to disintegrate shortly after World War II. The United States emerged as the new hegemonic power, the dominant state within the world-system core. This core was called the "First World." The Soviet Union and China, opting for alternative paths of development for themselves and their satellite countries, were seen as a "Second World," withdrawn from the capitalist world economy. Their pursuit of alternative political economies was based on radically different values.

By the 1950s, many of the European colonies were seeking political independence. Some of the early independence struggles were very bloody because the colonial powers were initially reluctant to withdraw from colonies where strategic resources or large numbers of European settlers were involved. By the early 1960s, however, the process of peaceful decolonization had gained momentum, and more and more colonies achieved independence. (See Chapter 9.) The periphery of the world-system now consisted of a "Third World" of politically independent states that were not formally aligned with or against either of the major power blocs of the First or Second Worlds. They were nevertheless still highly dependent, in economic terms, on the world's core countries.

From the 1960s onward, the peripheral states struggled to achieve economic independence through industrialization, modernization, and trade, but at the same time the capitalist world-system changed yet again to adapt to the new global situation. The old imperial patterns of international trade were replaced by more complex patterns that resulted in more interdependence and integration. However, many of the old colonial links and legacies remained intact, and so the former colonial powers continued to influence the newly independent states. The result was a neo-colonial pattern of international development.

Neo-colonialism refers to economic and political strategies by which powerful states in core economies indirectly maintain or extend their influence over other areas or people. Instead of formal, direct rule (colonialism), control is exerted through such strategies as international financial regulations, commercial relations, military aid and co-operation, and covert intelligence operations. Through neo-colonialism, the human geographies of peripheral countries continue to be heavily shaped by the linguistic, cultural, political, and institutional influences of the former colonial powers as well as their investment and trading activities.

At about the same time, a new form of imperialism was emerging. This was the *commercial imperialism* of giant corporations. These corporations had grown within the core countries through the elimination of smaller firms by mergers and takeovers. By the 1960s, quite a few of them had become so big that they were *transnational* in scope, having established overseas subsidiaries, taken over foreign competitors, or simply bought into profitable foreign businesses.

These **transnational corporations** have investments and activities that span international boundaries, with subsidiary companies, factories, offices, or facilities in several countries. Examples of transnational corporations include Airbus, Alcan, Barrick Gold, BP, Halliburton, News Corporation, Siemens, and Virgin Group. By 2009, over 80 000 transnational corporations were operating, 90 percent of which were headquartered in the core states. These corporations control about 790 000 foreign affiliates and account for the equivalent of 11 percent of world Gross Domestic Product (GDP) and one-third of world exports.

Transnational corporations have been portrayed as imperialist by some geographers because of their ability and willingness to exercise their considerable power in ways that adversely affect peripheral states. They have certainly been central to a major new phase of geographical restructuring that has been underway for the last 35 years or so. This phase has been distinctive because an unprecedented amount of economic, political, social, and cultural

activity has spilled beyond the geographic and institutional boundaries of states. It is a phase of *globalization*, a much fuller integration of the economies of the worldwide system of states and a much greater interdependence of individual places and regions from every part of the world-system.

> **APPLY YOUR KNOWLEDGE** Provide an example of how neo-colonialism reinforces the power and influence of core countries. Please be specific with your example. (Hint: You might want to consider milk production in Jamaica or oil extraction in Nigeria.) What is the role of transnational corporations in neo-colonialism? ∎

CONTEMPORARY GLOBALIZATION

Globalization is the increasing interconnectedness of various parts of the world through common processes of economic, environmental, political, and cultural change. As we have seen, globalization has been underway since the inception of the modern world-system in the sixteenth century. In the nineteenth century, when the competitive system of states fostered the emergence of international agencies and institutions, global networks of communication, a standardized system of global time, international law, and internationally shared notions of citizenship and human rights, the basic framework of modern globalization came into being. Global connections today, though, differ in at least four important ways from those in the past.

First, they function at much greater *speed* than ever before. Second, globalization operates on a much larger *scale*, leaving few people unaffected and wielding its influence in even the most remote places. Third, the *scope* of global connections is much broader and has *multiple dimensions*: economic, technological, political, legal, social, and cultural, among others. Fourth, the interactions and interdependencies among numerous global actors have created a new level of *complexity* for the relationships between places and regions.

Over the past 35 years, telecommunication technologies, corporate strategies, and institutional frameworks have combined to create a dynamic new geographical framework. Emerging information technologies have helped create a complex and frenetic international financial system, while transnational corporations are now able to transfer their production activities from one part of the world to another in response to changing market conditions and changing transportation and communications technologies. (See Chapter 7.) Now products, markets, and organizations are both spread and linked across the globe. Governments, in their attempts to adjust to this situation, have sought new ways of dealing with the consequences of globalization, including unprecedented international political and economic alliances such as NAFTA and the European Union. (See Chapter 9.)

The economic basis of contemporary globalization depends on myriad commodity chains that crisscross global space. **Commodity chains** are networks of labour and production processes that originate in the extraction or production of raw materials and whose end result is the delivery and consumption of a finished commodity.

VIRTUAL GEOGRAPHIES

The current technology system has helped create a globalized economy in which smaller businesses usually find it hard to compete. However, the recently developed concept of the virtual "Logistics Mall" combines several ICT solutions in ways that allow small and medium-sized businesses to operate worldwide. The Logistics Mall is an online gateway to international logistics services ranging from export permits and international customer support services to customs clearing and shipping, services that are usually too complex or expensive for small businesses to cover in-house. Through a single interface, a business can purchase, combine, and pay for customized solutions from a variety of providers—and the integration of technologies goes even further: using cloud computing technology and an integrated web interface, the Logistics Mall frees the individual business from having to purchase any hardware or software beyond a simple personal computer. As geographers, we are thus reminded that the current technology system, depending on how it is employed, can work both up and down the scale, and can emphasize or minimize the importance of physical location.

(See Box 2.4, "Visualizing Geography: Commodity Chains.") These networks often span countries and continents, linking into vast global assembly lines the production and supply of raw materials, the processing of raw materials, the production of components, the assembly of finished products, and the distribution of finished products. As we shall see in Chapter 7, these global assembly lines are increasingly important in shaping places and regions—not least because they directly affect people's lives at every stage.

Globalization also has important cultural dimensions. (See Chapter 5.) One is quite simply the diffusion around the world of all sorts of cultural forms, practices, and artifacts that had previously been confined to specific places or regions. Examples include "ethnic" and regional cuisine, "world" music, and Caribbean carnivals. Another dimension of cultural globalization derives from consumer culture: everything that is sold in international markets, from sneakers, replica soccer shirts, and automobiles to movies and rock concert tours. This has led some observers to believe that globalization is producing a new set of universally shared images, practices, and values—literally, a global culture.

All this adds up to an intensified global connectedness and the beginnings of the world as an interdependent system. Or, to be more precise, this is how it adds up for the one billion or so of the world's people who are directly tied to global systems of production and consumption and who have access to global networks of communication and knowledge. All of us in this globalizing world are in the middle of a major reorganization of the world economy and a radical change in our relationships to other people and places.

At first glance it might seem that globalization will render geography obsolete—especially in the more developed parts of the world. High-tech communications and the global marketing of standardized products seem as if they might soon wash away the distinctiveness of people and places, permanently diminishing the importance of differences between places. Far from it. The new mobility of money, labour, products, and ideas actually increases the significance of place in some very important ways:

- The more universal the diffusion of material culture and lifestyles, the more cherished regional and ethnic identities become. One example of this is the way in which the Quebec government is legislating against the Anglicization of the Quebecois language and culture.

- The more time people spend in virtual environments, the more they feel the need for a subjective setting—a specific place or community—they can call home. Examples are residential developments that have been carefully designed to create (or fake) a sense of community, identity, and heritage.

- The greater the reach of transnational corporations, the more easily they are able to respond to place-to-place variations in labour markets and consumer markets and the more often and more radically that economic geography has to be reorganized. Athletic shoe and apparel manufacturers, for example, frequently move production from one peripheral country to another in response to the changing international geography of wage levels and currency exchange rates.

- The greater the integration of transnational governments and institutions, the more sensitive people have become to localized cleavages of race, ethnicity, religion, or other markers of identity. Examples include the resurgence of Quebec nationalism and the rise of regionalist movements in Alberta.

In summary, there is no one experience of globalization. Although some places and regions have become more closely interconnected and interdependent as a result of globalization, others have been bypassed or excluded. All in all, the reality is that globalization is variously embraced, resisted, subverted, and exploited as it makes contact with specific cultures and settings. In the process, places are modified or reconstructed rather than destroyed or homogenized. Geography is the discipline that helps us understand exactly how globalization and places interact.

Key Issues in a Globalizing World

The integrated global system has also increased awareness of a set of common problems that many see as a consequence of globalization: climate change, transboundary pollution, drug trafficking, environmental diseases, crime, poverty, and inequality, to name but a few. This globalization of the contemporary world—its causes and effects on specific aspects of human geographies at different spatial scales—is a recurring theme through the rest of this book. Here, we note in broad outline the principal issues associated with contemporary globalization.

Environmental Issues

The sheer scale and capacity of the world economy means that humans are now capable of altering the environment at the global scale. The "footprint" of humankind extends to more than four-fifths of Earth's surface (**Figure 2.18** on p. 60). Many of the important issues facing modern society are the consequences—intended and unintended—of human modifications of our physical environment.

Humans have altered the balance of nature in ways that have brought economic prosperity to some areas and created environmental dilemmas and crises in others. For example, clearing land for settlement, mining, and agriculture provides livelihoods and homes for some but also transforms human populations, wildlife, and vegetation. The inevitable by-products—garbage, air and water pollution, hazardous wastes, and so forth—place enormous demands on the capacity of physical systems to absorb and accommodate them.

Climate change as a result of human activity—in particular, our burning of fossil fuels, agriculture, and deforestation that cause emissions of carbon dioxide (CO_2) and other "greenhouse" gases—also has profound implications for environmental quality. Without concerted action to reduce greenhouse gas emissions, the global average surface temperature is likely to rise by a further 1.8–4.0°C this century. Even the lower end of this range would take the temperature increase since preindustrial times to above 2°C, the threshold beyond which irreversible and possibly catastrophic changes become far more likely. Projected global warming this century is likely to trigger serious consequences for humanity and other life forms. These consequences may include a rise in sea levels of between 18 and 59 centimetres, which will endanger coastal areas and small islands, (see Chapters 3 and 4) and a greater frequency and severity of extreme weather events.

In addition to the spectre of global warming, we are facing serious global environmental degradation through deforestation, desertification, acid rain, loss of genetic diversity, smog, soil

Global commodity chains link the progression of a commodity from design through procurement of raw materials and production to import or export to the point of sale, distribution for sale, marketing, and advertising. They are often entirely internal to the global operations of transnational corporations.

Advances in telecommunications, management techniques, transportation, finance, and other services to industry have made possible the segmentation of corporate production lines, as well as services, across multiple settings. Manufacturing companies now design a product in one country, have it produced by contractors in various countries continents apart, sell the product with its brand name by telephone or Internet almost anywhere in the world, and have other contractors deliver it. The services involved—design, sales, financing, and delivery—can be undertaken without the various actors ever meeting face to face. Advances in technology and management have also permitted the reproduction and standardization of services and products on a global basis. Certain patented services, such as fast-food restaurants (McDonald's, KFC, Burger King), rely on computer-regulated technology to deliver a standard service and product over time and geographic space.

Almost every mass-marketed manufactured product involves a complex commodity chain. Take, for example, the manufacture of Lee Cooper jeans (**Figure 2.E**). Designed in the United States, advertised globally, retailed in stores across Europe, the United States, and the metropolises of semiperipheral and peripheral countries, their manufacture draws on labour and products from around the world. The final stages of the commodity chain of one particular pair of jeans sold in a large discount store of a provincial British city were "in a van that came up the A12 [road] from Lee Cooper's warehouse at Staples Corner, just at the bottom of the M1 [highway] in North London. . . . Before that they came through the Channel Tunnel in a lorry from similar warehouses in Amiens, France and before that, by boat and train from Tunis in Tunisia . . . ."[2]

The flows and activities associated with globalization have also helped spread new values around the world. These new values range from superficial and resource-intensive consumer lifestyle preferences to deeper, altruistic concerns with global resources, global environmental changes, and famine relief. The ambiguities associated with globalization mean that the term is often controversial because it has different meanings for different people. Most broadly, globalization is the expansion and intensification of linkages and flows of capital, people, goods, ideas, and cultures across national borders. To some this process implies a serious decline in the importance of local communities and national governments. Globalization has produced a more complex system of interdependent states in which transnational rules and organizations have gained influence. States pursuing their national interests are still a major force, but corporations and international nongovernmental

[2]F. Abrams and J. Astill, "Story of the Blues," *The Guardian*, 29 May 2001, p. 2; quoted in L. Crewe, "Unravelling Fashion's Commodity Chains." In A. Hughes and S. Reimer (eds.), *Geographies of Commodity Chains*. London: Routledge, 2004, p. 201.

organizations (INGOs) can now critically influence world politics. World society therefore contains many centres of power and has no single power hierarchy. As power disperses and goals diverge, yet another new pattern of complex interdependence is emerging.

There are three broad types of global commodity chains. The first is *producer-driven*, in which large, often transnational, corporations coordinate production networks. A good example of this is the U.S. pharmaceutical industry. Research and development of drugs are conducted in the United States; materials and components are produced in a global production line; and the drugs are assembled and marketed out of a semiperipheral site (particularly in Puerto Rico, but also in Ireland), where companies enjoy certain competitive advantages not only in the industrial segment of the assembly but in marketing, financial, and management services.

A second type of commodity chain is *consumer-driven*, where large retailers, brand-name merchandisers, and trading companies influence decentralized production networks in a variety of exporting countries, often in the periphery. One good example is the case of Lee Cooper jeans described in this box. Another example is the discount chain-store company Wal-Mart, which contracts directly with producers in low-wage countries (China, in particular) for the bulk of its merchandise. Ironically, this merchandise is sold in the U.S. to the accompaniment of advertising that invokes community-oriented and even patriotic themes. In Canada, there has been no similar attempt to obscure the off-shore origin of the merchandise.

The third type, the *marketing-driven* commodity chain, represents a hybrid of the first two types. It involves the production of inexpensive consumer goods—such as colas, beers, breakfast cereals, candies, cigarettes, and infant formula—that are global commodities and carry global brands yet are often manufactured in the periphery and semiperiphery for consumption in those regions. These commodities take their globalized status not only from their recipes and production techniques but, even more important, from their globally contrived cultural identities.

Commodity chains provide varying opportunities for firms and national economies to enter into and improve their position within the global division of labour. Commodity chains are an important dimension of the complex transnationalization of economic space. They are also an important dimension of the complex currents of cultural globalization. In addition to facilitating the standardization of products and services (for those who can afford them) around the world, commodity chains also reflect the inequalities of the global economy. If core-country consumers stop to think about the origins of many of the products they consume, they may recognize what is happening "down the line," where poverty wages and grim working and living conditions are a precondition for the feasibility and profitability of many commodity chains. In contrast, those who work on the farms and plantations and in the workshops and factories at the beginning of commodity chains are acutely aware—thanks to contemporary media—of the dramatically more affluent lifestyles of those who will eventually consume the fruits of their labour.

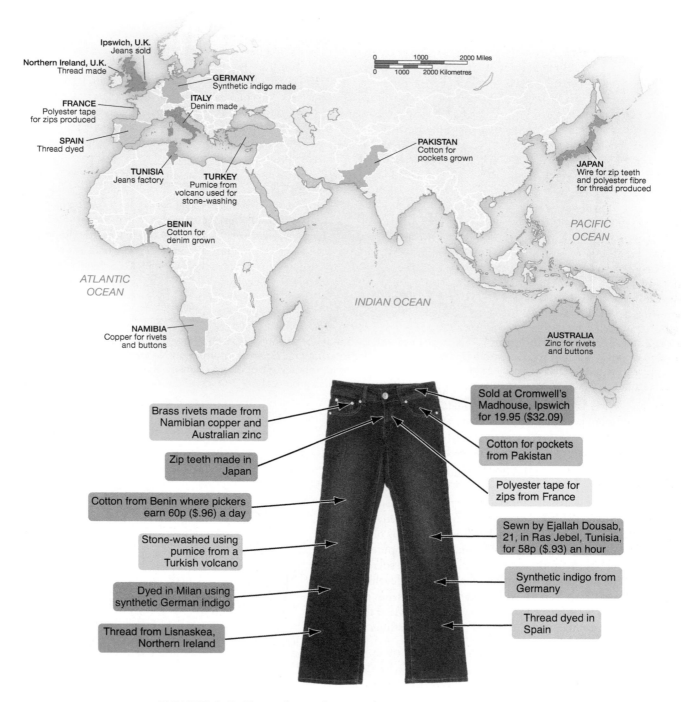

FIGURE 2.E The making of a pair of Lee Cooper jeans *(Source:* Adapted from A. Hughes and S. Reimer, eds., *Geographies of Commodity Chains.* New York: Routledge, 2004. *Photo source:* Oleksiy Maksymenko/Alamy)

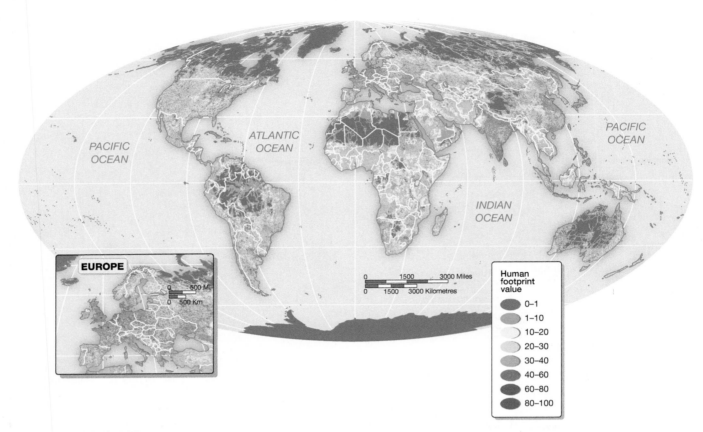

FIGURE 2.18 The human "footprint" This map, prepared by a team of scientists from the New York-based Wildlife Conservation Society and Columbia University's Center for International Science Information Network (CIESIN), shows the extent and intensity of human influence on the land, reflecting population density, agricultural use, access from roads and waterways, electrical power infrastructure, and urbanization. The lower the number, the lesser the overall degree of human influence. (*Source:* www.wcs.org/humanfootprint/)

erosion, groundwater depletion, and the pollution of rivers, lakes, and oceans.

Environmental issues such as these point to the importance of sustainability. **Sustainability** is about the interdependence of the economy, the environment, and social well-being. This is often couched in terms of the "three Es" of sustainable development, referring to the environment, the economy, and equity in society (**Figure 2.19**). The oft-quoted definition of sustainable development from the Brundtland Report, which examined the issues on the international scale, is "development that meets the needs of the present without compromising the ability of future generations to meet their own needs."[3]

> **APPLY YOUR KNOWLEDGE** Give an example of an environmental concern that affects your home region and suggest how it relates to issues of economic development and social equity. ∎

[3]World Commission on Environment and Development, *Our Common Future* (Brundtland Report), Oxford, UK: Oxford University Press, 1987, p. 40.

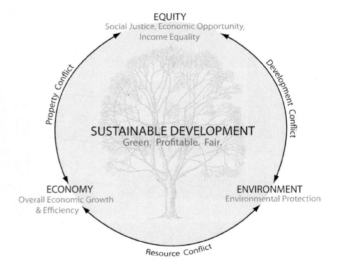

FIGURE 2.19 Sustainability There are three key aspects of sustainability in the long run—the physical environment, equity, and economic efficiency—and there are tensions between each of these.

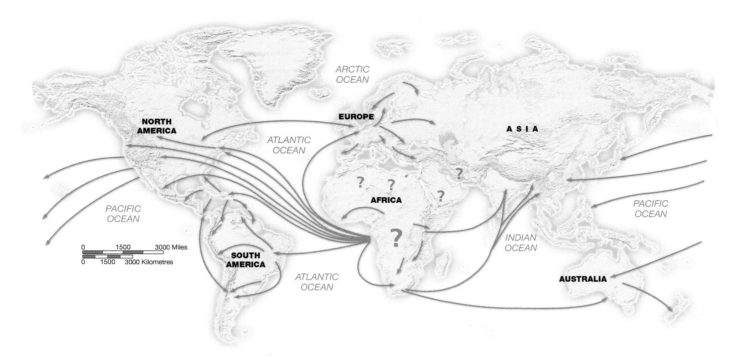

FIGURE 2.20 **Diffusion of the HIV virus** Medical geographers have concluded that the human immuno-deficiency virus (HIV), which causes AIDS, spread in a hierarchical diffusion pattern from a single hearth area in Central Africa in the late 1970s. The virus initially appeared almost simultaneously in the major metropolitan areas of North and South America, the Caribbean, and Europe. These areas then acted as localized diffusion poles for the virus. Today, HIV/AIDS affects sub-Saharan Africa more severely than any other part of the world. It has become the main cause of death in Africa, killing more people than malaria and warfare combined. (*Source:* Adapted from M. Smallman-Raynor, A. Cliff, and P. Haggett, *London International Atlas of AIDS*. Oxford: Blackwell Reference, 1992, Fig. 4.1[c], p. 146.)

Health Issues

The increased intensity of international trade and travel has also heightened the risk and speed of the spread of disease. A striking example of the health risks associated with increasing interdependency was the outbreak of H1N1 influenza ("swine flu") in 2009 that quickly spread from Mexico to become a global pandemic that lasted until August 2010. By the time the outbreak had been contained, it had caused widespread panic and serious disruption to business and tourism. The pandemic resulted in more than 14 000 deaths, some as far afield as Australia and Southeast Asia. Experts fear that similar threats are currently building from avian flu varieties that emerge in Asia and diffuse worldwide via air travel. Canada is likely to be among the first countries to which such a virus may spread because of its extensive transnational connections (as shown by the highly publicized H5N1 fatality in Alberta in January 2014).

Health care professionals are concerned that a new strain of influenza virus is likely to result in an influenza pandemic. A **pandemic** is an epidemic that spreads rapidly around the world with high rates of illness and death. Entirely new flu strains develop several times each century. Because no one has a chance to develop immunity to a new flu strain, it can spread rapidly and widely—especially so in today's globalized and highly interconnected world. Similarly, there is serious concern about the possibility of epidemics in the human population resulting from zoonotic diseases (diseases

originating with other species, e.g., anthrax, avian flu, Ebola, West Nile virus). The most significant international health issue so far, however, has been the spread of HIV/AIDS (**Figure 2.20**).

Security Issues

As sociologist Ulrich Beck has pointed out, the high degree of interdependence that is now embedded in a globalizing and highly interconnected world has brought about all sorts of security issues. In traditional societies, the risks faced by individuals and groups were associated mostly with hazards generated by nature (disease, flood, famine, and the like), along with socially determined hazards such as invasion and conquest and regressive forms of thought and culture. The industrial societies of the nineteenth and twentieth centuries, with more powerful technologies and weaponry, faced still more hazards, but they were mostly local and regional in nature.

Contemporary society, Beck points out, is characterized by the *production* of hazards, many of them uncontrollable and with a global reach. Examples include climate change as a result of human activity; the spread of weapons of mass destruction (i.e., nuclear and biological warfare); the risk of radioactive contamination from nuclear accidents; the risk of epidemics in the human population resulting from zoonotic diseases; and the risk of catastrophic instability in global financial markets (for example, the global financial "meltdown" of 2008: see Chapter 7).

FIGURE 2.21
Communication flows between major world regions This diagram shows the flows, in billions of minutes of telecommunications traffic over public telephone networks, between major regions. Note the absence of Africa. (*Source:* Adapted from G. C. Staple, ed., *TeleGeography 1999*. Washington, DC: TeleGeography Inc., 1999, Fig. 4, p. 255.)

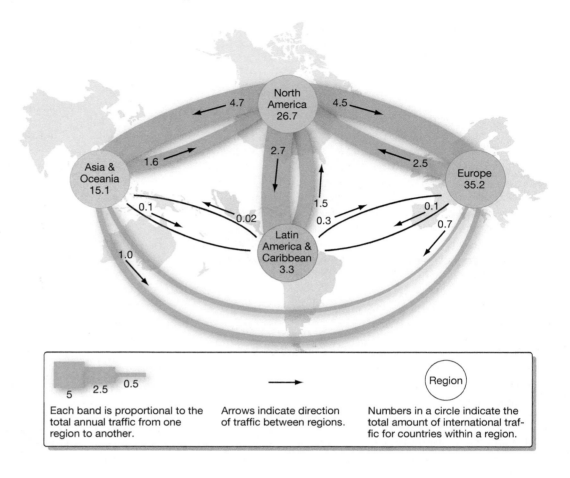

Overall, Beck argues, we are moving toward a **risk society,** in which the significance of wealth distribution is being eclipsed by the distribution of risk and in which politics—both domestic and international—is increasingly about avoiding hazards. As a result, knowledge—especially scientific knowledge—becomes increasingly important as a source of power, while science itself becomes increasingly politicized—as, for example, in the case of global warming.

International terrorism, another important security issue, can also be attributed in part to globalization. While terrorism has a long history, it is only recently that terrorist attacks have spilled beyond the sites of local conflict. This is largely a result of another set of issues: the cultural and political fallout from the Westernization that is associated with contemporary globalization.

Core–Periphery Disparity Issues

One of the most striking outcomes of contemporary globalization is the consolidation of the core of the world-system. The core is now a close-knit triad of the geographic centres of North America, the European Union, and Japan. These three geographic centres are connected through three main circuits, or flows, of investment, trade, and communication: between Europe and North America, between Europe and the Far East, and among the regions of the Pacific Rim. **Figure 2.21**, for example, shows just how dominant North America has become in accounting for flows of international telephonic communication.

Globalization, although incorporating more of the world more completely into the capitalist world-system, has intensified differences in prosperity between the core and the periphery. (See Box 2.5, "Window on the World: Worlds Apart.")

According to the United Nations Development Program, the gap between the poorest fifth of the world's population and the wealthiest fifth increased more than threefold between 1965 and 2005. Some parts of the periphery have almost slid off the economic map. In 55 countries, per capita income actually fell during the 1990s. In sub-Saharan Africa, economic output fell by one-third during the 1980s and stayed low during the 1990s, so that people's standard of living there is now, on average, lower than it was in the early 1960s. In 2010, the fifth of the world's population living in the highest-income countries had:

- 75 percent of world income (the bottom fifth had just 1 percent)
- 84 percent of world export markets (the bottom fifth had just 1 percent)

While 3 billion people around the world struggle to live on less than US$2.00 a day, the world's billionaires—only 1000 or so people—were together worth $3.5 trillion (equivalent to more than 5 percent of world GDP). OECD countries (the Organization for Economic Co-operation and Development, an association of 34 industrialized countries), with 19 percent of global population, control more than 75 percent of global trade in goods and services and consume 86 percent of the world's goods.

Such enormous differences lead many people to question the equity of the geographical consequences of globalization. The concept of **spatial justice** is important here because it requires us to consider the distribution of society's benefits and burdens at different spatial scales, taking into account both variations in people's need and in their contribution to the production of wealth and social well-being.

Many people, nations, and ethnic groups around the world feel marginalized, exploited, and neglected as a result of the quickening pace of change. Across much of the peripheral world, the perception of injustice has been brewing for a long time. Resentment at past colonial and imperial exploitation has been compounded as the more affluent places and regions of the world have become increasingly dependent on the cheap labour and resources of the periphery and as transnational businesses have displaced the traditional economic and social practices of peripheral and semiperipheral regions under the banner of modernization. Thinking about spatial justice is an important aspect of the "geographical imagination" described in Chapter 1 and is a recurring theme in the remainder of this book.

> **APPLY YOUR KNOWLEDGE** Why do you think Africa is absent from Figure 2.21? Name three ways in which globalization is contributing to increasing global inequality. Why is it so difficult to achieve a higher degree of spatial justice? ∎

Westernization and Cultural Imperialism

At the heart of many of the cultural tensions associated with contemporary globalization is a marked disillusionment with the West, especially within traditional Islamic societies. Across much of the world, modernization is now taken to mean Westernization and, more specifically, Americanization (**Figure 2.22**). Most Westerners may think of modernization as necessary and good but many other people see it as the cause of their exploitation. In most peripheral countries, only a minority can enjoy Western-style consumerism, and the impoverished majority is acutely aware of the affluence of the core countries. While the gap between rich and poor countries has been widening for several decades, the U.S. aid budget—already low compared to the aid budgets of other developed countries—has been declining substantially. The United States, as a result, tends to be easily portrayed as a swaggering superpower, rigging the world-system to serve its own interests and doing relatively little by way of economic or humanitarian aid.

The current phase of globalization thus involves a distinctive new geopolitical element that has been described as the "new imperialism": the imperialism of the United States, the world's only superpower. Although Americans do not like to think of their country as territorially aggressive or exploitative, the "war on terror" and invasion of Afghanistan and Iraq following the al-Qaeda attacks in 2001 are widely interpreted elsewhere in the world as an exercise in imperialism, motivated in large part by a desire for military control over global oil resources. This interpretation of the United States as the instigator of a new imperialism has been reinforced by military threats against Iran and North Korea, deployment of special forces around the globe (for instance in the killing of Osama Bin Laden in Pakistan in 2011), use of "extraordinary rendition" (the apprehension or kidnapping of suspects followed by their transfer to countries known to employ harsh interrogation techniques or torture), and unilateral rejection of international environmental treaties and international aid agreements. What is less widely discussed in the world's newspapers is that this new imperialism is also viewed by some academics as the result of a highly competitive global economic environment in which the United States is no longer able to achieve superiority through innovation, product design, productivity, and marketing and so has had to resort to military intervention.

FIGURE 2.22 Westernization Turkish Muslims chat near an illuminated billboard advertising a Turkish Internet company at Istanbul airport. (*Source:* Jim Hollander/Reuters/)

Worlds Apart

Meet Paul Rust and his family, who live and enjoy life in Zug, Switzerland, the richest canton in the world's richest country. And meet Hussein Sormolo and his family, who live in Addis Ababa, capital of the world's poorest country, Ethiopia.

Hussein Sormolo left the village where he was born for the big city in 1978. He left his eight brothers and seven sisters behind, as the land that the family farmed was being forcibly collectivized by a new regime. Hussein, then 16, travelled 160 kilometres north to the city in the back of a truck. A kinsman from the same village took him in until he found a job in a bakery. Paul Rust left his village in Switzerland when he was 17 and also ended up in a bakery. The two men are similar in other ways. Both are friendly, hospitable, and generous and love their families. Both work hard. Both like to watch the news. Both are active worshippers, without being religious dogmatists.

Yet their lives are different. Hussein lives with his wife, sons, and daughters in a leaky shack of corrugated asbestos and steel in the Nefas Silk district of Addis Ababa (**Figure 2.F**). Paul lives with his wife in a six-room house (not counting the ground-floor apartment where his son, Martin, lives with his girlfriend) overlooking the lustrous green waters and steep wooded slopes of Lake Aegeri in Zug (**Figure 2.G**).

The income difference is huge. Hussein supports his wife and three young children on wages of about US$280 a year (more than twice the average income in Ethiopia). Paul and his wife, Hedi, draw roughly US$68 000 between them each year from their bakery, though the Rusts are not affluent by Swiss standards. (The average income per head in Zug is about US$50 000.)

It is the rainy season in Addis. Fat raindrops drum against, and often through, the rusting grooves of the corrugated roofs of the houses in Nefas Silk. Nights can be chilly and dank. From Debre Zeit road, the busy street lined with small businesses, including the bakery where Hussein works, it's a 10-minute walk to the alley where he lives. Inside the Hussein shack, a single bare light bulb always burns. There is little natural light: There are no glass windows, and the openings punched in the asbestos walls are covered to keep out drafts. Hussein pays his neighbour 18 birr (about US$2) a month, almost a tenth of his 200-birr salary, to sublet an electricity supply for the bulb in the shack. The family has no other electrical appliances, apart from a battery-operated radio. Neither Hussein, his wife, Rukia, nor his eldest daughter, Fate, 17, who is lucky enough to be at school, has ever used a computer, taken a photograph, or made a phone call. Hussein and Rukia have a pair of shoes each. They buy new ones every two years. They have no savings and the family doesn't take holidays.

Except for feast days, the family eats the same dish every meal—a grey, spongy, bread called injera, spread out like a cloth, and a spicy vegetable stew. Meat, fish, cheese, and eggs are luxuries. They

FIGURE 2.F Hussein Sormolo and his family in Addis Ababa, Ethiopia. (*Source:* Guardian News and Media Limited)

FIGURE 2.G Paul Rust and his family in Zug, Switzerland. (*Source:* Guardian News and Media Limited)

buy fruit only when one of the children is sick. Just under a quarter of the family income is spent on cooking charcoal and cans of water. In a country where only a quarter of the people in the countryside have access to safe drinking water, Hussein's family is lucky. There is a standpipe around the corner with reasonably clean water. That's about where their luck ends. While they used to have a toilet they shared with 26 neighbours, now they have no toilet at all.

The Rust house, not counting the apartment, has three toilets, one each in the bathroom and two shower rooms of the four-storey building. On the balconies under its broad, dark, solid eaves are cascades of red flowers. The well-used furnishings inside are not ostentatious, but the building is roomy and comfortable. There is a loft, four bedrooms, two living rooms, a kitchen, an office, a small wine cellar, a workroom, garage parking for three cars (Paul, Hedi, and Martin Rust each have a car) with room for another five on the forecourt. The house has its own elevator.

Paul and Hedi are going on vacation for two weeks in Austria this month and usually take another week off at Easter. Each has a mobile phone. The home office has computers and Internet access. They have a TV, a VCR, and a dishwasher. They eat what they want, although their tastes are plain—meat with several vegetables, salad, sometimes a little wine.

Switzerland is a rich country landlocked by other rich countries. Ethiopia is a poor country landlocked by other poor countries.

Unlike other African nations, Ethiopia was not a European colony, but its people have endured regular European military incursions, proxy superpower duels, and local wars that have exacerbated the ravages of famine and disease. Famines in the 1970s, 1980s, and 1990s killed 1.3 million people. Through the 1970s and 1980s, the country was embroiled in ideological and ethnic civil war. Today, almost a million Ethiopians are living with HIV/AIDS, and 44 percent of the country's population live below the national poverty line.

Hussein knows little about Switzerland. "I heard about Switzerland on the radio but I don't know. I heard it was a rich country, they help poor countries," he said.

Paul thought he could find Ethiopia on the map. Switzerland is not as aloof from the world as it was, he points out: they joined the boycott of apartheid South Africa. He said his brother helped build a dairy in Nepal 20 years ago. His church has adopted a village in Romania, giving it money for a new church and a school. When the talk turns to immigration, daughter Andrea says, "The really poor people, they can't come to Switzerland, they need money to get here. We work, and have our life, we have our own problems," she concludes. "So we don't think very often of other people's problems. It's a little bit selfish."

Source: Based on an article by James Meek, *The Guardian*, 22 August 2002.

FIGURE 2.23 Broadband affordability, 2011 Africans pay a disproportionately high share of their salary for broadband Internet access. In several countries, the cost is higher than the average annual salary. However, as the graph shows, the cost has also been dropping dramatically over the last few years. (*Source:* Graham, M., and De Sabbata, S. 2014. Information Geographies. geography.oii.ox.ac.uk.)

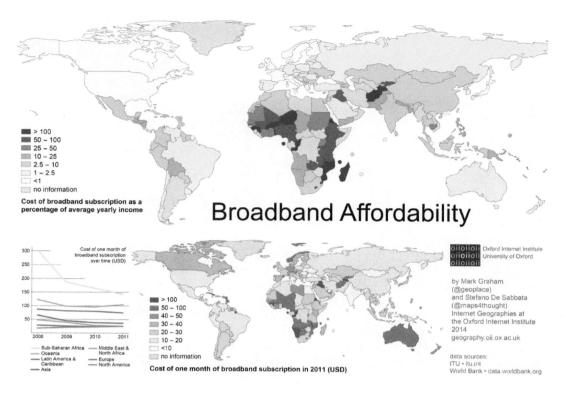

The Internet

No discussion of contemporary globalization would be complete without a look at the effects of the Internet. Like all previous revolutions in transportation and communications, the Internet is effectively reorganizing space. Geographers are now making a distinction between the "fast world" and the "slow world." The **fast world** consists of people, places, and regions directly involved, as producers and consumers, in transnational industry, modern telecommunications, materialistic consumption, and international news and entertainment. The **slow world** consists of the people, places, and regions whose participation is limited. Until recently, this slow world consisted chiefly of the impoverished periphery. Now, however, it also includes many places and regions in core countries that have been bypassed by this latest phase in the evolution of the modern world-system: rural backwaters, declining manufacturing regions, and disadvantaged slums, to name a few. Such inequalities between the fast world and the slow world are the result of a **digital divide** (the inequality of access to telecommunications and information technology, particularly broadband access to the Internet), that exists at *every* spatial scale.

Several factors influence levels of connectivity across the world, with cost obviously being a very important "gatekeeper." **Figure 2.23** shows the same pattern we have encountered several times already: in general, people in the core countries enjoy a locational advantage over people in peripheral countries in that the relative cost of broadband Internet access is dramatically lower. Africans, for instance, have to pay ten times as much (as a percentage of their salary) for Internet access than people elsewhere. And yet we also have to look beyond the national scale with its average figures and examine the regional and local levels, for it is here that we find other important reasons for differential access to the fast world: the presence of the necessary network infrastructure in one's neighbourhood, the ability to afford personal access devices, or simply the availability of reliable electricity to run them. All of these can vary greatly from place to place, which means that the digital divide literally extends to the local level. For example, in China the penetration rates of Internet and smartphone usage vary vastly between eastern urban areas and the western rural interior (**Figure 2.24**).

The local dimension of the differences between the fast and the slow worlds allows us to see the uneven spatial development of "informational capitalism" that sociologist and planner Manuel Castells has identified in his study *The Information Age.* Because access to networks and people is crucial in the Information Age, Castells argues that denial of such access means exclusion from "the powerhouse of global capitalism" and instead means becoming relegated to one of the "multiple black holes of social exclusion throughout the planet."[4]

Finally, we can also interpret this as yet another indication that the framework of the nation-state is increasingly unable to capture the "messy" reality of a globalizing world. When looking at national statistics or averages, we always need to remind ourselves that great variations exist *within* countries, and that these variations can be greater than the variations *between* countries. Although the centre of gravity of the fast world continues to be the tri-polar core of the world-system, the fast world also extends throughout the world to the more affluent regions, neighbourhoods, and households in the periphery that are "plugged in" to the contemporary world economy; the fast world now encompasses almost *everywhere* but not *everybody*.

APPLY YOUR KNOWLEDGE Find a story in a national newspaper that addresses an issue associated with contemporary globalization. Provide three examples from the article that illustrate the increasing interdependence of places and regions. ■

[4]Manuel Castells, *The Information Age: Economy, Society and Culture. Volume 3, End of Millennium,* rev. ed. Oxford: Blackwell, 1999, pp. 164 and 165.

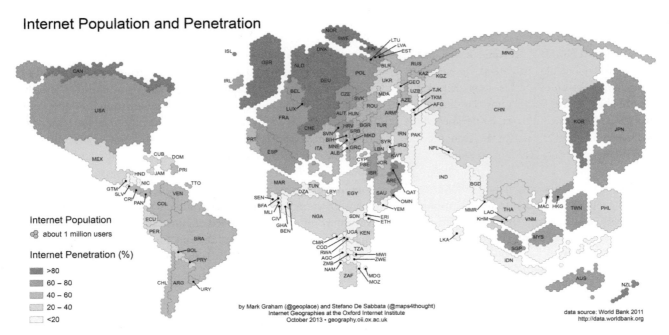

Internet Population and Penetration

Internet Population

🌐 about 1 million users

Internet Penetration (%)

- >80
- 60 – 80
- 40 – 60
- 20 – 40
- <20

by Mark Graham (@geoplace) and Stefano De Sabbata (@maps4thought)
Internet Geographies at the Oxford Internet Institute
October 2013 • geography.oii.ox.ac.uk

data source: World Bank 2011
http://data.worldbank.org

FIGURE 2.24 Number of Internet users and Internet penetration rates, 2011 While China has the greatest absolute number of Internet users, its Internet penetration rate is still quite low, a result of the great differences between eastern urban areas and the western rural interior. Note the relative modest participation of Russians in Internet communication (despite the relative affordability seen in Figure 2.23), as well as the growing participation in some African countries. (*Source:* Graham, M., and De Sabbata, S. 2014. Information Geographies. geography.oii.ox.ac.uk.)

Future Geographies

The globalization of the capitalist world-system involves processes that have been occurring for at least 500 years. But since World War II, world integration and transformation have been remarkably accelerated and dramatic. How will the forces of broadening global connectivity—and the popular reactions to them—change the fates and fortunes of world regions whose current coherence owes more to eighteenth- and nineteenth-century European colonialism than to the forces of integration or disintegration in the twenty-first century? To answer this and related questions, we need to understand what the experts think about the processes behind globalization and its future potential. But first we need to understand the very risky issue of predicting the future, how predictions are made, and how useful predictive exercises can be.

There is no shortage of visionary scenarios. Broadly speaking, futurists' projections can be divided into two kinds: optimistic and pessimistic. Optimistic futurists stress the potential for technological innovations to discover and harness new resources, to provide faster and more effective means of transportation and communication, and to make possible new ways of living. This sort of futurism is often characterized by science-fictional cities of mile-high skyscrapers and spaceship-style living pods, by ecological harmony, and by unprecedented social and cultural progress. It projects a world that will be stabilized and homogenized by supranational or even "world" governments. The sort of geography implied by such scenarios is rarely spelled out. Space and place, we are led to believe, will be transcended by technological fixes.

To pessimistic futurists, however, this is just "globaloney." They stress the finite nature of Earth's resources, the fragility of its environment, and population growth rates that exceed the capacity of peripheral regions to sustain them. Such doomsday forecasting scenarios include irreversible environmental degradation, increasing social and economic polarization, and the breakdown of law and order. The sort of geography associated with these scenarios is also rarely explicit, but it usually involves the probability of a sharp polarization between the haves and have-nots at every geographical scale.

Fortunately, we don't have to choose between the two extreme scenarios of optimism and pessimism. Using our geographical imagination, we can suggest a more grounded outline of future geographies. To do so, we must first glance back at the past. Then, looking at present trends and using what we know about processes of geographic change and principles of spatial organization, we can begin to map out the kinds of geographies that the future most probably holds.

Looking back at the way that the geography of the world-system has unfolded, we can see that a fairly coherent period of economic and geopolitical development occurred between the outbreak of World War I (in 1914) and the collapse of the Soviet Union (in 1989). Some historians refer to this period as the "short twentieth century." It was a period when the modern world-system developed its triadic core of the United States, Western Europe, and Japan. Geopolitics was based on an East–West divide, and geoeconomics was based on a North–South divide. The geographies of specific places and regions within these larger frameworks were shaped by the needs and opportunities of **technology systems** based on the internal combustion engine, oil and plastics, electrical engineering, aerospace industries, and electronics. In this short century, the modern world was established, along with its now-familiar landscapes and spatial structures: from the industrial landscapes of the core to the unintended metropolises of the periphery; from the voting blocs of the West to the newly independent nation-states of the South.

Looking around now, much of the established familiarity of the modern world and its geographies seems to be disappearing. We have entered a period of transition, triggered by the end of the Cold War in 1989 and rendered more complex by the geopolitical and cultural repercussions of the terrorist attacks of September 11, 2001, and the global financial "meltdown" of 2008. Obviously, we cannot simply project our future geographies from the landscapes and spatial structures of the past. At the same time, we can only guess at some aspects of the future. But we can draw some conclusions from a combination of existing structures and budding trends. We have to anticipate how the shreds of tradition and the strands of contemporary change might be rewoven into new landscapes and new spatial structures. Among the relative certainties over the next decade or so are the increasing power and influence of China and India, a general shift in relative wealth and economic power from the West to the East, an increased probability of conflict in the Middle East, and an intensification of problems resulting from pressure on food, water, and energy resources. Among the key uncertainties are the speed of climate change, the resolution of the Arab–Israeli conflict, and the effectiveness of alternative energy technologies (**Table 2-1**). In subsequent chapters, we examine these and related issues in detail.

TABLE 2-1 The 2025 Global Landscape

Relative Certainties	Likely Impact
A global multipolar system is emerging with the rise of China, India, and others. The relative power of non-state actors—businesses, tribes, religious organizations, and even criminal networks—also will increase.	By 2025 a single "international community" composed of nation-states will no longer exist. Power will be more dispersed, with the newer players bringing new rules to the game, and the risks will increase that the traditional Western alliances will weaken. Rather than emulating Western models of political and economic development, more countries may be attracted to China's alternative development model.
The unprecedented shift in relative wealth and economic power roughly from West to East now underway will continue.	As some countries become more invested in their economic well-being, incentives toward geopolitical stability could increase. However, the transfer is strengthening states like Russia that want to challenge the Western order.
The United States will remain the single most powerful country but will be less dominant.	Shrinking economic and military capabilities may force the U.S. into a difficult set of trade-offs between domestic and foreign policy priorities.
Continued economic growth—coupled with 1.2 billion more people by 2025—will put pressure on energy, food, and water resources.	The pace of technological innovation will be key to outcomes during this period. All current technologies are inadequate for replacing traditional energy architecture on the scale needed.
The number of countries with youthful populations in the "arc of instability"[5] will decrease, but the populations of several youth-bulge states are projected to remain on rapid growth trajectories.	Unless employment conditions change dramatically in youth-bulge states such as Afghanistan, Nigeria, Pakistan, and Yemen, these countries will remain ripe for continued instability and state failure.
The potential for conflict will increase owing to rapid changes in parts of the greater Middle East and the spread of lethal capabilities.	The need for the U.S. to act to balance power in the Middle East will increase, although other outside powers—Russia, China, and India—will play greater roles than today.
Terrorism is unlikely to disappear by 2025, but its appeal could lessen if economic growth continues in the Middle East and youth employment increases. For those terrorists who are active, the diffusion of technologies will put dangerous capabilities within their reach.	Opportunities for mass-casualty terrorist attacks using chemical, biological, or less likely, nuclear weapons will increase as technology diffuses and nuclear power (and possibly weapons) programs expand. The practical and psychological consequences of such attacks will intensify in an increasingly globalized world.

[5]Countries with youthful age structures and rapidly growing populations mark a crescent or "arc of instability" stretching from the Andean region of Latin America across Sub-Saharan Africa, the Middle East and the Caucasus, and through the northern parts of South Asia.

TABLE 2-1 The 2025 Global Landscape *(Continued)*

Key Uncertainties	Potential Consequences
Will an energy transition away from oil and gas—supported by improved energy storage, biofuels, and clean coal—be completed during the 2025 time frame?	With high oil and gas prices, major exporters such as Russia and Iran will substantially augment their levels of national power, with Russia's GDP potentially approaching that of the U.K. and France. A sustained plunge in prices, perhaps underpinned by a fundamental switch to new energy sources, could trigger a long-term decline for producers as global and regional players.
How quickly will climate change occur and in what locations will its impact be most pronounced?	Climate change is likely to exacerbate resource scarcities, particularly water scarcities.
Will mercantilism stage a comeback and global markets recede?	Descending into a world of resource nationalism increases the risk of great power confrontations.
Will advances toward democracy occur in China and Russia?	Political pluralism seems less likely in Russia in the absence of economic diversification. A growing middle class increases the chances of political liberalization and potentially greater nationalism in China.
Will regional fears about a nuclear-armed Iran trigger an arms race and greater militarization?	Episodes of low-intensity conflict and terrorism taking place under a nuclear umbrella could lead to an unintended escalation and broader conflict.
Will the greater Middle East become more stable, especially will Iraq stabilize, and will the Arab–Israeli conflict be resolved peacefully?	Turbulence is likely to increase under most scenarios. Revival of economic growth, a more prosperous Iraq, and resolution of the Israeli–Palestinian dispute could engender some stability as the region deals with a strengthening Iran and global transition away from oil and gas.
Will Europe and Japan overcome economic and social challenges caused or compounded by demography?	Successful integration of Muslim minorities in Europe could expand the size of the productive workforces and avert social crisis. Lack of efforts by Europe and Japan to mitigate demographic challenges could lead to long-term declines.
Will global powers work with multilateral institutions to adapt their structure and performance to the transformed geopolitical landscape?	Emerging powers show ambivalence toward global institutions like the UN and IMF, but this could change as these powers become bigger players on the global stage. Asian integration could lead to more powerful regional institutions. NATO faces stiff challenges in meeting growing out-of-area responsibilities with declining European military capabilities. Traditional alliances will weaken.

CONCLUSION

Places and regions everywhere carry the legacy of a sequence of major changes in world geography. The evolution of world geography can be traced from the prehistoric hearths of agricultural development and human settlement, through the trading systems of the precapitalist, preindustrial world, to the modern world. The foundations of the modern world are industrialization, colonization, and the international market economy. Today, these foundations are being altered by the emerging geography of the Information Age, a geography that provides a truly global context for places and regions.

Today's world is highly integrated. Places and regions have become increasingly interdependent, linked through complex and rapidly changing commodity chains that are orchestrated by transnational corporations. Using new technology systems that allow for instantaneous global telecommunications and flexible patterns of investment and production, these corporations span the world. This integration blurs some national and regional differences as the global marketplace brings about a dispersion of people, tastes, and ideas. The overall result, though, has been an intensification of differences between the core and the periphery. Within this new global context, local differences in resource endowments remain, and people's territorial impulses endure. Many local cultures continue to be resilient or adaptive. Fundamental principles of spatial organization also continue to operate.

The emergence of globalization—with its transnational architectural styles, dress codes, retail chains, and popular culture and ubiquitous immigrants, business visitors, and tourists—seems as if it might inevitably impose a sense of placelessness and dislocation, a loss of territorial identity, and an erosion of the distinctive sense of place associated with certain localities. Yet the common experiences associated with globalization are still modified by local geographies. The structures and flows of globalization are variously embraced, resisted, subverted, and exploited as they make contact with specific places and specific communities. In the process, places and regions are reconstructed rather than effaced. Often this involves deliberate attempts by the residents of a particular area to create or recreate territorial identity and a sense of place. Human geographies change, but they don't disappear.

Learning Outcomes Revisited

- Summarize the distinctive stages of the evolution of the modern world-system.

  Premodern geographies were organized around minisystems and regional empires. The modern world-system was established over a long period that began in the late fifteenth century. More and more peoples around the world have become exposed to one another's technologies and ideas since the fifteenth century. Different resources, social structures, and cultural systems resulted in quite different pathways of development, however. Some societies were incorporated into the new, European-based international economic system faster than others; some resisted incorporation; and some sought alternative systems of economic and political organization.

- Analyze how and why the new technologies of the Industrial Revolution helped bring about the emergence of a global economic system.

  The new technologies of the Industrial Revolution brought about the emergence of a global economic system that reached into almost every part of the world and into virtually every aspect of people's lives. New transportation technologies triggered successive phases of geographic expansion, allowing for an intensive period of external colonization and imperialism. The core of the world-system (Europe) grew to include the United States and Japan, while most of the rest of the world was systematically incorporated into the capitalist world-system as a dependent periphery.

- Examine the changing patterns of interdependence among different world regions.

  Each place and region carries out its own particular role within the competitive world-system. Because of these different roles, places and regions are dependent on one another. The development of each place affects, and is affected by, the development of many other places. Since the seventeenth century, the world-system has been consolidated, with stronger economic ties between countries. It has also been extended, with all the world's countries eventually becoming involved to some extent in the interdependence of the capitalist system and the consequent flows of resources, capital, goods, ideas, and people among places and regions.

- Compare the three tiers that constitute the modern world-system.

  Today, the world-system is highly structured and is characterized by three tiers: core regions, semiperipheral regions, and peripheral regions. The core regions of the world-system are those that dominate trade, control the most advanced technologies, and have high levels of productivity within diversified economies. Peripheral regions are characterized by dependent and disadvantageous trading relationships, by primitive or obsolescent technologies, and by undeveloped or narrowly specialized economies with low levels of productivity. Semiperipheral regions are able to exploit peripheral regions but are themselves exploited and dominated by the core regions. This three-tiered system is fluid, providing a continually changing framework for geographical transformation within individual places and regions.

- Explain how the growth and internal development of the world's core regions could take place only with the foodstuffs, raw materials, and markets provided by the colonization of the periphery.

  Peripheral regions were originally developed and exploited in order to provide the raw materials for industrializing regions and the food supplies for their rapidly growing populations. In the eighteenth and nineteenth centuries, the industrial core nations embarked on the inland penetration of the world's mid-continental grassland zones in order to exploit them for grain and livestock production. At the same time, as the demand for tropical plantation products increased, most of the tropical world came under the political and economic control—direct or indirect—of one or another of the industrial core nations. For these peripheral regions, European overseas expansion meant political and economic dependency.

- Identify an example of each of the four key issues caused by globalization—environmental, health, core–periphery disparity, and security issues.

  Many of the important issues facing modern society are the consequences—intended and unintended—of human modifications of our physical environment. In addition, the increased intensity of international trade and travel has also heightened the risk and speed of the spread of disease. Globalization has also intensified differences in prosperity between the core and the periphery, and contemporary society is characterized by new hazards, many of them uncontrollable and with a global reach.

KEY TERMS

capitalism *(p. 40)*

climate change *(p. 57)*

colonialism *(p. 48)*

colonization *(p. 39)*

commodity chain *(p. 56)*

comparative advantage *(p. 53)*

core regions *(p. 48)*

digital divide *(p. 66)*

division of labour *(p. 53)*

environmental determinism *(p. 55)*

ethnocentrism *(p. 55)*

external arena *(p. 43)*

fast world *(p. 66)*

globalization *(p. 56)*

hearth areas *(p. 38)*

hegemony *(p. 51)*

hinterland *(p. 41)*

hydraulic empire *(p. 40)*

imperialism *(p. 48)*

import substitution *(p. 45)*

law of diminishing returns *(p. 39)*

leadership cycles *(p. 51)*

minisystem *(p. 38)*

neo-colonialism *(p. 55)*

pandemic *(p. 61)*

peripheral regions *(p. 48)*

plantation *(p. 43)*

risk society *(p. 62)*

semiperipheral regions *(p. 48)*

slow world *(p. 66)*

spatial justice *(p. 63)*

staples thesis *(p. 51)*

staples trap *(p. 51)*

sustainability *(p. 60)*

technology systems *(p. 68)*

transnational corporations *(p. 56)*

world-empire *(p. 39)*

world-system *(p. 43)*

REVIEW AND DISCUSSION

1. In a group, discuss whether China should be considered a core, semi-peripheral, or peripheral country. What statistical evidence can you find that supports your argument? How much does the scale of your analysis (national, regional, local) influence your conclusions? What difficulties might emerge from only looking at the national scale?

2. Some analysts would classify Canada as a semiperipheral country. Do you think that is justified? Explain your position.

3. Identify two major events that had significant impacts on places and regions in the past few years (e.g., the Egyptian revolution of 2011 or the financial crisis of 2008) and discuss how they are related to globalization. On the whole, do you think globalization is more of a positive or more of a negative force? Provide three reasons for your position.

4. Consider the core, the semiperiphery, and the periphery, not from the perspective of states, but from the viewpoint of transnational corporations. Research two corporations and find out where their corporate headquarters are located, develop a list of what they produce, and, if possible, find out where their products come from. Take into consideration any raw materials and manufacturing that are involved. For example, your group might want to consider cell phone companies. Where are the companies located? Are they in the core, semiperiphery, or periphery? Where do they get the material to make cell

phones? Where do they manufacture and where do they sell them—in the core, semiperiphery, or periphery? Once you have compiled this information, develop a world map displaying your information and the ways the transnational corporations' products move among the core, semiperiphery, and periphery.

5. The idea of an international division of labour is based on the observation that different countries tend to specialize in the production or manufacture of particular commodities, goods, or services. In what commodities do the following countries specialize: Bolivia, Ghana, Guinea, Libya, Namibia, Peru, and Zambia? Take one product that you use in your everyday life and examine how any of the commodities you identified as originating in those countries has contributed to its production. Analyze the process it underwent until it finally came into your possession. Along the way, who has benefited most from this process, and are these beneficiaries located in the core, semiperiphery, or periphery?

6. Consider the division of labour in your place of work (either as a student or outside the university). How are tasks divided and who is responsible for what types of work? Is there an apparent division of labour? What principles do you think govern the distribution of work? How do these principles resemble those that govern the global division of labour?

Mastering GEOGRAPHY™

Log in to www.masteringgeography.com for MapMaster™ interactive maps, geography videos, RSS feeds, flashcards, weblinks, an eText version of *Human Geography: Places and Regions in Global Context*, and self-study quizzes to enhance your study of the changing global context.

MapMaster™ presents 13 Place Name and 13 Layered Thematic interactive maps to help students practise and master their geographic literacy, spatial reasoning, and critical thinking skills.

3 POPULATION GEOGRAPHY

Iraq has not conducted a national count of its population in over two decades. Most countries assess their population every 10 years. The last population count in Iraq, in 1987, occurred during the rule of Saddam Hussein and was used to conscript a majority of the male population into the army to fight in the Iran–Iraq war. At the time, international observers believed that the census was inaccurate, not only because the bureaucracy needed to conduct a national population count had been seriously dismantled under the dictatorship but also because the recorded numbers were misreported so that some ethnic populations would appear more numerous than others in parts of the country. Since the war against Iraq by the United States and its allies and the deposing of Hussein in 2003, hundreds of thousands of war casualties have occurred and millions of refugees have left the country. More recently, hundreds of thousands of Syrians fleeing the civil war in their country have been flooding *into* Iraq. Yet the current regime is still reluctant to launch a full national count of the population. Why? Because numbers have a wider impact besides knowing "how many": they are inherently political.

A census—a count of the number of people in a country, region, or city—is not only a practical undertaking answering basic demographic questions (how many people there are, where they live, how old they are, and what their ethnic backgrounds are), it is also a political undertaking. For instance, the number of eligible voters in a population routinely determines the

Iraqi officials distribute water to refugees of the Syrian civil war as they cross into Iraq at the Peshkhabour border point in Dahuk, on August 20, 2013. (*Source:* Hadi Mizban/AP Images)

number of officials that can be elected from that region to represent them in a national government. Population numbers also often decide the amount of tax revenues or transfer payments a region receives.

In Iraq, the current administration is wary of conducting a census because questions important to the future of the oil fields will be answered by the census. As a result of the census, some groups that currently have control over oil may lose it and others will gain control. At the centre of this dispute is Kirkuk Province, where an unstable ethnic mix of Arabs, Kurds, Turkmen, and others, sits atop 4 percent of the world's oil reserves. The census will statistically establish the majority population in these territories, which are contested between the Arab-dominated government in the capital city of Baghdad and the semiautonomous Kurds of the northeast. Once it is established by the official census, the majority population in this province will have a great deal of control over the future of that oil and be a significant political force not just in Iraq but in the world.

What the Iraq example illustrates is that it's not just the numbers that are important, it's where those numbers are located that matters too. The *where* of population is what drives geographers' interests in **demographics**, the characteristics of a *human population* including elements such as gender, race, age, income, disabilities, educational attainment, and migration patterns among different groups and death rates among others. ▪

THE DEMOGRAPHER'S TOOLBOX

Demography, the study of the characteristics of human populations, is an interdisciplinary undertaking. Geographers study population to understand the areal distribution of Earth's peoples. They are also interested in the reasons for, and the consequences of, the distribution of populations from the international to the local level. Historians study the evolution of demographic patterns and sociologists the social dynamics of human populations, but it is geographers who focus special attention on the spatial patterns of human populations, the implications of such patterns, and the reasons for them. Using many of the same tools and methods of analysis as other population experts, geographers think of population in terms of the places that populations inhabit. They also consider populations in terms of the way that places are shaped by populations and in turn shape the populations that occupy them.

Censuses and Vital Records

Population experts rely on a wide array of instruments and institutions to carry out their work. The most widely known instrument for assessing the state of the population is the census, a survey originally developed to obtain information for tax collection. Essentially, a **census** is a straightforward count of the number of people in a country, region, or city, but most censuses also gather additional information about the population, such as previous residence, marital status, occupation, income, and other personal data.

In Canada, the earliest census dates from 1666 when the population of New France (Quebec) was recorded on the orders of Louis XIV. Beginning in 1851, a nationwide census was conducted every 10 years. In 1956, a mid-decade census was added to keep up with the quickly changing population characteristics. The next censuses in this country will therefore take place in 2016 and 2021.

In addition to the census, population experts also employ other data sources to assess population characteristics. One such source is **vital records** (from the Latin word *vita*, meaning "life"), which report births, deaths, marriages, divorces, and the incidence of certain infectious diseases. These data are collected and recorded by all levels of government. Churches, schools, hospitals, and international organizations such as the World Health Organization also collect demographic statistics that are useful to population experts. In parts of Quebec, for example, parish registers date back to the beginning of the seventeenth century, allowing us to reconstruct the demographic experience of entire communities along the St. Lawrence River nearly 400 years ago.

Censuses and vital record information complement each other: census data produce a wealth of data, yet can record only a snapshot view (or cross-section) of a population on the particular day the census was conducted. On the other hand, vital records track changes over time, yet they can do so for only a limited number of individuals and variables. Recently, governments have begun linking a number of databases to not only build up a very detailed picture of individuals but also update this picture very regularly. Canada is a world leader in this respect and has, for the purposes of research, combined tax files with records of employment and immigration data to produce a very rich source of information on large samples of the population.

Upon looking more closely, however, we can see that there are problems with this method: it holds much greater potential for data leakage, loss of privacy, and identity theft than the traditional census, and it collects fewer data points per person. Notwithstanding such concerns, some Scandinavian countries have already replaced the census by interlinking residential databases with business registers and tax records to track information about their population. In the United Kingdom, the government is considering cutting the census for budget reasons and relying on data sources such as credit card information and mail records. In 2010, Canada replaced the mandatory long-form census with a less-detailed, voluntary online household survey. As a result, the response rate dropped from 95 percent to 68 percent. Many researchers—among them many geographers who depend on the rich census data for their research—have criticized the resulting loss in data coverage and accuracy. For instance, it stands to reason that those groups about whom the government needs the most information—First Nations, recent immigrants, low-income Canadians—are not necessarily reached by the voluntary survey.

Limitations of the Census

Censuses are extremely expensive and labour-intensive undertakings (the 2011 census cost $660 million, or roughly $20 per Canadian) and take several years to tabulate fully, which means that more detailed information from each census is not published until some years later. (You can check for Statistics Canada's latest releases of 2011 census data and related statistics at **www.statcan.gc.ca.**) Even so, censuses are not entirely comprehensive as most tend to underrepresent nonmainstream households and overrepresent wealthy mainstream households. For example, the homeless are hard to enumerate in a census that is based on place of residence, and some of Canada's First Nations reserves have declined to participate in recent surveys.

Despite such shortcomings, the census is an indispensable basis for government planning. The capturing of the spatial distribution of the population and its demographic characteristics allows governments to provide appropriate levels of public services such as education, transportation, and health care; delineate electoral districts; and determine the proper number of members of parliament. Moreover, the financial relationships between different levels of government are often based on census data. For instance, when the 2011 census in Germany revealed that big cities like Berlin and Hamburg had nearly 5 percent fewer inhabitants than was thought, transfer payments worth billions of dollars had to be reallocated. In total, the census showed that there were 1.6 million fewer Germans than was thought.

In many peripheral and semiperipheral countries, governments are not always able to finance a decennial census such as the comprehensive surveys undertaken in more developed countries like France or Germany. Cambodia conducted its first complete census in 1962 and did not conduct another until 1998. Liberia conducted its first census in 24 years in 2008. Pop stars were enlisted and billboards about the census were erected by the government to remind villagers to stay home for three days and be counted.

On the other hand, the example of India shows that a census can be at once technologically advanced and cost-effective. In 2011, India launched its first **biometric census**, a census in which individuals are photographed and fingerprinted to create a national

FIGURE 3.1 Biometric census taking in India, 2011 India became the first country in the world to collect photographs and fingerprints of all of its population as part of its decennial census exercise. Populations in many western countries have refused to participate in a biometric census count as they are reluctant to have the government possess such information about them.

(*Source:* Manpreet Romana/Newscom)

database. In addition to physically counting the country's over 1.2 billion people, the government photographed, fingerprinted, and scanned the irises of every individual over the age of five, creating a national biometric database that will be used to issue 12-digit official identification numbers and microchip-enabled identity cards. To collect this information, 2.7 million census officials visited households in almost 8000 towns and 600 000 villages (**Figure 3.1**). The count also gathered, for the first time, information about the availability of drinking water and toilets across the country as well as the use of the Internet. All this was accomplished at the comparatively low cost of less than $400 million, or thirty cents per enumerated person.

APPLY YOUR KNOWLEDGE Give an example, other than the Iraq case, of how the census is more than just counting people and why this might lead to controversy. Why is the current debate about the census in Canada so politically charged? ■

POPULATION DISTRIBUTION AND STRUCTURE

Because human geographers explore the interrelationships and interdependencies between people and places, they are interested in demography. Population geographers bring to demography a special perspective—the spatial perspective—that describes and explains the spatial differentiation of population distribution, patterns, and processes. Thus, when geographers look at population numbers, they ask themselves two questions: where are these populations concentrated, and what are the causes and consequences of such a population distribution?

Population Distribution

Many geographic reasons exist for the distribution of populations throughout the globe. As the world population density map demonstrates (**Figure 3.2**), some areas of the world are heavily inhabited, others only sparsely. Some areas contain no people whatsoever. Degree of accessibility, topography, soil fertility, climate and weather, water availability and quality, and type and availability of other natural resources are some of the factors that shape population distribution. Other factors are also crucial—first and foremost are a country's political and economic experiences and characteristics. For example, the high population concentrations along Brazil's Atlantic coast date back to the trade patterns set up during Portuguese colonial control in the sixteenth and seventeenth centuries. (See Chapter 2.) Another important factor is culture as expressed in religion, tradition, or historical experience. One of the key reasons the desert cities of Medina and Mecca, in the Middle East, comprise important population concentrations is because they are Islamic sacred sites. **Table 3-1** lists population estimates in terms of continental distributions. Asia is far and away the most populous continent. Running a distant second and third are Africa and Europe.

The population clusters that take shape across the globe have a number of physical similarities. Almost all of the world's inhabitants live on 10 percent of the land. Most live near the shores of oceans and seas or along rivers. Approximately 90 percent live north of the equator, where the largest proportion of the total land area (63 percent) is located. Finally, most of the world's population lives in temperate, low-lying areas with fertile soils.

Population numbers are significant not only on a global scale. Population concentrations within countries, regions, and even metropolitan areas are also important. Bangladesh and the Netherlands, for example, have high population densities throughout. Egypt, on the other hand, displays a pattern of especially high population concentrations along the coasts and the Nile River but a relatively low population density elsewhere (**Figure 3.3**). Meanwhile, most Canadians live along the border to the U.S. (**Figure 3.4** on p. 78).

APPLY YOUR KNOWLEDGE Name three factors that shape population distribution, and assess how they may have influenced the population of a city in your province over the last 50 years. ■

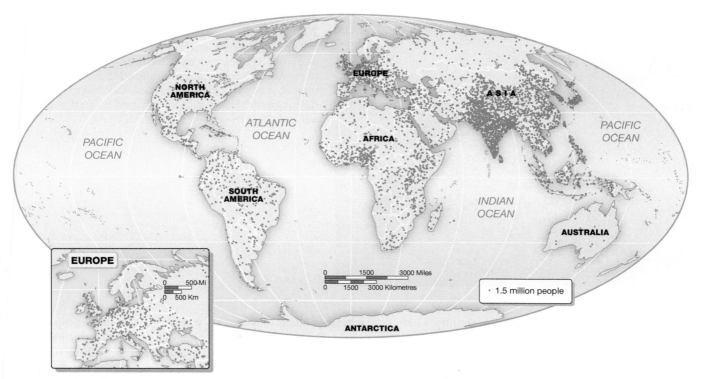

FIGURE 3.2 World population density by country, 2011 Maps such as this one are useful in understanding the relationships between population distribution and the national contexts within which they occur. The population of each country is represented by an equivalent number of dots, which are then distributed evenly over the area of the country to give a visual impression of density. Thus, while China's population is greater than India's in terms of absolute numbers, we can see that India actually has the higher population density of the two.

(*Source:* Adapted from World Bank, World Development Indicators, 2007, World Bank: Washington, DC. Updated data from 2011 World Data Sheet: http://www.prb.org/Publications/Datasheets/2010/2010.wpds.aspx)

TABLE 3-1   World Population Estimates by Continents

Continent	Number of Inhabitants (in millions)	% of Total Population
Asia	4302	60
Africa	1100	15.5
Europe	740	10.5
Latin America and Caribbean	606	8.5
North America	352	5
Oceania	38	0.5
Total	7138	100

(*Source:* Carl Haub and Toshiko Kaneda, 2013 World Population Data Sheet (Washington, DC: Population Reference Bureau, 2013). Reprinted with permission.)

Population Density and Composition

Another way to explore population is in terms of **density**, a numerical measure of the relationship between the number of people and some other unit of interest expressed as a ratio. Crude density is probably the most common measurement of population density. **Crude density**, also called **arithmetic density**, is the total number of people divided by the total land area. The metropolitan area of Mexico City, one of the most populous cities in the world with over 21 million residents, is a classic high-density urban settlement with a population density of approximately 8400 persons per square kilometre (**Figure 3.5**). By comparison, the population density of Vancouver is 802, that of Ontario 14, and that of Canada less than 4 persons per square kilometre.

The limitation of the crude density ratio—and hence the reason for its "crudeness"—is that it is one-dimensional. It tells us very little about the variations in the relationship between people and land. Yet, as we saw in the uneven distribution of the Canadian population, these variations can be substantial. To better understand those variations, we need other tools for exploring population density, such as nutritional density or health care density. **Nutritional density** is the ratio between the total population and the amount of land under cultivation. **Health care density** is the ratio between the total population and the number of physicians. **Figure 3.6** shows a cartogram that combines health care density with total population size for each country.

In addition to exploring patterns of distribution and density, population geographers also examine population in terms of composition—that is, the subgroups that constitute it. Understanding population composition enables geographers to gather important information about population dynamics. For example, knowing the composition of a population in terms of the total number of males and females, number and proportion of senior citizens and children, and number and proportion of people active in the workforce provides valuable insights into the ways in which the population behaves now and how it might behave in the future.

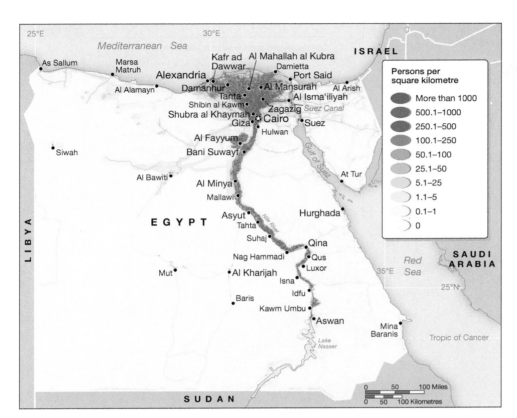

FIGURE 3.3 Population distribution of Egypt Egypt's population distribution is closely linked to the proximity of water. In the north, the population clusters along the Mediterranean, and in the interior, along the banks of the Nile River. (*Source:* Gridded Population of the World [GPW], Version 2. Palisades, NY: CIESIN, Columbia University.)

For example, countries with populations that contain a high proportion of older people face unique challenges. This is a situation most core countries will soon be facing as their "baby boom" generation ages. In Canada, the **baby boom** generation includes those individuals born between 1946 and 1966. A considerable share of a country's resources and energies will be necessary to meet the needs of a large number of people who may no longer be contributing in any significant fashion to the creation of the wealth necessary for their maintenance. There might also be a need to attract foreign workers to supplement the shrinking working-age population.

Similarly, knowing the number of women of childbearing age in a population, along with other information about their status and opportunities, can provide valuable information about the future growth potential of that population. For example, populations in core countries, such as Denmark (which has a small number of women of childbearing age relative to the total population), will generally grow very slowly, if at all. The reason is not only the small proportion of young women, but also their socioeconomic status: women with high levels of education, socioeconomic security, and wide opportunities for work outside the home tend to have fewer children. By contrast, peripheral countries, such as Kenya, will likely continue to experience relatively high rates of population growth because there a large number of women of childbearing age have low levels of education and socioeconomic security, and relatively few employment opportunities. Evidently, the social and economic opportunities that are available to groups within a country's population very much shape the opportunities and challenges that the country faces on a national, regional, and local scale.

Understanding population composition not only can tell us much about the potential future demographics of regions but is also quite useful in the present. For example, businesses use population composition data to make marketing decisions and to decide where to locate. For many years, businesses used laborious computer models to help target their markets. With the development of geographic information systems (GIS), however, this process has been greatly simplified. The practice of assessing the location and composition of particular populations is known as **geodemographic analysis**. As with all efforts to connect personal data with spatial information, there are both benefits and dangers. Obviously, businesses, planners, and governments can make better decisions on how and where to provide services and infrastructure if they have better information about the needs of various population groups. On the other hand, this information might also be used in ways that discriminate against certain population groups merely on the basis of where they live.

Age–Sex Pyramids

The most common way for demographers to graphically represent the composition of the population is an **age–sex pyramid**, which is a representation of the population based on its composition according to age and sex. An age–sex pyramid is actually a bar graph displayed horizontally. Ordinarily, males are portrayed on the left side of the vertical axis and females on the right. Age categories are ordered sequentially from the youngest at the bottom of the pyramid to the oldest at the top. By moving up or down the pyramid, one can compare the opposing horizontal bars in order to assess differences in frequencies for each age group.

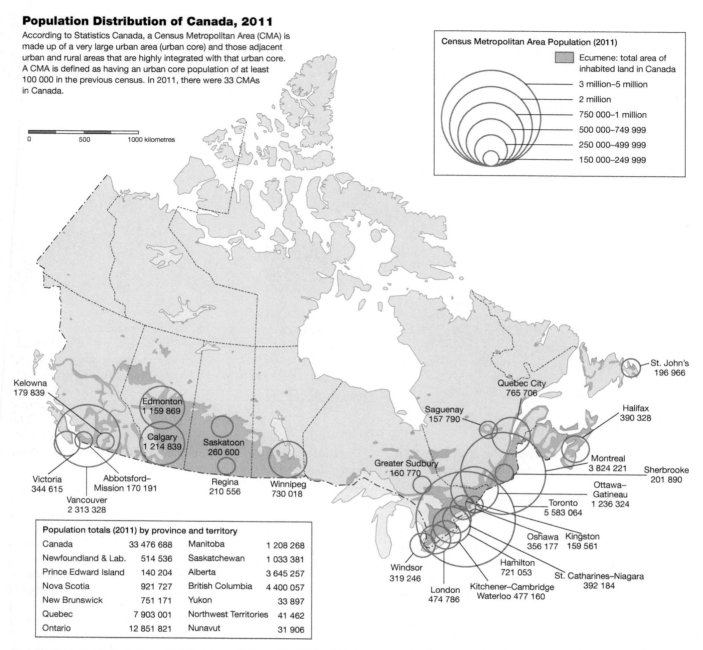

Population Distribution of Canada, 2011

According to Statistics Canada, a Census Metropolitan Area (CMA) is made up of a very large urban area (urban core) and those adjacent urban and rural areas that are highly integrated with that urban core. A CMA is defined as having an urban core population of at least 100 000 in the previous census. In 2011, there were 33 CMAs in Canada.

Census Metropolitan Area Population (2011)

Ecumene: total area of inhabited land in Canada

3 million–5 million
2 million
750 000–1 million
500 000–749 999
250 000–499 999
150 000–249 999

Kelowna 179 839
Edmonton 1 159 869
Calgary 1 214 839
Saskatoon 260 600
Victoria 344 615
Abbotsford–Mission 170 191
Regina 210 556
Winnipeg 730 018
Vancouver 2 313 328
Greater Sudbury 160 770
Saguenay 157 790
Quebec City 765 706
St. John's 196 966
Halifax 390 328
Montreal 3 824 221
Sherbrooke 201 890
Ottawa–Gatineau 1 236 324
Toronto 5 583 064
Oshawa 356 177
Kingston 159 561
Hamilton 721 053
St. Catharines–Niagara 392 184
Windsor 319 246
London 474 786
Kitchener–Cambridge Waterloo 477 160

Population totals (2011) by province and territory			
Canada	33 476 688	Manitoba	1 208 268
Newfoundland & Lab.	514 536	Saskatchewan	1 033 381
Prince Edward Island	140 204	Alberta	3 645 257
Nova Scotia	921 727	British Columbia	4 400 057
New Brunswick	751 171	Yukon	33 897
Quebec	7 903 001	Northwest Territories	41 462
Ontario	12 851 821	Nunavut	31 906

FIGURE 3.4 Population distribution of Canada, 2011 As shown by this map, Canada's population distribution has a number of unusual characteristics. First, the *ecumene* (the inhabited area of Canada) encompasses only a small part of the total land area. Second, even across much of the ecumene, the population density is rather low, with more than 70 percent of the total population highly concentrated in urban areas situated within 150 kilometres of the U.S. border, mainly in the three provinces of British Columbia, Ontario, and Quebec. In fact, despite its large size and relatively small population, Canada has become an urban (even metropolitan) country: more than 81 percent of the total population now lives in towns and cities of more than 1000 people. (*Sources:* The extent of the ecumene is from John Warkentin, *A Regional Geography of Canada*, 2nd ed. Scarborough: Prentice Hall, 2000, p. 71; 2011 census figures are from Statistics Canada, "Population and dwelling counts, for census metropolitan areas, 2011 and 2006 censuses." [http://www12.statcan.gc.ca])

Age–sex pyramids allow demographers to identify changes in the age and sex composition of populations. For example, an age–sex pyramid depicting Germany's population in the year 2000 clearly revealed the impact of the two world wars, especially the loss of large numbers of males of military age and the deficit of births during those periods (**Figure 3.7**). Demographers call population groups like these cohorts. A **cohort** is a group of individuals who share a common *temporal* demographic experience. A cohort is not necessarily based only on time of birth—it may also be based on criteria such as time of marriage or time of graduation.

In addition to revealing the demographic implications of war or other significant events, age–sex pyramids can provide information necessary to assess the potential impacts that growing or declining populations might have. The shape of an age–sex pyramid varies

FIGURE 3.5 Population density, Mexico City, Mexico Urban form and density in Mexico City are the result of many factors. While natural features such as a surrounding lake basin and the presence of seismic activity are important, social and economic factors, including population size and the city's role as a central node in the worldwide system of cities, are also key. (*Source*: Moreno Novello/Shutterstock)

depending on the proportion of people in each age cohort. The pyramid for the peripheral countries, shown in **Figure 3.8**, reveals that many dependent children, ages 0 to 14, exist relative to the rest of the population. The considerable narrowing of the pyramid toward the top indicates that the population has been growing very rapidly in recent years. The shape of this pyramid is typical of peripheral countries with high birth rates and low death rates.

Serious implications are associated with this type of pyramid. First, in the absence of high productivity and wealth, resources are increasingly stretched to their limit to provide even elemental schooling, nutrition, and health care for the growing number of children. Furthermore, when these children reach working age, a large number of additional jobs would have to be created to enable them to support themselves and their families. Also, as they form their own families, the sheer number of women of childbearing age will almost guarantee that the population expansion will continue. This will be true unless strong measures are taken, such as intensive and well-funded birth-control campaigns, improved education, and outside

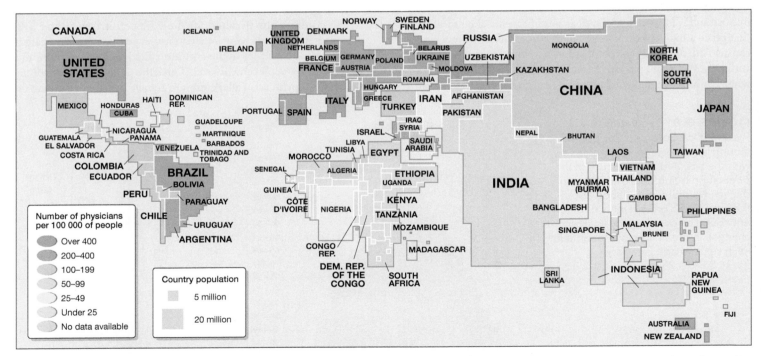

FIGURE 3.6 Health care density Another measure of population density is reflected in this map, which shows the number of people per physician in the total population. Most of the core countries as well as Cuba, the former Soviet Union, and some Central Asian and South American countries have the highest ratio of doctors to overall population. Most of the continent of Africa, except South Africa and Egypt, Libya, and Morocco in North Africa, has the lowest ratio, reflecting another dimension of core–periphery inequality. (*Source*: Adapted from H. Veregin [ed.], *Goode's World Atlas*, 22nd ed. Chicago, IL: Rand McNally & Co, 2010, p. 55. Updated data from NationMaster.com)

FIGURE 3.7 Population of Germany, by age and sex, 2000 Germany's population profile is that of a wealthy core country that has passed through the post-war baby boom and currently possesses a low birth rate. It is also the profile of a country whose population has experienced the ravages of two world wars.

(*Source:* Adapted from J. McFalls, Jr., "Population: A Lively Introduction," 5th ed., *Population Bulletin, 62* [1], 2007, p. 20.)

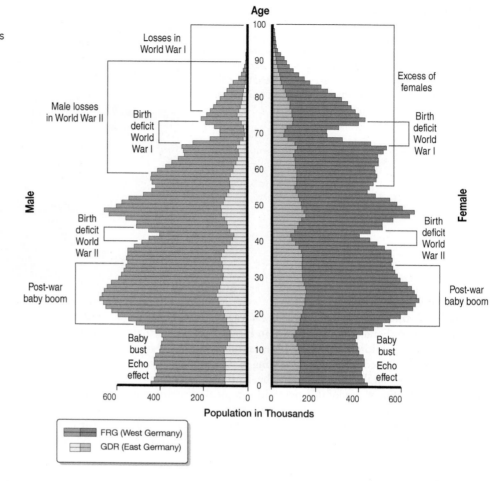

opportunities for women, as well as modifications of cultural norms that place a high value on large family size. Alternatively, a country can also implement coercive measures to control population growth. India, for example, has used controversial sterilization programs, while China had a one-child policy in place between 1979 and 2014.

In contrast, the pyramid for the core countries **(Figure 3.8)** illustrates the typical shape for a country experiencing a slow rate of growth. Most countries in the core are experiencing birth rates that are at or below replacement level. Thus, the pyramid is very columnar, hardly a pyramid at all. People are equally distributed among the

FIGURE 3.8 Population Pyramids of Core and Peripheral Countries Population pyramids vary with the age and sex structure of the population being depicted. We can derive important information about the population growth rates of different countries over time by analyzing changes in the numbers of people in each sex and age category.

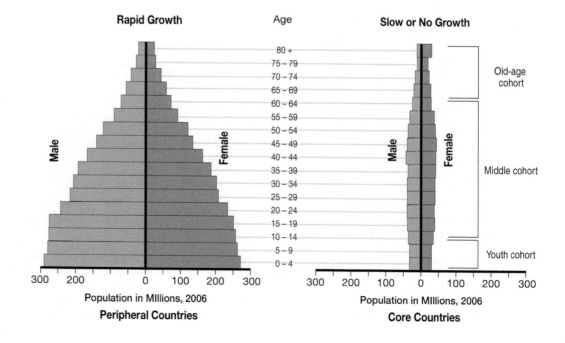

cohorts, though the base is perceptibly narrower. Many of the core European countries, such as Denmark, Spain, and Germany, as well as North America, will face similar demographic challenges, including an extremely large elderly population. In all these countries, however, high levels of production and wealth, combined with low birth rates, translate into a generally greater capacity to provide not only high levels of health, education, and nutrition but also jobs, as those children grow up and join the workforce. Whether these opportunities are equitably distributed among individual members of the population remains to be seen. It is important to note that age–sex pyramids can be constructed at any level from the national to the neighbourhood.

Table 3-2 and **Figure 3.9** show the present state and potential future impact of the baby boom cohort, the largest population

TABLE 3-2 Baby Boomer Population Structure

The baby boom demographically dominated the last half of the twentieth century, but its influence will begin to wane in the first half of the new one.

Year	% of Population Who Are Baby Boomers	Age
1990	30	25–44
2000	20	35–59
2020	15	55–79
2040	7	75–85+

Canadian Population Pyramids 1951–2026

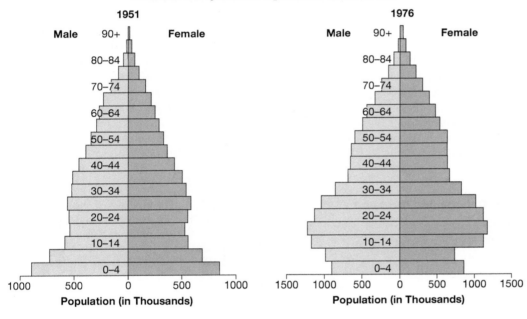

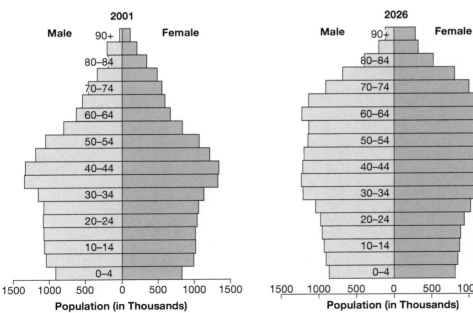

FIGURE 3.9 Population of Canada, by age and sex, 1951, 1976, 2001, and 2026 The profound effects of the baby boom (1946–1966) on Canada's population structure are seen in this series of age–sex pyramids. The four pyramids chart the baby boom's initial impact on a population shaped by low fertility rates of the Depression years and show how the baby boom has subsequently become a major factor in the aging of the Canadian population as the relative size of older age groups has increased over time. The decline in fertility rates since the end of the boom has accentuated the impact of aging on the population because, as the pyramids show, it has led to a relative decline in the size of younger age groups in the population. (*Sources:* "Canadian Population Pyramids," adapted from the Statistics Canada publication *The Daily*, Catalogue 11–001, 16 July 2002, available at www12.statcan.ca/english/census01/products/Analytic. A 30-second animated graphic showing how Canada's age–sex pyramids change over time can be seen at www12.statcan.ca/english/census01/Products/Analytic/companion/age/cda01pymd.cfm.)

The Baby Boom and the Aging of the Population

The baby boom generation—individuals born between 1946 and 1966—is the dominating demographic influence in Canada: almost one in five Canadians is a baby boomer. If we look back over a century of population change in Canada, we see that there has been a long-run (or secular) decline in the birth rate since the 1870s (**Figure 3.A**). We also notice a temporary reversal of that decline beginning in the 1940s—the baby boom.

Why so many births between 1946 and 1966? Most demographers cannot give a definitive answer to this question. Although increases in births following a war are expected, the two-decade surge in births that followed the end of World War II came as a surprise to population experts and policymakers. Sociological theories and predictions based on past trends could not explain the unprecedented phenomenon of the baby boom. To understand it, then, we need to examine a whole host of factors.

Demographic Factors

While the Great Depression of the 1930s and World War II (1939–1945) caused many couples to forego or delay having children, demographers insist that the baby boom not be seen as a direct or indirect result of the end of the war. In fact, although marriages did increase dramatically after the war, the accompanying rise in births accounts only for the very early part of the baby boom. By the early 1950s, the birth rate actually dipped before resuming to climb through the 1950s, reaching a peak in 1960, and returning to average levels by 1966 (**Figure 3.B**). During the peak years of the baby boom, twice as many babies were born in Canada as during the late 1930s.

Demographers have also demonstrated the presence of a "baby bust" generation, the result of lower-than-average birth rates from 1967 to 1979. The baby bust was caused by the economic recession at the time, the availability of birth control, and the changing roles of women in both family and workplace. When the sizable baby boom cohort became parents themselves in the 1980s, they created the so-called baby boom echo (also called "boomlet" because it was not nearly as pronounced as the original boom).

Cultural Factors

At least partially the baby boom was also the consequence of changing attitudes toward marriage and parenthood: couples got married earlier (on average at age 21!), had more children, and had them earlier in their marriage than cohorts before or after. Some scholars attribute this to the optimistic outlook for the future that pervaded the 1950s: an expanding economy seemed to promise progress and wealth for everyone. One job was enough to provide a comfortable family income, and few women entered the workforce. Conversely, the baby boom came to an end in the mid-sixties when women did enter the workforce—and when contraceptives became widely available.

Crude Birth Rate per 1000 Population, Canada and Quebec,* 1801–1989

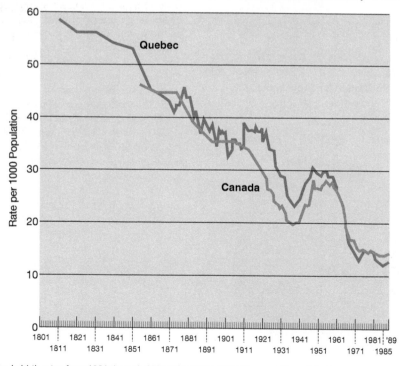

*Crude birth rates from 1801 through 1867 refer to the Catholic population of Quebec.

FIGURE 3.A The decline of the birth rate in Canada This graph shows the decline in the crude birth rate, measured as a rate per 1000 population, for Canada and Quebec from 1801 to 1989. (*Sources:* Anatole Romaniuc, "Fertility in Canada: Retrospective and Prospective." *Canadian Studies in Population* 18[2], 1991, p. 59. (c) 1991 Canadian Population Society. Reprinted by permission.)

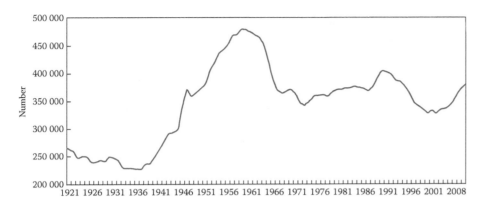

FIGURE 3.B Number of Births in Canada, 1921 to 2008 The graph shows that the number of babies born in Canada was well above the trend line during the 1940s and 1960s: the years of the baby boom. Also visible is the "boomlet" in the late 1980s. (*Source:* Statistics Canada, CANSIM table 102-4502, Births, Catalogue no. 84F0210X and Selected Birth and Fertility Statistics, Canada, 1921-1990, Catalogue no. 82-553-X.)

Political and Economic Factors

During the 1940s, the North American economy went through a phenomenal expansion as industrial production was ramped up for the war effort. Once the war was over, a considerable excess industrial capacity had to be repurposed. The solution was the creation of the consumer society in which marketing constantly fashioned new needs and wants. Production was shifted to consumer products and further stimulated by significant transformations in transportation (cars) and technology (television, household appliances).

Additionally, government expanded and created programs for education and housing that helped returning veterans start married life with property and the opportunity to improve their economic status by attending university. Cheaper mass and individual transportation helped fuel suburbanization, which in turn meant growth in the construction industry, in automobile manufacturing, and in the production of durable goods for the newly built homes. Not surprisingly, demand for labour was high in a growing economy, and young people were able to obtain good jobs with relatively high wages, decent benefits, and attractive prospects for promotion. They responded to the good outlook by starting families earlier and having more children. Now, decades later, these children have become aging baby boomers.

The Aging of the Population

It is important to recognize that something like the baby boom occurred also in parts of the periphery, if on a smaller scale. The result is a very large cohort of individuals worldwide, currently in their late forties to mid-sixties, that has had and will continue to have tremendous impacts on the rest of the population, especially as they enter old age. In fact, the most fundamental demographic transformation of the twenty-first century is the aging of the population worldwide (**Figure 3.C**), the result not only of the aging of the baby boom cohort but also of longer life expectancies and falling fertility rates. In 1980, the median age of the world's population was 23. By 2013, it had risen to 30, and by 2050 it is expected to increase to 38.

FIGURE 3.C Retired women enjoying a game of pool In core countries, men and women are living longer through lifestyle changes and improved health care. (*Source:* Blend Images/Shutterstock)

(Continued)

In the core countries, the number of older persons (60 and over) now exceeds the number of children under the age of 15, which will increase the median age of the population from 37.5 in 2000 to 45.6 in 2050. In many cases there will be a resulting decrease in national populations, which means there will be fewer working-age people to support the needs of the aging population. For countries like Italy, Japan, and Germany (where the median age has already reached 44 and one-fifth of the population is over the age of 65), this raises some very serious concerns about employment, economic growth, health care, pensions, and social support services. One possible counter measure that could have immediate effects is increasing immigration opportunities for young migrants from countries that are experiencing rapid population growth: the median age of new immigrants to Canada is less than 32.

Although the aging of the population has been slower in peripheral countries because of high twentieth-century birth rates, the next 50 years will see the median age rise there as well. By 2050, the median age in countries of the periphery is expected to be 36.7 years, up from 24.4 years in 2000. This is actually a bigger jump than in the core. East and Southeast Asia are the regions whose populations are aging most rapidly, with Africa aging the slowest.

The Impact on Canadians

Every day, 1000 Canadians turn 65. By 2030, the entire baby boomer cohort will be between the ages of 64 and 84, the phase of life when health care costs are highest. At the same time, Canada will find it harder to pay for those exploding costs: as the baby boomers retire, they pay considerably lower taxes.

Public pensions will also be strained because there will soon be more people receiving these pensions and fewer that are paying into pension plans. To cover the shortfall, the federal government has already increased the premiums and raised the age of retirement. Moreover, because the aging baby boomers will comprise more women than men (because average female life expectancies are higher), questions of gender disparities will become more prominent.

In economic terms, boomers still occupy the best jobs and the upper ranks of many institutions and corporations. (They also control most of Canada's personal wealth—as much as 50 percent by some estimates.) Only when the boomers retire in large numbers,

from about 2020 onward, will the younger generation be able to move up in the ranks.

As the Canadian population ages and its physical abilities change, our economy, society, and physical infrastructure will have to adjust as well. What will happen to the value of large multi-storey homes in car-dependent suburbs once ailing baby boomers are unable to climb stairs and no longer have drivers' licences? Will our inner cities experience a renaissance when retiring baby boomers move to downtown condos within walking distance to public transit and health care facilities? At a small scale, we are seeing the beginnings of these adjustments: in Vancouver, for instance, the 2014 building code requires handles instead of knobs on all doors and faucets in new construction to accommodate persons with arthritis or other limitations.

At the sociocultural level, Canada's young generation will increasingly live in a country where the teenage demand for music, fashion, and recreation that used to drive the marketplace is being replaced by the consumer preferences of a much older demographic. Already, the average Canadian new car buyer is 51, the average CBC television viewer is 49 years old.

The aging of the Canadian baby boomers also has a spatial dimension. For instance, Victoria (British Columbia) and Kingston (Ontario) have a higher-than-average population of those aged over 65 because of their attractiveness to retirees. This obviously means increased financial strain for these cities as the demand rises for age-appropriate medical facilities, retirement homes, and wheelchair-accessible public transit. Other parts of Canada, such as rural Saskatchewan and Newfoundland and Labrador, have been aging not because of in-migration of the elderly but because of out-migration of the young. Meeting the needs of the elderly in isolated rural communities poses an even greater problem than in cities.

In conclusion, as the baby boomers move through retirement and old age, Canada will face various challenges. The tremendous size of the baby boom cohort continues to affect the career and job mobility of younger generations, as well as labour costs, which in turn affect taxes, health care, pensions, and other benefit costs. The actual impact that the baby boom generation will have into the first half of the twenty-first century remains to be seen. We are all part of this demographic experiment.

cohort in Canadian history. **Figure 3.9** provides a series of pyramids that illustrate how the configuration changes as the boomers age. The narrower column of younger people rising below the boomer cohort in these pyramids reveals the biggest problem facing this population: a significantly smaller cohort moving into its main productive years having to support a growing cohort of aging and decreasingly productive boomers. Political wrangling over the need for pension reform, delaying retirement age, and expanding health care at the expense of university funding is only the tip of the iceberg with regard to this problem. (See Box 3.1, "Geography Matters: The Baby Boom and the Aging of the Population".)

As you might guess based on these discussions, a critical aspect of the population pyramid is the **dependency ratio**, which is a measure of the economic impact of the young and old on the more economically productive members of the population. In order to assess this relation of dependency in a particular population, demographers divide the total population into three age cohorts, sometimes further dividing those cohorts by sex. The **youth cohort** consists of those members of the population who are less than 15 years of age and generally considered to be too young to be fully active in the labour force. The **middle cohort** consists of those members of the population aged 15 to 64, who are considered economically active and productive.

Finally, the **old-age cohort** consists of those members of the population aged 65 and older, who are considered beyond their economically active and productive years. By dividing the population into these three groups, it is possible to obtain a measure of the dependence of the young and old upon the economically active and the impact of the dependent population upon the independent (Figure 3.8).

> **APPLY YOUR KNOWLEDGE** Why do researchers divide the population of a country into youth, middle, and old-age cohorts? What do these categories indicate about the potential of a country's population? What might be an "ideal" proportion of the three cohorts? ■

POPULATION DYNAMICS AND PROCESSES

In order to arrive at an understanding of population growth and change, experts look first at two significant factors: fertility and mortality. Birth and death rates, as they are also known, often are also indirect indicators of a region's level of development and its place within the world economy. To understand population growth overall, however, they must also look at the movement of the population. A simple equation for calculating population growth is $G = B - D + (I - E)$, where G (growth) equals B (births) minus

D (deaths) plus I (immigration) minus E (emigration). We look at each of these key population dynamics in turn.

Birth (or Fertility) Rates

The **crude birth rate (CBR)** is the number of live births in a single year for every thousand people in the population. The crude birth rate is indeed crude, because it measures the birth rate in terms of the total population and not with respect to a particular age-specific group or cohort. For instance, the CBR of the entire Canadian population in 2011 was 11 per 1000 people (which is only half of Mexico's CBR of 21). However, this value hides great differences among ethnicities in Canada: the rate for Aboriginal women is more than twice the rate for Korean and Chinese women, for example. Clearly, differences exist when we look at specific groups and especially at age and sex cohorts at their reproductive peak.

Although the level of economic development is a very important factor shaping the CBR, other, often equally important, influences also affect it. In particular, it may be heavily affected by the demographic structure of the population, as graphically suggested by age–sex pyramids. In addition, as we mentioned previously in this chapter, an area's CBR is influenced by women's educational achievement, religion, social customs, and diet and health, as well as by politics, war, civil unrest, and, increasingly, environmental degradation. Most demographers also believe that the availability of birth-control methods is critically important to a country's or region's birth rate. A world map of the CBR (**Figure 3.10**) shows high levels of fertility in

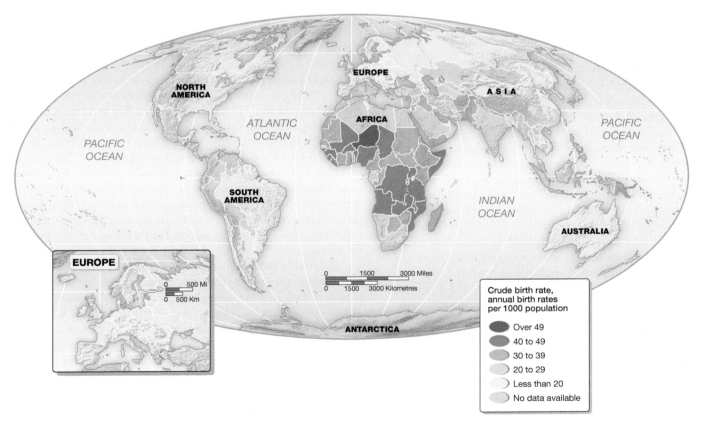

FIGURE 3.10 World crude birth rates, 2013 Crude birth rates and crude death rates are often indicators of the levels of economic development in individual countries. For example, the CBR of Australia offers a stark contrast to that of Ethiopia, a very poor and underdeveloped peripheral country. (*Source:* Data from Population Reference Bureau, *World Population Data Sheet, 2013.*)

TABLE 3-3 Total Fertility Rates for Selected Countries, 2013

Country	TFR
Somalia	6.8
Congo (DR)	6.3
Afghanistan	5.4
Iraq	4.3
Pakistan	3.8
Haiti	3.5
World	2.5
India	2.4
U.S.	1.9
Canada	1.6
China	1.5
Germany	1.4
Singapore	1.3

(*Source:* Carl Haub and Toshiko Kaneda, 2013 World Population Data Sheet (Washington, DC: Population Reference Bureau, 2013). Reprinted with permission.)

most of the periphery and low levels of fertility in the core. The highest birth rates occur in Africa, the poorest region in the world.

The crude birth rate is only one indicator of fertility and in fact is somewhat limited in its usefulness, telling very little about the potential for future fertility levels. Two other indicators formulated by population experts—the total fertility rate and the doubling time—provide more insight into the potential future dynamics of a population. The **total fertility rate (TFR)** is a measure of the average number of children a woman will have throughout the years that demographers have identified as her childbearing years, approximately ages 15 through 49 (**Table 3-3**). Whereas the CBR indicates the total number of births per 1000 people in a given year, the TFR is a more predictive measure that attempts to portray what birth rates will be among a particular cohort of women over time. A population with a TFR of slightly higher than 2 has achieved replacement-level fertility. This means that birth rates and death rates are approximately balanced and there is stability in the population.

Closely related to the TFR is the doubling time of the population. The **doubling time**, as the name suggests, is a measure of how long it will take the population of an area to grow to twice its current size. A country whose population increases at 1.1 percent per year will have doubled in about 63 years. In fact, world population is currently increasing at this rate. By contrast, a country whose population is increasing at 3.18 percent annually will double in only 22 years—the doubling time for the Gaza Strip. Birth rates and the population dynamics we can project from them, however, tell us only part of the story of the potential of the population for growth. We must also know the death (mortality) rates.

Death (or Mortality) Rates

Countering birth rates and shaping overall population numbers and composition is the **crude death rate (CDR)**, the number of deaths in one year for every thousand people in the population. As with crude birth rates, crude death rates often roughly reflect levels of economic development (**Figure 3.11**).

Although often associated with economic development, CDR is also significantly influenced by other factors. A demographic structure with more men and elderly people, for example, usually means higher death rates. Other important influences on mortality include health care availability, social class, occupation, and even place of residence. For example, poorer groups in the population have higher death rates than the middle class and mortality of First Nations populations living on reserves is higher than in urban areas. The net difference between the CBR and CDR is the rate of **natural increase**—the surplus of births over deaths—or the **natural decrease**—the deficit of births relative to deaths (**Figure 3.12**).

Death rates can be measured for sex and age cohorts; one of the most common measures is the **infant mortality rate**, which reflects the annual number of deaths of infants under 1 year of age per 1000 live births. The infant mortality rate has been used by researchers as an important indicator both of the adequacy of a country's health care system and of the general population's access to health care. Global patterns show that infant mortality rates are high in the peripheral countries of Africa and Asia and low in the more developed countries of Europe and North America (**Figure 3.13**). Generally, the core's low rates reflect adequate maternal nutrition and the wider availability of health care resources and personnel.

However, when patterns are examined at the level of countries, regions, and cities, infant mortality rates are far from uniform. In east central Europe, the Czech Republic has a 2.6 per-thousand infant mortality rate, yet nearby Bulgaria has a rate of 7.8. In Israel, the infant mortality rate is 3.5, while in the neighbouring Palestinian Territories it is 20. And when war is introduced into the equation, the infant mortality rate skyrockets: Afghanistan has 71 infant deaths per 1000 live births. Finally, in Canada, First Nations reserves and the overwhelmingly Inuit population in Nunavut suffer infant mortality rates that are two to three times higher than the national average of 4.9. The point is that global patterns and national averages often mask regional and local variations in mortality rates. The same, incidentally, holds true for many other indicators we use in this book: regional and local variations in culture, wealth, traditions, and resources, to name but a few factors, can lead to considerable deviations from the average.

Related to infant mortality and the crude death rate is **life expectancy**, the average number of years an infant newborn can expect to live. Not surprisingly, life expectancy varies considerably from country to country, region to region, and even from place to place within cities and among different classes and racial and ethnic groups. In the United States, a child entering grade 1 in 2014 can expect to live more than 78 years. If we begin to specify the characteristics of that infant by sex and race, however, variation emerges. An African-American male entering grade 1 has a life expectancy of 69.5 years, while a six-year-old Anglo-American female can expect to live, on average, 81 years. Canada, too, exhibits considerable variations in life expectancy across the country and among groups. Aboriginal communities, for example, record some of the lowest average life expectancies in Canada.

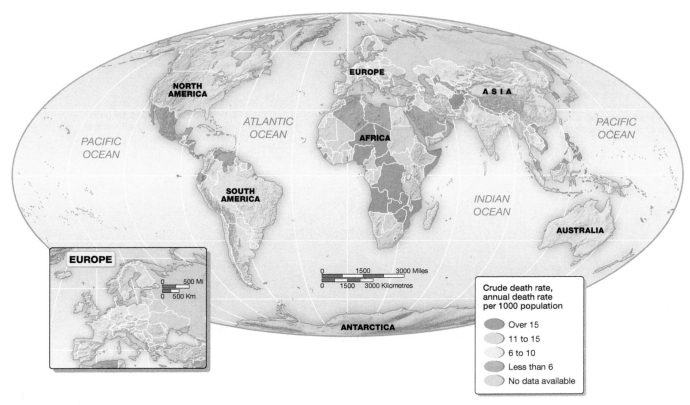

FIGURE 3.11 World crude death rates, 2013 The global pattern of crude death rates varies from crude birth rates. Most apparent is that the difference between highest and lowest crude death rates is relatively smaller than the difference for crude birth rates, reflecting the fact that nutrition and basic health care have improved almost everywhere in the world. *(Source: Data from Population Reference Bureau, World Population Data Sheet, 2013.)*

(See "Population, Health, and the Environment" section later in this chapter.)

Another key factor influencing life expectancy is epidemics, which can quickly and radically alter population numbers and composition. In our times, epidemics can spread rapidly over great distances, largely because people and other disease carriers can travel from one place to another rapidly. Epidemics can have profound effects, from the international to the local level, and reflect the increasing interdependence of a shrinking globe. They may affect different population groups in different ways and, depending on the quantity and quality of health and nutritional care available, may have a greater or lesser impact on different localities.

One of the most widespread epidemics of modern times is HIV/AIDS (human immunodeficiency virus/acquired immunodeficiency syndrome). The disease is a serious problem in regions ranging from Southeast Asia to sub-Saharan Africa and also affects certain populations in many core countries. In the United States, for example, HIV/AIDS first arose largely among male homosexuals and intravenous drug users who shared needles. Geographically, early concentrations of AIDS occurred in places with high concentrations of these two subpopulations. It has had perhaps the most severe impact in inner-city areas but has cropped up in every region of the United States, increasingly appearing in the male and female heterosexual population. The rate for blacks is roughly eight times the rate for whites

(67.7 per 100 000 versus 8.2 per 100 000). African-American males continue to bear the greatest burden of HIV/AIDS infection. Similarly, not all Canadians are uniformly affected by HIV/AIDS as their susceptibility to infection is to a large degree influenced by their relative position in society. For instance, among the more than 71 000 Canadians stricken with the disease, Aboriginals are more than three times overrepresented, while prison inmates are ten times overrepresented.

The spatial and social pattern of the disease is markedly different in Africa, where it is overwhelmingly associated with heterosexual, nondrug users and affects both sexes equally. Overall, of the 34 million people worldwide infected with HIV/AIDS, more than 22 million live in Africa (**Figure 3.14**) Once again, a closer look allows us to better appreciate the regional variability of the phenomenon. In the northern African nations from Morocco to Egypt and Sudan, cultural and religious norms that discourage many of the high-risk behaviours associated with the spread of HIV/AIDS have kept the prevalence of the infection below 1 percent of the population. By contrast, the further south we look on the continent, the higher the rates are, reaching 15 percent in South Africa and 25 percent in Botswana. Neighbouring Swaziland holds the sad distinction of having the world's highest rate, reaching more than 50 percent in certain subgroups of the population, such as pregnant women. As a result of the high mortality due to HIV/AIDS, life expectancy in Swaziland has dropped to from 61 years to 32 years over the past decade. The United Nations Development

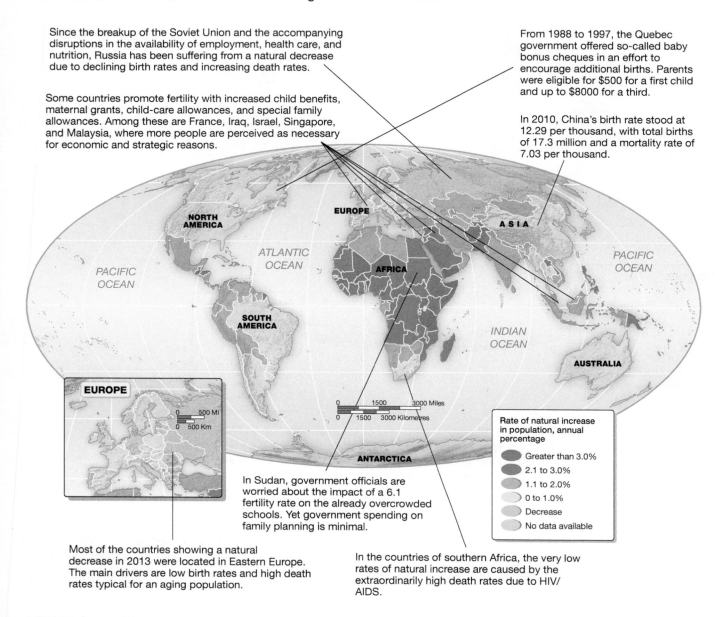

Since the breakup of the Soviet Union and the accompanying disruptions in the availability of employment, health care, and nutrition, Russia has been suffering from a natural decrease due to declining birth rates and increasing death rates.

Some countries promote fertility with increased child benefits, maternal grants, child-care allowances, and special family allowances. Among these are France, Iraq, Israel, Singapore, and Malaysia, where more people are perceived as necessary for economic and strategic reasons.

From 1988 to 1997, the Quebec government offered so-called baby bonus cheques in an effort to encourage additional births. Parents were eligible for $500 for a first child and up to $8000 for a third.

In 2010, China's birth rate stood at 12.29 per thousand, with total births of 17.3 million and a mortality rate of 7.03 per thousand.

Rate of natural increase in population, annual percentage

Greater than 3.0%
2.1 to 3.0%
1.1 to 2.0%
0 to 1.0%
Decrease
No data available

In Sudan, government officials are worried about the impact of a 6.1 fertility rate on the already overcrowded schools. Yet government spending on family planning is minimal.

Most of the countries showing a natural decrease in 2013 were located in Eastern Europe. The main drivers are low birth rates and high death rates typical for an aging population.

In the countries of southern Africa, the very low rates of natural increase are caused by the extraordinarily high death rates due to HIV/AIDS.

FIGURE 3.12 World rates of natural increase, 2013 As the map shows, rates of natural increase are highest in sub-Saharan Africa, the Middle East, and parts of Asia, as well as parts of South and Central America. While many core countries have slow to stable rates of natural increase, parts of Europe as well as Russia now show a natural decrease. (*Source:* Data from Population Reference Bureau, *World Population Data Sheet, 2013.*)

Programme (UNDP) has warned that if the spread of HIV/AIDS continues unabated, the "longer-term existence of Swaziland as a country will be seriously threatened."

Medical geographers have made important contributions to the study of the diffusion of HIV/AIDS. **Medical geography** is a subarea of the discipline that specializes in understanding the spatial aspects of health and illness. This spatial perspective includes disease mapping as well as the distribution and diffusion of health and illness. For instance, the geographical diffusion of HIV/AIDS in Africa has occurred along roads, rivers, and coastlines, all major transportation routes associated with regional marketing systems. Accordingly, the impact is worst in

urban areas, though no area has been immune to the disease's spread. Meanwhile, in core countries with their well-integrated urban systems and intensive transportation networks, HIV/AIDS has been able to spread even more rapidly because of hierarchical diffusion. (See Chapter 1.)

The importance of medical geography is heightened by the fact that the landscape of disease that we are seeing today is changing rapidly. Diseases we thought were eradicated, such as tuberculosis, are coming back; diseases that were previously unknown are emerging, such as Ebola; and diseases that have maintained geographic limitations, such as dengue hemorrhagic fever, are spreading. This latter process will only accelerate with global climate change.

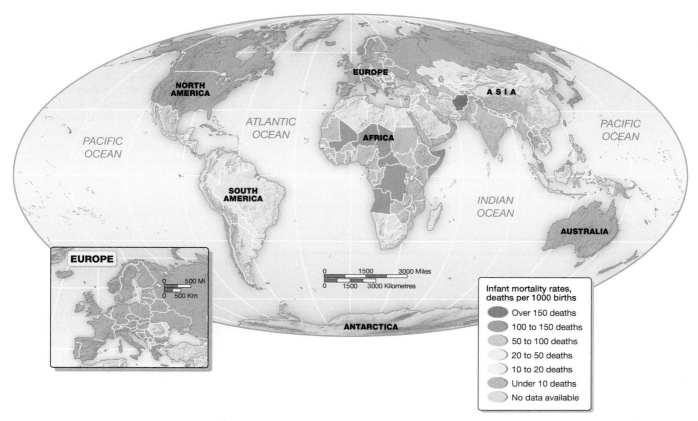

FIGURE 3.13 World infant mortality rates, 2013 The geography of poverty underlies the patterns shown in this map and allows us to analyze the linkages between population variables and social conditions. Infant mortality rates generally parallel crude death rates, with sub-Saharan Africa generally reporting the highest rates. These rates reflect a number of factors, including inadequate or completely absent maternal health care as well as poor nutrition for infants. (*Source:* Data from Population Reference Bureau, *World Population Data Sheet, 2013.*)

APPLY YOUR KNOWLEDGE How does the level of wealth of a country affect its ability to respond to health issues like HIV/AIDS, infant mortality, or life expectancy in general? Why do some wealthy countries, such as the U.S. or Saudi Arabia, score relatively low on those parameters? ∎

Demographic Transition Theory

Many demographers believe that fertility and mortality rates are directly tied to the level of economic development of a country, region, or place. Pointing to the history of demographic change in core countries, they contend that many of the economic, political, social, and technological transformations associated with

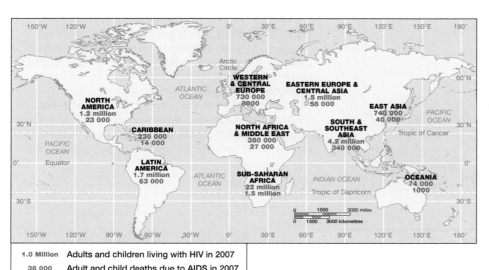

FIGURE 3.14 Adults and children living with and dying from HIV/AIDS, 2007 HIV/AIDS infections are concentrated in the periphery and semiperiphery, with 86 percent of people with HIV/AIDS living in Asia and sub-Saharan Africa. Compare the number of adults and children living with HIV/AIDS in Africa with those in North America or Europe. Deaths from HIV/AIDS have also been highest in Africa.

(*Source:* Joint United Nations Programme on HIV/AIDS [UNAIDS], "Annex 1," *Report on the Global AIDS Epidemic 2008.* Geneva: UNAIDS, 2008, www.unaids.org/en/dataanalysis/epidemiology/2008rep ortontheglobalaidsepidemic/.)

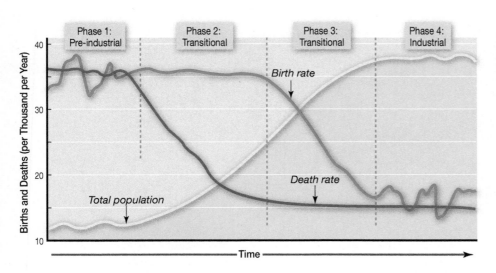

FIGURE 3.15 **Demographic transition model** The transition from a stable population based on high birth and death rates to one based on low birth and death rates progresses in clearly defined stages, as illustrated by this graph. With basic information about a country's birth and death rates, it is possible to identify that country's position within the demographic transition process. Population experts disagree about the usefulness of the model, however. Many insist it applies only to the demographic history of core countries.

industrialization and urbanization lead to a demographic transition. A **demographic transition** is a model of population change in which high birth and death rates are replaced by low birth and death rates. Once a society moves from a pre-industrial economic base to an industrial one, population growth slows. According to the demographic transition model, the slowing of population growth is attributable to improved economic production and higher standards of living brought about by better nutrition, health care, education, and sanitation.

As **Figure 3.15** illustrates, the high birth and death rates of the pre-industrial phase (Phase 1) are replaced by the low birth and death rates of the industrial phase (Phase 4) only after passing through a critical transitional stage. During these transitional Phases 2 and 3, birth and death rates fall at different speeds. During Phase 2, simple improvements in hygiene produce a rapid decline in mortality, whereas fertility remains at the high levels characteristic of a place that has not yet industrialized. The resulting lag leads to a high rate of natural increase of the population until finally, during Phase 3, the birth rate drops, too.

Some demographers have observed that many peripheral and semiperipheral countries appear to be stalled in the transitional stage—caught in a "demographic trap." **Figure 3.16** illustrates the disparity between birth and death rates for core and peripheral countries. Despite a sharp decline in mortality rates, most peripheral countries retain relatively high fertility rates. What causes this lag of the birth rate? Essentially, the reason is that mortality rates react quickly to relatively simple improvements in hygiene (e.g., availability of clean water and basic sanitation), nutrition, and health care. On the other hand, fertility rates are mostly the result of social attitudes about the desirability of large families that are relatively slow to change.

Although the demographic transition model is based on actual birth and death statistics of core countries during their period of industrialization (**Table 3-4**), many population geographers and other experts increasingly question whether it is generalizable to the experience of countries and regions in the periphery today. Among other things, critics note that industrialization—which, according to the theory, is central to moving from Phase 2 to Phases

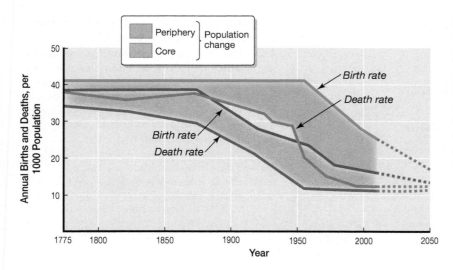

FIGURE 3.16 **World trends in birth and death rates, 1775–2050** The graph is an illustration of the impact of increasing affluence on reproductive choices. It also portrays an optimistic view of the future, in which peripheral regions will continue to experience falling birth rates as we move closer to the midpoint of this century. For the core, the projection is that birth and death rates will stay low. (*Source:* Adapted from T. Allen and A. Thomas, *Poverty and Development in the 1990s.* London: Oxford University Press, 1992; updates from *CIA World Factbook 2011,* https://www.cia.gov/library/publications/the-world-factbook/geos/xx.html.)

TABLE 3-4 Birth and Death Rates for England and Scotland, 1870–1920

The CBRs and CDRs for England and Scotland for the period between 1870 and 1920 illustrate countries moving between Phase 2 and Phase 3 of the demographic transition, in which death rates are lower than birth rates. England and Scotland are clear examples of the way in which the demographic transition has been theorized to operate in the core countries. During the 50-year period covered in the table, both countries were completing their transformation into key industrial regions.

	1870	1880	1890	1900	1910	1920
Crude Birth Rate						
England	35.2	35.4	32.5	29.9	27.3	22.7
Scotland	35	34.8	32.3	30.2	28.4	24
Crude Death Rate						
England	22.5	21.4	19.2	18.2	15.4	14.6
Scotland	22.1	21.6	19.2	18.5	16.6	15.3

(*Source:* M. Anderson and D. Morse, "High Fertility, High Emigration, and Low Nuptuality Adjustment Processes in Scotland's Demographic Experience, 1861–1914, Part I." *Population Studies, 47,* 1993, p. 8.)

3 and 4—is seldom domestically generated in the peripheral countries. Instead, it is foreign investment from core countries and transnational corporations that seems to drive peripheral industrialization. As a result, the rise in living standards and other features of demographic change witnessed in core countries—where industrialization was largely a result of domestic capital investment—have not occurred in many peripheral countries. Other critiques of the demographic transition model point to several factors undermining a demographic transition fuelled by economic growth: the shortage of skilled labour, the absence of advanced educational opportunities for all members of the population (especially women), and limits on technological advances. In other words, the demographic transition model reflects how the core countries were able to take advantage of their privileged starting position as early industrializers, yet today's peripheral countries may find it impossible to repeat this development as they are in a much more difficult starting position. (See Chapter 2.)

APPLY YOUR KNOWLEDGE Give an example of why a country might be concerned about its national population being too small. How could this affect its population characteristics? What might a country gain by increasing the birth rate? What might it lose? ∎

POPULATION MOVEMENT AND MIGRATION

In addition to the population dynamics of death and reproduction, the third critical influence on population is the movement of people from place to place. Individuals may make far-reaching international or intraregional moves, or they may simply move from one part of a city to another. For the most part, mobility and migration reflect the interdependence of the world-system. For example, global shifts in industrial investment result in local adjustments to those shifts as populations move or remain in place in response to the creation or disappearance of employment opportunities.

Mobility and Migration

One way to describe such movement is with the broader term **mobility**, the ability to move from one place to another, either permanently or temporarily. Mobility may be used to describe a wide array of human movement, ranging from a journey to work (for example, a daily commute from suburb to city or suburb to suburb) to an ocean-spanning permanent move.

The second way to describe population movement is with the more narrowly defined term of **migration**, a long-distance move to a new location. Migration involves a permanent or temporary change of residence from one neighbourhood or settlement to another. Moving from a particular location is defined as **emigration**, also known as out-migration. Moving to a particular location is defined as **immigration** or in-migration. For example, a person from China who moves to Canada *emigrates* from China and *immigrates* to Canada. This type of move, from one country to another, is termed **international migration**. Moves may also occur within a particular country or region, in which case they are called **internal migration**. Both permanent and temporary changes of residence occur for many reasons but most often involve a desire for economic betterment or an escape from adverse political conditions, such as war or oppression. Increasingly, people are also forced to migrate because of environmental degradation.

Governments are concerned about keeping track of migration numbers, migration rates, and the characteristics of the migrant populations because these factors can have profound consequences for political, economic, and cultural conditions at all scales. For example, a peripheral country, such as Cuba, that has experienced substantial out-migration of highly trained professionals may find it difficult to provide services to its population. On the other hand, such core countries as the United States, Germany, and France have received large numbers of low-skilled in-migrants willing to work for low wages, which leads to social friction. And the situation is even more complicated than that: Germany, for instance, in turn experiences a "brain drain" of highly qualified doctors and academics to the United Kingdom, Switzerland, and Scandinavia and has recently become a net exporter of population.

Demographers have developed several calculations of migration rates. The in-migration and out-migration rates provide the foundation for gross and net migration rates for an area under study. **Gross migration** refers to the total number of migrants moving into and out of a place, region, or country. **Net migration** refers to the gain or loss in the total population of that area as a result of migration.

Migration rates, however, provide only a small portion of the information needed to understand the dynamics of migration and its effects from the local to the national level. In general terms, migrants make their decisions to move based on push factors and pull factors. **Push factors** are events and conditions that impel an individual to move from a location. They include a wide variety of possible motives, from the idiosyncratic, such as dissatisfaction with the amenities offered at home, to the dramatic, such as war, economic dislocation, or ecological deterioration. **Pull factors** are forces of attraction that influence migrants to move to a particular location.

Usually, the decision to migrate is a combination of both push and pull factors. In **voluntary migration**, an individual chooses to move, mainly in response to pull factors (**Figure 3.17**). When push factors produce **forced migration**, migration occurs against the individual's will. We will look at both types of migration in the next two sections.

APPLY YOUR KNOWLEDGE Identify three push and three pull factors that shape the decisions by university students to migrate for employment opportunities. Do you suspect that you will migrate after graduation? If so, will you be doing it out of necessity or choice? Please provide specific reasons for both the pull and push factors. ■

International Voluntary Migration

Canada is a nation made up entirely of successive waves of voluntary immigrants, adding their own contributions to the development of this country, progressively inhabiting its spaces, and constructing their own places. Canada continues to receive approximately 250 000 immigrants each year, which in proportion to the total population amounts to the highest rate in the world. Archaeological evidence suggests that Canada was first settled from the west by small bands of hunter-gatherer peoples migrating from Asia at least 11 500 years ago. More than 10 000 years later, the first known migration from the east came in the form of the short-lived Viking settlement in L'Anse aux Meadows in Newfoundland (about 1000 C.E.). Another 500 to 600 years passed before permanent European immigration to Canada began, led by French ambitions to settle the gulf and lower valley of the St. Lawrence River. Only after the loss of its American colonies after 1783 and the flight of 100 000 Loyalists into Ontario, Quebec, and New Brunswick did Britain step up its efforts to settle Canada.

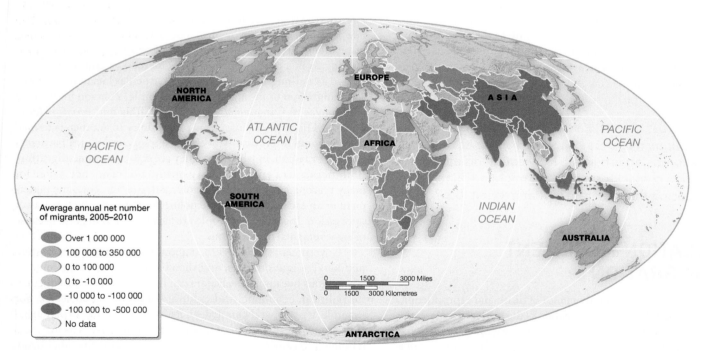

FIGURE 3.17 Global voluntary migration This snapshot map shows those countries that are largely receiving and those that are largely sending migrants. In 2011, 214 million people, over 3 percent of the world's population, lived outside their country of origin. (*Source:* United Nations Dept. of Economic and Social Affairs, Population Division, *International Migration 2009.* www.unmigration.org, www.unpopulation.org.)

For the next century or so, the agricultural lands of Ontario and Quebec attracted various migrant groups. It is estimated that from 1815 to 1865, over 1 million immigrants from the British Isles entered what was then known as British North America, many moving on to the United States. Approximately 60 percent of that flow was made up of migrants from Ireland, prompted to leave by disasters such as the famine of 1846 to 1849. By the 1860s, little arable land remained to be colonized in the east, and Canada began to experience a net emigration. Many of those who stayed in this country chose to move internally, either to Canada's developing cities or to its agricultural frontiers. Indeed, it was in the west that Canada's policymakers saw the solution to the flagging population numbers. The purchase of Rupert's Land, in 1870, and treaty negotiations with the First Nations opened up the Prairies for European settlement. The completion of the transcontinental Canadian Pacific Railroad in 1885 made it feasible to establish in Canada an economy based on western agriculture.

There followed a 30- to 40-year period of substantial immigration from eastern and central Europe to Alberta, Saskatchewan, and Manitoba. The twentieth century, with the exception of the war years and the Depression, continued this trend. Two major changes in the patterns of immigration occurred as the century progressed. First, immigration increasingly focused on urban rather than rural areas as destinations. Second, once a nonracist selection policy was introduced in the 1960s, the main sources of Canada's immigrants shifted from Europe to Asia. After 12 000 years, immigration to Canada has come full circle.

Of course, the full story of Canadian immigration lies buried beneath such statistics and generalizations. For many of us, the hopes and hardships, the memories of countries left behind, and the communities and cultures created in Canada form the real immigration experience. In places all across this country, we can see the indelible effects of that story. Contributions are evident from the Chinese workers brought in to build the railways in the 1870s; the pacifist Doukhobors who moved to Saskatchewan from Russia in the 1890s to flee religious persecution; the British gentlemen farmers trying to plant apple orchards at Walkachin in pre–World War I British Columbia; the Czech and Yugoslav miners who, from the 1930s, extracted minerals from the mines of Flin Flon, Manitoba; the waves of post–World War II settlers from Western Europe who arrived at Pier 21 in Halifax, Nova Scotia, in the 1950s; the Jamaicans coming to Toronto to seek a more prosperous life in the 1960s; the Chilean, Ugandan, and Vietnamese refugees who fled persecution in their own countries to settle in Toronto and Montreal in the 1970s; the Central Americans who sought refuge in the 1980s; and the latest wave of immigrants from Hong Kong that have become a significant economic presence in Vancouver. It is impossible to sum up these experiences, but it is obvious that the resulting combined contribution has reshaped this country.

Of course, these processes of immigration and settlement are by no means unique to Canada: they are major themes of human history and have, to a greater or lesser extent, affected all parts of the globe. Recognizing that we share such common experiences with other countries enables us to better understand other regions.

Besides outright immigration, international voluntary migration also comprises non-permanent changes of residence, such as for purposes of work. Higher wages or better job opportunities elsewhere can lead to temporary labour migration. An increasingly important category of international migrants are **transnational migrants**, so called because they set up homes or work in more than one country. Transnational migrants maintain ties with their country of origin while taking advantage of the opportunities offered by another country. Sometimes these migrants are low-paid workers, as in the case of millions of South Asian migrants who take up jobs in the unskilled sectors of the construction and service industries in Kuwait and other Gulf States. Other transnational migrants occupy the higher end of the socioeconomic spectrum, such as the Canadians who work in the Gulf States as engineers, teachers, and doctors. Another example from Canada is the Hong Kong Chinese who have established substantial investments and residences in Vancouver and Toronto while maintaining their citizenship status in Hong Kong. Transnational migrants seek destinations all over the world, with substantial communities occurring in France (from North Africa), Germany (from Turkey), the Gulf States (from South Asia), and South Africa (from neighbouring countries). Transnational migrants are an expression of increasing **transnationalism**, the multitude of processes between people and organizations that extend beyond national boundaries. As such, transnationalism can be seen as one aspect of increasing globalization.

Temporary labour migration has long been an indispensable part of the world economic order and has at times been actively pursued by governments and companies alike, as the example of Mexican and Caribbean farm labourers in Canada shows. (See "Geography Matters 3.2: Migrant Farm Workers in Canada.") Sending workers abroad is an important economic strategy for many peripheral and semiperipheral countries: it not only lessens local unemployment but also enables workers to send substantial amounts of money home to their families (called *remittances*). This arrangement helps support the workers' families left behind in their home countries, but it also continues the dominance of the core in global economic activities.

International Forced Migration

While many migrations are voluntary, forced migration (both international and internal) is a critical and growing problem in the contemporary world. Many forced migrants are refugees, but an even greater number are internally displaced persons (IDPs). On World Refugee Day 2013, the United Nations High Commissioner for Refugees (UNHCR) reported that 2011 and 2012 had been the most challenging years in its history, with multiple conflicts (for instance in Syria and Congo) forcing more people to flee than in the previous seven years combined. The UNHCR estimated that there were more than 43 million uprooted people worldwide, of which more than 26.4 million were IDPs. (See Box 3.3, "Window on the World: Internal Displacement.") On top of those numbers there were approximately 12 million stateless persons and 4.8 million Palestinian refugees (for whom the UNHCR has no official mandate).

Forced migrants may be fleeing a region or country for many reasons, but some of the most common are war, famine (often war-induced), or governmental coercion or oppression. For instance,

Migrant Farm Workers in Canada

Migrant labourers, or "guest workers" as they are sometimes called, have played an important part in the economy of many countries. For example, Jonathan Crush, a geographer at Wilfrid Laurier University, has written extensively about how South Africa's gold mines have depended on cheap migrant labour from neighbouring countries. Yet the host countries are not the only beneficiaries of this process, as the example of the Philippines shows. Filipinos working in other countries send a substantial amount of money back to the Philippines, thus supporting a good part of the population at home. Nevertheless, the reliance of one country on migrant labour recruited from another is a controversial policy as the migrants are often exploited and their home countries drained of labour and talent.

In view of such controversy, it is perhaps surprising to learn that Canada has long had a migrant labour program, albeit a small and relatively unpublicized one. The program, known as the Seasonal Agricultural Workers Program (SAWP), began in 1966 when 264 men were recruited from Jamaica to work temporarily in Canada. Since then, the number of recruits has grown to 20 000 men and women from the Caribbean and Mexico who spend from six weeks to eight months working on one of 1600 farms across Canada (**Figure 3.D**).

The program certainly has a number of benefits. First, the program helps Canadian farmers remain competitive as it allows them to pay only minimum wage for physically demanding jobs that many Canadians are no longer willing to perform. Second, the localities in Canada where SAWP workers temporarily reside benefit from their presence. One Simcoe, Ontario, farmer involved in the program estimates that the farm output generated by every migrant labourer he employs supports the jobs of three Canadians in related packing and transport activities. He estimates that SAWP migrants spend two-thirds of their income in the area—a "$32 million bounty each year for local shopkeepers, restaurateurs, and providers of telephone, banking and other services." A Simcoe discount store manager told researchers from the University of Guelph that the period when SAWP migrants are making purchases before they return home is "literally like Christmas in September."

Third, many of the SAWP workers state that the program benefits them economically. Despite the fact that migrant farm workers usually earn only minimum wage in Canada, the economic disparity between the economies of Canada and Mexico or the Caribbean makes the migrant labour program financially worthwhile for them. As an example, consider the remarks of Irena Gonzalez, a migrant farm worker who has come from Mexico to pick tomatoes for four months in Ontario every year since 1989:

> In Mexico, we're paid by the day, thirty pesos ($6 to $7 a day). But we have to fill fifteen or twenty pails. The time it takes depends on how fast you move your hands. But in Canada, we're paid by the hour, $7 an hour, and you can work as many hours as you want. If we work eight hours, which is what the contract says, we get $56, which is seven times as much as we get in Mexico.[1]

[1]Deborah Barndt, *Tangled Routes: Women, Work and Globalization on the Tomato Trail.* Aurora, ON Garamond Press, 2002, p. 162.

FIGURE 3.D Migrant farm workers (*Source: Rudy Umans/Shutterstock*)

Not all commentators agree that the program is so beneficial, and some have pointed to several major disadvantages with Canada's guest worker program. First, the dependence on low-wage employment may harm Canadian farmers in the long run by making the industry less efficient and harm Canadian farm workers by depressing the average wages in the agricultural sector.

Second, migrants often do not speak up when they are not treated properly for fear of losing their contract, which is governed by strict terms of employment. Under the SAWP, workers do not have the rights of Canadian citizens and are unable to gain immigrant status in Canada. Assigned a specific employer (who provides accommodation), they can change jobs only if their embassy and both the original and the new employer agree. Although they pay employment insurance in Canada (amounting to $3.4 million per year), workers cannot collect benefits because unemployed SAWP workers are usually repatriated within 24 hours. Workers in the SAWP are not covered by Ontario's health and safety legislation, and they do not have the right to bargain collectively. Professor Kerry Preibisch, a University of Guelph sociologist who has examined the program, calls these rules "extra-economic coercions" that make workers dependent on the subjective goodwill of their employers.

Complaints filed at the Simcoe migrant workers' support centre illustrate that such concerns are justified: substandard accommodations, unhealthy conditions, and unfair wage differences between SAWP workers and Canadian workers are frequent complaints; others include a man who almost lost a leg to an infection he was told to ignore, workers forced to escape their lodgings at night and walk an hour to phone home, and supervisors berating employees. Given these concerns, the fact that many continue to return to Canada year after year cannot be seen as a complete vindication of the program: SAWP workers are simply taking the best of a series of poor options available to them, options that diminish year by year as globalization and trade liberalization continue to erode agricultural wages both in this country and abroad.

Since the end of World War II, the global humanitarian community has monitored and aided **refugees**—individuals who cross national boundaries to seek safety and asylum. By contrast, the problem of internally displaced persons has only recently begun to draw international attention. **Internally displaced persons (IDPs)** are individuals who were uprooted within their own countries due to civil conflict or human rights violations, sometimes by their own governments. At the end of 2011, there were an estimated 26.4 million internally displaced persons worldwide, a slight decline from the 2007 numbers shown in **Figure 3.E**. Most of the decrease was due to successful returns in Africa, but at the same time the ongoing conflicts in other regions, particularly in Syria and Afghanistan, produced 3.5 million new IDPs in 2011 alone. At any time in the recent past, the total number of IDPs has been more than double the global refugee population, and it is frequently the case that the plight of IDPs is actually worse than that of the refugees. This is because the IDPs' governments are either unable to provide or deliberately withhold the protection or assistance they owe to their citizens. It is also the case that the international community is either unaware of them or has not secured the resources needed to help them.

As it has been for decades, Africa was the global region with the most IDP challenges in 2011. Africa harbours nearly ten million IDPs due to rebel activities and intercommunal violence as well as direct abuse by national governments. National security forces and government-backed militias have deliberately displaced large numbers of people in Zimbabwe, the Democratic Republic of Congo, and Côte d'Ivoire. In Liberia and Somalia, IDPs had virtually nowhere to go to escape attacks and find safe shelter; many were killed or died of hunger and disease. In Sudan, more than 2.5 million people have fled the western state of Darfur since 2003 to escape from attacks by government troops and raids by militias reportedly backed by the government. In the newly independent country of South Sudan, ethnic clashes flared up in 2013, sending hundreds of thousands to seek refuge in UN camps within mere weeks.

In the Middle East, ongoing conflicts have produced a dramatic worsening of both IDP and refugee numbers. In post-war

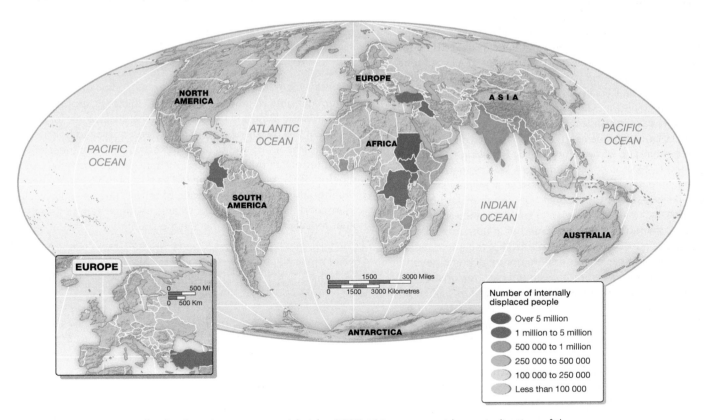

FIGURE 3.E Internally displaced persons worldwide, 2007 This map provides an indication of the geographical extent and numbers of people displaced from their livelihoods and homes but still living within their own countries, often in temporary camps provided by humanitarian organizations or the UN. As of December 2007, the Internal Displacement Monitoring Centre estimated that 27.5 million people had been displaced within their own countries. (*Source:* Adapted from Internal Displacement Monitoring Centre, http://www.internal-displacement.org/8025708F004BE3B1/(httpInfoFiles)/9 251510E3E5B6FC3C12572BF0029C267/$file/Global_Overview_2006.pdf.)

(Continued)

Iraq, over 2.5 million people continue to live in internal displacement, while another 2 million people have fled the country. Further east, in Afghanistan, the conflict has displaced 1 million people internally, and pushed 3 million out of the country. It is the civil war in Syria, however, that has produced the greatest humanitarian crisis of our time. By the end of 2014, the UN estimated that the conflict had pushed 3.5 million Syrian refugees into neighbouring countries, some of which can barely provide for their own populations. At the same time, an estimated 6.5 million Syrians were internally displaced, which means that almost half the Syrian population has lost their homes and livelihoods.

Until the recent explosion of IDP numbers in Syria, the country with the highest number of IDPs in the world was in South America. In Colombia, almost 5 million people continue to be displaced by the decades-old turf wars of drug cartels, guerrillas, and paramilitary gangs (**Figure 3.F**). All sides target civilian populations through arbitrary killings, looting, and destruction of property in order to depopulate rural areas for political and economic gains and to control or regain strategic territories.

Information about IDPs is gathered on behalf of the UN by the Internal Displacement Monitoring Centre (IDMC), which keeps a watchful eye on the critical situation of IDPs in over 50 countries worldwide. This means that fully one-quarter of all countries worldwide are grappling with a substantial IDP population, among them Congo (1.7 million IDPs in 2012), Pakistan (1 million), Somalia (1.5 million), Sudan (at least 2.2 million), and Turkey (1 million).

We have already mentioned several of the factors that drive the uprooting of both refugees and IDPs, but we must also recognize that the ramping up of security globally following the attacks of September 11, 2001, is contributing to a worldwide displacement crisis by encouraging governments to seek military solutions to conflicts. As a result, international humanitarian and human rights standards, including those relating to the protection of IDPs, have been undermined or ignored altogether in numerous places around the globe. In fact, there is little doubt that the international antiterrorism campaign has enabled some nondemocratic governments to characterize opposition movements as "terrorists" and to present their own counterinsurgency operations as part of an

FIGURE 3.F Resettlement camp, Bogota, Colombia
Pictured here is a displaced family camped in a park in the capital city. This family as well as many others also gathered to protest the government's failure to attend to the needs of Colombia's millions of displaced persons. (*Source:* Alejandra Vega/Newscom)

international "war on terror." This posture has earned these governments—many with a long history of instability, military coups, and human rights violations—substantial military support, mainly from the United States. In Indonesia and the Philippines, for example, tens of thousands of people have been displaced because of counterinsurgency operations conducted under the banner of the "war on terror." Importantly, these military campaigns were ongoing before 2001, but were relabelled as part of the "war on terror" thereafter. By invoking the rhetoric of terror, they have, ironically, undermined the protection of civilians, causing them to flee their homes for safe havens elsewhere in the country.

Source: Adapted from *Internal Displacement: A Global Overview of Trends and Developments in 2010*, by the Internal Displacement Monitoring Centre (IDMC), Geneva, Switzerland, 2010. Updated with 2011 figures from *The Global Overview 2011, People Displaced by Conflict and Violence*, and 2013 figures from the IDMC website: http://www.internal-displacement.org.

the "war or terror" following the attacks of September 11, 2001, has caused large forced migrations not only in Iraq, Afghanistan, and Pakistan, but also globally (**Figure 3.18**). More recently, the civil strife and state violence associated with the so-called Arab Spring have forced large numbers of people to flee unstable situations in Tunisia, Libya, Egypt, and in particular Syria, where they have sparked the largest movement of migrants the world has seen since World War II. Some of these refugees have tried to reach Italy and Spain by crossing the Mediterranean Sea in makeshift boats operated by criminal human smuggling rings. It is estimated that more than 25 000 people from the Middle East and Africa have drowned since the beginning of the century while trying to reach European shores.

Looking back in history, the African slave trade is a classic example of international forced migration. This migration stream was integral to European economic expansion from the seventeenth through the nineteenth centuries. The huge fortunes made in the sugar trade, for example, were earned on the backs of African slaves working the sugar plantations of Brazil, Guyana, and the Caribbean. **Figure 3.19** shows those regions of the world to which slaves from Africa were transported from the seventeenth to the nineteenth centuries.

Other prominent examples of international forced migration include the deportation of Armenians from Eastern Anatolia to other parts of the Ottoman Empire during World War I and the

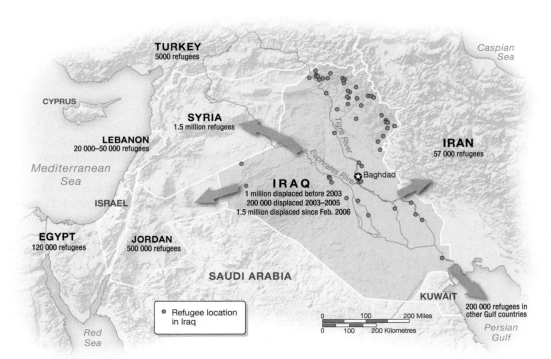

FIGURE 3.18 Iraqi diaspora before 2003 and since Over the past century, increasing numbers of refugees have fled Iraq and settled throughout the world. Some left because of persecution, like the Iraqi Jews who fled in 1950–1952. Others left because of wars such as the First and Second Kurdish Wars in the 1960s and 1970s. The most recent war in Iraq has caused the greatest mass exodus, however, with the United Nations High Commissioner on Refugees estimating the number at 4.7 million (as well as nearly 2 million internally displaced persons) since the 2003 U.S.-led invasion. Since the beginning of the civil war in Syria, Iraq in turn has become a destination for hundreds of thousands of Syrian refugees.

(*Source:* Data from United Nations High Commission for Refugees. http://www.unhcr.org/487ef7144.pdf.)

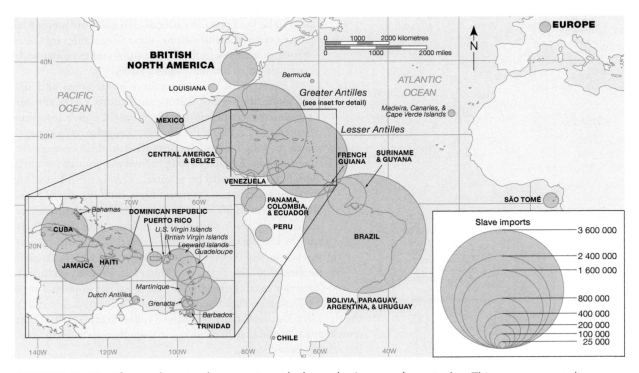

FIGURE 3.19 African slave trade, seventeenth through nineteenth centuries This map portrays the numbers of Africans who were carried off into slavery to Europe and various regions in the New World, mainly Brazil (3 647 000 slaves), the Greater Antilles (2 421 000), and the Lesser Antilles (1 619 000). It should also be noted that a substantial number of Africans died during the transatlantic crossing. (*Source:* Philip D. Curtin, *The Atlantic Slave Trade,* ©1969. Reprinted by permission of The University of Wisconsin Press.)

expulsion of Jews from Germany preceding World War II. At the end of that war in 1945, 12 million people of more than 20 nationalities found themselves scattered across Europe as displaced persons. An additional 14 million ethnic Germans fled or were deported from Eastern Europe to what would become West Germany. During the first Arab–Israeli War of 1948, almost one million Palestinian Arabs fled from the territory of the new state of Israel. Their second- and third-generation descendants still live in refugee camps in surrounding countries, where high birth rates have swelled their numbers to almost five million (**Figure 3.20**). Clearly, forced migration is a sad reality throughout history—and it continues: **Figure 3.21** shows those countries where residents have recently been forced from their homelands by war, abuse, and fear.

Finally, we must acknowledge the shadowy existence of modern slavery and its connection with forced migration. In 2013, two studies by the International Labour Organization (ILO) and the Walk Free Foundation (WFF) put the number of modern slaves between 21 and 30 million worldwide. In the periphery, slaves are often drawn from the native-born population, and it is in peripheral countries such as Mauritania, Haiti, Pakistan, and India that we find the highest number of slaves in proportion to the total population: in India alone, 14 million people are living in slavery. In core countries, however, slaves are overwhelmingly illegal migrants from poorer countries that are forced into prostitution or work as **undocumented workers**—individuals who arrive in the country without official entry visas and are considered by the government to be in the country illegally. To gain protection from discovery by the authorities, these illegal migrants must submit themselves to the total control and exploitation by criminals—they become modern slaves.

Faced with rising numbers of refugees and illegal migrants, several European countries have recently tightened their previously liberal asylum policies. Since September 11, 2001, the immigration issue has frequently been reconfigured as a security issue, and national governments across Europe have tightened the conditions under which asylum would be granted. This is despite the fact that many European countries were, until the global recession began in 2008, in need of immigrants to help counter labour shortages in skilled and unskilled jobs. Since 2010, xenophobic parties have been elected into coalition governments in the Netherlands, Norway, Denmark, Austria, Switzerland, Italy, Hungary, and Poland. In France and the UK, anti-foreigner parties garnered a quarter of the popular vote in the 2014 European Parliament elections. The remarkable shift to the right in a Europe usually considered rather liberal makes it quite clear that Europeans are becoming increasingly resistant to absorbing refugee populations.

FIGURE 3.20 Palestinian refugees in the Middle East This map shows the dispersion of Palestinian refugees—in camps and elsewhere—in the states around Israel. One of the biggest sticking points in negotiations between Israelis and Palestinians has been the question of whether refugees will be allowed to return and, if so, where they will be allowed to settle, given that most of their land has been occupied by Israeli settlers.

(*Source:* Adapted from *The Guardian*, October 14, 2000, p. 5.)

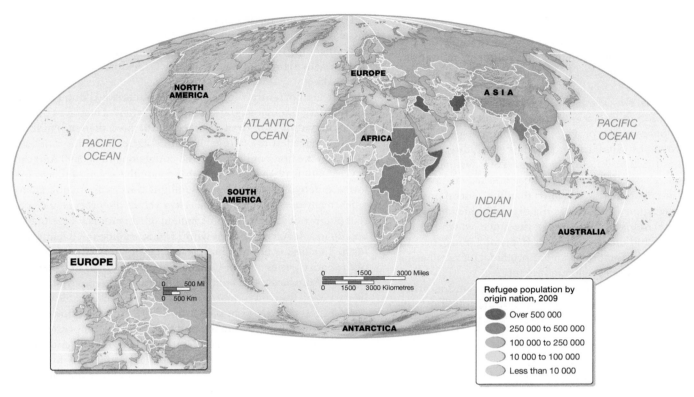

FIGURE 3.21 Refugee-sending countries War is certainly the most compelling factor in forcing refugee migration. Shown are the sending countries, those whose internal situations propelled people to leave. What is perhaps most distressing about this graphic is that refugee populations have increased over the past decade, and almost exclusively in the periphery. (*Source:* Data from United Nations High Commission for Refugees, *UNHCR Statistical Yearbook 2009*, page 24. http://www.unhcr.org/4ce5317d9.pdf)

So far, our discussion of the drivers of forced migration has focused on conflict and violence. Yet, an increasing number of people worldwide are also being forced to migrate by natural hazards and disasters. Geophysical events such as earthquakes and volcanic eruptions, as well as extreme weather events such as floods push many people off their homelands. In Bangladesh, for example, increasingly frequent and severe flooding of the floodplains (that were settled in the 1960s in response to growing population pressure) is routinely forcing huge numbers of people to temporarily relocate. On a smaller scale, the earthquake and subsequent tsunami in Japan in March 2011 caused both natives and foreigners to leave the affected region and even Tokyo in large numbers in response to radiation fears and rolling blackouts caused by the destroyed Fukushima nuclear plant.

Finally, there is also forced **eco-migration**—population movement caused by the degradation of land and essential natural resources. At the local scale, each year dams and irrigation projects are forcing between 1 million and 2 million people worldwide to move (by conservative estimates, the Three Gorges Dam in China alone displaced more than 1.3 million people). At the global scale, climate change threatens the homes and livelihoods of millions of people, particularly through the effects of storm surges and permanent sea-level increases. The International Federation of Red Cross and Red Crescent Societies has stated that eco-migrations related to climate change currently cause more population displacement than war and persecution. While the growth of eco-migration has

been greatest in sub-Saharan Africa, other areas are also teetering on the brink of environmental disaster. For example, Yemen is rapidly running out of water, China is experiencing dramatic desertification, as are Morocco, Tunisia, and Libya. In Egypt and Turkey, farm lands are being affected, and in Louisiana and Alaska shorelines are retreating at about 3 m per year.

Some low-lying island states such as Tuvalu, the Seychelles, and the Maldives may be permanently flooded by mid-century, prompting their governments to plan for a grim future in which leaving their islands may be the only option left. The Maldives, for example, have contacted Sri Lanka, India, and Australia to buy a new homeland for their population. Meanwhile, Tuvalu already has an agreement with New Zealand to accept all 11 600 of its citizens when sea-level rise makes the island uninhabitable. At the 2010 Climate Summit in Cancun, an "Alliance of Small Island States" (AOSIS) representing forty-three countries (remember that there are only 195 states in the world!) urged global leaders to prevent further sea-level increases that would wipe their islands off the map. Looking ahead, the large-scale forced migrations that could be triggered by climate change may pose one of the most difficult problems your generation will have to deal with.[2]

[2]A Google Earth simulation of how rising sea levels would affect the coastlines and cities of Caribbean islands is available through the extensive climate change website of *The Guardian* (www.guardian.co.uk/environment/video/2010/dec/01/cancun-climate-change-conference). The site also features many other videos and reports on the effects of climate change around the world.

Internal Voluntary Migration

Interprovincial migration in Canada is a good example of how economic structures can underlie internal voluntary migration. Every year, about one percent of Canadians move between provinces, often in response to job opportunities created by changing economic conditions. For example, while Newfoundland for many years suffered from out-migration due to the collapsing fishing industry, the oil boom in that province is now attracting Canadians from other provinces. Similarly, booming commodity markets have made potash-rich Saskatchewan an attractive destination for Canadians in search of employment. Because internal migrants are often younger and more highly educated than the general population, internal migration also changes the demographic characteristics of the populations at both ends of the move, which in turn affects the tax base and the public service demand, for instance. In short, interprovincial migration is an important factor in the constant reworking of Canada's economic structure.

In other countries, economic restructuring (among other factors) has led to much bigger internal population shifts. In the U.S., for example, the Sunbelt emerged as a migration destination after the end of World War II. Between 1950 and 1990, this region, which includes fifteen states and extends from North Carolina in the east to southern California in the west and Florida and Texas to the south, doubled in population. Beginning in the late 1970s and early 1980s, the West also began to grow dramatically. At the same time that the West and the South were booming, the Midwest and Northeast, known variously as the Snowbelt, Frostbelt, or Rustbelt, were languishing. **Figure 3.22** is one illustration of the relative decline and disinvestment experienced in the Rustbelt.

The most compelling explanation for the large-scale population shift was the pull of economic opportunity. Rather than investing in upgrading the aged and obsolescent urban industrial areas of the Northeast and Midwest, venture capitalists invested in Sunbelt locations, where cheaper land, lower labour costs, and the absence of labour unions made manufacturing and service-sector activity more profitable. The resulting new population distribution illustrates the way in which political and economic transformations play an especially significant role in shaping individual choice and decision making.

We are currently witnessing a particularly striking example of voluntary internal migration in China, where a massive rural to urban migration is underway. Since 1980, more than 400 million Chinese have left the country's mainly agricultural interior and moved to the burgeoning industrial cities along the coast. And the government is planning to further increase the speed of this transformation: by 2025, another 400 million citizens are to migrate to cities, many of which do not even exist yet. In the process, the current number of 120 cities with 1 million inhabitants is set to double, and up to a dozen mega cities with 15 to 20 million inhabitants will form. The task is nothing but gigantic: every year, the equivalent of the entire population of Canada is to be resettled; housing and infrastructure have to be built; and industrial and service jobs must be created.

Contrary to the examples from North America, this migration is not a result of economic pull factors, but a deliberate effort by the Chinese government to create a new economic and social structure. The goal is to increase industrial productivity by merging smaller facilities into massive complexes; improve the efficiency of infrastructure in the energy, communication, transportation, and health care sectors by increasing the service density; and simplify the bureaucratic surveillance of the population. As such, it is on the borderline between voluntary and forced migration.

Internal Forced Migration

One of the most infamous internal forced migrations occurred in the U.S. on the so-called "Trail of Tears," a tragic episode in which the Cherokee, Creek, Seminole, Chickasaw, and Choctaw nations were forced to leave their once treaty-protected homelands in the American Southeast for what is now western Oklahoma.

FIGURE 3.22 U.S. Rustbelt: the abandoned Packard automobile plant in Detroit, Michigan In the mid-twentieth century, the most important automobile manufacturers in the United States located their factories in the Midwest, where skilled labour and raw materials were readily available. By the late 1970s and 1980s, they increasingly moved out of the region either to the South or to foreign locations, such as Mexico, where labour is far cheaper and environmental laws less stringent.

(*Source:* Atomazul/Fotolia)

Approximately 16 000 Cherokees were forced to march across the continent in the winter of 1838, suffering from hunger, bitterly cold weather, violence, and sickness along the way. By some estimates at least a quarter of the Cherokees died as a result of the removal. Placed within the national and international context, the movement of Native American populations during the nineteenth century can be seen as a response to larger political and economic forces. European populations were migrating to the U.S. in massive numbers, and the national economy was on the threshold of an urban-industrial revolution. The eastern Native American populations posed an obstacle to economic expansion, which was dependent upon geographic expansion. Growing Anglo-American prosperity, it was believed, had to be secured by taking Native land.

More than a century later, Canada regrettably acted in a similarly callous way toward the Inuit. In 1953, at the height of the Cold War, the Canadian government relocated Inuit families from several communities in Northern Quebec to barren islands in the High Arctic. The move situated the Inuit in drastically different ecological conditions where their traditional knowledge about hunting, weather, and overland travel was inadequate for survival. As a result, the relocated families suffered considerably. In fact, without support from the government, they would have perished. After several government inquiries and independent reports, the relocation still remains controversial. The Inuit claim that the government used them to "populate" the High Arctic and so assert Canadian sovereignty, while the government maintains that it intended to help the Inuit escape from the deteriorating conditions in their original communities and provide them with a better life. In 1989, the federal government finally agreed to fund a return program, but it took until 2010 to issue an official apology.

Other recent examples of internal forced migration are provided by China and South Africa. In the late 1960s and 1970s, as part of the Cultural Revolution, the government of China forcibly relocated 10 to 17 million of its citizens to rural communes in order to enforce Chinese Communist dogma and to ease pressures arising from high urban unemployment. The policy has since been disavowed, but the effects on an entire generation of Chinese young people were profound. Another example took place in South Africa between 1960 and 1980, when apartheid policies forced some 3.6 million blacks to relocate to government-created homelands, resulting in much suffering and dislocation. Indeed, civil war, ethnic conflict, famine, deteriorating economic conditions, and political repression have produced an extraordinary series of internal forced migrations in several sub-Saharan countries (**Figure 3.23**).

These forced migrations, both internal and international in scope, become particularly significant in light of changing population. Forecasts predict that 80 percent of the world population increase in the next decade will take place within the poorest countries of the world. Many of these countries have some of the highest rates of forced migration. The combination bodes ill for these countries' prospects for economic and political improvement.

APPLY YOUR KNOWLEDGE Identify an environmental or economic issue in your region. Summarize two ways that this issue might result in push and pull factors that affect migration to and from your community. ∎

FIGURE 3.23 Acute malnutrition in Ethiopia A casualty of ecological catastrophe was Ethiopia, where late rains, failure of crops, and soaring food prices led to a severe food crisis and dislocation in 2008. Shown here are individuals congregating for international food aid. (*Source:* Mike Goldwater/Alamy)

POPULATION DEBATES AND POLICIES

One big question occupies the agenda of population experts studying world population trends today: how many people can Earth sustain without depleting or critically straining its resource base? The relationship between population and resources, which lies at the heart of this question, has been a point of debate among experts since the early nineteenth century.

Population, Resources, and the Environment

The debate about population and resources originated in the work of an English cleric named Thomas Robert Malthus (1766–1834). In his 1798 book, *An Essay on the Principle of Population,* he theorized that food supply was the critical factor limiting population growth. He insisted that "the passion between the sexes … is indefinitely greater than the power of the earth to produce subsistence." Inevitably, the population would thus grow faster than the food supply and eventually exhaust it. In turn, the ensuing famine would then prevent further growth. Fifty years later, Darwin saw in the work of Malthus the key to how evolution worked—the struggle for existence.

We must see the work of Malthus in the historical context within which it was written. Technological innovations in English agriculture and industry were eliminating traditional forms of employment faster than new ones could be created. This led to a widespread belief among wealthy members of English society that a surplus of unnecessary workers existed in the population. The displaced and impoverished farmworkers became a heavy burden on charity, and the so-called Poor Laws were introduced to control begging and regulate public behaviour. After centuries of authorities trying to "people" lands and increasing the population so as to have more agricultural labour available, a new perspective was forming: one that saw population as a potential problem that needed to be carefully managed.

The debate about the relationship between population and resources continues to this day, with the term *resources* now being conceived more broadly to include food, water, land, energy, minerals, etc. **Neo-Malthusians**—people today who share Malthus's perspective—predict a population doomsday: they believe that growing human populations the world over, with their potential to exhaust Earth's resources, pose the most dangerous threat to the environment. Although they acknowledge that the people of core countries consume the vast majority of resources, they and others argue that only strict demographic control everywhere, even if it requires severely coercive tactics, will solve the problem.

A more moderate approach argues that people's behaviours and governmental policies have a much greater impact on the condition of the environment and the state of natural resources than population size in and of itself. Proponents of this approach reject casting the population issue as a biological one in which an ever-growing population will inevitably create ecological catastrophe. They also reject framing it as an economic issue in which technological innovation and the sensitivities of the market will regulate population increases before a catastrophe can occur. Rather, they see the issue as a political one—one that governments have tended to avoid dealing with because they lack the will to redistribute wealth or the resources to reduce poverty, a condition strongly correlated with high fertility. Conversely, some analysts have recently argued that ecological problems may exacerbate or even cause political crises.

The question of whether too many people exist for Earth to sustain has bedevilled population policymakers and political leaders since the middle of the twentieth century. This concern led to the formation of international agencies that monitor and often attempt to influence population change. It also led to the organizing of a series of international conferences that attempted to establish globally applicable population policies. The underlying assumption of much of this policymaking, which has continued into the twenty-first century, is that countries and regions have a better chance of achieving improvement in their level of development if they can keep their population from outstripping the supply of resources and jobs.

Population Policies and Programs

Contemporary concerns about population—especially whether too many people exist for Earth to sustain—have led to the development of international and national policies and programs. A **population policy** is an official government strategy designed to affect any or all of several objectives, including the size, composition, and distribution of population. The implementation of a population policy takes the form of a population program. Whereas a policy identifies goals and objectives, a program is an instrument for meeting those goals and objectives.

Most of the international population policies of the last three decades have attempted to reduce the number of births worldwide through family-planning programs. The desire to limit fertility rates is a response to concerns about rapidly increasing global population—an increase that is being experienced overwhelmingly in the periphery and semiperiphery. Currently, Germany and Ethiopia each has 80 million inhabitants; by 2050, Germany's population will have shrunk to 72 million, but Ethiopia's will have ballooned to 174 million. Accompanying this situation of imbalanced population growth between the core and the periphery are gross social and economic inequalities as well as overall environmental degradation and destruction.

Figure 3.24 provides a picture of the recent history of world population growth by region and a reasonable projection of future growth. The difference between the core and the periphery is dramatically illustrated. Also striking is the acceleration of growth during the twentieth century, illustrated in **Table 3-5**. It currently takes only 12 years to add an additional billion people to the planet's population. In comparison, over the course of the entire nineteenth century, fewer than one billion people were added to the population. As the table shows, a dramatic decline in the infant mortality rate accompanies this accelerated growth.

By the year 2050, the world is projected to contain nearly 9 billion people. The geography of projected population growth is noteworthy. Over the next century, population growth is predicted to occur almost exclusively in Africa, Asia, and Latin America, while most core countries will experience low or negative population growth. In fact, several countries in Europe as well as Japan are set to experience population decline. In 2013, the core contained 35 countries with zero or negative population growth. By contrast, the periphery contained 30 countries with rates of natural increase of 3.0 or more. A sustained rate of natural increase of 3.0 per year means a population will double in less than 24 years.

Since 1954, the United Nations has sponsored several international conferences to develop population policy at the global level. Each conference produced explicit population policies aimed at lowering fertility rates in the periphery and semiperiphery, but they also placed the debates on overpopulation into the larger contexts of poverty, education, economics, ecology, and women's rights. Importantly, the world population conferences have recognized that the history, social and cultural practices, development level and goals, and political structures of countries, and even regions within countries, are highly variable and that one rigid and overarching policy to limit fertility will not work for all. Whereas some programs and approaches will be effective for some countries seeking to cut population numbers, they will be fruitless for others.

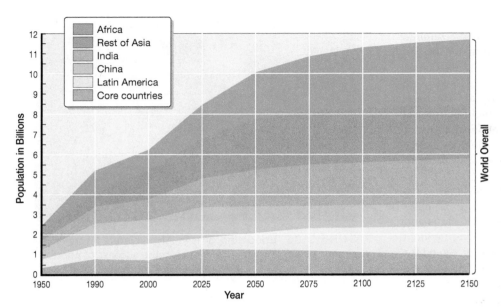

FIGURE 3.24 World population projection by region, 1950–2050 In the projection, population continues to expand in the periphery, though in some regions more than others. Africa is projected to experience the greatest growth, followed by Asia (not including China and India), where growth is expected to level off by 2150. Less dramatic growth is expected to occur in Latin America, while in the core population, numbers remain constant or drop slightly. Though the total number of people in the world will be dramatically greater by 2050, the forecast indicates a gradual levelling off of world population. (*Source*: Adapted from I. Hauchler and P. Kennedy [eds.], *Global Trends: The World Almanac of Development and Peace.* New York: Continuum, 1994, p. 109.)

For instance, China had a restrictive family-planning policy between 1979 and 2014 that allowed only one child per couple. More than half a million bureaucrats were needed to enforce the policy, and the sanctions ranged from fines and job loss all the way to enforced abortion late in the pregnancy. The policy appears to have been effective in driving down the birth rate and damping the country's overall population growth by averting up to 400 million births. When we look at the issue only in terms of such numbers, the policy could be called a success. However, when we also look at the human suffering caused by it, we must recognize that the policy violates basic human rights and could be implemented only in an authoritarian state such as China, where individual rights are routinely sacrificed to the national interest.

Moreover, while China's TFR did indeed drop from 5.5 in 1970 to 1.7 in 2013, countries such as Thailand and Brazil achieved the same reduction without coercive policies. In other words, China's TFR may have dropped regardless or even despite the one-child policy, and not because of it. Could it be that China's TFR has been dropping because China is rapidly urbanizing? This view is supported by studies of urban Chinese women who qualified for an exemption to the one-child policy: less than half of them actually planned to make use of the exemption, and even fewer ultimately did. It appears that high rents and cost of living are highly

effective means of birth control. In Shanghai, for example, the TFR now sits at 0.9, one of the lowest in the world. More than 80 percent of Shanghai residents in the reproductive age cohort are themselves products of the one-child policy and so we may also wonder about the imprint their upbringing has left on their own family plans.

One underestimated consequence of the one-child policy was how rapidly China's population as a whole would age as a result. In 1970, the median age of the population in both China and India was 20 years. By 2010, India was sitting at 25 years, but China had surpassed 35 years. Consequently, China now has twice as many old people as India, which need to be supported by a working-age population that is shrinking by about 3 million each year. Economists have calculated that, just to maintain the current pension levels—which can be as low as US$10 a month—taxation levels must more than double. The looming economic consequences of such an aging population are a sputtering economy, deflation, and a contracting real estate market—none of which are good news for a Chinese government that depends on substantial growth to offer its citizens more wealth in exchange for accepting the continued one-party rule. All the Chinese government has to do is look east if it wants to study the dangerous economic effects of an aging population: the persistent economic crisis that has plagued Japan for almost two decades is at least partially a demographic crisis, caused by its extremely old population, with a median age of almost 45 years.

Finally, the younger Chinese generation is experiencing a severe gender imbalance as a result of the one-child policy. In China, as in many other countries, there is a pronounced cultural preference for sons over daughters. The one-child policy tempted many couples to commit **female infanticide** by aborting, killing, or abandoning female babies and so retain their chances of having a male baby with the next pregnancy. As a result, there were 17 percent more boys than girls in 2012; in rural areas, the imbalance can be as high as 37 percent. With time, this lack of females brings a slew of problems: there are between 25 and 30 million young men who are unable to find a woman with whom to start a family, with all the social, cultural, and economic consequences this will produce.

TABLE 3-5   Global Population Growth and Global Infant Mortality Rates

Year	World Population (Billions)	Years Needed to Add 1 Billion	Infant Mortality (per 1000 Live Births)
1800	1		500 (est.)
1927	2	127	165
1960	3	33	115
1974	4	14	90
1987	5	13	65
1999	6	12	60
2011	7	12	55

For all these reasons, the Chinese one-child policy is not just a population policy, it is also a gigantic sociological and economic experiment that was possible only under the specific circumstances. In 2014, the Chinese government began to retract the most drastic aspects of the policy and use alternative methods to achieve a more balanced population growth. Such methods have already been employed with success by other countries and include offering free contraceptives, family-planning counselling, and incentives for couples to have only one child. Other approaches do not regulate the family size but increase access to social resources such as health care and education, particularly for women.

Indeed, as discussed earlier in the chapter, it is now a widely accepted belief among demographers and policymakers that a close relationship exists between women's status and fertility. Women who have access to education and employment tend to have fewer children because they have less of a need for the economic security and social recognition that children are thought to provide (**Figure 3.25**). In Botswana, for instance, women with no formal education have, on average, six children, while those with four to six years of schooling have just three children. The numbers are comparable for countries in Asia and South America.

More equality between men and women inside and outside the household is also believed to have a significant impact on reducing fertility. Giving both men and women choices about birth control, and educating them about the implications of such choices, appears to be especially successful in small island populations with historically high population growth, such as those of Bali, Barbados, and Mauritius. In Mauritius in just 24 years (between 1962 and 1986) the introduction of voluntary constraints lowered the total fertility rate from 5.8 to 1.9.

Ultimately, successful family-planning programs rely on the widespread availability of contraceptive commodities and practices. And while 40 years ago contraception was socially and culturally unacceptable to many women in both core and peripheral countries, today the challenge is a different one: there is far more demand for it than there is funding available. Ironically, family-planning and reproductive health programs are a victim of their own success. Today, over 92 percent of all countries support family-planning programs and contraceptives, either directly through government facilities or indirectly through support of nongovernmental activities, such as nonprofit family-planning associations.

Sustainable Development, Gender, and Population Issues

Governments worldwide are recognizing how important sustainable development and the reduction of poverty are for the goal of limiting births and improving quality of life for every human being. At the UN Millennium Summit held in 2000, world leaders proclaimed eight Millennium Development Goals (MDGs) that aim at reducing poverty by improving economic development through aid, trade, and debt relief and through the enhancement of democratic governance institutions and careful attention to the impact of development on the environment (see **Table 3-6**). The goals are to be achieved through a partnership between core and peripheral countries. With respect to

FIGURE 3.25 Educating girls in Afghanistan Improving the economic status of women is central to the success of controlling population growth. Access to education and employment security are seen as critical factors shaping a woman's decisions about how many children to have and when to have them.

(*Source:* Danita Delimont/Gallo Images/Getty Images)

governance transformations, for instance, the United Nations Development Programme (UNDP) is working with an oil company and Amnesty International in Venezuela to provide the country's judges with a comprehensive understanding of human rights laws, regulations, and issues. With respect to the environment, UNDP is working with farmers in Ethiopia by supporting the planting and marketing of traditional crops and, in the process, strengthening the country's Biodiversity Research Institute and encouraging farmers to create biodiversity banks, while the crops make their incomes more secure.

It is no coincidence that the eight MDGs reflect the neoliberal turn in international development. **Neoliberalism** promotes a reduction in the role and budgets of governments, including reduced subsidies and the privatization of formerly publicly owned and operated concerns such as utilities. The goal of neoliberal

---

TABLE 3-6 Millennium Development Goals (MDGs)

The goals and targets are based on the UN Millennium Declaration, and the UN General Assembly has approved them as part of the Secretary General's road map toward implementing the declaration. UNDP worked with other UN departments, funds, and programs, the World Bank, the International Monetary Fund, and the Organisation for Economic Co-operation and Development to identify over 40 quantifiable indicators to assess progress.

Goals and Targets
Goal 1: Eradicate extreme poverty and hunger
Goal 2: Achieve universal primary education
Goal 3: Promote gender equality and empower women
Goal 4: Reduce child mortality
Goal 5: Improve maternal health
Goal 6: Combat HIV/AIDS, malaria, and other diseases
Goal 7: Ensure environmental sustainability
Goal 8: Develop a global partnership for development

FIGURE 3.26 UN Summit, 2010
The UN Summit on the Millennium Development Goals met again in September 2010 and concluded with a further commitment to the global action plan to achieve the eight antipoverty goals by the 2015 target date. It also announced a major new initiative for women's and children's health and other initiatives against poverty, hunger, and disease. (*Source:* Emmanuel Dunand/Newscom)

development policies—such as the one being widely advanced by the UNDP—is to enable peripheral countries to achieve core economic standards of wealth and prosperity while recognizing that pre-existing conditions will have to be taken into account to construct a place-specific development path. As the goals imply, enabling more sustainable economic development worldwide is seen as a way of shaping population growth and the quality of life for populations in the periphery. At the same time, it is also a way of opening up new markets for core products and services and extending the capitalist world-system.

The MDGs also reflect the notion that the issues of population, economy, human rights, and environment all interrelate, and if progress is required on one issue (such as population policy), it must inevitably involve progress on almost all of the other goals if change is to be truly effective, sustainable, and fair. To monitor global progress toward achieving the MDGs, world leaders met again in follow-up UN summit meetings in 2005 and 2010 (**Figure 3.26**). They conceded that progress has been slow and that several goals will not be reached in many countries; nonetheless, the international community reaffirmed their commitment to strive toward achieving these goals by 2015. Regardless of whether the goals will be met or not, one beneficial outcome of the campaign is that debates on overpopulation are finally placed in the larger contexts of poverty, education, economics, ecology, and women's rights.

In summary, success at slowing population growth in the periphery appears to be very much tied to enhancing the possibility for a good quality of life and empowering people, especially women, to make informed choices. But, as citizens of a core country, we must realize that a better quality of life for everyone will require altering—even reducing—our consumption practices in the core to make more resources available to populations in the periphery. (See the discussion of the Ecological Footprint in Chapter 4.)

APPLY YOUR KNOWLEDGE What do you consider to be the most pressing issue with respect to global population growth? List five reasons why, in your opinion, this is a key issue. ▪

POPULATION, HEALTH, AND THE ENVIRONMENT

The study of the interconnections among population, health, and the environment is the subject of medical geography. At the global scale, geographers use the world-system approach to help explain the differences between the health experiences of populations in the core and the periphery. To this purpose, medical geographers use the **epidemiological transition** model, a theory stating that the prevailing forms of illness changed from infectious to degenerative types as the demographic transition occurred (**Figure 3.27**).

According to this theory, during the first phases of the epidemiological transition, high death rates are caused mainly by very high rates of infectious and parasitic diseases. This contrasts with the situation after the transition, when mortality is mainly the result of degenerative diseases caused by aging, changing lifestyles, and environmental toxicity. It will be part of the periphery's challenge to see if it can pass through the demographic transition without bringing on itself these so-called diseases of modernization.

The connection between disease incidence and spatial patterns is explored by medical geographers who examine the diffusion of diseases. (Remember the diffusion patterns of HIV/Aids from Chapter 2.) A contemporary Canadian example is the work of Professor Rowland Tinline of Queen's University in Kingston, Ontario. Using advanced diffusion theory, combined with GIS techniques, he has been able to develop computer models that predict the spread of rabies outbreaks in Ontario, thereby aiding

FIGURE 3.27 The epidemiological transition As societies move through the demographic transition, the prevailing form of illness changes from infectious and parasitic diseases to the degenerative diseases caused by modernization and urban life: those of aging, changing lifestyle, and toxic substances in the environment.

(*Sources:* Diagram based on a written description in Dhruva Nagnur and Michael Nagrodski, "Epidemiologic Transition in the Context of Demographic Change: The Evolution of Canadian Mortality Patterns." In Frank Trovato and Carl F. Grindstaff [eds.], *Perspectives on Canada's Population: An Introduction to Concepts and Issues.* Toronto: Oxford University Press, 1994, pp. 118–135.)

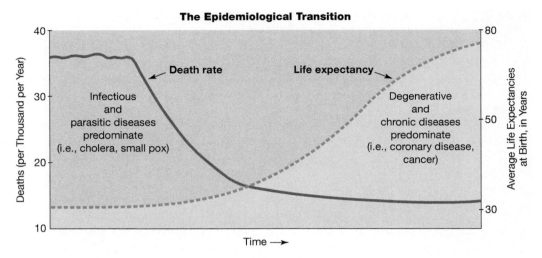

The Epidemiological Transition

the provincial government's attempts to control such outbreaks. Other diseases such as West Nile virus and Lyme disease, which have been spreading northward into Canada recently, are also being investigated by geographers (**Figure 3.28**).

Finally, medical geographers also examine the considerable spatial discrepancies in health care provision that exist across this country. For example, Alun Joseph and Mark Rosenberg have studied the locations of hospitals, physicians, clinics, and nurses across

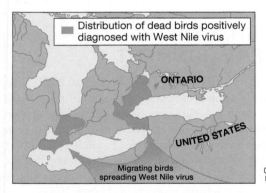

FIGURE 3.28 The beginnings of West Nile virus in Canada West Nile virus (WNV) is carried by mosquitoes and is spread when they bite any of several bird and mammal species. Crows, ravens, blue jays, and magpies are particularly susceptible, as are horses and human beings. In humans, WNV can cause West Nile fever and, in rare cases, develop into fatal inflammations of the brain or spinal cord. WNV was first identified in the West Nile district of Uganda in 1937. Since then, it has slowly spread throughout the Mediterranean and the temperate parts of Europe. The first reported cases in North America occurred in New York City in August 1999. By 2002, the disease had already spread to Ontario. Since then, the number of new cases reported annually in that province has oscillated between 4 and 400, mainly depending on summer temperatures: the warmer the summer, the higher the incidence rates. Most experts suggest that WNV is in Canada to stay because global warming will likely increase the range of infected mosquitoes and birds. (*Source: Vector-Borne Diseases 2013 Summary Report,* Public Health Ontario.)

Canada at a variety of scales. Simply put, urban areas have a better provision of health care than do rural areas, and richer urban areas have a better provision of services than do poorer urban areas. These discrepancies have raised questions about the social justice of such spatial inequalities and prompted analyses of their ultimate causes. They also prompted further research into the provision of health care for disadvantaged groups, such as single parents, people with disabilities, and Aboriginal communities, who find themselves further marginalized by where they live. These types of discrepancies between core and periphery also exist at a world scale, as in the global distribution of doctors we saw in the map of global health care density. (See **Figure 3.6**.)

The Geography of Canadian Health[3]

Population experts regard life expectancy as one of the basic indicators of the overall health of a population, and one that allows reliable comparisons to be made between places and over time. Life expectancy is also one of the parameters flowing into the UN Human Development Report ranking (together with educational attainment, standard of living, and quality of life). With 81 years, Canada has one of the highest life expectancies in the world, and it therefore is no surprise that Canada is among the top countries in this ranking. In fact, for most of the 1990s, it ranked first; by 2013, however, Canada had slipped to eleventh place. The reason is not that conditions in this country worsened (in fact, all measured indicators continue to improve), but that other countries have seen more improvement and that this improvement has been more even across all segments of the population.

This statement about equality points us to the single most significant point to be made about the geography of health in Canada (or elsewhere for that matter): people with higher incomes generally live longer than people with lower incomes. In other words,

---

[3]Parts of this section are based on *Toward a Healthy Future: Second Report on the Health of Canadians,* prepared by the Federal, Provincial, and Territorial Advisory Committee on Population Health for the Meeting of Ministers of Health, Charlottetown, PEI, September 1999. Health Canada: Ottawa, 1999, pp. ix, 14, and 41. Canada's current ranking can be checked in the latest United Nations Human Development Report, available at http://hdr.undp.org.

the geography of health is simply one manifestation of the spatial inequalities generated by Canada's economic geography. Let us look at two such inequalities. In 2006, Canadian men in the highest fifth of the income distribution could expect to live 7.1 years longer than those in the lowest fifth. (For women, the difference was 4.9 years.) Similarly, the life expectancy of the Status Indian population in 1990 was seven years less than that for the overall Canadian population. Sadly, by 2010, that difference had narrowed by only 1 year—one of the reasons why Canada has slipped in the Human Development Index ranking.

The geography of Canadian health can be examined at a number of scales. At the national level, we can once again see great regional differences. For heart attack, stroke, and cancer, for example, the mortality in Nunavut is twice as high as in British Columbia. Among the provinces, mortality for these diseases declines from east to west, with British Columbia having a 25 percent lower mortality than Newfoundland and Labrador. That is not to say, however, that all health districts in British Columbia have equally low mortalities: for breast cancer, the mortality in the Peace River health district in B.C. is 50 percent higher than the national average.

Clear patterns are thus not easy to identify. Indeed, one of the highest breast cancer mortality rates occurs in the South Eastman district of Manitoba, while neighbouring North Eastman district has only half that rate. Similar spatial variations exist in life expectancy across the country (**Figure 3.29**). For example, life expectancy in the Edmonton Health Region is significantly above average, while all surrounding health regions have life expectancies significantly below average. What might be the cause of such differences? We can sharpen our focus on the geography of health by moving to a smaller scale and examining, as a case study, the city of Montreal.

Data for average life expectancies at birth, calculated for Montreal's Centre local de services communautaires (CLSC) regions, for the years 2006 to 2010, indicate that people on the west of the island can expect to live, on average, almost a decade

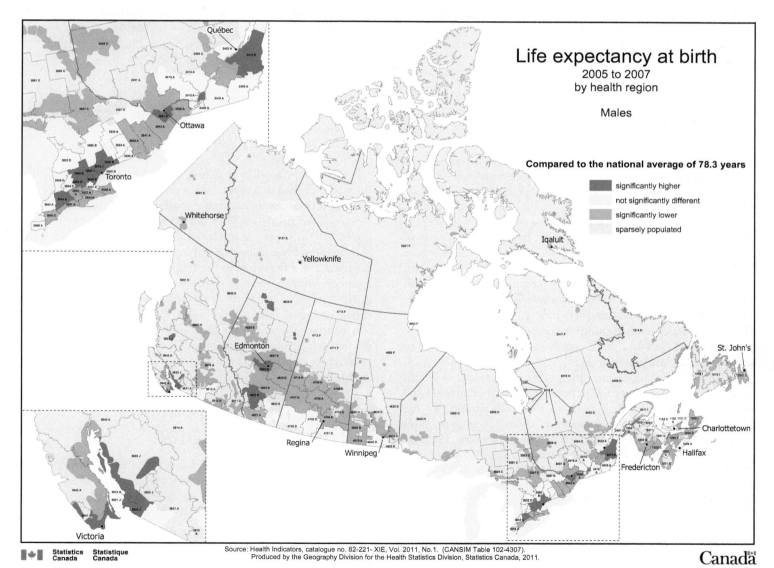

FIGURE 3.29 Life expectancy at birth for Canadian males, 2005–2007, by health region. As this map shows, life expectancy can vary considerably, even between neighbouring health regions. (*Source*: Statistics Canada,

Health Indicators, December 2013, Catalogue No. 82-221-XWE, available online at www.statcan.ca.)

FIGURE 3.30 Life expectancies on the island of Montreal This map shows life expectancies at birth, for both sexes combined, using 2006–2010 data for the 29 CLSC health districts of the island of Montreal. Considerable variations across the city can be seen, and the 10-year difference between the city centre and the western suburbs is a long-standing feature. For men, this gap can reach 11 years. (*Source:* The Centre local de services communautaires [CLSC] data are given on "Les CLSC d'un coup d'oeil," Direction de la santé publique de Montreal-Centre at www.santepub-mtl.qc.ca/Portrait/Les29/carteesperance.html. Updated information from the Foundation of Greater Montreal's annual publication *Greater Montreal's Vital Signs: 2012* is at http://www.signesvitauxmontreal.ca/.)

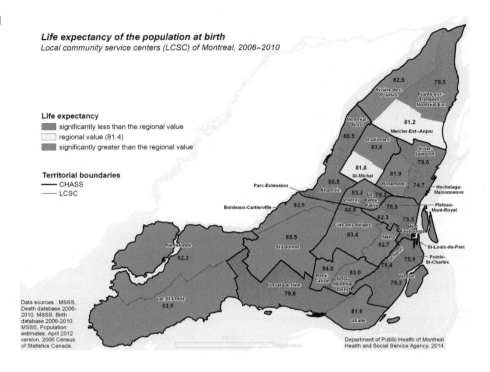

longer than those in some east-end communities (**Figure 3.30**). This variation, from a life expectancy of 83.9 years in the Lac Saint-Louis CLSC region to one of 75.5 years in the Des Faubourgs CLSC region, is one that closely follows patterns of income. In the Lac Saint-Louis area, only 1 percent of all age groups rely on social assistance, whereas in the Des Faubourgs region, as many as 40 percent receive welfare.

In seeking to explain the existence and persistence of these patterns, medical geographers have generally favoured two types of explanation. The first, a behavioural (or lifestyle) hypothesis, argues that these geographical differences (or spatial inequalities) in health arise because certain groups of people more commonly engage in health-threatening activities (such as smoking) and less commonly participate in health-promoting activities (such as sports or eating a healthful diet) than other groups in the population. As a headline in the *Montreal Gazette* bluntly explained it, "Poor people tend to smoke more, eat less healthy food."[4]

The second explanation approaches the pattern of health inequalities from a structuralist perspective and challenges the assumptions of the lifestyle hypothesis. From this perspective, the operation of the economy and society as a whole dictates people's quality of life. For example, less wealthy people are often exposed to health hazards where they live or work, and may find themselves effectively denied access to high-quality health care facilities simply because such resources tend to be located in more wealthy parts of town. As the medical geographer S. Martin Taylor has observed, "the higher mortality rates for men in the north end of Hamilton, for example, raise questions about exposure to hazards in the local workplace, a heavily industrial area. Equally, they may reflect limits in discretionary time and income as well as limited access to resources and facilities which would support engagement in positive health behaviour."[5]

Certainly, Canadian medical geographers have observed that there are marked discrepancies in the provision of medical services and that a more equitable spatial pattern, across city and country alike, is one possible and necessary step toward improving health for everyone in Canada. The search for the underlying causes of the patterns shown in Canada's medical geography brings us back full circle to the traditional medical geographer's concerns with patterns of spatial association. A provisional list must surely put the various advantages and disadvantages of urban and rural living in the balance, together with the spatial inequalities inherent in the basic differences that are embedded in Canada's economic geography. Once again, we clearly see the importance of place, this time in our consideration of Canadians' health.

Future Geographies

In 2013, the world contained more than 7 billion people. The population division of the UN Department of Social and Economic Affairs projects that the world's population will continue to increase by 1.2 percent annually to mid-century, resulting in 9.3 billion people by 2050. The distribution of this projected

[4]*Montreal Gazette*, May 30, 2001. See also "Montrealers Die Younger: Life Span among Lowest in Canada." *Montreal Gazette*, July 5, 2002, A1, A4.

[5]S.M. Taylor, "The Geography of Urban Health." In L. Bourne and D. Ley (eds.), *The Changing Social Geography of Canadian Cities.* Montreal and Kingston: McGill-Queen's University Press, 1993, pp. 309–325, p. 317.

population growth is noteworthy: over the next half-century, population growth is predicted to occur overwhelmingly in regions least able to support it. Just six countries will account for half the increase in the world's population, including Bangladesh, China, India, Indonesia, Nigeria, and Pakistan (**Figure 3.31**). Meanwhile, Europe and North America will experience very low population growth and in some cases even lose population. Collectively, the periphery will grow by 58 percent, as opposed to 2 percent for the core regions through 2050. The periphery will account for 99 percent of the expected increment in world population in this period.

Nevertheless, it is increasingly clear that the human population will not continue to grow indefinitely, even in countries with already high populations. Demographic transition theory has prompted some population analysts to suggest that many of the economic, political, social, and technological transformations associated with continued urbanization and industrialization across the globe will shift the world's population from a period of high growth to one of low growth, or even population decline. This will be due to falling fertility. Current total fertility of 3.11 children per woman will fall to 2.04 by mid-century—just below replacement level but still above the current rate in core regions.

FIGURE 3.31 Shanghai, China Considered to be the world's largest city by the UN, Shanghai has between 18 and 24 million people, depending on where one draws its boundaries. This difficulty alone suggests the scope of recent urbanization in China. The populations of cities like Shanghai are expected to continue to grow through the first half of the twenty-first century, though urban planners raise serious concerns about how urban systems like water, sewer, transportation, and energy supply—to name a few—will be able to keep up. (*Source:* fuyu liu/Shutterstock)

CONCLUSION

The geography of population is directly connected to the complex forces that drive globalization. And since the fifteenth century, the distribution of the world's population has changed dramatically as the capitalist economy has expanded, bringing new and different peoples into contact with one another and setting into motion additional patterns of national and regional migrations.

When capitalism emerged in Europe in the fifteenth century, the world's population was experiencing high birth rates, high death rates, and relatively low levels of migration or mobility. Four hundred years later, birth, death, and migration rates vary—sometimes quite dramatically—from region to region, with core countries experiencing low death and birth rates and peripheral and semiperipheral countries generally experiencing high birth rates and fairly low

death rates. Migration rates vary within and outside the core. These variations may be seen as reflections of the level and intensity of political, economic, and cultural connectedness between core and periphery and are difficult to predict.

The example of formerly colonized peoples migrating to their former ruling countries in search of work provides insights into the dynamic nature of the world economy and shows the important role that people play in acting out the dynamics of geographic variety.

In the final analysis, death rates, birth rates, and migration rates are the central variables of population growth and change. These indicators tell us much about transforming regions and places as elements in a larger world-system. Globalization has created many new maps as it has unfolded; the changing geography of population is just one of them.

- Understand the census and other sources of population data and how they are used to describe the geography of population.

  Geographers think of population in terms of the places that populations inhabit. They also consider populations in terms of the way that places are shaped by populations and in turn shape the populations that occupy them. Population experts employ the census as well as other data sources such as vital records and health statistics to assess population characteristics. All levels of government as well as international organizations collect the data and maintain the records that are produced from them. This information can help show the way the population of any area—from the national level down to the individual census tract or neighbourhood—is changing.

- Recognize why populations change, where those changes occur, and what the implications of population change are for the future of different places around the globe.

  Population geographers bring to demography a special perspective—the spatial perspective—that emphasizes description and explanation of the "where" of population distribution, patterns, and processes.

The distribution of population is a result of many factors, such as employment opportunities, culture, water supply, climate, and other physical environment characteristics. Geographers explore these patterns of distribution and density, as well as population composition in order to understand the complex geography of populations. Understanding the reasons for and implications of variation in patterns and composition provides geographers with insight into population change and the potential impacts that growing or declining populations might have.

- Identify the two most important factors in population dynamics—birth and death—and explain how they shape population characteristics.

  In order to arrive at a dynamic understanding of population growth and change, experts look first at two significant factors: fertility and mortality. Birth and death rates are simple but central indicators of a place's level of economic development. Fertility and mortality rates provide key insights into how well a country, region, or city is able to provide for its population, especially in terms of income, education, and health care. Population geographers also consider how life expectancy, immigration, and emigration affect population dynamics.

- Realize that demographic patterns can be explained within a world-system framework.

  Demographic patterns are influenced by the very different economic and social "spaces" that the world-system produces. Low birth rates and death rates are a feature of today's core; high birth rates and death rates are a feature of the periphery. As countries make the economic transition from (semi)periphery to core, it is hoped that they also go through the demographic transition. On the other hand, continued globalization may accentuate these differences rather than remove them. For the time being, the discrepancy between core and periphery generates substantial migration flows.

- Demonstrate how the movement of population is affected by both push and pull factors, and explain how these factors are key to understanding new settlement patterns.

  A third crucial factor in population dynamics is migration. In general terms, migrants make their decisions to move based on push factors and pull factors. Push factors are events and conditions that impel an individual to move from a location. Pull factors are forces of attraction that influence migrants to move to a particular location. Mobility is the capacity to move from one place to another, either permanently or temporarily. Migration, in contrast, is a long-distance move to a new location. Permanent and temporary changes of residence can occur for a variety of reasons. Striving for economic betterment or escaping from adverse political conditions, such as war or oppression, are the most frequent causes. Push factors can produce forced migration, but it is usually the case that the decision to migrate reflects both push and pull factors.

- Evaluate the challenges of providing for the world's growing population with adequate food and safe drinking water, as well as a sustainable environment.

  A moderate response to the question "How can the global economy provide the world's growing population with adequate food and safe drinking water, as well as a sustainable environment?" rejects casting the population issue as a biological one in which an ever-growing population will inevitably create ecological catastrophe. It also rejects framing it as an economic issue in which technological innovation and the sensitivities of the market will regulate population increases before a catastrophe can occur. Importantly, the response to this question is more convincingly understood as a political one. Yet governments across the globe tend to avoid dealing with the population–resource problem because they lack the will to redistribute wealth or the resources to reduce poverty. This leaves the burden on citizens to organize to force government to address the problem and to change their own behaviours to lessen its effects.

- Recognize that there can be considerable spatial variations in health within a population and that these variations are largely the result of different income levels.

  From the international to the neighbourhood scale, the work of health geographers shows that many variations in life expectancy, disease incidence, and access to health care can be traced back to income differences within the population. In general, the higher the income, the longer an individual can expect to live.

KEY TERMS

age–sex pyramid *(p. 77)*	cohort *(p. 78)*	demographics *(p. 73)*	eco-migration *(p. 99)*
arithmetic density *(p. 76)*	crude birth rate (CBR) *(p. 85)*	demography *(p. 74)*	emigration *(p. 91)*
baby boom *(p. 77)*	crude death rate (CDR) *(p. 86)*	density *(p. 76)*	epidemiological transition *(p. 105)*
biometric census *(p. 74)*	crude density *(p. 76)*	dependency ratio *(p. 84)*	female infanticide *(p. 103)*
census *(p. 74)*	demographic transition *(p. 90)*	doubling time *(p. 86)*	forced migration *(p. 92)*

geodemographic analysis *(p. 77)*	**international migration** *(p. 91)*	**neoliberalism** *(p. 104)*	**refugees** *(p. 95)*
gross migration *(p. 92)*	**life expectancy** *(p. 86)*	**neo-Mathusians** *(p. 102)*	**total fertility rate (TFR)** *(p. 86)*
health care density *(p. 76)*	**medical geography** *(p. 88)*	**net migration** *(p. 92)*	**transnational migrant** *(p. 93)*
immigration *(p. 91)*	**middle cohort** *(p. 84)*	**nutritional density** *(p. 76)*	**transnationalism** *(p. 93)*
infant mortality rate *(p. 86)*	**migration** *(p. 91)*	**old-age cohort** *(p. 85)*	**undocumented workers** *(p. 98)*
internal migration *(p. 91)*	**mobility** *(p. 91)*	**population policy** *(p. 102)*	**vital records** *(p. 74)*
internally displaced persons (IDPs) *(p. 95)*	**natural decrease** *(p. 86)*	**pull factors** *(p. 92)*	**voluntary migration** *(p. 92)*
	natural increase *(p. 86)*	**push factors** *(p. 92)*	**youth cohort** *(p. 84)*

REVIEW AND DISCUSSION

1. Pick two major Canadian cities and examine them from the perspective of migration. What have been the migration patterns of people in and out of these cities? Where did they come from? Were they international or internal migrants? Forced or voluntary migrants? List three reasons for these migration patterns. How has migration changed over the past 20 years? Which larger political, economic, or environmental processes might be responsible for these changes? How has Canada as a whole benefited from these migrations?

2. Use the Internet resources referenced in this chapter to research the characteristics of the populations of a core country and a peripheral country. Find out their age–sex structure, TFR, rate of natural increase, and any other characteristic you need to know to discuss the past and future development of those populations. What caused the current population structure? What are the challenges and opportunities these countries face because of their population structures? Be sure to address at least one economic, political, and social aspect for each country.

3. The distribution of population is a result of many factors, such as employment opportunities, culture, water supply, climate, and other physical environmental characteristics. Look at the distribution of population in your province. Is it evenly distributed, or are the majority of people found in only a few cities? What role do you think these various factors have played in influencing where people live in your province? Can you think of other reasons for this distribution? How has the effect of the various factors changed with technological innovation, for example in communication and transportation? Can you detect influences of globalization and trade liberalization on the distribution of population?

4. Do an Internet search and find a current example each of refugees and internally displaced people. Compare and contrast these different categorizations. What similarities do these groups share? What are their primary differences? Develop a list of two reasons for each situation. Also, consider how refugees and internally displaced people have changed the population characteristics of their given place. For

example, have these factors had an effect on birth rates or infant mortality rates? Please be as specific as possible in your answer by citing data that support your conclusion.

5. Immigration is an important factor contributing to the increase in the population of Canada. Chances are your great-grandparents, grandparents, parents, or even you immigrated to, or migrated within, this country. Construct your family's immigration or migration history. Identify push and pull factors influencing your family's decision to immigrate to or migrate within Canada. What barriers to integration, if any, did they face: language difficulties, racial discrimination, ethnic prejudice, religious segregation, economic exclusion? How did they adapt to life in their new country? Did they use strategies similar to those described in this chapter?

6. Think about the effects immigration has had on your own life. What are the new experiences, insights, discoveries, hardships, or successes immigration has meant for you? Now try to flip your perspective: if you are from a recently immigrated family, imagine how you would answer this question from the perspective of a native-born Canadian; if you are a native-born Canadian, try to answer it from the perspective of a recent immigrant. Do you find it difficult to imagine this? What might be the reasons you find it difficult?

7. The civil war in Syria has created the largest forced migration since the end of World War II. Using the resources referenced in this chapter, inform yourself about the dimensions and the characteristics of the refugee streams fleeing to neighbouring countries. Taking into account their age, gender, and other characteristics such as education or wealth, what are the effects of this migration on the populations of Syria and the countries receiving the refugees? Discuss some of the demographic implications for both sides if the refugee population cannot return to Syria in the foreseeable future. What would be the impact on the age–sex structure of the populations, their dependency ratios, and their future dynamics? How would this affect the economies of the countries?

Mastering**GEOGRAPHY**™

Log in to www.masteringgeography.com for MapMaster™ interactive maps, geography videos, RSS feeds, flashcards, weblinks, an eText version of *Human Geography: Places and Regions in Global Context,* and self-study quizzes to enhance your study of population geography.

MapMaster™ presents 13 Place Name and 13 Layered Thematic interactive maps to help students practise and master their geographic literacy, spatial reasoning, and critical thinking skills.

MapMaster™

4

PEOPLE AND NATURE

Learning Outcomes

- Recognize how people and nature form a complex relationship such that nature is both a physical realm and a social construct.

- Compare and contrast the many views of nature operating both historically and in society today, from the traditional Western approach to the radical left and contemporary ecotheological ones.

- Assess how European colonization as well as contemporary globalization transformed nature in the New World on an unprecedented scale.

- Appraise how the globalization of the capitalist political economy has affected the environment so that environmental problems, often predicated on industrialization and its attendant energy needs, are increasingly global in scope.

- Evaluate the ways sustainability has become a predominant approach to global economic development and environmental transformation.

In early November 2013, a massive tropical cyclone brewed over the Pacific Ocean southeast of the Philippines. Gathering strength from the unusually warm waters, it was named Haiyan and soon became a so-called category-five super typhoon, with sustained wind speeds rising beyond 200 km/h. On November 8, it slammed into the Philippines with winds howling at 315 km/h, the strongest tropical cyclone ever recorded.

Haiyan hit a country already weakened by an earthquake that had forced many thousands out of their homes three weeks earlier. Now the storm's high winds simply blew away the tent cities, tore down wooden buildings, shredded the vegetation, and whipped up a two-storey storm surge that washed over the coastal areas, heaving entire neighbourhoods into the sea in some areas and depositing ocean-going ships up to one kilometre inland in others. Within minutes of the storm's landfall, power was knocked out across the three Philippine islands in the path of Haiyan; communication lines were down; and landslides and twisted debris had buried roadways. For 13 million people, the lives they had built for themselves were literally turned upside down.

In the cities of Guiuan and Tacloban, and other areas hardest hit, up to 90 percent of the infrastructure was destroyed. As of spring 2014, the final death toll was not yet known as bodies continue to be discovered below the tangled wreckage. Current estimates are that

A family sifts through the remains of their destroyed house on the outskirts of Tacloban on Leyte Island after tropical cyclone Haiyan hit the Philippines on November 8, 2013. *(Source: Eoghan Rice/Trócaire/Caritas)*

8000 people lost their lives and that another 30 000 were injured. Two million people were made homeless.

Within hours of the storm's passing, people in the worst-hit areas began to experience how crucial a functioning technical infrastructure is for modern humanity's interaction with nature—and for the peaceful workings of society: without a functioning water supply, water bottles became something to be fought over. Food supplies diminished rapidly, and survivors were reduced to looting to try to feed their children. Without electricity, the few intact stores or gas stations were not operational, hospitals could not lessen the pain of the injured, and thousands of corpses were left to decompose in the heat, spreading stench and disease. Within hours, the storm had pushed a functioning society to the brink of anarchy.

The hardships of immediate survival were only the beginning, though. Even before the disaster, almost half of the people in the affected areas lived in poverty. As is often the case with natural disasters, the poor are the ones who bear the brunt of the damage because their homes were built in the most exposed locations. Many also depended on the now smashed fishing boats and splintered coconut palms for their livelihood. Without them, and without money to replace them, they face a life of permanent destitution, and many decided to leave the islands

113

altogether. Those who stay will be in an even more precarious position when the next natural disaster strikes because they have to rebuild their houses in the same dangerous flood-prone locations, and often with fewer resources and more flimsy materials.

The societal breakdown and economic collapse that occurred in a matter of days in November 2013 are powerful reminders of how fragile humanity's systems are, particularly when faced with the awesome power of natural systems. This relationship, the fragile balance between humans and their environments, is perhaps the most central of all relationships within the discipline of geography. Indeed, the discipline unites those who study natural systems, those who study human systems, and those who study the connections between them. ∎

NATURE AS A CONCEPT

As discussed briefly in Chapter 2, a simple model of the nature–society relation is that nature limits or shapes society. This model is known as environmental determinism. An alternate model posits that it is society that shapes and controls nature, largely through technology and social institutions. This second model emphasizes the complexity of nature–society interactions. In this chapter, we use this model to explore how society uses technology to transform and adapt to nature, and how those technological adaptations in turn affect humans and the environment.

Interest in the relationship between nature and society started to grow in the 1970s, when environmental problems began to be felt on a global scale. An important milestone was the Earth Summit held in Stockholm in 1972, when world leaders for the first time acknowledged that human rights, poverty, environmental protection, and economic development had to be seen in conjunction. At a second Earth Summit held in 1992 in Rio de Janeiro, more than 100 world leaders and 30 000 other participants tried to ensure a sustainable future for Earth by establishing treaties on global environmental issues. Among the outcomes were such important agreements as the Kyoto Protocol, Agenda 21, and the Convention on Biological Diversity.

In 2012, a third Earth Summit, called Rio+20, brought all 192 UN member states back to Rio de Janeiro to assess progress and renew their commitment to sustainable development. Discussions focused on two specific themes: a green economy in the context of poverty eradication and sustainable development, and an institutional framework for sustainable development. The 45 000 delegates reaffirmed the goals of the second Earth Summit and discussed some nonbinding initiatives, but there were no concrete agreements—which led Greenpeace to call the summit a failure of epic proportions (**Figure 4.1**). Indeed, the need for action is growing with every passing day: in the twenty years since the second Earth Summit, the world's population has ballooned by another 25 percent, annual global carbon dioxide emissions have increased by another 50 percent, and another 300 million hectares of forest have been cleared—the equivalent of all of Canada's forest. On a global scale, humanity now uses 1.5 times as many resources as in 1992.

These statistics underline the great irony of our time: we may be living in the "environmental age," but humanity's impact on the global environment has never been more widespread and detrimental. Canada's best-known environmental campaigner, David Suzuki, expressed it in three gloomy words: "Environmentalism has failed." Global resource consumption and pollution are soaring, not only

FIGURE 4.1 NGO protest at the Rio+20 Summit Activists cover a model of a tank with loaves of bread to symbolize the connection between widespread hunger and the global armaments trade. They point out that 10 percent of global military spending would be sufficient to realize all Millennium Development Goals. (See Chapter 3.) (*Source: Adriane MacDonald*)

because of the growing number of people on the planet, but also because changes in consumption and lifestyle patterns in many core countries require increasing amounts of resources per capita. In Canada, for instance, the average house size has doubled since 1970, whereas the average number of people living in a house has dropped from 4 to 2.5.

Since the turn of the century, however, it is the rising middle class in semiperipheral countries such as Brazil, China, and India that has been the greatest driver of another sharp increase in global resource consumption and pollution. One in four cars worldwide is now sold in China, and to provide roads for those additional 20 million cars per year, China is building a new highway network that already is more extensive than that of North America. Meanwhile, in India, the middle class is set to grow from 50 million to 600 million people over the next 20 years—more than the current population of the European Union.

Do these increases in consumption and resource use reflect parallel improvements in equality, health, and well-being? Sadly, the answer is no: the benefits of economic development and the damages arising from environmental deterioration are more unevenly distributed than ever before. For instance, according to the United Nations, more people have access to a cell phone than to a toilet. More generally, since 1970, the debt load of peripheral countries has increased eightfold, and the income gap between rich and poor nations has doubled, leaving more of the world's poor population to disproportionately suffer the effects of environmental degradation.

This is not to deny that some very important improvements have occurred since the first summit 40 years ago. One change has been the creation of national ministries and international institutions to facilitate and monitor environmental improvements. Another is the move toward phasing out leaded gasoline, DDT, and ozone-depleting chemicals, for example (**Figure 4.2**). A third has been the growing scientific and popular interest in global environmental issues—chances are, you are taking this course because of your own interest in the environment. Perhaps most significant has been the proliferation of concern for sustainability, especially as it has broadened out from being a conference theme to a set of practices being taken up by governments, corporations, public and private organizations, and individuals. Among these new practices and objectives are recycling (**Figure 4.3**), sustainable buildings, green

FIGURE 4.2 Rachel L. Carson (1907–1964) Rachel L. Carson was a professional biologist who worked for the U.S. Fish and Wildlife Service. Many people regard her as a key figure in the emergence of what is now known as the *environmental movement.* Her 1962 book, *Silent Spring* (alluding to a future in which songbirds are poisoned by pesticides), was instrumental in changing attitudes toward the widespread and carefree use of synthetic pesticides such as DDT. Carson called these substances "biocides" to stress the emerging realization that their poisonous effects cannot be limited to "pests" but harm other organisms, too. In birds, exposure to DDT causes brittle eggshells that break under the weight of the brooding bird; in humans it is believed to cause cancer. The United States and Canada banned DDT in 1972 and 1974, respectively, but Mexico did not follow until 2000. Carson did not live to see the bans: she died in 1964—of cancer. (*Source:* Erich Hartmann/Magnum Photos)

FIGURE 4.3 Recycling In some core countries, recycling has become so widespread that it now is a social norm as well as a revenue generator. Pictured on the left are collection bins for seven different recyclable materials in a park in Germany. The photo on the right shows a 500 kg bale of crushed aluminum cans that generated $1003.10 in revenue for the municipality that collected it. (*Source:* M. Imort)

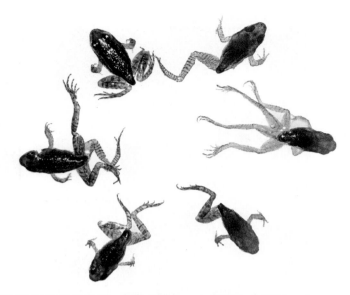

FIGURE 4.4 **Deformities in frogs** Although DDT and other substances now known to be harmful have been banned, many others continue to be used, even if we are not certain of their possible systemic effects. A 2005 study published in the *Proceedings of the National Academy of Sciences* found that the combination of pesticide contamination and parasite infection has caused missing legs and extra legs in wood frogs in 43 states in the United States and 5 provinces in Canada. It is believed that exposure to agricultural chemicals may weaken amphibian immune systems, making the frogs more vulnerable to parasitic infection leading to limb deformities. Worldwide, populations of amphibians have been decreasing at an alarming rate, and scientists believe that pesticides, global climate change, and other human-induced factors are responsible for this decline. (*Source:* Joseph Kiesecker/AP Images)

urban development, renewable energy technologies, sustainable tourism, environmental restoration, sustainable agriculture, promotion of biomass and biofuels, the emergence and growth of carbon markets, and "green" marketing and government practices.

As people the world over are becoming increasingly concerned about environmental problems, they are also beginning to wonder whether the reason for the situation worsening so rapidly is that humans have a flawed view of the nature–society relationship. In the past, technology was viewed as the apparent solution to most environmental problems, but today's technological progress often seems to aggravate rather than to solve such problems (**Figure 4.4**). As a result, researchers and activists have begun to ask different questions and to abandon the assumption that technology is the *only* solution. For instance, philosopher and environmental activist Vandana Shiva has led a global movement advocating changes in agriculture and food production practices (**Figure 4.5**). In 1991, she founded Navdanya, a social movement with the goal of promoting the use and preservation of native seeds, organic farming, and fair trade. In India, Navdanya has so far successfully conserved more than 5000 crop varieties, has created awareness of the hazards of genetic engineering, and has defended people whose food rights are under threat from globalization and biopiracy. A controversial practice with many conflicting definitions, *biopiracy* involves the commercial appropriation (including patenting) of traditional indigenous knowledge of naturally occurring substances.

FIGURE 4.5 **Vandana Shiva** Indian environmental activist Vandana Shiva was trained in Canada as a physicist before becoming a philosopher of science and ecofeminist. She is also a leading figure in the global solidarity movement known as the alter-globalization movement. (*Source:* SFM Press Reporter/Alamy)

Navdanya and other movements like it have influenced environmental experts, including a number of geographers, to conceptualize nature not as something apart from humans but as inseparable from us. These experts believe that nature and questions about the environment need to be considered in conjunction with society because the latter shapes our attitudes toward nature and how we identify sources of and solutions to environmental problems. Such an approach—thinking of nature and society as interactive components of a complex system—enables us to ask new questions and consider new alternatives to our current practices with respect to nature.

In this chapter we examine the nature–society relationship by looking first at different approaches to it. We then examine how changing conceptions of nature have translated into very different human uses of nature as well as human adaptations to nature. We conclude the chapter with an examination of sustainable development as a way of addressing global environmental problems and a discussion of the new institutional frameworks and activist organizations that are emerging to promote sustainability.

Nature and Society Defined

The central concepts of this chapter—nature and society—have very specific meanings. Although we discuss the changing conceptions and understandings of nature in some detail, we hold to one basic conception here, namely that **nature** is a social creation as much as it is the physical universe that includes human beings. This means that understandings of nature change because they are the product of different times and different needs: they are a reflection of society because people's philosophies, belief systems, and ideologies also shape the way they think about and use nature.

Society is the sum of the inventions, institutions, and relationships created and reproduced by human beings across particular places and times. Society's relationship with nature varies from place to place and among different social groups. Moreover, the relationship between nature and society is two-way: society shapes people's understandings and uses of nature at the same time that nature shapes society.

The relationship between society and nature is usually mediated through technology. **Technology** is defined as

- physical objects or artifacts (for example, the plow)
- activities or processes (for example, steelmaking to produce a plow)
- knowledge or know-how (for example, plow-based agriculture)

This definition recognizes tools, applications, and understandings equally as critical components of technology. The manifestations and impacts of technology can be measured in terms of such concepts as level of industrialization and per capita energy consumption. We now look at two methods of quantifying the human impact on the environment in those terms.

The first method is the **ecological footprint**, which is a measure of the biologically productive land area (biocapacity) required to support a given population by providing for its needs and absorbing its wastes. It allows us to visualize the growth and scale of the impact humans have on Earth in terms of sustainability (**Figure 4.6**). Because people use resources from all over the globe, the ecological footprint calculation includes all the cropland and natural resources required to produce the products consumed by a population, wherever on the planet they may be drawn from. According to the *Ecological Footprint Atlas 2010*, Canada's footprint is 7.01 hectares per capita, a figure exceeded only by seven other countries in the world, including the United States (8.0 hectares) and the United Arab Emirates (at the top of the list with 10.68 hectares). At the other extreme we find countries such as Afghanistan and Bangladesh with 0.62 hectares. The global average is 2.7 hectares—but there are only 1.8 hectares of biocapacity available for each person on the planet, which means that the global population currently uses 50 percent more resources than is sustainable. Finally, because the ecological footprint is measured per capita, we also need to take into consideration the size of national populations to appreciate its true dimensions: half the total global footprint can be attributed to only 10 countries, with the United States using 21 percent and China using 24 percent of the global biocapacity.[1]

The second method is the $I = PAT$ formula, an attempt to distinguish the various sources of social impacts on the environment. The formula relates human population pressures on environmental resources to the level of affluence and access to technology in a society. More specifically, the formula states that $I = PAT$, where I (impact on Earth's resources) is equal to P (population) times A (affluence, as measured by per capita income) times T (a technology

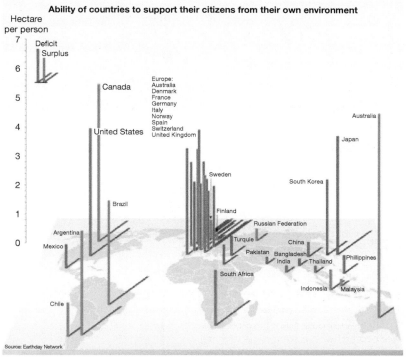

FIGURE 4.6 Ecological footprint The ecological footprint measures the amount of productive land area needed to support a nation's consumption and waste. This map shows that in many countries the demand for natural resources exceeds the amount available. Countries that are not able to support their national consumption with their own natural resources are running an ecological deficit (shown by the red bars). Therefore these countries have to either import biocapacity from other places or take it from future generations. (*Source:* Philippe Rekacewicz, UNEP/GRID-Arendal, "Ability of countries to support their citizens from their own environment," © 2005 GRID-Arendal. Reprinted by permission.)

factor). For example, the impact on the environment of a household's food consumption would equal the number of people per household times the per capita income of the household times the type of technology and energy used in producing foodstuffs for that household.

Each of the variables in the formula—population, affluence, and technology—is complex. For example, with regard to population numbers, it is generally believed that fewer people on the planet will result in fewer direct pressures on resources. Some argue, however, that increased world population is quite desirable, since more people means that more minds and more labour can be put toward solving present and future problems. Clearly, there is no simple answer to the question of how many people are too many people.

Affluence also cannot simply be assessed in terms of "less is better." Certainly, increasing affluence is a drain on Earth's resources and a burden on Earth's ability to absorb waste. Yet how much affluence is too much is difficult to determine. For instance, evidence shows that the core countries, with high levels of affluence, are more effective than the poor countries of the periphery at protecting their environments. Unfortunately, core countries often do so by exporting their noxious industrial processes and waste

[1]The latest version of the atlas is available at www.footprintnetwork.org, a website that also allows you to calculate your personal ecological footprint.

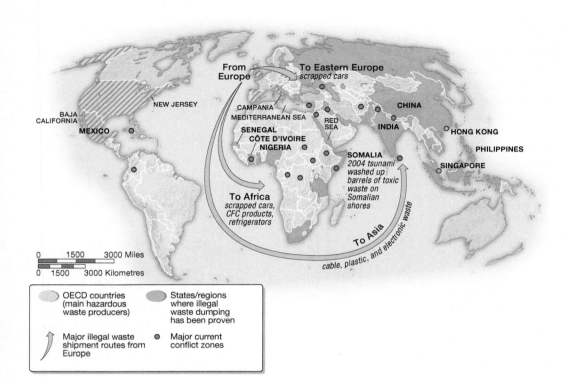

FIGURE 4.7 Electronic waste This map shows the major illegal waste shipment routes for electronic garbage produced in Europe. It also shows which countries are the major waste producers. (*Source:* Adapted from Figure 8.7, Waste Trafficking in Global Environment Outlook 4 [GEO4], 2009. Cartographer/designer Bounford.com and UNEP/GRID-Arendal, compiled from multiple sources in UNEP 2006c. http://maps.grida.no/graphic/wastetrafficking.)

products to peripheral countries (**Figure 4.7**). By exporting polluting industries and the jobs that go with them, however, core countries may also be contributing to increased affluence in the receiving countries. Given what we know from the historical development in core countries, such a rise may foster a set of social values, attitudes, and behaviours that ultimately leads to better protection of the environment in a new place. Evidently, the role of affluence in terms of environmental impacts is, like that of population, difficult to assess.

Not surprisingly, the technology variable is no less complicated. Technology affects the environment in three ways, through

- the harvesting of resources
- the emission of wastes in the manufacture of goods and services
- the emission of waste in the consumption of goods and services

A technological innovation can shift demand from an existing resource to a newly discovered, more plentiful one. An example would be the recent shift from oil to natural gas for home heating in Canada. In addition, technology can sometimes be a solution and sometimes a problem. Both principles can be seen in the case of nuclear energy, widely regarded as a cleaner and more efficient alternative to fossil fuels. Producing this energy creates hazards, however, as we will discuss later in this chapter.

It is therefore clear that increases in human numbers, in levels of wealth, and in technological capacity are key components of social and economic progress that have had an extremely complex impact on the environment. In the past 100 years, this complexity has come to be seen as a triple-barreled threat to the quality of the natural world and the availability and quality of environmental resources. Before we look more carefully at the specific impacts of populations, affluence, and technology on nature, we need to look first at how differing social attitudes toward nature shape the human behaviours that are a basis for *I=PAT*. This will help us understand that humankind, in its uses and abuses of the environment, is as much influenced by prevailing ideas about nature as by the realities of nature.

Nature–Society Interactions

The concept of human *adaptation* to the natural environment is part of the geographical subfield of cultural ecology. **Cultural ecology** is the study of how human society has adapted to environmental challenges such as aridity and steep slopes through technologies such as irrigation and terracing and organizing people to construct and maintain these systems. (See the discussion of hydraulic empires in Chapter 2.) These adaptations can be seen clearly in the agricultural terraces of the Incas in Peru or the irrigation canals and reservoirs of the modern southwestern United States (**Figure 4.8**). More recent adaptations include the use of biotechnology and agricultural chemicals to increase agricultural production and the development of new pharmaceuticals to cope with diseases.

Human adaptation has involved more than simply responding to natural constraints though. In addition, we have produced widespread modifications of environments and landscapes. In some cases, the human use of nature has resulted in environmental degradation or pollution. For example, overcultivation of steep slopes can erode the soil, and the use of toxic agricultural chemicals can contaminate rivers and lakes. The Industrial Revolution produced a dramatic growth in waste emissions and resulted in serious air pollution and health problems in many areas. These emissions and the associated pollution persist to this day.

The massive transformation of nature by human activity led geographers such as Neil Smith and Margaret Fitzsimmons to claim that there are no more "natural" environments or untouched wildernesses. They used the phrase "social production of nature"

FIGURE 4.8 Agricultural terraces in Machu Picchu, Peru The Inca civilization adapted to the extremely steep slopes in the Andes by constructing elaborate agricultural terraces that required high levels of social organization and engineering skills. (*Source:* M. Imort)

to describe the refashioning of landscapes and species by human activity, especially capitalist production and labour processes. Geographers have played a major role in highlighting the global scope of this transformation through their discussions of the human dimensions of global environmental change and their explorations of the social causes and consequences of changes in global environmental conditions. Recently, one global transformation has come to be seen as a particularly grave threat: the global patterns of fossil-fuel use and changes in land use that are producing serious changes in climate and biodiversity through carbon dioxide–induced global warming or deforestation (**Figure 4.9**).

Global climate change is causing sea levels to rise as polar ice caps melt and ocean temperatures rise. Because warmer oceans surrender greater quantities of water and energy in the form of water vapour, weather systems will intensify and produce fiercer cyclones and hurricanes. In fact, many observers have connected the unprecedented severity of Haiyan to exactly this phenomenon. We already mentioned that the social and economic standing of people greatly influences how severely they are affected by natural disasters. Given that human-induced global change contributes to such disasters, and that the level of impact also depends greatly on social and political factors, are we really justified in calling them "natural" disasters?

In the summer of 2005, the twin disasters of violent storms and flooding came together in the United States as Hurricane Katrina bore down on a wide swath of the Gulf Coast that extended from Pensacola, Florida, to New Orleans, Louisiana. The hurricane destroyed extensive sections of the built environment and caused the flooding of low-lying areas, especially Greater New Orleans, where thousands died or were injured and more than 1 million people were displaced. Hurricane Katrina was quickly labelled the worst natural disaster the United States ever experienced.

It is now largely accepted, however, that the root causes of the calamity were far from "natural." While there is no doubt that the force of the winds slamming the Gulf Coast were extreme, the fact that districts and parishes in and around New Orleans (where the most dramatic impacts occurred) flooded and so many people (who had not evacuated) died was the result of avoidable political and social factors. The event is instructive because it provides insight into the ways that global climate change can have catastrophic effects because of the social as well as the environmental vulnerability of populations.

In New Orleans, critically needed improvements to the levees—a system of dikes that hold back the Mississippi River and Lake Ponchartrain and enable large parts of the city to sit more than a metre below sea level—had been repeatedly postponed. When Katrina made landfall in New Orleans, the strong winds first brought down power and communication lines, leaving the region without electricity or phone service. The storm surge then breached the levees and flooded over 80 percent of the city. The city's evacuation plan worked well for many who could leave the city in their own cars, but tens of thousands of people were too poor, disabled, uninformed, or fearful to leave the city before the storm hit, and they were left in harm's way. The result was that these people suffered disproportionately from this "natural" disaster. The level of vulnerability of people thus depended more on social, economic, and political factors (many of which were beyond their control) than on anything else.

The 2010 earthquake in Haiti is another instance of the impact of a natural disaster being dramatically intensified by poverty and political problems. The quake that hit Haiti on January 12 was a catastrophic 7.0 moment magnitude, with the epicentre approximately 25 km west of Port-au-Prince, Haiti's capital. More than 200 000 people were killed by the earthquake and 2.3 million were made

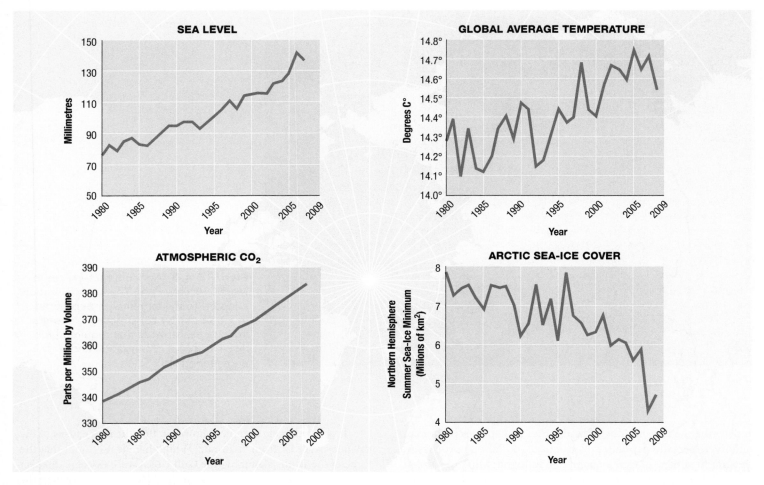

FIGURE 4.9 Composite graphs of climate change The International Geosphere-Biosphere Programme (IGBP) considers the four elements shown here—temperature, carbon dioxide level, sea level, and Artic sea ice cover—to represent how climate change is affecting the planet. The IGBP was launched in 1986 by the International Council of Scientific Unions to study global change. (*Source:* Adapted with permission from *IGBP Climate Change Index: Global-change trends for the public and policy makers.* Global Change: International Geosphere-Biosphere Programme [IGBP].)

homeless (out of a total population of 10 million). The government of Haiti estimated that 250 000 residences and 30 000 commercial buildings collapsed or were severely damaged. Inadequate building codes and poor emergency response increased the impact of the earthquake significantly. Four years later, the situation is still critical. According to the UN, three-quarters of Haitians have no electricity, more than half a million are food-insecure, and 25 percent of children are out of primary schools (**Figure 4.10**). Because of persistent poor sanitation, Haiti accounts for half of the world's cholera cases. Long after the quake, corruption and inefficiency ensure that people's lives will not return to normalcy anytime soon. As a result, tens of thousands of Haitians still live in tents in over 300 displacements camps, dependent on handouts from international aid organizations.

Atmospheric scientists have been arguing for over two decades that global warming is putting cities on the Gulf and Atlantic coasts in a vulnerable position as higher-than-normal ocean temperatures intensify hurricanes and tropical storms. Many believe that Hurricanes Katrina and Sandy are not examples of a "perfect storm," where essential meteorological elements combine to produce an extreme and devastating event. Instead, they are perfect examples of

how global climate change in combination with human practices is transforming Earth's environment in dramatic and devastating ways.

During the twentieth century, global sea level rose by 20 centimetres, and a recent report by Britain's Meteorological Office warned that flooding will increase more than nine-fold over the twenty-first century, with four-fifths of the increase occurring in South and Southeast Asia. Any rise in sea level would be disastrous for some countries. About 70 percent of Bangladesh, for example, is at sea level, as is much of Egypt's most fertile land in the Nile delta. On the other hand, farmers in much of Europe and North America would welcome a local rise in mean temperatures, since it would extend their options for the kinds of crops that they could profitably raise.

The causes and consequences of these global climate changes vary considerably by world region. For example, the industrial countries have higher carbon dioxide emissions. Increased carbon dioxide emissions are contributing to rising temperatures through the trapping of heat in Earth's atmosphere. In order to survive in many of the world's peripheral regions, the rural poor are often impelled to degrade and destroy their immediate environment by cutting down forests for fuelwood. Not only does this add carbon dioxide and soot

FIGURE 4.10 Haiti, one year after the earthquake Less than 5 percent of debris had been cleared on the one-year anniversary of the earthquake, January 11, 2011. The amount of rubble still on the ground would fill dump trucks parked bumper to bumper halfway around the world. Even today the rebuilding efforts remain stalled by a lack of funds, indecision, political infighting, corruption, and a host of other factors that are exacerbating the lingering effects of the disaster. (*Source:* AP Images)

to the atmosphere but it also leads to the destruction of forests that otherwise could help counteract global warming. Thus, both the core and the periphery are contributing to the problem of global change in different, but equally significant, ways (**Figure 4.11**).

Population growth patterns and the changing geography of economic development allow us to predict with some confidence that the air and water pollution generated by (semi)peripheral countries will more than double in the next 10 to 15 years as they rapidly industrialize. Clearly, environmental problems are already inseparable from processes of demographic change, economic development, and human welfare. In addition, regional environmental problems are becoming increasingly enmeshed in matters of national security and regional conflict.

Before the 1980s, the principles of cultural ecology did not include the political dimensions of ecological questions, but since then cultural ecologists have moved away from a strict focus on particular cultural groups' relationship with the environment, placing that relationship within a wider context instead. The result is political ecology, the merging of political economy with cultural ecology. **Political ecology** stresses that human–environment relations can be adequately understood only by relating patterns of resource use to political and economic forces. (See Box 4.1, "Geography Matters: Water Politics.")

APPLY YOUR KNOWLEDGE List three examples of cultural ecology from your own community or campus. (Hint: how specifically has your town or campus adapted to environmental challenges over the past 20 years?) ■

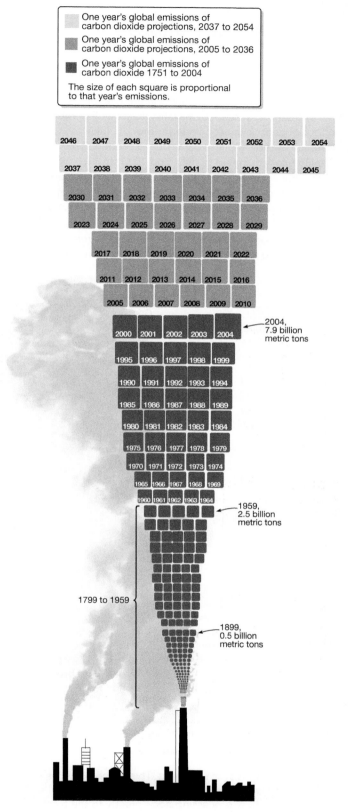

FIGURE 4.11 Global emissions of carbon dioxide Each square represents one year's global emissions of carbon dioxide, measured by the weight of carbon it contains.

(*Source:* Adapted from *New York Times*, December 16, 2007. http://www.nytimes.com/interactive/2007/12/16/weekinreview/20071216_EMISSIONS_GRAPHIC.html, accessed May 16, 2011.)

Water Politics

One of the most crucial elements in the relationship between people and their environment is water. We can't live without it, and all of our economic practices depend on it. Take your breakfast, for instance: it took 140 litres of water to produce your cup of coffee, 250 litres for your glass of milk, and 1000 litres for the orange juice. That means that by 8 am you have already consumed 14 bathtubs full of water—and you haven't even eaten yet! Put on your new T-shirt and you are adding another 25 bathtubs that were used in the production of the garment. The water embedded in the production of the food or other things we consume is referred to as **virtual water** (**Figure 4.A**), and Canadians use more than twice the global average. Much of this virtual water is "imported" to Canada along with the product: thus the orange juice we consume in Canada puts a strain on the water supply in California, Spain, Morocco, or wherever the oranges were grown in irrigated groves.

Evidently, this makes (virtual) water one of the most heavily traded resources worldwide—but does that mean that water should also be treated as a commodity, that is, a tradable resource with a market price determined by supply and demand? Without abundant water, people in the core could not live the high-quality lives they currently enjoy; without clean water, those in the periphery die. It is therefore important to question what our lives would be like if the price of water were as volatile as, for example, oil. The price of oil has risen and fallen repeatedly, most recently due to the Arab Spring, but also because OPEC (a cartel of 12 oil exporting countries known as the Organization of Petroleum Exporting Countries) has the power to set oil production schedules and prices. What would happen if water were subject to similar conditions and price effects?

While this may seem a far-fetched question for people in the core who often enjoy artificially low water costs, populations in the periphery have been feeling the effects of escalating water prices for nearly a decade, and in some places far longer. The *2013 UN Human Development Report* states that 1 billion people in peripheral countries do not have adequate access to water, and that another 1.5 billion face economic water shortages (**Figure 4.B**). Almost two-thirds of the people lacking access to clean water survive on less than US$2 a day, and they simply cannot afford high-priced water. In fact, these statistics are two sides of the same coin: poor people in urban areas of the periphery rarely have access to piped water and therefore must pay horrendous prices to mobile water merchants, whereas their neighbours in the wealthier parts of town pay low rates for piped municipal water.

Experts around the world have begun to talk about a global "water crisis," which is occurring not only because there is a looming shortage of clean water, but also because water is being turned from a public good into a privatized commodity with steeply rising prices. The privatization of water (as opposed to the provision of water through publicly owned utilities) was touted as a way of bringing equitable access and efficiency to all water users, but has instead led to increased prices and accessibility problems for poor and marginalized peoples not only in the global periphery but in peripheral areas of many core countries as well. Nearly two decades ago, many governments—national as well as local—looked to the privatization of water provision as a way of unburdening themselves of a relatively expensive service in response to the public's demand for smaller, leaner government. Corporations—mostly multinational ones—began buying up municipal water providers and offering water provision based on profit-and-loss considerations.

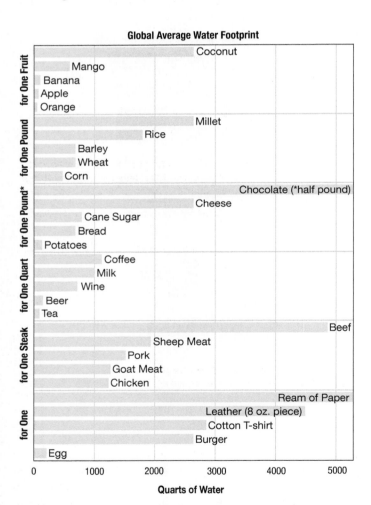

Global Average Water Footprint

FIGURE 4.A Water footprint This graph provides examples of the virtual water expended to produce some of our everyday foods. Notice how processing adds greatly to the total amount of virtual water involved. (*Source*: Data from A.Y. Hoekstra and A.K. Chapagain [2008] *Globalization of water: Sharing the planet's freshwater resources.* Oxford, UK: Blackwell Publishing; and www.waterfootprint.org.)

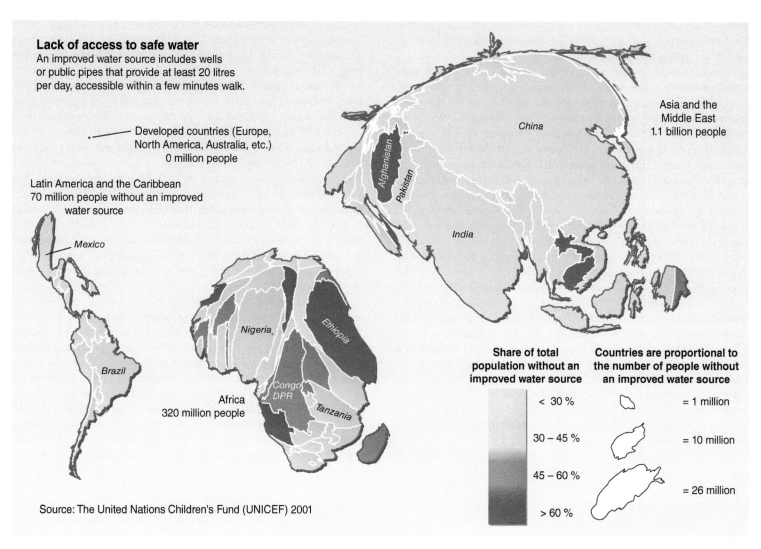

Lack of access to safe water
An improved water source includes wells or public pipes that provide at least 20 litres per day, accessible within a few minutes walk.

• —— Developed countries (Europe, North America, Australia, etc.) 0 million people

Latin America and the Caribbean 70 million people without an improved water source

Mexico

Brazil

Africa 320 million people

Nigeria

Ethiopia

Congo DPR

Tanzania

China

Afghanistan

Pakistan

India

Asia and the Middle East 1.1 billion people

Share of total population without an improved water source

< 30 %

30 – 45 %

45 – 60 %

> 60 %

Countries are proportional to the number of people without an improved water source

= 1 million

= 10 million

= 26 million

Source: The United Nations Children's Fund (UNICEF) 2001

FIGURE 4.B Lack of access to safe water This cartogram shows that many people in the periphery do not have access to safe, clean water. Note the complete absence of core countries from this cartogram. (*Source:* Hugo Ahlenius, UNEP/GRID-Arendal, "Lack of access to safe water," © 2005 GRID-Arendal. Reprinted by permission.)

An illustration of the kinds of problems that the privatization of water can create is the case of Cochabamba in Bolivia. Recently the subject of an internationally acclaimed motion picture, *Even the Rain/También la lluvia*, starring Gabriel García Bernal, explores the real-life conflict that erupted around a European water company's attempt to privatize water in this lush valley community at the entrance to the Amazon rain forest. In 1998, the International Monetary Fund (IMF) approved a US$138 million loan for Bolivia to help the country control inflation and bolster economic growth. To qualify for the loan, Bolivia had to agree to structural reforms that reduced the role of the state and opened the country to international competition. Bolivia agreed to sell off a wide range of public utilities, including Cochabamba's local water agency, SEMAPA. Cochabamba in central Bolivia has a metropolitan population of about 1 million. It is a prosperous place with an economic base dedicated to commerce, industrial

(Continued)

production, and services. It has a large indigenous population—Quechua people—and enjoys a reputation for being economically and socially progressive.

Water rates in most municipalities around the world are subsidized because water is absolutely essential to life and the "real" cost of water—acquisition, treatment, delivery, waste management—can be prohibitive. Moreover, subsidies exist not just for households but also for agriculture and industries. However, when water prices increased in Cochabamba, due to the sale of its municipal water supply to Aguas del Tunari, a multinational consortium of private investors, including a subsidiary of the multinational Bechtel Corporation, the population received no subsidies that would allow it to afford the new, much higher water rates. Water rates doubled and tripled, forcing many residents to discontinue water service. Eventually, citizens assembled to protest against the difficult situation. The result was four days of conflict where members of The Coalition for the Defense of Water and Life (La Coordinadora) went on strike and erected roadblocks throughout the city (**Figure 4.C**). The protests in Cochabamba spread to Bolivia's administrative capital, La Paz, and other cities and outlying rural communities. Across the country, thousands clashed with riot police, erected roadblocks, and protested not only the water-rate hikes but also high unemployment. The violence culminated in a historic victory for the residents of Cochabamba and their supporters that guaranteed the withdrawal of Aguas del Tunari, granted control of Cochabamba's water to La Coordinadora, assured the release of detained protesters, and promised the repeal of water privatization legislation.

But stories similar to that of Cochabamba continue to unfold across municipalities globally. Large international water companies such as Paris-based Suez, the largest water company, Veolia (formerly Vivendi), also French and the world's second-largest water giant, and RWE, a German utility conglomerate, are competing for control of water supplies across the world. For instance, in 1999, the German capital of Berlin sold half of its water works to RWE and Veolia—and water rates began to rise immediately. The contract governing the sale was never fully disclosed, and citizen activists—suspecting that Berliners were overcharged for water—mobilized. In 2001, they forced a referendum, and Berliners overwhelmingly supported them. The contracts were made public, revealing that they contained contractual guarantees for certain profit levels. In response, the German Federal Competition Bureau ordered a cut of almost 20 percent in water rates as well as refunds. In the roughly ten years of operating the Berlin water supply, the two transnationals reportedly made almost CDN$2 billion.

Reports abound across the globe of private purchases of local water supplies and resulting rate hikes, negative economic impacts, inadequate customer service, and harm to natural resources. The bottom line is that water—clean, drinkable water—like many other natural resources, is becoming increasingly scarce and an attractive investment opportunity. Chile has become the most water-privatized country in the world. But unlike other places, it undertook privatization through careful staging that unfolded over many years. By the time private companies actually assumed control of water provision across Chile's urban areas, strict rules

FIGURE 4.C Water conflict in Cochabamba, Bolivia Pictured here are protesters running from tear gas fired by national police attempting to disperse thousands of demonstrators on the streets of Cochabamba, Bolivia, during the action against the hike in water rates. (*Source:* Jeff Schonberg/AP Images)

and regulations were in place to increase efficiency, improve service quality, and mobilize capital to extend wastewater treatment. Most importantly, in Chile privatized water provision is regulated by a public, autonomous entity, and the system provides subsidies for those unable to afford higher water rates.

One of the most significant challenges of the twenty-first century will be how to ensure access to adequate supplies of quality drinking water for everyone. In response to the global water privatization movement, individuals as well as governments and nongovernmental organizations are increasingly arguing that access to safe and adequate supplies of water should be seen as a human right and that large corporations are not capable of guaranteeing that right (because it runs counter to their objective of generating profits). It is important to be aware that the conflict over who should provide safe water is occurring in cities and towns throughout the core as well as in the periphery. Besides issues of access and public safety, many of those opposing water privatization argue that conflicts over water are really about fundamental questions of democracy. In particular, if water is no longer a public good, who will make the decisions that affect our future access to it, and who will be denied access? This question is an especially significant one as climate change is expected to have dramatic impacts on water quality and quantity throughout the world. Water, then, is an apt illustration of the many ways in which humans interact with their environment and how this interaction is mediated by society, mainly through technology, but also through politics, economics, culture, religion, and consumption.

ENVIRONMENTAL PHILOSOPHIES AND POLITICAL VIEWS OF NATURE

As we mentioned at the beginning of this chapter, nature is a construct that is very much shaped by social ideas, beliefs, and values. As a result, different societies and different cultures have different views of nature. In the contemporary world, views of nature are dominated by the Western (also known as Judeo-Christian) tradition that understands humans to be superior to nature. In this view, nature is something to be tamed or dominated. But other views of nature have emerged that depart dramatically from the dominant view. These include the environmental philosophies that became popular in the nineteenth and early twentieth centuries and the more radical political views of nature that gained prominence in the late twentieth century. Among the latter are approaches based on ecotheology—including Christianity, Hinduism, Islam, and Judaism—which reject the long-standing Western tradition. We examine these and other well-known approaches to nature in this section.

Our review of environmental philosophies begins with Henry David Thoreau (1817–1862), an American naturalist and activist, whose ideas represent one of the first alternatives in the English-speaking world to the "humans-over-nature" approach that characterized his times. He embraced European notions of **romanticism**, a philosophy that emphasized interdependence and relatedness between humans and nature and saw all creatures (and not just humans) as infused with a divine presence.

Thoreau studied the natural world around the town of his birth, Concord, Massachusetts. He is most famous for his book *Walden*, which chronicles the two years he spent living and observing nature in solitude in a cabin he built at nearby Walden Pond. Thoreau regarded the natural world as an antidote to the negative effects of technology on the landscape and the human character. The Industrial Revolution was in full force all around Thoreau, and he was keenly aware of its impacts. In fact, Thoreau's approach to the natural world was very much a response to the impacts of the early forces of globalization. His research on the animals and plants that surrounded Concord was an attempt to reconstruct the landscape as it had existed before colonization and massive European immigration.

The first to explicitly argue that human beings are significant agents of environmental change was the American diplomat George Perkins Marsh. In 1874, he published *The Earth as Modified by Human Action*, in which he concluded that the denuded landscapes he had seen on his mission to the Mediterranean were the result of human overuse. His book is considered one of the most important advances in what would later be called geography, ecology, and resource management. Like Thoreau, Marsh cautioned that humans should not damage the natural environment through reckless exploitation.

Early in the twentieth century, writers like Gifford Pinchot and politicians like Theodore Roosevelt drew on the ideas of Thoreau, Marsh, and others to advocate the wise use of natural resources and the conservation of natural environments. Their view that nature should be conserved has survived to the present. **Conservation** holds that natural resources should be used thoughtfully and that humans should serve as stewards, not exploiters, of the natural world. Conservation implies responsibility to future generations as well as to the natural world itself in the utilization of resources. These ideas eventually helped inspire a wide range of environmental organizations, including the Environmental Defense Fund, World Watch Institute, the Nature Conservancy, and the Sierra

Club. The latter is a well-established private organization with chapters throughout Canada and the United States and an extensive legal division that litigates cases of corporate or individual violations of environmental regulations.

Those who espouse a more radical approach to nature regard the conservation approach as too passive to be truly effective in protecting the environment. Such individuals believe that conservation leaves intact the political and economic system that drives the exploitation of nature in the first place. They believe that nature is sacred and should be preserved, not used at all. This more extreme position, **preservation**, advocates that certain habitats, species, and resources should remain off-limits to human use, regardless of whether the use maintains or depletes the resource in question.

The philosophy of such groups as the Sea Shepherd Conservation Society is closely aligned with the preservationist perspective. Whereas the Sierra Club takes its opponents to the courtroom, the Sea Shepherd Conservation Society, under its leader, Canadian environmentalist Paul Watson, actively promotes the use of "quick strike" actions to protect the biodiversity of the oceans and halt what they regard as government or corporate abuses of the environment, such as dolphin "harvesting" in Japan, sealing in Canada, bluefin tuna fisheries in the Mediterranean, or whaling in the Pacific (**Figure 4.12**).

Founded in Vancouver in 1979, Greenpeace is an environmental organization that combines the strategies of the Sierra Club and the Sea Shepherd Conservation Society: it conducts research and awareness campaigns, uses oppositional tactics, and initiates formal legal actions. In its membership (with the world headquarters in Amsterdam and regional offices in most major industrial countries) as well as its objectives (halting environmental pollution worldwide), Greenpeace articulates the belief that places are interdependent and that what happens in one part of the globe affects us all.

These and other environmental organizations are practical illustrations of approaches to understanding human interactions with nature that have developed since the publication of *Silent Spring* over 50 years ago. These, as well as other new approaches—including environmental ethics, ecofeminism, deep ecology, environmental

justice, ecotheology, and an animistic approach to nature—take the view that nature is both a physical universe and a product of social thought. Each provides a different way of understanding how society shapes our ideas about nature.

Environmental ethics is a philosophical perspective that prescribes moral principles as guidance for our treatment of nature. What exactly these principles are is a matter of controversy among the different schools of thought in environmental ethics, but all agree that society has a moral obligation to treat nature according to the rules of moral behaviour that exist for humans. An aspect of environmental ethics that has caused a great deal of controversy is the idea that animals, trees, rocks, and other elements of nature have rights in the same way that humans do. If the moral system of our society insists that humans have the right to a safe and happy life, then, it is argued, the same rights should be extended to nonhuman nature. Such a perspective would, of course, have far-reaching consequences for the way in which humans treat and use nature.

Ecofeminism holds that patriarchy—a system of social ideas that values men more highly than women—is at the root of our present environmental malaise. Ecofeminists argue that patriarchy has not only equated women with nature but also established the subordination and exploitation of both. Ecofeminism has been widely embraced in the periphery, where women are primarily responsible for the health and welfare of their families in environments that are being rapidly degraded. The unifying objective in all of ecofeminism is to dismantle the patriarchal biases in Western culture and replace them with a perspective that values social, cultural, and biological diversity.

Deep ecology is an approach to nature revolving around two key components: self-realization and biospherical egalitarianism. The first idea sees humans as identifying with a larger organic unity or "self" that transcends their individual being. In this view, the universe is not merely a collection of matter and energy, but just as much a complex and diverse set of relationships. Or, as a deep ecologist might say: you *are* the universe, and the universe is you. The second idea regards humans as no more valuable or important than any other species: humans and their interests should not be given preferential treatment. In sum, deep ecologists hope that the belief that all things are

FIGURE 4.12 Sea Shepherd Society protest Using direct-action as a form of protest, the Sea Shepherd Conservation Society has been involved in scuttling and disabling whaling vessels and intervening in Canadian seal hunts, in an attempt to halt these practices. This photograph shows members of the organization interfering with the progress of a large Japanese whaling ship. (*Source:* Simon Ager/Sea Shepherd Conservation Society/AP Images)

FIGURE 4.13 Conflicting environmental perceptions Pictured here is a member of the Algonquin First Nation attempting to prevent a logging truck from passing along a forest road. In conflict here are opposing perceptions of the forest: some members of the band see it as a place of spiritual renewal, whereas lumber companies see it as the source of harvestable commodities. (*Source:* Mike Greenlar/The Image Works)

internally related can enable society to treat the nonhuman world with respect and not simply as a source of raw materials for human use.

Activists in the **environmental justice** movement consider the pollution of their neighbourhoods by, for example, factories and hazardous-waste dumps to be the result of a structured and institutionalized inequality that is pervasive in both the capitalist core and the periphery. They see their issues as distinct from those of middle-class mainstream groups like the Sierra Club or even Greenpeace. Environmental justice activists see their struggles as uniquely rooted in their economic status. Thus, theirs are not quality-of-life issues, such as whether any forests will be left for recreational hiking, but sheer economic and physical survival today and the next day. As a result, the questions raised by environmental justice activists involve the distribution of economic and political resources. Such questions are not easily resolved in courts of law but speak to more complex issues such as the nature of racism and sexism and of capitalism as a class-based economic system. Like ecofeminism, the environmental justice movement is not restricted to the core. Indeed, poor people throughout the world are concerned that the negative impacts of economic development consistently affect them more than the rich.

Ecotheology calls for a re-evaluation of the Western relationship to nature. The term came into prominence in the late twentieth century—mainly in Christian circles, though it has since spread to other religions—in association with the scientific field of ecology. Within religious circles, there is a fear that science may not be capable of inspiring the changes in behaviour necessary to thwart continuing environmental destruction. Ecotheologists also argue that capitalist political and economic institutions actively contribute to environmental degradation. In their view, it has become necessary, therefore, to address the current environmental crisis through belief systems that will overcome the inadequacies of humanly created institutions. Ecotheology recognizes the value of other creatures and God's intent for the cosmos as the basis for developing ethical models that take into account politics, economics, and practical issues in the quest for intelligent environmental policies.

Animistic approaches to nature are widespread among the indigenous religious traditions in the Americas and Africa. They build on the belief that natural phenomena—both animate and inanimate—possess an indwelling spirit or consciousness. For many indigenous peoples, humans cannot be separated from nature, and the natural cannot be separated from the supernatural (**Figure 4.13**). The Cree, for instance, believe in an unending cycle of reciprocity between humans and animals based on respect. According to this worldview, a hunter is successful because the animal chooses to give itself to the hunter who has behaved with respect toward the animal and its spirit. Through this spirit, the animal may then become part of the hunter, "dissolving any discernable boundary between person and the animal and between the natural and spirit worlds," anthropologist Naomi Adelson writes.[2]

All of these approaches attest to a growing concern over the environmental effects of globalization. Acid rain, deforestation, the disappearance of species, nuclear accidents, and toxic waste have all been important stimuli for newly emerging philosophies about the relationships between society and nature within a globalizing world. While none of these philosophies is a panacea to our environmental problems, each one offers an important critique of our current relationship with nature. More than anything, however, each serves to remind us that environmental crises are complex and that simple, technology-based solutions will no longer suffice to mitigate humanity's ever-growing impact on the environment. With a better understanding of how ideas can shape human behaviour toward the environment, we are now ready to examine the effects humans have wrought on the environment over the course of their history.

APPLY YOUR KNOWLEDGE Which approach to the relationship between humans and nature comes closest to your own personal views? Illustrate your choice with the help of three examples of environmental issues and explain how your chosen perspective interprets them. ∎

[2]Naomi Adelson, *"Being Alive Well": Health and the Politics of Cree Well-Being.* Toronto: University of Toronto Press, 2000, pp. 67–70, p. 68.

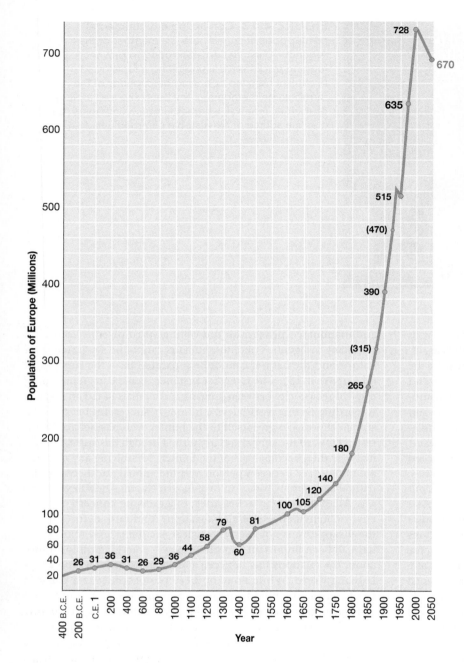

FIGURE 4.14 Population growth in Europe
This graph shows growth and change in the European population from 400 B.C.E. to 2050 C.E. The growth in European population has been especially dramatic in the past 500 years as a result of technological innovations and capitalist globalization. The increase in human numbers after 1500 gave an important push to exploration and colonization beyond the confines of the continent. The dip in the graph from 1300 to 1500 is partially explained by the bubonic plague epidemic and food shortages. The dip around the mid-twentieth century shows the effect of the two world wars. European population is expected to decline over the next four decades. (*Source:* Updated from C. McEvedy and R. Jones, *Atlas of World Population History.* London: Allen Lane, 1978, Fig. 1.2, p. 18.)

more forest land was cleared for agriculture, more animals were killed for food, and more minerals and other resources were exploited for a variety of needs. At the end of the period of internal expansion—around 1300—the forest cover of Western and Central Europe had been reduced from 90 percent to barely 20 percent.

The bubonic plague, also known as the Black Death, temporarily slowed population growth by wiping out over a quarter of Europe's people in the mid-fourteenth century. By then, agricultural settlement had taken up all readily available land and had even extended into less desirable areas. In England, Italy, France, and the Netherlands, for example, marshes and fens had been drained and the sea pushed back or the water table lowered to reclaim and create new land for agriculture and settlement.

In the fifteenth century, Europe underwent its second phase of expansion. This phase was external and not only changed the global political map but launched a period of environmental change that continues to this day. European external expansion—colonialism—was the response to several impulses, ranging from discovery to self-interest to altruism. Europeans were fast running out of land, and as we saw in Chapter 2, explorers were being dispatched by monarchs to conquer new territories, enlarge their empires, and collect tax revenues from new subjects (**Figure 4.15**). Many of these adventurous individuals were also searching for fame and fortune or avoiding religious persecution. Behind European external expansion was also the impulse of Christian missionaries to bring new souls into the kingdom of God. Other forces behind European colonialism included the need to expand the emerging system of trade by creating new markets, which ultimately meant increased wealth and power for a new class of people—the merchants—as well as for the aristocracy.

Over the centuries, Europe came to control increasing areas of the globe. The two examples we will discuss in the next sections illustrate how the introduction of European people, ideologies, technologies, plant species, pathogens, and animals changed the

EUROPEAN EXPANSION AND GLOBALIZATION

The history of European expansion provides a powerful example of how a society possessing new environmental attitudes was able to radically transform nature. These new attitudes drew upon a newly emerging science and its contribution to technological innovation as well as the capitalist political and economic system.

Initially, European expansion was internal—largely contained within continental boundaries. The most obvious reason for expansion was population increase: from 36 million in the year 1000 to over 44 million in 1100, nearly 60 million in 1200, and about 80 million by 1300 (**Figure 4.14**). As population increased,

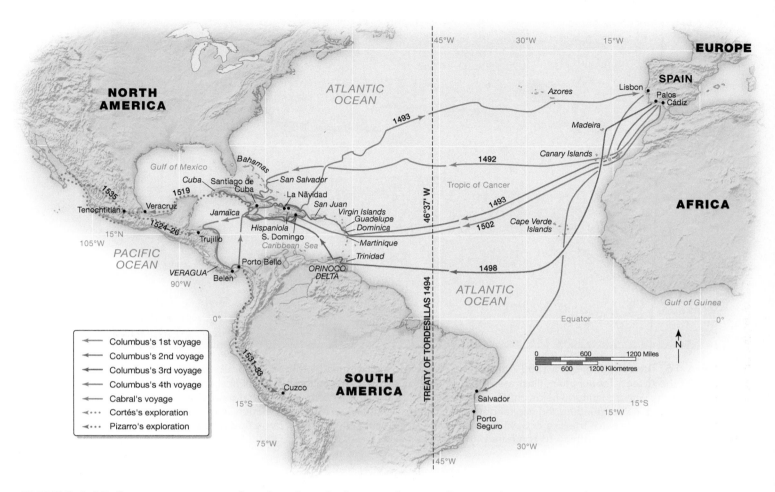

FIGURE 4.15 European voyages of exploration The lines on this map illustrate the voyages and missions of Columbus, Pizarro, Cabral, and Cortés. Departing from Portugal and Spain, Columbus encountered several of the islands of the Caribbean as well as the coastal areas of present-day Honduras and Venezuela. (*Source:* Adapted from *The Penguin Atlas of the Diasporas*, by G. Chaliand and J. P. Rageau, translated by A. M. Berrett. Translation copyright © 1995 by G. Chaliand and J. P. Rageau.)

Disease and Depopulation in the Spanish Colonies

Historians generally agree that the European colonization of the New World was ultimately responsible for the greatest loss of human life in history, primarily through diseases the colonizers brought with them. New World populations, including Canada's First Peoples, had been isolated for millennia from the Old World and so their immune systems had never encountered some of the most common European diseases. **Virgin soil epidemics**—in which the population at risk has no natural immunity or previous exposure to the disease within the lifetime of the oldest member of the group—were common in the so-called Columbian Exchange. The **Columbian Exchange** was the interaction between the Old World (Europe) and the New World (the Americas) initiated by the voyages of Columbus. Diseases such as smallpox, measles,

chicken pox, whooping cough, typhus, typhoid fever, bubonic plague, cholera, scarlet fever, malaria, yellow fever, diphtheria, influenza, and others were unknown in the pre-Columbian New World. Conversely, the population of the Old World was defenceless against syphilis introduced by sailors returning from voyages to the New World.

Geographer W. George Lovell, of Queen's University in Kingston, Ontario, has examined the role disease played in the depopulation of some of Spain's New World colonies from the time of initial contact until the early seventeenth century, using several cases to illustrate his point.[3]

In one example, Lovell describes how Hernán Cortés made contact with the Aztecs, a complex civilization in Central Mexico whose achievements in architecture, mathematics, and astronomy easily surpassed those of the Spanish colonizers. In 1521, Cortés

---

[3]W.G. Lovell, "Heavy Shadows and Black Night: Disease and Depopulation in Colonial Spanish America." *Annals, Association of American Geographers* 82, 1992, pp. 426–443.

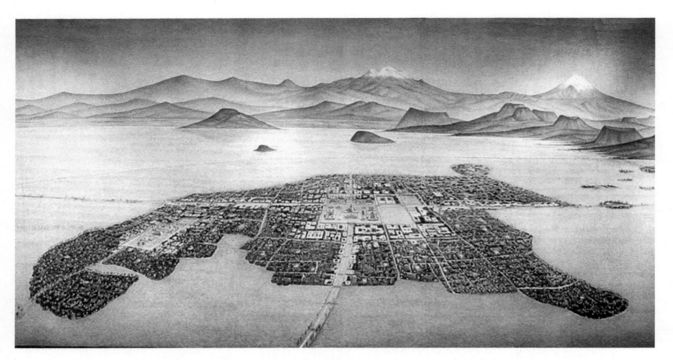

FIGURE 4.16 Tenochtitlán, circa 1500 This famous contemporary painting by Miguel Covarrubias of the capital city of the Aztecs, Tenochtitlán, illustrates the existence of dense social, cultural, and political activity in the core of the city with agricultural fields on the periphery, particularly to the north. Agricultural goods were also imported from the area surrounding the capital beyond the shores of the lake. With a population of two hundred thousand, it was roughly twice the size of Seville, then Spain's largest city. When Cortés came upon the capital he noted that "in Spain there is nothing to compare with it." *(Source: Schalkwijk/Art Resource, NY)*

captured their capital city, Tenochtitlán, a sprawling city of 200 000 inhabitants located on an island in a lake (**Figure 4.16**). The presence of the Spaniards triggered a devastating outbreak of smallpox among the virgin soil population. An Aztec text provides a graphic description of the disease:

> While the Spaniards were in Tlaxcala, a great plague broke out here in Tenochtitlán. It began to spread during the thirteenth month [30 September–19 October 1520] and lasted for 70 days, striking everywhere in the city and killing a vast number of our people. Sores erupted on our faces, our breasts, our bellies; we were covered with agonizing sores from head to foot. . . .
>
> A great many died from this plague, and many others died of hunger. They could not get up and search for food, and everyone else was too sick to care for them, so they starved to death in their beds.[4]

In another example, Lovell describes the Jesuits' missionizing efforts in northern Mexico during a slightly later period. Contact with Spanish conquistadors in advance of the missionaries had already reduced the indigenous Maya population by perhaps 30 percent to 50 percent. Now that the Jesuits gathered previously dispersed groups of the population into single locations around a mission, conditions for the outbreak of disease were created, and

mortality climbed to 90 percent. Sadly, missionizing seems to have killed the Aboriginal people whose souls it was claiming to save. Eventually, the disease was diffused beyond the initial area of contact as traders carried it across long-distance trade routes to the periphery of the Maya empire. The Maya were not defeated by European technological superiority but by the ravages of diseases against which they possessed no natural defences.

Lovell provides similar descriptions of disease impacts in Mayan Guatemala and the Central Andes of South America that led to devastating depopulation, a phenomenon scholars refer to as **demographic collapse.** The ecological effect of the population decline was the transformation of many regions from productive agriculture to abandoned land. Many of the Andean terraces, for example, were abandoned, often leading to soil erosion and landslides (**Figure 4.17**). In the lowlands, large expanses of cleared land returned to forest (**Figure 4.18**).

Old World Plants and Animals in the New World

A second case study of the environmental effects of European colonization involves the introduction of Old World plants and animals into New World ecosystems, and vice versa. (An **ecosystem** is a community of different species interacting with each other and with the larger physical environment that surrounds it.) The introduction of exotic plants and animals into new ecosystems is called **ecological imperialism,** a term now widely used by geographers,

[4]W.G. Lovell, 1992, p. 429, quoting from M. Leòn-Portilla, *The Broken Spears: The Aztec Account of the Conquest of Mexico.* Boston: Beacon Press, 1962, pp. 92–93.

FIGURE 4.17 Andean landscape with partly abandoned terraces
The photo shows agricultural terraces in various states of maintenance: abandoned and partly eroded on the left, still under cultivation on the right. The bottom of the valley is partly filled with eroded material from the hillsides. (*Source:* M. Imort)

ecologists, and other scholars of the environment. The interaction between the Old and the New Worlds resulted in both the intentional and unintentional introduction of new crops and animals on both sides of the Atlantic.

Europeans brought from their homelands many plants and animals that were exotics, that is, unknown to American ecosystems. For example, the Spanish introduced wheat and sugarcane, as well as horses, cattle, and pigs. On the other hand, New World crops and animals as well as pathogens were introduced into the Old World—often with beneficial, other times with devastating, effects. Corn, potatoes, tobacco, cocoa, tomatoes, and cotton were all taken back to Europe; so was syphilis, which spread rapidly throughout the European population.

In addition, ecological imperialism inadvertently introduced exotic species that were more hardy and soon crowded out the less competitive indigenous species. As with the human population, the indigenous populations of plants, birds, and mammals had few defences against newcomers and were sometimes seriously reduced or even made extinct through contact. In New Zealand, for example, newspapers described a "sparrow pest" within 12 years of their introduction. Other examples include pigeons and starlings; mammals, such as rats and pigs; and weeds, such as the dandelion and thistle.

FIGURE 4.18 The ruins of a Maya pyramid at Altun Ha, Belize The pre-Columbian Maya civilization supported population densities of up to 400 people per square kilometre (the equivalent of modern-day Netherlands) through a variety of crops and cultivation practices, including irrigation. After the collapse of the Maya populations, the agricultural landscapes and temple sites quickly returned to forest land. This temple site was excavated by Dr. David Pendergast of the Royal Ontario Museum.

(*Source:* Alan E. Nash)

On the other hand, ecological imperialism also added to the types and amounts of foods available worldwide. It is estimated that it may have tripled the number of cultivable food plants in the New World. It certainly enabled new types of food to grow in abundance where they had never grown before, and it introduced animals as an important source of dietary protein.

As Europe's colonial empires grew, plant transfers increasingly occurred within the periphery (**Figure 4.19**). By 1600, the pineapple had been spread across Spanish and Portuguese colonies and was virtually ubiquitous across the tropics. By 1800, the British had transferred the breadfruit from Tahiti to St. Vincent to feed the slaves on their Caribbean plantations more efficiently. One result of the exchange of flora and fauna was that the world's landscapes became increasingly homogenized. The "typical" tropical landscape of today is made up of introduced species such as bananas, royal palm trees, and pineapples. By the same token, Canadian gardens are made up almost entirely of introduced species, and yet they are now so familiar to us that we can no longer sense how "out of place" they really are.

The introduction of animals provided the New World with both additional sources of protein and additional animal power.

Before the Columbian Exchange, the only important sources of animal energy were the llama and the dog. The introduction of the horse, the ox, and the ass created a virtual power revolution in the New World. These animals also provided fibres and, after slaughter, hides and bones to make various tools, utensils, and coverings. Most significant in its environmental impact, however, was the ox. Land that had escaped cultivation because the indigenous digging sticks and tools were unable to penetrate the heavy soil and matted root surface became workable with an ox-drawn plow. The result was that the indigenous form of intensive agricultural production (small area, many labourers) was replaced by extensive production (large area, fewer labourers). This transformation often produced negative impacts, such as deforestation and soil erosion.

When discussing the impact of exchange, it is important to acknowledge the impact of native New World peoples on their environment prior to European contact. The popular image of indigenous peoples living in harmony with nature, having only a minimal effect on their environment, is flawed. In reality, different groups had different impacts, and it is erroneous to conflate the thousands of groups into one romanticized caricature. In eastern North

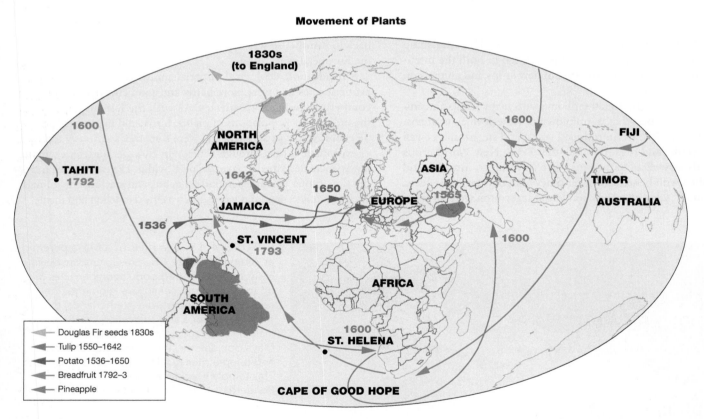

Movement of Plants

Douglas Fir seeds 1830s
Tulip 1550–1642
Potato 1536–1650
Breadfruit 1792–3
Pineapple

FIGURE 4.19 Ecological imperialism The movement of plants occurred on an ever-increasing scale as the core of the world-system extended its grasp into the periphery. Early transfers, such as the diffusion of the tulip from Central Asia to Holland, satisfied Europeans' aesthetic desire for the novel and exotic. As the core developed overseas colonies, the emphasis quickly shifted to plants with agricultural or commercial value. (*Sources:* Map compiled by author from the following: R.A. Howard, "Captain Bligh and the Breadfruit." *Scientific American* 188[3], March 1953, pp. 88–94; W.H. McNeill, "American Food Crops in the Old World." In H.J. Viola and C. Margolis [eds.], *Seeds of Change*. Washington, DC: Smithsonian, 1991, pp. 43–59; Anna Pavord, *The Tulip*. London: Bloomsbury, 1999; K.F. Kiple and K.C. Ornelas [eds.], *The Cambridge World History of Food*, vol. 2. Cambridge: Cambridge University Press, 2000, p. 1834; J. Grimshaw, *The Gardeners Atlas*. Willowdale, ON: Firefly, 1998, p. 11.)

America, for example, some groups hunted for wild game and gathered wild foods. More sedentary groups, living in permanent and semipermanent villages, cleared and planted small areas of land. Hunter-gatherers were mobile, moving with the seasons to obtain fish, migrating birds, deer, wild berries, and plants. Agriculturalists planted corn, squash, beans, and tobacco and used a wide range of other natural resources. The economy was a fairly simple one based on personal use or on barter (trading corn for fish, for example). The idea of a surplus was foreign: people cultivated or exploited only as much land and resources as they needed to survive. Land and resources were shared, without concepts such as private property or land ownership. Fire was used to clear land for planting as well as for hunting. Although vegetation change did occur, it was minimal and not irreversible.

The Aztecs of Mexico and the Incas of Peru altered their environment as well, though perhaps in more dramatic ways. They had developed complex urban systems—some of them more sophisticated and highly populated than any European cities—that were supported by intensive agricultural techniques that included the irrigation of dry regions and the terracing of steep slopes. Irrigation over several centuries resulted in the salinization of soils, however. In the lowland tropics, intensive agricultural practices resulted in widespread deforestation as people cut and set fire to patches of forest, planted crops, and then moved on when soil fertility declined. A surplus had to be generated by the operations of both societies, as the urbanized political and religious elites required tribute in the form of food, animals, labour, or precious metals. Concentrated populations and the demands of urbanization meant that widespread environmental degradation existed prior to European contact.

APPLY YOUR KNOWLEDGE Identify three plant or animal species you might find in your own garden or in a nearby park that can serve as examples of ecological imperialism. When and why were these species transplanted to Canada? What advantages did they have over native species? What unexpected negative effects (if any) did they have? ∎

HUMAN ACTION AND RECENT ENVIRONMENTAL CHANGE

No other transition in human history has had the impact on the natural world that industrialization has. When we couple industrialization with its frequent companion, urbanization, we have the two processes that, more than any others, have revolutionized human life and effected far-reaching ecological changes. The changes wrought by industrialization have moved beyond a local or a regional level and are now affecting the entire globe. Nobel-prize-winning atmospheric chemist Paul Crutzen has coined a term, **anthropocene**, to describe the modern geological era during which humans have dramatically affected the global environment. While some scientists assert, from atmospheric evidence, that the era began with the Industrial Revolution, others see its beginnings in the rise of agriculture approximately 10 000 years ago. The concept is so new that these disagreements have not yet been settled. In this book we follow the lead of Crutzen and use it to explore some of the dramatic contemporary environmental impacts that industrial technology produced. In doing so, we highlight the two issues most central to environmental geography today: energy-use and land-use change.

The Impact of Energy Needs on the Environment

Certainly the most central and significant technological breakthrough of the Industrial Revolution was the discovery and utilization of fossil fuels: coal, oil, and natural gas. The first factories in Europe and the United States still relied on waterpower to drive the machinery, but it was the shift to the more constant, concentrated and also more mobile energy source of hydrocarbon fuels that enabled large-scale mechanization. A steady increase in power production and demand since the beginning of the Industrial Revolution has been paralleled, not surprisingly, by an increase in resource extraction and conversion.

At present, the world's population relies most heavily on nonrenewable energy resources, which include fossil fuels and nuclear ones, but renewable resources, such as wood and solar, hydroelectric, wind, and geothermal power, are beginning to increase in importance.

Fossil Fuels

The International Energy Agency (IEA) estimates that the largest proportion of the world's current supply of primary energy, 32 percent, comes from oil (see Box 4.2, "Window on the World: Peak Oil"); 29 percent from coal (and related materials, such as peat); 21 percent from natural gas; 10 percent from wood, biofuel, and waste; 5 percent from nuclear power; 2 percent from hydroelectricity; and only 1 percent from a mixture of renewable sources that includes wind, solar, and geothermal sources.[5] The production and consumption of these available resources, however, is geographically uneven, as **Figure 4.20** shows.

Until recently, almost half of the world's oil production occurred in the Middle East. This is changing, however, as the Alberta oil sands ramp up production and as extensive fracking is greatly expanding the exploitable reserves in the U.S. Most of the coal is extracted in China (which accounts for half of the global coal production), followed by the United States. Nuclear reactors are predominantly a phenomenon of the core: France and the United States together produce more than 40 percent of all the nuclear-generated electricity in the world.

The consumption of energy also varies geographically. Globally, annual energy consumption is equal to 13 billion tonnes of oil—the equivalent of a million years' worth of fossil fuel accumulation. Except for a brief slowdown during the 2008 financial crisis, energy consumption continues to increase year after year, with most of the increase now occurring in BRICS countries. What is most remarkable is that global energy consumption now is four times higher than in 1950. And according to the $I = PAT$ formula,

[5]International Energy Agency, *Key World Energy Statistics 2013*. Paris: International Energy Agency, 2013, p. 6 (available at www.iea.org). © OECD/IEA 2013 World Energy Outlook, IEA Publishing.

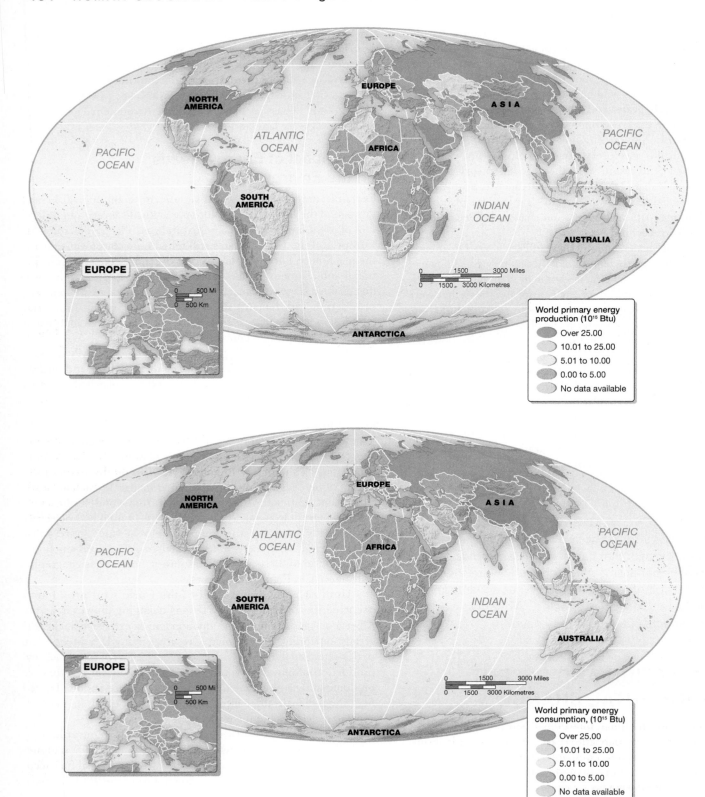

FIGURE 4.20 World production and consumption of energy, 2008 These paired maps provide a picture of the uneven distribution of the production and consumption of energy resources around the world. The United States is the largest producer and consumer of a range of energy resources. Notice that although the Middle East and North African countries as well as Nigeria are important producers of energy resources, their consumption (as well as that of the rest of the African continent, excluding South Africa) is very low. Japan produces a negligible amount of the total of world energy resources but consumes a relatively high share. (*Source:* International Energy Agency, Key World Energy Statistics 2013. Paris: International Energy Agency, 2013, p. 6 (available at www.iea.org). © OECD/IEA 2013 World Energy Outlook, IEA Publishing.)

by Ian G. R. Shaw (updated in 2014 by M. Imort)

Any finite resource has a midway point between the growth and decline of its availability. If we were to plot the rates of oil extraction on a graph, it would loosely resemble a bell-shaped curve and we could label the halfway point, or peak, of this imaginary graph as "Peak Oil." In this sense, Peak Oil refers to the point at which the highest global rate of oil production is reached. Many experts believe that if world consumption of petroleum-derived products is not slowed, the arrival of Peak Oil is likely to bring with it a worldwide energy crisis. Keep in mind that, in order to determine the point of Peak Oil, it is necessary to know something about existing oil reserves. It is generally agreed that the summit of new oil discovery was passed in the 1960s, and the world started using more oil than was contained in new fields in 1981. The calculations that predict the point of Peak Oil are premised not only on current use data but also on the known global oil reserves (**Figure 4.D**).

Oil is the lifeblood of most economies, and the increasing dependence on oil in core, semiperipheral, and peripheral countries—especially rapidly developing and highly populous ones like China and India—means that Peak Oil will dramatically affect the global economy, demanding proactive mitigation measures by businesses, governments, and individuals. Optimistic predictions place Peak Oil somewhere in the next few decades, whereas pessimistic predictions indicate that Peak Oil has already occurred—or is imminent. Two well-respected scientific networks, the Association for the Study of Peak Oil and Gas (ASPO) and Energy Watch Group (EWG), have projected fairly similar peaks. ASPO argues that Peak Oil was reached in 2010, whereas

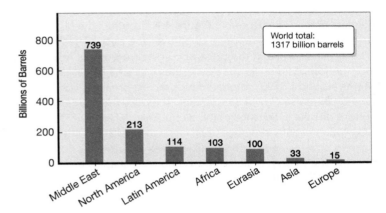

FIGURE 4.D Oil reserves by region, 2007 To reasonably project future oil production, it is necessary to have reliable data on known oil reserves. (*Source*: Adapted from "Worldwide Look at Reserves and Production," *Oil and Gas Journal*, *104* [47], 2006, pp. 24–25.)

EWG believes Peak Oil production occurred in 2006. There are some others—mostly influential corporations and government entities—who believe that Peak Oil is a problematic theory that cannot be substantiated by the evidence (**Figure 4.E**). Whatever one's position on Peak Oil, the other aspect of oil production and consumption that will unarguably affect both the global economy and our individual practices is the rapidly escalating demand for and price of oil.

FIGURE 4.E Predictions of future oil production This figure illustrates Energy Watch Group's prediction for global oil supply through 2030. The prediction is dramatically different from the International Energy Agency's (IEA) World Energy Outlook (plotted on the graph as WEO 2006). This divergence reflects not only differences in methodology but also contradictory attitudes to future ambiguity—with the IEA opting for a far more optimistic and "business-as-usual" scenario. Muddying these predictions further is the notorious difficulty of obtaining accurate estimations of oil reserves from corporations and governments.

(*Source*: Adapted from Energy Watch Group, *Crude Oil: The Supply Outlook*, 2007, p. 12. http://www.energywatchgroup.org/fileadmin/global/pdf/EWG_Oilreport_10-2007.pdf, accessed May 16, 2011.)

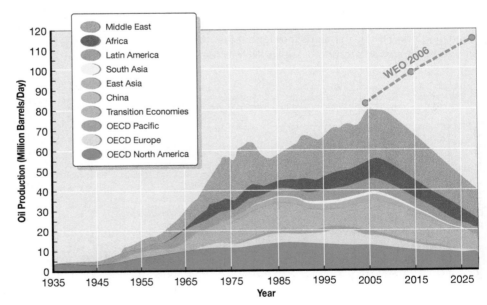

(*Continued*)

The forecasts in demand for oil must be considered alongside the increasing cost of oil. **Figure 4.F** illustrates the history of fluctuations in the barrel price of oil over the past 30 years. The most significant rise in the price of oil occurred over a relatively short period of time—in June 2003 the price of a barrel of crude oil was around US$30, compared to a record-breaking US$130 in June 2008—a rise of over 333 percent. The price then began a precipitous decline in advance of the global financial crisis of October 2008. More recently, the price of oil has increased again, though its movement is unsteady, with significant rises and declines occurring monthly due to both political and economic instability around the globe. This fluctuation in price illustrates how sensitively entwined oil production and worldwide economies are.

The underlying causes of rising oil prices are highly contested. First are the economic explanations: record demand for oil is outstripping available supplies, leading to surging prices. Currently, world consumption of oil is at around 83 million barrels per day, but this is predicted to jump to 118 million barrels in 2030, with two-thirds of this rise coming from increased use in the transportation sector. Other explanations for high prices vary. The Organization of the Petroleum Exporting Countries (OPEC), comprising 12 countries and responsible for two-thirds of the international oil supply, has been criticized by some for restricting the levels of supply. Many commentators also blame "speculators" for "betting" on rising prices of oil. We can add to our list of economic explanations the falling value of the U.S. dollar. Geopolitical explanations for rising prices are also important: there are fears about the political stability of oil-producing countries like Libya, Algeria, Nigeria, and Venezuela, as well as sanctions against Iranian oil. Wars and skirmishes can also drive up the price of oil by compromising supply, as happened during the U.S.-led war in Iraq and the lingering insurgency. Given these economic and geopolitical driving forces, combined with increased population growth, urbanization, and rising living standards throughout the world, what are some of the impacts and responses we are likely to see?

The arrival of Peak Oil is likely to affect people and places differently—and it depends on policies and responses made right *now*. This urgency to act sooner rather than later is created by the huge time lags involved with mitigation responses. The *Hirsch Report*, published in 2005 for the U.S. Department of Energy, investigated the likelihood of Peak Oil and the necessary mitigation responses. Crucially, if governments wait for Peak Oil production to arrive before taking action, the consequences will be severe, with liquid-fuel deficits for over two decades. Even a response 10 years in *advance* of Peak Oil would likely leave the world in deficit for over a decade. What is further cause for concern is the rapidity with which oil reserves are predicted to potentially dwindle once the Peak is reached. For example, supplies in the North Sea oil fields might more or less "crash" after the Peak, rather than follow a smoother bell-shaped curve. Similarly, indications are that the so-called "tight" oil fields recently opened up with the new extraction technology of fracking are most productive in the first few years and then rapidly deplete. All this points to the need to initiate a response *now* rather than later.

We must also realize that Peak Oil is not just a momentary "energy crisis." Right now, there are simply no alternatives for the modes of transportation we use every day, such as cars, trains, planes, and ships. Similarly, our food supply relies on large-scale agriculture, which will become increasingly expensive due to the huge oil-based energy inputs required. This may lead to increased reliance on smaller, local, and organic farms. Perhaps we will also see the reshaping of the urban landscape in the core countries and the so-called "end of suburbia." Low-density housing tracts built around the use of the automobile will become increasingly costly places to reside. Migration back to inner cities may occur, or, at the very least, there will be surging demand for public transportation. In summary, it is likely that the transition through Peak Oil will be difficult, contested, and fraught with social and political upheaval.

Ian Shaw is a post-doctoral researcher in the School of Geographical and Earth Sciences at the University of Glasgow.

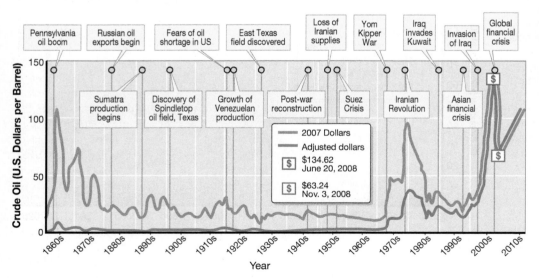

FIGURE 4.F Price of crude oil, 1986–2011 As this figure shows, the barrel price of oil was relatively stable until 2003. Production, consumption, and political factors all contributed to its recent instability. (*Source:* Adapted from M. Janofsky, "Forecasts of $250 Oil Finds Few Believers," *Arizona Daily Star*, June 22, 2008. http://www.azstarnet.com/allheadlines/244867.php, accessed June 22, 2008.)

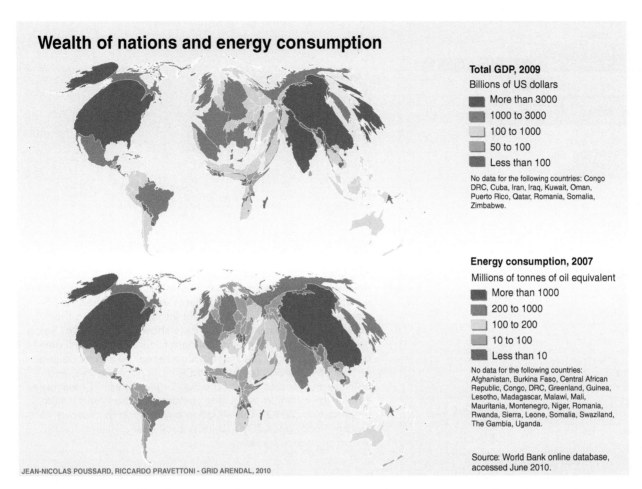

Wealth of nations and energy consumption

Total GDP, 2009
Billions of US dollars

- More than 3000
- 1000 to 3000
- 100 to 1000
- 50 to 100
- Less than 100

No data for the following countries: Congo DRC, Cuba, Iran, Iraq, Kuwait, Oman, Puerto Rico, Qatar, Romania, Somalia, Zimbabwe.

Energy consumption, 2007
Millions of tonnes of oil equivalent

- More than 1000
- 200 to 1000
- 100 to 200
- 10 to 100
- Less than 10

No data for the following countries: Afghanistan, Burkina Faso, Central African Republic, Congo, DRC, Greenland, Guinea, Lesotho, Madagascar, Malawi, Mali, Mauritania, Montenegro, Niger, Romania, Rwanda, Sierra, Leone, Somalia, Swaziland, The Gambia, Uganda.

Source: World Bank online database, accessed June 2010.

JEAN-NICOLAS POUSSARD, RICCARDO PRAVETTONI - GRID ARENDAL, 2010

FIGURE 4.21 **Wealth of nations and energy consumption** As the two cartograms show, there is a linear relationship between a nation's wealth and its energy consumption. This suggests that, as semiperipheral nations industrialize and become more wealthy, their energy consumption will rise. (*Source:* Riccardo Pravettoni, UNEP/GRID-Arendal, "Wealth of nations and energy consumption," © 2012 GRID-Arendal. Reprinted by permission.)

the affluent core regions of the world still far outstrip the peripheral regions in energy consumption (**Figure 4.21**). With nearly four times the population of the core regions, the peripheral regions still account for less than one-third of global energy expenditures. Yet consumption of energy in the peripheral regions is rising quite rapidly as globalization spreads industries, energy-intensive consumer products such as automobiles and air conditioners, and energy-intensive agricultural practices into regions of the world where they were previously unaffordable. It is projected that within the next decade or so, the peripheral regions will become the dominant consumers of energy (**Figure 4.22**). *India & China*

Most relevant to our discussion in this chapter, however, is that every stage of the energy conversion process—from discovery to extraction, processing, and utilization—has an impact on the physical landscape and the atmosphere. In the coalfields of the world, from China to Germany to Australia, mining results in a loss of vegetation and topsoil, in erosion and water pollution, and in acid and toxic drainage (**Figure 4.23**). It also contributes to cancer and lung disease in coal miners. In addition, coal burning is associated with relatively high emissions of environmentally harmful gases, such as carbon dioxide and sulphur dioxide, and the emission of smog-producing soot (**Figure 4.24**).

The burning of home heating oil, along with the use of petroleum products for fuel in internal combustion engines, also launches harmful chemicals into Earth's atmosphere—causing air pollution and related health problems, and contributing to the rising carbon dioxide levels in the atmosphere. On the local and regional levels, the production and transport of oil have resulted in oil spills and substantial pollution of water and ecosystems.

Natural gas is one of the least noxious of the hydrocarbon-based energy resources because its combustion is relatively clean. Now supplying nearly one-quarter of global commercial energy, natural gas is predicted to be the fastest-growing energy source in this century. Reserves are still being discovered, with Russia holding the largest amount—about one-third of the world's total (**Figure 4.25**). Significant deposits of natural gas have also been discovered in Alberta and off the coast of Nova Scotia. Plans are currently being made to pipe liquefied gas from these sources to the urban markets in Canada and the United States. While regarded as a preferred alternative to oil and coal, natural gas is not produced or consumed without environmental impacts. The risk of explosions at natural gas conversion facilities is significant; groundwater contamination and leakages and losses of gas from distribution systems contribute to the deterioration of Earth's atmosphere.

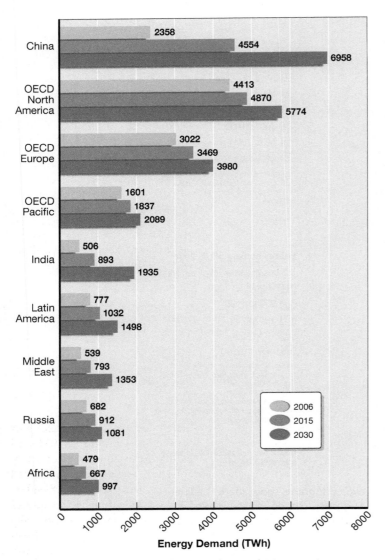

Energy Demand (TWh)

FIGURE 4.22 Increase in energy demand This graph projects rising demand for energy across key world regions from 2006–2030. (*Source:* Adapted from "New Challenges in Power Generations," October 27, 2009. *Energy – European Energy Trends.* OECD/IEA [2008].)

FIGURE 4.24 Air pollution, Shanghai, China With China relying heavily on burning coal, it is particularly affected by the resulting smog. Coal-powered plants and home heating chimneys pour sulphur dioxide and soot into the air, causing the urban photochemical smog and haze shown in this photo. Smog has become a significant impediment to further industrial development in China: in 2013, smog smothered the capital Beijing on 189 days, forcing factory shutdowns, school closures, and traffic restrictions. In fact, of the 500 largest cities in China, only 5 meet the minimum air quality standards of the World Health Organization (WHO). This situation is not going to improve anytime soon: since 2000, Chinese total coal consumption has almost tripled. (*Source:* hxdbzxy/Shutterstock)

FIGURE 4.23 Coal mining This coal-mining operation in western Germany is typical of the surface-mining technologies used to exploit shallow deposits in most parts of the world. After deposits are located, the vegetation and overburden (rocks and dirt overlaying the coal seam) are removed by bulldozers and discarded as waste material. With the coal seam exposed, heavy equipment is used to mine the deposit. Some countries have laws that require restoration of newly mined landscapes. Successful restoration can make it difficult to tell that an area was once a mining site (at least on the surface, as the groundwater regime remains disturbed). Sites exploited before these laws were introduced remain unrestored, however. Unfortunately, many such sites are in arid or semiarid areas where soil and climate prevent full restoration. In addition to substantial land disturbance, the mining and processing of coal resources often cause soil erosion and water and air pollution. (*Source:* VanderWolf Images/Shutterstock)

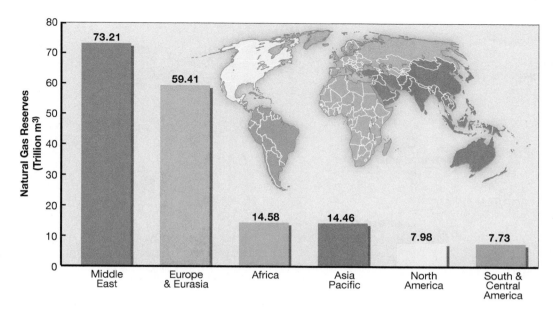

FIGURE 4.25 Global natural gas reserves, 2010 Almost three-quarters of the world's natural gas reserves are located in the Middle East and Eurasia. Together, Russia, Iran, and Qatar account for about 55 percent of the world's natural gas reserves. Four major natural gas producers in the Middle East—Qatar, Iran, Saudi Arabia, and the United Arab Emirates—account for 84 percent of the natural gas produced in the Middle East. North American reserves are currently growing substantially as the oil and gas industries employ hydraulic fracturing to open up previously inaccessible deposits. (*Source:* Adapted from BP World Energy Report.)

The recent use of hydraulic fracturing (commonly called *fracking*) has greatly expanded the exploitable reserves of oil and gas in North America. **Hydraulic fracturing (fracking)** injects a highly pressurized mixture of water, sand, and chemicals into bedrock layers to create artificial fractures that allow oil and gas to flow to the borehole and be extracted. The technique is highly controversial as critics argue that it uses large quantities of water, employs poisonous chemicals that can enter the groundwater, leads to earthquakes, and releases noxious gases. In response, some countries (France and Germany, for instance) have imposed a moratorium on fracking.

In Canada, fracking is regulated provincially. Alberta, British Columbia, and New Brunswick permit fracking, while Nova Scotia is reviewing the practice and Quebec has declared a moratorium. With roughly 11 000 new fracking wells being drilled in Canada every year, the discussion is gaining momentum. In the U.S., with its roughly half a million fracking wells, the controversy already is in full swing, including public relation campaigns, court cases, and even acts of sabotage. Proponents argue that fracking is enabling the country to meet its energy demands from domestic sources. In fact, oil production from fracking wells in the U.S. is increasing so rapidly (by almost 20 percent in 2013 alone) that the country will become the world's largest producer by 2015.

Nuclear Energy

At the midpoint of the twentieth century, nuclear energy was widely promoted as a cleaner and more efficient alternative to fossil fuels. It was also seen by many as the answer to the expanding energy needs of core countries, especially as the supply of uranium worldwide was thought to be more than adequate for centuries of use. Although nuclear war was a pervasive threat, and there were certainly critics of nuclear energy even in the early years of its development, the civilian "atomic age" was widely seen as

a triumphant technological solution to the energy needs of an expanding global economic system.

It was not until the devastating accidents and meltdowns at nuclear power plants at Chernobyl in Ukraine in 1986 and Fukushima in Japan in 2011, that concerns about reactor safety led to a questioning of the nuclear option. Some countries decided to go nuclear-free, such as Denmark, Finland, Germany, Sweden, Switzerland, and New Zealand. And yet, while some core countries have moved away from nuclear energy, many more—and especially populous—peripheral countries are moving in the opposite direction, even in the wake of the Fukushima disaster (**Figure 4.26**). Given that world energy consumption is predicted to increase by more than 50 percent between now and 2030, it is not surprising that rapidly developing countries like India and China have growing nuclear energy programs. And in Eastern Europe, countries like the Czech Republic and Romania, as well as Russia and Belarus, are continuing to invest in nuclear power. Another problem is the disposal of nuclear waste generated in the reactors: to this day, no permanent storage site for highly radioactive waste exists anywhere on the planet.

Biomass Fuels

While nuclear power problems are still largely confined to the core, the periphery is not without its own energy-related environmental problems. Because a large proportion of populations in the periphery relies on biomass for energy needs, the demand for fuelwood has risen in tandem with population growth. One of the most immediate environmental impacts of wood burning is air pollution, but the most alarming environmental problem is the rapid depletion of forest resources. With the other conventional sources of energy (coal, oil, and gas) being too costly or unavailable to most peripheral households, wood or other forms of biomass—dried animal dung, for example—are the only alternative. The demand for fuelwood has been so great in many

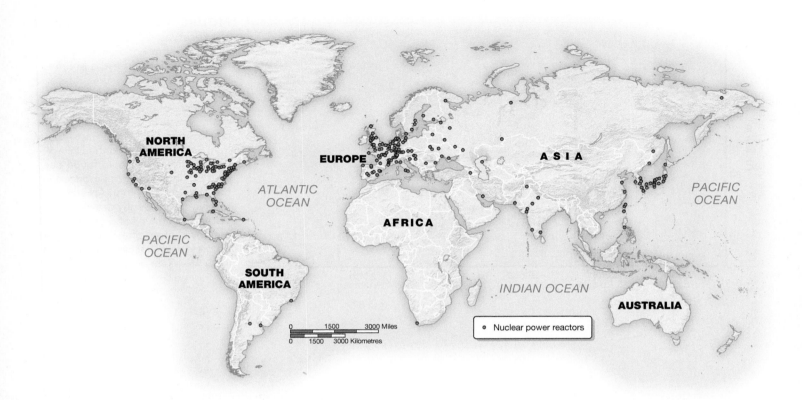

FIGURE 4.26 World distribution of nuclear reactors, 2011 Most of the dependence on nuclear power is concentrated in the core countries. South America and Africa together contain only four nuclear reactors. With the recent accident in Japan, some countries, such as France, that were very enthusiastic supporters of nuclear energy, are now experiencing popular opposition to them. Although just five years ago nuclear power was experiencing new popularity, a reconsideration of its ultimate value, when disasters cannot be 100 percent prevented, is now taking place. (*Source: International Nuclear Safety Center, http://www.insc.anl.gov/pwrmaps/.*)

peripheral regions that forest reserves are being rapidly used up (**Figure 4.27**).

Fuelwood depletion is extreme in the highland areas of Nepal, as well as in the Andean mountains of Bolivia and Peru (**Figure 4.28**). The clearing of forests for fuelwood in these regions has led to serious steep-slope soil erosion. In sub-Saharan Africa, where 90 percent of the region's energy needs are supplied by wood, overcutting of the forests has resulted in denuded areas, especially around rapidly growing cities. And although wood gathering is usually associated with rural life, it is not uncommon for city dwellers to use wood to satisfy their household energy needs as well. In Niamey, the capital of Niger, the zone of overcutting is expanding as the city itself expands. It is estimated that city dwellers in Niamey travel from 50 to 100 kilometres to gather wood. The same goes for inhabitants of Ouagadougou in Burkina Faso, where the average haul for wood is also over 50 kilometres. And fuelwood use in Asian and South American highland regions as well as in sub-Saharan Africa is expected to continue to increase by a third over the next decade.

Hydropower

Hydroelectric power was also once seen as a preferred alternative to polluting and nonrenewable fossil-fuel sources. It is true that the wave of dam building that occurred throughout the world over the course of the twentieth century improved the overall availability, quality, cost, and dependability of energy (as well as harnessed water resources for food production, energy generation, flood control, and domestic use) (**Figure 4.29**). Unfortunately, however, dams built to provide hydroelectric power (as well as water for irrigation, navigation, and drinking) for the burgeoning cities of the core and to encourage economic development in the periphery and semiperiphery have also had profound negative environmental impacts. Among the most significant of these impacts are changes in downstream flow, evaporation, sediment transport and deposition, mineral quality and soil moisture, channelling and bank scouring, and aquatic plants and animals, as well as changes in human health.

The construction of dams also dramatically alters the surrounding landscape, sometimes with serious consequences, such as geological tremors caused by the enormous weight of the water behind the dam. Furthermore, as the rising waters of the reservoir drown the vegetation, decomposition processes in the increasingly acidic water produce methyl mercury, a poisonous substance that bioaccumulates in the aquatic food chain and ultimately harms humans that eat fish caught in the reservoir or downstream. The impounded waters can also incubate mosquitoes, which carry diseases, such as malaria and West Nile virus. In light of these and various other environmental and social problems, many argue that new dam projects should not be undertaken without a clear strategy for preventing or alleviating the associated challenges.

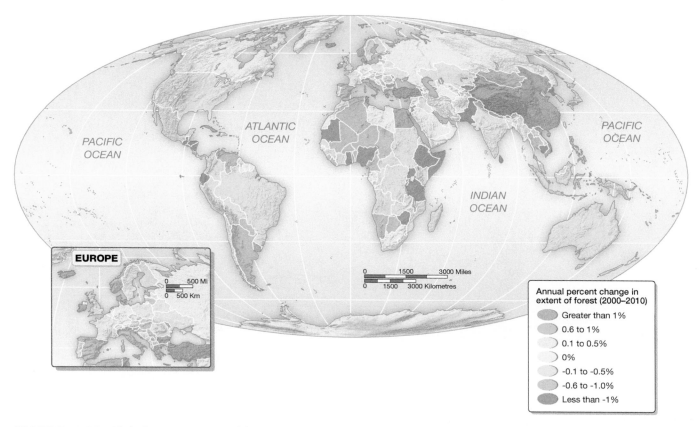

FIGURE 4.27 Global consumption of fuelwoods, 2010 Firewood, charcoal, and dung are considered traditional fuels, and although their availability is decreasing, dependence upon them is increasing. Dependence on traditional sources of fuel is especially high in the periphery. In Africa, for example, they are the most important energy source for cooking and heating. Wood and charcoal, although renewable sources, are replenished very slowly. Acute scarcity will be a certainty for most African households in the twenty-first century. (*Source:* Data from UN Food and Agricultural Organization, *State of the World's Forests 2011*, Annex, Tab. 4, Rome, 2011.)

FIGURE 4.28 Deforestation, erosion, and reforestation in Peru This photo shows the effects of deforestation (on the hillside on the right), severe gully erosion (in the centre), and reforestation efforts (in the foreground). (*Source:* M. Imort)

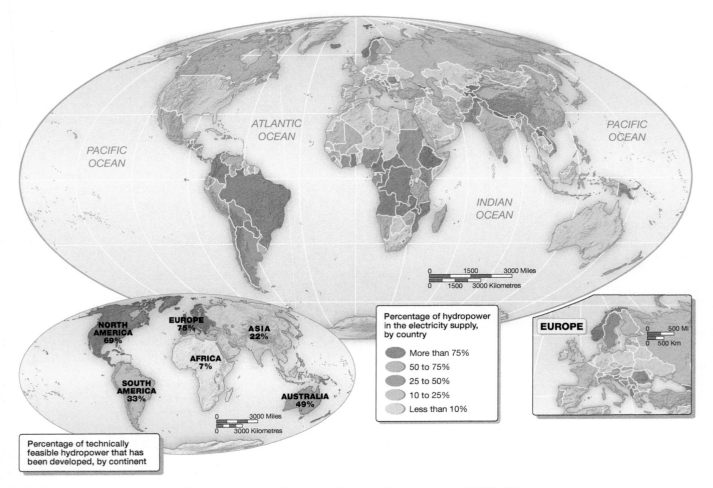

FIGURE 4.29 Percentage of hydropower in the electricity supply by country, 2010 Although the great dam-building era for core countries is now largely completed, many peripheral countries, in a bid to participate more actively in the world economy, are building dams. A few countries are almost exclusively dependent on the hydropower produced from dams. These include Norway, Nepal, Zambia, Ghana, Paraguay, and Costa Rica. Although the power produced by dams is environmentally benign in terms of emissions, the construction of large dams can be extremely destructive to the environment and can dislocate large numbers of people. Still, given the increasing need for electricity in rapidly developing peripheral countries, hydropower is becoming a more attractive energy option for many of them because of the uncertain supply of oil in the future. The larger map shows the amount of hydropower that is currently available; the smaller one shows the potential for hydropower development, especially for peripheral regions. (*Source:* U.S. Energy Information Administration, U.S. Department of Energy.)

To make matters more complex, many large-scale dam projects are located on Aboriginal lands, which means that these problems disproportionally affect indigenous populations, whereas the produced electricity benefits mainly urban populations. An example of the increasing controversy over dam construction is the James Bay Project in Quebec, approximately 1000 kilometres north of Montreal. Begun in the 1970s, the expansive system of dams now produces as much electricity as Belgium, but it pits the interests of electricity consumers as far away as New York City against the concerns of the Cree whose livelihood is altered by the reservoirs (**Figure 4.30**).

Despite these problems and in response to the rising cost of fossil fuels, the use of hydroelectricity is expected to continue to expand, particularly where its use is supported by government policies and incentives, such as in Asia and South America. The construction of the Three Gorges Dam, as well as several other large-scale hydroelectric projects in China, illustrates this trend

(**Figure 4.31**). In contrast, most of the increase in core energy production is expected to be in the form of renewable resources, such as wind, solar, geothermal, municipal solid waste, and biomass.

Energy-Related Pollutants

One reason hydroelectric power continues to be appealing in the periphery is that it produces fewer atmospheric pollutants than fossil fuels. Indeed, coal and gas power stations as well as factories, automobiles, and other forms of transportation are largely responsible for the increasingly acidic quality of Earth's atmosphere. Although it is true that people as well as other organisms naturally produce many gases, including oxygen and carbon dioxide, increasing levels of industrialization and motor vehicle use have destabilized the natural balance of such gases, leading to serious atmospheric pollution (see Box 4.3, "Visualizing Geography: Global Climate Change"). Sulphur dioxide, nitrogen oxides, and

FIGURE 4.30 Dam construction in Quebec Using an extensive system of large dams in the James Bay and Great Whale watersheds, Quebec has become an important producer of hydroelectricity. Once considered an environmentally friendly source of power, dam projects are becoming increasingly controversial as people learn more about their drawbacks. These include the destruction of Aboriginal lands, the disruption of fish stocks, and the problems of silt accumulation. Other critics observe that more stringent energy conservation would remove the need for any further dam construction. (*Source:* Photos.com/Thinkstock)

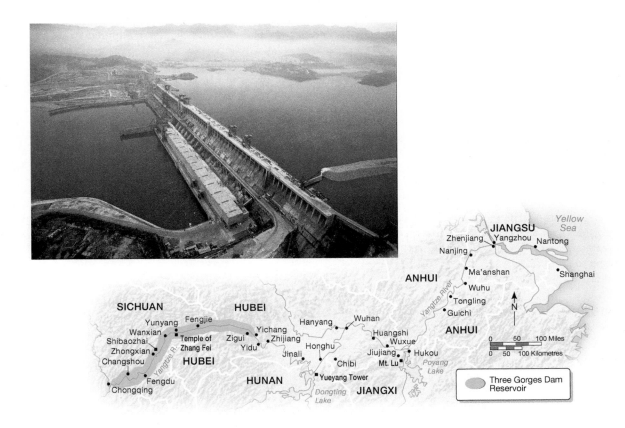

FIGURE 4.31 Three Gorges Dam, China In May 2006, the world's largest dam was completed in Yichang, central China's Hubei Province. The axis of the dam is over 2.3 kilometres, the longest in the world. Begun in 1993, the project proceeded with the backing of the communist leadership despite objections to its US$22 billion cost and projected environmental and social impacts. More than 1.3 million people have been relocated to make way for the dam and its reservoir; environmentalists and engineers warned that the reservoir risks becoming polluted with waste from cities and towns upriver. The shore of the reservoir has already collapsed in 91 places, a total of 36 km, killing scores of people. The inset map shows the 477 km extent of the reservoir that is impounded behind the dam. (*Photo source:* Xinhua Press/Corbis)

Global Climate Change

The issue of a human-induced (anthropogenic) change in Earth's climate, which is distributed *unevenly* across the planet, has become a growing concern for scientists and policymakers since the 1980s. By 1992, at the Earth Summit in Rio de Janeiro, the international community had begun to seek a way to increase the pace of economic development without further threatening the global environment. The biggest potential threat to the global environment then and now is the impact that increased energy use will have on global climate. Extensive climate changes may alter and threaten the living conditions of much of humankind. These changes may induce large-scale migration and lead to greater competition for the earth's resources. Such changes will place particularly heavy burdens on the world's most vulnerable countries. Increased danger of violent conflicts and wars, within and between states, is one possible consequence.

At the Rio Earth Summit, 167 nations ratified the UN Framework Convention on Climate Change with the aim of reducing the amount of **greenhouse gases (GHGs)** generated by energy use. A GHG is any gas that absorbs infrared radiation in the atmosphere, including, but not limited to, water vapour, carbon dioxide (CO_2), methane (CH_4), and nitrous oxide (N_2O). An equally critical aim of the convention is to ensure that the burden of protecting the environment is shared equitably across all nations.

In December 1997, the nations that attended the 1992 Earth Summit began to confront the problem of balancing global economic development and environmental protection more substantively by forging the Kyoto Protocol. The protocol marked the first attempt to limit the amount of greenhouse gas emissions generated by core countries. The aim of the protocol was to cut the combined emissions of greenhouse gases from core countries by roughly 5 percent from their 1990 levels by 2012—a goal that generally has not been reached (Canadian emissions actually went up). Sadly, halting or even reversing GHG emissions now seems more unlikely than ever as more and more semiperipheral countries are increasing their GHG emissions to fuel their industrialization process.

Despite annual UN climate change conferences, no further binding agreement has been reached. In fact, at the 2011 Durban conference, Canada even withdrew from the Kyoto Protocol. In

FIGURE 4.G Schematic framework of climate change drivers, impacts, and responses This diagram represents human-induced drivers, impacts of and responses to climate change, and their linkages. (*Source:* Philippe Rekacewicz, UNEP/GRID-Arendal.)

"recognition" of its persistent role in impeding progress at international climate-change negotiations, Canada was subsequently awarded the "Lifetime Unachievement Fossil Award" at the Warsaw climate talks in November 2013.

As the collected scientific evidence continues to make increasingly clear, human-induced climate change is affecting a wide range of Earth systems. This change can be addressed only if we begin to modify human behaviour as individuals and as members of local, national, and international communities. **Climate change** is defined by the Intergovernmental Panel on Climate Change (IPCC) as "a change in the state of the climate that can be identified (e.g., using statistical tests) by changes in the mean and/or the variability of its properties, and that persists for an extended period, typically decades or longer. It refers to any change in climate over time, whether due to natural variability or as a result of human activity." **Figure 4.G** provides a schematic understanding of the complex process of climate change and its effects.

The IPCC's *Fourth Assessment Report: Climate Change Synthesis Report: Summary for Policymakers* provides helpful data about the state of the world's climate in a format that is easily accessible to a lay audience. We draw directly from that report as well as synthesize some of its finding in the following content. (The fifth report is expected to be finalized in 2014, and early

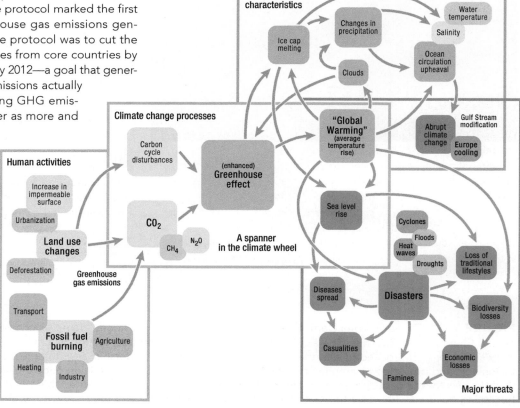

indications are that it will show that the scope and the speed of change exceed scientists' earlier predictions.)

Observations of Climate Change

2013 was the thirty-seventh consecutive year in which the global temperature was above average. Even worse, nine out of the ten hottest years since the beginning of record-keeping (1850) have occurred since 2000. The temperature increase is greatest at higher northern latitudes, where warming is proceeding at twice the global rate.

Increases in sea level are consistent with warming. Global average sea level rose at an average rate of 1.8 (ranging from 1.3 to 2.3) mm per year over 1961 to 2003 and at an average rate of about 3.1 (2.4 to 3.8) mm per year from 1993 to 2003.

Satellite data since 1978 show that annual average Arctic sea ice extent has shrunk by 2.7 (2.1 to 3.3) percent per decade, with larger decreases in summer of 7.4 (5.0 to 9.8) percent per decade. Mountain glaciers and snow cover have declined on average in both hemispheres.

Trends in precipitation amounts from 1900 to 2005 have been observed in many large regions. Over this period, precipitation increased significantly in eastern parts of North and South America, northern Europe, and northern and central Asia, whereas precipitation declined in the Sahel, the Mediterranean, southern Africa, and parts of southern Asia. Globally, the area affected by drought has likely increased since the 1970s.

Average Northern Hemisphere temperatures during the second half of the twentieth century were very likely higher than during any other 50-year period in the past 500 years and likely the highest in at least the past 1300 years.

Some Projected Impacts

Continued GHG emissions at or above current rates will cause further warming and induce many changes in the global climate system during the twenty-first century that will very likely be larger than those observed during the twentieth century.

Snow cover area is projected to contract. Widespread increases in thaw depth are projected over most permafrost regions. Sea ice is projected to shrink in both the Arctic and Antarctic.

Based on a range of models, it is likely that future tropical cyclones (typhoons and hurricanes) will become more intense, with larger peak wind speeds and more heavy precipitation associated with ongoing increases of tropical sea-surface temperatures.

Anthropogenic warming and sea level rise would continue for centuries due to the time scales associated with climate processes and feedbacks, even if GHG concentrations were stabilized (see **Figure 4.H**). Coasts are projected to be exposed to increasing risks, including coastal erosion, due to climate change and sea level rise.

The resilience of many ecosystems is likely to be exceeded this century by an unprecedented combination of climate change, associated disturbances (e.g., flooding, drought, wildfire, insects, ocean acidification), and other global change drivers (e.g., land-use change, pollution, fragmentation of natural systems, overexploitation of resources).

Crop productivity is projected to increase slightly at mid to high latitudes for local mean temperature increases of up to 1° to 3°C, depending on the crop, and then decrease beyond that in some regions. At lower latitudes, especially in seasonally dry and tropical regions, crop productivity is projected to decrease for even small local temperature increases (1° to 2°C), which would increase the risk of hunger.

The health status of millions of people is projected to be affected through, for example, increases in malnutrition; increased deaths, diseases, and injury due to extreme weather events; increased burden of diarrheal diseases; increased frequency of cardio-respiratory diseases due to higher concentrations of ground-level ozone in urban areas related to climate change; and the altered spatial distribution of some infectious diseases.

Climate change is expected to exacerbate current stresses on water resources from population growth and economic and land-use change, including urbanization.

Figure 4.I provides an overview of the possible effects of climate change on global food production through a number of the pathways mentioned above.

Mitigation Efforts

There are many ways that individuals can begin to address the effects of climate change as described above, such as driving less, using compact fluorescent and LED light bulbs, taking shorter showers, buying local produce, and using refillable water bottles instead of disposable ones. More concentrated efforts are the responsibility of corporations, governments, and large organizations.

One increasingly popular strategy for reducing GHGs is emissions trading. Already an established practice, emissions trading allows governments to regulate the amount of emissions produced in aggregate by setting the overall cap but allowing corporations the flexibility of determining how and where the emissions reductions will be achieved. Corporations that want to limit their emissions are allocated allowances, with each allowance representing a tonne of the relevant emission, such as carbon dioxide. Corporations can emit in excess of their allocation of allowances by purchasing allowances from the market. Similarly, a company that emits less than its allocation of allowances can sell its surplus allowances.

Emissions trading is believed to be a more desirable mitigation strategy than strict regulation because it gives companies the flexibility to meet emission reduction targets according to their own strategies, for example, by reducing emissions on-site or by buying allowances from other companies that have excess allowances because they invested in installing newer, cleaner technologies. The important outcome is that an overall reduction is achieved, regardless of whether and how much an individual company contributes to that reduction.

(Continued)

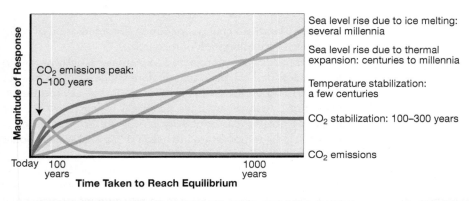

Sea level rise due to ice melting: several millennia

Sea level rise due to thermal expansion: centuries to millennia

Temperature stabilization: a few centuries

CO_2 stabilization: 100–300 years

CO_2 emissions

CO_2 emissions peak: 0–100 years

Magnitude of Response

Today 100 years — 1000 years

Time Taken to Reach Equilibrium

FIGURE 4.H Projected sea level rise This graph shows the changes in sea level rise over varying time scales. The maps show the impact of five metres of sea level rise on Florida (l) and Southeast Asia (r). (*Source:* From *Vital Geo Graphics*, published by UNEP/GRID-Arendal based on UNEP's *Global Environment Outlook: environment for development [GEO4]*. Copyright 2009 © UNEP, UNEP/GRID-Arendal.)

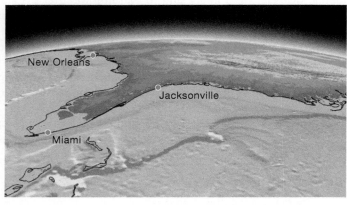

New Orleans

Jacksonville

Miami

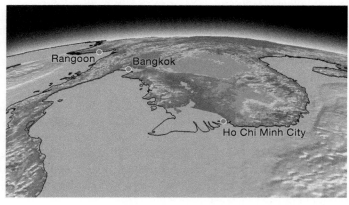

Rangoon   Bangkok

Ho Chi Minh City

FIGURE 4.I Projected impacts of climate change on food production Food production is a complex process that can be affected by a variety of factors, each of which can be impacted by climate change.
(*Source:* Hugo Ahlenius, UNEP/GRID-Arendal, "Projected impacts of climate change," © 2009 GRID-Arendal. Reprinted by permission., www.grida.org.)

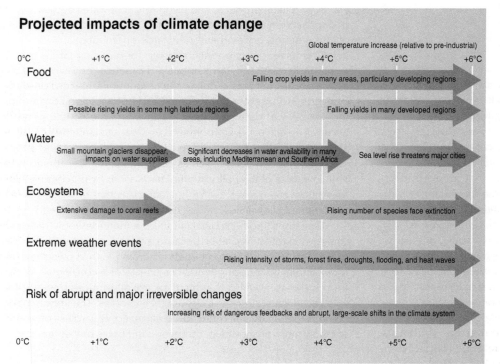

Projected impacts of climate change

Global temperature increase (relative to pre-industrial)

0°C   +1°C   +2°C   +3°C   +4°C   +5°C   +6°C

Food

Falling crop yields in many areas, particulary developing regions

Possible rising yields in some high latitude regions

Falling yields in many developed regions

Water

Small mountain glaciers disappear, impacts on water supplies

Significant decreases in water availability in many areas, including Mediterranean and Southern Africa

Sea level rise threatens major cities

Ecosystems

Extensive damage to coral reefs

Rising number of species face extinction

Extreme weather events

Rising intensity of storms, forest fires, droughts, flooding, and heat waves

Risk of abrupt and major irreversible changes

Increasing risk of dangerous feedbacks and abrupt, large-scale shifts in the climate system

0°C   +1°C   +2°C   +3°C   +4°C   +5°C   +6°C

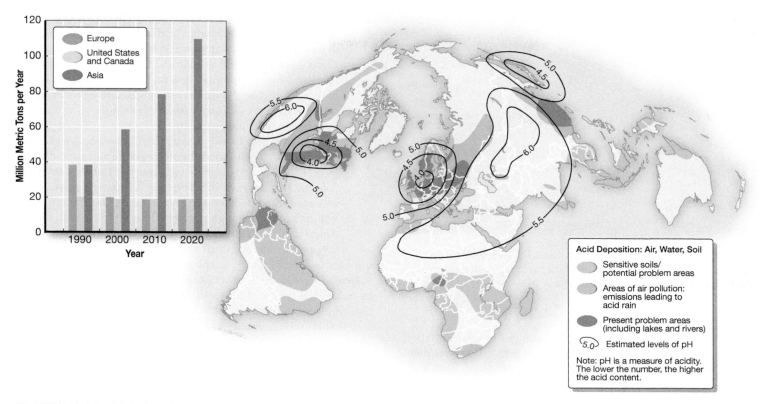

FIGURE 4.32 Global acid emissions Acid emissions affect various elements of the natural and the built environment. In some parts of the world, the damage to soils is especially severe. In others, acid emissions cause serious lake acidification. Large amounts of acid-producing chemicals may be generated in one place but transported to another by prevailing winds. Most industrialized countries have cut sulphur dioxide emissions from fossil fuel burning to help mitigate the damage of acid rain to ecosystems. But the acid rain problem is not yet solved, as it is emerging as a major problem in the developing world, especially in parts of the Asia and the Pacific region where energy use has surged. It is likely that the acid emissions experienced in the core countries in the twentieth century will be repeated in the periphery in the twenty-first century. (*Source:* Adapted from J.L. Allen, *Student Atlas of Environmental Issues*, Guilford, CT: Duskin/McGraw-Hill: 1997, p. 45; World Resources Institute, "Acid Rain: Downpour in Asia," *World Resources 1998–1999*, 1998; The International Energy Agency.)

hydrocarbons, among other gases, which are released into the atmosphere from motor vehicle exhaust, industrial processes, and power generation (based on fossil fuels), are increasing the level of acids in the atmosphere. If these gases reach sufficient concentrations and are not effectively dispersed in the atmosphere, acid rain can result.

Acid rain or acid deposition, as it is known scientifically, is the wet deposition of acids upon Earth through the natural cleansing properties of the atmosphere. The term acid rain also includes acid mists, acid fogs, and smog. Acid rain occurs as the water droplets in clouds absorb certain gases that later fall back to Earth as acid precipitation. **Figure 4.32** illustrates the widespread nature of acid depositions. The problem first emerged in the industrial countries of the Northern Hemisphere, especially Germany, Scandinavia, Canada, and the United States. Acid deposition poisons soils and water bodies that subsequently become too acidic to support life. In urban areas, acid rain corrodes marble and limestone structures, affecting iconic buildings such as the Parthenon in Athens and St. Paul's Cathedral in London. By the late 1990s, however, acid deposition became far less of a problem in Europe and North America as decades of environmental

regulations and co-operative agreements diminished the release of environmental pollutants into the atmosphere.

The problem has not gone away entirely, however, and is emerging with great negative effect in South Asia, especially China, where few governmental limits on industrial pollution are in place. In fact, because of rapid industrial growth and the explosion in automobile ownership, China has some of the world's worst air pollution. In the past decade, the intensifying pollution and the prevailing weather patterns have caused the so-called Asian Brown Cloud to hover over large parts of Asia during the winter months (**Figure 4.33**). It consists of sulphates, nitrates, organic substances, black carbon, and fly ash, along with several other pollutants. It is an accumulated cocktail of contamination resulting from a dramatic increase in the burning of fossil fuels in vehicles, industries, and power stations in Asia's megacities, from forest fires used to clear land, and from the emissions from millions of inefficient stoves burning wood or cow dung.

A study of the Asian Brown Cloud sponsored by the UN Environment Programme and involving more than 200 scientists suggests that the Asian Brown Cloud not only influences local weather but also may have worldwide consequences. The smog

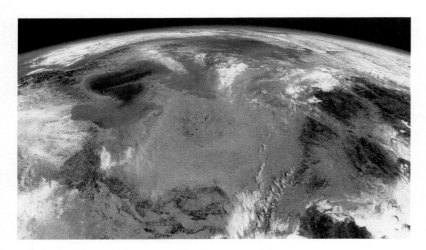

FIGURE 4.33 The Asian Brown Cloud This satellite view shows a dense haze over eastern China, looking eastward across the Yellow Sea toward Korea. (*Source:* NASA)

of the Asian Brown Cloud reduces the amount of solar radiation reaching the Earth's surface by 10 to 15 percent, with a consequent decline in the productivity of crops. But it can also trap heat, leading to warming of the lower atmosphere. It suppresses rainfall in some areas and increases it in others, while damaging forests and crops because of acid rain. The haze is also believed to be responsible for hundreds of thousands of premature deaths from respiratory diseases.

Alternative Energy Sources

Before giving up all hope that the production and use of energy can ever be anything but detrimental to the environment, it is important to realize that alternatives to fossil fuels, hydroelectric power, and nuclear energy do exist. Renewable energy derived from the sun, the wind, Earth's interior (geothermal sources), and the tides has been found to be clean, profitable, and dependable. Japan, the United States, and Germany all have large-scale solar energy production facilities, whereas Iceland, Italy, Japan, the United States, Mexico, New Zealand, and the Philippines all derive some of their energy production from geothermal sources. Tidal power barrages are currently operating in France, China, Russia, and Annapolis Royal, Nova Scotia. With the commissioning of the Sihwa Lake tidal power station in South Korea in 2011, the global production of electricity from tidal power has doubled. The biggest success story in renewable energy, however, is wind energy.

Wind power generation has enjoyed a meteoric rise over the past two decades. From its beginnings in Denmark and Germany in the 1980s, the wind power industry has now developed into a globalized business with remarkable growth rates: wind power generating capacity worldwide now doubles roughly every three years. China is the leader, producing half of all wind energy worldwide. The example of the rapid emergence of India is equally instructive: it is the fifth-largest producer of wind energy in the world and its Suzlon Energy—a company founded only in 1995—now is the third-largest manufacturer of wind turbines in the world.

A similar story could be told about solar energy. Since 2010, China has been literally flooding the global market with low-priced solar panels, enabling a remarkable expansion of solar energy generation worldwide. China itself is aiming to double its solar power-generating capacity every year. China finds itself in an ironic situation, then: due to its relentless hunger for coal, it is the worst offender in terms of increasing greenhouse gas emissions. On the other hand, China also is the country with the fastest-growing alternative energy generating capacity.

Meanwhile, in the established core countries, it is becoming increasingly difficult to get public approval for large-scale energy projects (witness the debates over the Alberta Tar Sands or the Keystone XL pipeline), which is why efforts are often focusing on reducing energy consumption, primarily through greater efficiency of use. In North America, for example, average household energy use has dropped by about a third since 1980. More energy-efficient appliances—refrigerators, washing machines, heating and cooling systems—have helped, as have better insulation and construction to reduce the escape of heat and cooling through the walls, roofs, and windows of homes.

It should be pointed out, however, that the increased use of electronic devices—cell phones, televisions, computers—is partly offsetting these greater efficiencies. Energy consumption to fuel the increasing use of these devices is expected to double over the next 10 years. A similar trend is noticeable with regard to automobiles: each car generation is more fuel efficient than the previous one, but we buy more cars and drive more kilometres, thus negating any fuel savings.

APPLY YOUR KNOWLEDGE The renewable energy sector is in rapid transition. Research the current global distribution of renewable energy production. Which countries (other than China) are leading in the production of solar and wind energy? Can you identify geographical reasons (e.g., location, resource endowment, weather patterns) why these countries are pushing renewable energy sources? ∎

The Impact of Land-Use Change on the Environment

In addition to industrial pollution and steadily increasing demands for energy, the environment is also being dramatically affected by land use. As human populations have increased and the need for land for settlement and cultivation has also increased, changes to the land have followed. The clearing of land for fuel, farming, grazing, resource extraction, highway building, energy generation, or war all have significant impacts. Geographers classify land into five categories: forest, cultivated land, grassland, wetland, and areas of settlement. Geographers understand land-use change as occurring in either of two ways: conversion or modification. *Conversion* is the wholesale transformation of land from one use to another (for example, the conversion of forest to settlement). *Modification* is an alteration of existing land use (for example, when a grassland is overlaid with railroad tracks or when a forest is thinned but not clear-cut).

TABLE 4-1   Estimated Area Cleared (1000 km²)

Total Region or Country	Pre-1650	1650–1749	1750–1849	1850–1978	1990–2000	2000–2005	Estimate
North America	6	80	380	641	0	1	1108
Central America	15	30	40	200	+4*	3	288
Latin America and Caribbean	12	100	170	637	42	45	1006
Oceania	4	5	6	362	4	4	385
Former USSR	61	150	260	575	—	—	1046
Europe	176	54	186	18	+9	+7	481
Asia	732	190	606	1220	8	10	2766
Africa	126	24	72	469	44	40	775
Total Estimate	**1132**	**633**	**1720**	**4185**	**85**	**96**	**7855**

*"Plus" sign indicates a growth, not loss, of total forest area (1000 km²).
(*Source:* Adapted from B. L. Turner II, W. C. Clark, R. W. Kates, J. F. Richards, J. T. Mathews, and W. B. Meyer, *The Earth as Transformed by Human Action: Global and Regional Changes in the Biosphere over the Past 300 Years.* Cambridge: Cambridge University Press, 1990, p. 180; UN Food and Agricultural Organization, *State of the World's Forests, 2007*, pp. 109–115.)

One of the most dramatic impacts is loss or alteration of forest cover, which humans have cleared for millennia to make way for cultivation and settlement, and to extract the vast timber resources they contain. The approximate chronology and estimated extent of the clearing of the world's forests are listed in **Table 4-1**, which shows that the forested area of the world has been reduced by about 8 million square kilometres (four-fifths of the size of Canada) since preagricultural times. **Figure 4.34** shows the global extent of deforestation in recent years.

Forests

The permanent clearing and destruction of forests, **deforestation**, is currently occurring most alarmingly in the world's rain forests. The UN Food and Agricultural Organization has estimated that

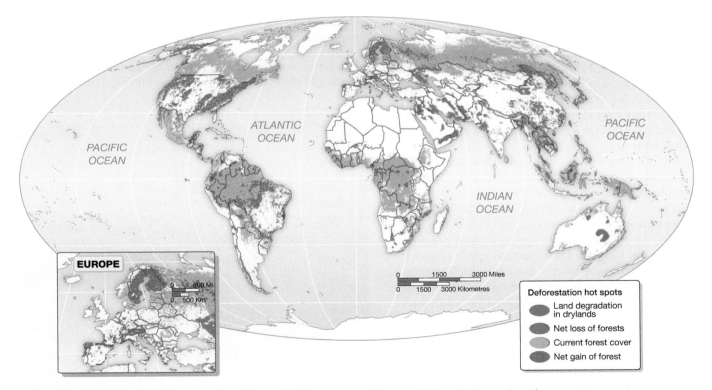

FIGURE 4.34 Global deforestation The world's forests are disappearing or being reduced or degraded everywhere, but especially in tropical countries. Since agriculture emerged about 10 000 years ago, human activities have diminished the world's forest resources by about 25 percent. Whereas forests once occupied about one-third of Earth's surface, they now take up only one-quarter. Playing an important role in the global ecosystem, forests filter air and noise pollution, provide a habitat for wildlife, and slow down water runoff, helping to recharge streams and groundwater. They also influence climate at local, regional, and global levels. (*Source:* World Resources Institute, http://images.wri.org/sdm-gene-02-deforestation.jpg or http://www.wri.org/image/view/10981/_original.)

FIGURE 4.35 Deforestation in Mato Grosso, Brazil Brazil's Amazonian rain forest is increasingly converted to agricultural land. The cleared areas are used for the cultivation of soybeans (for feedstuff exports or domestic biofuel production) or livestock grazing (for beef exports). (*Source:* Frontpage/Shutterstock)

rain forests globally are being destroyed at the rate of one football field (0.5 hectare) per second (**Figure 4.35**).

Today, rain forests cover less than 7 percent of the land surface, half of what they covered only a few thousand years ago. Destruction of the rain forests, however, is not just about the loss of trees, a renewable resource that is being eliminated more quickly than it can be regenerated. It is also about the loss of the biological diversity of an ecosystem, which translates into the potential loss of biological compounds that may have great medicinal value. The destruction of rain forests is also about destabilizing the oxygen and carbon dioxide cycles of the forests, which may have long-term effects on global climate.

Much of the destruction of the South American rain forests is the result of peripheral countries' attempts at economic development. In the Bolivian Amazon rain forest the introduction of coca production has become an important source of revenue for farmers in the region and has led to the removal of small tracts of forest. The pressure of economic development persists in the region such that net rain forest and forest land more generally are continuing to decline in Central and South America at a faster rate than in the 1990s. The same is occurring in Indonesia for palm oil plantations, in Brazil for livestock grazing, and in Madagascar for subsistence slash-and-burn agriculture.

Figure 4.36 illustrates another aspect of the problem—the clear-cutting of forests as part of regular forestry operations. In Canada, demands for more sustainable forestry practices have long dogged this industry, and yet for many parts of Canada's periphery, the clear-cutting of forests for lumber or pulp and paper is still a crucial economic activity. In Canada alone, 1 million hectares are harvested (90 percent by clear-cutting) and replanted each year. Forest practices in the vast interior of Russia are even less sustainable.

Great geographical variability exists with respect to human impacts on the world's forests. In most of the core regions, the forests that were once cleared have been replanted. In some regions of Europe, the forest is even expanding as more and more farmers give up (see Table 4.1). For most of the periphery, in contrast, clearance has accelerated to such an extent that one estimate shows a 50 percent reduction in the amount of forest cover since the early 1900s. It is estimated that deforestation and its effects contribute about 20 percent to global warming.

Cultivated Lands

Cultivation is another important component of global land use, which we will deal with extensively in Chapter 8. In this section, we briefly cover one or two points about the environmental impacts of cultivation that are particularly pertinent to our current discussion. During the past 300 years the land devoted to cultivation has expanded globally by 450 percent. In 1700, the global stock of land in cultivation took up an area about the size of Argentina. Today, it occupies an area roughly the size of the entire continent of South America. While the most rapid expansion of cropland since the mid-twentieth century has occurred in the peripheral regions, the amount of cropland in the core regions has either held steady or been reduced. The expansion of cropland in peripheral regions is partly a response to growing populations and rising levels of consumption worldwide. It is also due to the globalization of agriculture (see Chapter 8), which has "outsourced" some of the food production destined for core populations to regions in the periphery. Conversely, the reduction of cropland in some core regions is partly a result of this globalization.

The phenomenon of corporations and rich governments investing in the agricultural land of peripheral countries is often

FIGURE 4.36 Clear-cutting in New Zealand Views like this one have mobilized groups, such as Greenpeace, against clear-cutting forestry practices worldwide. Although making some concessions and supporting research into more environmentally acceptable methods, the forest industry continues to log large parts of its timber licences in this way. (*Source:* M. Imort)

Africa, a global market for large-scale land acquisitions

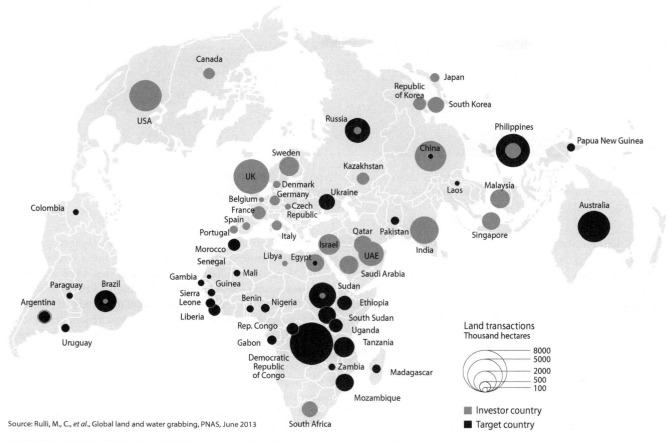

Source: Rulli, M., C., *et al.*, Global land and water grabbing, PNAS, June 2013

FIGURE 4.37 Global land grab This graphic illustrates the patterns of the investment in land across the world. In general terms, countries and private companies in Asia and the Middle East are investing in Africa and Latin America—but there are some interesting exceptions, notably Russia and Australia. (*Source:* GRID-Arendal, www.grida.org.)

called a "land grab." While it is impossible to know exactly how much peripheral land is being sold to investors (because land deals are often secret), the UN estimates that, by 2013, almost 50 million hectares of farmland in the periphery were bought up by foreign governments and agribusiness—the equivalent of a third of Europe's farmland. Much of this land is situated in Africa, where food insecurity is a frequent reality (**Figure 4.37**). Big investors are countries with concerns about feeding their own people that purchase farmland abroad as a guarantee of future food supplies. China is the largest of these investors, buying or leasing twice as much land as anyone else, usually in Africa. The most worrying aspect of these land grabs is the high levels of corruption among the buyers and low levels of benefit for the sellers.

APPLY YOUR KNOWLEDGE Examine Figure 4.37 more closely. Can you identify geographical and economic reasons for the pattern you see? What is the connection between the semiperipheral status of Brazil, the Philippines (and Russia?) and the fact that they are both investors and targets of investment? ■

Grasslands

Grasslands—distinct from agricultural land—are also used productively the world over, either as rangeland or pasture for livestock grazing. Most grasslands are found in arid and semiarid regions that are unsuitable for farming due to lack of water or poor soils. Some grasslands, however, occur in more rainy regions where tropical rain forests have been removed. Others are at the mid-latitudes, such as the tall- and short-grass prairies of Canada and the central United States (**Figure 4.38**). Approximately 68 million square kilometres of global land surface is currently taken up by grasslands—an area seven times the size of Canada. African grasslands, also called savannahs, contain extensive herds of hoofed animals, including gazelles, giraffes, zebras, wildebeests, antelopes, and elephants.

Human impacts on grasslands are largely of two sorts. The first is the clearing of grasslands for other uses, most frequently settlement. As the global demands for beef production have increased, the use of the world's grasslands has intensified. Widespread overgrazing of grasslands has led to acute degradation. In its most severe form, overgrazing has led to desertification.

Desertification is the spread of desert conditions resulting from deforestation, overgrazing, and poor agricultural practices, as well as reduced rainfall associated with climatic change. Until recently, one

FIGURE 4.38 North American tall-grass prairie Grasslands include scattered shrubs and isolated small trees and are normally found in areas with high-to-average temperatures and low-to-moderate precipitation. They occur in an extensive belt on both sides of the equator. (*Source:* Ricardo Reitmeyer/Shutterstock)

of the most severe examples of desertification has been occurring in the Sahel region of Africa. The degradation of the grasslands bordering the Sahara Desert has not been a simple case of careless overgrazing by thoughtless herders, however. Severe drought, land decline, recurrent famine, and the breakdown of traditional systems for coping with disaster have all combined to create increased pressure on fragile resources, resulting in a loss of grass cover and extreme soil degradation since the 1970s. However, increasing evidence is suggesting that between 1982 and 2000 the desertification in this region has been declining (**Figure 4.39**). Scientists believe they are seeing signals that the Sahara Desert and surrounding regions are actually **greening**—adding biomass including grasses as well as trees—due to increasing rainfall. The increased rainfall may be the result of global climate change, which is leading to warmer temperatures. Warmer air can hold more moisture, which in turn creates more rain. Aerial photographs as well as ground studies have confirmed the greening phenomenon. The most optimistic projection of the various climate models that attempt to better understand the impacts of the greening is that the rains could continue to revitalize drought-ravaged regions, providing new grazing lands for farming communities.

Wetlands

The wetlands category covers swamps, marshes, bogs, peatlands, and the shore areas of lakes, rivers, oceans, and other water bodies. Wetlands can be associated either with saltwater or freshwater. Most

of Earth's wetlands are associated with the latter. The human impacts on wetland environments are numerous. The most widespread has been the draining or filling of wetlands and their conversion to other land uses, such as settlement or cultivation. One reliable estimate places the total area of the world's wetlands at about 8.5 million square kilometres, with about 1.5 million square kilometres lost to drainage or filling. For example, Australia has lost all of its original 20 000 square kilometres of wetlands to conversion. For the last 400 years or so, people have regarded wetlands as nuisances and as sources of disease. In core countries, technological innovation made modification and conversion of wetlands possible and profitable.

In San Francisco, California, for example, the conversion of wetlands in the mid-nineteenth century allowed speculators and real estate developers to extend significantly the central downtown area into the once marshy edges of San Francisco Bay. The Gold Rush in the Sierra Nevada sent millions of tonnes of sediment down the rivers into the bay, filling in its marshland and reducing its nearshore depth. By the 1960s the conversion and modification of the wetlands (as well as the effects of pollution pouring directly into the bay) had so dramatically transformed water quality and the habitats of fish, fowl, and marine life that the viability of the ecosystem was seriously threatened. Since then, restoration activities have been undertaken and parts of the bay have returned to something approximating their former state, but large parts are heavily urbanized and cannot be restored.

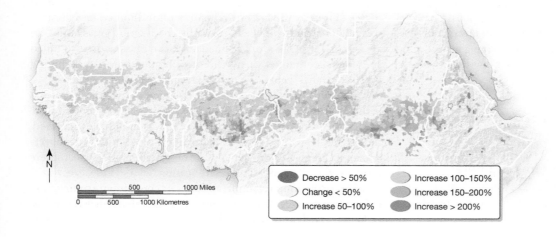

FIGURE 4.39 Greening of the Sahel Desertification has been a significant problem in many parts of the world, particularly in Africa south of the Sahara Desert. Overgrazing of fragile arid and semiarid rangelands and deforestation without reforestation have been the chief causes. Recently, however, there is growing evidence of increasing biomass production in this region as a result of increasing rainfall. This figure is based on trend analyses of time series over the Sahel region from 1982 to 1999. (*Source:* NOAA AVHRR NDVI-data from 1982 to 1999.)

Identify a core country and a peripheral country that share a common environmental concern relating to threats to forests, grasslands, or wetlands. Compare and contrast the different ways core and peripheral countries are addressing the same issue. What are the reasons for the difference in approaches? ■

THE GLOBALIZATION OF THE ENVIRONMENT

The combustion of fossil fuels, the destruction of forest resources, the damming of watercourses, and the massive change in land-use patterns brought about by the pressures of globalization—industrialization being the most extreme phase—contribute to environmental problems of enormous proportions. It is now customary to speak of the accumulation of environmental problems we, as a human race, experience as global in dimension. Geographers and others use the term **global change** to describe the combination of political, economic, social, historical, and environmental problems with which human beings across Earth must currently contend. Very little, if anything, has escaped the embrace of globalization, least of all the environment.

In fact, no other period in human history has transformed the natural world as profoundly as the anthropocene. While we enjoy the benefits of a modern way of life, it is important to recognize that these benefits have not been without cost. Fortunately, the costs have not been accepted uncritically. Over the past two to three decades, responses to global environmental problems have been on the increase as local groups have mobilized internationally.

Global Environmental Politics

The increasing importance of flows and connections—economic, political, social, and cultural—means that contemporary globalization has resulted in an increasingly shrinking world. In addition to allowing people and goods to travel farther faster and to receive and send information more quickly, a smaller world means that political action has also become global. It can now move beyond the confines of the state into the global political arena, where rapid communications enable complex supporting networks to be developed and deployed, facilitating interaction and decision making. Good examples can be seen in the protests that occurred in June 2009 in Copenhagen, Denmark, around the UN climate negotiations conference, and again in December 2010 in Cancún, Mexico, during the UN climate conference. Telecommunications as well as Facebook, Twitter, and other social media enable protest leaders to organize and deploy demonstrators from interested groups all over the world. Such political protests reflect attempts to match the political reach of institutions like the World Trade Organization (WTO), the International Monetary Fund (IMF), the World Bank, and the United Nations.

One indication of the expanding influence and geographical extent of popular political groups is the growth of environmental organizations whose purview and membership are global. These organizations have emerged in response to the global impact of such contemporary environmental problems as the depletion of fisheries, global warming, genetically modified seeds, and the decline in global biodiversity. Since the 1990s, these groups—ranging from lobbying organizations and nongovernmental organizations (NGOs) to direct-action organizations and political parties like the Green Party in Canada, and drawing on distinctive traditions and varying levels of resources—have become an important international force.

Increasingly, agreements and conventions protecting biodiversity are being created, and not a moment too soon. The decline in the diversity of simple foodstuffs, such as lettuce, potatoes, tomatoes, and squash, occurred most dramatically over the course of the twentieth century. For instance, in 1903 there were 13 known varieties of asparagus; by 1983 there was just one. There were 287 known varieties of carrots in 1903; this number today is just 21. A decline in the diversity of foodstuffs means that different resistances to pests inherent in these different varieties have also declined, as have their different nutritional values and tastes. It should be pointed out, however, that a growing local food movement in the core countries is working hard to recover some of these lost varieties.

Moreover, new sources of medicine may be lost not only because of deforestation in tropical forests but also because of the decline in indigenous languages, cultures, and traditions. Recognizing that many indigenous people have extensive knowledge of local plants and animals and their medicinal uses, the Convention on Biological Diversity that emerged from the Rio Summit in 1992 is attempting to protect global biodiversity by preserving and protecting these cultures and traditions. Traditional knowledge and practices are being lost as globalization homogenizes languages and draws more and more people into a capitalist market system. The UN Environment Program devotes a great deal of its energies to biological and cultural diversity. Even the WTO has begun to recognize the value of indigenous knowledge and the promise of biodiversity through its advocacy of intellectual property rights of both corporations and indigenous peoples. For the latter, this means protection against **bioprospecting**, the scientific or commercial practice of searching for a useful application, process, or product in nature, often in extreme environments such as deserts, rain forests, and cold places like the Arctic and Antarctic (**Figure 4.40**).

Clearly, global environmental awareness is on the rise from both ends of the political spectrum: the conservative (such as the WTO) as well as the progressive (such as Navdanya and other organizations devoted to preserving genetic diversity in seed strains). This increasing awareness is directly responsible for the staging of global environmental conferences like Rio in 1992, Kyoto in 1997, Johannesburg in 2002, and Rio+20 in 2012, which have not only affected international laws but continue to shape the debates about and responses to environmental problems. Most recently, these debates have centred on the concept of sustainability.

Research two different environmental policies that demonstrate co-operation on an environmental problem across national boundaries. How successful have they been? What were the factors influencing the success? ■

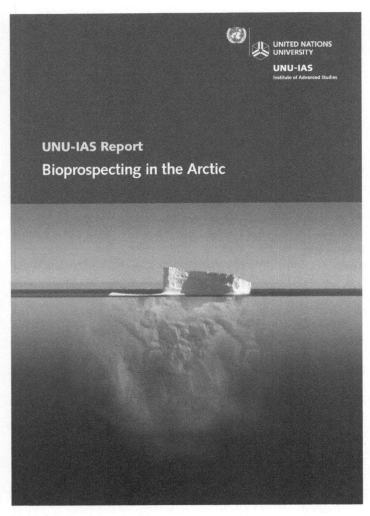

FIGURE 4.40 Bioprospecting in the Arctic The combination of extreme temperatures and special light conditions has led to the evolution of organisms with unique properties and potentially valuable bioactive compounds in the Arctic as well as the Antarctic. The United Nations is currently exploring bioprospecting in the cold regions of the globe in an attempt to establish governance standards that protect those resources from reckless exploitation. (*Source:* Puppim de Oliveira, Jose A.)

Environmental Sustainability

The interdependence of economic, environmental, and social problems, often located within widely different political contexts, means that some parts of the world are ecological time bombs.

Most environmental threats are greatest in the world's periphery, where daily environmental pollution and degradation amount to a catastrophe that will continue to unfold in slow motion in the coming years.

In the peripheral regions there is simply less money to cope with environmental threats. The poverty endemic to peripheral regions also adds to environmental stress. In order to survive, the rural poor are constantly impelled to degrade and destroy their immediate environment, cutting down forests for fuelwood and exhausting soils with overuse. In order to meet their debt repayments, governments generate export earnings by encouraging the harvesting of natural resources. In the cities of the periphery, poverty encompasses so many people in such concentrations as to generate its own vicious cycle of pollution, environmental degradation, and disease. (See Chapter 11.) Even climate change, an inherently global problem, seems to pose its greatest threats to poorer, peripheral regions.

A more benign relationship between nature and society has been proposed under the principle of *sustainable development*, a term that incorporates the ethic of intergenerational equity, with its obligation to preserve resources and landscapes for future generations. Sustainable development involves employing ecological, economic, and social measures to prevent environmental degradation while promoting economic growth and social equality. Sustainable development insists that economic growth and change should occur only when the impacts on the environment are benign or manageable and the impacts (both costs and benefits) on society are fairly distributed across classes and regions. This means finding less-polluting technologies that use resources more efficiently and managing renewable resources (those that replenish themselves, such as water, fish, and forests) to ensure replacement and continued yield. In practice, sustainable development policies of major international institutions, such as the World Bank, have promoted reforestation, energy efficiency and conservation, and birth control and poverty programs to reduce the environmental impact of rural populations. At the same time, however, the expansion and globalization of the world economy has resulted in increased use of resources and inequality, contradicting many of the goals of sustainable development.

APPLY YOUR KNOWLEDGE Research an international institution, such as the World Bank, that implements programs that strive to promote sustainable development. Evaluate the effectiveness of one of its programs in a peripheral region by identifying the reasons for both its successes and failures. ■

Future Geographies

The continued expansion of the global economy and the globalization of industry will undoubtedly boost the overall demand for raw materials and energy and continue to shape the relationship between people and nature. While the extraction of raw materials will be important in the future, the most concerning issue, by far, will be energy resources. World energy consumption has been increasing steadily. As the periphery is industrialized and its population increases further, the demand for energy will expand even more rapidly. Basic industrial development tends to be highly energy-intensive. The International Energy Agency, assuming

FIGURE 4.41 Containers Recyclable paper and metal, half-processed forest products and other raw materials as well as agricultural products account for most of the goods that are shipped from North America to China and other ports in Northeast Asia. Those that come from China to North America are largely manufactured commodities such as clothing, shoes, toys, furniture, appliances and other household goods. (*Source:* Andy Wong/AP Images)

(fairly optimistically) that energy in peripheral countries will be generated in the future as efficiently as it is in developed ones now, estimates that developing-country energy consumption will more than double by 2025, lifting total world energy demand by almost 50 percent. Unless peripheral countries are able to limit the degradation associated with energy use, the globe will continue to feel the negative public health and environmental effects of air, water, and terrestrial pollution.

Despite the threat to people and the environment, industrialization geared to meeting the growing worldwide market for consumer goods, such as automobiles, air conditioners, refrigerators, televisions, and household appliances, will continue (**Figure 4.41**). Without higher rates of investment in exploration and extraction than at present, production will be slow to meet the escalating demand. Many experts believe that current levels of production in

fact represent "Peak Oil" and that the world is at the halfway point of depleting its finite reserves of crude oil.

The past 25 years have seen a growing public awareness of how continued globalization will affect the world in which we live. Increasingly, citizens, nongovernmental organizations, and environmental policymakers are expressing concern over the negative outcomes of rapid and enduring global economic growth. However, because growth is so critically tied to improving the lives of poor people around the world, governments are reluctant to limit it. The response from the global community, hammered out during international meetings, through academic publications, and in response to social protest, is to link globalization to governmental co-operation across states, with the assumption that global challenges will require international political and economic co-operation.

CONCLUSION

The relationship between people and nature is very much mediated by institutions and practices, from technology to religious beliefs. In this chapter, we have seen how the nature–society relationship has changed over time and how the globalization of the capitalist world economy has had a more widespread impact on attitudes and practices than any cultural or economic system that preceded it.

The expansion of European trade, followed by colonization and eventually industrialization, broadcast worldwide the belief that humans should take their place at the apex of the natural world. The Western attitude toward nature as manifested by the capitalist economic system is the most pervasive shaper of nature–society interactions today.

In addition to exploring the history of ideas about nature and contemporary environmental philosophies and organizations, this chapter has

also shown that people and nature are interdependent and that events in one part of the global environmental system affect conditions in the system elsewhere. Finally, we have shown that events in the past have shaped the contemporary state of society and nature.

In short, as economies have globalized so has the environment. We can now speak of a global environment in which not only the people but also the physical environments where they live and work are linked in complex and essential ways.

Along with the recognition of a globalized environment have come new ways of thinking about global economic development. Sustainable development, one of these new ways of thinking, has come to dominate the agenda of international institutions, as well as environmental organizations, as the new century unfolds.

Learning Outcomes Revisited

■ Recognize how people and nature form a complex relationship such that nature is both a physical realm and a social construct.

Nature is not only an object, it is a reflection of society in that the philosophies, belief systems, and ideologies people produce shape the way we think about and employ nature. Society is the sum of the inventions, institutions, and relationships created and reproduced by human beings across particular places and times. The relationship between nature and society is two-way: Society shapes people's understandings and uses of nature at the same time that nature shapes society.

■ Compare and contrast the many views of nature operating both historically and in society today, from the traditional Western approach to radical left and contemporary ecotheological ones.

In the contemporary world, views of nature are dominated by the Western (also known as Judeo-Christian) tradition that understands humans to be superior to nature. In this view, nature is something to be tamed or dominated. But other views of nature have emerged that depart dramatically from the dominant view. These include the environmental philosophies that became popular in the nineteenth and early twentieth centuries and the more radical political views of nature that gained prominence in the late twentieth century. Among the latter are approaches based on ecotheology, which reject the long-standing consumption-based Western tradition.

■ Assess how European colonization as well as contemporary globalization transformed nature in the New World on an unprecedented scale.

In the fifteenth century, Europe initiated territorial expansion that changed the global political map and launched dramatic environmental change. Europeans were fast running out of land, and explorers were dispatched to conquer new territories, enlarge their empires, and collect tax revenues from new subjects. European people, ideologies, technologies, plant species, pathogens, and animals changed the environments into which they were introduced and the societies they encountered.

■ Appraise how the globalization of the capitalist political economy has affected the environment so that environmental problems, often predicated on industrialization and its attendant energy needs, are increasingly global in scope.

No other transition in human history has had the impact on the natural world that industrialization and urbanization have. The combustion of fossil fuels, the destruction of forest resources, the damming of watercourses, and the massive change in land-use patterns brought about by the pressures of globalization contribute to environmental problems of enormous proportions. Geographers and others use the term *global change* to describe the combination of political, economic, social, historical, and environmental problems with which human beings across Earth must currently contend.

■ Evaluate the ways that sustainability has become a predominant approach to global economic development and environmental transformation.

Sustainable development involves employing ecological, economic, and social measures to prevent environmental degradation while promoting economic growth and social equality. Sustainable development insists that economic growth and change should occur only when the impacts on the environment are benign or manageable and the impacts (both costs and benefits) on society are fairly distributed across classes and regions. This means finding less-polluting technologies that use resources more efficiently and managing renewable resources (those that replenish themselves, such as water, fish, and forests) to ensure replacement and continued yield.

KEY TERMS

REVIEW AND DISCUSSION

1. Consider the relationship between industrialization and physical geography by examining mountain top removal in Appalachia. Visit the Beehive Collective graphic campaign entitled "The True Cost of Coal" at **www.beehivecollective.org/english/coal.htm**. Describe the environmental philosophies that the Beehive Collective most closely adheres to. (*Hint:* Is it the collective part of the environmental justice or ecofeminist movements? Or a combination of a variety of different theories?) Explain your choice. Be specific in the reasons you give by citing examples from the organization's website. List four examples of how the graphics on the site depict the complex relationship between nature and society.

2. Universities have become much more involved in sustainability over the past decade. In order to know where your institution fits into the larger university sustainability movement, visit the College Sustainability Report Card website at **www.greenreportcard.org/about/faq** and determine how your institution is rated. Discuss how it compares to other institutions and how your institution might improve or how sustainability practices engaged in at your institution could be transferred to other colleges or universities.

3. The concept of the anthropocene is being debated in scientific circles around the world. Geologists are divided on this issue. To mirror this situation, set up a debate in which half of the group is tasked with providing reasons for accepting the anthropocene as a new geological era and the other half of the group is arguing against its adoption.

4. Read a natural history of the place where your university is located. What sorts of plants and animals dominated the landscape there during the Paleolithic period? Do any plants or animals continue to survive in altered or unaltered forms from that period? What new plants have been introduced and how extensive are they? What sorts of tending and maintenance do these new species require, and how have they changed the landscape?

5. Universities are large generators of waste, from plain-paper waste to biomedical and other sorts of wastes, that can have significant environmental impacts. Identify how your campus handles this waste stream and how you, as a member of the academic community, contribute to it. Where does the waste go when it leaves the campus? Is it locally deposited? Does it go out of province?

Log in to www.masteringgeography.com for MapMaster™ interactive maps, geography videos, RSS feeds, flashcards, weblinks, an eText version of *Human Geography: Places and Regions in Global Context,* and self-study quizzes to enhance your study of people and nature.

MapMaster™ presents 13 Place Name and 13 Layered Thematic interactive maps to help students practise and master their geographic literacy, spatial reasoning, and critical thinking skills.

5 CULTURAL GEOGRAPHIES

Antarctica is simultaneously deeply connected to the rest of the world as well as practically remote. Earth's southernmost continent, it is also its coldest place. The only plant and animal life that can survive in Antarctica is cold-adapted, including whales, penguins, and seals as well as tundra vegetation.

Antarctica's remoteness at the "bottom of the world" is linked to its climate, where temperatures average −51°C during the six-month winter. By the end of the southern winter in September, half the surrounding ocean is frozen, creating a vast ice-covered area almost three times the size of Canada. The cold, ice, lack of air pollution, and towering mountains render Antarctica one of the most visually striking landscapes in the world. In the clear, bright light, the snow and ice fields seem endless. In summer, the Antarctic pack ice breaks up, and the coastal glaciers calve off huge icebergs that drift and change shape by the hour.

There is growing concern that global warming is threatening Antarctica. Temperatures are warming and changing the ecology, and ice cover is disappearing. As a result, travel companies have begun to capitalize on the urge of the more than 40 000 tourists every year who want to see Antarctica—before it is forever changed.

Tourists photographing emperor penguin chicks at Snow Hill Island, Antarctica, in summer. *(Source: david tipling/Alamy)*

Tourism enables the traveller to experience new places by direct contact with the sounds, sights, smells, and feel of a place. Tourists travel to Antarctica to appreciate firsthand this extreme landscape; but these visitors must transform themselves—"become polar"—in order to encounter the landscape without harming themselves. Special thermal clothing must be worn to guard the body against the extreme cold. This includes special eyewear. Snow blindness—a serious, painful, and possibly disabling condition—can occur when unprotected human eyes are exposed to excessive light generated where snow and ice reflect 85 percent of ultraviolet radiation. Alcohol consumption is discouraged here, where unforeseen events may require swift, intelligent action, and a person's ability to deal effectively with a mishap is reduced by intoxication.

Tourism in Antarctica illustrates a new way of thinking about culture and nature in human geography today. In this view, people and land (or culture and nature) are not to be understood as separate entities but entwined in such a way that in the encounter, each brings the other into being. From this perspective, we can see the Antarctic landscape not as some totality of air, land, and water that can be observed, but as a world that creates the tourist as a human subject seeking to know. In this way, the Antarctic makes tourists out of thrill seekers just as the tourist creates an imaginary Antarctic that shapes his or her experience of it. ■

CULTURE AS A GEOGRAPHICAL PROCESS

Anthropologists, geographers, and other scholars who study culture, such as historians, sociologists, and political scientists, agree that culture is a complex concept. Over time, our understanding of culture has been changed and enriched. A simple definition of culture is that it is a particular way of life, such as a set of skilled activities, values, and meanings surrounding a particular type of practice. Scholars also describe culture in terms of classical standards and aesthetic excellence in, for example, opera, ballet, or literature.

The term *culture* also describes the range of activities that characterize a particular group, such as working-class culture, corporate culture, or teenage culture. Although all these understandings of culture are accurate, for our purposes they are not inclusive enough. Broadly speaking, **culture** is a shared set of meanings that is lived through the material and symbolic practices of everyday life. Our understanding in this book is that culture is not something that is necessarily tied to a place and thus a fact to be discovered. Rather, we regard the connections among people, places, and cultures to be social creations that can be altered and are therefore always changing, sometimes in subtle and other times in more dramatic ways. The "shared set of meanings" can include values, beliefs, practices, and ideas about religion, language, family, gender, sexuality, and other important identities **(Figure 5.1)**. These values, beliefs, ideas, and practices are routinely subject to re-evaluation and redefinition and can be, and very frequently are, transformed from both within and outside a particular group. As with many other processes discussed in this book, globalization can greatly increase the speed and frequency with which such transformations are occurring.

Nothing perhaps better illustrates this than music, which has both the formalism to preserve traditional cultural forms and the fluidity to adopt new characteristics. For example, the traditional French lyrics and tunes of the Acadians deported from Nova Scotia in the eighteenth century were merged with African and Aboriginal-American rhythms of Louisiana and produced Cajun music played on a variety of instruments—including the French fiddle, the German accordion, and the washboard, a local addition. This distinctive style, with variants such as zydeco, was altered yet again and became part of "world music" in the late twentieth century. Another example that shows how traditional forms of culture are continually adapted and recombined to produce new meanings is the practice of tattooing. Originating in Aboriginal cultures, it was first adopted by certain subcultures within Western culture (e.g., sailors, soldiers, prison inmates) before expanding into youth culture **(Figure 5.2)**. Finally, at least in some countries of the West, tattooing has found its way into the mainstream: one in five Canadians now has a tattoo.

In short, culture is a dynamic concept that revolves around and intersects with complex social, political, economic, and even historical factors. For much of the twentieth century, geographers, like anthropologists, have focused most of their attention on material culture, as opposed to its less tangible symbolic or spiritual manifestations. For example, they have explored the spatial extent of particular religious practices such as the global distribution of Buddhism, and the physical expression of religiosity, such as the practice of installing crosses along roadways where fatal traffic accidents have occurred **(Figure 5.3)**. This understanding of culture is part of a longer, evolving tradition within geography and other disciplines. We will look more closely at the development of the cultural tradition in geography in the following section, in which we discuss the debates surrounding culture within the discipline.

FIGURE 5.1 Maori men with traditional tattoos These indigenous men of New Zealand are dancing a *haka*, a traditional war dance meant to display aggressiveness and fearlessness. The dancers use facial contortions to deride their enemy. The tattoos, known as *ta moko*, can signify identification, rank, genealogy, tribal history, eligibility to marry, beauty, and ferocity. (*Source:* Dave G. Houser/Corbis)

FIGURE 5.2 Youth culture The term *culture* is also used to describe a range of practices characterizing a group. This photo illustrates a youth culture known as *goth*, who have adopted the traditional indigenous practices of tattooing and body piercing as a cultural marker of their own, together with hairstyle and dress, as well as a distinctive philosophy and music. Yet culture is more than just the physical distinguishing aspects of a group. It is also a way in which groups derive meaning and attempt to shape the world around them. (*Source:* John Rensten/Stone/Getty Images)

Like agriculture, politics, and urbanization, globalization has had complex effects on culture. Terms such as *world music* and *international television* are a reflection of the sense that the world seems a smaller place now as people everywhere are sharing aspects of the same culture through the widespread influence of the Internet, television, and other media. Yet, as pointed out in Chapter 2, although powerful homogenizing forces are certainly at work, the world has not become so uniform that place no longer matters. With respect to culture, the opposite is true. Place matters more than ever in the negotiation of global forces, as local forces confront globalization and translate it into unique place-specific forms. For example, Box 5.1, "Geography Matters: The Culture of Hip Hop," illustrates

that while hip-hop music has spread globally, it is produced differently in different places.

The place-based interactions occurring between culture and global political and economic forces are at the heart of cultural geography today. **Cultural geography** focuses on the way space, place, and landscape shape culture at the same time that culture shapes space, place, and landscape. As such, cultural geography demarcates two important and interrelated parts. Culture is the ongoing process of producing a shared set of meanings and practices, while geography is the dynamic context within which groups operate to shape those meanings and practices and, in the process, to form an identity and act. Geography in this definition can be a space that is as small as the body and as large as the globe—or indeed as pervasive as the virtual space of the Internet.

An example of the two-way relationship between geography and culture in a non-physical space is the ubiquity of Facebook, Twitter, and other social media. These virtual networks have revolutionized the way we communicate with each other, as friendship groups and circles obscure the boundaries between online and offline domains. Cultural scholars who study them believe that social media are not turning us into "virtual creatures" that exist only in the ether of the Internet but rather into hybrid creatures with a foot in both the virtual and the real worlds. This hybridity enables us to be in more than one place at any one time and to connect to others whom we may never meet in person but with whom we may form significant relationships or merely passing ones. In fact, it may even enable us to be more than one person: you could be a student sitting in class or reading this text and at the same time be a more or less different "online" person that exists only through the notebook or smartphone in front of you. Whatever the degree of overlap between our "real" and "virtual" characters, these virtual interactions change us, perhaps only in small ways, but those ways can and often do add up to something quite substantial. Even virtual spaces are thus venues where cultural identities and practices can emerge and flourish.

FIGURE 5.3 Road accident memorial Originating in Spain and exported to Mexico, these road shrines are known as *descansos*—memorials that mark the place where the soul has left the body in a fatal accident. *Descansos* are ubiquitous in Mexico and Spain and have begun, over the past several decades, to appear in non-Hispanically influenced areas. (*Source:* Paul Souders/Corbis)

Hip hop is a popular manifestation of contemporary cultural practices developed among U.S. big-city and inner-city youth. Characterized to some extent by graffiti art, and earlier by breakdancing, hip hop is understood globally through rap music and a distinctive idiomatic vocabulary. Like most nations, hip hop has its forebears. These include American boxer Muhammad Ali, Jamaican Rastafarian and reggae musician Bob Marley, Black Panther founder Huey Newton, and funksters James Brown and George Clinton. The hip-hop nation has its recognized origins in the Bronx, in New York City. But it also has much older roots in the West African storytelling culture known as *griot*. Hip hop in the United States enlarged upon those origins, and now hip hop is both appreciated and produced on six continents.

Hip hop is a cultural practice that is truly globalized, not because its practitioners have migrated far and wide but because its culture has migrated via telecommunications and the music and film industries. Hip hop has become a cultural phenomenon that exists beyond geography in the music, the clothes, and the language of its practitioners.

Predominantly black and male, hip hop also crosses colour lines and includes women and gays, though the latter two groups have also been the targets of entrenched sexism and homophobia by a wide range of rappers. In addition to the founding fathers mentioned previously, its pioneers include white graffiti artists and Latinos who influenced breakdancing as well as hip-hop DJ (disk jockey) and MC (rapper) styles.

Music is the heart and soul of hip-hop nation and the geography of U.S. hip hop—its hearth area—can be crudely divided into East Coast, West Coast, South Coast, and a region in and around Detroit where white rap-metal groups became popular. But hip hop has broken out of its regional boundaries and transcended national boundaries as well, for example, spreading from the U.S. West Coast region into Vancouver. Today, hip-hop graffiti art can be found in urban areas as distant as Austria and South Africa, and rap music is as popular in the Philippines as it is in Paris.

Hip hop is about how space and place shape the identities of rappers in particular but also African Americans more generally. It demonstrates how race, space, and place come together to produce the contradiction of "home" not only as a locus of roots and the foundation of personal history but also as a site of devaluation vis-à-vis the dominant white society. And as hip-hop cultural theorist Murray Forman argues, "Virtually all of the early descriptions of hip-hop practices identify territory and the public sphere as significant factors, whether in visible artistic expression and appropriation of public space via graffiti or b-boying [breakdancing], the sonic impact of a pounding bass line, or the discursive articulation of urban geography in rap lyrics [and films]."[1] Hip hop, then, is very much about claiming space and place!

The most controversial variant of U.S. hip hop is "gangsta rap," pioneered in the late 1980s by artists like Ice T and groups such as N.W.A. For more than a decade, gangsta rap was one of the most popular and lucrative hip-hop genres in the United States. The element that has drawn the most condemnation from both the left and the right is the lyrics, which can be interpreted as glorifying promiscuity, violence, misogyny (hatred of women), gang culture, rape, drug dealing, and other acts of criminal behaviour both major and minor. Gangsta artists respond, however, by arguing that they merely retell the real inner-city life of young African Americans. Gangsta rap artists include Snoop Dog, Lil Wayne, Dr. Dre, and Jay-Z, all of whom have achieved global success. Nicki Minaj, a more eclectic rapper, frequently incorporates gangsta lyrics as well **(Figure 5.A)**.

Cultural critic bell hooks turns the condemnation of gangsta rap on its head by pointing out that gangsta rap does not exist in a vacuum but is an extension of white, male-dominated, capitalist society.[2] She argues that it is far easier to attack gangsta rap than the culture that produces and reproduces it (the white middle-class that consumes the music). Simultaneously, hooks points out that while we are repelled by the misogyny promoted by gangsta rappers, we fail to see it everywhere else—including within mainstream U.S. culture. For instance, who's to say which is more misogynist, *Mad Men* or Lil Wayne?

[1]M. Forman, "Ain't No Love in the Heart of the City: Hip-Hop, Space, and Place." In M. Forman and M.A. Neal (eds.), *That's the Joint! The Hip Hop Studies Reader*. New York: Routledge, 2004, p. 155.

[2]b. hooks, "Sexism and Misogyny: Who Takes the Rap?" *Z Magazine*, February 1994, pp. 26–29, http://race.eserver.org/misogyny.html, accessed June 29, 2008.

Hip hop is a youth-oriented cultural product that has become widely commercialized in core countries by multinational corporations. However, in other parts of the world, it is a fully homegrown phenomenon. Interestingly, rather than homogenizing local cultures, the global spread of hip hop from the United States outward has tended to create hybrid and synthetic forms of music, adjusting to local cultures and expressing local struggles. What is most consistent about the rap music that is being produced in the periphery is that it has become a focal point for the underprivileged around the world to unite and challenge the oppression of the status quo.

Social struggle seems to be the single strongest thread that weaves together the disparate sounds, cultures, and artists of global hip hop. The British, Pakistani-born, Muslim rapper Aki Nawaz is well-known for his controversial lyrics that attack the hypocrisy and immorality of the West. In Sudan, Emmanuel Jal, a former child soldier in Sudan's People's Liberation Army, uses rap as a way of educating the world about the struggles that oppressed people face in Africa: political injustice, government terror, war, as well as the hope of freedom from these tyrannies.

Indeed, rap may be the most pervasive music among young people the world over. There are Islamic rappers in the United Kingdom and France protesting the racist treatment of Muslims there. The children of Turkish immigrants in Germany rap about racism and the experiences of second-class citizenship there. In Sydney, Australia, the rap group Def Wish Cast composes its rap around an attempt to forge a white, Australian-accented, nationalistic hip-hop culture. There are also revolutionary rhetoric "combat" Italian rappers like Onda Rossa Posse and Assalti Frontali, rappers in mainland China, like Cui Jian, who questions the 1997 handover of Hong Kong, and artists in New Zealand who combine rap, soul, and reggae with traditional Maori music.

At the same time that rap has become global, worldwide sales of its U.S. variant have been dropping. It is not clear whether this signals the decline of rap as a popular music style, whether audiences have simply gotten tired of the U.S.-dominated scene, or whether this music is often downloaded from the Web illegally and the sales therefore reflect only part of its popularity. Whatever the reason or reasons, it is doubtful that rap as a musical form and hip hop as a cultural complex will disappear entirely any time soon.

FIGURE 5.A Rapper Nicki Minaj She was born in Trinidad and Tobago but grew up in Queens, New York, where she began her musical career. She is the most-charted female rapper in the history of the *Billboard* Hot 100. (*Source*: Helga Esteb/Shutterstock)

VIRTUAL GEOGRAPHIES

Beyond the virtual space, Facebook and the Internet are also perfect examples of the two-way relationship between physical space and culture. Consider how our virtual cultural practices can change the arrangement and use of physical space: the more time we spend online shopping or "meeting" with friends, the less busy our stores and streets become, which reduces both our shopping opportunities and our feeling of personal safety. In turn, the changed space now changes our cultural practices: with fewer brick-and-mortar stores to go to and our feeling less safe on the less busy streets, we elect to do even more socializing or shopping online.

We should also mention the increasing privacy concerns arising from our intense use of social media. Their open access means that users as diverse as stalker, employers, marketing companies, and the police can use the sites to gain access to members' personal information. Not surprisingly, because these networking sites allow users from all over the world to express their opinions and engage with other users, the same cultural fault lines that occur in everyday spaces are also drawn within cyberspace, though the connections can be far more extensive and immediate.

Before we proceed any further in our discussion of culture, it is important to discuss a significant difference between our view and that of more traditional cultural geographers. Many introductory human geography texts divide culture into two major categories: folk and popular culture. Specialists see **folk culture** as the traditional practices of small groups, especially rural people with a simple lifestyle (compared with modern, urban people), such as the Mennonites in Canada or the Roma (also known as Gypsies or Travellers) in Europe, who are seen as homogeneous in their belief systems and practices. **Popular culture,** by contrast, is viewed by some cultural geographers as the practices and meaning systems produced by large groups of people whose norms and tastes are often heterogeneous and change frequently, often in response to commercial products. Hip hop would be seen by these theorists as an example of popular culture.

In this text, we do not divide culture into categories. We see culture as an overarching process that is shaped by and shapes politics, the economy, and society and cannot be neatly demarcated by reference to the number of characteristics or degree of homogeneity of its practitioners. We see culture as something that can be enduring as well as newly created, but always influenced by a whole range of interactions as groups maintain, change, or even create traditions from the material of their everyday lives. For us, there is no purpose served in categorically differentiating between hip hop and Hinduism, as both are significant expressions of culture and both are of interest to geographers. (Note, though, how the capitalization of the word *Hinduism* expresses the persistence of traditional evaluations.)

APPLY YOUR KNOWLEDGE In your own words define what cultural geography is and what it tries to do. Once you have done this, identify three aspects of your own culture and the ways that place and space have shaped it. ■

BUILDING CULTURAL COMPLEXES

Geographers are interested in the interactions between people, culture, space, place, and landscape. One of the "founding fathers" of what we now call cultural geography was Carl Sauer, who taught at the University of California, Berkeley, in the early to mid-twentieth century (**Figure 5.4**). Sauer was largely responsible for creating the "Berkeley School" of cultural geography, which rejected environmental determinism as a way of understanding human geography and saw landscape as the unique product of both cultural and physical processes. He was particularly interested in trying to understand how a culture expresses itself in the **cultural landscape**, which we can define as a characteristic and tangible outcome of the complex interactions between a human group—with its own practices, preferences, values, and aspirations—and a natural environment (**Figure 5.5**).

Sauer differentiated the cultural landscape from the natural landscape. He emphasized that the former was a "humanized" version of the latter, such that the activities of humans resulted in an identifiable and understandable alteration of the natural environment. In making such connections, Sauer was influenced by the work of George Perkins Marsh, whose 1874 book, *The Earth as Modified by Human Action,* was one of the first to explore the links between human action and environmental change (see Chapter 4). **Figure 5.6** illustrates Sauer's notion of the differences between a natural and a cultural landscape.

For roughly five decades, scholars working in cultural geography largely followed Sauer's important ideas about the role of culture. His approach to the cultural landscape was ecological, and his many published works reflect his attempts to understand the

FIGURE 5.4 Carl Sauer (1889–1975) Carl Sauer spent his career as a geographer at the University of California, Berkeley. He rejected environmental determinism as a way of understanding human geography and emphasized the uniqueness of landscape through the impact of both cultural and physical processes.

(*Source:* University of California, Berkeley Department of Geography)

FIGURE 5.5 Masai village, Kenya The cultural landscape, as defined by Carl Sauer, reflects the way that cultural and environmental processes come together to create a unique product as they do in the small village pictured here, where herding is the major occupation. The village is enclosed by thorny brambles and branches harvested from the surrounding area. Within the enclosure, the dwellings are arranged in a unique circular pattern, with the animal pens in the middle of the settlement for easy observation by the residents. This cultural landscape reflects the needs of the herder society that created it by modifying the natural landscape. (*Source:* Gavriel Jecan/Terra/Corbis)

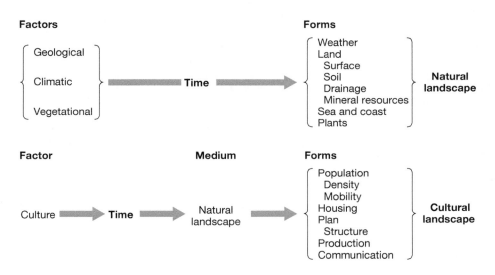

FIGURE 5.6 Sauer's cultural landscape This illustration is a graphic representation of the ways in which the natural landscape is formed and then transformed into a specific cultural landscape. First, physical factors shape the natural landscape. Then people—through culture—reshape the natural landscape into a cultural landscape that meets their needs. This reshaping creates specific cultural forms (such as population distributions, patterns, and housing) that together make up the characteristics of a cultural landscape that is specific to a particular group of people.

(*Source:* Adapted from C. Sauer, "The Morphology of Landscape." In J. Leighly (ed.), *Land and Life: Selections from the Writings of Carl Ortwin Sauer.* Berkeley and Los Angeles: University of California Press, 1963, pp. 315–350.)

myriad ways that humans transform the surface of Earth. In his own words

> The cultural landscape is fashioned from a natural landscape by a cultural group. Culture is the agent, the natural area is the medium, the cultural landscape is the result. Under the influence of a given culture, itself changing through time, the landscape undergoes development, passing through phases, and probably reaching ultimately the end of its cycle of development. With the introduction of a different—that is an alien—culture, a rejuvenation of the cultural landscape sets in, or a new landscape is superimposed on remnants of an older one.[3]

[3]C. Sauer, "The Morphology of Landscape." In J. Leighly (ed.), *Land and Life: Selections from the Writings of Carl Ortwin Sauer.* Berkeley, CA: University of California Press, 1964, pp. 315–350.

In Europe, geographers interested in human interactions with the landscape developed slightly different approaches. For example, in Great Britain the approach to understanding the human imprint on the landscape was termed *historical geography*, while in France it was conceptualized as *genre de vie*. **Historical geography,** very simply defined, is the geography of the past. Its most famous practitioner was Henry Clifford Darby (1909–1992), who attempted to understand how past geographies changed, or evolved, into more recent geographies. In France, Paul Vidal de La Blache (1845–1919) developed an approach to cultural geography that centred on the livelihood practices of a group that were seen to shape physical, social, and psychological bonds. Called ***genres de vie*** (or "ways of living"), it refers to a functionally organized way of life characteristic of a particular culture group **(Figure 5.7)**. This approach emphasizes the need to study small, homogeneous areas to uncover the close relationships that exist between people and their immediate surroundings. What unifies

FIGURE 5.7 Alpine pasture dairy farming as a *genre de vie* These images show a typical alpine way of life and a landscape shaped by so-called seasonal pasturing. In fall and spring, cows graze on individually owned low-altitude pastures in the valley (a). In late spring, the animals are moved to a communal summer pasture on high-altitude alpine meadows (b). All summer long, their milk is rendered into cheese on site (c). At the end of the summer, when the cows return to their owners' farms, the cheese is transported down to the valley and sold. While the valley pastures are empty over the summer months, farmers produce hay on them, which they store for the winter in the dispersed hay barns. The resulting landscape is a functional unit that is common across the Alps, and it reflects the way of life—the *genre de vie*—of a population that bases its livelihood on alpine pasture dairy production. Settlements, land tenure, and infrastructure all reflect the requirements and opportunities of this way of life. (*Source:* M. Imort)

all of these approaches is that they place the cultural landscape at the heart of their study of human–environment interactions. They differ, however, in the emphasis they place on different landscape components and the importance of the role they assign to the physical environment.

Cultural Traits

Geographers' interest in culture as a geographical factor ranges from single attributes to complex systems. One simple aspect of culture of interest to geographers is the idea of special traits, which include such things as distinctive styles of dress, dietary habits, and styles of architecture (**Figure 5.8**). A **cultural trait** is a single aspect of the complex of routine practices that constitute a particular cultural group. For example, canon law for Catholics requires fasting during the holy season of Lent. This practice may be said to be a cultural trait of Catholic people. Geographers are interested in learning how cultural traits come together to form larger frameworks for living in the world. Ultimately, though, cultural traits are not necessarily unique to one group, and understanding them is only one aspect of the complexity of culture. For instance, there are a number of

cultural groups, including Hindus, Muslims, and Jews, who avoid pork in their diet (**Figure 5.9**).

Many cultures also recognize the passage from childhood into adulthood with a celebration or ceremony. Called **rites of passage,** these are acts, customs, practices, or procedures that recognize key transitions in human life—birth, menstruation, and other markers of adulthood such as sexual awakening and marriage. Such rites of passage are not uncommon among many of the world's cultures. Some non-Western cultures, for example, send adolescent boys away from the village to experience an ordeal—ritual scarring or circumcision, for example—or to meditate in extended isolation on the new roles they must assume as adults (**Figure 5.10**).

Cultural Complexes and Regions

In Roman Catholicism, the passage of boys and girls into adulthood, traditionally around the age of 12, is celebrated by confirmation. In this religious ceremony, the confirmed chooses a new name to mark this important spiritual transition. Jews mark the passage of adolescent boys and girls into adulthood with separate religious ceremonies: a *bar mitzvah* for boys and a *bat mitzvah* for

FIGURE 5.8 Tuareg men in Niger The Tuareg are also known as the Blue Men of the Sahara because of their distinctive indigo blue robes and veils. Tuareg women do not wear veils but men do when they reach maturity. (*Source:* Paul Harris/John Warburton-Lee Photography/Alamy)

FIGURE 5.9 Halal butcher For Muslims, there is a prescribed method of slaughtering all animals except for fish and most sea life. (Prohibited flesh includes pork, carnivorous animals, and birds of prey.) Flesh that is butchered in the prescribed manner is considered *halal* or "permissible" to eat. (*Source:* Alex Segre/Alamy)

FIGURE 5.10 A coming-of-age ceremony, South Korea The coming-of-age ceremony for girls in South Korea is held every May 15 in Seoul. There, young women who are turning 20 participate in dances and a citywide celebration that is meant to remind them of the responsibilities they face as adults. In South Korea, people who turn 60 are also ritually celebrated. This ritual is not so much a coming-of-age celebration as it is a coming-*to*-an-age celebration. Called *hwan-gap*, this celebration is considered one of the larger celebrations in a person's life. It is significant because it marks the day on which an individual has completed a full zodiacal cycle. But, more importantly, it is also celebrated, because to live to be 60 is seen as a great accomplishment. In the past, most people in South Korea died before their 60th birthday. (*Source:* Shin Young-kyun/Yonhap/AP Images)

girls. Although marking the passage into adulthood is a trait of both religious groups, they do not exhibit the trait in exactly the same way. This and other traits always occur in combination. The combination of traits characteristic of a particular group is known as a **cultural complex.** The avoidance of pork, the celebration of *bar* and *bat mitzvahs,* and other dietary, religious, and social practices constitute the cultural complex of Judaism, although it is important to note that even within the cultural complex of Judaism, variation exists among regions and sects.

Another concept key to traditional approaches in cultural geography is the cultural region. Although a cultural region may be quite extensive or very narrowly described and even discontinuous in its extension, it is the area within which a particular cultural system prevails. A **cultural region** is an area where certain cultural practices, beliefs, or values are practised by more or less the majority of the inhabitants.

Illustrations of cultural regions abound in Canada. For example, parts of New Brunswick, Nova Scotia, and Prince Edward Island compose the Acadian cultural region (**Figure 5.11**). The population of this cultural region is made up mainly of a long-settled community of French-speaking, Roman Catholic people who have a series of distinct cultural traits in connection with music, folk architecture, and language.

To take another example, the Manitoba lowlands were settled by hundreds of thousands of immigrants from continental Europe in the years before 1914. The settlers' adherence to an agricultural way of life and to their Central European traditions serves to define this area as a cultural region. At a finer scale of analysis, this region is, in fact, made up of a great variety of subregions—each the home of a distinctive culture, which gives a specific flavour to a particular cluster of communities. For instance, when Mennonites came to the area from southern Russia in the 1870s, they created very distinctive agricultural landscapes around Winkler, Altona, and Steinbach, in which they recreated a European-style nucleated village form.

On the other hand, cultural regions can also be quite extensive. For example, the state of Utah in the U.S. is considered to be a Mormon cultural region because the population of the state is dominated by people who practise the Mormon religion and presumably adhere to its beliefs and values. **Figure 5.12** illustrates the extent of the Mormon cultural region in the overall religious geography of the United States, a country with a remarkable religious diversity. (See also Figure 1.25.)

We can use the work of Peter Ennals and Deryck Holdsworth to show how a single cultural trait, such as architecture, can contribute to identifying cultural regions (**Figure 5.13**). In the areas of Canada first occupied by Europeans, settlers built houses that were very similar in style and building technique to those found in the areas of Europe from which they had come. In Newfoundland and Labrador, versions of English and Irish cottages were erected. In Acadia and Quebec, houses were built that copied the regional patterns found in France at the time.

Obviously, having no time to experiment and being heavily conditioned by their own images of what a house should look like, these early settlers simply replicated the styles they knew. In this way, at least, Canada was "a simplification of Europe overseas," as some Canadian cultural geographers have described it. Certainly, as we shall see in Chapter 6, these settlers were engaged in their own version of "place making" and recreating in this country a world they knew.

From about 1850, however, another element was added to the mix—that of fashion. By then, many Canadian settlers had become a little more prosperous and could afford to rebuild their houses in the styles affected by new ideals of domestic privacy and by the "refined" architecture of the neo-Georgian houses that Canada's elite were building for themselves. In this way, Ennals and Holdsworth argue, earlier folk styles were replaced by what they call vernacular architecture. This everyday, or common, architecture, developed in Canada, maintains a set of distinct regional styles, ranging from the exuberance of the porches of Lunenburg, Nova Scotia, to the "eyebrow" designs of the nineteenth-century Ontario farmhouse with its distinctive dormer window. The latter has become so quintessentially Ontarian that its design elements are echoed in many contemporary subdivisions (**Figure 5.14**).

Increased immigration and growing urbanization in the nineteenth century did little to erode these patterns. In fact, these phenomena added their own distinctive contributions, because the need to adapt vernacular styles to the high-density demands of Canada's cities was met in different ways. In Montreal, for example, the duplex and triplex styles were developed, designs almost unique in North America, possibly inspired by the city's Scottish immigrants with their memories of Glaswegian tenement life. In Toronto, the classic farmhouse morphed into the gothic row house. During early twentieth-century expansion in Vancouver, the bungalow, perhaps inspired by immigrants from California, was the leading suburban form of housing.

FIGURE 5.11 The Acadian cultural region The Acadian region of Canada preserves its cultural heritage through many visual reminders, as this picture of the Acadian flag at Grand Pré illustrates. The Acadian flag consists of the French *tricolore* flag with a gold star, representing the *Stella Maris* (Star of the Sea). The national park at Grand Pré, Nova Scotia, is a memorial to the deportation of the Acadians by the British Crown in 1755.

(*Source:* Courtesy of Alan E. Nash)

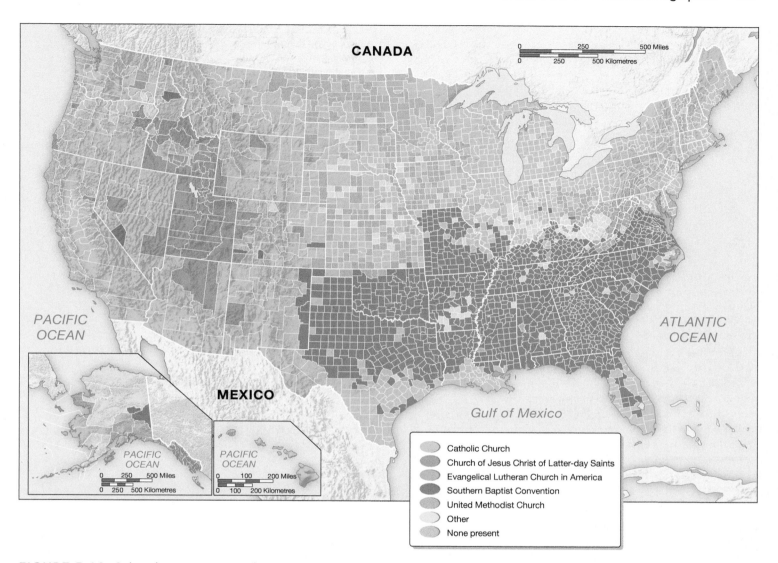

FIGURE 5.12 Cultural systems: U.S. religious population distribution by county, 2000 This map shows the majority religion by county for the United States and illustrates the concept of cultural regions based on religion. However, at such a scale, it would be erroneous to assume too much homogeneity within these regions. In each aggregation of counties or region, there are likely to be substantial variations in belief systems and practices at the local level. Note that the Mormon religion is labelled "Church of Jesus Christ of Latter-day Saints." (*Source: Adapted from D. E. Jones, S. Doty, C. Grammich, J. E. Horsch, R. Houseal, M. Lynn, J. P. Marcum, K. M. Sanchagrin, and R. H. Taylor, Religious Congregations and Membership in the United States 2000: An Enumeration by Region, State and County Based on Data Reported for 149 Religious Bodies. Nashville, TN: Glenmary Research Center, 2000, p. 562.)*

Meanwhile, on the Prairies, history was repeating itself with new waves of immigration. By the late nineteenth century, settlers from Central Europe were building farmhouses in the styles of their homelands. From Verigin, Saskatchewan, to Dauphin, Manitoba, the farm architecture of Ukraine, Poland, and Russia was adopted as the design for barns, houses, and churches. Prosperity, when it occurred, was marked this time by the purchase of plans or prefabricated houses from mail-order companies. The vernacular architecture of the Prairies thus arose from a literally off-the-shelf, central Canadian design made in Toronto that could be seen in countless small towns across the West.

A preference for rational planning and the lure of profit from mass production erased regional differences in new construction styles during the second half of the twentieth century. However, postmodernism's rejection of uniformity (see Chapter 6) and the real estate industry's realization that "difference sells" have rekindled interest in Canadian regional patterns of vernacular architecture in recent times.

APPLY YOUR KNOWLEDGE Identify two traits that are characteristic of the cultural group to which you belong. Could the traits be considered characteristic of the country or region in which you live? Describe the relationship between trait and region or explain why there is none. ∎

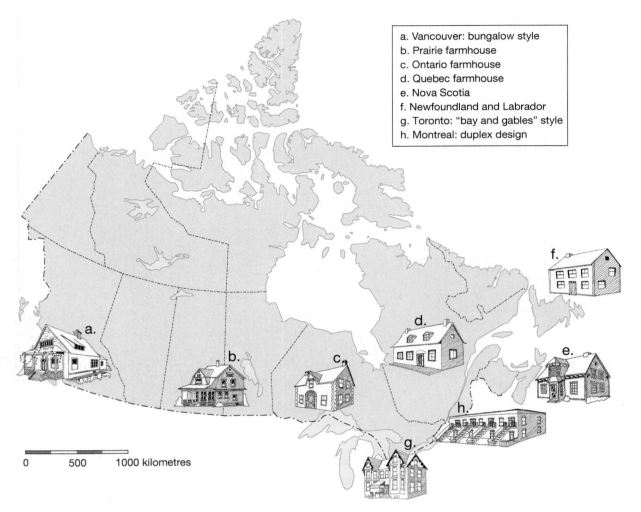

a. Vancouver: bungalow style
b. Prairie farmhouse
c. Ontario farmhouse
d. Quebec farmhouse
e. Nova Scotia
f. Newfoundland and Labrador
g. Toronto: "bay and gables" style
h. Montreal: duplex design

0   500   1000 kilometres

FIGURE 5.13 Vernacular architectural regions in Canada Geographers have shown that architectural style is an important characteristic of the cultural region and that differences in architecture are one way of distinguishing different cultural regions. This map shows the major types of *vernacular* (that is, everyday) residential architecture found in Canada at the end of the nineteenth century. The pattern reflects the traditional, or folk, architectural styles of Canada's major European colonizers, adapted to this country's environment and modified over time as more recent ideas about fashionable style diffused across Canada. (*Sources:* Based on redrawings by Karine Arakelian. House types a and c–f based on Peter Ennals and Deryck W. Holdsworth, "The Look of Domestic Building, 1891." In William Dean et al., *Concise Historical Atlas of Canada.* Toronto: University of Toronto Press, 1998, Plate 30. House types b, g, and h from Peter Ennals and Deryck W. Holdsworth, *Homeplace: The Making of the Canadian Dwelling over Three Centuries.* Toronto: University of Toronto Press, 1998, pp. 195–196, 210.)

FIGURE 5.14 The present preserves the past These houses in a new Orangeville, Ontario, subdivision echo architectural elements from earlier styles.

(*Source:* Courtesy of Alan E. Nash)

CULTURAL SYSTEMS

Broader than the cultural complex concept is the cultural system, a collection of interacting components that, taken together, shape a group's collective identity. A **cultural system** includes traits, territorial affiliation, and shared history, as well as other, more complex elements, such as language and religion. In a cultural system it is possible for internal variations to exist in particular elements at the same time that broader similarities lend coherence. For example, Christianity unites all Protestant and Catholic faith traditions, yet the practices of particular denominations—Lutherans, Anglicans, and Quakers, etc.—vary. And while Mexicans, Bolivians, Cubans, and Chileans exhibit variations in pronunciation, pitch, stress, and other aspects of vocal expression, they all speak Spanish. This means they share a key element of a cultural system (which, for these nationalities, also includes Roman Catholicism and a Spanish colonial heritage).

Geography and Religion

Two key components of a cultural system for most of the world's people are religion and language. **Religion** is a belief system and a set of practices that recognize the existence of a power higher than humankind. Although religious affiliation is on the decline in some parts of the world's core regions, it still acts as a powerful shaper of daily life, from eating habits and dress codes to coming-of-age rituals and death ceremonies, holiday celebrations, and family practices, in both the core and the periphery. And, like language, religious beliefs and practices change as new interpretations are advanced or new spiritual influences are adopted.

The most important influence on religious change has been conversion from one set of beliefs to another. From the Arab invasions following Muhammad's death in 632, to the Christian Crusades of the Middle Ages and the onset of globalization in the fifteenth century, religious missionizing—propagandizing and persuasion—as well as forceful and sometimes violent conversion have been key elements in changing geographies of religion. Especially in the 500 years since the onset of the Columbian Exchange (Chapter 4), conversion of all sorts has escalated throughout the globe. Since 1492, traditional religions have become dramatically dislocated from their sites of origin not only through missionizing and conversion but also by way of diaspora and emigration. Whereas missionizing and conversion are deliberate efforts to change the religious views of a person (or an entire people), diaspora and emigration involve the involuntary and voluntary movement of persons who bring their religious beliefs and practices to their new locales.

Diaspora is the spatial dispersion of a previously homogeneous group. The processes of global political and economic change that led to the massive movement of the world's populations over the past five centuries have also meant the dislodging and spread of the world's many religions from their traditional sites of practice. Religious practices have become so spatially mixed that it is a challenge to present a map of the contemporary global distribution of religion that reveals more than it obscures. This is because the globe is too gross a level of resolution to portray the wide variation that exists among and within religious practices. **Figure 5.15** identifies the contemporary distribution of what religious scholars consider to be the world's major religions because they contain the largest number of practitioners. As with other global representations, the map is useful in that it helps present a generalized picture.

Figure 5.16 identifies the source areas of four of the world's major religions and their diffusion from those sites over time. The map illustrates how the world's major religions originated and diffused from two fairly small areas of the globe. The first, where Hinduism and Buddhism (as well as Sikhism) originated, is an

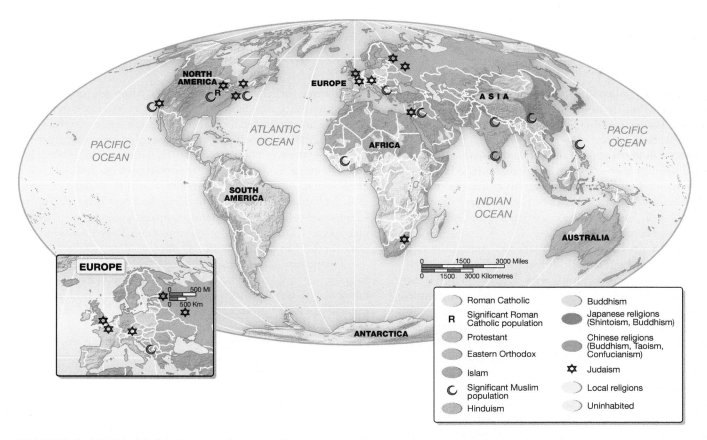

FIGURE 5.15 World distribution of major religions Most of the world's peoples are members of these religions. Not evident on this map are the local variations in practices, as well as the many smaller religions that are practised worldwide. Although known in the West primarily as philosophies, Taoism and Confucianism both also developed religious traditions and so are included on this map.

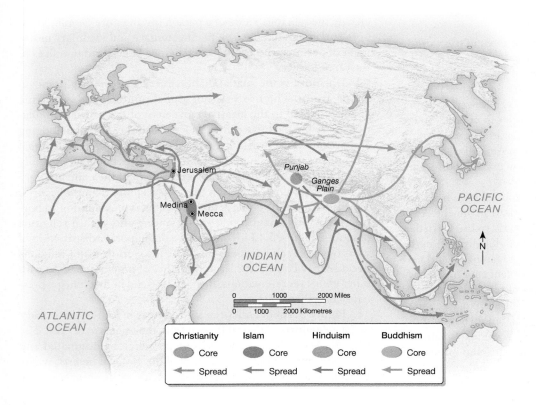

FIGURE 5.16 Origin areas and diffusion of four major religions The world's major religions originated in a fairly small region of the world. Judaism and Christianity began in present-day Israel and Jordan. Islam emerged from western Arabia. Buddhism originated in India, and Hinduism in the Indus region of Pakistan. The source areas of the world's major religions are also the cultural hearth areas of agriculture, urbanization, and other key aspects of human development.

area of lowlands in the subcontinent of India drained by the Indus and Ganges rivers (Punjab on the map). The second area, where Christianity and Islam (as well as Judaism) originated, is in the deserts of the Middle East.

Religious beliefs are organized and codified, often based on the teachings and writings of one or more founders. And it is important to recognize that each of the world's religions contain all sorts of variation. For example, Christians may be Catholics or Protestants, and even within these large groups there exists a great deal of variation. The same is true for all religions.

Hinduism emerged about 4000 years ago among the peoples of the Indo-Gangetic Plain. Buddhism and Sikhism evolved from Hinduism as reform religions, with Buddhism appearing around 500 B.C.E. and Sikhism developing in the fifteenth century. Buddhism dispersed to other parts of India and was carried by missionaries and traders to China (100 B.C.E. to 200 C.E.), Korea and Japan (300–500 C.E.), Southeast Asia (400–600 C.E.), Tibet (700 C.E.), and Mongolia (1500 C.E.). Not surprisingly, as Buddhism spread, it developed many different regional forms, such that Tibetan Buddhism is distinct from Japanese Buddhism.

Christianity, Islam, and Judaism all developed among the Semitic peoples of the deserts of the Middle East. And like the Indo-Gangetic religions, these three religions are related. Judaism originated about 4000 years ago, Christianity about 2000 years ago, and Islam about 1300 years ago. Judaism developed out of the cultures and beliefs of Bronze Age peoples and was the first monotheistic (belief in one God) religion. Although Judaism is the oldest monotheistic religion, and one that spread widely and rapidly, it is numerically small because it does not seek converts.

Christianity developed in present-day Israel and Jordan and is now the world's largest religion, with approximately 2 billion adherents. Early Christianity spread through Europe largely because of missionary efforts by monks, and monasteries were especially important as hubs of diffusion in the larger network. During later periods of European expansion, Spanish colonizers, in particular, spread Christianity by forced conversion, to save souls but also often for the purposes of political control.

Islam is an Arabic term that means "submission," specifically submission to God's will. A **Muslim** is a member of that community of believers, whose duty is obedience and submission to the will of God. The Islamic world includes very different societies and regions, from Southeast Asia to Africa. Muslims comprise over 85 percent of the populations of Afghanistan, Algeria, Bangladesh, Egypt, Indonesia, Iran, Iraq, Jordan, Pakistan, Saudi Arabia, Senegal, Tunisia, Turkey, and most of the independent republics of Central Asia and the Caucasus (including Azerbaijan, Tajikistan, Turkmenistan, and Uzbekistan). In Albania, Chad, Ethiopia, and Nigeria, Muslims make up 50 to 85 percent of the population. In India, Burma (Myanmar), Cambodia, China, Greece, Slovenia, Thailand, and the Philippines, significant Muslim minorities exist. After Christianity, Islam possesses the next largest number of adherents worldwide—about 1.5 billion.

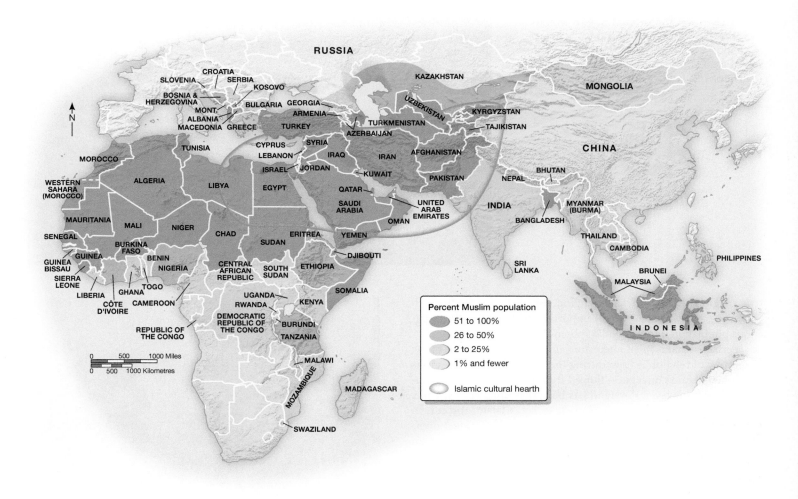

FIGURE 5.17 Muslim world Like the Spanish colonial effort, Muslim colonization was accompanied by the diffusion of the colonizers' religion. The distribution of Islam in Africa, Southeast Asia, and South Asia that we see today testifies to the broad reach of Muslim cultural, colonial, and trade activities. But the heart of the Muslim culture remains the Middle East, its original cultural hearth. (*Source:* Adapted from D. Hiro, *Holy Wars.* London: Routledge, 1989.)

The map in **Figure 5.17** shows the relative distribution of Muslims throughout Europe, Africa, and Asia as well as the heartland of Islamic religious practice.

While these are the world's major religions, many others figure prominently in the cultural lives of people around the world. Among them are Confucianism, Taoism, Shintoism, Mormonism, Zoroastrianism, and Jansenism, as well as Voodoo, Rastafarianism, and animism. The point is that faith, a trusting belief in a transcendent reality or a supreme being, is a profoundly powerful force in human life. It can guide people's actions and attitudes and shape the worlds in which they live.

Religion and Globalization

Faith is a significant element of globalization. As disparate belief systems come into contact, in some cases causing tension and even violent conflict, new religions are introduced among populations who are adherents of a different one. An excellent illustration of the global forces behind the changing geography of religious faith is the Columbian contact with the New World. Before Columbus and later Europeans reached the continents of North and South America, the people living there practised, for the most part, various forms of animism and related rituals. They viewed themselves holistically, as one part of the wider world of animate and inanimate nature. Shamanism, in which spiritually gifted individuals are believed to possess the power to control preternatural forces, is one important aspect of the belief system that existed among Native American populations at the time of European contact.

European contact with the New World was, from the beginning, accompanied by Christian missionizing efforts directed at changing the belief systems of the Aboriginal peoples and converting them to what the missionizers believed to be "the one

FIGURE 5.18 Mission at Sainte-Marie-Among-the-Hurons This historically exact recreation was built in the 1960s on the actual site of a seventeenth-century Jesuit mission to the Hurons, in what is now Midland, Ontario. (*Source:* Courtesy of Alan E. Nash)

true religion" (**Figure 5.18**). Religion, especially for the Spanish colonizing agents, was especially important in integrating the indigenous population into the feudal system (**Figure 5.19**).

Perhaps what is most interesting about the present state of the geography of religion is how, during the colonial period, religious missionizing and conversion flowed from the core to the periphery. Recently, however, the trend has been reversing. For example, the fastest-growing religion in Canada today is Islam, and it is in the core countries where Buddhism is making the greatest numbers of converts. Not surprising, many recent efforts of the Roman Catholic church are directed at dissuading conversion to other belief systems, such as Protestant evangelicalism in the United States and Latin America. In fact, the election of the first South American pope, Francis, is seen by many observers as an element of that strategy: if present population growth trends continue, the bulk of the world's Roman Catholics will be located in Latin America. Meanwhile, the Dalai Lama promotes conversion to Buddhism by carrying its message to new places, especially in the core. At the same time, he advocates sovereignty for Tibet, a region once independent but currently controlled by China (**Figure 5.20**).

FIGURE 5.19 Lima Cathedral, Peru Religious affirmation and missionizing were important motivators for the Spanish colonizers. Conquistador Pizarro himself laid the first stone of Lima Cathedral in 1535. (*Source:* M. Imort)

FIGURE 5.20 Tibetan monks protest in Nepal China's refusal to acknowledge an independent Tibet has sent the fourteenth Dalai Lama on numerous international tours to broadcast the plight of Tibetans, who are experiencing extreme persecution. Pictured here are Tibetan monks in exile in Nepal protesting outside the Chinese embassy to mark the anniversary of the failed 1959 uprising against China and to demand that China grant sovereignty to Tibet. (*Source:* Brian Sokol/Getty Images)

FIGURE 5.21 Megachurch, South Barrington, Illinois Willow Creek Community Church is typical of the megachurch phenomenon that has come to characterize certain evangelical Christian sects in many places across the United States. A Sunday service at Willow Creek often draws 20 000 or more. According to a recent survey, there are 1200 Protestant churches that claim more than 2000 weekly worship attendees in the United States. There are megachurches in 45 out of 50 states; Texas has 174 (14 percent), California has 169 (13.7 percent), Florida 83 (6.7 percent), and Georgia 64 (5.2 percent). Houston and Dallas alone host 56 megachurches, or 4.5 percent of the total. The following states do not have megachurches: Maine, New Hampshire, Rhode Island, South Dakota, Vermont, Wyoming. (*Source:* John Gress/Reuters/Corbis)

One other impact of globalization upon religious change occurs through the electronic media. The rise of television evangelism, or *televangelism*—especially in the United States—has contributed to the conversion of large numbers of people to Christian fundamentalism, which is a term popularly used to describe strict adherence to Christian doctrines based on a literal interpretation of the Bible. Today, Christian fundamentalism is strong and growing stronger, with a trend toward megachurches as popular sites of worship in the United States **(Figure 5.21)**. Christian televangelism is also widespread in other countries, including Brazil, Argentina, and Chile, as well as India, Kenya, and China. (Meanwhile, Muslim "televangelism" is just beginning to emerge.)

APPLY YOUR KNOWLEDGE Review the information about the distribution of U.S. megachurches given in Figure 5.21 and cross-reference it with the map in Figure 5.12. Now obtain population numbers for each of the named states. On the basis of this enlarged information, re-evaluate the geographical distribution of megachurches. Has your impression changed? What other geographical information might be important to take into consideration? ■

The Geography of Canada's Religions

The geography of Canada's religions is—as you might expect—a product of this country's history of colonialism and recent immigration. Following European contact, the original pattern of Aboriginal faiths and belief systems found across Canada was slowly replaced by the dominant Christian faiths of the French and British colonizing powers. For instance, New France (Quebec and Acadia) was peopled by settlers who brought the Roman Catholic faith of France with them. Conversely, substantial parts of Newfoundland and Labrador were settled by Protestant fishing people from England. When Britain gained control of Canada after 1760, immigrants from Britain and the United States brought with them into Ontario the Protestant denominations of Christianity that they practised **(Figure 5.22)**.

FIGURE 5.22 Protestant religion in Canada Established by dissident Quakers in Ontario in the early nineteenth century, the small community of Sharon still retains the original Quaker meeting house constructed in what was believed to be the image of Solomon's Temple. (*Source:* Courtesy of Alan E. Nash)

TABLE 5-1 Canada's Religions by Affiliation Numbers for Major Religious Denominations, 1991 to 2011

Religious Affiliation	2011	%	2001	%	1991	%	% Change 1991–2011
Roman Catholic	12 728 885	38.7	12 793 125	43.2	12 203 625	45.2	−14.4
Protestant*	5 225 865*	15.9*	8 105 640*	27.3*	8 798 730*	32.6*	−51.2
Christian Orthodox	550 690	1.7	479 620	1.6	387 395	1.4	21.4
Muslim	1 053 945	3.2	579 640	2.0	253 265	0.9	355.5
Jewish	329 500	1.0	329 995	1.1	318 185	1.2	−16.6
Buddhist	366 830	1.1	300 345	1.0	163 415	0.6	183.3
Hindu	497 960	1.5	297 200	1.0	157 015	0.6	250.0
Sikh	454 965	1.5	278 415	0.9	147 440	0.5	300.0
No religion	7 850 605	23.9	4 796 325	16.2	3 333 245	12.3	194.3

*Because this reporting category changed in the 2011 census, the 1991 and 2001 numbers were recalculated using the new 2011 category.
(Source: Compiled from Statistics Canada data. Census data for 2011 is from Statistics Canada's *The Daily*, 8 May, 2013.)

The legacy of this history can be seen to this day at the national level (**Table 5-1**) as well as on the provincial level: census data from 2011 show that in Newfoundland and Labrador, 35.8 percent of people record their religious affiliation as Roman Catholic, while in Quebec that number is 74.6 percent. In Ontario, we find that 31.4 percent are Roman Catholics and 21 percent Protestants. Since the inception of the non-discriminatory immigration policy in 1967, people from a wide variety of religious backgrounds have immigrated to Canada, and many of them have settled in Ontario, changing the map of religious affiliation considerably. Thus, we now find that non-Christian religions now make up more than 12 percent of Ontario's population. Ontario is home to almost three-quarters of Canada's Hindu population, and more than half of Canada's Muslim population. We should also note that 23.1 percent of Ontarians record no religious affiliation. In broad terms, the Roman Catholic and Protestant denominations of Christianity still dominate in most parts of the country, except for British Columbia,

where those individuals expressing no religious affiliation form the largest single group in the population. In fact, in Vancouver, 41.5 percent of the population are not affiliated with any religion.

As Table 5-1 shows, immigration has greatly changed the reported religious affiliations of Canadians. Over the past two decades, Muslims and Sikhs have tripled their share among the population, while Buddhists and Hindus have doubled (**Figure 5.23**). At the same time, however, the share of persons reporting no religious affiliation has doubled as well.

Geography and Language

Languages are another aspect of cultural systems that interest geographers. Language is an important focus for study because it is a central aspect of cultural identity. Without language, cultural accomplishments could not be transmitted from one generation to the next. And language itself reflects the ways that different groups

FIGURE 5.23 Sikh temple, Surrey, **British Columbia** Almost half of Canada's Sikh population live in British Columbia, while another 40 percent live in Ontario.

(*Source:* Courtesy of Alan E. Nash)

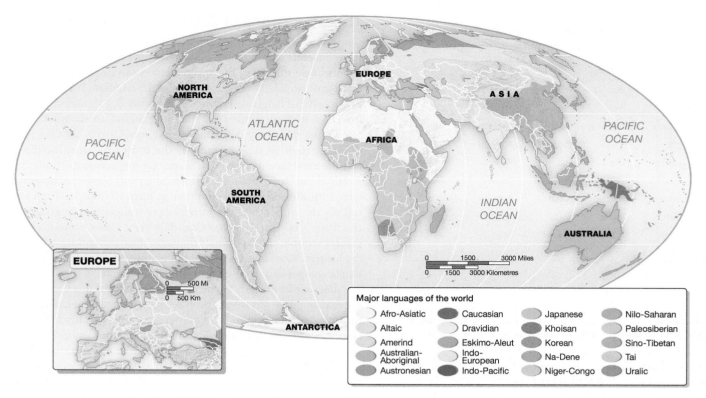

FIGURE 5.24 World distribution of major languages and major language families Classifying languages by family and mapping their occurrence across the globe provide insights about human geography. For example, we may discover interesting cultural linkages between seemingly disparate cultures widely separated in space and time. We may also begin to understand something about the nature of population movements across broad expanses of time and space. Note that the map shows the situation before European expansion and globalization carried the languages of the colonizers around the world. The present global distribution of Indo-European languages is much greater than shown here. (*Source:* Adapted from E. F. Bergman, *Human Geography: Cultures, Connections, and Landscapes.* Upper Saddle River, NJ: Prentice Hall, 1994; Western Hemisphere after J. H. Greenberg, *Language in the Americas.* Stanford, CA: Stanford University Press, 1987; Eastern Hemisphere after D. Crystal, *The Cambridge Encyclopedia of Language.* Cambridge: Cambridge University Press, 1997.)

regard and interpret the world around them. Finally, the distribution and diffusion of languages tell much about the changing history of human geography, European expansion, and the impact of globalization on culture. Before looking more closely at the geography of language and the impact of globalization on the changing distribution of languages, it is necessary to become familiar with some basic vocabulary.

Language is a way of communicating ideas or feelings by means of a conventionalized system of signs, gestures, marks, or articulate vocal sounds. Communication is symbolic, based on commonly understood meanings of signs or sounds. Within standard languages (also known as official languages because they are maintained by offices of government such as schools and the courts), regional variations, known as **dialects,** exist. Dialects feature differences in pronunciation, grammar, and vocabulary that are place-based in nature.

For the purposes of classification, languages are grouped into families, branches, and groups. A **language family** is a collection of individual languages believed to be related in their prehistoric origin. About 50 percent of the world's people speak a language that is in the Indo-European family. A **language branch** is a collection of languages that possesses a definite common origin but has split into

individual languages. A **language group** is a collection of several individual languages that is part of a language branch, shares a common origin in the recent past, and has relatively similar grammar and vocabulary. For instance, Spanish, French, Portuguese, Italian, Romanian, and Catalan are a language *group,* classified under the Romance *branch* as part of the Indo-European language *family.*

Traditional approaches in cultural geography have identified the source areas of the world's languages and the paths of diffusion of those languages from their places of origin. Carl Sauer identified the origins of certain cultural practices with the label "cultural hearth." (See Chapter 2.) **Cultural hearths** are the geographic origins or sources of innovations, ideas, or ideologies. Language hearths are a subset of cultural hearths; they are the source areas of languages. **Figure 5.24** shows the distribution of the world's major languages and language families.

Language is a sophisticated cultural creation that retains a memory of its past within its present form. In the late eighteenth century, scholars recognized the close similarities between Sanskrit (an extinct East Indian language) and many European languages, both extinct (such as Latin) and extant (such as English or French). **Table 5-2** illustrates the often astonishing similarities in vocabulary among these languages.

TABLE 5-2 Vocabulary Comparisons between Some Indo-European and Non–Indo-European Languages

English	French	Greek	Sanskrit	P-I-E[†]	Japanese
two	deux	duo	dva	*duwo	ni
three	trois	treis	tryas	*treyes	san
four	quatre	tettares	catvaras	*kwetwores	yon
ten	dix	deka	dasa	*dekmt	jyu
cow [ox]	vache	bous	gauh	*kwou	usi
field	champ	agros	ajras	*agras	hatake
water	eau	hudor	udan	*wedor	mizu
father	père	pater	pita	*pater	chichi
god	dieu	theos	devas	*dyeus	kami
wheel	roue	roda	ratha	*roto	sharing

[†]P-I-E: Proto-Indo-European
*denotes a reconstructed word in P-I-E
The Proto-Indo-European language may have originated about 6000 years ago somewhere between the Black Sea and the Caspian Sea, or in Anatolian Turkey. Its vocabulary (here shown by the use of an asterisk to denote a reconstructed word) has been reconstructed by linguistic experts on the basis of correspondences between daughter languages (the name given to languages that are descended from a common original) and known rules of linguistic change over time. P-I-E is believed to be the ancestor of extinct languages (such as Latin and Sanskrit) and many languages of the Indo-European family (such as English, French, and Hindi) spoken in the world today. The difference between these languages and those from other language families can be seen in the comparison with Japanese.

(*Sources:* J.P. Mallory, *In Search of the Indo-Europeans.* London: Thames and Hudson, 1989; Colin Renfrew, *Archaeology and Language: The Puzzle of Indo-European Origins.* London: Cape, 1987; T.V. Gamkrelidze and V.V. Ivanov, "The Early History of Indo-European Languages," *Scientific American*, March 1990, pp. 110–16; and P. Tieme, "The Indo-European Language," *Scientific American*, October 1958, pp. 63–74.)

Scholars assert that all of these languages are related to one another and belong to the "Indo-European" language family (Figure 5.24) and that they have all descended from a now lost language called "Proto-Indo-European." The passage of time and the migration of peoples, who then lost contact with one another, have been sufficient to change Proto-Indo-European into the many languages of the Indo-European language family we hear today.

We do not know exactly where the Proto-Indo-European language had its cultural hearth; we do know, however, that it spread across almost all of Europe, missing only four areas. (See Figure 5.24.) Finnish, Estonian, and Hungarian are members of the Uralic language family (a non-Indo-European language believed to have originated in the northern Urals around 6000 B.C.E.). By contrast, the Basque language of northeastern Spain and southwest France is an **isolate,** a language that has no known relationship with any other language and cannot be assigned to any language family. We can gain an impression of how different Basque is from its vocabulary for the numerals 1 through 10, which are *bat, bi, hiru, lau, bost, sei, zazpi, zortzi, beheratzi,* and *hamar.* The linguistic distinctiveness of the Basques is mirrored by the fact that they are genetically distinct from all other Europeans. One intriguing possibility is that they are descended from a pre-Neolithic people who were not completely absorbed by a westward-moving, Indo-European–speaking Neolithic people.

The Geography of Canada's Languages

Let us now consider Canada. Historical linguists speculate that the thousands of indigenous languages that probably existed in the Americas on the eve of European contact can be divided into just three groups. These are known as the Amerindian, Na-Dene, and Eskimo-Aleut language families (see Figure 5.24), and languages from each of these families can still be found in Canada today.

Of the three language families, Eskimo-Aleut is both the least differentiated (its only member is the Inuit language, Inuktitut) and the most recent arrival in Canada, moving across the Canadian Arctic about 4000 years ago. Amerindian and Na-Dene, however, were introduced into this continent at least 10 000 years ago and rapidly developed into the hundreds of indigenous languages of the Americas. The fact that Canada's West Coast contains a far greater number of Aboriginal languages than either the Prairies or the Eastern Woodlands is probably a result of the much longer time that languages had to develop in British Columbia.

Because language is an intrinsic part of culture, it is not surprising that language has always been seen as an important characteristic of the cultural region. Many groups strongly identify with their language and use it as a means to establish ethnic, regional, and national differences. Canada is no exception in this regard. Indeed, many see disputes over language as a particularly distressing part of this country's identity. Canada has two **official languages,** English and French, in which the business of the federal government is conducted. Government policies of "multiculturalism" indicate a tolerance of other languages, but the reality of the workplace shows that a proficiency in English or French is an important determinant of an individual's economic success. As a result, many immigrants quickly learn either English or French if neither of the two is their **mother tongue**—the first language learned at home in childhood and still understood. Nonetheless, more than 200 languages are spoken as mother tongue in Canada, and one-fifth of Canadians speak a language other English or French at home.

In Quebec, the use of French is very much seen as an intrinsic part of the "nationalist project" and is also an established part of provincial government policy. All of the leading provincial political parties have been conscious of the minority position of the French language in Canada and North America as a whole. Realizing that this position was further weakened by a decline in the provincial birth rate among francophones and an increase in the number of **allophone** immigrants to the province (those whose mother tongue is neither English nor French) who chose to adopt English, the Quebec government has taken steps to encourage the greater use of French in Quebec. Through such legislation as Bill 101, the government has acted to ensure the use of French in government, in public schools, and even on street signs. A provincial agency (Office québécois de la langue française) has the responsibility for monitoring public compliance (**Figure 5.25**). Although initially the target of much opposition, especially from Quebec's large anglophone and allophone communities (each representing about 10 percent of Quebec's population), this policy has now become accepted as a fact of life in the province, one that no political party can afford to oppose. However, as the example of Montreal shows, it takes more than government policy to create a truly integrated, bilingual society **(Figure 5.26)**.

Outside of Quebec, the francophone population totals just over one million, and is found mainly in the two provinces of Ontario and

FIGURE 5.25 Office québécois de la langue française Quebec's watchdog on language monitors compliance with provincial legislation promoting French. Among the most publicized prosecutions in recent years have been cases where store signs did not use French or, if more than one language was used, French did not have the largest font size.

(*Source:* Courtesy of Alan E. Nash)

New Brunswick, where it is declining in relative size. The 2011 census records that 17.5 percent (5.8 million) of the country's population were bilingual in English and French, up from 13 percent in 1971. Most of that increase (71 percent) is due to an increase in the bilingual population of Quebec aged 15 to 49. In other words: more and more younger francophones in Quebec elect to become bilingual. The highest rates of bilingualism were recorded in Quebec (42.6 percent of the population) and New Brunswick (33 percent). Urban centres, such as Montreal (50 percent), Ottawa-Hull (44 percent), and Sudbury (40 percent) also have sizable bilingual populations.

In terms of Canada's allophone population, the 2011 census records that 20.6 percent of the population spoke neither English nor French as the mother tongue. This represents an increase from 13 percent in 1971, fuelled by Canada's large immigration flows from countries where neither English nor French is spoken. (See Chapter 3.) The numbers also show the changing geographical range of immigration: in 1971, the leading allophone languages were German, Italian, Ukrainian, and Greek. By 2011, the top four were Punjabi, Chinese, Spanish, and Tagalog (Filipino). Given the patterns of immigration discussed in Chapter 3, it is not surprising to see that Toronto and Vancouver have the highest proportions of allophones, with just over 30 percent. Montreal, however, reports only 16.5 percent allophones.

The 2011 census also records approximately 213 000 persons who speak an Aboriginal language as a mother tongue. Of these, the majority spoke Cree (83 475), Ojibway (19 275), or Inuktitut (34 110). Over the years, the number of Aboriginal language speakers has been reduced through the economic and political necessity of learning English or French. As a result, Canada's Aboriginal languages are among the most endangered in the world: only a handful of the 50 Aboriginal languages currently spoken in this country can be considered as thriving, and at least a dozen are on the brink of extinction. For example, most of the 30 Aboriginal languages spoken in British Columbia have fewer than 1000 speakers left.

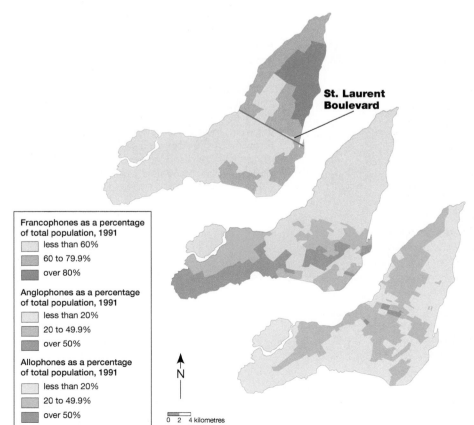

Francophones as a percentage of total population, 1991
- less than 60%
- 60 to 79.9%
- over 80%

Anglophones as a percentage of total population, 1991
- less than 20%
- 20 to 49.9%
- over 50%

Allophones as a percentage of total population, 1991
- less than 20%
- 20 to 49.9%
- over 50%

0   2   4 kilometres

St. Laurent Boulevard

FIGURE 5.26 The language divide in Montreal As these maps based on 1991 census data show clearly, the English- and French-speaking populations of Montreal (the anglophone and francophone communities) maintain separate existences. The traditional boundary of St. Laurent Boulevard can still be seen as demarcating these two groups. Straddling the "two solitudes," the allophone communities have developed language geographies of their own. (*Sources:* L. Lo and C. Teixeira, "If Quebec Goes . . . The 'Exodus' Impact," *Professional Geographer* 50, 1998, pp. 481–498. The material is used by permission of Blackwell Publishing Ltd. Further information, including mother tongue maps for 1996, can be found in Julie Archambault, Damaris Rose, and Anne-Marie Séguin, "ATLAS: Immigration and Metropolis," on the website of the Montréal Centre for Interuniversity Research on Immigration, Integration and Urban Dynamics at http://im.metropolis.net. Reproduced by permission of the Association of American Geographers: http://www.aag.org.)

While the loss of language does not equate with the death of a culture, it can severely handicap its future. The vocabulary that each language develops is unique, and its loss therefore diminishes a people's ability to describe phenomena in terms most appropriate to it. Perhaps the most famous illustration of this point is the considerable number of words that the Inuit have for *snow*, a range of vocabulary brought about by the importance of the many varieties of snow in their daily lives.

Given how important language is to a sense of cultural identity, the issue of continuing language diversity is of great concern to people both in the global core and in the periphery. In the recent census in India (see Chapter 3), people reported the use of over 1600 languages. Overall, no single language is spoken or understood by more than 40 percent of the Indian people. Since the country became independent, there have been efforts to establish Hindi, the most prevalent language, as the national language, but this has been resisted by many of the states within India, whose political identity is closely aligned with a different language.

English, spoken by fewer than 6 percent of the people, serves as the link language among India's multilingual states and regions. As in other former British colonies in South Asia, English is the language of higher education, the professions, and national business and government. Without English, there is little opportunity for economic or social mobility. Most poor children attend only primary school, where they are taught only their local language and so are inevitably restricted in their prospects. Guards, sweepers, cooks, or drivers who speak only Hindi or Urdu will likely do the same work all their lives. In contrast, those who can speak English—by definition the upper middle classes—are able to practise their profession or do business in any region of their country and in most parts of the world.

With globalization, the geography of language has become even more dynamic. The plethora of languages and dialects in a region like South Asia makes communication and commerce among different language speakers difficult. It may, furthermore, create problems in governing a population. For this reason developing states create one national language to facilitate communication and enable the efficient conduct of state business. In general, where official languages are put into place, indigenous languages are threatened **(Figure 5.27)**.

Yet the actual unfolding of globalizing forces—such as official languages—works differently in different places and in different times. The overall trend appears to be toward the loss of indigenous language (and other forms of culture). Language can also serve as an important means of challenging the political, economic, cultural, and social forces of globalization—as occurs right here in Canada around the Québecois movement but also in places like Belgium (among the Flemish people), Spain (with the Basque and Catalonian separatist movements), as well as other countries.

Another way to examine the geography of language is to consider the proportion of people around the world whose mother tongue is not their country's official language. In places like China, where the dominant language is often not the mother tongue, simple communication may pose considerable challenges. Mandarin is the

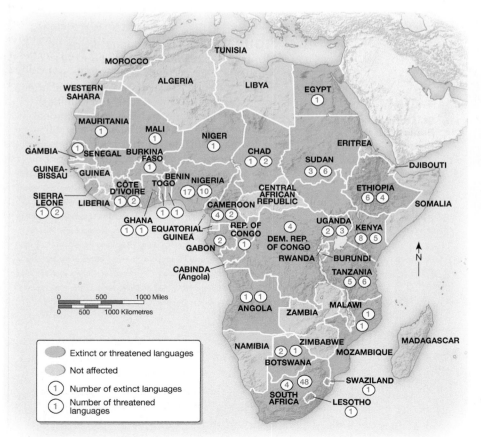

FIGURE 5.27 African countries with extinct and threatened languages It is not absolutely certain how many languages are currently being spoken worldwide, but the estimates range between 4200 and 5600. While some languages are being created through the fusion of an indigenous language with a colonial language, such as English or Portuguese, indigenous languages are mostly dying out. Although only Africa is shown in this map, indigenous languages are dying throughout the Americas and Asia as well. Also, remember the disappearance of the Canadian Aboriginal languages we examined earlier.

official language, but there are 6 major regional dialects of Mandarin as well as another 41 distinct languages spoken by ethnic minorities in China. In other cases, the disparity between the official language and the mother tongue is the result of colonization. For instance, in South Africa before apartheid was dismantled, there were 2 official languages, English and Afrikaans—both languages of the colonizers—but over 50 indigenous languages. Since the election of Nelson Mandela in the early 1990s, the number of official languages has grown to 11. The increase gives more residents access to public information and is intended to expand participation in civil society as well as preserve the cultural diversity of the country.

> **APPLY YOUR KNOWLEDGE** Given what you have read about immigration and language so far, can you speculate why Montreal, despite being a preferred destination for immigrants to Canada, has a comparatively low share of allophones? ∎

Culture and the Nation

The protection of regional languages as a way of resisting globalization is just one part of a larger movement that interests geographers and other scholars. The movement, known as **cultural nationalism,** is an effort to protect regional and national cultures from the homogenizing impact of globalization, especially from the penetrating influence of U.S. culture. Two aspects of U.S. culture that are particularly widespread are movies and television programming. Although many of these cultural products are welcomed abroad, many others are not. Australia, Britain, Canada, and France all have formally attempted to erect barriers to U.S. cultural products. This is especially true for Canada, which continues to struggle to maintain an independent cultural identity beyond the shadow of the United States (**Figure 5.28**). To this purpose, Canada has developed an extensive and very public policy of cultural protection against the onslaught of U.S. music, television, magazines, movies, and other art and media forms. Besides regulating how much and

what type of U.S. culture can travel north across the border, the Canadian government also sponsors a sort of "affirmative action" grant program for this country's own cultural industries.

Nations can respond to the homogenizing forces of globalization and the spread of U.S. culture in any number of ways. Some groups attempt to seal themselves off from undesirable influences. Other groups attempt to legislate the flow of foreign ideas and values.

One of the most widespread forces of cultural resistance is Islamism (more popularly, although incorrectly, known as Islamic fundamentalism). Whereas *fundamentalism* is a general term that describes the desire to return to strict adherence to the fundamentals of a religious system, **Islamism** is an anticolonial, anti-imperial political movement. In Muslim countries, Islamists resist core, especially Western, forces of globalization—namely modernization and secularization. It is important to note that not all Muslims are Islamists, although Islamism is the most militant movement within Islam today.

The basic intent of Islamism is to create a model of society that protects the purity and centrality of Islamic precepts through the return to a universal Islamic state—a state that would be religiously and politically unified. Islamists object to modernization because they believe the corrupting influences of the core place the rights of the individual over the common good. They view the popularity of Western ideas as a move away from religion to a more secular (nonreligious) society. Islamists desire to maintain religious precepts at the centre of state actions, such as introducing principles from the sacred law of Islam into state constitutions.

Islamism—a radical and sometimes militant movement—should not be regarded as synonymous with the practices of Islam, any more generally than Christian fundamentalism is with Christianity. Islam is not a monolithic religion, and even though all adherents accept the basic pillars of the faith, specific practices vary according to the different histories of countries, nations, and tribes. Some expressions of Islam allow for the existence and integration of Western styles of dress, food, music, and other aspects of culture, while others call for the complete elimination of Western influences. (See Box 5.2, "Window on the World: Fashionable Veiling.")

FIGURE 5.28 **The United States in Canada** This image of a Kentucky Fried Chicken restaurant in Quebec illustrates the influence of U.S. products on Canadian society and culture. Because Canada is the nearest northern neighbour to the United States, it is not surprising that Canada is probably more heavily influenced by U.S. culture than any other country in the world. It should be pointed out, however, that the flow is not one way.
(*Sources:* Steve Liss/The LIFE Images Collection/Getty Images)

VIRTUAL GEOGRAPHIES

For an impression of how diverse and controversial various views within Islam can be (particularly as regards the issue of fashionable veiling), check out the heated online discussion about a video released by an amateur group of young American Muslim women calling themselves "Mipsterz" (Muslim Hipsters) that features fashionably veiled young women skateboarding to the tune of Jay-Z.

> **APPLY YOUR KNOWLEDGE** Locate online the video titled "Lifting the Veil: Muslim Women Explain Their Choice." Before watching, write down your current understanding and knowledge of the *hijab*. After viewing the segment, describe how your impressions changed or stayed the same in response to the content of the program. ∎

Why do some Muslim women wear headscarves or veils when they are in public? In large part because the Muslim holy book, the Qur'an, instructs them, as well as men, to be modest in their public comportment. Some Muslim women wear headscarves to demonstrate their piety and to publicly identify themselves as people who adhere to Muslim religious beliefs. For them, covering one's head is an expression of religious conviction. But being religious doesn't mean a Muslim woman must also be unfashionable. And just because many Muslim women wear headscarves (or other forms of more modest dress such as full-length skirts and long sleeves) does not mean that they all dress the same.

In fact, fashionable Muslim dress has grown increasingly popular since the 1980s. This move toward more fashion choices for Muslim women is connected to globalization and the growth in consumer culture in increasingly liberal democracies in Muslim nations that encourage more personal freedom. A complex, widespread Islamic consumer culture includes well-educated, upwardly mobile Islamic young women who are active in moderate Islamist politics and possess personal disposable income.

Geographers Banu Gökariksel and Anna Secor have studied the veiling fashion industry in Istanbul, Turkey, a particularly interesting place to explore because of the over 200 firms operating there. With retail outlets in the Middle East, Europe, and North America, these firms clearly have a global reach. One such firm, Tekbir (meaning "God is great"), has outlets in Germany, the Netherlands, France, England, Belgium, Austria, Switzerland, Bosnia Herzegovina, Macedonia, Azerbaijan, Dubai, Lebanon, Jordan, Syria, Palestine, Libya, Egypt, Sudan, Algeria, South Africa, Australia, the United States, and Canada. In addition to Istanbul, other Islamic fashion centres have formed in Beirut, Cairo, Dakar, Dubai, Kuala Lumpur, and Jakarta.

Turkish veiling-fashion designers visit the annual fashion shows in Paris to find inspiration for their new styles in emerging Western trends of fabric, colour, cut, and style. Veiling fashion is little different from Western fashion in that it is part of a larger system of production, consumption, and changing cultural tastes. The Turkish veiling-fashion industry takes these elements and combines them with a commitment to modest dress and head covering to produce women's everyday wear, though some haute couture (high fashion) is also retailed.

While fashionable veiling in Turkey looks to the modern Western fashion world for inspiration, some Muslim women are looking in the opposite direction. An interesting contrast is found in Indonesia, where fashionable young women who previously did not cover their hair are now wearing headscarves, while those who have been wearing headscarves for most of their lives have started to adopt more fashionable styles of covered dress.

Indeed, fashionable veiling is a trend that exists throughout most of the Islamic world, from the Islamic states of Saudi Arabia or Oman to Muslim immigrant communities in Canada, the United States, Europe, Australia, the United Kingdom, Japan, and the Philippines.

In the Netherlands, Islamic fashion researcher Annelies Moors explored the trend of young women, children of immigrant guest workers, moving toward wearing headscarves. Though it is important to appreciate that not all Muslim women wear headscarves, these young women, who are usually better educated than their mothers, have taken an interest in Islamic dress in response to an increasing commitment to their religion. In exploring this phenomenon, Moors interviewed three Muslim women to understand their reasons for these choices:

While all three women are immediately recognizable as Muslim, wearing a headscarf that covers the hair completely, the outfits that they currently wear are strikingly different. Feride [who is in her mid-thirties and is the daughter of working class Turkish immigrant parents] is most comfortable in elegant suits, combinations of floor-length skirts and well-cut jackets of high-quality materials, often brought from Turkey. She pays much attention to wearing matching headscarves, but does not like the style that many younger Turkish girls have adopted, who use underscarves and other materials to produce a high and voluminous head shape. Her style is more personal, playing with the various ways that are common in eastern Turkey. Lisa [a 22-year-old college student whose father is from Pakistan and mother is a Hindu from Suriname who converted to Islam], in contrast, is not interested in elegance, sophistication, or, for that matter, high-heeled shoes. She describes her style as casual, sporty, urban, and cool. She usually wears jeans with a tunic or a blouse over them, [a headscarf], and "always a hoodie, combined with a cool bag and Nikes." It is only on special occasions amongst Pakistanis that she can be spotted wearing shalwar qamiz [a set consisting of a long shirt or tunic and a pair of loose trousers] often brought from Pakistan. Malika [a 24-year-old college student whose parents were Moroccan immigrants] wears an outfit that shows the least variety. She wears a long, loose, all-covering dress, made by a seamstress who specializes in such outfits, and combines this with a three-quarter-length, all-enveloping veil (khimar); sometimes she also wears gloves. Underneath, however, she wears very fashionable styles, including brand-name jeans.

Although Feride considers herself very much a religious person, she also explained that she had to grow into wearing these styles of covered dress. "You have your own personal taste, and also fashion plays a role. If long splits are fashionable, you buy skirts with long splits . . . Covering is a form of worship, and you are not really supposed to draw attention to yourself or to make yourself beautiful. That is a thin line . . ." Feride is outspoken about why she wears covered dress. "For

(b)

(c)

(d)

(a)

FIGURE 5.B Islamic veiling fashion These images make it clear that veiling fashion among Muslim women is highly variable. (a) shows a style created by an Indonesian designer. The silken fabric of the body covering is feminine and attention getting, reflecting both sartorial trends and spiritual dictates. (b) shows teenage girls with brightly coloured veils worn with one or two underscarves wrapped around the neck. (c) shows young women entering Regent's Park Mosque in London, England. Though they are dressed in full-length body covering, their veils are only loosely worn, exposing their hair, which would not be an acceptable style among the more conservative and older Syrian women shown in (d). Notice, however, that the young woman in the middle of (d) is modestly but also more fashionably veiled than the older others. (*Source:* Lai Seng Sin/AP Images [5.Ba] Kamarulzaman Russali/Alamy [5.Bb] Sally and Richard Greenhill/Alamy [5.Bc] dbtravel/dbimages/Alamy [5.Bd])

(*Continued*)

me, covering is a form of worshipping the Creator, a form of devotion. Some would say that you need to cover to avoid arousing sexual feelings in men, but I do not do it for that reason. If they have a problem with their feelings, that is their problem, not mine.

Malika began wearing her veil almost a year ago. Although to an outsider this shift in clothing may look like a huge change, she said: "I do not think it is that much of a change. I still love fashion, but now it is halal [permissible according to Islamic law]. I simply wear a long dress over my jeans. Sometimes people who know me from before say what a pity, all those curls, what happened, you were always so free. Then I say that was my appearance, but what you see is not the same as what is inside. I had always been practicing. I used to pray off and on, but I started to do this more consistently during the last three years, especially last year during Ramadan. Now I fast extra days, do not listen to music, and do not shake hands with men. For me, this has become normal, but people around me find it rather extreme. I first wanted to change my behavior and only when I had done that, to start to veil. My veil has made it [the transition] complete.

Lisa . . . likes brand names: "G-Star, for instance. The quality is much better." She often goes to the smaller stores where they have different brands. "But for simple things, I go to Vero Moda or H&M." Thinking about what she finds Islamically acceptable, she says: "I would not say everything except the face and the hands, but I do cover my chest and the section between my waist and my knees. Also, it should not be too tight or too short. If I wear skirts, it is a long skirt, or I wear trousers underneath. With skinny jeans, I make sure that they do not fit too tightly around my legs. I wear such styles with my headscarf, because of [my] love for God. It is not that it makes you less attractive, because your eyes or your face can also do that." Lisa stresses that in the first place it is "a personal relation with God." At the same time, it is an attempt not to attract attention "so that men do not look [at you] twice. But nowadays they also think that the headscarf is beautiful and they make comments about that. But I do feel better. It is clear that I have committed myself and that is visible to all."[4]

The stories these very different women tell about themselves and their personal choices indicate that traditional cultural traits, such as dressing the female body consistent with religious strictures, are never static. Fashion, as a mass-produced cultural product, is always open to interpretation. As the different veiling styles shown in the composite figure (**Figure 5.B**) demonstrate, Muslim women are as capable of producing their own sense of style as manufacturers are of capitalizing on them. Indeed, the websites of Islamic fashion designers make it clear that while a great deal of inspiration for their work comes from international fashion trends, they also look to the street and what everyday women are wearing for their new ideas.

[4]From Annelies Moors, 2009, "Islamic Fashion in Europe: Religious Conviction, Aesthetic Style and Creative Consumption," *Encounters*, 1:175–200. Reprinted by permission of *Encounters* and the author.

CULTURE AND IDENTITY

In addition to exploring cultural forms, such as religion and language, and movements, such as cultural nationalism, geographers have increasingly begun to ask questions about other forms of identity. This interest largely has to do with the fact that certain long-established and some more recently self-conscious cultural groups are beginning to use their identities to assert political, economic, social, and cultural claims.

Sexual Geographies

Sexuality is a set of practices and identities that a given culture considers related to each other and to those things it considers sexual acts and desires. One of the earliest and most effective examples of the geographic study of sexuality is the examination of the spatial expression of prostitution. Research on prostitution in California found that sex work—as it is now more commonly known—is spatially differentiated based upon the target clientele as well as systems of surveillance. More typical contemporary work on sexuality explores the spatial constraints on homosexuality and the ways in which lesbian, gay, bisexual, and transgendered (LGBT) people respond to and reshape them. Two particular areas of research have emerged: gay and lesbian consumerism, and the body as a site of performance of sexuality and gender identities.

Montreal's Gay Village provides an example of how gay and lesbian consumerism is contributing to the transformation of the urban landscape. In this case, the higher-than-average income that many gay Canadian couples enjoy has enabled an extensive rejuvenation of the area's housing stock and the emergence of an

FIGURE 5.29 Montreal's "Gay Village" This building, known as the Complexe Bourbon, incorporates a café and a restaurant. It is located on the corner of rue St. Catherine and rue Alexandre de Sève in the heart of Montreal's "Gay Village." The building flies multicoloured flags recalling the rainbow, an emblem of gay culture.
(*Source*: Courtesy of Alan E. Nash)

increasingly expensive range of restaurants (**Figure 5.29**). Indeed, in its promotional tourist literature, the city of Montreal is trying to capitalize on the attractiveness of the village as a destination for high-end gay tourism.

Geographers also research and write on the body and the ways in which individuals literally perform their sexual identities through clothing, attitude, body language, and grooming, such as hairstyles and bodily adornments. Research on the body has also been used to decode the social and cultural practices that express other kinds of social identity, such as gender and class. But the work has been most fully developed in its application to sexuality.

The central theoretical position of this research is that sexual identities are learned and performed through standard, taken-for-granted practices. Using gender as a starting point and recognizing it as a key feature of all human identity that marks and defines humans as "sexed" beings, researchers in this area contend that gender is not something people essentially are (because of a given set of physical characteristics), but something people do (something we enact by the way we present our bodily selves to the world).

Research on sexuality and the body in geography recognizes that space is central to understanding. *Where* gay or straight identities can be performed plays a central role in *who* occupies those spaces, *how* they are occupied, and even *what* sexual identity people might be performing if they occupy one space or another. But issues of sexuality and space go beyond the performance of sexual identity to the emergence of new political cultures that are being constructed to protect the rights of lesbian, gay, and transgendered people in particular national and international spaces (**Figure 5.30**).

Ethnicity and Territory

Ethnicity is another area in which geographers explore cultural identity. **Ethnicity** is a socially created system of rules about who belongs to a particular group based upon actual or perceived commonalities, such as language or religion. A geographic focus on ethnicity is an attempt to understand how it shapes and is shaped by space and how ethnic groups use space with respect to mainstream culture as well as other ethnic groups. For cultural geographers, territory is also a basis for ethnic group cohesion. (See Chapter 9 for more on territory.) For example, cultural groups—ethnically identified or

FIGURE 5.30 Gay pride parade, São Paulo, Brazil Almost 2 million LGBT people and their supporters—many in lavish Carnival costumes and waving rainbow-coloured flags—paraded in Brazil's biggest city in May 2005 to celebrate gay pride and call for the legalization of civil unions between homosexuals. In comparison, San Francisco's gay pride parade typically attracts tens of thousands of people, and the 2004 World gay pride day celebrations in Berlin attracted between 200 000 and 500 000 participants. (*Source*: AP Images)

FIGURE 5.31 Uyghur protest Uyghur residents protest in the city of Urumqi, following bloody riots in the capital of China's Xinjiang region. One hundred fifty-six people died and over 1400 people were arrested.
(*Source:* Kyodo/Newscom)

otherwise—may be spatially segregated from the wider society in areas that can be as small as individual neighbourhoods and ghettos, or as large as ethnic enclaves, homelands, and tribal areas.

In China, for example, 91 percent of the population is Han, while 55 other ethnic groups make up the remainder. These are mostly residual groups of indigenous people such as the Miao, the Dong, Li, Naxi, and Qiang, who are economically disadvantaged and found in relatively remote border regions, removed from central authority in Beijing. Tensions exist between the dominant Han and several of the larger minority groups such as the Tibetans and the Uyghurs. The latter are a Turkic Muslim minority group living in western China. They demand greater control over their territory in order to practise self-governance and to follow their own cultural traditions and not those of mainstream (Han-dominated) society. The Uyghur ethnic identity is fragmented, however. Some Uyghur support a Pan-Islamic vision, exemplified in the East Turkestan Islamic Movement; others support a Pan-Turkic vision, as in the East Turkestan Liberation Organization; and a third group—the East Turkestan independence movement—promotes a "Uyghurstan" state. As a result, Uyghurs do not speak with one voice, and members of each of these groups have committed violence against other Uyghurs whom they view as too assimilated to Chinese society or not religious enough (**Figure 5.31**).

Ethnicity is a complex cultural category constituted through shared history and often through language, religion, and an attachment to a particular place or homeland. And though there are many examples of ethnic groups who share a cohesive sense of community and belonging, not all do. As with any identity, variation exists in practice.

Race and Place

Geographers also use prevailing ideas and practices with respect to race to understand places.[5] **Race** is a problematic classification of human beings based on skin colour and other physical characteristics.

Racialization is the practice of creating unequal castes based on the norm of whiteness. Biologically speaking, no such thing as race exists within the human species. Yet consider the categories of race and place that correspond to "Chinese" and "Chinatown." Powerful Western ideas about Chinese as a racial category have enabled the emergence and perpetuation of Chinatowns in many North American cities (**Figure 5.32**). In this and other cases, the visible characteristics of hair, skin, and bone structure made race into a category of difference that was (and still is) widely accepted and often spatially expressed.

The mainstream approach views neighbourhood as a spatial setting for systems of affiliation more or less chosen by *minority* people with similar skin colour. Cultural geographers have overturned this approach in order to see neighbourhoods as spaces that affirm the *dominant* society's sense of identity. For example, from the perspective of white Canadian society, the nineteenth-century Chinatown in Vancouver was the physical expression of what set the Chinese apart from whites. The distinguishing characteristics revolved around the way the Chinese looked, what they ate, their non-Christian religion, opium consumption, gambling habits, and other "strange" practices (**Figure 5.33**).

A recent study of the history of the Chinese laundry in Canada, by Ban Seng Hoe, shows that discrimination against the Chinese often worked at spatial scales even smaller than that of a Chinatown. He shows that many Chinese immigrants established laundries in a large number of communities across Canada during the early part of the twentieth century; however, this way of making a living almost always caused antagonism from the local residents:

> The City of Calgary, for example, stipulated that no Chinese laundries would be allowed to operate on certain streets. In 1905, the Calgary Central Labour Union condemned Chinese laundries as a menace to public health, and *The Calgary Herald* demanded that the Chinese laundries be cleared in order to avoid an epidemic.[6]

[5]Adapted from K. Anderson, "The Idea of Chinatown: The Power of Place and Institutional Practice in the Making of a Racial Category," *Annals of the Association of American Geographers* 77(4), 1987, pp. 580–598.

[6]Ban Seng Hoe, *Enduring Hardship: The Chinese Laundry in Canada*. Gatineau: Canadian Museum of Civilization, 2003, p. 55.

FIGURE 5.32 Chinatown, San Francisco
Chinatowns have been portrayed as places
voluntarily chosen by immigrant Chinese. But
they can also be seen as places of exclusion and
racism created by the dominant society that
prefers to segregate people different from the
wider society. (*Source:* Panoramic Images/Getty Images)

Chinatown, Vancouver, 1907 — The marginalization of the Chinese
population of Vancouver, British Columbia, had strong racial and
ethnic undercurrents that surfaced in illustrations such as this one,
published in 1907. Note how the white settlements are pictured
as airy, light, and single-family, whereas the Chinese domiciles
are labelled as "warrens" "infested" by thousands of Chinese.

FIGURE 5.33 Chinatown, Vancouver, 1907 Rather than
depicting the real conditions in Vancouver's Chinatown, this illustration reflects what the "Vancouver white workingman" thought
Chinatown looked like. In other words, it reflects the notions and
prejudices of the mainstream Canadian society at the time. (*Source:* K.
Anderson, "The Idea of Chinatown: The Power of Place and Institutional Practice in the Making of a
Racial Category," *Annals of the Association of American Geographers* 77[4], 1987, pp. 580–598.)

Place—in this case Chinatown—maintained and manifested
differences between white and Chinese society. Place continues to
be a mechanism for creating and preserving local systems of racial
classification and for containing geographical difference within
defined geographical confines. The homelands of South Africa and
the dismantling of apartheid there also illustrate the interaction of
race and place on a much larger scale.

Unexamined in the kinds of perceptions and practices that
create racialized places as different as Chinatown and the homelands of South Africa is the taken-for-grantedness of whiteness.
Whiteness is seen to be the norm or the standard against which
all other visible differences are compared. But whiteness, as geographers and other scholars have shown, is itself a category of difference that depends on visible distinctions, not biological ones,
and is always constructed in relation to other categories. Recently,
researchers in the humanities and social sciences have begun to
"denaturalize" whiteness by investigating the way whiteness has
been constructed as a social category in different periods and
places as well as the ways that whiteness operates in particular
sites such as classrooms, on the street, and in boardrooms. It is
only when we begin to challenge the "naturalness" of whiteness
and the spaces that enable it that we can truly begin to undo racist
practices.

APPLY YOUR KNOWLEDGE In your community, are
whiteness and heterosexuality the taken-for-granted
"normal"? Can you identify spaces that express
different ethnic, religious, or sexual identities? How
do these identities and "their" spaces overlap or
contrast with other categories such race, class, and
economic wealth? For instance, do they seem to
exclude or reinforce each other? ∎

FIGURE 5.34 Indian women in the informal sector Many women in South Asia are self-employed as small vendors in the daily markets. Others do home-based work such as weaving and dyeing cloth or embroidering or sewing garments. Nearly all workers in the informal sector, whether male or female, lack any sort of social protection such as health or unemployment insurance.
(Bob Krist/Corbis)

Gender and Other Identities

Gender has received a great deal of attention from cultural geographers within the last three decades. **Gender** is a category reflecting the social differences between men and women. As with other forms of identity, gender implies a *socially constructed* difference in power between groups, meaning it is not biologically determined but socially and culturally created (or learned). In the case of gender, the power difference gives males an advantage over females. Gender interacts with other forms of identity and can intensify power differences among and between groups. The implications of these differences are played out differently in different parts of the world.

For example, although gender differences play an important part in shaping social life for men and women in the Middle East, as elsewhere around the globe, there is no single Islamic, Christian, or Jewish notion of gender that operates exclusively in the region. Many in the West have formed stereotypes about the restricted lives of Middle Eastern women because of the operation of rigid Islamic traditions. It is important to understand, however, that these do not capture the great variety in gender relations that exists in the Middle East and North Africa across lines of class, generation, level of education, and geography (urban versus rural origins), among other factors.

In South Asia, gender is greatly complicated by class such that among the poor, women bear the greatest social and economic burden and the most suffering. Generally speaking, South Asian society—India, Pakistan, Afghanistan, Nepal, Bhutan, and Bangladesh—is intensely patriarchal, though the form that patriarchy takes varies by region and class. The common denominator among the poor throughout South Asia is that women not only have the constant responsibilities of motherhood and domestic chores but also have to work long hours in informal-sector occupations **(Figure 5.34)**. In many poor communities, 90 percent of all production occurs outside of formal employment, more than half of which is the result of women's efforts. In addition, women's property rights are curtailed, their public behaviour is restricted, and their opportunities for education and participation in the waged labour force are severely limited.

Women's subservience to men is deeply ingrained within South Asian cultures, and it is manifested most clearly in the cultural practices attached to family life, such as the custom of providing a dowry to daughters at marriage. The preference for male children is reflected in the widespread (but illegal) practice of selective abortion and female infanticide. Within marriage, many (but by no means all) poor women are neglected and maltreated. More extreme are the cases—usually reported only when they involve middle-class families—of "bride burning," whereby a husband or mother-in-law fakes the accidental death (kitchen fires are favoured) or suicide of a bride whose parents had defaulted in their dowry payments. Several thousand such deaths are reported in India each year, and this is almost certainly only a fraction of the real incidence.

The picture for women in South Asia, the Middle East, and elsewhere is not entirely negative, however, and one of the most significant developments has been the increasing education of girls. Because women's education is so closely linked to improvements in economic development, more and more countries are investing in their education. As more and more women become educated, they have fewer children and greater levels of economic independence and political empowerment.

Turning to examples from the core, we can see that geographical studies in Canada have paid special attention to how our city spaces have become gendered and how this has affected our use and appreciation of place. These studies have shown that the suburbs were seen as "female" space; the downtown and industrial areas as "male" space.[7] This simple dichotomy has its roots in nineteenth- and twentieth-century constructions of gender in which residential

[7]See, for example, Suzanne Mackenzie, "Restructuring the Relations of Work and Life: Women as Environmental Actors, Feminism as Geographic Analysis," *Gender, Place and Culture* 6(4), 1999, pp. 417–430.

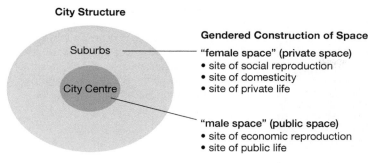

City Structure

Suburbs

City Centre

Gendered Construction of Space

"female space" (private space)
• site of social reproduction
• site of domesticity
• site of private life

"male space" (public space)
• site of economic reproduction
• site of public life

FIGURE 5.35 The gendered construction of space This simple model shows the ways in which nineteenth- and twentieth-century constructions of gender in Western societies affected how those societies created and used landscapes, such as the city. Men, as breadwinners, inhabited a very different social world from that of women, and this affected not only their economic roles but also their geographic experiences in our cities.

space was seen as the site of social reproduction and private life, and commercial and industrial space as the site of economic reproduction and public life. Under gender stereotypes prevalent at the time, the former site became identified as female space; the latter site as male space (**Figure 5.35**).

Although such constructions of gender relations are entirely artificial, their existence has a series of real implications. For example, the unquestioning assumption by city planners that the suburbs are still a domestic or female space means that city by-laws often forbid the creation of small businesses in suburban zones. These rules are based on old preconceptions that there is no need for economic activity ("male" work) in residential areas ("female" space). These preconceptions could not envisage the need for people to create paid employment where they live (the mixture of private or domestic and public or economic spheres). Home businesses, for example, are precluded because they are "male" use of "female" space—despite the obvious opportunities for home-based work in the Information Age.

In discussing questions of geography and identity, one last point should be made. In the 1990s, cultural theorists began to point out that identities were not fixed and a more nuanced and subtle understanding of the formation of human beings as cultural subjects—man, woman, homosexual, heterosexual, etc.—was required. To appreciate this flexibility in identity, the term *hybridity* was introduced. **Hybridity** is meant to convey a mixing of different types. In cultural geography, hybridity is most often associated with movements across a binary of, for instance, the racial categories of black and white such that identities are more multiple and ambivalent. U.S. President Barack Obama, as a child of a white mother and a black father, characterizes this notion of hybridity: his identity can be seen as neither white nor black but both (though he does self-identify as black).

APPLY YOUR KNOWLEDGE Make a list of gender constructions that are characteristic of your own culture. Now compare them to those of the mainstream (dominant) culture in your region. If there are differences, how do they affect your personal life? If there are no differences, what does that tell you about the status of your culture in your society? ■

EMERGENT CULTURAL GEOGRAPHIES

In the past decade, cultural geography has experienced, again, a transformation in the way its practitioners think about the relationship between people and their worlds. These new ways of conceptualizing culture and space are still developing, but they hold the promise of opening up a wide range of previously ignored aspects of daily life that could advance our attempts at explanation.

Actor-Network Theory

Perhaps the most important influence on cultural geography in the twenty-first century has been actor-network theory, which is actually less of a theory and more of an orientation. **Actor-network (ANT)** theory views the world as composed of "heterogeneous things," including humans and nonhumans and objects. What makes ANT so interesting is that the approach attributes to nonhumans and objects as much force in the composition of social life as humans have. Rather than elevating humans as the superior species that determines all social practice and action, ANT recognizes that humans coexist with nonhumans (who may be other living species or inert objects) in a network that includes all sorts of social and material bits and pieces. In an actor network, things are just as important to social life as are humans.

An example of an actor network is a family. According to ANT, a family is both a network *and* an actor that hangs together and for certain purposes acts as a single entity. A family is connected through all sorts of objects: cell phones, houses, automobiles, family dinners, the family pet, etc. Nonhumans help constitute the fabric of "family" and enable it to persist, though its contours are always changing. It is not only the humans who make the family what it is, it is also the nonhumans that help the assemblage come together as a recognizable and coherent entity. Agency—the ability to make things happen—thus resides not only in the human members of the assemblage but also in the nonhuman (the house, the dog, the barbeque grill, the flat-screen television) (**Figure 5.36**).

Non-Representational Theory

One of the criticisms of ANT has been that it treats humans as undifferentiated and lacking in affect and emotion as they go about the business of social life. In attempting to go further into what it means to be human, and particularly into what is present in human experience, cultural geographers have become increasingly interested in non-representational theory. In brief, **non-representational theory (NRT)** understands human life as a process that is always unfolding, always becoming something different, even if only slightly so. It recognizes that much of this becoming occurs outside of conscious thought. Because much of human existence is precognitive (decisions are made before the conscious self is aware of them), NRT is interested in those moments of indeterminacy when events emerge that produce new orderings that may persist or give way to older, more settled ones. These are moments we have all experienced, when something happens that no one expected and yet in which everyone participated in enabling the new ordering. This focus on indeterminacy means that NRT's task is a difficult one in that it attempts to attend to things that words (as representations) cannot express.

FIGURE 5.36 Family watching television in China Grandparents, parents, and their one child gather around their flat-screen television to enjoy time together. Seen from the perspective of ANT, it is the television set that "acts" to bring together the family on this occasion. (*Source:* Blue Jean Images/Alamy)

Geographer Ben Anderson has used non-representational theory to explore memory and music. His work is concerned with how the process of listening to music produces both remembering and forgetting within the context of ordinary living. He describes a young woman (whom he interviewed) listening to music as background to her getting ready for work. As she sits flipping through a magazine and eating breakfast with a Frank Sinatra tune playing in the background, she suddenly hears her mother (who died several years before) singing along to the music. It's a moment from her past; her mother would frequently sing along to all music, and this song was one of her favourites. And in that moment, the young woman is transported from her apartment back in space and time to her family home. The woman notes that when this happened she got "shivery feelings really suddenly."[8] Anderson identifies that "shivery feeling" as **affect**—emotions that are embodied reactions to the social and physical environment. Affect is also about the power of these emotions to result in or enable action.

NRT is keenly interested in events in which things suddenly shift and something involuntary occurs. And it is particularly interested in events when whole groups experience something not anticipated in advance. These are moments that hold significant political potential. For example, in Tunisia in the spring of 2011 the self-immolation of a fruit seller ignited a city's anger at their political dispossession, launching a political event that spread across the Middle East as the Arab Spring. In Madison, Wisconsin, that same year, thousands of people swarmed the state Capitol to protest Governor Scott Walker's intention to eliminate collective bargaining rights for public workers. Both actions can be interpreted from the perspective of NRT. (See Box 5.3, "Visualizing Geography: Geographies of Protest and Care.")

The demonstrations on Maidan Square in Kiev, Ukraine, in the winter of 2013/2014 can also be interpreted from the perspective

of non-representational theory. In December 2013, pro-Western demonstrators took over the iconic square in the centre of Kiev to protest the refusal of pro-Russian President Yanukovych to sign an association agreement with the EU. They vowed to keep the square occupied until the government would allow a popular vote on which direction Ukraine should take (**Figure 5.37[a]**). As the occupation drew into January, the protesters established ad-hoc rules of autonomous self-regulation to structure their protest: soup kitchens, dormitories, communication centres, first-aid posts, and even surgical rooms were staffed and stocked by volunteers; regular clean-up blitzes were organized to tidy up the square and remove garbage; and citizen patrols tried to maintain civic order and safety. Meanwhile, solidarity addresses and visits from supporters established a worldwide circle of awareness and support.

By mid-February 2014, the events on Maidan square suddenly escalated and spun out of control as unmarked snipers fired shots, killing both protesters and government forces. Within hours, the situation grew "chaotic" in the sense that no one group had control over the events any more, and further developments unfolded "unscripted" in a cascading sequence of actions and reactions (**Figure 5.37[b]**). As violence escalated, an outcome began to take shape that neither side had anticipated: President Yanukovych fled to Russia, an interim government that included questionable right-wing groups formed and broke ties with Russia, which in turn used the affront to send in military forces and annex the geopolitically important Crimean peninsula from Ukraine. This action was roundly condemned by the West and, by summer 2014, a new Cold War threatened to freeze relationships between Russia and the West as both sides moved military forces to the area, stepped up belligerent rhetoric, and imposed sanctions on each other. At the time of writing, it is not clear whether Ukraine will survive as a country or whether it will split into an independent western half and an eastern half that will become associated or even amalgamated with Russia. At this moment, it is anyone's guess how extensive and long-lasting the damage to international relationships will turn out to be.

[8]B. Anderson, "Recorded Music and Practices of Remembering," *Social and Cultural Geography,* 5(1), 2004, pp. 3–18.

FIGURE 5.37 Protests on Maidan Square in Kiev, Ukraine Over the winter months of 2013/2014, peaceful protests turned into chaotic violence with unanticipated global outcomes. (*Source:* OlegMit/ Alamy [5.37a] Nosach Vitaliy/Ukrafoto/Polaris/Newscom [5.37b])

APPLY YOUR KNOWLEDGE Can you apply non-representational theory to the events in Ukraine? In other words, can you identify "those moments of indeterminacy when events emerge that produce new orderings that may persist or give way to older, more settled ones"? ■

Materialism

Both ANT and non-representational theory share an interest in matter and materiality. **Materialism** emphasizes that the material world—its objects and nonhuman entities—is at least partly separate from humans and possesses the power to affect humans. A materialist approach is about attempting to understand the ways

that specific properties of material things affect the interactions between humans and nonhuman entities. What materialism adds to NRT and ANT is a commitment to understanding the material world as it unfolds in unpredictable ways. Both theories point to real physical and mental entities as significant in our attempts to explain the world. And they both recognize that humans are not separate from or in any way superior to the world of things. The aim of these new ways of thinking about cultural geography is to rethink how material objects work in the world so that they come to be seen as "lively"—having real force and intensity in the world.

When seen in terms of cultural geography, the materialism that is at the centre of these new ways of thinking directs our attention to how cultural beliefs and values gain permanence and power through material form. Buildings, symbols, commodities, or rituals—the

Geographies of Protest and Care

The 2011 Wisconsin Protests

based on The 2011 Wisconsin Protests by Mario Bruzzone, Abigail H. Neely, Sigrid Peterson, and Keith Woodward (updated in 2014 by M. Imort)

Throughout February and March 2011, hundreds of thousands of people journeyed to the State Capitol building in Madison, Wisconsin, to voice opposition to State Senate Bill 11—the "Budget Repair Bill." Hastily announced and scheduled to be voted on with little time for debate, the bill sought to strip most collective bargaining rights from public sector employees and curtail benefits for poor and elderly Wisconsinites. Within weeks, the daily demonstrations at the Capitol grew into one of the largest sustained protests in the U.S. since the Vietnam War. By March 13th, a month into the protests, attendance swelled to an estimated 100 000—an extensive mobilization for a state with a population of 5.3 million people.

For cultural geographers, the significance of these protests extends beyond their historic size. Positioned in the centre of a large public square and frequently traversed by residents and visitors, the Capitol building came to exemplify the fraught relation between popular protest and public space. During the first week of protests, state workers, students, teachers, farmers, activists, organizers, and concerned citizens who had made their way to the Capitol began to camp overnight on its marble floors. This peaceful "occupation"—and the "rotunda community" it created—offered a glimpse at how political cultures can grow spontaneously out of novel organizational forms and unique uses of places and spaces (**Figure 5.C[a]**). Normally the location of legislative meetings, the spaces inside the Capitol—its walls, hallways, and rotunda area—were re-imagined and transformed by citizens into living, sleeping, and working spaces suited to the practical needs of the community, complete with food preparation and distribution areas, meeting centres, an information station, a first-aid table, and a family space for children to play.

Many different groups and individuals made up the Capitol community. They collectively developed rules, etiquette, decision-making structures, and shared labour, and maintained and cared for the common space. The Capitol thus became a new cultural space. Once bare, polished marble, the walls were now covered with signs posted by citizens. These signs not only voiced protests but also offered strategies for peaceful protest, announced collective decisions concerning practices for keeping the space clean, and displayed the general schedule for Capitol living (announcing "quiet" sleeping times for example). Citizens also re-imagined and transformed the Capitol through their practical use of its spaces for meetings, teach-ins, and, later in the night, sleeping spaces. A large group of college-aged Capitol residents, for example, came to be known as the "cuddle puddle" because they slept closely together to stave off the cold of the marble floors (**Figure 5.C[d]**).

Some of the most striking elements of the Wisconsin protests were the visual and sensory challenges to the traditional, political characteristics of the Capitol space. State capitols almost invariably represent power through the prominent visual display of statues, figures, paintings, murals, and other objects that blend political ideology with local and national cultural ideals. By contrast, in Madison, the visual sensation of the signs, the massive number of protesters filling the multiple floors of the Capitol building, and their loud chants of "Whose House? Our House!" echoing through the hallways, transformed Capitol space from a scene of representational democratic governance into a site of direct democratic practice.

At the same time, the dissemination of protest events through social and popular media enmeshed the emerging Capitol culture with more "global" struggles. The Wisconsin protests unfolded during the same period that the "Arab Spring" was at its height in the Middle East and across North Africa. From Egypt, the union leader Kamal Abbas posted an expression of solidarity on YouTube. Soon after that, a photo went viral that expressed street-level solidarity: it showed a protester in Egypt holding a sign that read "Egypt supports Wisconsin: One World, One Pain" (**Figure 5.C[b]**). On a very practical level, people around the world showed support for the Wisconsin protests by purchasing food online for delivery to the protesters (**Figure 5.C[c]**).

Finally, the transformation of Capitol space can also be understood through the novel kinds of physical movements that the occupation enabled and restricted. How bodies move—or are moved—through a place often informs how that place is perceived, embraced, or contested. For protesters, free movement through the Capitol allowed them to develop increasing feelings of ownership and pride in the space they had helped create.

At the same time, the movement of bodies through the building was also connected to practices of governance and security. As the 2011 protests progressed, the Wisconsin Department of Administration responded by heightening security within the building, introducing airport-style metal detectors, closing building entrances (which created long lines for building access), and restricting items that could be carried in by citizens. As a consequence, movement through the Capitol slowed substantially.

After several months of occupation, the protest community withdrew to a tent city on the square surrounding the Capitol before fizzling out. Since then, the space of the Capitol has continued to undergo transformation while remaining a space for transformative political practice.

Mario Bruzzone, Abigail H. Neely, Sigrid Peterson, and Keith Woodward are all either students or faculty members at the University of Wisconsin, Madison.

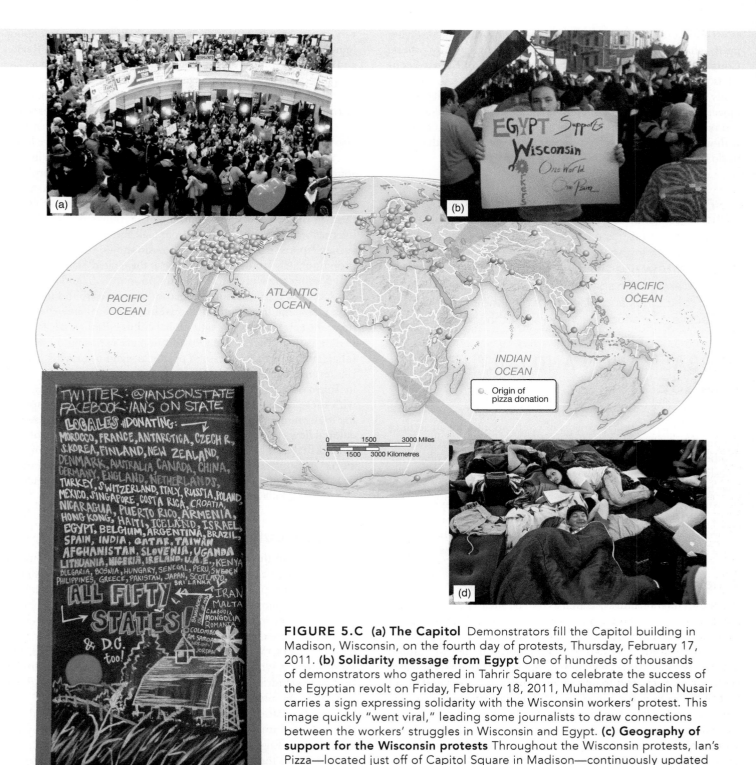

FIGURE 5.C (a) The Capitol Demonstrators fill the Capitol building in Madison, Wisconsin, on the fourth day of protests, Thursday, February 17, 2011. **(b) Solidarity message from Egypt** One of hundreds of thousands of demonstrators who gathered in Tahrir Square to celebrate the success of the Egyptian revolt on Friday, February 18, 2011, Muhammad Saladin Nusair carries a sign expressing solidarity with the Wisconsin workers' protest. This image quickly "went viral," leading some journalists to draw connections between the workers' struggles in Wisconsin and Egypt. **(c) Geography of support for the Wisconsin protests** Throughout the Wisconsin protests, Ian's Pizza—located just off of Capitol Square in Madison—continuously updated a restaurant chalkboard listing the countries from which thousands of pizza donations for the Capitol-bound protesters originated. **(d) The Cuddle Puddle** By February 23, 2011, the occupation of Wisconsin's Capitol had transformed much of the first two floors to accommodate the lives of the protesters. Likewise, they had to adapt to the strange living conditions of the space. Here, many gather together in a nightly "cuddle puddle," sleeping close together to fight off the cold of the building's marble floors. (*Source:* Trent Dietsche/Alamy [5.Ca] Bahgat Ahmed Mahmoud [5.Cb] Ian's Pizza [5.Cc] PhotoLibrary/Index Stock Imagery [5.Cd])

CN Tower, the Star of David, the diamond ring, the Thanksgiving meal—shape us and affect the way we are recognized by others. Consider the cell phone as an example. This mobile device connects people to family and friends, nearly instantaneously and certainly in ways that a landline never could. The materiality of that object—its thingness—is not inert; it has an active forcefulness that can produce significant outcomes such that we are often at a loss without them. In a way, cell phones have become objects that make us do things we might not or could not otherwise.

APPLY YOUR KNOWLEDGE Identify an object (other than a cell phone, which has already been discussed in the text) that has a powerful influence over the way you operate in the world. How does that object work on you? How does it affect your relationships to others and to the space around you? Are there particular times and places in which the object is effective or ineffective? Why might that be? ■

GLOBALIZATION AND CULTURAL CHANGE

Anyone who has ever travelled between major world cities will have noticed the many familiar aspects of contemporary life in settings that until recently were thought of as being quite different from one another. Airports, offices, and international hotels have become notoriously alike, and their similarities of architecture and interior design have become reinforced by the near-universal dress codes of the people who frequent them. For example, the business suit, especially for males, has become the norm for office workers throughout much of the world. Jeans, T-shirts, and sneakers, meanwhile, have become the norm for young people, as well as those in lower-wage jobs.

Americanization and Globalization

It is these commonalities—as well as others, such as the same automobiles, television shows, popular music, food, and global brands, such as Apple and Coca-Cola—that provide a sense of familiarity to core travellers abroad. From the point of view of cultural nationalism, the "lowest common denominator" of this familiarity is often seen as the culture of fast food and popular entertainment that emanates from the United States. Popular commentators have observed that cultures around the world are being Americanized (see Chapter 2). Could this process represent the beginnings of a single global culture based on material consumption, with the English language as its medium?

U.S. culture is increasingly embraced by individuals around the world, largely through consumer goods that are valued as much for their symbolism of a particular way of life as for their intrinsic value. McDonald's burgers, along with Coca-Cola, Hollywood movies, rock music, and NBA insignia, have become associated with a lifestyle package that features luxury, youth, fitness, beauty, and freedom.

It is important to recognize, however, that U.S. products often undergo changes when they travel across the globe. For instance, Revlon, a U.S.-based international corporation and a leading mass-market producer of cosmetics, skin-care products, and fragrances, is very much aware of the need to vary its products for their consumption in non-U.S. markets. Modi Revlon, a joint venture between Revlon and the Indian company Modi Mundipharma, provides a product line of colour cosmetics that complement Indian women's skin tones and appeal to upper-income markets. The success of Modi Revlon, which has captured 80 percent of the Indian cosmetics market, is remarkable.

The economic success of the U.S. entertainment industry has also helped reinforce the idea of an emerging global culture based on Americanization. Today the entertainment industry is the leading source of foreign income in the United States, with a trade surplus of over US$25 billion. The originals of over half of all the books translated in the world (more than 25 000 titles) are written in English, the majority of which are produced by U.S. publishers. In terms of international flows of everything from mail and phone calls to press-agency reports, television programs, radio shows, and movies, a disproportionately large share originates in the United States.

Neither the widespread consumption of U.S. and U.S.-style products nor the increasing familiarity of people around the world with global media and international brand names, however, adds up to the emergence of a single global culture. Rather, what is happening is that processes of globalization are exposing the world's inhabitants to a common set of products, symbols, myths, memories, events, cult figures, landscapes, and traditions. People living in Tokyo or Tucson, Turin or Timbuktu, may be perfectly familiar with these commonalities without necessarily using or responding to them in uniform ways. It is also important to recognize that cultural flows take place in all directions, not just outward from the United States. Think, for example, of European fashions in U.S. stores; of Chinese, Indian, Italian, Mexican, and Thai restaurants in U.S. towns and cities; and of U.S. and European stores selling exotic craft goods from the periphery.

A Global Culture?

The answer to the question of whether there is a global culture must therefore be "no," or at least there is no indisputable sign of it yet. While people around the world share an increasing familiarity with a common set of products, symbols, and events (many of which originate in the U.S. culture of fast food and popular entertainment), these commonalities are configured in different ways in different places, rather than constituting a single global culture. The local interacts with the global, often producing hybrid cultures. Sometimes traditional local cultures become the subject of global consumption; sometimes it is the other way around.

An illustration of the absence of a homogenous global culture is **world music**, the musical genre defined largely by the surge of non–English-language recordings released in the United Kingdom and the United States during the 1980s. There are at least two major views on the effect of globalization on indigenous musical productions. The first emphasizes how the Western music industry has enabled indigenous music to be more widely disseminated and therefore more widely known and appreciated. This position sees local roots mixing with Western popular musical styles, with a hybrid sound resulting. The second view worries that the influence of Western musical styles and the Western music industry has transformed indigenous musical productions to the point where their authenticity has been lost and global musical heterogeneity diminished. Despite their fundamental

FIGURE 5.38 Bossa nova dancers Both a musical style and a dance, *bossa nova* (Portuguese for "new style" or "new beat") originated in Brazil in the late 1950s and was a fad until the mid-1960s, when it faded out. The music style is a blend of cool jazz and hot Latin rhythms accompanied by intimate vocals and instrumental improvisation. It is well suited for listening but failed to become widespread dance music—many felt it was too slow to dance to—despite heavy promotion. Yet in the twenty-first century, *bossa nova* has been experiencing resurgence as a popular dance form as shown here. It has even been merged with four-wall country line dancing performed as a group, rather than in couples.

(Source: Matt Crossick/EMPPL PA Wire/AP Images)

disagreement, holders of both positions recognize that world music has enabled cultural diversity to flourish, and they hope that indigenous performers will be able to resist the power of the Western music industry to homogenize their work and that at the same time hybrid forms will emerge that are satisfying to a wide audience (**Figure 5.38**).

Another example of the variation that exists despite the globalization of commercial cultural products can be found in the film industry. The commercial film industry has become global; the sites of production vary, and the products themselves are significantly different aesthetically and practically. Many Canadians are aware of Bollywood films, made in India and distributed widely because of the large global diaspora of Indian peoples. No one would mistake a Bollywood film for one made in Hollywood, largely because Indian audiences have different expectations for a film experience. Less well-known among Canadians, however, but arguably more globally popular than either Hollywood or Bollywood, is Nollywood, the film industry centred in Lagos, Nigeria. Nollywood produces over 1000 films a year that are viewed avidly not only by Nigerians but across the globe by the large diasporic African population (**Figure 5.39**). Unlike Hollywood films, with their high production values, Nollywood video films are made on inexpensive Chinese cameras with short production schedules and a minimum of editing. Within about a three-week period, the video film is shot and edited and is available for retail consumption. Canadians watching the films might complain about the quality of the lighting and sound, among other things, but Africans appreciate the video films as reflections of their own lives and experiences. As with music, the world film industry translates into anything but homogeneity in this instance.

APPLY YOUR KNOWLEDGE What is your own experience of the processes of globalization and Americanization? Do they enrich or limit your choices in terms of food, education, entertainment, or consumption? Do you resist or welcome these effects? ∎

FIGURE 5.39 On the set of *Nollywood* Nollywood video films are popular the world over and rival Hollywood and Bollywood in numbers produced. The video films are unlike those of either of the other two leading film industries, using different production techniques and invoking different kinds of stories, ultimately resulting in a different aesthetic. Despite the name, Nollywood is *not* a cheap imitation of Hollywood, but a unique cultural form. (*Source:* Tadej Znidarcic/Redux)

Future Geographies

In 2005, the United Nations adopted the Convention on the Protection and Promotion of the Diversity of Cultural Expressions. The convention "is a legally binding international agreement that ensures artists, cultural professionals, practitioners, and citizens worldwide can create, produce, disseminate, and enjoy a broad range of cultural goods, services, and activities, including their own."[9] This UN convention is just one of the ways that governing bodies are actively working to encourage and protect culture and creativity in a rapidly changing world. Given this

growing commitment to recognizing and proactively appreciating the relevance of cultural diversity to the global community, it is fair to predict that culture—in both its material as well as less tangible manifestations—will continue to be the focus of formal attention and support well into the future (**Figure 5.40**).

Importantly, connections across global space are making it increasingly possible for distant groups to share their ideas, cultural practices, and products in a way that helps both to circulate and sustain them. Geographers who work with culture as their research focus are beneficiaries of these trends as they seek to understand how culture is produced and maintained and how it morphs as it is practised and shared across distances that once would have prohibited contact.

[9]UNESCO, accessed May 22, 2011, from http://www.unesco.org/new/en/culture/themes/cultural-diversity/2005-convention/the-convention/.

CONCLUSION

Culture is a complex and exceedingly important concept within the discipline of geography. A number of approaches exist to understanding culture. It may be understood through a range of elements and features, from single traits to complex systems. Cultural geography recognizes the complexity of culture and emphasizes the roles of space, place, and landscape and the ecological relationships between cultures and their environment. It distinguishes itself from other disciplinary approaches, providing unique insights that reveal how culture shapes the worlds we live in at the same time that the worlds we inhabit shape culture.

Cultural geography is a diverse subfield that incorporates three general approaches. The first, traditional cultural geography, is a reflection of the work of Carl Sauer, who understood landscape as the definitive unit of geographic study. The second approach is centred on identity,

ideology, power, and meaning. Gender and sexuality, race and ethnicity, as well as media are frequent empirical objects of this approach. Most recently, cultural geography has been influenced by what has come to be known as the "non-representational" approach. Cultural geographers who are non-representationalists reject what they see as static views of space inherent in more conventional approaches and turn instead to an empirical focus on embodied practices and dynamic processes and how best to comprehend them and their effects without sacrificing their dynamism.

Cultural geographers continue to embrace all of these approaches in their attempts to understand how culture is the product of humans' relationships with the world around them, a world that is alive with symbols, artifacts, practices, and discourses.

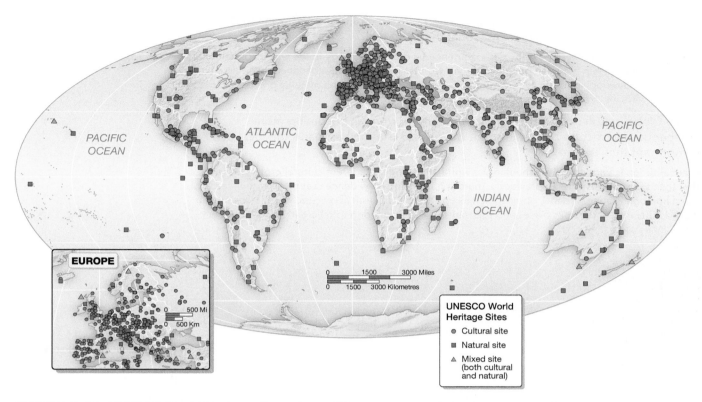

FIGURE 5.40 UNESCO World Heritage Sites The World Heritage List includes 981 properties forming part of the cultural and natural heritage that the World Heritage Committee considers as having outstanding universal value. (*Source:* UNESCO World Heritage List, http://whc.unesco.org/pg.cfm?cid=31&l=en&&&&mode=table.)

Learning Outcomes Revisited

- Interpret how place and space shape culture and, conversely, how culture shapes place and space.

  A simple understanding of culture is that it is a particular way of life, such as a set of skilled activities, values, and meanings surrounding a particular type of economic practice. Geographers understand culture to be shaped by the places in which people live and make meaning from their lives. This means that social relations, politics, and economy all play a role in the production of cultural practices by different groups in different places.

- Compare and contrast the different ways that contemporary approaches in cultural geography interpret the role played by politics and the economy in establishing and perpetuating cultures and cultural landscapes.

  Culture is not something that is necessarily tied to a place and thus a fact waiting to be discovered. Rather, the connections among people, places, and cultures are social creations that can be altered by new impulses from the economy or politics, for example, and are therefore always changing, sometimes in subtle and other times in more dramatic ways. As a result, a particular ethnic landscape may change dramatically after only a decade as the economy improves or declines and members of the group have access to additional or fewer resources that then shape their homes, vehicles, businesses, etc.

- Probe the ways that differences—especially gender, class, sexuality, race, and ethnicity—are both products of and influences upon geography, producing important variations within, as well as between, cultures.

  Like most social scientists, geographers understand that cultural groups are not homogeneous. All women are not alike, just like all working-class people are not alike. Where people live can have an important impact on their sexual identity, for instance, when they are living in a place that is homophobic.

- Appreciate the conceptual changes that are taking place in cultural geography that include actor-network theory and non-representational theory.

  Over the past decade, cultural geography has experienced a dramatic change in the way its practitioners think about the relationship between people and their worlds. These new ways of conceptualizing culture and space are still developing, but they focus on the importance of objects and material practices and how they shape the ways we experience and conduct our daily lives.

- Show that globalization does not necessarily mean the world is becoming more homogeneous, and recognize that in some ways, globalization has made the local even more important than before.

  While globalization is undoubtedly reshaping the world and bringing different cultural groups closer together than they have ever been previously, there is no conclusive evidence that globalization leads to cultural homogenization. Instead, globalization seems to be a differential process, which means that it is deployed differently in different places and experienced and responded to differently by the people who live in those places.

KEY TERMS

actor-network theory (ANT) *(p. 189)*

affect *(p. 190)*

allophone *(p. 178)*

cultural complex *(p. 168)*

cultural geography *(p. 161)*

cultural hearth *(p. 177)*

cultural landscape *(p. 164)*

cultural nationalism *(p. 181)*

cultural region *(p. 168)*

cultural system *(p. 170)*

cultural trait *(p. 166)*

culture *(p. 160)*

dialect *(p. 177)*

diaspora *(p. 171)*

ethnicity *(p. 185)*

folk culture *(p. 164)*

gender *(p. 188)*

genre de vie *(p. 165)*

historical geography *(p. 165)*

hybridity *(p. 189)*

Islam *(p. 172)*

Islamism *(p. 181)*

isolate *(p. 178)*

language *(p. 177)*

language branch *(p. 177)*

language family *(p. 177)*

language group *(p. 177)*

materialism *(p. 191)*

mother tongue *(p. 178)*

Muslim *(p. 172)*

non-representational theory (NRT) *(p. 189)*

official language *(p. 178)*

popular culture *(p. 164)*

race *(p. 186)*

racialization *(p. 186)*

religion *(p. 171)*

rites of passage *(p. 166)*

sexuality *(p. 184)*

world music *(p. 194)*

REVIEW AND DISCUSSION

1. Make a list of movies that members of your group have viewed recently. Pick two of the films on which to conduct research. If possible, watch the trailers for each film. While watching the trailers, identify three different aspects of culture that are depicted. In terms of cultural geography, how do the aspects of culture you identified interact with space, place, and landscape?

2. Variations in gender identities are often the result of the different spaces in which they are enacted. In your group, discuss what this means by creating a list of how gender might be performed in different spaces by members of your group. For instance, in what spaces are you likely to project a highly feminized or masculinized identity? In what spaces might you project an identity that is not traditionally feminine or masculine? How does the space—for example, a venue for a job interview, a date, a sports competition, a place of worship—shape your gender performance? Finally, do time of day or time of year (e.g., Mardi Gras or St. Patrick's Day) make any difference?

3. Find a description of a coming-of-age ceremony in any part of the world that is different from the one that can be found in your own culture. What are the differences and the similarities between your experience and the one you read about? What might be some of the reasons for these?

4. University campuses generate their own cultural practices and ideas that shape behaviours and attitudes in ways that may not be so obvious at first glance. Observe a particular practice that occurs routinely at your institution. (For example, fraternity and sorority initiations are important rituals of student life, as are sports events and political discussions.) Who are the participants in this practice? What are their levels of importance? Are there gender, age, or status differences in those who carry out this practice? What are the time and space aspects of the practice? Who controls its production? What are the intended outcomes? How does the practice contribute to or detract from the maintenance of order both in your institution and in the larger culture?

Log in to www.masteringgeography.com for MapMaster™ interactive maps, geography videos, RSS feeds, flashcards, weblinks, an eText version of *Human Geography: Places and Regions in Global Context*, and self-study quizzes to enhance your study of cultural geographies.

MapMaster™ presents 13 Place Name and 13 Layered Thematic interactive maps to help students practise and master their geographic literacy, spatial reasoning, and critical thinking skills.

6

INTERPRETING PLACES AND LANDSCAPES

Learning Outcomes

- Investigate how environment shapes people and how people shape environments.

- Recognize that place-making stands at the centre of issues of culture and power relations and that it is a key part of the systems of meaning through which humans make sense of the world.

- Identify how different cultural identities and status categories influence the ways people experience and understand landscapes, as well as how they are shaped by—and are able to shape—landscapes.

- Understand how codes signify important information about landscapes, a process known as semiotics.

- Describe how globalization has occurred in parallel with a transition from modernity to postmodernity and assess how those two periods differ.

The Memorial to the Murdered Jews of Europe offers little guidance on how we "should" interpret it—and yet that very ambiguity may be its greatest contribution to Holocaust remembrance in Germany. This memorial landscape in the centre of Berlin, right next to the Brandenburg Gate, is devoid of any of the symbols we usually associate with death, loss, absence, grief, violence, or remorse. In fact, it is almost without *any* symbolism and obvious meaning, which prevents visitors from "performing" a rehearsed, formulaic form of remembrance. Instead, each individual must probe for his own interpretation of the memorial landscape and the events it seeks to memorialize. Whether that memorialization happens is thus negotiated between the visitor and the memorial, rather than simply "done" by the memorial on behalf of the visitor.

For us as human geographers the interesting question is, how can a landscape and a human observer "negotiate" the construction of meaning? A simple answer could be, negotiation occurs when the visitor reacts to the memorial landscape she encounters, and when she in turn changes the memorial landscape with her reaction. This is best explained with the help of an example. As the visitor enters the memorial landscape, she is quickly engulfed by hundreds of regularly spaced, but variously tall, concrete slabs and blocks. The blocks are set in slightly uneven cobblestones, and some are a touch off kilter. If she perceives this labyrinth of blocks as overwhelming, confining, and confusing, she might feel lost, crowded, or even buried alive—and so come to imagine in some small way the dread of each of the six million

The Memorial to the Murdered Jews of Europe, in central Berlin, stretches over a 2-hectare undulating cobbled square. It comprises 2711 concrete slabs and blocks arranged in a grid pattern, ranging in height from 20 centimetres to almost 5 metres. (*Source:* Carsten Medom Madsen/Shutterstock)

Jews as they realized they were facing death. In that case, her own comportment would be pensive and serious, adding a reflective mood to the atmosphere of the memorial landscape around her. The landscape has made her someone who remembers; in turn, she has made the landscape function as a somber memorial. Together, they have constructed a meaning for the landscape that revolves around remembrance.

If, however, our visitor perceives the arrangement mainly as an architecturally unique stop on the "must-see" list in Berlin, or as a place offering relative quiet and refuge from the big-city bustle, she might react to the landscape by snapping a selfie among the blocks or sitting on one of the lower slabs to rest up and update her Facebook status. In that case, the landscape has not only failed to elicit remembrance in the visitor, but her casual behaviour is also shifting the atmosphere of the landscape toward leisure use, in turn making it more difficult for other visitors to engage in reflection and remembrance and thus perceive and socially construct the landscape as a memorial.

The Memorial to the Murdered Jews of Europe is a compelling illustration of the power of landscape to affect us and of our power to construct various meanings for landscape. In this chapter, we take up the concepts and processes that are captured in this example and explore places and landscapes as the manifestation of multifaceted two-way relationships between people and space.

BEHAVIOUR, KNOWLEDGE, AND HUMAN ENVIRONMENTS

Geographers, as we learned in Chapter 5, attempt to understand how the environment shapes and is shaped by people. In this chapter, we will see that geographers also seek to learn how the environment is perceived and understood by people. Asserting that there is an interdependence between people and places, geographers explore how individuals and groups acquire knowledge of their environments and how this knowledge shapes their attitudes and behaviours. Some geographers focus their research on natural hazards as a way of learning about environmental knowledge, while others try to understand how people ascribe meaning to landscape and places. In this chapter, we consider the key geographical concepts of place, landscape, and space, and we explore the ways in which people understand them, create them, and operate within them. Our goal is to understand how individuals and groups experience their environments, create and struggle within places, and find meaning in the landscapes they create.

In their attempts to understand environmental perception and knowledge, geographers share a great deal with other social scientists, but especially with psychologists. Human cognition and behaviour are at the centre of psychology. What makes environmental knowledge and behaviour uniquely geographical is their relation to both the environmental context and the humans who struggle to understand and operate within it. Much of what we as humans know about the environment we live in is learned through direct and indirect experience. Our environmental knowledge is also acquired through a filter of personal and group characteristics, such as race, gender, stage of the life cycle, religious beliefs, and where we live (**Figure 6.1**).

For instance, children have interesting and distinct relationships to the physical and cultural environment. How do children acquire knowledge about their environments? How do boys and girls differ in the ways they learn about and negotiate their environments? What kind of environmental knowledge do children acquire, and how do they use it? What role do cultural influences play in the process? What happens when larger social, economic, and environmental changes take place?

Geographer Cindi Katz conducted research in rural Sudan to find answers to these questions. Working with a group of 10-year-old children in a small village, she sought to discover how they acquired environmental knowledge. What she also learned was how the transformation of agriculture in the region changed not only the children's relationships to their families and community but also their perceptions of nature.[1] In this Sudanese village, as in similar communities elsewhere in the periphery, children were important contributors to subsistence activities, especially planting, weeding, and harvesting. The villagers were strict Muslims and thus had stringent rules about what female members of the community were allowed to do and where they were allowed to go. Many of the subsistence activities that required leaving the family compound were customarily delegated to male children. Within the traditional subsistence culture, boys predominated in all agricultural tasks except planting and harvesting and were responsible for herding livestock as well. Many boys (and occasionally girls) were also responsible for fetching water and helping gather firewood. Both boys and girls collected seasonal foods from lands surrounding the village. Work and

FIGURE 6.1 Conflicting environmental perceptions This bear is one of several that can be seen almost every day at dusk on a primitive garbage dump in northern Ontario. The bears have learned that the waste is an easy and reliable food source during the summer months, when seasonal cottagers supply a constant stream of fresh refuse. For the locals, the daily bear presence is a nuisance and possible source of danger as they go about their everyday outdoor activities. By contrast, the seasonal cottagers see the bears as a symbol of the "wild North" they came to experience during their vacation. From the safety of their parked cars, they toss food at the bears to get a better "wildlife" snapshot. (*Source:* M. Imort)

[1] C. Katz, *Growing Up Global: Economic Restructuring and Children's Everyday Lives.* Minneapolis: University of Minnesota Press, 2004.

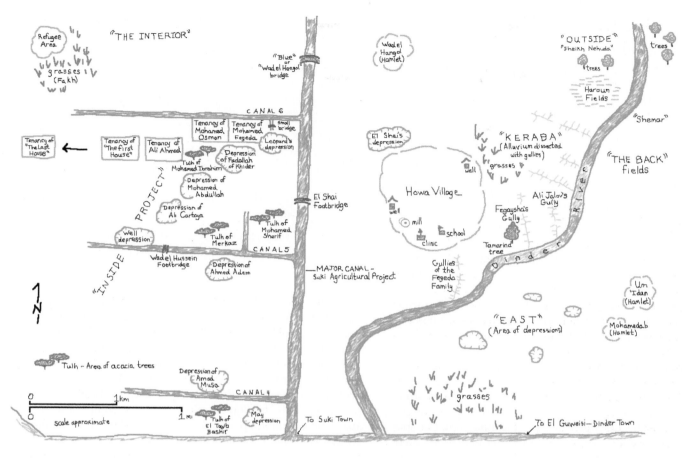

FIGURE 6.2 Shepherd's map This map, drawn by a 10-year-old Sudanese boy, shows the area over which the sheep are herded. It illustrates the detailed environmental knowledge Sudanese children possess of the landscape that surrounds their village. The village is an Islamic one, and norms determine the kinds of tasks in which boys and girls can participate. Only boys are allowed to tend sheep, which requires a particular environmental knowledge about grazing areas and water availability. (*Source:* Image courtesy of C. Katz.)

play were often mixed together, and play, as well as work, provided a creative means for acquiring and using environmental knowledge and for developing a finely textured sense of the home area (**Figure 6.2**).

What happens when the agricultural production system is thoroughly changed, as it was in this village when irrigated cash-crop cultivation was introduced? Through an international development scheme, with the financial assistance of outside donors, a Sudanese government project transformed the agriculture of the region from subsistence livestock raising and cultivation of sorghum and sesame to cultivation of irrigated cash crops such as cotton. The new cash-crop regime, which required management of irrigation works, application of fertilizers, herbicides, and pesticides, and more frequent weeding, required children as well as adults to work longer and harder. Parents were often forced to keep their children out of school because many of the tasks had to be done during the school term.

Destruction of local forests required children to range farther afield to procure fuelwood and to make gathering trips more frequently. Soon wealthier households began buying wood rather than increasing the demands on their children or other household members. For the children of poor households, the selling of fuelwood,

foods, and other items provided a new means of earning cash to support their families, but it also placed increasing demands on their energies and resourcefulness and changed their whole experience of their world.

For the children of this village, globalization (in the form of the transition to cash-crop agriculture) altered their relationships with their environment and with their future. The kinds of skills the children had learned for subsistence production were no longer useful for cash-crop production. As they played less and worked longer hours in more specialized roles, their experience of their environment became narrowed. At the same time, as their roles within the family changed, they attended school less and learned less about their world through formal education. As a result, their perceptions of their environment transformed, along with their values and attitudes toward the landscape and the place they knew as home.

APPLY YOUR KNOWLEDGE Scrutinize how globalization has shaped the environment you operate in as a student. How has it shaped you—the buildings, the people, the climate, the social life, etc.—and how do you shape it by interacting with it? ■

PLACE-MAKING

Places are *socially constructed*—given different meanings by different groups for different purposes. Most people identify with places as part of their personal identity, drawing on particular images and particular histories of places in order to lend distinctiveness to both their individuality and their sense of community. But identifying with place may also imply the exclusion of other people and the stereotyping of other places. People often reinforce their sense of place and of who they are by contrasting themselves with places and people they feel are very different from them. Seen in this context, place-making stands at the centre of issues of culture and power relations, a key part of the systems of meaning through which we make sense of the world.

Territoriality

Some social scientists believe that wanting to have a place where you feel you belong is a natural human attribute, part of a strong territorial instinct. Humans, it is argued, have an innate sense of territoriality, just like many other species. The concept of **territoriality** refers to the persistent attachment of individuals or peoples to a specific location or territory. The concept is important to geographers because it can be related to fundamental place-making forces.

The specific study of people's sense of territoriality is part of the field of **ethology**, the scientific study of the formation and evolution of human customs and beliefs. The term also refers to the study of the behaviour of animals in their natural environments. According to ethologists, humans carry genetic traits resulting from our species' need for territory. Territory provides a source of physical safety and security, a source of stimulation (through border disputes), and a physical expression of identity. These needs add up to a strong territorial urge that can be seen in people's behaviour: claims to space in reading rooms or on beaches, for example, and claims made by gangs to neighbourhood turf (**Figure 6.3**). Ethologists argue that the territorial urge also can be observed when people become frustrated because of overcrowding. They become stressed and, in some circumstances,

begin to exhibit aggressive or deviant behaviour. Ethologists and environmental psychologists link crowding to everything from vandalism and assault to promiscuity, listlessness, and clinical depression.

VIRTUAL GEOGRAPHIES

One (tongue-in-cheek) illustration of the force of the territorial instinct in humans: territorial "marking" can now also be done in the virtual world with the help of smartphone apps that allow users to "mark their territory" digitally on a public map. Users compete for rankings by marking (and overmarking) locations through the GPS function of their smartphones.

While such claims are difficult to substantiate (as is the whole notion that humans have an inborn sense of territoriality), the idea of territoriality as a product of *culturally* established meanings is supported by a large body of scientific evidence. Some of this evidence comes from the field of **proxemics**, the study of the social and cultural meanings that people give to personal space. These meanings make for unwritten territorial rules that can be seen in the micro-geography of people's behaviour. It has been established, for example, that people develop unwritten protocols about how to claim space. One common protocol is simply regular use, as in students always choosing the same seat in a classroom. Another is through the use of spatial markers such as a bag or a towel to reserve a space in a reading room or on a beach. There are also bubbles, or areas, of personal space that we try not to invade (or allow to be invaded by others). Varying in size and shape according to location and circumstance, these bubbles tend to be smaller in public places and in busier and more crowded situations, to be larger among strangers and in situations involving members of different social classes, and to vary from one social class or cultural group to another.

FIGURE 6.3 Tags as territorial markers in a wealthy suburban neighbourhood Tags and graffiti have left behind their inner-city and gang-related origins and are now found even in wealthy neighbourhoods. (*Source:* M. Imort)

VIRTUAL GEOGRAPHIES

The ubiquitous use of smartphones is destabilizing some of our carefully ordered bubbles because a larger personal space is required to keep phone conversations private. Similarly, when we text or check our Facebook account in the presence of another person, we unilaterally introduce a third, "virtual person" to the shared personal space. Just like we had to learn about spatial privacy when entering PINs at ATMs or passwords on computers, we now have to develop new spatial protocols for "properly" using smartphones. These examples show how important the spatial dimension is to social interaction, even in the age of instant telecommunications across great distances. In fact, far from eliminating the importance of space, place, and distance, the new technologies actually present us with an entirely new set of challenges to the way we order space.

On larger spatial scales, territoriality is mostly a product of political relations and cultural systems. This aspect of territoriality underpins a great deal of human geography. All social organizations and the individuals who belong to them are bound at some scale or another through formal or informal territorial limits. Many organizations—nations, corporations, unions, clubs—actually claim a specific area of geographic space to be under their influence or control. In this context, territoriality can be seen as an attempt to assert control over other people, resources, or relationships over a specific geographic area. Territoriality also fulfills socially produced needs for identity, defence, and stimulation. Territoriality covers many phenomena, including the property rights of individuals and private corporations; the neighbourhood covenants of homeowners' associations; the market areas of commercial businesses; the heartlands of ethnic or cultural groups; the jurisdictions of local, provincial, and national governments; and the reach of transnational corporations and supranational organizations.

Territoriality thus provides a means of meeting three social and cultural needs:

- the regulation of social interaction
- the regulation of access to people and resources
- the provision of a focus and symbol of group membership and identity

Territoriality fulfills these needs because, among other things, it facilitates classification, communication, and enforcement. We can classify people and/or resources in terms of their location in space much more easily than we can classify them in relation to personal or social criteria. All that is necessary to communicate territory is a simple marker or sign that constitutes a boundary. This, in turn, makes territory an efficient device for determining whether or not people are subject to the enforcement of a particular set of rules: if they are inside the boundaries, the rules apply; if they are outside, the rules do not.

Territoriality also gives tangible form to power and control but does so in a way that directs attention away from the personal relationships between the controlled and the controllers. In other words, rules and laws become associated with particular spaces and territories rather than with the particular individuals or groups who created those rules and whose interests they serve. Finally, territoriality allows people to create and maintain a framework through which to experience the world and give it meaning. Bounded territories, for example, make it easier to differentiate "us" from "them."

APPLY YOUR KNOWLEDGE Describe the relationship between the concepts of ethology, territoriality, and proxemics. Next, examine three examples of proxemics from your everyday life (beyond the classroom). How are these "unwritten territorial rules" that guide your behaviour an expression of power and culture? ■

People and Places, Insiders and Outsiders

Places are constantly under social construction as people respond to the opportunities and constraints of their particular locality. What this means is that, as people live and work in places, they gradually impose themselves on their environment, modifying and adjusting it to suit their needs and express their values. But at the same time they gradually adapt both to their physical environment and to the values, attitudes, and comportment of the people around them. People are constantly modifying and reshaping places, and places are constantly coping with change and influencing their inhabitants. For instance, your student cohort is influenced and shaped by the constraints and opportunities presented by your university campus. At the same time, your cohort also leaves its unique imprint on the institution and its campus, making it a little bit your own.

Places are therefore both centres of meaning for people and the frameworks for their actions and behaviour. It is important to remember that places are constructed by their inhabitants from their own subjective internal point of view and that they are simultaneously constructed and seen as an external "other" by outsiders. A neighbourhood, for example, is both an area of special meanings to its residents as well as an area containing houses, streets, and people that others may view from an outsider's perspective.

As we saw in Chapter 1, a key concept is that of the *lifeworld*, the taken-for-granted pattern and context through which people conduct their day-to-day lives without having to make it an object of conscious attention. People's familiarity with one another's vocabulary, speech patterns, dress codes, gestures, and humour, and with shared experiences of their physical environment, often carries over into people's attitudes and feelings about themselves and their locality and to the symbolism they attach to that place. When this happens, the result is a collective and self-conscious "structure of feeling": a sociocultural frame of reference generated among people as a result of the experiences and memories that they associate with a particular place.

Experience and Meaning

The interactions between people and places raise some fundamental questions about the meanings that people attach to their experiences: How do people process information from external settings? What kind of information do they use? How do new experiences affect the way they understand their worlds? What meanings do particular environments have for individuals? How do these meanings influence behaviour? How do people develop and modify their sense of a place, and what does it mean to them? The answers to these questions are by no means complete. It is clear, however, that people filter information from their environments through neurophysiological processes and also draw on personality and culture to produce cognitive images of their environment, representations of the world that can be called to mind through the imagination (**Figure 6.4**). Cognitive images are what people see in the mind's eye when they think of a particular place or setting.

Cognitive images both simplify and distort real-world environments. Research has suggested, for example, that many people tend to organize their cognitive images of particular parts of their world in terms of several simple elements (**Figure 6.5**):

Paths: the channels along which they and others move; for example, streets, walkways, transit lines, canals

Edges: barriers that separate one area from another; for example, shorelines, walls, railroad tracks

Districts: areas with an identifiable character (physical and/or cultural) that people mentally "enter" and "leave"; for example, a business district or an ethnic neighbourhood

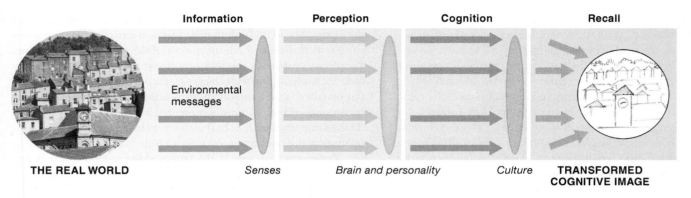

FIGURE 6.4 The formation of cognitive images People form cognitive images as a product of information about the real world, experienced directly and indirectly, and filtered through their senses, brain, personality, and the attitudes and values they have acquired from their cultural background. (*Source:* Adapted from R. G. Golledge and R. J. Stimson, *Analytical Behavioural Geography.* Beckenham, UK: Croom Helm, 1987, Fig. 3.2, p. 3. *Photo source:* M. Imort)

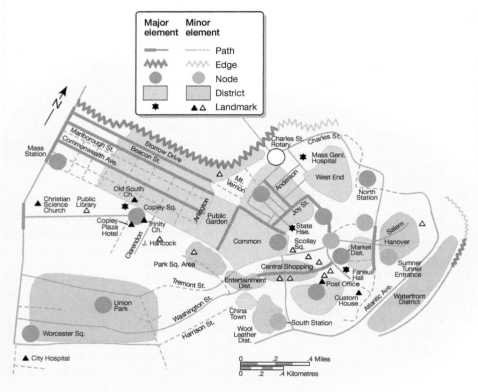

FIGURE 6.5 Cognitive image of Boston This map was compiled by Kevin Lynch from interviews with a sample of Boston residents. Lynch found that the residents of Boston tended to structure their cognitive images of the city with the same elements. He produced ingenious maps, such as this one, to demonstrate the collective "mental map" of the city, using symbols of different boldness or colour to indicate the proportion of respondents who had mentioned each element. (*Source:* Adapted from K. Lynch, *The Image of the City.* Cambridge, MA: M.I.T. Press, 1960, p. 146.)

Nodes: strategic points and foci for travel; for example, street corners, traffic junctions, city squares

Landmarks: physical reference points; for example, distinctive landforms, buildings, or monuments

Individual landscape features may function as more than one kind of cognitive element. A freeway, for instance, may be perceived as both an edge and a path in a person's cognitive image of a city. Similarly, a train station may be seen as both a landmark and a node.

Distortions in our cognitive images are partly the result of incomplete information. Once we get beyond our immediate living area, we know few spaces in complete detail. Yet our worlds are increasingly large in geographic scope—especially for those of us in developed countries who are directly tied into global networks of communication and knowledge. As a result, these extended worlds are not directly experienced by us and must instead be conceived, or understood, with limited direct stimuli. Thus we have to rely on fragmentary and often biased information from other people, from books, magazines, television, and the Internet. Distortions in cognitive images are also partly the result of our own biases. What we remember about places, what we like or dislike, what we think is significant are all functions of our personalities, our experiences, and the cultural influences to which we have been exposed.

APPLY YOUR KNOWLEDGE Use the five elements noted in this section of the chapter to map out your cognitive image of your university campus—the mental map that you use to navigate around. What are the key paths, edges, districts, nodes, and landmarks that make up your mental map? ∎

Images and Behaviour

Cognitive images are compiled, in part, through behavioural patterns. Environments are "learned" through experience. Meanwhile, cognitive images, once generated, influence future behaviour. Via this two-way relationship, cognitive images are constantly changing. Each of us also generates—and draws on—different kinds of cognitive images in different circumstances.

Elements such as districts, nodes, and landmarks are important in the kinds of cognitive images that people use to orient themselves and to navigate within a place or region. The more of these elements an environment contains—and the more distinctive they are—the more legible that environment is to people and the easier it is to get oriented and navigate. In addition, the more firsthand information people have about their environment and the more they are able to draw on secondary sources of information, the more detailed and comprehensive their images are.

This phenomenon is strikingly illustrated in **Figure 6.6**, which shows the collective image of Los Angeles as seen by the residents of three neighbourhoods: Westwood, an affluent neighbourhood; Avalon, a poor, inner-city neighbourhood; and Boyle Heights, a poor, immigrant neighbourhood. The residents of Westwood have a well-formed, detailed, and comprehensive image of the entire Los

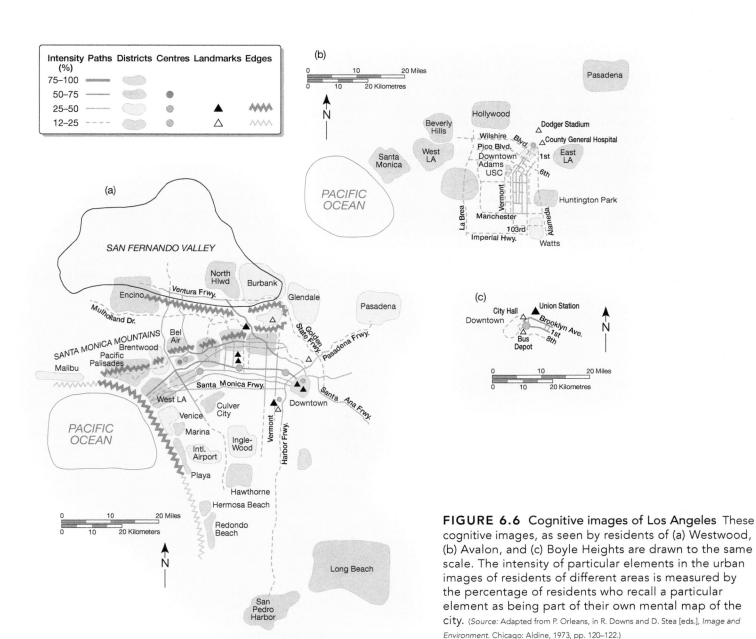

FIGURE 6.6 Cognitive images of Los Angeles These cognitive images, as seen by residents of (a) Westwood, (b) Avalon, and (c) Boyle Heights are drawn to the same scale. The intensity of particular elements in the urban images of residents of different areas is measured by the percentage of residents who recall a particular element as being part of their own mental map of the city. (*Source:* Adapted from P. Orleans, in R. Downs and D. Stea [eds.], *Image and Environment.* Chicago: Aldine, 1973, pp. 120–122.)

Angeles basin. At the other end of the socioeconomic spectrum, residents of the Black ghetto neighbourhood of Avalon, near Watts, have a much more vague image of the city, structured only by the major east–west boulevards and freeways and dominated by the gridiron layout of streets between Watts and the city centre. The Hispanic residents of Boyle Heights—even less affluent, less mobile, and more isolated by language—have an extremely restricted image of the city. Their world consists of a small area around Brooklyn Avenue and First Street, bounded by the landmarks of city hall, the bus depot, and Union Station.

The importance of these images goes beyond people's ability simply to navigate around their environments. The narrower and more localized people's images are, for example, the less they will tend to venture beyond their home area: their behaviour becomes circumscribed by their cognitive imagery. People's images of places also shape particular aspects of their behaviour. Research on shopping in cities, for example, has shown that customers do not necessarily go to the nearest store or to the one with the lowest prices; they are influenced by the configuration of traffic, parking, and pedestrian circulation within their imagery of the environment.

In addition, shopping behaviour, like many other aspects of behaviour, is influenced by people's values and feelings. A district in a city, for example, may be regarded as attractive or repellent, exciting or relaxing, fearsome or reassuring, or, more likely, a combination of such feelings. As is the case with all cognitive imagery, such images are produced through a combination of direct experience and indirect information, all filtered through personal and cultural perspectives. Images such as these often exert a strong influence on behaviour. Returning to the example of consumer behaviour, one of the strongest influences on shopping patterns relates to the imagery evoked by retail environments—something else that has not escaped the developers of malls, who spend large sums of money to establish the "right" atmosphere and image for their projects.

Shopping behaviour is one narrow example of the influence of place imagery on behaviour. Additional examples can be drawn from every aspect of human geography and at every spatial scale. The settlement of North America, for example, was strongly influenced by the changing images of the Prairies. In the early 1800s, the Prairies were perceived as arid and unattractive, an image reinforced by early atlases that labelled them as "desert." In the late 1800s, when the railroad companies wanted to encourage settlement in these regions, they changed people's image of the Prairies with advertising campaigns that portrayed them as fertile and hospitable regions. The images associated with different regions and localities continue to shape settlement patterns. People draw on their cognitive imagery, for example, in making decisions about migrating from one area to another. **Figure 6.7** shows the composite image of the United States held by a group of Virginia Tech university students, based on the perceived attractiveness of cities and states as places in which to live.

Another example of the influence of cognitive imagery on people's behaviour is the way that people respond to environmental hazards, such as floods, droughts, earthquakes, storms, and landslides, and come to terms with the associated risks and uncertainties. Some people attempt to change the unpredictable into the knowable by imposing order where none really exists (resorting to folk wisdom about weather, for example), while others deny all predictability and take a fatalistic view.

Finally, one aspect of cognitive imagery is of special importance in modifying people's behaviour: the sentimental and symbolic attributes ascribed to places. Through their daily lives and the cumulative effects of cultural influences and significant personal events, people develop bonds with places. They do this simultaneously at different geographic scales: from the home, through the neighbourhood and locality, to the provincial and national scale. The tendency for people to do this has been called topophilia. **Topophilia** literally means "love of place." Geographers use the term to describe the complex emotions and meanings associated

FIGURE 6.7 Preference map of the United States This isoline map illustrates collective preferences for cities in the coterminous United States as places in which to live and work, as expressed by architecture students at Virginia Tech in 1996. It is a generalization based on the scores the students gave to the 150 largest cities in the U.S.

Preference Index
High preference
90 and above
70 to 89
50 to 69
30 to 49
Less than 30
Low preference

with particular places that, for one reason or another, have become significant to individuals.

LANDSCAPES AS HUMAN SYSTEMS

Landscape is a term that means different things to different people. For some, the term signifies a bucolic countryside or the spatial arrangement of houses, roads, and fields. For others, it brings to mind the design of formal gardens and parks, as in landscape architecture. For still others, landscape calls to mind the artistic rendering of scenery, as in landscape painting.

As we learned in Chapter 1, geographers study a variety of landscapes. They study "landscapes of power," such as clusters of corporate office towers; "landscapes of despair," such as homeless encampments; and **derelict landscapes**—landscapes that have experienced abandonment, misuse, disinvestment, or vandalism. Geographers are particularly interested in symbolic landscapes because they reflect certain values or ideals—mainly those intended by their builders or financiers, but also those perceived by other groups (**Figures 6.8** and **6.9**). In the extreme, individual buildings and landscape elements can become so closely identified with "their" city that they now are seen as iconic: the Eiffel Tower

FIGURE 6.8 The Canadian National Vimy Memorial Set on Vimy Ridge, this monument commemorates the Canadian soldiers killed in World War I. At the time of its construction in the 1920s, the overtly pacifist symbolism of its statuary was criticized as a sign of "meekness." In later years, its muteness and absence of overt militarism came to be reinterpreted as representing Canadian virtues of peacefulness, sympathy, and mediation. (*Source*: M. Imort)

FIGURE 6.9 Statue of Mother Canada at Vimy Ridge A statue representing the mourning young nation of Canada overlooks the former battlefield of Vimy Ridge. Visible in the background are the tailings of the coal mines that were the reason for the battle: controlling the coal fields was vitally important for producing arms and ammunition. (*Source*: M. Imort)

in Paris, the Colosseum in Rome, and Sugarloaf Mountain in Rio de Janeiro, for example (**Figure 6.10**). Most interesting to geographers, however, are the everyday landscapes that people create in the course of their lives together because these so-called vernacular (ordinary) landscapes reflect the distinctive attributes of particular places or regions.

Ordinary Landscapes

Vernacular landscapes can be seen to express the "character" of a particular nation, region, or culture. For example, the stereotypical Atlantic Canadian townscape with its painted wooden buildings and the colonial façades of Ontario towns are easily recognized as types of regional Canadian architecture (**Figure 6.11**). At the same time, however, they are widely understood to represent a simpler, more wholesome life that is based on community, family values, and a slower pace of life. Signifying neither affluence nor poverty, these landscapes have come to symbolize the Canadian ideal of a balanced community populated by property-minded, law-abiding citizens devoted to economic self-reliance and a certain kind of social morality.

A counterpoint is provided by the landscapes of contemporary Canadian suburbia. They are conservative utopias of seemingly casual displays of wealth, characterized by master-planned developments, simulated settings, and conspicuous consumption (**Figure 6.12**). Rather than suggesting local rootedness or regional identity, these generic suburban landscapes express individual success through size: the bigger the house/lot/car, the higher the presumed social status of the owner. In this sense, they signify Canada's sharing in the Western ideal of a neoliberal society in which individual rights and accomplishments are paramount.

The key point is that ordinary landscapes, as geographers such as Don Mitchell have established, are powerful complexes of signs that perform vital functions of social regulation: they are instruments of social and cultural power that *naturalize* political-economic structures (making them appear as if they were simply given and inevitable).

FIGURE 6.10 Iconic landmarks Some cities are immediately recognizable because of certain buildings, landmarks, or cityscapes that have come to symbolize them. These examples—the Colosseum in Rome, Sugarloaf Mountain in Rio de Janeiro, the Eiffel Tower in Paris, and the London skyline along the Thames—are known worldwide. (*Source :* Doug Pearson/Jon Arnold Images Ltd/Alamy [top left] David R. Frazier Photolibrary, Inc./Alamy [top right] M. Imort [bottom left] Julian Love/John Warburton-Lee Photography/Alamy [bottom right])

FIGURE 6.11 Ordinary landscapes Some ordinary cityscapes are powerfully symbolic of particular kinds of civic values. The quiet small town in Atlantic Canada (left) and the renovated colonial main street of Ontario towns are in this category, so much so that they are often seen as symbolizing Canada and Canadian values. (*Source:* M. Imort)

FIGURE 6.12 Vulgaria In Canada, and even more so in the U.S., upscale residential development increasingly employs the symbolic language of size and ostentation to express competitive notions of individual economic success and social standing. (*Source:* M. Imort)

In our examples, the Atlantic townscape with its tight but shared public spaces encourages notions of community, but also social control. By contrast, the landscape of upscale Canadian suburbia with its emphasis on privacy and exclusion naturalizes the primacy of individual rights, but it also promotes cocooning—the disengagement from civic affairs and a focus on competitive consumption.

Conceptualization of Landscape

Since 1925, when Carl Sauer advocated the study of the *cultural landscape* as a uniquely geographical pursuit, new generations of geographers have been expanding the concept. The fact that different people comprehend the landscape differently is central to the humanistic approach in geography. **Humanistic approach** places the individual—especially individual values, meaning systems, intentions, and conscious acts—at the centre of analysis. As the Sudanese example given earlier in the chapter suggests, children's perceptions of their worlds are different from those of their parents, and girls may perceive their world differently from boys, even in the same family.

Environmental perception and its close relative, behavioural geography, are interdisciplinary, drawing together geographers, landscape architects, psychologists, architects, and others. Professionals in these disciplines investigate what preferences people have in landscapes, how they construct cognitive images of their worlds, and how they find (or fail to find) their way around in various settings. Here the humanistic approach with its focus on the perceptions of individuals is an important counterweight to the tendency to talk about a social group or society more generally. In other words, the humanistic approach avoids the stereotyping of people. On the other hand, some critics argue that humanistic research has limited utility because the results apply only to the individual and thus are hard to generalize to the level of the group or population. The tension between these viewpoints reminds us that there is not one single correct approach and that we need to be open to a variety of perspectives when studying any phenomenon in human geography.

How would we do this in the case of studying landscape? We could combine the humanistic focus on individual motivations and actions with an approach that considers the role of larger forces, such as culture, gender, and the state, and the ways in which these forces enhance or constrain individuals' lives. Much recent cultural geographical work therefore conceptualizes the relationship between people and the environment as *interactive*, not one-way, and emphasizes the role that landscapes play in shaping and reinforcing human practices. This most recent conceptualization of landscape is more dynamic and complex than the one Carl Sauer advanced, and it encourages geographers to look outside their own discipline—to anthropology, psychology, sociology, and even history—to fully understand its complexity.

CODED SPACES

A dynamic and complex approach to understanding landscape is based on the conceptualization of **landscape as text**, by which we mean that, like a book, landscape can be read and written by groups and individuals. This approach departs from traditional attempts to systematize or categorize landscapes based on the different elements they contain. The landscape-as-text view holds that landscapes do not come ready-made with labels on them. Rather, there are "writers" who produce landscapes and give them meaning, and there are "readers" who consume the messages embedded in landscapes. Those messages can be read as signs about values, beliefs, and practices, though not every reader will take the same message from a particular landscape (just as people may differ in their interpretation of a passage from a book).

In short, landscapes both produce and communicate meaning, and one of our tasks as geographers is to interpret those meanings. In order to interpret or read our environment, we need to understand the language in which it is written. We must learn how to recognize the signs and symbols that go into the making of landscape. The practice of writing and reading signs is known as **semiotics**.

Semiotics asserts that innumerable signs are embedded or displayed in landscape, space, and place, sending messages about identity, values, beliefs, and practices. These signs may have different meanings for those who produce them and those who read, or interpret, them. Some signs are so subtle as to be recognizable only when pointed out by a knowledgeable observer; others may be more readily available and more ubiquitous. For example, semiotics enables us to recognize that university students, simply by the way they dress, send messages to one another and the wider world about who they are and what they value. For some of us, certain groups, such as jocks, preps, emos, gamers, hipsters, or tree-huggers, are readily identifiable by their clothes, hairstyles, or footwear; by the bags they carry; or even by the food they eat.

Commercial Spaces

Semiotics, however, is not only about the concrete signs that people convey with their bodies or their behaviours. Messages are also deployed through the landscape and embedded in places and spaces. Consider the very familiar landscape of the shopping mall. In a society where just about every aspect of life has become a commodity, shopping defines who we are more than ever before, and what we consume sends signals about who we want to be. Advertising and social media tell us what to consume, equating ownership of products with happiness, a good sex life, social standing, and success in general. Within the space of the mall, these signals are collected and re-sent.

Malls are complex semiotic sites, transmitting important signals not only about what to buy but also about who should shop there and who should not. The placement and mix of stores and their interior design, the arrangement of products within stores, the amenities offered to shoppers, and the ambient music all combine to send signals to the consumer about style, taste, and self-image. Most malls therefore are "anchored" on the outer corners by middlebrow stores like The Bay and Sears, while the more expensive and luxurious shops and boutiques occupy interior locations. Similarly, many malls possess a kind of socioeconomic geology, where the lower level of the mall

FIGURE 6.13 The Forum Mall, Caesar's Palace, Las Vegas Investors in Las Vegas have developed integrated complexes in which hotel, casino, and opulent mall create a themed "experience" of another time and place, in this case Ancient Rome. Other complexes pretend to take the visitor to nineteenth-century Paris, Ancient Egypt, or Renaissance-era Venice. The purpose of focusing the visit on the fake experience is to mask the real act of consumption. (*Source:* M. Imort)

provides for the mundane needs of middle-class patrons (dry cleaners, lottery kiosks, and the food court), whereas the upper level offers a more diverse and pricey selection of vendors associated with conspicuous consumption (jewellers, boutiques, and the Apple Store).

Shopping malls play a fundamental role in the Canadian economy: there are almost 5000 shopping centres in Canada, which together account for almost half of all non-automotive retail sales. They employ more than 1.2 million people, representing almost 10 percent of Canada's non-agricultural work force. Ninety-two percent of Canadians visit a mall at least once a month, with the average being 2.25 visits per month.[2] Evidently, shopping is an integral part of Canadian life. Yet, as much as we seem to enjoy shopping, there persists for a great many of us an explicit disdain for shopping and the commercialism and materialism that accompany it. Thus, shopping is a complicated activity that is full of ambivalence. It is not surprising, therefore, that developers have promoted shopping as a kind of escape from the ordinary. The mall is a "pseudoplace" meant to encourage one sort of activity—shopping—by projecting the illusion that something else besides shopping (and spending money) is actually going on (**Figure 6.13**).

Jon Goss has written that to conceal the contradiction in our society between conspicuous consumption and contempt for consumerism, a mall needs to disconnect us from the reality of shopping. We do not want to know about the true circumstances in which the objects we buy were made or distributed, for to do so will diminish the object's value in our eyes, and our own value as discriminating purchasers in the eyes of other people. Malls must therefore mystify the true connection between the ideals and reality

[2]International Council of Shopping Centres (icsc.org).

of consumption—a "trick" that many successful malls perform by creating a "sense of place."[3] Consequently, malls provide an excellent opportunity to see "place-making" at work.

In a detailed study of the West Edmonton Mall, Jeff Hopkins shows us how to read some of the semiotics embedded in the retail landscape.[4] By 2011, this mega-mall just outside Edmonton, Alberta, consisted of more than 800 stores, 100 restaurants, two hotels, and numerous recreational facilities (including a wave pool, dolphin lagoon, and ice rink), and the world's largest parking lot. Every year, more than 30 million visitors find their way to the mall. (Obviously, much more than shopping is going on in this mall.) Hopkins writes that the mall creates a sense of place through the following:

- *Simple allusion to place names.* Thus, one part of the West Edmonton Mall is called "Bourbon Street." The name alone makes the link with any associations we may have of the real city of New Orleans.

- *A general allusion to a distant time period*—such as the 1920s— or general type of place—such as "the Wild West"—through statues, other decorative details, or music.

- *The replication of a specific place.* The West Edmonton Mall's "Fantasyland" makes direct reference to Disneyland. Again, this is achieved through architecture and design, colour, lighting, statues, and so on.

Depending on our perspective, however, we can each interpret the landscape quite differently, and a mall is no exception in this regard. Not surprisingly, the homeless will be less concerned with how a mall creates a sense of place than with how it can provide warmth and shelter. It would be a mistake, however, to interpret the park benches and open spaces of the mall as an indication of public space in which one can remain. Malls are private space, and security personnel will soon appear to move people who misinterpret the signals.

In fact, ambiguities about public and private space are deliberately fostered by malls to make us feel at home when we make our purchases. These ambiguities have been strengthened by the recent development in Canada of covered, combined retail and pedestrian spaces, such as the skywalks of Halifax and Calgary and the "underground cities" of Montreal and Toronto (**Figure 6.14**).

Officially called the "PATH: Downtown Walkway," Toronto's underground city in 2014 comprised 30 kilometres of tunnels beneath the city core, lined with over 1200 stores and services and frequented by over 200 000 pedestrians a day. Montreal's underground city is even more extensive, with more than 1700 shops and services. Both networks are linked to underground transit systems via a number of stations and so draw on considerable hinterlands of nearby office towers as well as distant residential neighbourhoods.

These forms of underground retailing make it difficult to clearly separate public from private space. For example, although the tunnels of the Toronto underground city seem to be a continuous public space, they actually are a mosaic of 35 private spaces that

FIGURE 6.14 Toronto's underground city A network of underground tunnels lined with shops and services below the streets enables pedestrians to avoid the discomforts of the Canadian winter and summer. Five thousand people now work in Toronto's underground city, which started with a single tunnel as early as 1900. (*Source:* City of Toronto Economic Development—Small Business & Local Partnerships Office. Reproduced by permission.)

are individually owned and controlled. On their property, owners have the right to evict "undesirables," such as skateboarders or street people. On the other hand, recent legal decisions have shown that public right can be extended to such private spaces. This is because, in Canadian law, a public space need not be public property. This means that, even in such underground mosaics of privately owned spaces, individuals enjoy constitutionally guaranteed freedoms of expression and peaceful assembly.

Commercial spaces are thus not merely utilitarian spaces with clear functionality. Instead, they embody various codes of meaning that can vary across time and space, as well as among individuals.

> **APPLY YOUR KNOWLEDGE** Apply what you just learned about codes to provide a description of the systems of signification that operate in your neighbourhood mall. Appraise what information the various sections of the mall convey through coded means. ■

Sacred Spaces

Religious places can also be read and decoded. **Sacred spaces** are areas of the globe recognized by individuals or groups as worthy of special attention because they are the sites of special religious experiences and events. They do not occur naturally; rather, they are assigned sanctity through the values and belief systems of particular groups or individuals. Geographer Yi-Fu Tuan insists that what defines the sacredness of a space goes beyond the obvious shrines and temples. Sacred spaces are those that rise above the commonplace and interrupt ordinary routine.

[3]Jon Goss, "The Magic of the Mall: An Analysis of Form, Function, and Meaning in the Contemporary Retail Built Environment," *Annals of the Association of American Geographers* 83, 1993, pp. 18–47.
[4]Jeffrey S.P. Hopkins, "West Edmonton Mall: Landscape of Myths and Elsewhereness," *Canadian Geographer* 34, 1990, pp. 2–17.

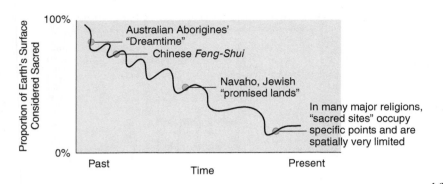

FIGURE 6.15 A model of sacred space This diagram shows how views of sacred spaces may have changed over time.

If we want to make geographical sense of the phenomenon of sacred space, it is useful to consider a very simple model (**Figure 6.15**). In this model, we hypothesize a very early time when almost all of Earth's surface was considered sacred, in contrast with the present day, when very little of its surface is so considered. In between lies a long period of transition, affected by many changes in religion and spirituality. We should note that many other changes were occurring during this transition period, including changing attitudes to nature (see Chapter 4) and to material wealth (Chapter 7).

The Australian Aborigine interprets the entire surface of Earth as embodying aspects of the Creation, an event occurring during the Dreamtime. Hills and caves, for example, are where creatures of the Dreamtime have slept or hidden. The Dreamtime can be called to mind by travelling through the landscape on prescribed routes known as "Songlines," celebrating the landscape (and creation) in song.

Similarly, Chinese *feng shui* practitioners recognize the sacredness of the entire Earth's surface as they seek to interpret its energy lines and identify the most propitious landscapes. University of Victoria geographer David Lai describes how *feng shui* was used to locate the first Chinese cemetery in Victoria: nearby hills that resembled a dragon and a tiger promised to be auspicious for houses or graves located nearby. This is because these two animals symbolize respectively the yang and yin energies present in nature, and their occurrence together at such locations shows that these two energies will be kept in abundance and harmony.[5]

Other groups believe that they have been given their homeland as a sacred trust, to inhabit it as a chosen people. This division of Earth in some way implies that not all space is seen as sacred, at least in the eyes of the group in question. Jewish belief in the "promised land" is one example. Another is the North American Navaho belief that their appointed territory lies between four sacred mountains. For the Blackfoot, certain locations in the Alberta foothills, where Spirit Beings changed into human form and gave them their sacred ceremonies, are considered special places. As the Blackfoot people explained at a recent exhibition at Calgary's Glenbow Museum that they curated, "These places provide physical evidence that the events really happened and are part of Blackfoot history. Sacred places connect the Blackfoot to our territory, are part of our identity and are the basis of our claim to this territory."[6]

With the development of Islam, Christianity, and Buddhism, ideas of sacred space becomes more focused into specific locations. Those

parts of Earth touched by the deity are more valued than those places that were not. A geography of sacred and profane spaces begins to unfold. Places of pilgrimage and shrines articulate that space and serve to connect us with the sacred. Indeed, it is worth noting that it is necessary to *go to* church, temple, synagogue, or mosque because these are more sacred places than the everyday or profane world in which we live.

Such segregated sacred spaces are often permanent sites, meaning that they are maintained as such generation after generation. The range of sacred spaces includes sites as different as an elegant and elaborate temple in Cambodia, Angkor Wat, sacred first to Hindus and then to Buddhists (**Figure 6.16**), and the Black Hills of South Dakota, the sacred mountains of the Lakota Sioux.

Often, members of a specific religion are expected to journey to especially important sacred spaces to renew their faith or to demonstrate devotion. A pilgrimage is a journey to a sacred space, and a pilgrim is a person who undertakes such a journey. For Hindus, the Ganges is India's holiest river, and many sacred sites are located along its banks (**Figure 6.17**). Hindus visit sacred pilgrimage sites for a variety of reasons, including seeking a cure for sickness, washing away sins, and fulfilling a promise to a deity.

Perhaps the most well-known pilgrimage is the **hajj**, the obligatory once-in-a-lifetime journey of Muslims to Mecca. For one month every year, the city of Mecca in Saudi Arabia swells from its base population of 150 000 to over 1 000 000 as pilgrims from all over the world journey to fulfill their obligation to pray in the city and receive the grace of Allah. **Figure 6.18** shows the principal countries that send pilgrims to Mecca.

Pilgrimages to sacred sites are made all over the world, including Christian Europe. The most-visited sacred site in Europe is Lourdes, at the base of the Pyrenees in southwest France, not far from the Spanish border (**Figure 6.19**). Another sacred site that attracts pilgrims throughout the world is Jerusalem, and the Holy Land more generally, which is visited by Jews, Orthodox, Catholics, Protestants, Christian Zionists, and followers of many other religions. (See Box 6.1, "Geography Matters: Jerusalem, the Holy City.") As with most sacred spaces, the codes that are embedded in the landscape of the Holy Land may be read quite differently by

FIGURE 6.16 Angkor Wat, Cambodia Built for the king Suryavarman II in the early twelfth century, Angkor Wat was dedicated to the Hindu god Vishnu. In the late thirteenth century, the temple became a sacred site for Buddhists, and continues as such to this day. (*Source:* Vladimir Wrangel/Shutterstock)

[5]Chuen-yan David Lai, "A *Feng Shui* Model as a Location Index," *Annals Association of American Geographers* 64, 1974, pp. 516–513.
[6]*Nitsitapiisinni: The Story of the Blackfoot People.* Toronto: Key Porter, 2001, p. 50.

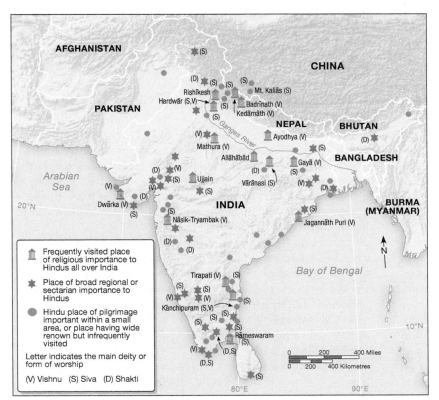

FIGURE 6.17 **Sacred sites of Hindu India** India's many rivers are holy places within the Hindu religion, so sacred sites are located along the country's many riverbanks. Shrines closer to the rivers are regarded as holier than those farther away. (*Source:* Adapted from Ismail Ragi al Farugi and David E. Sopher, *Historical Atlas of the Religions of the World.* New York: Macmillan, 1974.)

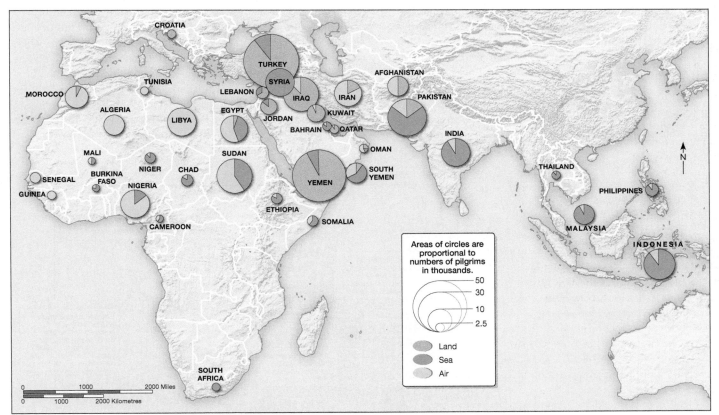

FIGURE 6.18 **Source areas for pilgrims to Mecca** Islam requires that every adult Muslim perform the pilgrimage to Mecca at least once in a lifetime. This obligation is deferred for four groups of people: those who cannot afford to make the pilgrimage; those who are constrained by physical disability, hazardous conditions, or political barriers; slaves and those of unsound mind; and women without a husband or male relative to accompany them. The pattern of actual pilgrimages to Mecca (located close to the Red Sea coast in Saudi Arabia) suggests a fairly strong distance-decay effect, with most pilgrims travelling relatively short distances from Middle Eastern Arab countries. More-distant source areas generally provide smaller numbers of pilgrims, though Indonesia and Malaysia are notable exceptions. (*Source:* After C. C. Park, *Sacred Worlds.* London: Routledge, 1994, p. 268.)

Although many cities in the world have been the object of struggle and conflict over the centuries, none has been as endlessly beset as Jerusalem. Visitors, writers, and residents believe Jerusalem to be the most beautiful city in the world. If there are other serious competitors to that coveted beauty title, Jerusalem certainly has few rivals for the title of the most sacred city in the world, possessing as it does an unmatched Christian, Jewish, and Islamic history. Jerusalem began as a small settlement on the slopes of Mount Moriah. In 997 B.C.E., it was captured by David, king of the Israelites, who made Jerusalem the capital of Israel. Solomon, David's son and successor, built the Great (First) Temple on Mount Moriah to commemorate the place where Abraham offered to sacrifice his son. Though the temple was destroyed centuries ago, the site is central to the Jewish faith.

The history and the map of the city reflect the histories of the various empires that dominated and were succeeded by new and yet more powerful empires (**Figure 6.A**). Nebuchadnezzar, king of Babylon, destroyed the Great Temple in 586 B.C.E. and banished the Jews. But the Babylonian control of Jerusalem eventually gave way to the Persians, under whose rule the Jews were allowed to return and rebuild their temple, known as the Second Temple. The Romans entered the scene around 63 B.C.E., installing Herod the Great to command the Roman Kingdom of Judea from Jerusalem.

The Jews revolted openly against the Roman occupiers, and in 70 C.E., the Romans responded by destroying the Second Temple and banishing all Jews from Jerusalem and Palestine. As a result, the Jews scattered north into Babylon and later into Europe and North Africa. The popular myth is that this ancient Jewish diaspora remained in exile until 1948, when the state of Israel was created.

The major Christian influence on Jerusalem began when Constantine I (285–337 C.E.), the emperor of the Eastern Roman Empire, converted to Christianity in 313 C.E. This event led to the construction of churches and other buildings dedicated to celebrating the life of Jesus Christ. But Christian influence over the city ceased when Jerusalem eventually succumbed to Islam. In 638 C.E. Jerusalem was designated a holy city of Islam because it was believed that Muhammad's spirit had once made a visit to heaven while he was in the city.

Although for several centuries Jews, Christians, and Muslims were all allowed access to the city of Jerusalem, by the tenth century the persecution of non-Muslims had become common. From the eleventh century until the thirteenth, European Christians undertook military expeditions—called the Crusades—to the Holy Land in an attempt to wrest control of Jerusalem from the Muslims. In 1099, Crusaders captured the city; Christians lost it again to the Muslim military leader Saladin in 1187. In 1517, Jerusalem was absorbed into the Ottoman Empire, and the city was ruled from Istanbul for more than 400 years. The Ottomans, however, had little interest in Jerusalem, and Jewish immigrants began returning to the city and Palestine starting in the mid-nineteenth century.

The contemporary history of the city derives from the political and geographical implications of a British statement of policy, which stipulated that Jerusalem should be an international city with no one state claiming it as entirely its own. Today, Jerusalem is a highly contested city as Palestinians, Christians, Muslims, and Jews fight for control of it. An example of this contest for control is the continuing dispute over the Dome of the Rock, which was constructed between 688 and 691 C.E. Muslims claim the Dome as one of their most sacred

FIGURE 6.A Jerusalem, the Holy City This map of Jerusalem demarcates the main sections of the city. Over the many years of the Israeli–Palestinian peace process, numerous proposals have been advanced about how to divide the city to satisfy the wishes of both Arabs and Israelis. The disposition of Jerusalem is one of the major issues in the ongoing peace process. (*Source:* Redrawn from *The Guardian*, 14 October 2000, p. 5.)

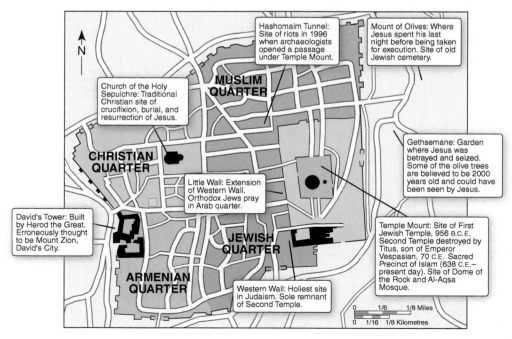

Hashomaim Tunnel: Site of riots in 1996 when archaeologists opened a passage under Temple Mount.

Mount of Olives: Where Jesus spent his last night before being taken for execution. Site of old Jewish cemetery.

Church of the Holy Sepulchre: Traditional Christian site of crucifixion, burial, and resurrection of Jesus.

MUSLIM QUARTER

CHRISTIAN QUARTER

Gethsemane: Garden where Jesus was betrayed and seized. Some of the olive trees are believed to be 2000 years old and could have been seen by Jesus.

Little Wall: Extension of Western Wall. Orthodox Jews pray in Arab quarter.

David's Tower: Built by Herod the Great. Erroneously thought to be Mount Zion, David's City.

JEWISH QUARTER

Temple Mount: Site of First Jewish Temple, 956 B.C.E. Second Temple destroyed by Titus, son of Emperor Vespasian, 70 C.E. Sacred Precinct of Islam (638 C.E.– present day). Site of Dome of the Rock and Al-Aqsa Mosque.

ARMENIAN QUARTER

Western Wall: Holiest site in Judaism. Sole remnant of Second Temple.

0 1/6 1/8 Miles

0 1/16 1/8 Kilometres

sites (**Figure 6.B**). Yet the Dome sits on a site sacred to the Jews, the Temple Mount, the site where the Great Temple and Second Temple were built and later destroyed. Indeed, the Dome is believed to enclose the sacred rock upon which Abraham prepared to sacrifice his son, according to Jewish tradition, and, according to Islamic tradition, is the same rock from which the prophet Muhammad launched his spirit on a heavenly visit. Also located on the Temple Mount is the Al-Aqsa Mosque, a central sacred site to Muslims.

While nationalist Israelis maintain that Jerusalem will be the "eternal and undivided capital" of Israel, Palestinians believe that Jerusalem is the future capital of the Palestinian state. In fact, the 1992 Oslo peace accords that led to a declaration of principles between Israel and Palestine hint at the possibility of negotiating a future for Jerusalem that includes some control by the Palestinians. However, subsequent peace negotiations, including those at Wye River, Maryland, in 1998; at Sharm al-Shaykh in the Egyptian Sinai Desert in 1999; in Camp David, Maryland, in 2000; in Washington, D.C., in 2001; in Geneva in 2003; in Annapolis, Maryland, in 2007; and, most recently, in Washington in 2014 have not yet brought about a resolution. At present, Jerusalem is entirely controlled by Israel.

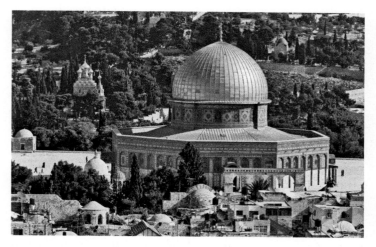

FIGURE 6.B Dome of the Rock Located in Haram al-Sharif, or Temple Mount, the Dome of the Rock sits in the part of Jerusalem that is technically neither Jewish nor Muslim, but both. The Muslims want this entire holy site. The Israelis also want it because the Western Wall, sacred to Jews, forms part of the basis of the Temple Mount. (*Source:* Vladimir Khirman/iStock/Getty Images Plus/Getty Images)

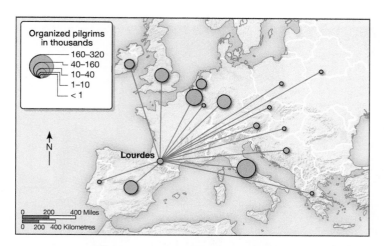

FIGURE 6.19 Source areas for pilgrims to Lourdes This map shows the points of origin of European group-organized pilgrims to Lourdes in 1978. These represent only about 30 percent of all pilgrims to Lourdes, most of whom travel to the shrine on their own. Improved transportation (mainly by train) and the availability of organized package trips have contributed to a marked increase in the number of pilgrims visiting. Many of the 5 million pilgrims who visit the town each year do so in the hope of a miraculous cure for medical ills at a grotto where the Virgin Mary is said to have appeared before 14-year-old Bernadette Soubirous in a series of 18 visions in 1858. (*Source:* After C. C. Park, *Sacred Worlds*. London: Routledge, 1994, p. 284.)

different religious and even secular visitors. Two scholars studying the phenomenon of pilgrimage observed

> Each group brings to Jerusalem their own entrenched understandings of the sacred; nothing unites them save their sequential—and sometimes simultaneous—presence at the same holy sites. For the Greek Orthodox pilgrims, indeed, the precise definition of the site itself is largely irrelevant; it is the icons on display which are the principal focus of attention. For the Roman Catholics, the site is important in that it is illustrative of a particular biblical text relating to the life of Jesus, but it is important only in a historical sense, as confirming the truth of past events. Only for the Christian Zionists does the Holy Land itself carry any present and future significance, and here they find a curious kinship with indigenous Jews.[7]

APPLY YOUR KNOWLEDGE Choose a religious or spiritual landscape and dissect the semiotic code that helps explain how it operates. ∎

---

[7]J. Eade and M. Sallnow (eds.), *Contesting the Sacred.* London: Routledge, 1991, p. 14.

PLACE AND SPACE IN MODERN SOCIETY

While memorials, malls, and sacred places illustrate the way that places are coded within *specific* settings or contexts, there are also *broader* dimensions of social, economic, and political life that shape the ways people think about themselves and about the places they inhabit. One of these broader forces is the philosophy of modernity, which for the past century has been a major influence on the interdependencies among culture, society, space, place, and landscape throughout much of the world.

Modernity is a forward-looking view of the world that emphasizes reason, scientific rationality, creativity, novelty, and progress. Its origins can be traced to the European Renaissance and the emergence of the world-system of competitive capitalism in the sixteenth century. At that time, scientific discovery and commerce began to displace traditional sociocultural views of the world that emphasized mysticism, romanticism, and fatalism. These origins were consolidated into a philosophical movement during the eighteenth century, when the Enlightenment established the widespread belief in universal human progress and the sovereignty of scientific reasoning over religious dogma.

At the beginning of the twentieth century, this philosophy developed into a more widespread intellectual movement. A series of sweeping technological and scientific developments not only triggered a new round of spatial reorganization but also transformed the underpinnings of social and cultural life. These developments included the telegraph, the telephone, the X-ray, the motion picture, the radio, the bicycle, the internal combustion engine, the airplane, the skyscraper, relativity theory, and psychoanalysis. Universal human progress suddenly seemed to be a realistic prospect, to be achieved through the consequent application of technology.

Nevertheless, the pace of economic, social, cultural, and geographic change was unnerving and the outcomes uncertain. The intellectual response, developed among a cultural avant-garde of painters, architects, novelists, and photographers, was a resolve to promote modernity through radical changes in culture. These ideas were first set out in the "Futurist Manifesto" by the Italian poet Filippo Marinetti in 1909. Gradually, the combination of new technologies and radical design contributed to the proliferation of landscapes of modernity. Among the most striking of these were modernist urban landscapes whose design was guided by such principles as "form follows function," a preference for linearity and angularity, and a call for simple forms without "unnecessary detail." In a general sense almost all of the place-making and landscapes of the twentieth century are the products of modernity, and as a result they often resemble each other, no matter where they are or what purpose they serve (**Figure 6.20**).

For most of the twentieth century, the confident and forward-looking, modernist philosophy remained virtually unquestioned. Places and regions everywhere were heavily shaped by people acting out their notions of rational behaviour and progress. Rural regions, for example, were reorganized into efficient monocultures of agricultural modernization. The hedgerows of traditional European field patterns were torn up to make way for landscapes of large, featureless fields in which heavy machinery could operate more effectively (**Figure 6.21**). On a different scale, peripheral countries sought to remake traditional landscapes through economic modernization. Economic development and social progress were to be achieved through a modern infrastructure of highways, airports, dams, harbours, and industrial parks.

FIGURE 6.20 Landscapes of modernity These photographs show modernist urban landscapes on two continents: one is at La Défense, an office district in Paris designed to be emblematic of the aspirations of Paris to compete as a major world city in the global economy. The other is a Las Vegas cluster of condo and hotel buildings whose flawless surfaces give expression to the ideal of hedonist consumption. You cannot tell where each photo was taken and whether the buildings serve residential or office purposes. That is the point: modernist landscapes across the world have an interchangeable look to them because they all follow the same design rules.

(*Source:* Paul L. Knox [left]. M. Imort [right])

FIGURE 6.21 Rural landscape of modernity Circular bales of hay dot the "gutted" agricultural landscape of East Anglia in the United Kingdom. (*Source:* jlynx/Shutterstock)

Globalization and Place-Making

The spread of modernity to peripheral regions can be seen as another aspect of globalization. These globalization processes have not only brought about a generalization of forms of industrial production, market behaviour, trade, and consumption but also reinforced and extended the commonalities among places. Three factors are especially important in this context.

First, mass communications media have created global culture markets in print, film, music, television, and the Internet. Indeed, the Internet has created an entirely new *kind* of space—cyberspace—with its own "landscape" and its own embryonic cultures. (See Box 6.2, "Visualizing Geography: The Cultural Geography of Cyberspace and Social Media.") The instantaneous character of contemporary communications has also made possible the creation of a shared, global consciousness from the staging of global events such as the Olympic Games and the World Cup. Second, mass communications media have diffused certain values and attitudes toward a wide spectrum of sociocultural issues, including citizenship, human rights, child rearing, social welfare, and self-expression. Third, international legal conventions have increased the degree of standardization and level of harmonization not only of trade and labour practices but of criminal justice, civil rights, and environmental regulations.

These commonalities have been accompanied by the growing importance of material consumption within many cultures. Increasingly, people around the world are eating the same foods, wearing the same clothes, and buying the same consumer products. Yet the more people's patterns of consumption converge, the more fertile the ground for countercultural movements. The more transnational corporations undercut the authority of national and local governments to regulate economic affairs, the greater the popular support for regionalism. The more universal the diffusion of material culture and lifestyles, the more local and ethnic identities are valued. The more time people spend in virtual environments, the more they feel the need for a subjective setting—a specific place or community—they can call their own. The faster the pace of life in search of profit and material consumption, the more people

value family and leisure time. And the faster their neighbourhoods acquire the same generic supermarkets, gas stations, shopping malls, big-box stores, office parks, and suburban subdivisions, the more people feel the need for enclaves of familiarity, centredness, and identity. The United Nations Centre for Human Settlements (UNCHS) notes

> In many localities, people are overwhelmed by changes in their traditional cultural, spiritual, and social values and norms and by the introduction of a cult of consumerism intrinsic to the process of globalization. In the rebound, many localities have rediscovered the "culture of place" by stressing their own identity, their own roots, their own culture and values and the importance of their own neighborhood, area, vicinity, or town.[8]

One example of the impulse for people to recover a sense of place is provided by the Cittaslow (slow city) movement. The Cittaslow movement is a grassroots response to globalization and is closely related to the longer-established and better-known slow food movement. The aims of the two movements are different but complementary: in broad terms, both organizations are in favour of local, traditional cultures, a relaxed pace of life, and conviviality. Both are a response to the quickening pace of everyday life associated with the acceleration of money around local, national, and global circuits of capital. Both are hostile to big business and globalization, though their driving motivation is not so much political as ecological and humanistic. Slow food is devoted to a less-hurried pace of life and to the true tastes, aromas, and diversity of good food. The movement also serves as a rallying point against globalization, mass production, and the kind of generic fast food represented by U.S.-based franchises. Its campaigns cover a range of specific causes, from protecting the integrity of chocolate to promoting the cultivation of traditional crop varieties and livestock breeds and opposing genetically engineered foods.

[8]United Nations Centre for Human Settlements, *Global Report on Human Settlements 2001*. London: Earthscan, 2001, p. 4.

The rapid growth of the Internet and of social media like Facebook and Twitter is of great cultural significance. It has created the basis for a massive shift in patterns of social interaction, a seedbed for new forms of human consciousness, and a new medium for cultural change. Culture is fundamentally based on communication, and in cyberspace we now have an entirely new form of communication: at once written, visual, and aural, but also multidirectional and open to all (**Figure 6.C**).

At face value, the Internet represents the leading edge of the globalization of culture. The Internet portends a global culture based on English as the universal world language, with a heavy emphasis on core-area cultural values, such as novelty, spectacle, fashionableness, material consumption, and leisure. When we look more closely, however, we see that this globalization bears the hallmarks of Americanization, or at least Westernization, as much

of the content originates in and deals with Western core countries. (**Figures 6.D** and **6.E**).

Despite the core bias of the Internet, it is unlikely that the Internet will simply be a new medium through which core-area values and culture are spread. To begin with, the impact of the Internet is likely to be highly uneven because of the **digital divide**—the inequality of access to telecommunications and information technology—which applies particularly to Internet services (see Figures 2.23 and 2.24). Moreover, there is resistance in some places and regions to the cultural globalization associated with an Anglophone and Americanized cyberspace. For example, authorities in France and Quebec, already sensitive about the influence of English-language popular culture, have actively sought ways to give francophones access to the Internet without submitting to English.

Furthermore, in much of Asia, the Internet's basic function as an information-exchange medium clashes with local cultures in which information is a closely guarded commodity. Whereas many government and corporate websites in Western core countries feature lengthy reports and scientific studies, as well as lively debates about policy, comparable Asian sites typically offer little beyond public relations materials. The reluctance of major Asian organizations to put important information on their websites—along with the need for Westerners to use special software to read any local-language documents that do exist—has resulted in a largely one-way flow of information, from North America and Europe to Asia (**Figure 6.F**).

In addition, some Asian countries actively put barriers in place to control even that one-way flow of information. For example, the connection between China and the global Internet is tightly controlled and can be severed at a moment's notice to prevent the spreading of unwelcome information. Services such as YouTube, Google, Facebook, and Twitter are blocked by the "Great Firewall," and censored Chinese substitutes have been established. Over 600 million Chinese use this "domestic" Internet—more than the online population of North America and Europe combined.

Despite these biases and limitations, the greatest potential of the Internet and social media in terms of cultural change resides in the liberating and empowering potential of their vast resource of dispersed knowledge and information. By its very nature the Internet empowers individuals (rather than social groups or institutions), allowing millions to say whatever they want to each other, free from state control (for the first time in history). As such, it also is an important vehicle for the spread of participatory democracy to much of the world, as demonstrated by the political upheavals of the Arab Spring.

But authoritarian regimes are fully aware of this potential, too, and so they launch their own propaganda through paid mouthpieces. A prominent example is the so-called 50-Cent Army. For about ten years now, the Chinese authorities have hired tens of thousands of Internet commentators to post favourable comments about their policies and steer online discussions away from sensitive or critical subject matters. For each posting, the commentators are paid 50 Renminbi cents—hence the name.

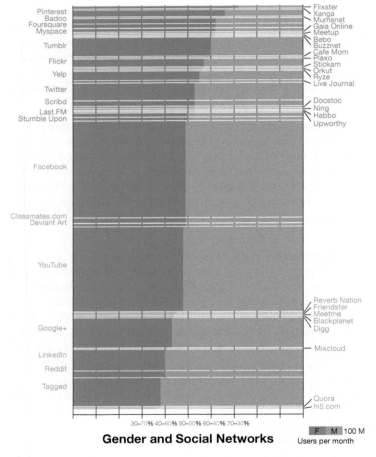

Gender and Social Networks

FIGURE 6.C Gender and social media Probably for the first time in human history, access to public channels of communication appears to be relatively gender neutral. In fact, on most of the platforms graphed in this figure, women outnumber men. The graph uses 2013 data and shows both the total number of users per month (area) and their gender distribution (colour). (*Source:* Graham, M., S. Hale & M. Stephens. 2011. Geographies of the World's Knowledge. Convoco! Edition. Available from geography.oii.ox.ac.uk.)

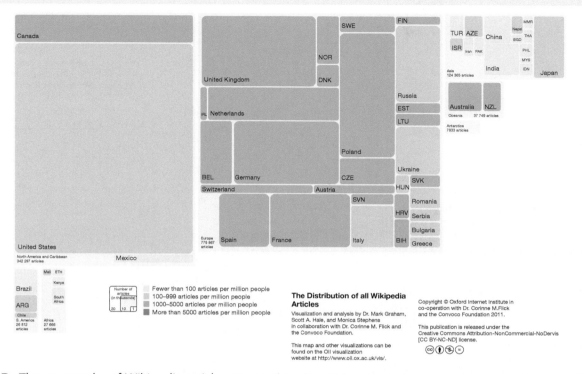

The following labels appear within the cartogram:

Canada · United Kingdom · Netherlands · IRL · BEL · Germany · Switzerland · United States · Mexico · Brazil · ARG · Chile · S. America 26 512 articles · Mali · ETH · Kenya · South Africa · Africa 27 668 articles · North America and Caribbean 342 297 articles · SWE · NOR · DNK · Spain · France · Austria · Europe 775 867 articles · Italy · FIN · Russia · EST · LTU · Poland · Ukraine · SVK · HUN · SVN · HRV · CZE · BIH · Greece · Bulgaria · Serbia · Romania · TUR · AZE · ISR · Iran · PAK · China · Nepal · BGD · THA · MMR · PHL · MYS · IDN · India · Japan · Asia 124 365 articles · Australia · NZL · Oceania 37 749 articles · Antarctica 7833 articles

Number of articles (in thousands) 20 10 1

Fewer than 100 articles per million people
100–999 articles per million people
1000–5000 articles per million people
More than 5000 articles per million people

The Distribution of all Wikipedia Articles
Visualization and analysis by Dr. Mark Graham, Scott A. Hale, and Monica Stephens in collaboration with Dr. Corinne M. Flick and the Convoco Foundation.

This map and other visualizations can be found on the OII visualization website at http://www.oii.ox.ac.uk/vis/.

Copyright © Oxford Internet Institute in co-operation with Dr. Corinne M.Flick and the Convoco Foundation 2011.

This publication is released under the Creative Commons Attribution-NonCommercial-NoDervis [CC BY-NC-ND] license.

FIGURE 6.D The geography of Wikipedia articles Most Wikipedia articles about places, events, or any other locatable subject matter are geotagged with longitude and latitude coordinates. This cartogram uses 2010 data to show the number of such geotagged Wikipedia articles for each country. Assuming that Wikipedia reflects the Internet's "swarm knowledge," the cartogram shows how utterly uneven the distribution of that knowledge is: almost 85 percent of all articles deal with North America and Europe. By contrast, fewer than 1 percent of all articles are about China, the country with the world's largest online population. Less surprising is the fact that most small nations have less than 100 articles dealing with them—which not only restricts the amount of information that is available about them on Wikipedia, but also focuses attention disproportionately on those few sources. Because so many opinions and resulting decisions are founded on Wikipedia information, this asymmetric geography of representation can have far-reaching, real-life consequences through travel preferences, investment decisions, political views, and cultural biases. (*Source:* Graham, M., Hogan, B.,Straumann, R. K., and Medhat, A. 2014. Uneven Geographies of User-Generated Information: Patterns of Increasing Informational Poverty. Annals of the Association of American Geographers (forthcoming).)

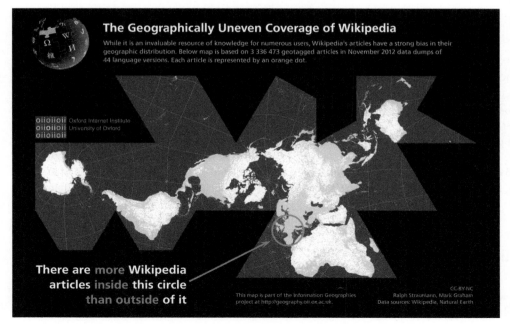

FIGURE 6.E The geographically uneven coverage of Wikipedia This dot map on a Buckminster Fuller's Dymaxion projection shows the distribution of Wikipedia articles in November 2012. Most articles are from or about countries inside the red circle, thus showing the considerable geographic and informational bias of Wikipedia. (*Source:* Graham, M., and De Sabbata, S. 2014. Information Geographies. geography.oii.ox.ac.uk.)

(Continued)

221

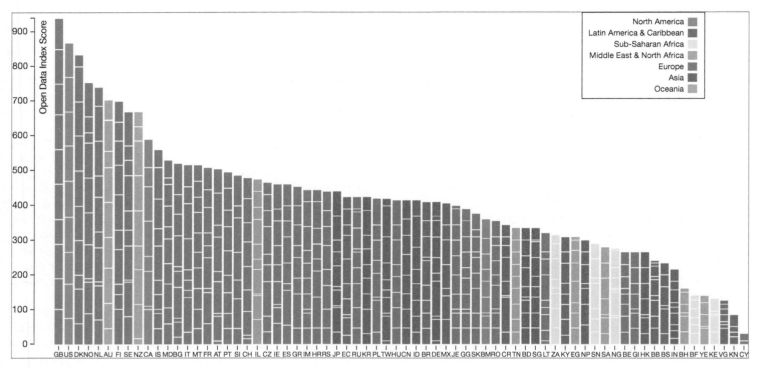

FIGURE 6.F **Data "openness" of countries** This chart visualizes how "open" countries were in 2013 when it came to providing access to open datasets on the Internet. The datasets range from government spending and national statistics to election results and pollutant emissions. On average, the scores of North American and European countries are twice as high as those of Asian countries. *(Source: Graham, M., and De Sabbata, S. 2014. Information Geographies. geography.oii.ox.ac.uk.)*

The Cittaslow movement, formed in 1999, commits to working toward calmer and less-polluted physical environments, conserving local aesthetic traditions, and fostering local crafts, produce, and cuisine. The goal is to foster the development of places that enjoy a robust vitality based on good food, healthy environments, sustainable economies, and the seasonality and traditional rhythms of community life. (See Box 6.3, "Window on the World: Waldkirch, Germany.") Currently, there are two member towns in Canada, both on the B.C. coast: Cowichan Bay and Naramata.

Places as Objects of Consumption in Postmodern Society

The slow city movement is but one way in which people resist the increasing speed and homogeneity brought about by the dual forces of modernity and globalization. As early as the 1980s, modernity's unrelenting emphasis on rationality, uniformity, and efficiency began to be mocked by an emerging postmodernist perspective that valued playfulness and diversity instead. **Postmodernity** is a view of the world that emphasizes openness to a range of perspectives in social inquiry, artistic expression, and political empowerment. It is often described in terms of cultural expressions that are playful, superficial, populist, pluralistic, and spectacular.

Postmodernity critiques modernity's emphasis on economic and scientific progress, arguing that modernity's failure to deliver such progress in a sustainable and equitable fashion to all people is indicative of its flaws. Because of this, postmodernity also rejects modernity's search for grand universal theories. Instead, postmodernity values difference and the unique—both aspects that appeal to human geographers and other students of

Waldkirch, a town of 12 500 inhabitants, sits astride the valley of the River Elz in southwestern Germany, where the river exits the Black Forest headed toward the Rhine. To the southwest of the town are the broad floodplains of the Elz and its tributaries, a region of intensive and prosperous agriculture—mainly dairy farming and orchards, viticulture, and market gardening **(Figure 6.G)**. To the north, east, and south of the town is the Black Forest, dotted with prosperous and immaculately kept farmsteads set in meadows bordered by fruit trees.

Waldkirch was once famous for the manufacture of barrel organs, and the name of the town was carried around the world on its products. The industry began, along with clock-making, as a winter craft for Black Forest farmers in the late 1700s. It grew to become internationally famous between 1850 and the 1930s, with several firms exporting all kinds of finely crafted organs—from small drawing-room models to larger versions for churches, fairgrounds, music halls, theatres, and ocean liners—all over the world.

Today, Waldkirch is a prosperous and lively town with a strong sense of place and a collective commitment to the quality of life of its residents **(Figure 6.H)**. Just 15 kilometres north of the regional capital of Freiburg, and connected to that city by light rail, Waldkirch has acquired a growing commuter population that has contributed to a high level of prosperity. Its vitality is reflected in its shops, services, clubs, and community organizations. Despite its relatively small population, there are scores of clubs and volunteer organizations, and the town is well endowed with stores; there are several optometrists, for example, plus a high-end furniture store (with customers from Freiburg and beyond), three shoe stores, a health food store, a good bookstore, a sportswear store, and several bakers, butchers, and pharmacists.

In addition to this general prosperity, Waldkirch has an unusually energetic and progressive group of community leaders that includes elected officials, bureaucrats, business owners, and company managers. In 1998, the city began a visioning process that resulted in a strong emphasis on quality of life and a parallel commitment to urban planning. Waldkirch joined the Cittaslow movement in 2002 as a natural outcome of this strategy. Policies that have been put in place to commit to the Cittaslow philosophy include a strong emphasis on using streets as social and play spaces **(Figure 6.I)**. Priority is given to pedestrians wherever possible, and on all residential streets there is a 30 kilometres per hour speed limit with radar enforcement. Storefronts on the main street, Lange Strasse, are being gradually restored to traditional windows and façades (reversing 1960s and 1970s plate-glass modernizations); and the local public utility company has installed a renewable energy system for public buildings, using locally sourced wood chips as the fuel source.

Complementing the Cittaslow philosophy is the town's involvement in the Austrian-based *Lebensqualität durch Nähe* movement with its "Live Here; Buy Local" slogan. The program

FIGURE 6.H Waldkirch, Germany The heart of the town is the Marktplatz, a broad street that slopes down from the site of the original hillside settlement, which dates from the early Middle Ages. Waldkirch began as a small ecclesiastical centre and country market that developed on the southern shoulder of the valley, guarded by a small castle built above town. As in many German municipalities, the town centre is off limits to vehicular traffic except for early morning deliveries. (*Source:* Paul L. Knox)

FIGURE 6.G The cultural landscape around Waldkirch, Germany The cultural landscape around Waldkirch is still dominated by small-scale, mixed-dairy family farms connected by a network of first-rate infrastructure. (*Source:* M. Imort)

(Continued)

has three elements: social networks (meaning face-to-face networking, rather than the virtual kind) and sense of place; lifestyle, food, and nutrition; and employment. The broad idea is to strengthen basic services in small settlements and to build local consciousness about the connections between quality of life and the availability of services and products that are locally produced and sold. An additional goal is to support surrounding farms and agriculture to maintain the traditional cultural landscape. As a result, Waldkirch has developed special zoning requirements to ensure minimum percentages of arable land and pastureland.

The town's leadership has also placed a great deal of emphasis on social sustainability. A recent project involved the revitalization of a house that had been serving as a residence for the homeless in a neglected and run-down neighbourhood. The city government spent about CDN$1.5 million on renovating the house—now known as the "Red House" because of its bright red façade. Today, the house functions as a multi generational meeting place and houses the office of a neighbourhood social worker and a drop-in kitchen. A farmers' market with local vendors takes place once a week in front of the house. Stalls feature fresh fruit and vegetables, bread, and fairtrade products **(Figure 6.J)**. Since the "Red House" opened, neighbourhood vandalism has dropped and residents of all ages and ethnic groups are strengthening social networks. To connect these social efforts with economic opportunities for the residents, Waldkirch initiated a program that provides local job opportunities for residents who have been long-term unemployed.

FIGURE 6.I **Social bonds** Waldkirch is an enthusiastic member of the Cittaslow (slow city) movement, which endeavours to support and encourage conviviality. Opportunities for regular casual encounters among pedestrians are an important means of developing a sense of conviviality in the town. (*Source:* Paul L. Knox)

FIGURE 6.J **Waldkirch farmers' market** A long-standing tradition, the weekly farmers' market is an important element in sustaining the rhythm of the town and its residents' sense of place. (*Source:* Paul L. Knox)

place making. (See Box 6.4 Visualizing Geography: Postmodern Architecture.)

Outside of architecture, postmodernity has contributed to the creation of a sociocultural environment in which the emphasis is on the *style* of consumption. In much of the world, people's enjoyment of material goods now depends not just on their physical consumption or use but also on the role of material culture as a social marker. A person's home, automobile, clothing, smartphone, reading, viewing, eating and drinking preferences, and choice of vacations are all seen as indicators of that person's status, social distinctiveness, and sense of style. Postmodern society has thus been interpreted as a "society of the spectacle," in which

the symbolic properties of material possessions and places have assumed unprecedented importance.

One result of these trends is that contemporary cultures rely much more than before not only on material consumption but also on *visual* and *experiential* consumption of *places*: the purchase of images and the experience of being in spectacular and distinctive places, physical settings, and landscapes. An important example of the increased economic importance of visual and experiential consumption of places is the growing heritage industry that exploits the histories of people and places worldwide. For instance, in the United Kingdom, more than 200 million tourists visit designated heritage sites every year, spending more than

Postmodern Architecture

Postmodernity is most recognizable in architecture and urban design in core areas, where it is expressed through eclecticism, decoration, parody, and a heavy use of historical and vernacular motifs—all rendered with a playful self-conscious stylishness. (**Figures 6.K, 6.L, 6.M, 6.N,** and **6.O**)

FIGURE 6.K Town Square Mall, Las Vegas This master-planned outdoor shopping mall blends architectural elements from different times and places to create a pastiche of "Old World" sense of place. Pastiche, or the celebration of style through imitation, is an integral part of postmodern aesthetics. (*Source:* M. Imort)

FIGURE 6.L Westerturm Ensemble, Duderstadt, Germany When the town of Duderstadt renovated part of its medieval fortifications, it added architectural elements of glass, steel frames, and cubic concrete to create a postmodern "ensemble" that is a playful architectural mashup of various eras. (*Source:* M. Imort)

FIGURE 6.M The Re:START Mall, Christchurch, New Zealand After the 2011 earthquake devastated the city's main shopping street, merchants set up temporary shops in a purpose-designed cluster of containers. Both the name and design of the mall play with its ephemerality in a self-referential manner typical for postmodernity: rather than hiding the provisional character of the containers, the development emphasizes them through contrasting colours and irregular stacking. (*Source:* M. Imort)

(Continued)

FIGURE 6.N "Borrowed heritage" inside Casino Niagara, Niagara Falls, Ontario When Casino Niagara was built in the mid-1990s, it enveloped part of the former outdoor streetscape into the building complex. However, the incorporated "historical" façades are anything but authentic: they had been purpose-built in 1979 for the Maple Leaf Amusement Park that used to occupy the site. Borrowing and intentional fakeness are prominent stylistic devices of postmodern architecture. (*Source:* M. Imort)

FIGURE 6.O Cellphone tower in Caiscais, Portugal Postmodern playfulness is often co-opted to hide more mundane technical necessities, as in this "camouflaged" cellphone tower in an upscale coastal neighbourhood. (*Source:* M. Imort)

$50 billion on entry fees, retail sales, travel, and hotel accommodations (**Figure 6.22**).

It is important to note that the images, signs, and experiences that are consumed do not necessarily have to be originals; they can also be copies or even simulations (as in the Edmonton Mall). This means that developers are tempted to imitate and even invent "heritage" landscapes that satisfy commercial considerations rather than principles of authenticity or heritage preservation. As a result, contemporary landscapes contain increasing numbers of inauthentic settings—what geographer David Harvey has called the "degenerative utopias" of global capitalism. These are as much the product of contemporary postmodern approaches to material and visual culture as they are of any cultural heritage. In the extreme, urban cultural environments are vulnerable to a debasing and trivializing "Disneyfication" process. The United Nations Centre for Human Settlements (UNCHS) *Global Report on Human Settlements 2001* notes

> The particular historic character of a city often gets submerged in the direct and overt quest for an international image and international business. Local identity becomes an ornament, a public relations artifact designed to aid marketing. Authenticity is paid for, encapsulated, mummified, located, and displayed to attract tourists rather than to shelter continuities of tradition or the lives of its historic creators.[9]

[9]United Nations Centre for Human Settlements, *Global Report on Human Settlements 2001*. London: Earthscan, 2001, p. 38.

FIGURE 6.22 Heritage tourism German tourists enjoying a preserved English heritage townscape in Rye, East Sussex. (*Source:* M. Imort)

FIGURE 6.23 Kimberley, B.C. This community in the interior of British Columbia has adopted a (Disneyfied) Austrian style of architecture to suggest an Alpine heritage. (*Source:* Courtesy of Alan E. Nash)

In Canada, we can find a number of towns that have "borrowed" another cultural heritage to heighten their tourist appeal. The Okanagan valley community of Osoyoos in British Columbia has adopted Spanish-American architecture to advertise its unusually warm microclimate. Kimberley, also in British Columbia, plays with Alpine heritage imagery on its "Austrian"-style town square (**Figure 6.23**).

The intriguing example of Shelburne, Nova Scotia, suggests that sometimes we value the replica at least as much as the authentic. Settled in 1783, the town still has a considerable number of genuine vernacular buildings of that period. Partly on the strength of this, Shelburne was chosen to be the location for the film *The Scarlet Letter*, set in seventeenth-century New England. To fully recreate the appearance of such a place, the filmmakers built a number of additional structures in the style of the period (**Figure 6.24**). These buildings were so "authentic" that, when shooting was over, the town petitioned the movie company to leave them standing. These replica buildings are now advertised on the town's website as "authentic": "Why not tour part of the remaining set and experience an authentic historic market square?"[10]

FIGURE 6.24 Shelburne, Nova Scotia Authentic or replica? Some of the "historic" buildings of Shelburne were built in 1994 as part of a film set. (*Source:* M. Imort)

FIGURE 6.25 Paris in Las Vegas The inauthentic "historic" settings of "places" in Las Vegas are inspired at least as much by movies and popular stereotypes as by historic realities. Shown here is the Paris Las Vegas hotel and casino, located on the Las Vegas Strip. The replica of the Eiffel Tower was planned to be the height of the original, but it had to be reduced to half scale because it is too close to the airport. (*Source:* M. Imort)

FIGURE 6.26 Venice in Las Vegas Contrary to appearances, this picture was taken *indoors*. The façades are part of a simulated St. Mark's Square inside the Venetian Hotel in Las Vegas, complete with a painted faux sky and simulated dusk. (*Source:* M. Imort)

The pinnacle of simulated places is probably found in Las Vegas. Here the leisure and entertainment industries have created copies of well-known places that allow tourists to consume a fake sense of place at reduced scale (**Figure 6.25**) and in air-conditioned comfort (**Figure 6.26**).

Our review of the visual and experiential consumption of places leaves us with an interesting question: if we are so often satisfied with consuming fake place experiences instead of the real ones, what exactly is it that we hope to find in such a place? Since we all know that we are "posers" in a fake place, there can be no cachet associated with being there. Is it simply the desire to be in a place that is out of the ordinary? Has our everyday world, build on the ideals of modernity, become so meaningless to us that we are happy to escape to a postmodern fiction? Is this the beginning of an "experience economy"? (See Chapter 7.)

APPLY YOUR KNOWLEDGE Compare and contrast modernity and postmodernity. Give specific examples of what each stands for and the ways they are different. ■

Future Geographies

Globalization has already brought a significant degree of homogenization of culture through the language of consumer goods. This is the material culture of the West, enmeshed in Airbus jets, CNN, YouTube, smartphones, and the Internet, and swamped by Coca-Cola, Budweiser, McDonald's, GAP clothing, Nikes, iPads, PlayStations, Toyotas, Disney franchising, and formula-driven Hollywood movies (**Figure 6.27**). Furthermore, sociologists have recognized that a distinctive culture of "global metropolitanism" is

FIGURE 6.27 McDonald's greeting customers with a traditional *wai* The McDonald's franchise has always been aggressive in marketing its brand, but many felt it went too far in Shanghai when in the mid-1990s a new branch of the fast-food restaurant was opened in the Zhongshan Guang Chang district featuring a gigantic fiberglass Ronald McDonald figure in the form of the Buddha seated in the lotus position. At the time, their attempt at co-opting the holy man (and dedicated vegetarian) to market McDonald's hamburgers was widely criticized and the icon was removed within one month. In 2005, however, the Ronald McDonald figure greeting guests with the traditional Thai *wai* gesture, pictured here, was introduced to restaurants around Thailand with no strenuous objections. (*Source:* Kristin Piljay/Danita Delimont/Alamy)

emerging among the transnational elite. This is simply homogenized culture at a higher plane of consumption (French wines instead of Budweiser, sushi and fusion cuisine instead of McDonald's, Hugo Boss clothes instead of Levis, BMWs instead of Toyotas, and so on). The members of this new culture are people who make international conference calls, make decisions and transact investments that are transnational in scope, edit the news, design and market international products, and travel the world for business and pleasure. Globally, this culture is likely to grow significantly in size and influence.

The idea of the emergence of a single global culture is too simplistic, but the pervasive emphasis on material, visual, and experiential consumption means that many aspects of contemporary culture will increasingly transcend local and national boundaries. More and more of the world's population are world travellers—either directly or via the Internet—and thus many are knowledgeable about aspects of others' cultures. This contributes to **cosmopolitanism**, an intellectual and aesthetic openness toward divergent experiences, images, and products from different cultures.

Cosmopolitanism is an important geographic phenomenon because it fosters a curiosity about all places, peoples, and cultures, together with at least a rudimentary ability to situate such places and cultures geographically, historically, and anthropologically. It also suggests an ability to reflect upon, and aesthetically appreciate, different places and cultures. Optimists would speculate that this bodes well for global peace and understanding: we can, perhaps, more easily identify and connect with people who use the same products, listen to the same music, and appreciate the same sports stars that we do. At the same time, however, focusing attention on material consumption obscures the emergence of other trends. As people's lives are homogenized through their jobs and their material culture, many of them want to revive subjectivity, reconstruct we/us feelings, and re-establish a distinctive cultural identity. One potential outcome of this is an increased probability of cultural and territorial conflict.

> **APPLY YOUR KNOWLEDGE** Elaborate on three examples of how globalization of culture shapes places and landscapes. ∎

CONCLUSION

Geographers study the interdependence between people and places and are especially interested in how individuals and groups acquire knowledge of their environments and how this knowledge shapes their attitudes and behaviours. People ascribe meanings to landscapes and places in many ways, and they also derive meanings from the places and landscapes they experience. Different groups of people experience landscape, place, and space differently. For instance, the experience that rural Sudanese children have of their landscapes and the ways in which they acquire knowledge of their surroundings differs from how

middle-class children in a Canadian suburb learn about and function in their landscapes. Furthermore, both landscapes elicit a distinctive sense of place that is different for those who live there and those who simply visit.

As indicated in previous chapters, the concepts of landscape and place are central to geographic inquiry. They are the result of intentional and unintentional human action, and every landscape is a complex reflection of the operations of the larger society. Geographers have developed categories of landscape to help distinguish the different types that exist.

Ordinary landscapes, such as suburban neighbourhoods, are ones that people create and experience in the course of their everyday lives. By contrast, symbolic landscapes represent the particular values and aspirations that developers and financiers want to impart to a larger public, as in the classical appearance of government buildings or the symbolism of war memorials.

More recently, geographers have come to regard landscape as a text, something that can be written and read, rewritten, and reinterpreted. This concept suggests that a landscape can have more than one author, and different readers may derive different meanings from what is written there. The idea that landscape can be written and read is further supported by the understanding that the language in which the landscape is written is a code. To understand the significance of the code is to understand its semiotics, the language in which the code is written. The code may be meant to convey many things, including a language of power or of playfulness, a language that elevates one group above another, or a language that encourages imagination or religious devotion and spiritual awe.

The global transition from modernity to postmodernity has altered cultural landscapes, places, and spaces differently as individuals and groups have struggled to negotiate the local impacts of this widespread shift in cultural sensibilities. The shared meanings that insiders derive from their place or landscape have been disrupted by the intrusion of new sights, sounds, and smells as values, ideas, and practices from one part of the globe have been exported to another. The Internet and the emergence of social media have meant that new spaces of interaction have emerged that have neither a distinct historical memory attached to them nor a well-established sense of place. Because of this, the virtual space of the Internet carries with it some unique possibilities for cultural exchange. It remains to be seen, however, whether access to this new space will be truly open—or whether the Internet will become another landscape of power and exclusion.

Learning Outcomes Revisited

- Investigate how environment shapes people and how people shape environments.

  People not only filter information from their environments through neurophysiological and psychological processes; they also draw on personality and culture to produce cognitive images of their environment—pictures or representations of the world that can be called to mind through the imagination. The human–environment relationship results in a variety of ways of understanding the world around us as well as different ways of being in the world as information about our environment is filtered by people.

- Recognize that place-making stands at the centre of issues of culture and power relations and that it is a key part of the systems of meaning through which humans make sense of the world.

  Places are the result of a wide range of forces from economic to social. Economically, places emerge through all sorts of transactions that result from the complexities of the land market. But places are also more than just real estate. They can reflect tensions between social groups as well as harmonious interaction.

- Identify how different cultural identities and status categories influence the ways people experience and understand landscapes, as well as how they are shaped by—and are able to shape—landscapes.

  Among the most important relations are the cultural identities of race, class, gender, ethnicity, and sexuality. Often these identities come together in a group, and their influence in combination becomes central to our understanding of how group identity shapes space and is shaped by it.

- Understand how codes signify important information about landscapes, a process known as semiotics.

  To interpret our environment, we must learn how to read the codes that are written into the landscape. Landscapes as different from each other as shopping malls and memorials can be understood in terms of their semiotics, although it is important to appreciate that even when certain landscapes have intended meanings by those who have created them, those who perceive them may make their own sense of that landscape.

- Describe how globalization has occurred in parallel with a transition from modernity to postmodernity and assess how those two periods differ.

  Material consumption has become central to the repertoire of symbols, beliefs, and practices of post-modern cultures. As a result, the "culture industries"—advertising, publishing, communications media, and popular entertainment—have also become important shapers of spaces, places, and landscapes as have global products. In this way, landscapes can become familiar in foreign places like a McDonald's in Bangkok, Thailand, or a fancy shopping mall in Istanbul, Turkey, that contains a wide array of global brands.

KEY TERMS

cosmopolitanism *(p. 229)*

derelict
   landscape *(p. 209)*

digital divide *(p. 220)*

ethology *(p. 204)*

hajj *(p. 214)*

humanistic
   approach *(p. 211)*

landscape as text *(p. 212)*

modernity *(p. 218)*

postmodernity *(p. 222)*

proxemics *(p. 204)*

sacred space *(p. 213)*

semiotics *(p. 212)*

territoriality *(p. 204)*

topophilia *(p. 208)*

REVIEW AND DISCUSSION

1. Consider the environment of your own town or campus. Conduct research exploring how the environment has been shaped or reshaped over the past 5 to 10 years. (*Hint:* you might want to research the building of new parking structures or sports complexes or consider how your university has expanded and bought more land or is not using all of its buildings.) Are there opposing perceptions regarding how your university has been shaped?

2. Conduct research to identify and explore the different elements (paths, edges, districts, nodes, and landmarks) within your campus or town. Begin by making a list of the different elements and who occupies these spaces. What are the territorial, social, and cultural markers of each space? List three of the proxemics you observe in these spaces. (*Hint:* you might start by considering the different coffee shops, bars, or restaurants at your university. Who hangs out at these different locations? List and assess the types of social interactions that are taking place. List the symbols or cultural behaviours that are associated with the location and the people who occupy it.) Once you have the information compiled, draw a territorial cognitive image map like the ones in Figures 6.5 and 6.6.

3. As a student on a campus, in what ways might your environmental perception of the campus landscape differ from that of the faculty or the maintenance staff working on campus? Give three examples of how these different groups will have different perceptions of the landscape. Also provide a detailed sketch of how each group would read the landscape as text. For example, what is the meaning of a classroom, hallway, bathroom, or office for each group? List the different semiotics that is involved for each group.

4. Describe, from your personal perspective, the sense of place that you associate with your hometown. Why are the places, buildings, sights, and sounds you describe so meaningful to you?

5. Draw up a list of the top 10 places in Canada in which you would like to live and work; then draw up a list of the bottom 10. How do these lists compare with the map of student preferences in the U.S., shown in Figure 6.7? Are there factors that apply on either side of the border? What differences are there that make it difficult to compare Canadian and U.S. preferences?

6. On a clean sheet of paper and without reference to maps or other materials, sketch a detailed map of the town or city in which you live. When you have finished, compare your sketch to Figure 6.5. Does your sketch contain nodes? Landmarks? Edges? Districts? Paths? How does your cognitive image map compare to your "real" town or city?

Mastering GEOGRAPHY™

Log in to www.masteringgeography.com for MapMaster™ interactive maps, geography videos, RSS feeds, flashcards, weblinks, an eText version of *Human Geography: Places and Regions in Global Context,* and self-study quizzes to enhance your study of interpreting places and landscapes.

MapMaster™

MapMaster™ presents 13 Place Name and 13 Layered Thematic interactive maps to help students practise and master their geographic literacy, spatial reasoning, and critical thinking skills.

7

GEOGRAPHIES OF ECONOMIC DEVELOPMENT

Learning Outcomes

- Scrutinize the nature and degree of unevenness in patterns of economic development at national and international scales.

- Analyze how geographical divisions of labour have evolved with the growth of the world-system and the accompanying variations in economic structure.

- Interpret how regional cores of economic development are created, following some initial advantage, through the operation of several basic principles of spatial organization.

- Explain how spirals of economic development can be arrested in various ways, including the onset of disinvestment and deindustrialization.

- Demonstrate how globalization has resulted in patterns and processes of local and regional economic development that are open to external influences.

A trip in China on National Highway 321 east from Chengdu in Sichuan province to Shenzhen in Guangdong is a journey through economic development. Migrating workers who travel these highways often leave their families behind. But they also help their families escape poverty and propel China upward through the ranks of middle-income countries. As they travel eastward, they leave an agrarian realm with few jobs and miserable wages and enter the realm of "agglomeration economies," in which a big labour market attracts manufacturers who offer better wages.

Shenzhen attracts young workers—90 percent of its 8 million residents are of working age, between 16 and 65 years old. Cao Bin, aged 20, from Chengdu in Sichuan left for Shenzhen in 2008 and hasn't been back. Chengdu is considered one of the most livable cities in China, but Cao Bin thought it was boring. "That town is too lazy," he says. "I wanted to go somewhere where life is faster." Peng Chunxia, 21, migrated from Hunan at 17, following her elder sister. "Where we are from, most people leave for work . . . I was young, and I thought it'd be fun to come here." Li Chunying, 34, started working at a toy factory when she was 16. She now works as a line manager for an LED maker and looks forward to her day off, when she can spend time shopping with friends or eating in restaurants that serve food from their native Hunan. "When was I happiest? I don't know. There were so many times here that I've been

Migrant workers queue to get on a specially arranged train from Beijing to Chongqing to go back home for the Spring Festival (also called Chinese New Year). (*Source:* Yan Sheng-CNImaging/Newscom)

happy," she says. Still, she longs for home, and would go back with her husband and two daughters if only she could be assured of finding a job.

With a ready supply of skilled and semiskilled young workers, Shenzhen is investing in better education and research facilities to ensure that the city supplies what industries need. The area specializes in electronic goods and it makes them in enormous quantities. In 2006, its exports exceeded India's, making the Shenzhen seaport the fourth busiest in the world. The port ships in intermediate inputs and ships out final products. It boasts expensive facilities, such as top-notch container ports and convention centres, and it matches workers to the growing number of jobs as firms rapidly expand their operations. Proximity to Hong Kong provides access to finance, though Shenzhen is also home to a rapidly expanding financial sector of its own. And competition for customers among the multiple suppliers of inputs produces cost savings. In many ways, what is happening in Shenzhen is a direct reflection of the local, regional, and international processes of economic change that we analyze in this chapter.

Based on *World Development Report 2009*, The World Bank, Washington, D.C., 2009, p. 13; and A. Ramzy and J. Jiang, "Person of the Year 2009: The Chinese Worker," *Time Magazine*, 174, December 28, 2009, p. 8. ■

PATTERNS OF ECONOMIC DEVELOPMENT

We often discuss economic development in terms of levels and rates of change in prosperity, as reflected in bottom-line statistical measures of productivity, incomes, purchasing power, and consumption. Increased prosperity is only one aspect of economic development, however. For human geographers and other social scientists, the term *economic development* refers to processes of change involving the nature and composition of the economy of a particular region as well as to increases in the overall prosperity of a region. These processes can involve three types of changes:

- changes in the *structure* of the region's economy (for example, a shift from agriculture to manufacturing)
- changes in forms of *economic organization* within the region (for example, a shift from socialism to free-market capitalism)
- changes in the availability and use of *technology* within the region. (See Box 7.1, "Visualizing Geography: Technological Change and Economic Development.")

Economic development is also expected to bring with it some broader changes in the economic well-being of a region. The most important of these are changes in the capacity of the region to improve the basic conditions of life (through better housing, health care, and social welfare systems) and to improve the physical framework, or infrastructure, on which the economy rests.

The Unevenness of Economic Development

Geographically, the single most important feature of economic development is that it is *uneven*. At the global scale, this unevenness takes the form of core–periphery contrasts within the evolving world-system (Chapter 2). These global core–periphery contrasts are the result of a competitive economic system that is heavily influenced by cultural and political factors. The core regions within the world-system—North America, Europe, and Japan—have the most diversified economies, the most advanced technologies, the highest levels of productivity, and the highest levels of prosperity. They are commonly referred to as *developed regions* (though processes of economic development are, of course, continuous, and no region can ever be regarded as fully developed).

Other countries and regions—the periphery and semiperiphery of the world-system—are often referred to as *developing* or *less developed*. Indeed, the nations of the periphery are often referred to as LDCs (less-developed countries). Another popular term for the global periphery, originally developed as a political label but now synonymous with economic development in popular usage, is the *Third World*. This term had its origins in the early Cold War era of the 1950s and 1960s, when the newly independent countries of the periphery positioned themselves as a distinctive political bloc, aligned with neither the First World of developed, capitalist countries nor the Second World of the communist Soviet Union and its satellite countries.

At the global scale, levels of economic development are usually measured by economic indicators such as gross domestic product and gross national income. **Gross domestic product (GDP)** is an estimate of the total value of all materials, foodstuffs, goods, and services that are produced by a country in a particular year. To standardize for countries' varying sizes, total GDP is normally divided by total population, which gives an indicator, *per capita* GDP, that is a reasonably good yardstick of relative levels of economic development. **Gross national income (GNI)** is a measure of the income that flows to a country from production, no matter where in the world that production occurs. For example, if a Canadian-owned mining company operating in Chile sends some of its income (profits) to its Canadian headquarters, this adds to the Canadian GNI (but not the Canadian GDP).

Comparing GDP or GNI internationally can be problematic if they are expressed in each nation's local currency. As a result, it is now common to compare such indicators in "international dollars" based on purchasing power parity. **Purchasing power parity (PPP)** means that one international dollar has the same local purchasing power as one U.S. dollar has in the United States; the PPP thus measures how much of a common "market basket" of goods and services each currency can purchase locally. When we use PPP-based indicators to compare levels of economic prosperity, we usually see lower GNI figures in wealthy countries (because of the generally higher cost of living) and higher GNI figures in poorer nations (because of the generally lower cost of living). Nevertheless, even if we take into account that people in wealthy countries often have to spend more of their money to afford a certain standard of living than people in poorer nations, we still must note that economic prosperity is very unevenly distributed among the world's nations.

As **Figure 7.1** shows, most of the highest levels of economic development are to be found in northern latitudes (very roughly, north of 30° N), which has given rise to another popular shorthand for the world's economic geography: the "North" (the core) and the "South" (the periphery). Viewed in more detail, the global pattern of per capita GNI (measured in PPP "international dollars") in 2012 is a direct reflection of the core-semiperiphery-periphery structure of the world-system. In many of the core countries of North America, northwestern Europe, and Japan, annual per capita GNI (in PPP$) exceeds $35 000 (Canada's GNI is $42 270). The only other countries that match these levels are Singapore ($60 110), Hong Kong ($52 190), and the United Arab Emirates ($41 430). Semiperipheral countries such as Brazil, China, and Thailand have an annual per capita GNI ranging between $9000 and $11 000. In the rest of the world—the periphery, accounting for almost half of the world's countries—annual per capita GNI (in PPP) is typically less than $5000.

The gap between the highest per capita GNIs in 2012 ($67 450 in Norway and $60 950 in Luxembourg) and the lowest ($390 in the Democratic Republic of the Congo and $550 in Eritrea) is huge. The gap between the world's rich and poor is also getting wider. In 1970, the average GNI per capita of the ten most prosperous countries in the world was 50 times greater than the average GNI per capita of the ten poorest countries. By 2009, the relative gap had increased to a factor of 67. Overall, more than 80 percent of the world's population lives in countries where income differentials are widening (**Figure 7.2**).

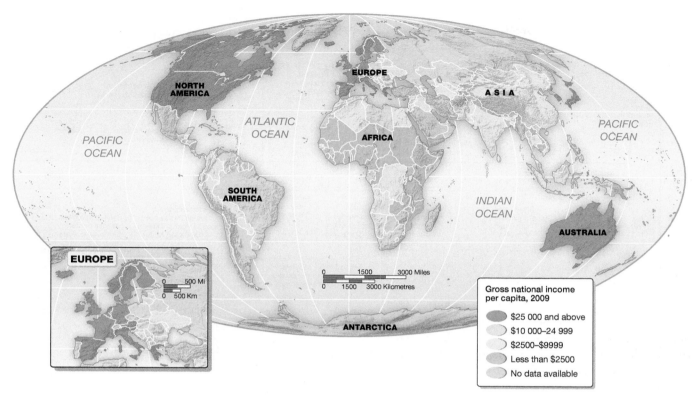

FIGURE 7.1 Gross national income (GNI) per capita GNI per capita is one of the best single measures of economic development. This map, based on 2009 data, shows the tremendous gulf in affluence between the core countries of the world economy—like Canada, the United States, Norway, and Switzerland, with annual per capita GNI (in PPP "international dollars") of more than $25 000—and peripheral countries like Angola, Haiti, and Mali, where annual per capita GNI was less than $2500. In semiperipheral countries like South Korea, Brazil, and Mexico, per capita GNI ranged between $5000 and $10 000. (*Source:* World Bank, International Comparison Program database.)

APPLY YOUR KNOWLEDGE What kind of statistics besides GNI or GDP provide an indication of international disparities in economic development? Find data on one such indicator and propose two possible reasons why the variations exist in the data you found. (*Hint:* good sources are the World Bank, **http://data.worldbank.org/**, and the United Nations Development Programme, **http://hdr.undp.org/en/statistics/**.) ■

Resources and Development

Current patterns of economic development are the result of many different factors. One of the most important is the availability of key resources such as cultivable land, energy, and valuable minerals. Unevenly distributed across the world are both key resources and—equally important—the *combinations* of energy and minerals crucial to economic development. A lack of natural resources can, of course, be remedied through international trade. (Japan's success is a prime example of this.) For most countries, however, the resource base remains an important determinant of development.

Energy

One particularly important resource in terms of the world's economic geography is energy. The major sources of commercial energy—oil, natural gas, and coal—are unevenly distributed across

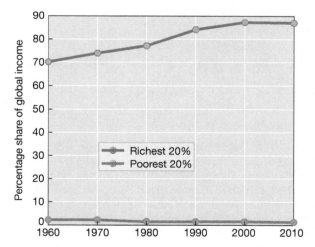

FIGURE 7.2 Long-term trends in per capita GNI This graph shows the steady divergence in income between the richest and poorest quintiles of the world's population. In 1960, the richest 20 percent of the world's population accounted for 70.2 percent of global income, whereas the poorest 20 percent accounted for 2.3 percent: a ratio of 30 to 1. By 2010, the ratio had increased to 55 to 1.

the globe. Most of the world's core economies are reasonably well off in terms of energy *production*, the major exceptions being Japan and parts of Europe. Most peripheral countries, on the other hand,

Technological Change and Economic Development

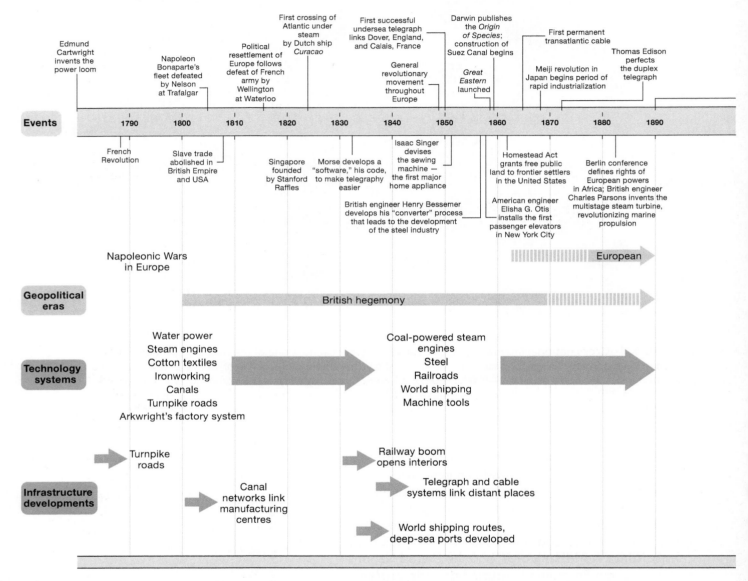

FIGURE 7.A Technological change and economic development The Industrial Revolution, which began in England at the end of the eighteenth century, was driven by a technology system based on water power and steam engines, cotton textiles, ironworking, river transport systems, and canals. It eventually resulted not only in the complete reorganization of the geography of the original European core of the world-system but also in an extension of the world-system core to the United States and Japan. Since then there have been several more technology systems, each opening new geographic frontiers and rewriting the geography of economic development while shifting the balance of advantages between regions. Overall, the opportunities for development created by each new technology system have been associated with distinctive economic epochs and long-term fluctuations in the overall rate of change of prices in the economy.

Beginning in the late eighteenth century, a series of technological innovations in power and energy, transportation, and manufacturing processes resulted in crucial changes in patterns of economic development. Each of these major clusters of technological innovations created new demands for natural resources as well as new labour forces and markets. The result was that each major cluster of technological innovations—called technology systems—tended to favour different regions and different kinds of places. **Technology systems** are clusters of interrelated energy, transportation, and production technologies that dominate economic activity for several decades at a time—until a new cluster of improved technologies evolves. What is especially remarkable about technology systems is that so far they have come along at about 50-year intervals. Since the beginning of the Industrial Revolution, we can identify four of them:

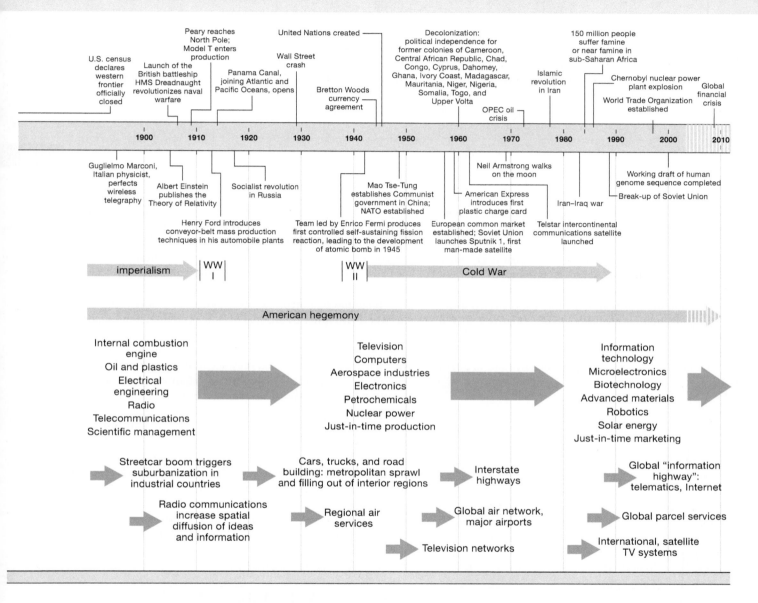

- *1790–1840*: early mechanization based on water power and steam engines; development of cotton textiles and ironworking; development of river transport systems, canals, and turnpike roads

- *1840–1890*: exploitation of coal-powered steam engines; steel products; railroads; world shipping; machine tools

- *1890–1950*: exploitation of the internal combustion engine; oil and plastics; electrical and heavy engineering; aircraft; radio and telecommunications

- *1950–1990*: exploitation of nuclear power, aerospace, electronics, and petrochemicals; development of limited-access highways and global air routes

A fifth technology system, still incomplete, began to take shape in the 1980s with a series of innovations that are now being commercially exploited:

- *1990 onward*: exploitation of solar energy, robotics, microelectronics, biotechnology, nanotechnology, advanced materials (fine chemicals and thermoplastics, for example), and information technology (digital telecommunications and geographic information systems, for example)

Each of these technology systems has rewritten the geography of economic development as it has shifted the balance of advantages between regions (**Figure 7.A**). From the mid-1800s, industrial development spread to new regions. The growth of

(Continued)

those regions then became interdependent with the fortunes of other regions through a complex web of production and trade.

Early technology systems diffused outward in a "pulse" of innovation that took changes outward from the core to the periphery. In the process, technology systems became part of broader economic forces that tied the global core and periphery together. However, by the time a technology eventually diffused to more remote locations, a newer technology had already supplanted it in the countries of the core. For instance, canals were still being built in Canada in the 1830s, at a time when they were being replaced by railroads in Britain. This "lag" illustrates one of the mechanisms that made it difficult for peripheral countries to simply "catch up" with core countries.

are energy poor. The major exceptions are Algeria, Ecuador, Gabon, Indonesia, Libya, Nigeria, and Venezuela—all major oil producers.

Because of this unevenness, energy has come to be an important component of world trade. As more of the world becomes industrialized and developed, demand for oil continues to increase. Yet, as we saw in Chapter 4, it is generally agreed that the peak of oil *discovery* was passed in the 1960s and that the world started using more oil than was contained in new fields in 1981 (**Figure 7.3**). Oil prices have risen sharply: more than 300 percent between 2005 and 2010. Oil is now the most important single commodity in world trade, making up more than 20 percent of the total by value in 2010.

of commercial energy *consumption* mirror the fundamental core–periphery cleavage of the world economy. (See Figure 4.20.) In 2008, energy consumption per capita in North America was 14 times that of India, 18 times that of Mozambique, and nearly 50 times that of Bangladesh. The world's high-income countries, with 15 percent of the world's population, use half its commercial energy.

It should be noted that these figures do not reflect the use of firewood and other traditional fuels for cooking, lighting, heating and, sometimes, industrial needs. In total, such forms probably account for around 20 percent of total world energy consumption. In parts of Africa and Asia, they account for up to 80 percent of energy consumption. This points to yet another core–periphery contrast. Whereas massive investments in exploration and exploitation are enabling more of the developed, energy-consuming countries to become self-sufficient through various combinations of coal, oil, natural gas, hydroelectric power, and nuclear power, 1.5 billion people in peripheral countries depend on collecting fuelwood as their principal source of energy. The collection of fuelwood causes considerable deforestation. The problem is most serious in densely populated locations, arid and semiarid regions, and cooler mountainous areas, where the regeneration of forests is particularly slow. Nearly 100 million people in 22 countries (16 of them in Africa) cannot meet their minimum energy needs even by overcutting remaining forests (see Chapter 4).

VIRTUAL GEOGRAPHIES

We can combine the ideas of "creating" space and technology systems by looking at the spatial changes enabled by cell phone technology. In many parts of northern and rural Canada, remote communities or individual homeowners for the longest time were disadvantaged when it came to accessing telecommunication systems because it was either physically impossible or prohibitively expensive to run cables to their locations. This not only reduced the attractiveness of those locations as residences but also limited what kind of businesses could locate there. Now, more advanced satellite systems make it possible for remote locations to connect to the "fast world" just as easily and quickly (and almost as cheaply) as a suburban business park in Calgary—which opens up new opportunities for businesses and jobs. Similarly, many peripheral countries are currently "leapfrogging" over the "wired" stage of telecommunications, thus skipping the expensive infrastructure requirements.

For many peripheral countries the cost of importing energy is a heavy burden. Consider, for example, the predicament of countries like India, Ghana, Paraguay, Egypt, and Armenia, where in 2010 the cost of energy imports amounted to more than one-quarter of their total export revenues. Few peripheral countries can afford to consume energy on the scale of the developed economies, so patterns

FIGURE 7.3 An oil exploration rig in shallow coastal waters
With new oil reserves to be found mostly under the seabed, oil exploration has moved offshore into an environment that is at once ecologically sensitive, accident-prone, and expensive to exploit. (*Source: Artur Synenko/Fotolia*)

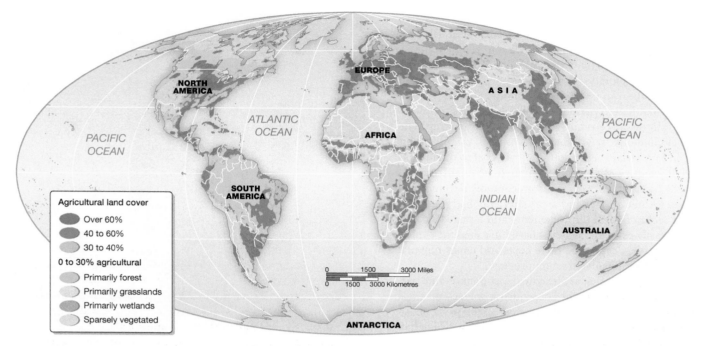

FIGURE 7.4 Agricultural land cover Some countries, like Canada and the United States, are fortunate in having a broad range of cultivable land, which allows for many options in agricultural development. Many countries, though, have a much narrower base of cultivable land and must rely on the exploitation of one major resource as a means to economic development. (*Source:* Adapted from World Resources 2000–2001: *People and Ecosystems.* Washington, DC: World Resources Institute, 2000, p. 57. Originally from Wood et al., 2000. The map is based on Global Land Cover Characteristics Database Version 1.2 [Loveland et al. (2000)] and USGS/EDC [1999a]. The figure is based on FAOSTAT [1999]).

Cultivable Land

The distribution of cultivable land is another important factor in international economic development. Much more than half of Earth's land surface is unsuitable for any productive form of arable farming, as shown in **Figure 7.4**. Poor soils, short growing seasons, arid climates, mountainous terrain, forests, and conservation limit the extent of agricultural land across much of the globe. As a result, the distribution of the world's cultivable land is highly uneven, being concentrated in Europe, west-central Russia, eastern North America, the Malay archipelago, Latin America, India, eastern China, and parts of Australia and sub-Saharan Africa. Some of these regions may be marginal for arable farming because of marshy soils or other adverse conditions, while irrigation or other factors sometimes extend the local frontier of productive agriculture. We also have to bear in mind that not all cultivable land is of the same quality. This leads to the concept of the **carrying capacity** of agricultural land: the maximum population that can be maintained in a place at rates of resource use and waste production that are sustainable in the long term without damaging the overall productivity of that or other places.

Industrial Resources

A high proportion of the world's key industrial resources—basic raw materials—are concentrated in Russia, the United States, Canada, South Africa, and Australia. The United States, for example, in addition to having 42 percent of the world's known resources of hydrocarbons (oil, natural gas, and oil shales) and 38 percent of the lignite ("brown coal," used mainly in power stations), has 38 percent of the molybdenum (used in metal alloys), 21 percent of the lead (used for

FIGURE 7.5 Mineral exports Rare earth being loaded at Lianyungang dock, Jiangsu province, China. (*Source:* Chinafotopress/ZUMApress/Newscom)

batteries, gasoline, and construction), 19 percent of the copper (used for electrical wiring and components and for coinage), 18 percent of the bituminous coal (used for fuel in power stations and in the chemical industry), and 15 percent of the zinc. Russia has 68 percent of the vanadium (used in metal alloys), 50 percent of the lignite, 38 percent of the bituminous coal, 35 percent of the manganese, 25 percent of the iron, and 19 percent of the hydrocarbons (**Figure 7.5**).

The concentration of known resources in just a few countries is largely a result of geology, but it is also partly a function of countries' political and economic development. Political instability in much of postcolonial Africa, Asia, and Latin America has seriously hindered their exploration and exploitation of resources. In contrast, the affluence and political stability in North America have led to a much more intensive exploration of resources.

We should also bear in mind that the significance of particular resources is often tied to particular technologies. As technologies change, so do resource requirements, and the geography of economic development is "rewritten." A Canadian example of this is the switch in industrial energy sources from coal to oil and gas in the twentieth century. When this happened, coalfield areas in Atlantic Canada found their prospects for economic development dashed, whereas Alberta's tar sand areas suddenly had potential. More recently, technological improvements and a post-Peak Oil decline in more easily exploited reserves have intensifed the exploitation of the tar sands, despite the huge costs and environmental impacts caused by the difficult extraction process.

Regions and countries that are heavily dependent on one particular resource are vulnerable to the consequences of technological change. They are also vulnerable to fluctuations in the price set for their product on the world market, as is the case for the Canadian industries of mining, forestry, fishing, and agriculture. You will recall from Chapter 2 that the staples thesis lists such vulnerability as one of the challenges of Canadian economic development. Globally, these vulnerabilities are particularly important for countries (many of them in Africa) whose economies are dependent on nonfuel minerals, such as the Democratic Republic of the Congo (copper), Mauritania (iron ore), Namibia (diamonds), Niger (uranium), Sierra Leone (diamonds), Togo (phosphates), and Zambia (copper).

Resources and Sustainability

The goal of **sustainable development** is to achieve a balance among economic growth, the environmental impacts of that growth, and the fairness, or social equity, of the distribution of the costs and benefits of that growth. The importance of sustainability is cogently illustrated by the concept of the ecological footprint, which is a measure of the human pressures on the natural environment from the consumption of resources and the production of pollution (see Chapter 4).

Humanity's footprint first grew larger than global biocapacity in the 1980s, and this overshoot has been increasing every year since. Currently, demand exceeds supply by about 50 percent. This means that it takes a year and a half for Earth to produce the ecological resources we use in one year.

Sustainable development means using renewable natural resources in a manner that does not deplete or degrade them—by making greater use, for example, of solar and geothermal energy and recycled materials. It means managing economic systems so that all resources—physical and human—are used optimally. It means regulating economic systems so that the benefits of development are distributed more equitably (if only to prevent poverty from causing environmental degradation). It also means organizing societies so that improved education, health care, and social welfare can contribute to environmental awareness and sensitivity and an improved quality of life. A final and more radical aspect of sustainable development involves moving away from wholesale globalization toward increased "localization": a return to more locally based economies where production, consumption, and decision making are oriented to local needs and conditions (**Figure 7.6**).

FIGURE 7.6 Promoting local economies Increasing awareness of the benefits of locally produced foods has encouraged many supermarkets, like this one in Lugano, Switzerland, to feature local products. (*Source:* Paul L. Knox)

We can contrast the "traditional" approach to economic growth (one that ignores the environment) with a "new" approach that endeavours to achieve economic growth through sustainable development, in the following manner:

The Traditional Economy	The New Economy
– consumes renewable and nonrenewable resources	– recycles, replaces, and reduces its use of renewable and nonrenewable resources
– treats the environment as a "free good"	– prices the use of the environment (through environmental audits)
– uses the environment to absorb pollution	– costs the price of pollution (through emission credits)
– considers any environmental action as a cost	– considers environmental action part of the price of doing business and, increasingly, as a business opportunity
– regards "place" as simply a location	– regards "place" as a locus of interconnections at the global, regional, and local scales
– regards "space" only in economic terms	– regards "space" as the arena in which those interconnections operate

Defined this way, sustainable development sounds eminently sensible yet impossibly utopian. A succession of international summit meetings on the topic has revealed deep disagreements between core countries and peripheral countries. One of the most serious roadblocks on the path to sustainable development is continued heavy reliance on fossil fuels as the fundamental source of energy for economic development. This not only perpetuates international inequalities but also leads to transnational problems such as climate change, acid rain, deforestation, health hazards, and, many would argue, war. The sustainable alternative—renewable energy generated from the sun, tides, waves, winds, rivers, and geothermal features—has been pursued half-heartedly because of the commercial interests of the powerful corporations and governments that control fossil-fuel resources.

A second important challenge to the possibility of sustainable development is the rate of population growth in peripheral countries. Sustainable development is feasible only if population size and growth are in harmony with the changing productive capacity of the ecosystem. Currently, 1.2 billion of the world's 7.1 billion people are undernourished and underweight.

But the greatest single obstacle to sustainable development is the inadequacy of institutional frameworks. Sustainable development requires economic, financial, and fiscal decisions to be fully integrated with environmental and ecological decisions. National and local governments everywhere have evolved institutional structures that tend to separate decisions about what is economically rational and what is environmentally desirable. International organizations, while better placed to integrate policy across these sectors and better able to address economic and environmental "spillovers" from one country to another, have (with the notable exception of the European Union) not acquired sufficient power to promote integrated, harmonized policies. Without radical and widespread changes in value systems and unprecedented changes in political will, "sustainable development" is likely to remain an embarrassing contradiction in terms.

APPLY YOUR KNOWLEDGE Find two examples of renewable energy projects in Canada. List three ways they can change this nation's ecological footprint and contribute to the sustainable development of the Canadian economy. Also consider reasons why their growth may be impeded. (*Hint:* you might want to consider what their funding source is and whether it is adequate.) ∎

THE ECONOMIC STRUCTURE OF COUNTRIES AND REGIONS

The relative share of primary, secondary, tertiary, and quaternary economic activities determines the *economic structure* of a country or region. **Primary activities** are those concerned directly with natural resources of any kind; they include agriculture, mining, fishing, and forestry. **Secondary activities** are those that process, transform, fabricate, or assemble the raw materials derived from primary activities or that reassemble, refinish, or package manufactured

goods. Secondary activities include steelmaking, food processing, furniture production, textile manufacturing, automobile assembly, and garment manufacturing. **Tertiary activities** are those involving the sale and exchange of goods and services; they include warehousing, retail stores, personal services such as hairdressing, and commercial services such as accounting, advertising, and entertainment. **Quaternary activities** are those dealing with the handling and processing of knowledge and information. Examples include data processing, information retrieval, education, and research and development (R&D).

Geographical Divisions of Labour

Variations in economic structure—according to primary, secondary, tertiary, or quaternary activities—reflect *geographical divisions of labour*. Geographical divisions of labour are national, regional, and locally based economic specializations that have evolved with the growth of the world-system of trade and politics and with the locational needs of successive technology systems. They represent one of the most important dimensions of economic development. For instance, countries whose economies are dominated by primary-sector activities tend to have a relatively low per capita GDP. The exceptions are oil-rich countries such as Saudi Arabia or Qatar. As **Figure 7.7** shows, the economic structure of much of the world is still dominated by the primary sector.

Where the **international division of labour** (the specialization, by countries, in particular products for export) has produced national economies with a large secondary sector, per capita GDP is much higher (as, for example, in Argentina and South Korea). The highest levels of per capita GDP, however, are associated with economies that are *postindustrial*: economies where the tertiary and quaternary sectors have grown to dominate the workforce, with smaller but highly productive secondary sectors.

The secondary sector is much larger in the core countries and in semiperipheral countries, where the world's specialized manufacturing regions are located (**Figure 7.8**). In 2010, core countries accounted for almost three-quarters of world manufacturing value added (MVA). MVA is the net output of secondary industries; it is determined by adding up the value of all outputs and subtracting the value of all intermediate inputs. This share has been slowly decreasing, however. Between 1990 and 2010, the core countries had an average MVA annual growth rate of around 2 percent, while the rest of the world was closer to 7 percent.

This growth has been concentrated in semiperipheral, newly industrializing countries. **Newly industrializing countries (NICs)** are countries, formerly peripheral within the world-system, that have acquired a significant industrial sector. Usually this industrialization is not financed domestically but through foreign direct investment. **Foreign direct investment (FDI)** occurs when a private company invests in business based outside of its own country. Of the 20 biggest manufacturing countries, seven are NICs: China, South Korea, Mexico, Brazil, India, Indonesia, and Thailand (listed here in order of importance). Indeed, China is now the world's largest exporter of manufactured goods; South Korea, Brazil, and India rank sixth to eighth. By contrast, the vast majority of peripheral countries have a very small manufacturing output. For example, the share of world MVA for Africa has changed little over the past two decades, remaining at about 1 percent.

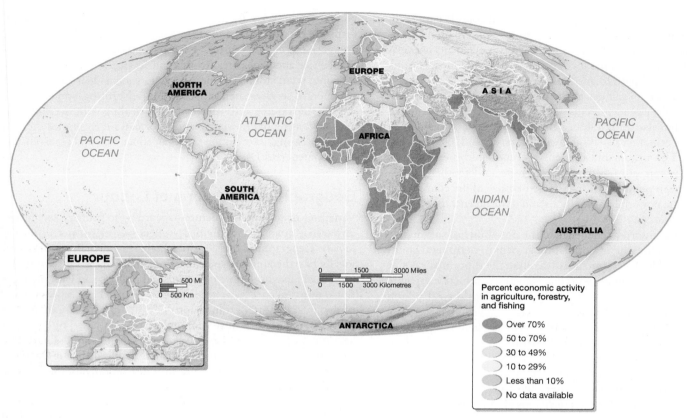

FIGURE 7.7 **The geography of primary economic activities** Primary economic activities are those that are concerned directly with natural resources of any kind. They include agriculture, mining, forestry, and fishing. The vast majority of the world's population, concentrated in China, India, Southeast Asia, and Africa, is engaged in primary economic activities. This map shows the percentage of the labour force in each country that was engaged in primary activities in 2002. In much of Africa, primary activities account for more than 70 percent of the workforce. In contrast, primary activities always account for less than 10 percent of the labour force in the world's core countries, and often for less than 5 percent.

The United States alone accounted for just over 22 percent of global MVA in 2010, and just five countries—the United States, Japan, Germany, China, and the United Kingdom—together produced over 60 percent of the world total MVA. Another important aspect of secondary activities concerns *productivity*. In general, the highly capitalized manufacturing industries of the developed countries have been able to maintain high levels of worker productivity, with the result that the contribution of manufacturing to their GDP has remained relatively high even as the size of their manufacturing labour forces has decreased.

Since the 1970s, China has experienced a dramatic increase in manufacturing production, achieving annual average growth rates of roughly 10 percent. (See Box 7.2, "Window on the World: China's Economic Development.") At such growth rates, the Chinese economy is doubling in size every seven years. Of the four Asian "Tigers"—South Korea, Hong Kong, Taiwan, and Singapore—only South Korea enjoyed a similarly spectacular increase in manufacturing production (**Figure 7.9**).

Rapid growth of manufacturing in Pacific Asia has generated agglomerations of economic activity at a scale that sometimes crosses national boundaries, as with the Southern China–Hong Kong–Taiwan triangle and the Singapore–Batam–Johor triangle (**Figure 7.10** on p. 246). The 1500-kilometre urban belt in

northeast Asia that runs from Beijing to Tokyo via Pyongyang and Seoul connects some 80 cities of over 200 000 inhabitants each, encompassing nearly 100 million urban dwellers altogether.

These shifts are part of a globalization of economic activity that has emerged as the overarching component of the world's economic geography. As we shall see, it has been corporate strategy, particularly the strategies of large transnational corporations, that has created this globalization of economic activity. **Transnational corporations (TNCs)** are companies that participate not only in international trade but also in production, manufacturing, and/or sales operations in several countries.

The tertiary and quaternary sectors are significant only in the most affluent countries of the core. In Canada, for example, the primary sector in 2010 accounted for under 5 percent of the labour force, the secondary sector for just over 20 percent, the tertiary sector for almost 50 percent, and the quaternary sector for just under 25 percent. In every core country, the tertiary sector has grown significantly in the past several decades as consumption and marketing became the hallmarks of postindustrial economies. More recently, globalization has meant that knowledge-based activities have become a critical aspect of economic development, resulting in the rapid growth of quaternary industries.

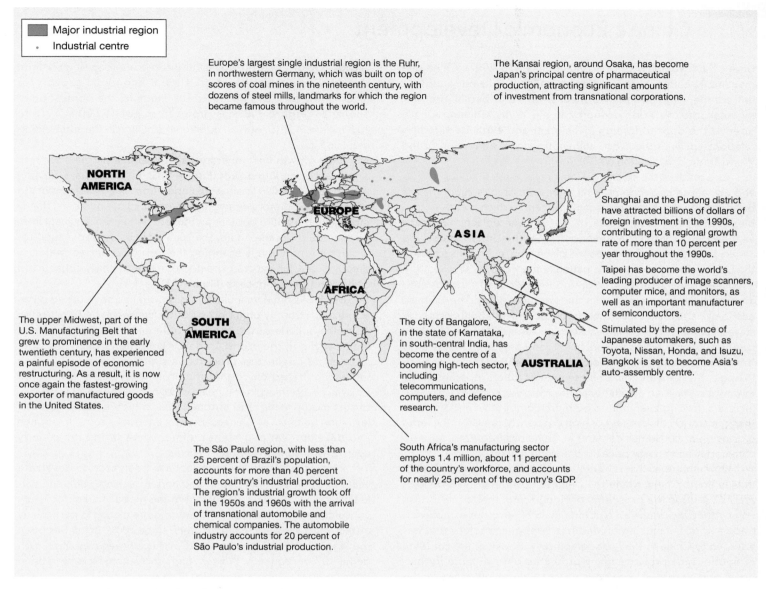

Major industrial region
Industrial centre

Europe's largest single industrial region is the Ruhr, in northwestern Germany, which was built on top of scores of coal mines in the nineteenth century, with dozens of steel mills, landmarks for which the region became famous throughout the world.

The Kansai region, around Osaka, has become Japan's principal centre of pharmaceutical production, attracting significant amounts of investment from transnational corporations.

Shanghai and the Pudong district have attracted billions of dollars of foreign investment in the 1990s, contributing to a regional growth rate of more than 10 percent per year throughout the 1990s.

Taipei has become the world's leading producer of image scanners, computer mice, and monitors, as well as an important manufacturer of semiconductors.

Stimulated by the presence of Japanese automakers, such as Toyota, Nissan, Honda, and Isuzu, Bangkok is set to become Asia's auto-assembly centre.

The upper Midwest, part of the U.S. Manufacturing Belt that grew to prominence in the early twentieth century, has experienced a painful episode of economic restructuring. As a result, it is now once again the fastest-growing exporter of manufactured goods in the United States.

The city of Bangalore, in the state of Karnataka, in south-central India, has become the centre of a booming high-tech sector, including telecommunications, computers, and defence research.

The São Paulo region, with less than 25 percent of Brazil's population, accounts for more than 40 percent of the country's industrial production. The region's industrial growth took off in the 1950s and 1960s with the arrival of transnational automobile and chemical companies. The automobile industry accounts for 20 percent of São Paulo's industrial production.

South Africa's manufacturing sector employs 1.4 million, about 11 percent of the country's workforce, and accounts for nearly 25 percent of the country's GDP.

FIGURE 7.8 **The geography of secondary economic activities** As this map shows, the world's largest and most productive manufacturing regions are in the core regions of Europe, North America, and Japan. Important concentrations of manufacturing industry are in semiperipheral countries, such as South Korea, Mexico, and Brazil, but the increasing globalization of manufacturing means that patterns are subject to rapid change. (*Source:* Data from Population Reference Bureau, World Population Data Sheet, 2013.)

For the world's core economies, knowledge has become more important than physical and human resources in determining levels of economic well-being. More than half of the GDP of major core countries is based on the production and distribution of knowledge. Soon, more Canadians will be engaged in producing and distributing knowledge than in making physical goods.

For the world's peripheral economies, lack of knowledge—along with a limited capacity to absorb and communicate knowledge—is an increasingly important barrier to economic development. Poor countries have fewer resources to devote to research, development, and the acquisition of information technology. They also have fewer institutions for providing high-quality education,

fewer bodies that can enforce standards and performance, and only weakly developed organizations for gathering and disseminating the information needed for business transactions. As a result, economic productivity tends to fall relative to the performance of places and regions in core economies, where new knowledge is constantly generated and rapidly and effectively disseminated.

APPLY YOUR KNOWLEDGE Consider a product that you own, such as a T-shirt, a pair of shoes, or your smartphone or tablet, and map out the product's development through the primary, secondary, and tertiary activities. ∎

China's Economic Development

Under the leadership of Deng Xiaoping (1978–1997), China dismantled its communist-style central planning in favour of private entrepreneurship and market mechanisms and began integrating itself into the world economy. In the 1990s, China gradually opened the door to foreign investment and expanded trading relationships with the West, culminating in its admission to the World Trade Organization (WTO) in 2001.

As a result of the opening, China has completely reorganized and revitalized its economy: year after year, China's economy has been growing by an average of 10 percent—which means it doubles in size every seven years. In 2010, China replaced Germany as the world's third-largest economy after the United States and Japan. In 2011, it took over second place, and in 2013 it surpassed the U.S. as the biggest trading nation in the world.

China's increased participation in world trade has created an entirely new situation within the world economy. The Chinese economy's size makes it a major producer, and its labour costs have stayed flat for many years because there seemed to be an endless supply of people willing to work for 60 cents an hour. (Only recently has the inflationary pressure forced the government to order a rise in wages.) This meant that Chinese manufacturers, operating with low wages, imposed a deflationary trend on world prices for manufacturers, forcing everyone to be more competitive and thus further intensifying the process of globalization. Meanwhile, the rapid expansion of consumer demand in China has begun to drive up commodity and energy prices in the world market.

Nowhere have China's "open-door" policies had more impact than in South China, where the Chinese government has deliberately built upon the prosperity of Hong Kong, the former British colony that was returned to China in 1997, and the established trade and manufacturing of Macão, a Portuguese colony that was returned to China in 1999. Geographically speaking, the coastline of South China provides many protected bays suitable for harbours, and a series of large ports now provide an interface with the world economy.

When Deng Xiaoping established his "open-door" policy, a third factor kicked in: capital investment from Hong Kong, Taiwan, and the Chinese diaspora. By 1993, more than 15 000 manufacturers from Hong Kong alone had set up businesses in neighbouring Guangdong Province, and a similar number established subcontracting relationships, contracting out processing work to Chinese companies. Today, the cities and special economic zones of South China's "Gold Coast" provide a thriving export-processing platform that has driven double-digit annual economic growth for much of the past two decades. For example, the population of Shenzhen (**Figure 7.B**) has grown from just 19 000 in 1975 to 10.5 million in 2010, with an additional 2 million in the surrounding municipalities.

Such growth has generated a substantial middle class with significant spending power (**Figure 7.C**). Over the past decade, the Chinese middle class has exploded from only 4 percent of the urban population to over two-thirds—in absolute numbers, that is more than the entire population of North America. Ten years from now, it could double again, thanks mainly to the rapid rural-to-urban transition that is changing the face of China: several hundred million Chinese are expected to move to newly constructed cities over the next decade (**Figure 7.D**).

Much of China's manufacturing growth has been based on an aggressive strategy of import substitution (see p. 247) that often operates outside of the confines of legality. In spite of China's membership in the World Trade Organization (which has strict rules about intellectual property), a significant share of China's industry is based on counterfeiting and reverse engineering. Copying everything from DVDs, designer clothes and footwear, drugs, motorcycles, and automobiles to high-speed magnetic levitation trains saves Chinese industry enormous sums in research and development and licensing fees, while saving the country even greater sums in imports.

Foreign investors, meanwhile, have been keen to develop a share of China's rapidly expanding and increasingly affluent market: China accounts for 40 percent of the global market for luxury consumer goods. The high-end automobile market is particularly attractive to Western manufacturers: since 2009, China has been the largest car market in the world, and luxury vehicles are in high demand. Consequently, Western high-end automakers have been ramping up their engagement in China considerably.

Initially, however, a large share of the foreign investment in China came from elsewhere within East Asia. Japan, Taiwan, and South Korea, having first developed manufacturing industries in their countries that undercut those of the United States, then in turn moved their production to even cheaper Chinese locations. This meant that they were facing deindustrialization at home through the inexorable process of "creative destruction" (see p. 254). For instance, Pusan, the centre of the South Korean footwear industry

FIGURE 7.B Shenzhen The city of Shenzhen, just across the border from the Special Administrative Region of Hong Kong. (*Source:* Digital Vision/Getty Images)

FIGURE 7.C New affluence A saleswoman waits for customers at an outlet of the French fashion brand Hermes in Shanghai. (*Source:* Liu Jin/Getty Images)

FIGURE 7.D Real estate boom In the rapidly growing regions of coastal China, house price inflation has risen as high as 9.5 percent a month. Shown here is a small fishing village near Sanya Harbor in Hainan province, where new luxury buildings are displacing the older homes and their inhabitants. (*Source:* Feng Li/Getty Images)

that in 1990 exported US$4.3 billion worth of shoes, is now full of deserted factories. South Korean footwear exports are down to less than US$700 million, while China's footwear exports have ballooned from US$2.1 billion to US$29 billion.

Similarly, Japanese electronics giants have expanded operations in China even as they have shed tens of thousands of workers at home. Toshiba's factory in Dalian illustrates the logic. Toshiba is one of about 40 Japanese companies that built large-scale production facilities in a special export-processing zone established by Dalian with generous financial support from the Japanese government and major Japanese firms. By shifting production of

digital televisions from its plant in Saitama, Japan, Toshiba cut labour costs per worker by 90 percent.

In the past few years, China too has begun to experience the effects of creative destruction (see p. 254). Wages for industrial workers have risen in the booming coastal regions of the South, making it more profitable for manufacturers to move production to less expensive interior regions further west.

International Trade

The geographical division of labour on a world scale means that the geography of international trade is very complex. One significant reflection of the increased economic integration of the world-system is that global trade has grown much more rapidly over the past few decades than global production. Between 1985 and 2008, the average annual growth rate of the value of world exports was twice that of the growth of world production and several times greater than that of world population growth.

The fundamental structure of international trade is based on a few **trading blocs**—groups of countries with formalized systems of trading agreements. Most of the world's trade takes place within and between four trading blocs:

- Western Europe, together with some former European colonies in Africa, South Asia, the Caribbean, and Australasia
- North America, together with some Latin American states
- the countries of the former Soviet world-empire
- Japan, together with other East Asian states and the oil-exporting states of Saudi Arabia and Bahrain

FIGURE 7.9 High-tech manufacturing in South Korea Employees work in a cleanroom semiconductor production facility in a Samsung plant in Suwon, south of Seoul. (*Source:* Samsung EElectronics Co/AP Images)

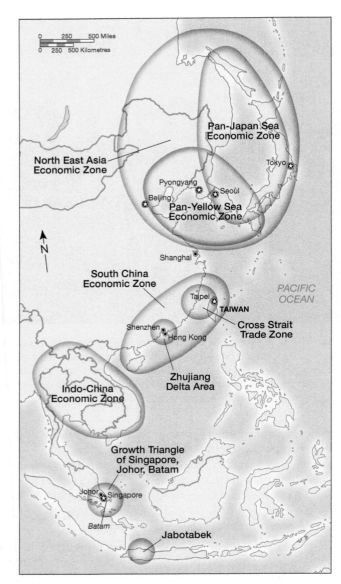

FIGURE 7.10 Emerging growth zones in Pacific Asia The globalization of manufacturing industries has spurred the growth of a series of extended metropolitan regions. (*Source:* Adapted from P. Dicken, *Global Shift*, 4th ed. New York: Guilford, 2003, Figure 3.28, p. 78.)

Nevertheless, a significant number of countries exhibit a high degree of **autarky** from the world economy. That is, they do not contribute significantly to the flows of imports and exports that constitute the geography of trade. Typically, these are smaller, peripheral countries, such as Bolivia, Burkina Faso, Ghana, Malawi, Samoa, and Tanzania.

Patterns of world trade have been shifting rapidly, however, in response to several factors. In general, the trend has been toward an intensification of the long-standing domination of trade within and between core regions at the expense of trade between core countries and peripheral countries—with the major exception of trade in oil. Innovations in transport, communications, and manufacturing technology have diminished the importance of distance between trading partners.

Shifts in global politics have also affected the geography of trade. One important shift was the breakup of the former Soviet

Union. Other significant geopolitical changes include the trend toward the political as well as economic integration of Europe and the increasing participation of China in the world economy. But perhaps the most important shift in global politics in relation to world trade has been the shift toward open markets and free trade through neoliberal policies propagated by core countries. **Neoliberal policies** are economic policies predicated on a minimalist role for the state that assume the desirability of free markets not only for economic organization but also for political and social life.

The globalization of economic activity has created new flows of materials, components, information, and finished products. As a global system of manufacturing has emerged, significant quantities of manufactured goods are now imported *and* exported across much of the world through complex commodity chains (as we saw in the case of blue jeans in Box 2.4, "Visualizing Geography: Commodity Chains"); no longer do developed economies exclusively export manufactures and peripheral countries import them. African countries are an important exception, with many of them barely participating in world trade in manufactures.

The most striking aspect of contemporary patterns of trade is the persistence of the dependence of peripheral countries on trade with core countries that are geographically or geopolitically close. For example, the United States is the central focus for the exports and the origin of the bulk of the imports of most Central American countries, while France is the focus for commodity flows to and from French ex-colonies such as Algeria, Cambodia, Benin, and the Ivory Coast. (These flows, however, represent only part of the action for the core economies, whose trading patterns are dominated by flows to and from other core countries.)

One implication of this situation is that the smaller, peripheral partners in these trading relationships find themselves in a situation of dependency. **Dependency** involves a high level of reliance by a country on foreign enterprises, investment, or technology. Dependency for a peripheral country can result in a narrow economic base in which the balancing of national accounts and the generation of foreign exchange depend on the export of only one or two agricultural or mineral resources (**Figure 7.11**).

Patterns of International Debt

In many peripheral countries, debt service—the annual interest payable on international debts—is a significant handicap to economic development. Peripheral countries owed almost US$4 trillion in 2010, and their debt service amounted to 1.5 billion—every single day. In many countries, 20 percent or more of all export earnings is swallowed up by debt service (**Figure 7.12**). Meanwhile, core countries are doing extremely well from this aspect of international finance: they receive about half a trillion dollars in interest annually.

At the root of the international debt problem is the *structured* inequality of the world economy. The role inherited by most peripheral countries within the international division of labour has been one of producing primary goods and commodities for which the price elasticity of demand is low. The **price elasticity of demand** is the degree to which levels of demand for a product or service change in response to changes in its price. Where a relatively small change in price induces a significant change in demand, price elasticity is high; where levels of demand remain fairly stable in spite of price changes, it is said to be inelastic. Demand for the products of

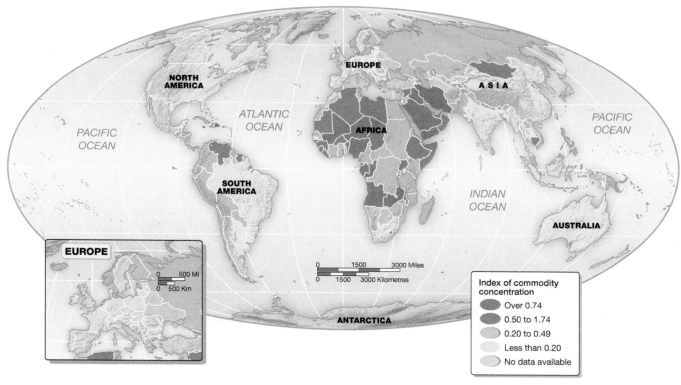

FIGURE 7.11 Index of commodity concentration of exports, 2002 Countries with low scores on this index have diversified export bases. They include Argentina, Brazil, China, India, and North and South Korea, as well as most of the core countries. At the other extreme are peripheral countries where the manufacturing sector is poorly developed and exports consist mainly of one or two agricultural or mineral resources, as is the case in Angola, Chad, the Dominican Republic, Iran, Iraq, Libya, and Nigeria, for example.

peripheral countries in their principal markets (the more developed countries) has a low price elasticity.

Consider, for example, the cocoa-producing regions of West Africa (**Figure 7.13**). No matter how they improve productivity in order to keep prices low, and no matter how much more affluent their customers in core countries become, there is a limit to the demand for cocoa products. In contrast, the price elasticity of demand for high-tech manufactured goods and high-order services (the specialties of core economies within the international division of labour) is high. As a result, the terms of trade are stacked against the producers of primary goods. The **terms of trade** are determined by the ratio of the prices at which exports and imports are exchanged. When the price of exports rises relative to the price of imports, the terms of trade reflect an improvement for the exporting country. No matter how efficient primary producers may become, or how affluent their customers, the balance of trade is tilted against them.

An obvious counterstrategy for peripheral countries is to attempt to establish a new role in the international division of labour, moving away from a specialization in primary commodities toward a more diversified manufacturing base. This strategy, known as **import substitution**, involves the replacement of goods and services previously imported from core regions with goods and services that are domestically produced. It is a difficult strategy to pursue, however, because building up a diversified manufacturing base requires vast amounts of start-up capital. With the terms of

trade running against them, it is extremely difficult for peripheral countries to accumulate this capital; so they have to borrow.

The debt problem has led to calls for affluent lending countries to provide debt relief to some of the poorest countries. In 2005, the world's richest countries—the G8 group—agreed to write off US$40 billion in debts owed by 18 of the world's poorest countries, most of them in Africa. Addressing the full magnitude of LDC debt, however, will require continued substantial and sustained efforts if the poorest countries are to break free of the crushing financial obligations of their accumulated debts.

APPLY YOUR KNOWLEDGE Conduct research to determine the current debt of three countries. List two main factors contributing to each of the specific countries' debt. ■

Fair Trade

The Fair Trade movement highlights the interdependencies involved in international trade. The movement is a result of increasing awareness within developed countries of the weak bargaining position of many small producers at the beginning of the commodity chains that underpin the global economy. Fair Trade has become part of the "mobilization against globalization," an attempt to raise consumers' consciousness about the relationships embodied in their purchases.

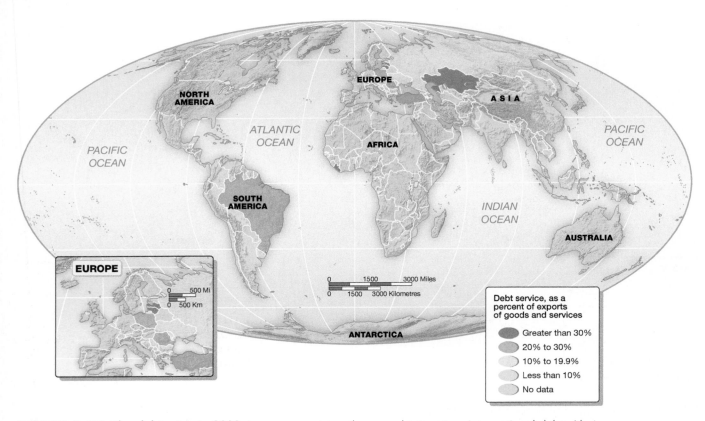

FIGURE 7.12 The debt crisis in 2008 In some countries, the annual interest on international debts (their "debt service") accounts for more than 20 percent of the annual value of their exports of goods and services. Many countries first got into debt trouble in the mid-1970s, when Western banks, faced with recession at home, offered low-interest loans to the governments of peripheral countries rather than being stuck with idle capital. When the world economy heated up again, interest rates rose and many peripheral countries had to take out new loans to pay the increased interest on the old loans: they slid into a debt crisis. The World Bank and the International Monetary Fund (IMF), in tandem with Western governments, worked to prevent a global financial crisis by organizing and guaranteeing programs that eased poor countries' debt burdens. Western banks were encouraged to swap debt for equity stakes in nationalized industries, while debtor governments were persuaded to impose austere economic policies. These policies have helped ease the debt crisis, but often at the price of severe hardship for ordinary people. In dark humour, among radical development theorists IMF came to stand for "imposing misery and famine." (*Source*: World Bank, Global Development Finance.)

FIGURE 7.13 Cocoa production Workers spread cocoa to dry in a Ghanaian hamlet.

(*Source*: marco vacca/Alamy)

represents a considerable improvement over what they usually receive. Fair Trade thus demonstrably enables producers in developing countries (**Figure 7.14**) to help themselves, not least because it typically involves democratic decision making over how the extra money earned is to be distributed.

Several types of Fair Trade organizations perform various roles along the commodity chains linking producers to consumers. At the beginning of the commodity chain are producer organizations—village or community groups or co-operatives, for example, often joined together under export marketing organizations. In 2009, there were more than 750 Fair Trade–certified producer groups (including many umbrella bodies) in 58 countries. These organizations typically sell their products to a second kind of Fair Trade organization: registered importers and wholesalers in more developed countries. In 2009, these existed in about 60 countries. They in turn sell to Fair Trade retailers: "world shops" and catalogue- or Internet-based retailers (**Figure 7.15**). In some countries, Fair Trade products are now mainstream, available in major supermarkets and independent shops and beginning to gain market share. In Switzerland, for example, Fair Trade bananas account for 20 percent of the retail market. In Canada, over 15 million pounds of certified Fair Trade coffee are sold annually, accounting for $200 million in sales in 2011.

Interpretations of International Patterns of Development

The overall relationship between economic structure and levels of prosperity makes it tempting to interpret economic development in distinctive stages. Each developed region or country, in other words, might be thought of as progressing from the early stages of development, with a heavy reliance on primary activities (and relatively low levels of prosperity), through a phase of industrialization and on to a "mature" stage of postindustrial development (with a diversified economic structure and relatively high levels of prosperity). This, in fact, has been a commonly held view of economic

FIGURE 7.14 Fair Trade coffee Susan Nangobi, aged 14, works with her father, a coffee farmer in the Kamuli region of Uganda. Their freshly picked coffee beans are ready to be dried before being taken to the Kulika Sustainable Organic Agricultural Training Program centre and then sold to Ibero Coffee company under Fair Trade guidelines. (*Source*: Andrew Aitchison/Alamy)

The Fair Trade movement is a global network of producers, traders, marketers, advocates, and consumers focused on building equitable trading relationships between consumers and the world's most economically disadvantaged artisans and farmers. As such, it is fundamentally a strategy for poverty alleviation and sustainable development. The key principles of Fair Trade include (1) creating opportunities for economically disadvantaged producers, (2) capacity building, (3) ensuring that women's work is properly valued and rewarded, (4) ensuring a safe and healthy working environment for producers, and (5) payment of a fair price—one that covers not only the costs of production but enables production that is socially just and environmentally sound.

Ultimately, only a very modest share of the retail price of Fair Trade goods in developed countries—only about 9 cents of the $3.10 cost of an average fairly traded 100-gram bar of chocolate—goes to producers in developing countries, but even this small share

FIGURE 7.15 Fair Trade retailing A Fair Trade shop in Canterbury, England. (*Source*: Chris Cooper-Smith/Alamy)

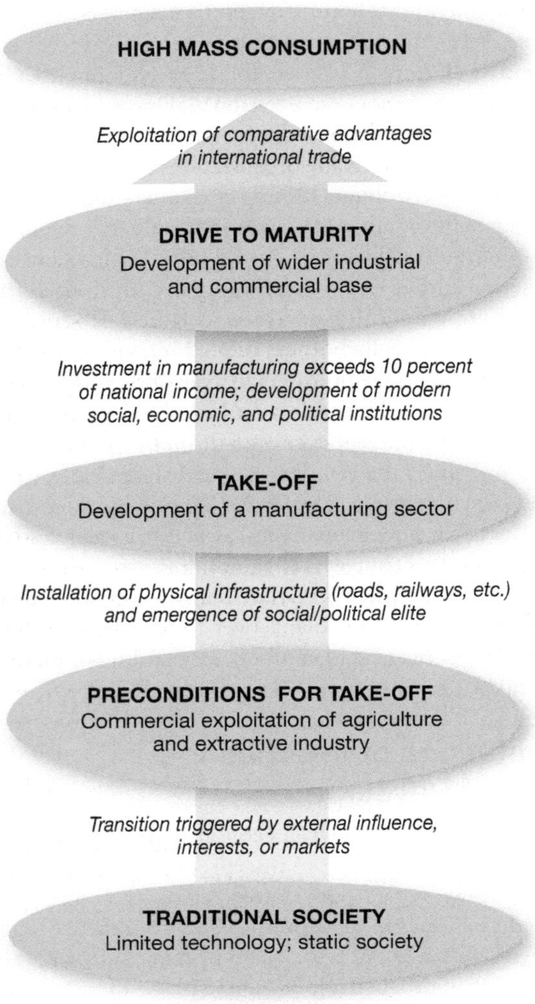

HIGH MASS CONSUMPTION

Exploitation of comparative advantages in international trade

DRIVE TO MATURITY
Development of wider industrial and commercial base

Investment in manufacturing exceeds 10 percent of national income; development of modern social, economic, and political institutions

TAKE-OFF
Development of a manufacturing sector

Installation of physical infrastructure (roads, railways, etc.) and emergence of social/political elite

PRECONDITIONS FOR TAKE-OFF
Commercial exploitation of agriculture and extractive industry

Transition triggered by external influence, interests, or markets

TRADITIONAL SOCIETY
Limited technology; static society

FIGURE 7.16 Stages of economic development This diagram illustrates a model based on the idea of successive stages of economic development. Each stage is seen as leading to the next, though some regions or countries may take longer than others to make the transition from one stage to the next. According to this view, now regarded as overly simplistic, places and regions follow parallel courses within a world that is steadily modernizing. Late starters eventually make progress, but at speeds determined by their resource endowments, their productivity, and the wisdom of their people's policies and decisions.

development, first conceptualized by a prominent economist, W. W. Rostow (**Figure 7.16**).

Rostow's model, however, is too simplistic to be of much help in understanding human geography. The reality is that places and regions are now interdependent. The fortunes of any given place are increasingly tied up with those of many others. Furthermore, Rostow's model perpetuates the myth of "developmentalism," the idea that every country and region will eventually make economic progress toward "high mass consumption" provided that they compete to the best of their ability within the world economy. The main weakness of developmentalism is that it is simply not reasonable to compare the prospects of late starters to the experience of places, regions, and countries that were among the early starters. For early starters the horizons were clear: free of effective competition, free

of obstacles, and free of precedents. For late starters the situation is entirely different. Today's less developed regions must compete in a crowded field while facing numerous barriers that are a direct consequence of the success of some of the early starters.

Indeed, many writers and theorists of international development claim that the prosperity of the core countries in the world economy has been based on *under*development and squalor in peripheral countries. Peripheral countries, it is argued, could not "follow" the previous historical experience of developed countries in stages-of-development fashion because their underdevelopment (that is, exploitation) was a structural requirement for development elsewhere. The development of Europe and North America, in other words, required the systematic underdevelopment of peripheral countries. By means of unequal trade, exploitation of labour, and profit extraction, the underdeveloped countries became increasingly rather than decreasingly impoverished.

The writings of economic historian and sociologist André Gunder Frank exemplify the explanations of international economic change that arose from this critique. Frank rejected the idea that underdevelopment is an original condition, equivalent to "traditionalism" or "backwardness." To the contrary, he argues, it is a condition created by integration into the worldwide system of capitalism. The world economy, Frank argues, has been unequally structured since Europeans first ventured out into the world in the sixteenth century. Although the form of the dominance of core over periphery has changed from colonialism and imperialism to neocolonialism, an overall transfer of wealth from periphery to core continues to fuel growth in some places at the expense of others.

Frank's approach is an example of "dependency theory." This has been a very influential approach in explaining global patterns of development and underdevelopment. Dependency theory states, essentially, that development and underdevelopment are reverse sides of the same process: *Development somewhere requires underdevelopment somewhere else.* Immanuel Wallerstein's world-system theory (see Chapter 2) takes this kind of dependency into account. According to this perspective, the entire world economy is to be seen as an evolving market system with an economic hierarchy of states—a core, a semiperiphery, and a periphery. The composition of this hierarchy is dynamic: individual countries can move from periphery to semiperiphery, core to periphery, and so on.

REGIONAL ECONOMIC DEVELOPMENT

Unevenness in economic development often has a regional dimension. Initial conditions are a crucial determinant of regional economic performance. Scarce resources, a history of neglect, lack of investment, and concentrations of low-skilled people all combine to explain the lagging performance of certain areas. In some regions, initial extreme disadvantages constrain the opportunities of individuals born there. A child born in the Mexican state of Chiapas, for example, has much bleaker prospects than a child born in Mexico City. The child from Chiapas is twice as likely to die before age 5, less than half as likely to complete primary school, and 10 times as likely to live in a house without access to running water. On reaching working age, he or she will earn 20 to 35 percent less than a comparable worker living in Mexico City and 40 to 45 percent less than one living in northern Mexico.

Other examples of regional inequality can be found throughout the world. Gansu, China, with an income per capita 40 percent below the national average, is one of the poorest and most remote regions in the nation. With poor soils highly susceptible to erosion, low and erratic rainfall, and few off-farm employment opportunities, a high proportion of its inhabitants live in poverty. Chaco Province, in Argentina, has a GDP per capita that is only 38 percent of the national average. Low educational attainment and lack of infrastructure, especially roads, explain much of this deviation.

Globalization has been associated with *increasing* regional inequality within many countries since the 1980s. In China, for example, disparities have widened dramatically between the interior and the export-oriented regions of the coast. The transition economies of the countries of the former Soviet Union and its Eastern European satellites have registered some of the largest increases in regional inequality. Some core countries—especially Sweden, the United Kingdom, and the United States—have also registered significant increases in regional inequality since the 1980s. At this regional scale, as at the global scale, levels of economic development often exhibit a fundamental core–periphery structure. Indeed, *within-country* core–periphery contrasts are evident throughout the world: in core countries such as France and the United States, in semiperipheral countries such as South Korea, and in peripheral countries such as Nigeria and Indonesia.

In Canada, the fortunes of coal-mining Cape Breton in Nova Scotia waned with the collapse of the coal industry and the increased importance of oil and gas in energy production in the late twentieth century. As a result, about one percent of the population is leaving the region every year, further accelerating the decline.

With roughly two-thirds of the average Canadian per capita GDP, it remains one of the poorest regions in Canada to this day.

Figure 7.17 shows the average individual earnings in each Canadian province and territory in 2013. The continuing importance of staple production is shown in the above-national-average earnings in the Northwest Territories, Saskatchewan, and Alberta, where booming resource extraction (based on gold and diamonds, phosphates, and oil) has become the mainstay of the regional economy. Meanwhile, earnings in "post-fisheries" Atlantic Canada are below the national average, illustrating the continuing importance of core and periphery relationships in the Canadian economy.

Patterns of regional economic development are historical in origin and cumulative in nature. Recognizing this, geographers are interested in **geographical path dependence,** the relationship between present-day activities in a place and the past experiences of that place. When spatial relationships and regional patterns emerge through the logic of fundamental principles of spatial organization, they do so in ways guided and influenced by pre-existing patterns and relationships, as the case of Ottawa illustrates. Initially a small and remote lumber town, Ottawa developed into a large administrative employment centre once it was designated as the capital of Canada. Its growing population provided both a market and a labour pool for a host of service and small manufacturing industries that were then able to develop in the area. Most recently, the Ottawa area has added high-tech industries to its activities, industries that developed on the basis of federal government grants and the presence of two universities.

These observations lead to an important principle of regional economic development, the principle of initial advantage. **Initial advantage** highlights the importance of an early start in economic development. It represents a special case of external economies. Other things being equal, new phases of economic development

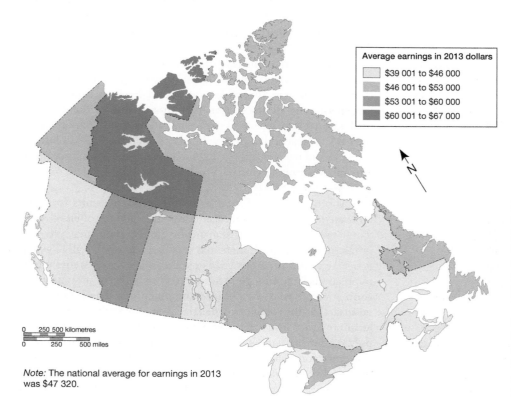

FIGURE 7.17 Average earnings in Canada's provinces and territories in 2013 In Canada, we find considerable differences in earnings among provinces and territories. The rising demand for resources (much of it from China) has caused a boom in Alberta, Saskatchewan, and the Northwest Territories, while the decline of fisheries in Atlantic Canada continues to depress the regional economy. Meanwhile, difficulties in the manufacturing sector have dampened Ontario's economy. Note that the numbers reflect only the earnings of people who are gainfully employed.

Average earnings in 2013 dollars

- $39 001 to $46 000
- $46 001 to $53 000
- $53 001 to $60 000
- $60 001 to $67 000

0   250 500 kilometres

0   250   500 miles

Note: The national average for earnings in 2013 was $47 320.

take hold first in settings that offer external economies: existing labour markets, existing consumer markets, existing frameworks of fixed social capital, and so on. **External economies** are cost savings that result from advantages beyond a firm's organization and methods of production. For example, a firm can locate close to similar businesses and so enjoy **localization economies**—cost savings that accrue to particular industries as a result of clustering together at a specific location. In turn, this will attract other similar firms and so form the basis for continuing economic growth (**Figure 7.18**).

Examples of localization economies include sharing a pool of labour with special skills or experience, supporting specialized technical schools, joining to create a marketing organization or a research institute, and drawing on specialized subcontractors, maintenance firms, suppliers, distribution agents, and lawyers. If such advantages lead to a reputation for high-quality production, localization is intensified because more producers want to cash in on the reputation. Examples include haute couture fashion in Paris, electronics and software industries in Silicon Valley, recording companies in Los Angeles, and the U.S. auto industry in Detroit. Examples from Canada are movie production in Vancouver, aerospace technology in Ottawa, and software development in Kitchener-Waterloo.

For places and regions with a substantial initial advantage, therefore, the trajectory of geographical path dependence tends to be one of persistent growth. This pattern reinforces, in turn, the core–periphery patterns of economic development found in every part of the world and at every spatial scale. That said, geographers recognize there is no single pathway to development. The consequences of initial advantage for both core and peripheral regions can be—and often are—modified. Old core–periphery relationships can be blurred, and new ones can be initiated.

FIGURE 7.18 The haute couture fashion district in Paris
Specialized fashion districts, such as this one on the Boulevard Saint-Honoré in Paris, provide good examples of how firms can benefit from a form of external economies called localization economies. By locating close to each other, the businesses form a narrow community of interest in which close rivalries breed innovation and easy contact among producers helps minimize uncertainty. (*Source:* Courtesy of Alan E. Nash)

APPLY YOUR KNOWLEDGE Identify an example of localization economies functioning in your own community. What industries are clustering together and how can this result in cost savings? ∎

The Development of Regional Economic Cores

Regional cores of economic development are created cumulatively, following some initial advantage, through the operation of several of the basic principles of economic geography. Commercial and industrial location decisions all take place within complex webs of *functional interdependence*. These webs include the relationships and linkages between different kinds of industries, different kinds of stores, and different kinds of offices. Particularly important here are the **agglomeration effects** associated with various kinds of economic linkages and interdependencies. These interdependencies include the cost advantages that accrue to individual firms because of their location among functionally related activities. The trigger for these agglomeration effects can be any kind of economic development—the establishment of a trading port or the growth of a local industry or any large-scale enterprise. The external economies and economic linkages generated by such developments are the initial advantages that stimulate a self-propelling process of local economic development.

A number of interrelated effects come into play when new economic activity begins in an area. *Backward linkages* develop as new firms arrive to provide the growing industry with components, supplies, specialized services, or facilities. *Forward linkages* develop as new firms arrive to take the finished products of the growing industry and use them in their own processing, assembly, finishing, packaging, or distribution operations. Together with the initial growth, the growth in these linked industries helps create a threshold of activity large enough to attract **ancillary industries** and activities (maintenance and repair, recycling, security, and business services, for example).

The existence of these interrelated activities establishes a pool of specialized labour with the kinds of skills and experience that make the area attractive to still more firms. Meanwhile, the linkages among all these firms help promote interaction between professional and technical personnel and allow the area to support R&D (research and development) facilities, research institutes, and so on, thus increasing the likelihood of local inventions and innovations that might further stimulate local economic development.

Another aspect of local economic growth results from the increase in population represented by the families of employees. Their presence creates a demand for housing, utilities, physical infrastructure, retailing, personal services, and so on—all of which generate additional jobs. This expansion, in turn, helps create populations large enough to attract an even wider variety and more sophisticated kinds of services and amenities. Last—but by no means least—the overall growth in local employment creates a larger local tax base. The local government can then provide improved public utilities, roads, schools, health services, recreational amenities, and so on—all of which serve to intensify agglomeration economies and so enhance the competitiveness of the area in attracting further rounds of investment.

Swedish economist Gunnar Myrdal, the 1974 Nobel Prize winner, was the first to recognize that any significant initial local advantage tends to be reinforced through geographic principles of agglomeration and localization. He called the process **cumulative causation (Figure 7.19)**. Cumulative causation refers to the spiralling buildup of advantages that occurs in specific geographic settings as a result of the development of external economies, agglomeration effects, and localization economies. Myrdal also pointed out that this spiral of local growth tends to attract people—enterprising young people, usually—and investment funds from other areas. According to the basic principles of spatial interaction, these flows tend to be strongest from nearby regions and areas with the lowest wages, fewest job opportunities, or least attractive investment opportunities.

In some cases this loss of entrepreneurial talent, labour, and investment capital is sufficient to trigger a cumulative negative spiral of economic disadvantage. With less capital, less innovative energy, and depleted pools of labour, industrial growth in peripheral regions tends to be significantly slower and less innovative than in regions with an initial advantage. This in turn tends to limit the size of the local tax base, making it difficult for local governments to furnish a competitive **infrastructure** of roads, schools, and recreational amenities. Myrdal called these negative impacts on a region (or regions) of the economic growth of some other region **backwash effects**. Negative impacts take the form, for example, of out-migration, outflows of investment capital, and the shrinking of local tax bases. Backwash effects are important because they help explain why regional economic development is so uneven and why core–periphery contrasts in economic development are so common. The processes that have led to the formation of heartlands and hinterlands in the Canadian context (see Chapter 2) are specific types of these general core–periphery processes.

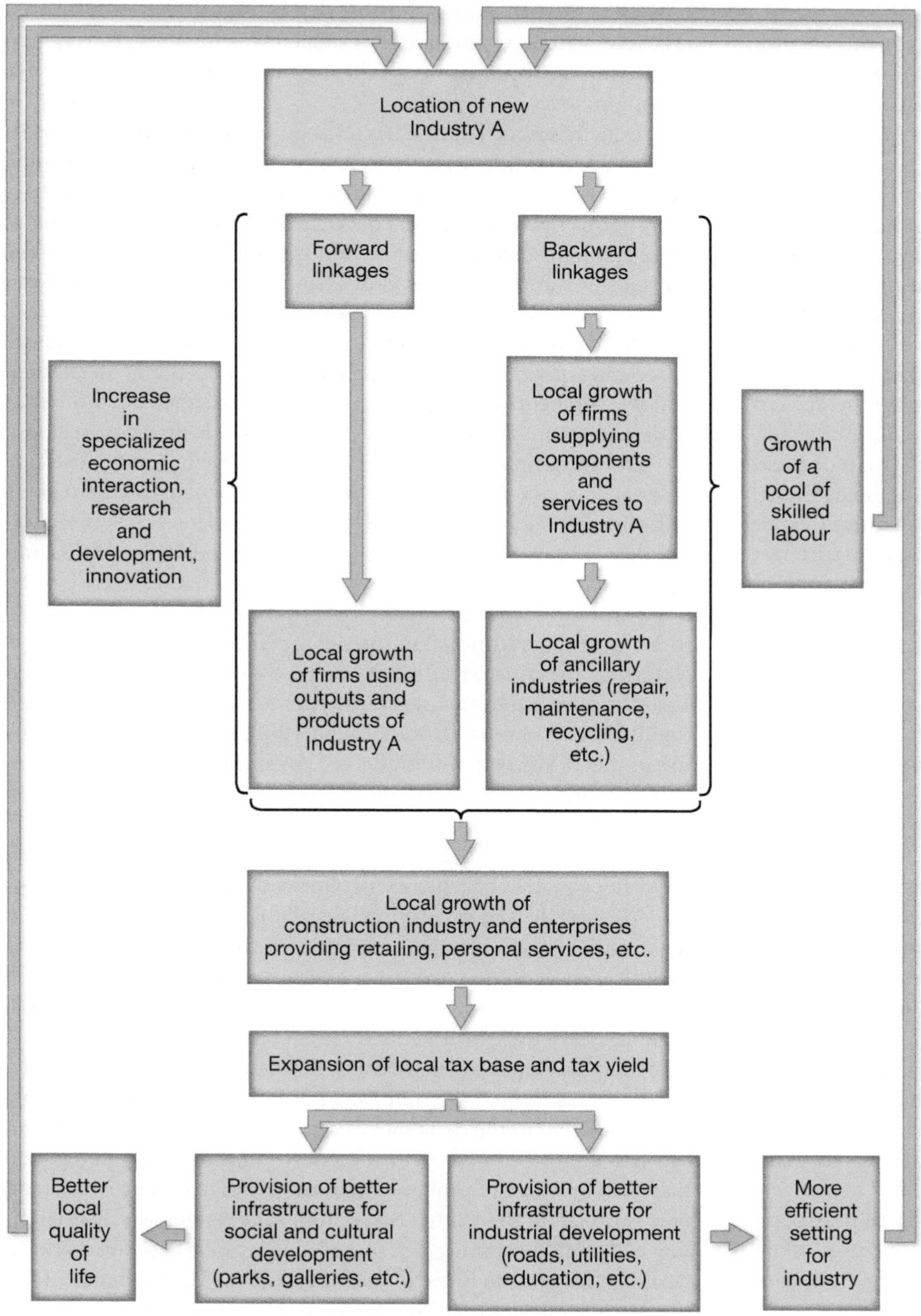

APPLY YOUR KNOWLEDGE

Identify and research three cities that have experienced a backwash effect. List three reasons for the backwash effect in each locale. ■

The Modification of Regional Core–Periphery Patterns

Although very important, cumulative causation and backwash effects are not the only processes affecting the geography of economic development. If they were, the world's economic geography would be even more starkly polarized than it is now. There would be little chance for the emergence of new growth regions, like Guangdong in Southeast China, and there would be little likelihood of stagnation or decline in once-booming regions, like northern England.

Myrdal himself recognized that peripheral regions do sometimes emerge as new growth regions, and he partially explained them in what he called *spread* (or trickle-down) effects. **Spread effects** are the positive

FIGURE 7.19 Processes of regional economic growth Once a significant amount of new industry becomes established in an area, it creates a self-propelling process of economic growth. As this diagram shows, the geographic principles of agglomeration and localization reinforce the initial advantages of industrial growth. The overall process is known as *cumulative causation*.

impacts on a region (or regions) from the economic growth of some other region, usually a core region. Growth creates levels of demand for food, consumer products, and other manufactures that are so high that local producers cannot satisfy them. This demand gives investors in peripheral regions (or countries) the opportunity to establish a local capacity to meet the demand. Entrepreneurs who participate are also able to exploit the advantages of cheaper land and labour in peripheral regions. If strong enough, spread effects can enable peripheral regions to develop their own spiral of cumulative causation, thus changing the interregional geography of economic patterns and flows. The economic growth of South Korea, for example, is partly attributable to the spread effects of Japanese economic prosperity. More recently, the Chinese economy benefited from the spread effects of the North American consumer society.

Another way in which peripheral regions can develop their own spiral of cumulative causation is by replacing imported goods and services with goods and services that are domestically produced—a process called import substitution we already encountered in the context of the international division of labour. Obviously, some things are hard to copy because of the limitations of natural resources or climate (Canada being a good example). However, many products and services *can* be copied by local entrepreneurs, thus capturing local capital, increasing local employment opportunities, intensifying the use of local resources, and generating profits for further local investment. The classic example is Japan, where import substitution, especially for textiles and heavy engineering, played an important part in the transition from a peripheral economy to a major industrial power in the late nineteenth century. Import substitution also figured prominently in the Japanese "economic miracle" after World War II, featuring the automobile industry and consumer electronics. Today, countries like Brazil, Peru, and Ghana are seeking to follow the same sort of strategy, subsidizing domestic industries and protecting them from outside competitors through tariffs and taxes.

Core–periphery patterns and relationships can change as a result of internal changes in core regions that can slow or modify the spiral of cumulative causation. The main factor that can have this effect is the development of agglomeration diseconomies. **Agglomeration diseconomies** are the negative economic effects of urbanization and the local concentration of industry, including the higher prices that must be paid by firms competing for land and labour; the costs of delays resulting from traffic congestion and crowded port and railroad facilities; the increasing costs of waste disposal; and the burden of higher taxes that eventually have to be levied by local governments in order to support services and amenities previously considered unnecessary—traffic police, city planning, and transit systems, for example.

Diseconomies imposed through taxes can often be passed on by firms to consumers in other regions and other countries in the form of higher prices. Charging higher prices, however, decreases the competitiveness of a firm in relation to firms operating elsewhere. Agglomeration diseconomies that cannot be "exported"— noise, air pollution, increased commuting costs, and increased housing costs, for example—require local governments to tax even more of the region's wealth in attempts to compensate for a deteriorating quality of life.

Deindustrialization and Creative Destruction

The most fundamental cause of change in the relationship between initial advantage and cumulative causation is longer-term shifts in technology systems and the competition between states within the world-system. The innovations associated with successive technology systems generate new industries that are not yet tied down by enormous investments in factories or allied to existing industrial agglomerations—they are free to choose their location. Combined with innovations in transport and communications, this creates *windows of locational opportunity* that can result in new industrial districts, with new generations of small towns or cities growing into dominant metropolitan areas through new rounds of cumulative causation.

Equally important as a factor in how core–periphery patterns change are the shifts in the profitability of old, established industries in core regions compared to the profitability of new industries in fast-growing new industrial districts. As soon as the differential is large enough, some disinvestment takes place within core regions. This disinvestment can take place in several ways. Manufacturers can reduce their wage bill by cutting back on production; they can reduce their fixed costs by closing down and selling off some of their factory space and equipment; or they can reduce their spending on research and development for new products. This disinvestment, in turn, leads to deindustrialization in formerly prosperous industrial core regions.

Deindustrialization involves a relative decline (and in extreme cases an absolute decline) in industrial employment in core regions as firms scale back their activities in response to lower levels of profitability (**Figure 7.20**). This is what happened in the 1960s and 1970s when the Manufacturing Belt in the northeastern United States turned into the "Rustbelt" (**Figure 7.21**). It also occurred in many of the traditional industrial regions of Europe: in France, Belgium, the Netherlands, Norway, Sweden, and the United Kingdom, manufacturing employment decreased by between one-third and one-half from 1960 to 1990. In Canada, restructuring in the 1980s and 1990s affected the industrial region between Windsor and Quebec City, and many isolated resource centres in Canada from Powell River (British Columbia) to Corner Brook (Newfoundland). Similarly, fishing centres on the Atlantic coast suffered an economic collapse as fish stocks dwindled.

Meanwhile, the capital made available from disinvestment in these core regions becomes available for investment by entrepreneurs in new ventures based on innovative products and production technologies. Old industries—and sometimes entire old industrial regions—have to be "dismantled" (or at least neglected) in order to help fund the creation of new centres of profitability and employment. This process is often referred to as creative destruction, something that is inherent to the dynamics of capitalism. **Creative destruction** involves the withdrawal of investments from activities (and regions) that yield low rates of profit in order to reinvest in new activities (and new regions). In the United States, for example, the deindustrialization of the Manufacturing Belt provided the capital and the locational flexibility for firms to invest in the Sunbelt of the United States and in semiperipheral countries like Mexico and South Korea.

The process does not stop there, however. If the deindustrialization of the old core regions is severe enough, the relative cost of their land, labour, and infrastructure may decline to the point where they once again become attractive to investors. As a result, a see-saw movement of investment capital occurs, which over the long term

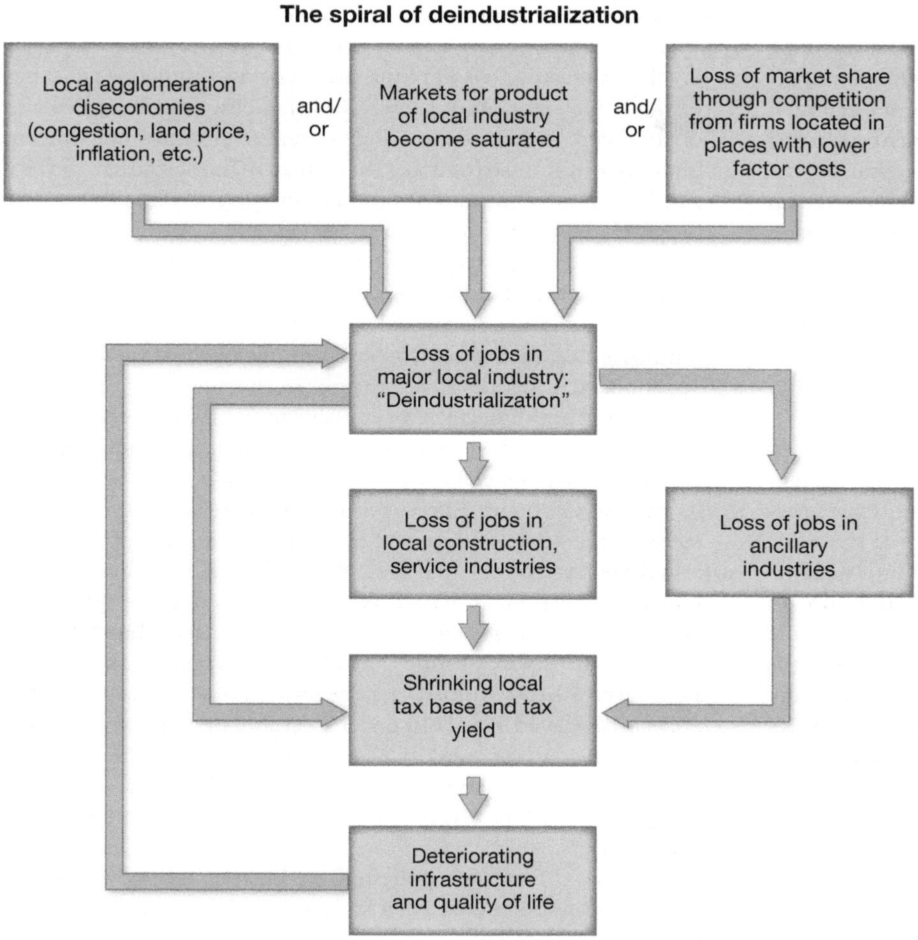

The spiral of deindustrialization

Local agglomeration diseconomies (congestion, land price, inflation, etc.)	and/ or	Markets for product of local industry become saturated	and/ or	Loss of market share through competition from firms located in places with lower factor costs

Loss of jobs in major local industry: "Deindustrialization"

Loss of jobs in local construction, service industries

Loss of jobs in ancillary industries

Shrinking local tax base and tax yield

Deteriorating infrastructure and quality of life

FIGURE 7.20 Regional economic decline
When the locational advantages of manufacturing regions are undermined for one reason or another, profitability declines and manufacturing employment falls. This can lead to a downward spiral of economic decline, as experienced by many of the traditional manufacturing regions of Europe and North America during the 1960s, 1970s, and 1980s. (*Source:* Reprinted with permission of Prentice Hall, from P. L. Knox, *Urbanization,* © 1994, p. 55.)

tends to move from developed to less-developed regions—then back again, once the formerly developed region has experienced a sufficient relative decline. A "has-been" region can become redeveloped and revitalized, given a new lease on life by the infusion of new capital for new industries. This is what happened, for example, to the Pittsburgh region in the 1980s, resulting in the creation of a postindustrial economy out of a depressed industrial setting. Steel mills reduced their workforce in the Pittsburgh region from more than 20 000 to less than 5000 between 1975 and 1995. These losses have been more than made up, however, by new jobs generated in high-tech electronics, specialized engineering, and finance and business services.

FIGURE 7.21 Deindustrialization: from Manufacturing Belt to Rust Belt This derelict steel mill in New Jersey is testament to the downward economic spiral in what was once one of the world's most important heavy manufacturing regions. Unfortunately, many such sites have to be remediated before being redeveloped because their soils and water tables have been contaminated by decades of industrial use. (*Source:* Vince Streano/Corbis)

Government Intervention

In addition to the processes of deindustrialization and creative destruction, core–periphery patterns can also be modified by government intervention. National governments realize that regional planning and policy can be an important component of broad economic strategies to stabilize and reorganize their economies, as well as to maximize their overall competitiveness. Without regional planning and policy, the resources of peripheral regions can remain underutilized, while core regions can become vulnerable to agglomeration diseconomies. For political reasons, too, national governments are often willing to help particular regions adjust to changing economic circumstances. At the same time, most local governments take responsibility for stimulating economic development within their jurisdiction, if only in order to increase the local tax base.

The nature and extent of government intervention has varied over time and by country. In some countries, special government agencies have been established to promote regional economic development and reduce core–periphery contrasts. Among the best-known examples are the Japanese MITI (Ministry of International Trade and Industry), and the Italian Cassa del Mezzogiorno (Southern Development Agency). In Canada, federal Economic Development Agencies exist for several regions. Some governments have sought to help industries in declining regions by undertaking government investment in infrastructure and providing subsidies for private investment; others have sought to devise tax breaks that reduce the cost of labour in peripheral regions. Still others have sought to deal with agglomeration diseconomies in core regions through increased taxes and restrictions on land use (**Figure 7.22**).

FIGURE 7.22 Congestion charges, London The London congestion charge was introduced in 2003 to reduce traffic congestion in the centre of the city. The standard charge is almost $20 per day for each non-exempt vehicle that travels within the zone between 7:00 am and 6:30 pm (Monday–Friday only); a penalty of up to $300 is levied for non-payment. The intent is to reduce time delays and costs that make city locations less attractive to businesses and their clients. (*Source:* Stephen Finn/Fotolia)

While each approach has its followers, one of the most widespread governmental approaches to core–periphery patterns involves the exploitation of the principle of cumulative causation through the creation of growth poles. **Growth poles** are places of economic activity deliberately organized around one or more high-growth industries that, given an artificial start, may develop a self-sustaining spiral of economic prosperity. The basic idea is for governments to promote regional economic growth by fostering propulsive industries in favourable locations. Economists have noted, however, that not all industries are equal in the extent to which they stimulate economic growth and cumulative causation. The ones that generate the most pronounced effects are known as "propulsive industries," and they have changed over time: in the 1920s, shipbuilding was a propulsive industry; in the 1950s and 1960s, it was automobile manufacturing; and today biotechnology and digital technologies are propulsive industries.

Many countries have used the growth-pole approach as a basis for regional development policies. For example, French governments have designated certain locations as *technopoles*—sites for the establishment of high-tech industries (such as computers and biotechnology)—under the assumption that these leading-edge activities will stimulate further development. In southern Italy various heavy industries were located in a number of remote areas after World War II in order to stimulate ancillary development. In Canada, a total of 23 growth poles were identified for federal subsidies, mainly in eastern Canada. The new industries, it was hoped, would trigger the geographic process of cumulative causation.

The results of such policies have been mixed, however. The French technopoles have been fairly successful because the French government invested large sums of money in establishing propulsive industries in favourable locations. But the Italian and Canadian growth-pole efforts, like many others, have been disappointing. In practice, governments often fail to invest in the right industries, and they nearly always fail to invest heavily enough to kick-start the process of cumulative causation.

The British Columbia town of Kitimat provides a Canadian example (**Figure 7.23**). Developed in the 1950s around an aluminum smelter that used hydropower created by a purpose-built dam, the townsite was carved out of old growth forest and laid out to accommodate 50 000 residents. However, the government's projections that the dam and the smelter would attract substantial industries and become one of the province's largest centres never materialized—perhaps because of its remoteness or perhaps because such large projects are rarely truly propulsive for the local community. In recent years, Kitimat has been proposed as the terminal for pipeline projects that would see Albertan oil and gas exported to Asia via new deepwater port facilities.

APPLY YOUR KNOWLEDGE Identify two regions that have experienced deindustrialization in addition to the regions referred to in the text. List the industries each lost. Did the regions you found experience creative destruction? If so, what industries were dismantled and which ones were created? Has government intervention played a role in core–periphery patterns in the regions you selected? ■

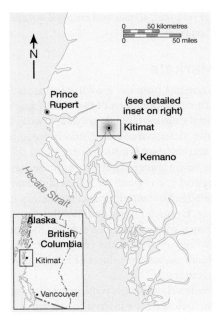

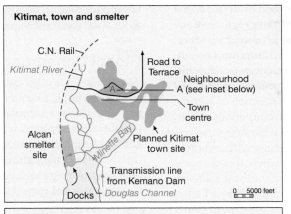

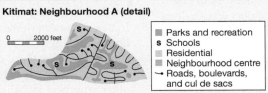

FIGURE 7.23 The town centre of Kitimat, British Columbia Originally established in the 1950s as a growth centre based on aluminum smelting, the town of Kitimat, British Columbia, has not seen any significant expansion since. In fact, Kitimat lost 12.6 percent of its population between 2001 and 2006—the census district with the largest population decline in Canada. The 2011 census noted another 7.3 percent decline to just over 8000 residents. (*Source for diagrams:* Based on Ira M. Robinson, *New Industrial Towns on Canada's Frontier.* University of Chicago Research Paper No. 73, 1962. *Photo source:* Courtesy of Alan E. Nash)

GLOBALIZATION AND ECONOMIC DEVELOPMENT

In the past 30 years, regional core–periphery patterns have been increasingly influenced by globalization and the economic interdependence of major world regions. This globalization has been caused by four important and interrelated factors: a new international division of labour, a new technology system, a homogenization of international consumer markets, and an internationalization of finance.

A New International Division of Labour

A major wave of corporate globalization took place in the 1970s, led by U.S.-based manufacturing giants like General Motors and General Electric that wanted to reduce labour costs, outflank national labour unions, and increase overseas market penetration. As they moved production facilities overseas, a new international division of labour developed that resulted in three main changes. The first of these is that the United States has declined as an industrial producer. A second and related change is that manufacturing production has been decentralized from the world's core regions to semiperipheral and peripheral countries. For example, in 2009, U.S.-based companies

employed about 31 million workers overseas, 80 percent of whom were in manufacturing jobs. An important reason for this trend has been the prospect of keeping production costs low by exploiting the huge differential in wage rates around the world.

The disparity between wages in the countries where these industries are headquartered and where their goods are manufactured is hard to overstate: in 2014, Nike offered US$1 billion over ten years for the right to outfit the English soccer club Manchester United with its shoes. Competitor Adidas paid NBA player Derrick Rose US$280 million over 14 years to secure his endorsement for his entire basketball career.

Meanwhile, the Asian workers who make the shoes and other sports gear worn by players are paid as little as 75 cents per hour—about $6 for a standard working day. Shopping at their cheapest local markets, the women producing brand-name sportswear in Indonesia need to work half a day to earn enough to purchase 1.5 kg of uncooked chicken, which for some is all the meat they can afford for a month.[1]

[1]Offside! Oxfam International, "Labour Rights and Sportswear Production in Asia," 2006, p. 2. Accessed April 27, 2011, www.oxfam.org.au/campaigns/labour/06report.

A third result of the new international division of labour is that new specializations have emerged within the core regions of the world-system: high-tech manufacturing and **producer services**, examples of which include information services, insurance, consulting, and market research that enhance the productivity or efficiency of other firms' activities or that enable them to maintain specialized roles. These producer services industries have themselves become globalized in response to the needs of their most important clients, the global manufacturing corporations. If, say, a law firm or advertising agency wished to keep the business of a major corporation, it had to be able to provide its services in places where that corporation needed them. Thus, advanced business service firms followed their clients along the globalization path in the late 1970s and especially in the 1980s. This meant creating an office network to match clients' needs. After a while, some advanced business service firms used their global office network to win more clients in new markets. By the 1990s, the leading business service firms themselves became global corporations that offer seamless service with offices in key cities around the world.

A New Technology System

The second factor contributing to the globalization of the economy is the new technology system, which is based on a combination of innovations, including solar energy, robotics, microelectronics, biotechnology, and digital telecommunications and information systems. This new technology system has required the geographical reorganization of the core economies. It has also extended the global reach of finance and industry and permitted a more flexible approach to investment and trade. Especially important in this regard have been new and improved technologies in transport and communications—the integration of shipping, railroad, and highway systems through containerization (**Figure 7.24**); the introduction of wide-bodied cargo jets that can be loaded with standardized skids in a matter of minutes; and the development of fibre-optic networks, communications satellites, cloud computing, and ubiquitous Internet access. Finally, many of these telecommunications technologies have also introduced a wider geographical scope and

faster pace to many aspects of political, social, and cultural change, as we shall see in subsequent chapters.

Global Consumer Markets

The third factor in globalization has been the growth of consumer markets. Among the more affluent populations of the world, a new and materialistic international culture has taken root, in which people save less, borrow more, defer parenthood, and indulge in affordable luxuries that are marketed as symbols of style and distinctiveness. This culture is easily transmitted through the new telecommunications media, and it has been an important basis for transnational corporations' global branding and marketing of "world products" (for instance, German luxury automobiles, Swiss watches, British raincoats, French wines, American soft drinks, and Italian shoes and designer clothes). Seven of the ten most trusted brands in India in 2009, for example, were products of European or American transnational corporations.

This materialistic international culture is reinforced through other aspects of globalization, including the internationalization of television, especially CNN, Sky, and Star Television, and the syndication of TV movies and light entertainment series. Yet, while multimedia industries have been booming, the global market for popular cultural products carried by these media is becoming more concentrated. At the core of the entertainment industry—film, music, and television—there is a growing dominance of U.S. products, and many countries have seen their homegrown industries wither. Hollywood obtains more than 50 percent of its revenues from overseas, up from just 30 percent in 1980. Movies made in the United States account for about 50 percent of the market in Japan, 70 percent in Europe, and 85 percent in Latin America. Similarly, U.S. television series have become increasingly prominent in the programming of other countries.

The Internationalization of Finance

The fourth factor contributing to today's globalization is the internationalization of finance: the emergence of globally integrated

FIGURE 7.24 The impact of containerization on world trade Containerization revolutionized long-distance transport by doing away with the slow, expensive, and unreliable business of loading and unloading ships with manual labour. Before containerization, ships spent one day in port for every day at sea; in the wake of containerization, they spend a day in port for every ten days at sea. By 1965, an international standard for containers had been adopted, making it possible to transfer goods directly from ship to rail to road and allowing for a highly integrated global transport infrastructure. The largest container ships today hold up to 18 000 containers. Containerization requires a heavy investment in both vessels and dockside handling equipment, however. As a result, container traffic has quickly become concentrated in a few ports that handle high-volume transatlantic and transpacific trade. This photograph shows the Harem container port in Istanbul, Turkey. (*Source: Ali Kabas/Alamy*)

financial markets. The pivotal moment was a "system shock" to the international economy that occurred in the mid-1970s. World financial markets, swollen with U.S. dollars by the U.S. government's deficit budgeting and by huge currency reserves held by the Organization of Petroleum Exporting Countries (OPEC) after it had orchestrated a four-fold increase in the price of crude oil, quickly evolved into a new and sophisticated system of international finance, with new patterns of investment and disinvestment.

Meanwhile, the capacity of computers and information systems to deal very quickly with changing international conditions added a speculative component to the internationalization of finance. International movements of money, bonds, securities, and other financial instruments have now become an end in themselves because they are a potential source of high profits from speculation and manipulation. The global banking and financial network handles trillions of dollars *every day*—yet only 10 percent of those transactions have anything to do with the traditional world economy of trade in goods and services. In other words, 90 percent of the transactions are speculative in nature, betting on future rate fluctuations.

The volume and complexity of international investment and financial trading has created a need for banks and financial institutions that can handle investments on a large scale, across great distances, quickly and efficiently. The nerve centres of the new system are located in just a few places—London, Frankfurt, New York, and Tokyo, in particular. Satellite communications systems and fibre-optic networks make it possible for firms to operate key financial and business services 24 hours a day around the globe (**Figure 7.25**), handling an enormous volume of transactions. Linked to these communications systems, computers permit the recording and coordination of the data. The world's fourth-largest stock market, the National Associated Automated Dealers Quotation System (NASDAQ), has no trading floor at all: telephone and fibre-optic lines connect its half-million traders worldwide.

This interconnectedness and complexity contributed to the global financial crisis of October 2008. The failure of several major private financial institutions in the U.S. prompted panic in international financial markets. Suddenly, the world's major economies were thrown into recession, and millions of households in affluent countries had to cope with the loss of jobs, savings, and pension funds. The governments of the leading economies intervened with hundreds of billions of dollars of support for private financial institutions in an attempt to prop up the international financial system and, with it, their national, regional, and local economies.

How could this have happened? Part of the explanation lies in the steady increase in debt that had been fuelling every aspect of the world economy and, in particular, the American economy, since the late 1970s. Consumer spending had been increasingly financed by credit card debt; a housing boom had been financed by an expanded and aggressive mortgage market; and wars in Iraq and Afghanistan had been financed by U.S. government borrowing from overseas. By mid-2008, private

debt in America had reached US$41 trillion, almost three times the country's annual Gross Domestic Product; the external debts of the United States meanwhile had reached US$13.7 trillion. All sorts of financial instruments had emerged in the speculative free-market climate engendered by neoliberalism: securitization, derivatives, hedge funds, collateralized debt obligations, mortgage-backed securities, and so on. Soon, banks and financial institutions in other countries were joining in, profiting immensely from a global credit binge. Everyone, it seemed, was borrowing from everyone else in an international financial system that had become extremely complex, increasingly leveraged, and decreasingly regulated.

Taking advantage of the relaxed controls on financial institutions resulting from neoliberal policies, mortgage lenders in core countries (and especially the United States) had been reselling their mortgages on bond markets and to investment banks in order to fund the soaring demand for housing. Few in the financial services industries fully understood the complexities of the booming mortgage market, and the various risk-assessment agencies were seriously at fault in underestimating the risks associated with these loans. Eventually, when interest rates increased, many households began to default on their monthly payments and, as the bad loans added up, mortgage lenders, in turn, found themselves in financial trouble.

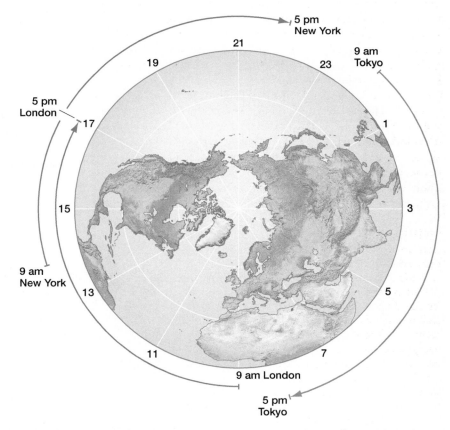

FIGURE 7.25 Twenty-four-hour trading among major financial markets
Office hours in the two most important financial centres—New York and London—overlap one another somewhat, even though the two cities are situated in broadly separated time zones. When these markets are both closed, Tokyo offices are open. This means that between them the world's three major financial centres span the globe with almost 24-hour trading in currencies, stocks, and other financial instruments.

Because the entire world economy is so interdependent, the problem quickly spread. As credit markets seized up, manufacturers and other businesses found it difficult to get the credit they needed in order to keep going. Understandably, investors big and small were shaken; stock markets collapsed (**Figure 7.26**). Consumer confidence also plummeted, prompting retailers to cut back on orders. The sophisticated flexible production system of global commodity chains meant that the impact was almost instantaneous and felt worldwide.

Within days of the U.S. stock market crash in mid-October 2008, workers in Chinese toy factories found themselves unemployed, as did garment workers in Thailand. Meanwhile, in Iceland, the entire economy collapsed almost immediately, a result of its banks having been overextended in their search for profit from the international credit binge. The domino effects of the crisis continued around the world. The U.S. and European governments have led a coordinated attempt to bolster the global financial system and provide a continuing flow of the credit needed to keep the global economy from falling into a deep depression, but in 2010 the Greek economy had to be propped up with a massive US\$146 billion loan from the European Union and International Monetary Fund, and a few months later the Irish economy was saved the same way with a loan almost as large. In 2013, Cyprus had to be bailed out, and there is growing concern that two of Europe's largest economies, Italy and France, may be headed for the same trouble. Clearly, the financial crisis is not over yet.

> **APPLY YOUR KNOWLEDGE** Choose a semiperipheral or peripheral country and determine the ways each of the four factors of globalization have affected its economic development process. ∎

THE GEOGRAPHY OF ECONOMIC GLOBALIZATION

In this section, we examine some specific impacts of three principal components of the global economy: global assembly lines and supply chains, resulting in large measure from the operations of transnational corporations; the global office, resulting mainly from the internationalization of banking, finance, and business services; and the pleasure periphery, resulting from the proliferation of international tourism. We also describe a key new trend in economic development: the increasing importance of places as part of consumers' experience.

Global Assembly Lines and Supply Chains

The globalization of the world economy represents the most recent stage in a long process of internationalization. At the heart of this process are private companies that participate not only in international trade but also in production, manufacturing, and/or sales operations in several countries. Almost 80 percent of Ford's workforce, for example, are employed outside of the U.S., and foreign sales account for 55 percent of its total revenues. Over 50 percent of IBM's workforce are employed overseas, and 61 percent of its revenues are derived from foreign sales; 82 percent of the workforce of Philips, the Dutch electronics firm, are employed overseas, and 95 percent of its revenues are derived from foreign sales. Many of these transnational corporations have grown large through mergers and acquisitions, and their activities span a diverse range of economic activities.

Corporations like these, which consist of several divisions engaged in quite different activities, are known as **conglomerate corporations**. Altria (formerly known as Philip Morris), for example, primarily known for its tobacco products (such as Marlboro cigarettes), also controls a large group of assets in the beverage industry (including Miller Brewing and several wine labels) and has extensive interests in real estate, import–export, publishing, and foods (including General Foods, Tobler, Terry's, and Suchard chocolate). Nestlé, the world's largest packaged-food manufacturer, is the largest company in Switzerland but derives less than 2 percent of its revenue from its home country. Its major North American product lines and brand names include beverages (Nescafé, Nestea,

FIGURE 7.26 Financial meltdown A trader in the Dow Jones Industrial Average stock index futures pit at the Chicago Board of Trade reacts to trading as a monitor above the trading floor broadcasts U.S. President George W. Bush addressing the nation about the financial crisis on October 10, 2008, in Chicago, Illinois.
(*Source:* Scott Olson/Staff/Getty Images)

Perrier, Pure Life), chocolate and candy (Butterfinger, Crunch, KitKat), culinary products (Carnation, Libby, Maggi), frozen foods (Delissio, Lean Cuisine), baby foods (Gerber), pet foods (Purina, Fancy Feast, Friskies), and drugs and cosmetics (L'Oreal, Garnier, Vichy, The Body Shop, Diesel perfume). In addition to its 480 factories in 63 countries around the world, Nestlé operates more than 40 Stouffer hotels.

Transnationals and Globalization

Transnational corporations first began to appear in the nineteenth century, but until the mid-twentieth century there were only a few. Most of these were U.S.- or European-based transnationals concerned with obtaining raw materials, such as oil or minerals, for their domestic manufacturing operations. The majority of Canada's current transnational corporations grew up as domestic mining companies that developed operations in other countries to increase market share of world trade in their particular commodity. Examples include Teck Resources (zinc), Rio Tinto Alcan (aluminum), and Barrick Gold—all among the world's largest companies in their sector. Canadian transnationals in other sectors include Magna International (auto parts) and Bombardier (trains and planes).

After World War II, an increasing number of large corporations began to invest in overseas production and manufacturing operations as a means of establishing a foothold in foreign consumer markets. Beginning in the 1970s, the growth of transnational conglomerates increased sharply, not only in the United States but also in Europe, Japan, and even some semiperipheral countries. By 2009, there were about 80 000 transnational corporations in the world. Of these, the top 300 controlled approximately one-quarter of the world's productive assets. Many of the largest transnational corporations are now more powerful, in economic terms, than most sovereign nations. General Motors' economy is larger than Portugal's; Toyota's is larger than Ireland's; and Walmart's annual sales exceed Norway's gross domestic product.

The reason for such growth in the number and scale of transnational conglomerate corporations is that international economic conditions have changed. A recession, triggered by a massive increase in the price of crude oil in 1973, meant that companies everywhere had to re-examine their strategies. At around the same time, technological developments in transport and communications provided larger companies with the flexibility and global reach to exploit the steep differentials in labour costs that exist between core countries and peripheral countries. Meanwhile, these same developments in transport and communications made for intensified international competition, which forced firms to search more intensely for more efficient and profitable global production and marketing strategies. Concurrently, a homogenization of consumer tastes (also facilitated by new developments in communications technologies) has made it possible for companies to more readily cater to global markets.

In effect, the playing field for large-scale businesses of all kinds had been marked out anew. Companies have had to reorganize their operations in a variety of ways, restructuring their activities and redeploying their resources *among different countries, regions, and places* in a global assembly line. Local patterns of economic development have been recast again and again as these processes of restructuring, reorganization, and redeployment have played out.

Manufacturers draw several advantages from a global assembly line. First, a standardized global product for a global market allows them to maximize economies of scale. Second, a global assembly line allows production and assembly to take greater advantage of the full range of geographical variations in costs. As noted earlier, basic wages in manufacturing industries, for example, are between 25 and 75 times higher in core countries than in some peripheral countries. Third, a global assembly line means that a company is no longer dependent on a single source of supply for a specific component, thus reducing its vulnerability to labour disputes and other disturbances. Fourth, global sourcing allows transnational conglomerates better access to local markets. For example, Boeing has pursued a strategy of buying a significant number of aircraft components in China, thus opening the Chinese market to its products. Similarly, Volkswagen has become the dominant foreign car maker in the Chinese market partly because it was one of the first to establish production facilities there.

The automobile industry was among the first to develop a global assembly line. In 1976, Ford introduced the Fiesta, the first "world car" designed to sell in Europe, South America, and Asia as well as North America. The Fiesta was assembled in several locations from components manufactured in an even greater number of locations. Today, the components of the successor models Focus and Escort are made and assembled in 15 countries across three continents. Ford's international subsidiaries, which used to operate independently of the parent company, are now functionally integrated, using supercomputers and video teleconferencing.

The other automobile companies followed suit and organized their own global assembly systems (**Figure 7.27**). The global production networks of these companies allow them to process raw materials near sources of supply, to undertake labour-intensive work where labour is cheap, and to complete final assembly close to major markets. They employ modular manufacturing for their world cars based on a common underbody platform, yet have the flexibility to adapt the interior, trim, body, and ride characteristics to preferences in different countries. Honda, for example, has produced three distinct versions of the Accord based on its world car platform—the bigger, family-oriented Accord for North American drivers; the smaller, sportier Accord aimed at young Japanese professionals; and the shorter and narrower Accord, offering the stiff and sporty ride preferred by European drivers.

More than two-thirds of the 60 to 70 million motor vehicles that roll off the production lines each year are made by just 10 transnationals. In order of size, they are Toyota, General Motors, Volkswagen, Ford, Honda, PSA Peugeot Citroën, Nissan, Renault, and Hyundai. A completely different picture emerges, however, if we ask *where* those cars are produced: China produces nearly as many as the United States, Japan, and Germany taken together. The fact that no Chinese car maker appears among the top 10 indicates the degree to which the core-based transnationals control the international car market.

The global assembly line is constantly being reorganized as transnational corporations seek to take advantage of geographical differences between places and regions and as workers and consumers in specific places and regions react to the consequences of globalization. Nike, the athletic footwear and clothing marketer, provides a good illustration. Nike once relied on its own manufacturing facilities in the United States and the United Kingdom.

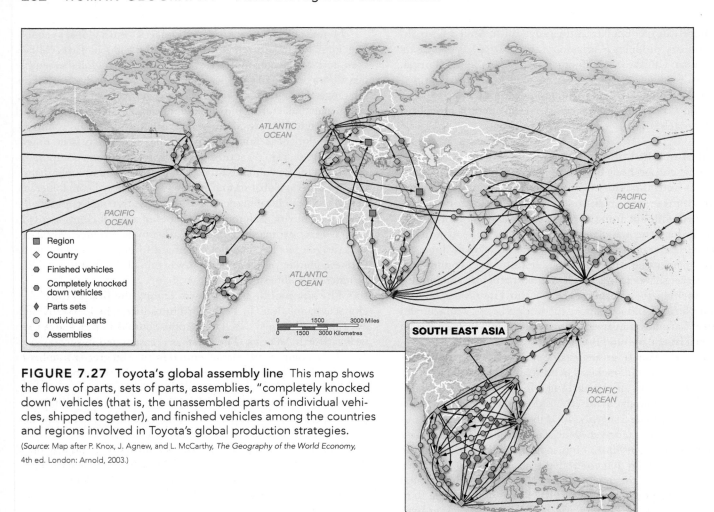

FIGURE 7.27 Toyota's global assembly line This map shows the flows of parts, sets of parts, assemblies, "completely knocked down" vehicles (that is, the unassembled parts of individual vehicles, shipped together), and finished vehicles among the countries and regions involved in Toyota's global production strategies.

(*Source*: Map after P. Knox, J. Agnew, and L. McCarthy, *The Geography of the World Economy*, 4th ed. London: Arnold, 2003.)

Today, however, most of its production is subcontracted to suppliers in East, South, and Southeast Asia. The geography of this subcontracting evolved over time in response to the changing pattern of labour costs in Asia. The first Asian production of Nike shoes took place in Japan. The company then switched most of its subcontracting to South Korea and Taiwan. As labour costs rose there, Nike's subcontracting spread across more and more peripheral countries in search of low labour costs. By 2006, Nike subcontractors employed more than 800 000 people in more than 680 factories. Nike was the largest foreign employer in Vietnam, where its factories accounted for 5 percent of Vietnam's total exports. China, Indonesia, and Thailand were also major components in Nike's expanded global assembly line because of their low wage costs—around US$60 per month.

Flexible Production Systems

The strategies of transnational corporations are an important element in the transition from Fordism to Neo-Fordism in much of the world. **Fordism** is named after Henry Ford, the automobile manufacturer who pioneered the principles involved: mass production, based on assembly-line techniques and "scientific" management, together with mass consumption, based on higher wages and sophisticated advertising techniques. In **neo-Fordism** the logic of mass production coupled with mass consumption has been modified by the addition of more flexible production, distribution, and

marketing systems. This flexibility is rooted in forms of production that enable manufacturers to shift quickly and efficiently from one level of output to another and, more importantly, from one product configuration to another.

Flexible production systems involve flexibility both within firms and between them. *Within* firms, new technologies now allow a great deal of flexibility. Computerized machine tools, for example, are capable of producing a variety of new products simply by being reprogrammed, often with very little downtime between production runs for different products. Different stages of the production process (sometimes located in different places) are integrated and coordinated through computer-aided design (CAD) and computer-aided manufacturing (CAM) systems. Computer-based information systems monitor retail sales and track wholesale orders, allowing producers to reduce the costs of raw materials stockpiles, parts inventories, and warehousing through sophisticated small-batch, just-in-time production and distribution systems. **Just-in-time production** employs vertical disintegration (see next page) within large, formerly functionally integrated firms, such as automobile manufacturers, in which daily and even hourly deliveries of parts and other supplies from smaller (often nonunion) subcontractors and suppliers now arrive "just in time" to maintain "last-minute" and "zero" inventories. The combination of computer-based information systems, CAD/CAM systems, and computerized machine tools has also given firms the flexibility to exploit specialized niches of consumer demand so that economies of scale in production can be applied to upscale but geographically scattered markets.

The Benetton clothing company provides an excellent case study of the exploitation of flexible production systems within a single firm. In 1965, the Benetton company began with a single factory near Venice. In 1968, it acquired a single retail store in the Alpine town of Belluno, marking the beginning of a remarkable sequence of corporate expansion. Benetton is now a global organization with over 5000 retail outlets in more than 120 countries and with its own investment bank and financial services organizations. It achieved this growth by exploiting computers, new communications and transportation systems, flexible outsourcing strategies, and new production-process technologies (such as robotics and CAD/CAM systems) to the fullest possible extent.

From the Benetton headquarters in Treviso, Benetton managers coordinate the activities of more than 250 outside suppliers in order to stock its worldwide network of retail outlet franchises (**Figure 7.28**). In Treviso, the firm's designers create new shirts and sweaters on CAD terminals, but their designs are produced only once orders have been received, allowing for the coordination of production with the purchase of raw materials. In factories, rollers linked to a central computer spread and cut layers of cloth in small batches according to the numbers and colours ordered by Benetton stores around the world. Sweaters, gloves, and scarves, knitted in volume in white yarn, are dyed in small batches by machines similarly programmed to respond to sales orders. Completed garments are warehoused briefly (by robots) and shipped out directly (via private package delivery firms) to individual stores to arrive on their shelves within 10 days of ordering.

Sensitivity to demand, however, is the foundation of Benetton's success. Niche marketing and product differentiation are central to this sensitivity, which requires a high degree of flexibility in exploiting new product lines. Key stores patronized by trendsetting consumers are monitored closely, and many Benetton stores' cash registers operate as point-of-sale terminals so that marketing data are available to company headquarters daily. Another notable feature of the company's operations is the way that different market niches are exploited with the same basic products. In Italy, Benetton products are sold through several retail chains, each with an image and decor calculated to bring in a different sort of customer.

Between firms, the flexibility inherent in neo-Fordism is achieved through the externalization of certain functions. One way of doing this is to reorganize administrative, managerial, and technical functions into flatter, leaner, and more flexible forms of organization that can make increased use of outside consultants, specialists, and subcontractors. This has led to a degree of vertical disintegration among firms. **Vertical disintegration** involves the evolution from large, functionally integrated firms within a given industry toward networks of specialized firms, subcontractors, and suppliers. In other words, many components and services are no longer produced "in-house," but are outsourced. Another route to externalization is participation in joint ventures, in the licensing or contracting of technology, and in strategic alliances involving design partnerships, collaborative R&D projects, and the like. **Strategic alliances** are commercial agreements between transnational corporations, usually involving shared technologies, marketing networks, market research, or product development. They are an important contributor to the intensification of economic globalization (**Figure 7.29**).

FIGURE 7.28 Headquarters of the Benetton Group, Villa Minelli, Treviso, Italy Only about 400 of Benetton's more than 9500 employees are located in the company's home base of Treviso, Italy. (*Source:* Courtesy of Benetton USA, Corp.)

FIGURE 7.29 Disneyland, Paris The Nestlé food company has a number of strategic alliances, including an alliance since 1990 with the Walt Disney Company in Europe, the United States, Latin America, and other markets that includes making Nestlé the main food company for Disneyland Paris. (*Source:* Yaghobzadeh Rafael/SIPA/Newscom)

Maquiladoras

The governments of many peripheral and semiperipheral countries encourage the type of subcontracting carried out by big transnational corporations. These governments see participation in global assembly lines as a pathway to export-led industrialization. They offer incentives such as tax "holidays" (not having to pay taxes for a specified period) to transnational corporations. In the 1960s, Mexico enacted legislation permitting foreign companies to establish "sister factories"—*maquiladoras*—within 20 kilometres of the border with the United States for the duty-free assembly of products destined for re-export (see **Figures 7.30** and **7.31**). By 2005, more than 3500 such manufacturing and assembly plants had been established, employing about a million Mexican workers, most of them women, and accounting for more than 30 percent of Mexico's exports. But since 2000, over 500 *maquiladoras* have closed, resulting in the loss of tens of thousands of jobs. The tax breaks that had favoured the establishment of the *maquiladoras* are due to expire under the terms of the North American Free Trade Agreement (NAFTA), while lower wage rates and better incentives in other countries—particularly China—have recently proved more attractive to manufacturers.

Export-Processing Zones (EPZs)

Export-processing zones (EPZs) are small areas where governments create especially favourable investment and trading conditions to attract export-oriented industries. These conditions include minimum levels of bureaucracy, the absence of foreign exchange controls, factory space and warehousing at subsidized rents, low tax rates, and exemption from tariffs and export duties. In 1985, the International Labour Organization (ILO) estimated there were 173 EPZs around the world, which together employed 1.8 million workers. The latest ILO estimate of 2007 puts the number of EPZs at 3500, which employed 66 million people. China alone had 164 EPZs with 40 million workers. The ILO has criticized these "vehicles of globalization" because very few of them have any meaningful links with the domestic economies around them, and most trap large numbers of people in low-wage, low-skill jobs.

FIGURE 7.30 Principal *maquiladora* centres on the United States–Mexico border Cheap labour and tax breaks for firms manufacturing and assembling goods for re-export have made many Mexican border towns attractive to U.S. companies. Around half a million workers are employed in these *maquiladora* plants, producing electronic products, textiles, furniture, leather goods, toys, and automotive parts. (*Source:* Adapted from P. Dicken, *Global Shift*, 4th ed. New York: Guilford, 2003; updated per Instituto Nacional de Estadista y Geographia [INEGI], 2011 data, http://dgcnesyp.inegi.org.mx/cgi-win/bdieintsi. exe/NIVR250110009001000370#ARBOL.)

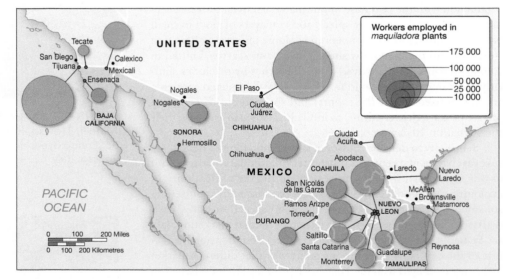

FIGURE 7.31 "Offshore" manufacturing The production floor at the Flextronics *maquiladora* in Guadalajara, Mexico.
(*Source:* Keith Dannemiller/Alamy)

In addition to tax incentives and EPZs, many governments also establish policies that ensure cheap and controllable labour. Sometimes countries are pressured to participate in global assembly lines by core countries and by the transnational institutions they support. The United States and the World Bank, for example, have backed regimes that support globalized production and have pushed for austerity programs that help keep labour cheap in peripheral countries. Countries pursuing export-led industrialization as an economic development strategy do not plan to remain the providers of cheap labour for foreign-based transnational corporations, however. They hope to shift from labour-intensive manufactures to capital-intensive, high-technology goods, following the path of semiperipheral Asian countries like Singapore and South Korea.

Retailing Chains and Global Sourcing

At the other end of the commodity chain from the farms, mines, *maquiladoras,* and factories of the world are the retail outlets and restaurants where the products are sold and consumed. Traditionally, retailing and food services in developed countries have been dominated by small, specialized, independent stores and local cafés, restaurants, pubs, and bars. But the logic of economic rationalization and economies of scale has displaced the traditional pattern of downtown department stores, main street shops, corner stores, and local bars with big-box superstores and national and international chains of retail outlets and restaurants. Town centres once filled with a thriving mix of independent and family-owned stores now have "cloned" settings consisting of standardized supermarket retailers, fast-food chains, coffee bars, cell phone shops, and fashion outlets of global conglomerates. With their cost advantages, these chains have become the economic equivalent of invasive species: voracious, indiscriminate, and often antisocial. Their big, centralized logistical operations have not only put small independent stores out of business but are driving the homogenization of consumption. The retail sector of most towns and cities is now characterized by external control. Decisions about hiring, labour policies, wages, stock, and menus are made in corporate headquarters hundreds or thousands of kilometres away.

Fast-food restaurants have become icons of this trend. McDonald's alone has some 31 000 restaurants worldwide and opens new ones at the rate of almost 2000 each year. It is the largest purchaser of beef, pork, and potatoes and the largest owner of retail property in the world. In Canada, 20 percent of meals are eaten outside of the home, most of them at fast-food restaurants. In the United States, that number is as high as 40 percent, with one in 3.5 adults visiting a fast-food restaurant every day. Not surprisingly, the majority of the North American population is overweight and the frequency of health problems associated with obesity—such as early-onset diabetes and high cholesterol—is rising rapidly. The cost of these problems to personal well-being and to health care systems is already daunting. Meanwhile, fast food's low-paying service sector has become an increasingly significant component of the economy.

Equally significant in terms of local economies, local development patterns, and global supply chains has been the success of "big-box" retail outlets such as Best Buy, Staples, Home Depot, Target, and Walmart. To many observers, Walmart has come to symbolize the worst characteristics of globalization, including corporate greed, low wages, the decline of small-town mom-and-pop stores, and the proliferation of sweatshops in less-developed countries. (See Box 7.3, "Geography Matters: Walmart's Economic Landscape.")

Supermarket chains have also become particularly influential. In the United Kingdom, for example, the top four supermarket chains—Tesco, Asda (owned by Walmart), Sainsbury, and Safeway—have come to dominate the retail food market through a combination of out-of-town superstores and convenience supermarkets along main streets. As a consequence, they have killed off small general stores in the United Kingdom at the rate of one a day and specialist shops—such as butchers, bakers, and fishmongers—at the rate of 50 per week.

The centralized supply chains of supermarket chains have not only killed off small local businesses but also affected local farmers. Supermarket chains rely on big suppliers in agribusiness. These suppliers are typically highly subsidized national and transnational firms whose global reach depends heavily on monoculture and extensive husbandry that, in turn, require the extensive use of antibiotics in animals and pesticides, fertilizer, and genetic engineering. As a result, small farmers and fishermen have been squeezed from the market. And with them many traditional local foods have disappeared or are in danger of disappearing. Meanwhile, supermarket shelves are lined with highly processed foods, out-of-season fruit and vegetables, and produce that has travelled a long way and, often, been stored for a while. When the average North American or European family sits down to eat, most of the ingredients have typically travelled at least 2000 kilometres from farm, processing, packing, distribution, to consumption.

> **APPLY YOUR KNOWLEDGE**   Consider three of the eateries you dine at most often in your community. Are they are locally owned or chains owned by large corporations? If they are chain outlets, research whether they belong to an even larger conglomerate. For you as a consumer, what are the pros and cons of local ownership? ∎

New Geographies of Office Employment

The globalization of production and the growth of transnational corporations have brought about another important change in patterns of local economic development. Banking, finance, and producer services are no longer locally oriented ancillary activities but important global industries in their own right. They have developed some specific spatial tendencies of their own—tendencies that have become important shapers of local economic development processes.

One of the most striking trends has been the geographic decentralization of office employment. This mainly involves "back-office" functions that have been relocated from metropolitan and business-district locations to small-town and suburban locations. Back-office functions such as record-keeping and analytical functions do not require frequent personal contact with clients or business associates. Developments in computing technologies, database access, electronic data interchanges, and telephone call routing technologies are enabling a larger share of back-office work to be relocated to specialized office space in cheaper settings, freeing space in the high-rent locations. For example, many postal services use optical character recognition software (OCR) to decipher addresses on letters, which are then bar-coded and automatically sorted to the

Walmart's Economic Landscape

Walmart (Wal-Mart until 2008) is the largest company in the world in terms of revenue, with sales exceeding US$250 billion in 2010. It is also the most highly rationalized, centralized retail chain in the world, designed to run like an assembly line. To some, Walmart represents what happens when the principles of economic geography are implemented in an effort to provide high-quality products at low cost in a global market economy. To others, Walmart illustrates the negative consequences of globalization and corporate power that are consequences of recent trends in the economic geography of the world.

Walmart was founded on a distinctive—and unusual—geographic marketing strategy, which was born in a network of stores in small, isolated towns in the American South. From the firm's headquarters in Bentonville, Arkansas, Walmart's founder, Sam Walton, built a retail empire that reflects the values embedded in the small-town rural South: conservatism, idealized views of family and community, and the principles of hard work, frugality, and competitiveness. The company has moved out of the small-town South and into metropolitan markets and international ventures, but it is still characterized by store locations on the outskirts (**Figure 7.E**), partly due to land costs and tax benefits and partly because of the NIMBYism (NIMBY stands for "not in my backyard") of established neighbourhoods.

From the start, Walmart's emphasis was on a business model that rests on high-volume turnover through low prices. This required a rapid expansion of stores in order to strengthen the firm's position with suppliers. This, in turn, meant that Walmart quickly developed expertise in **logistics**—the movement and storage of goods and the management of the entire supply chain, from purchase of raw materials through sale of the final product. Walmart put together its own distribution facilities, fleet of trucks, and satellite communications network to maximize the supplier discounts needed for this business model. Another key feature of Walmart's economic landscape is cost control: pressure is continuously exerted on local governments, employees, and suppliers to get the best deal possible for Walmart. Walmart's labour policies are virulently antiunion; the stores are deliberately understaffed; there is no grievance policy for employees; vendor agreements are tough; suppliers do not give up ownership of the goods until they are sold to the customer; and suppliers are required to drop prices by as much as 5 percent annually. Suppliers conform to this pressure because they depend on Walmart as their largest (or sole) customer.

The company's rapid expansion and tremendous profitability "allowed it a market power unequalled by any of its large corporate competitors, a power that is reshaping the nature of America's and the world's retail industry."[2] Walmart's low prices have reduced consumer inflation and brought many products within the reach of consumers previously unable to afford them. But there has been a great deal of concern over the impact of Walmart stores on smaller stores and towns as Walmart's predatory pricing has put numerous independent local stores out of business. The result is external control of the local economy. With fewer locally owned businesses, money spent on goods no longer stays within the community but instead is funnelled back to corporate headquarters. At the same time, Walmart wages tend to be significantly lower—in the region of 30 percent lower—than in independent, locally owned businesses, so that wages in local labour markets tend to be depressed.

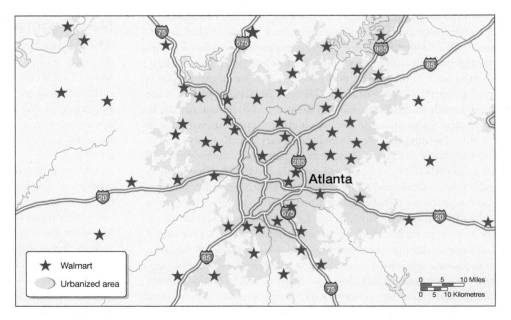

FIGURE 7.E Walmart locations in the Atlanta metropolitan region Note how they are overwhelmingly located in the suburbs beyond the ring road. Since U.S. low-income households are typically concentrated in the inner cities, they are not being served by Walmart's discount stores.

(*Source:* Adapted from Figure 2.6 in S. D. Brunn [ed.], *Wal-Mart World.* New York: Routledge, 2006, p. 23.)

[2]E. Rosen, "Wal-Mart: The New Retail Colossus." In S. Brunn (ed.), *Wal-Mart World*. New York: Routledge, 2006, p. 92.

FIGURE 7.F Walmart superstore (*Source:* Paul L. Knox)

Other concerns include the aesthetic and environmental impact of the big cinderblock boxes and their enormous adjoining parking lots (**Figure 7.F**). Also, although large retailers such as Walmart carry an extensive array of goods, they often stock only a limited variety of any specific product, thereby leaving the consumer with less choice overall. For example, whereas independent book and magazine retailers typically carry a broad range of titles, big-box chain stores typically concentrate on only the titles with the biggest turnover, in order to maximize profit. The same is true of CDs and DVDs. So, not only do corporate chains reduce the range of shops available in small towns, they also reduce the choice of goods readily available.

This lack of choice is compounded, in Walmart's case, by the company's censorship, "protecting" consumers from products that the management deems offensive. This includes refusing to sell CDs with parental warning stickers and obscuring the covers of popular magazines like *Redbook, Marie Claire, Cosmopolitan*, and *Rolling Stone*. Because of the enormous size of the Walmart network, some magazines willingly send advance copies to corporate headquarters in Bentonville for approval before publication and will even alter cover artwork to avoid losing sales. "Thus, far from being simply a store, Walmart is also a moral universe external to the community."[3] Walmart advertising campaigns have always emphasized happy staff, customers from cozy families, and support for local communities. Patriotism has been a strong theme.

However, the firm's Buy-American campaign rollout coincided with Walmart becoming China's sixth-largest trading partner. There are no references to Fair Trade, fair employment, ethical trading, or environmental consciousness.

The most recent development in Walmart's economic landscape has been internationalization. The company entered markets in Mexico, Puerto Rico, and Canada in the early 1990s, later expanding into Argentina, Brazil, China, El Salvador, Germany, Guatemala, Honduras, Indonesia, Japan, Nicaragua, and South Korea. Walmart's greatest global impact, though, is through its supply chains. Overall, 50 to 60 percent of the goods Walmart imports into the United States each year by ship come from China, and the home office of Walmart Global Procurement is in Shenzhen, China. The company has a network of over two dozen field offices in other countries and oversees the sourcing of products from more than 5000 factories in 65 countries, including Bangladesh, Brazil, Guatemala, India, Indonesia, Malaysia, the Philippines, Sri Lanka, and Thailand. The reason, of course, is labour costs. But the "natural" cheapness of labour in these countries is not enough for Walmart; the company systematically imposes pressure on suppliers to reduce costs still further. This has led to abuse and violations of labour laws.

China Labor Watch, for example, found that four apparel factories in China that supplied Adidas and Walmart were paying workers just 48 cents an hour—which was not enough to sustain employees unless they worked overtime. A 2007 report by the National Labor Committee, "A Wal-Mart Christmas,"[4] featured Guangzhou Huanya Gift Ltd. Company of Guangdong Province, China, where the 8000 workers must put in 10- to 15-hour shifts, seven days a week during the long, eight-month busy season manufacturing Christmas ornaments for Walmart. At least half the workers, some 4000 people, were working 95 hours, including 55 hours of (mandatory) overtime. The legal minimum wage in Guangzhou is 55 cents an hour, but workers were paid by a piece rate, with some workers earning just 26 cents an hour, half the legal minimum wage.

[3]B. Warf and T. Chapman, "Cathedrals of Consumption: A Political Phenomenology of Wal-Mart." In S. Brunn (ed.), *Wal-Mart World*. New York: Routledge, 2006, p. 165.

[4]National Labor Commmittee, 2007, "A Wal-Mart Christmas. Brought to You by a Sweatshop in China," http://www.nlcnet.org/article.php?id=498.

appropriate substation. Addresses that the OCR cannot read are digitally photographed and the image is transmitted to a computer screen in a back-office facility in a cheap rural location. There a worker deciphers the address and manually types it into a terminal for transmission back to the sorting facility.

Internationally, this trend has taken the form of offshore back offices. By decentralizing back-office functions to offshore locations, companies save even more in labour costs. For example, Australian mortgage applications can be processed in Bangalore, India, at a fraction of the cost by using cheaper labour and paperless processes.

The logical next step is outsourcing. The outsourcing of services is one of the most dynamic sectors of the world economy. Global outsourcing expenditures are expected to grow significantly as small and medium-sized enterprises follow the example of large transnational companies in taking advantage of low wages in semiperipheral and peripheral countries. Typically, international outsourcing in service industries involves the work of "routine producers" (who process data by following instructions, perform repetitive tasks, and respond to explicit procedures) rather than "symbolic analysts" (who work with abstract images, are involved with problem-identifying and problem-solving, and make decisions based on critical judgment sharpened by experience). Outsourced services range from simple business-process activities (for example, data entry, word processing, transcription) to more sophisticated, high-value-added activities (for example, architectural drawing, product support, financial analysis, software programming, and human resource services).

India has become one of the most successful exporters of outsourced service activities, ranging from call centres and business-process activities to advanced IT (information technology) services (**Figure 7.32**). More than 150 of the *Fortune* 500 companies, for example, now outsource software development to India. In the Philippines, special electronic "enterprise zones" have been set up with competitive international telephone rates for companies specializing in telemarketing and electronic commerce. Mexico, South Africa, and Malaysia have also become important locations for call centres and business-process activities.

FIGURE 7.32 Outsourcing: globalized office work Workers at a call centre in New Delhi, India, where business is outsourced from western companies. (*Source:* Fredrik Renander/Alamy)

Clusters of Specialized Offices

Decentralization is outweighed, however, by the tendency for a disproportionate share of the new jobs created in banking, finance, and business services to cluster in highly specialized financial districts within major metropolitan areas. The reasons for this localization are to be found in another special case of the geographical agglomeration effects that we discussed earlier in this chapter.

Metropolitan areas such as New York City, London, Paris, Tokyo, and Frankfurt have acquired the kind of infrastructure—specialized office space, financial exchanges, teleports (office parks equipped with satellite Earth stations and linked to local fibre-optic lines), and communications networks—that is essential for delivering services to clients with a national or international scope of activity (**Figure 7.33**). These metropolitan areas have also established a comparative advantage both in the mix of specialized firms and expert professionals on hand and in the high-order cultural amenities (available both to high-paid workers and to their out-of-town business visitors). Above all, these metro areas have established themselves as centres of authority, with a critical mass of people in the know about market conditions, trends, and innovations. These people gain one another's trust through frequent face-to-face contact, not just in business settings but also in the informal settings of clubs and office bars. These key cities have become **world cities**—places that, in the globalized world economy, are able not only to generate powerful spirals of local economic development but also to act as pivotal points in the reorganization of global space. They are control centres for the flows of information, cultural products, and finance that collectively sustain the economic and cultural globalization of the world. (See Chapter 10 for more details.)

Offshore Financial Centres

The combination of metropolitan concentration and back-office decentralization fulfills most of the locational needs of the global

FIGURE 7.33 Headquarters office space Office workers outside Lloyds of London, part of a specialized office district that accounts for a quarter of the world market for marine insurance and over a third of the market in aviation risks. (*Source:* Paul L. Knox)

financial network. There are, however, some needs—secrecy and shelter from taxation and regulation, in particular—that call for a different strategy. The result has been the emergence of a series of **offshore financial centres**: islands and microstates such as the Bahamas, Bahrain, the Cayman Islands, the Cook Islands, Luxembourg, Liechtenstein, and Vanuatu that are specialized nodes in the geography of worldwide financial flows.

The chief attraction of offshore financial centres is simply that they provide low-tax or no-tax settings for savings. They are havens for undeclared income and for hot money. They also provide discreet markets in which to deal currencies, bonds, loans, and other financial instruments without attracting the attention of regulating authorities or competitors. The U.S. Internal Revenue Service estimates that about US\$400 billion ends up in offshore financial centres each year as a result of tax-evasion schemes. Overall, about 60 percent of all the world's money now resides offshore.

The Pleasure Periphery: Tourism and Economic Development

Many areas of the world, including parts of the world's core regions, do not have much of a primary base (that is, in agriculture, fishing, or mineral extraction), are not currently an important part of the global assembly line, and are not closely tied into the global financial network. For these areas, tourism can offer the otherwise unlikely prospect of economic development. Geographers (with their interests in the movements of peoples, world regions, and the meaning of "place") have become important contributors to the interdisciplinary study of tourism and leisure and their contribution to economic development.

The globalization of the world economy has been paralleled by a globalization of the tourist industry. Tourism is now the world's largest nonagricultural employer, with 1 in every 12 workers worldwide involved in transporting, feeding, housing, guiding, or amusing tourists. Every year, international tourists take about a billion trips and spend about US\$ 1 trillion. The majority of these trips were taken by tourists from the more affluent countries of the world. Spending by German, U.S., U.K., and Chinese tourists alone accounted for more than 25 percent of total international tourist dollars in 2008. Tourists from France, Italy, Japan, and Canada accounted for another 12 percent. On a per capita basis, Canadians now rank third in the world when it comes to spending on international tourism.

What is most striking, though, is not so much the growth in the number of international tourists as the increased range of international tourism. Thanks largely to cheaper long-distance flights, a significant proportion of tourism is now transcontinental and transoceanic. While Europe (58 percent) and the Americas (18 percent) continue to be the main tourist destinations, visits to countries in Africa, Asia, and the Pacific have grown to account for almost one-quarter of the industry. This has made tourism a central component of economic development in countries with sufficiently exotic wildlife (Kenya), scenery (Nepal, Vietnam), beaches (the Seychelle Islands), shopping (Singapore, Dubai, and Hong Kong), culture (China, India, Japan, and Indonesia), or sex (Thailand).

In addition, "alternative" tourism has been widely advanced as a more sustainable strategy for economic development in peripheral regions (**Figure 7.34**). Alternative tourism emphasizes self-determination, authenticity, preservation of the existing environment, small-scale development, and greater use of local techniques, materials, and architectural styles. Alternative tourism includes ecotourism (bird-watching in Costa Rica, participating in a program to protect endangered sea turtles in Bali), cultural tourism (visiting Machu Picchu, the lost city of the Incas), industrial tourism (touring the Potteries district of northern England by canal boat), and indigenous tourism ("walking with spirits" in Australia). Such developments must be aimed, however, at tourists who are both wealthy and environmentally conscious. This is not, perhaps, a large enough market on which to pin hopes of significant increases in levels of economic development.

Tourism is by no means confined to the less developed ("unspoiled") peripheral regions. Canada is a safe and convenient destination for many American tourists. Conversely, Canadian tourists often spend their dollars domestically or in the U.S.—in national parks, specialized resorts, theme parks, casinos, and big cities. The growth of tourism and the economic success of renovated historic towns and districts in particular has meant that few localities exist in North America—or anywhere else in the developed world, for that matter—that do not encourage tourism as a central plank of

FIGURE 7.34 Ecotourism Birdwatchers in Darien National Park, Panama. (*Source:* Kevin Schafer/Alamy)

FIGURE 7.35 Quebec City One of Canada's leading heritage attractions, Quebec City is on UNESCO's list of world heritage sites. (*Source*: Photo by Stefan D. Bruda http://photography.bruda.ca)

consumption, depends very much on matters of style and fashion. Some places are sought out by tourists because of their remoteness and their "natural," undeveloped qualities, which are most vulnerable to shifts of style and fashion. Nepal and New Zealand are recent examples of this phenomenon: they are now too "obvious" as destinations and are consequently having to rebrand themselves. New Zealand is using its natural landscape to offer "thrill tourists" unique experiences such as "dam dropping" and "bungee dipping" (**Figure 7.36**). On the other hand, Bhutan, Bolivia, Estonia, Patagonia, and Vietnam have been discovered as new pristine destinations and are coping with their first significant growth in tourism. China, meanwhile, is rapidly growing into one of the most popular destinations.

Although tourism is a multibillion-dollar industry, the financial returns for tourist areas are often not as high as might be expected. The greater part of the price of a package vacation, for example, stays with the organizing company and the airline. Typically, only 40 percent is captured by the tourist region itself. If the package involves a foreign-owned hotel, this number may fall below 25 percent.

The costs and benefits of tourism are not only economic, of course. On the positive side, tourism can help sustain indigenous lifestyles, regional cultures, arts, and crafts, and it can provide incentives for wildlife preservation, environmental protection, and the conservation of historic buildings and sites. On the negative side, tourism can adulterate and debase indigenous cultures and bring unsightly development, pollution, and environmental degradation. In the Caribbean, for instance, raw sewage, garbage, and engine oil from cruise ships are damaging fragile marine ecosystems such as coral reefs and mangrove swamps. In the United States, many of the popular national parks are being choked by visitors: congestion in Yosemite National Park (with over

their economic development strategy (**Figure 7.35**). It has been estimated that because tourism requires only a basic infrastructure, no heavy plant, and little high-tech equipment, the cost of creating one new job in tourism is less than one-fifth the cost of creating a manufacturing job and less than one-fiftieth the cost of creating a high-tech engineering job.

Tourism can provide a basis for economic development, but it is often a mixed blessing. It certainly creates jobs, but they are often seasonal. Dependence on tourism also makes for a high degree of economic vulnerability. Tourism, like other high-end aspects of

FIGURE 7.36 "Bungee dipping" into a whitewater river in New Zealand As New Zealand experiences increasing competition from other "pristine" destinations, it is rebranding itself as "the home of outdoor adventure." (*Source*: M. Imort)

FIGURE 7.37 Yosemite Summer traffic jam on the road to Yosemite National Park. (*Source:* Curtis Martin/Getty)

4 million visitors per year) has become so acute that Park Service rangers frequently have to turn away as many as 1000 vehicles per day, and park administrators are considering the establishment of a strict advance reservation system (**Figure 7.37**). In the European Alps, where an incredible 40 000 ski runs attract a winter tourist population ten times greater than the resident population, forests have been ripped up, pastures obliterated, rivers diverted, and scenic valleys and mountainsides covered with chalets, cabins, and hotels (**Figure 7.38**).

Tourism can also involve exploitative relations that debase traditional lifestyles and regional cultural heritages as they become packaged for outsider consumption. In the process, the behaviours and artifacts that are made available to an international market of outsiders can lose much of their original meaning. Traditional ceremonies that formerly had cultural significance for the performers are now enacted only to be watched and photographed. Artifacts like masks and weapons are manufactured not for their original use but as curios, souvenirs, and ornaments. In the process, indigenous cultures are edited, beautified, and altered to suit outsiders' tastes and expectations.

APPLY YOUR KNOWLEDGE Choose a popular tourist location and list four of the costs and benefits of tourism for this place and its inhabitants. ■

The Experience Economy and Place Marketing

Tourism is part of what some observers claim is the fourth in a sequence of phases of economic organization. Over the past 200 years, they argue, there has been a shift from an agrarian economy based

FIGURE 7.38 Tourism development in Grindelwald, Switzerland A town of 4000 residents, Grindelwald also accommodates 8000 chalet renters, 2500 hotel guests, and up to 5000 day trippers. (*Source:* M. Imort)

on extracting commodities to an industrial economy based on manufacturing goods, then to a service economy based on delivering services, and now to an experience economy based on staging experiences. As profitability becomes more challenging in agrarian, industrial, and service enterprises, so businesses must orchestrate memorable events for their customers, with memory itself becoming the "product"—the experience. It is not what is sold that characterizes the experience economy, but rather the way it is sold. Experience thus becomes a competitive advantage for products and services.

James Gilmore, one of the originators of the concept of the experience economy, notes that "Vans has launched a network of Skateparks, where customers pay a $40 annual membership fee, plus $4 to $11 per two-hour skateboarding session. Atlantis, a resort in the Bahamas, charges people who aren't guests just to tour the place! In New Zealand, the country that introduced bungee jumping to the world, people pay to go zorbing, an adventure that involves being strapped into a huge ball and then pushed down a hill."[5]

The experience economy is by no means new. Think, for example, of sports entertainment, arena rock concerts, fancy megamalls with themed entertainment, and visits to museums and galleries, as well as a great deal of traditional tourism. But businesses are increasingly combining commodities, products, and services with compelling experiences. Restaurants organize their services around particular themes (providing marketers with a new term: "eatertainment"). Shops and malls organize shows, events, or expositions ("shoppertainment"), while some manufacturers have established flagship stores that have a significant experiential component (Nike Town and SegaWorld). In addition, some businesses are based on selling new kinds of experiences. In 11 U.S. locations, American Girl Place offers a combination of attractions specifically targeted at young girls and their dolls: a doll hair salon, a doll bistro with "formal dining atmosphere," a doll hospital, doll care classes, and of course a doll shopping mall with personal shopping services. Their website advertises "Café. Theater. Shops. *Memories*."[6]

In the experience economy it is important to capitalize on places because, as we saw in Chapter 6, places have the capacity to arouse distinctive feelings and attachments. At the same time, thanks to economic and cultural globalization, places and regions throughout the world are increasingly seeking to influence the ways

in which they are perceived by tourists, businesses, media firms, and consumers. As a result, places are increasingly being reinterpreted, reimagined, designed, packaged, and marketed. Through place marketing, sense of place has become a valuable commodity and culture has become an important economic activity.

Seeking to be competitive within the globalizing economy, many places have sponsored extensive makeovers of themselves, including the creation of pedestrian plazas, cosmopolitan cultural facilities, festivals, and sports and media events—what geographer David Harvey has described as the "carnival masks" and "businessmen's utopias" of global capitalism. Not surprisingly, the question of who does the reimagining and cultural packaging can become an important issue for local politics.

Central to place marketing is the deliberate manipulation of culture in an effort to enhance the appeal of places to key groups. These groups include the upper-level management of large corporations, the higher-skilled and better-educated personnel sought by expanding high-technology industries, wealthy tourists, and the organizers of business and professional conferences and other income-generating events. In part, place marketing strategies depend on promoting traditions, lifestyles, and arts that are locally rooted; in part, they depend on being able to tap into globalizing culture through new cultural amenities and specially organized events and exhibitions. Some of the most widely adopted strategies include funding for experiential settings for the arts, investment in public spaces, the recreation and refurbishment of distinctive settings like waterfronts and historic districts, the expansion and improvement of museums (especially with blockbuster exhibitions of spectacular cultural products that attract large crowds and can be marketed with commercial tie-ins), and the designation and conservation of historic landmarks.

APPLY YOUR KNOWLEDGE Determine if the location you cited in the previous Apply Your Knowledge on p. 271 is part of the experience economy. List two ways that manipulation of material and visual culture is used to create or enhance a sense of place for this location. ∎

Future Geographies

As we have seen, technological breakthroughs and the availability of resources have had a profound influence on past patterns of development, and the same factors will certainly be a strong influence on future economic geographies. The expansion of the world economy and the globalization of industry will undoubtedly boost the overall demand for raw materials of various kinds, and this will spur the development of some previously underexploited but resource-rich regions in Africa, Eurasia, and East Asia.

Raw materials, however, will represent only a fraction of future resource needs. The main issue, by far, will be energy resources.

World energy consumption has been increasing steadily over the recent past, and as the periphery is industrialized and its population increases, the global demand for energy will expand rapidly. Basic industrial development tends to be highly energy-intensive. The International Energy Agency, assuming (fairly optimistically) that energy in peripheral countries will be generated in the future as efficiently as it is today in core countries, estimates that developing-country energy consumption will increase dramatically, lifting total world energy demand by almost 50 percent by 2020. Peripheral and semiperipheral countries will then account for more than half of world energy consumption. Much of this will be driven by industrialization geared to meet the growing worldwide market for consumer goods, such as private automobiles, air conditioners, refrigerators, televisions, and household appliances (**Figure 7.39**).

[5]James H. Gilmore, Frontiers of the Experience Economy, Batten Briefings, Autumn, 2003.
[6]www.americangirl.com/stores/brand_agplace.php

FIGURE 7.39 Energy-consuming goods An Apple Store in Beijing, China. (*Source: Lou-Foto/Alamy*)

been quadrupled by the OPEC cartel), the outcome could be a major revision of patterns of industrial location and metropolitan areas. Significantly higher energy costs may change the optimal location for many manufacturers, leading to deindustrialization in some regions and to new spirals of cumulative causation in others. Higher fuel costs will encourage some people to live nearer to their place of work; others will be able to take advantage of telecommuting to reduce personal transportation costs.

If fracking in North America and Europe is indeed blocked by public opposition, almost all of the increase in oil production over the next 15 or 20 years is likely to come from outside the core economies. This would make the world economy increasingly dependent on OPEC governments, which control over 70 percent of all proven oil reserves, most of them in the politically unstable Middle East. If fracking proceeds, however, the scenario would be different as the largest core consumer of energy, the United States, could (at least temporarily) achieve energy independence.

Given what we know about past processes of geographic change and principles of spatial organization, it is clear that changes in transportation technology are also of fundamental importance. Consider, for example, the impact of oceangoing steamers and railroads on the changing geographies of the nineteenth century and the impact of automobiles and trucks on the changing geographies of the twentieth century. Among the most important of the next generation of transportation technologies that will influence future geographies are high-speed rail systems, smart roads, and smart cars.

Without higher rates of investment in exploration and extraction than at present, production will be slow to meet the escalating demand. As we saw in Box 4.2, many experts believe that current levels of production in fact represent Peak Oil and that by 2020 global oil production may be only 90 percent of its current level. While fracking technology has the potential to increase the exploitable reserves, the rising public opposition to fracking may also negate that potential. The result might well be a significant increase in energy prices. This would have important geographical ramifications: companies would need to seriously reconsider their operations and force core-region households into a re-evaluation of their residential preferences and commuting behaviour, while peripheral-region households would be driven deeper into poverty. If the oil-price crisis of 1973 is anything to go by (after crude oil prices had

CONCLUSION

The growth of alternative tourism in Costa Rica, like the growth of the Cayman Islands as an offshore financial centre, the emergence of India as a centre for back-office activities, and the decline of the northeastern U.S. as a manufacturing region, shows that economic development is not simply a sequential process of modernization and increasing affluence. Economic development involves not only using the latest technology to generate higher incomes but also improving the quality of life through better housing, health care, and social welfare systems and enhancing the physical framework, or infrastructure, on which the economy rests.

Local, regional, and international patterns and processes of economic development are of particular importance to geographers. Levels of economic development and local processes of economic change affect many aspects of local well-being and so contribute to many aspects of human geography. Economic development is an important place-making process that underpins much of the diversity among regions and nations. At the same time, it is a reflection and a product of variations in natural resources, demographic characteristics, political systems, and social customs.

Economic development is an uneven geographic phenomenon. Regional patterns of economic development are tied to the geographic distribution of resources and to the legacy of the past specializations of places and regions. A general tendency exists toward the creation of regional cores with dependent peripheries. Nevertheless, such patterns are not fixed

or static. Changing economic conditions can lead to the modification or reversal of core–periphery patterns, as in the stagnation of once-booming regions like northern England and the spectacular growth of Guangdong Province in Southeast China. Over the long term, core–periphery patterns have most often been modified as a result of the changing locational needs and opportunities of successive technology systems. Today, economic globalization has exposed more places and regions than ever to the ups and downs of episodes of creative destruction—episodes played out ever faster, thanks to the way that technological innovations have shrunk time and space.

At the global scale, the unevenness of economic development takes the form of core–periphery contrasts. Most striking about these contrasts today are the dynamism and pace of change involved in economic development. The global assembly line, the global office, and global tourism are all making places much more interdependent and much faster changing. Parts of Brazil, China, India, Mexico, and South Korea, for example, have developed quickly from rural backwaters into significant industrial regions. Countries like Costa Rica and Belize, with few comparative advantages, suddenly find themselves able to earn significant amounts of foreign exchange through the development of ecotourism. This dynamism has, however, brought with it an expanding gap between rich and poor at every spatial scale: international, regional, and local.

- Scrutinize the nature and degree of unevenness in patterns of economic development at national and international scales.

  At the global scale, unevenness takes the form of core–periphery contrasts. Similar core–periphery contrasts exist at the regional scale. The core regions within the world-system—North America, Europe, and Japan—have the most diversified economies, the most advanced technologies, the highest levels of productivity, and the highest levels of prosperity. Other countries and regions—the periphery and semi-periphery of the world-system—are often referred to as *developing* or *less developed*. The average GNI per capita of the ten most prosperous countries in the world is 67 times greater than the average GNI per capita of the ten poorest countries. Overall, more than 80 percent of the world's population live in countries where income differentials are widening.

- Analyze how geographical divisions of labour have evolved with the growth of the world-system and the accompanying variations in economic structure.

  Geographical divisions of labour are national, regional, and locally based economic specializations in primary, secondary, tertiary, or quaternary activities. The relationship between changing regional economic specialization and changing levels of prosperity has prompted the interpretation of economic development in distinctive stages. In reality, however, various pathways exist to development, as well as various processes and outcomes of development. A new international division of labour was initiated in the 1970s as a result of a major wave of corporate globalization. This new international division of labour has resulted in three main changes: the decline of the United States as an industrial producer, the decentralization of manufacturing production from the world's core regions to some semiperipheral and peripheral countries, and the emergence of new specializations in high-tech manufacturing and producer services within the core regions of the world-system.

- Interpret how regional cores of economic development are created, following some initial advantage, through the operation of several basic principles of spatial organization.

  Any significant initial local economic advantage—existing labour markets, consumer markets, frameworks of fixed social capital, and so on—tends to be reinforced through a process of cumulative causation, a spiral buildup of advantages that occurs in specific geographic settings as a result of the development of external economies, agglomeration effects, and localization economies. The agglomeration effects that are associated with various kinds of economic linkages and interdependencies—the cost advantages that accrue to individual firms because of their location among functionally related activities—are particularly important in driving cumulative causation. Spirals of local growth tend to attract people and investment funds from other areas. According to the basic principles of spatial interaction, these flows tend to be strongest from nearby regions and those with the lowest wages, fewest job opportunities, or least attractive investment opportunities.

- Explain how spirals of economic development can be arrested in various ways, including the onset of disinvestment and deindustrialization.

  Core–periphery patterns and relationships can be modified by changes that can slow or modify the spiral of cumulative causation. The main factor is the development of agglomeration diseconomies, the negative economic effects of urbanization, and the local concentration of industry. Spirals of cumulative causation can also be undermined by changes in the relative costs of the factors of land, labour, or capital; by the obsolescence of infrastructure and technology; or by the process of import substitution, whereby goods and services previously imported from core regions come to be replaced by locally made goods and locally provided services. The capital made available from disinvestment in core regions becomes available for investment by entrepreneurs in new ventures based on innovative products and innovative production technologies. This process is often referred to as creative destruction.

- Demonstrate how globalization has resulted in patterns and processes of local and regional economic development that are open to external influences.

  The globalization of the world economy involves a new international division of labour in association with the internationalization of finance, the deployment of a new technology system, and the homogenization of consumer markets. This new framework for economic geography has meant that the lives of people in different parts of the world have become increasingly intertwined. Transnational corporations now control a large fraction of the world's productive assets, and the largest of them are more powerful, in economic terms, than most sovereign nations. As these corporations have restructured their activities and redeployed their resources among different countries, regions, and places, they have created many new linkages and interdependencies among places and regions around the world. Even small and medium-sized companies are involved in the myriad global assembly lines and supply chains that characterize the contemporary world economy, linking the fortunes of diverse and often distant local economies.

KEY TERMS

agglomeration diseconomy *(p. 254)*

agglomeration effect *(p. 252)*

ancillary industry *(p. 252)*

autarky *(p. 246)*

backwash effect *(p. 253)*

carrying capacity *(p. 239)*

conglomerate corporation *(p. 260)*

creative destruction *(p. 254)*

cumulative causation *(p. 253)*

deindustrialization *(p. 254)*

dependency *(p. 246)*

export-processing zone (EPZ) *(p. 264)*

external economy *(p. 252)*

flexible production system *(p. 262)*

Fordism *(p. 262)*

foreign direct investment (FDI) *(p. 241)*

geographical path dependence *(p. 251)*

gross domestic product (GDP) *(p. 234)*

gross national income (GNI) *(p. 234)*

growth pole *(p. 256)*

import substitution *(p. 247)*

infrastructure *(p. 253)*

initial advantage *(p. 251)*

international division of labour *(p. 241)*

just-in-time production *(p. 262)*

localization economy *(p. 252)*

logistics *(p. 266)*

neo-Fordism *(p. 262)*

neoliberal policy *(p. 246)*

newly industrializing country (NIC) *(p. 241)*

offshore financial centre *(p. 269)*

price elasticity of demand *(p. 246)*

primary activity *(p. 241)*

producer service *(p. 258)*

purchasing power parity (PPP) *(p. 234)*

quaternary activity *(p. 241)*

secondary activity *(p. 241)*

spread effect *(p. 253)*

strategic alliance *(p. 263)*

sustainable development *(p. 240)*

technology system *(p. 236)*

terms of trade *(p. 247)*

tertiary activity *(p. 241)*

trading bloc *(p. 245)*

transnational corporation (TNC) *(p. 242)*

vertical disintegration *(p. 263)*

world city *(p. 268)*

REVIEW AND DISCUSSION

1. How could your group measure the ecological footprint of your university? What data would you need to make an informed statement? List three things that might contribute to sustainable or unsustainable development of your campus.

2. Research the businesses in the area connected to your campus. Create a list of the stores. Determine whether or not the stores are locally owned. What is the percentage of locally owned to big-box retail or chain stores? What does this say about the economic structure of your campus?

3. After rereading the section on Fair Trade in the chapter, walk with your group to your on-campus store and create a list of Fair Trade products. What is the percentage of Fair Trade products vs. not Fair Trade products in the store? What does this say about your campus store?

4. While India's per capita income is well below that of the United States (Figure 7.1), India has more people who earn the equivalent of US$70 000 or above a year than all of North America does. How can you explain this, and what might be some of the consequences from the point of view of economic geography?

5. Research any local specialized manufacturing region or office district with which you are familiar. Describe the different kinds of firms that are found there, and suggest the kinds of linkages between them that might be considered examples of agglomeration effects. (*Hint:* you might consider the example of car manufacturing. How many parts are needed to make an entire car? What other firms are needed in the production? Do they come from the same place or are they manufactured in different locations? Are the parts manufactured in one place, region, or country? How would this be an example of agglomeration effects?)

6. Consider the economic structure of the city or town you live in. List two primary, secondary, tertiary, and quaternary activities in your region. How might these activities lead to one part of your city or town being more economically developed than others? Finally, consider where you fit into these economic structures. If you work in a community business, what is your labour used to produce?

Mastering GEOGRAPHY™

Log in to www.masteringgeography.com for MapMaster™ interactive maps, geography videos, RSS feeds, flashcards, weblinks, an eText version of *Human Geography: Places and Regions in Global Context*, and self-study quizzes to enhance your study of geographies of economic development.

MapMaster™ presents 13 Place Names and 13 Layered Thematic interactive maps to help students practise and master their geographic literacy, spatial reasoning, and critical thinking skills.

8

FOOD AND AGRICULTURE

In Niger, Africa, one in every two children is malnourished and one in every six dies before the age of 5. *Growing a Better Future*, published by Oxfam International, describes the situation of the people of Niger people as they face drought, soil depletion, desertification, water scarcity, and predatory food traders.[1] The report sums up the global situation, of which Niger is just one part:

> At the start of 2011, there were 925 million hungry people worldwide. By the end of the year, extreme weather and rising food prices may have driven the total back to one billion, where it last peaked in 2008. Why, in a world that produces more than enough food to feed everybody, do so many—one in seven of us—go hungry? (p. 6)

The report argues that the globe is heading for a serious food crisis. One of the factors thought to be adding to it is that an increasing amount of cropland once dedicated to food production is now being redirected to raising **biofuels,** renewable fuels derived from biological materials that can be regenerated. Replacing even a fraction of fossil fuels with biofuels requires the acquisition and conversion of vast areas of land. National governments around the world have passed laws and are providing inducements for the conversion of tens of millions of hectares

[1]Oxfam, *Growing a Better Future: Food Justice in a Resource-Constrained World*. Oxfam International: Oxford, England, 2011, http://www.oxfam.org.uk/resources/papers/growing-better-future.html.

Peasants in Carchi, Ecuador, prepare sustainably grown potatoes for market.
(*Source:* Alejandro Balaguer/archivolatino/Redux)

to biofuel monocultures like corn, soy, sugarcane, cotton, and grains. Land conversion on this scale often results in evictions of small farmers and poor communities.

In addition to land speculation and the increase in biofuel production, other equally significant factors are increasing the probability of a global food crisis being in full force by 2030. *Growing a Better Future* argues that the global food system is already reeling from the impacts of climate change, ecological degradation, population growth, rising energy prices, and an increasing demand for meat and dairy products.

The Oxfam report also proposes some workable solutions for repairing the global food system, some of which are already in place. In order to enact these solutions the global community must first agree on a *global governance model* that will make hunger reduction its chief priority. Second, the global community must work toward a new *agricultural future* that puts small-scale farmers at the centre of food production. Major gains in productivity, sustainable intensification, and poverty reduction are already being accomplished in some places and can certainly be applied more widely. Finally, the global community must build a new *ecological future*, one that redirects investments and transforms the behaviours of both businesses and consumers toward more sustainable practices and a more even distribution of resources. All of these will require a global agreement on climate change. ∎

TRADITIONAL AGRICULTURAL GEOGRAPHY

In this chapter, we examine the geography of agriculture from the global to the household level. As the example in the chapter-opening discussion of the impending global food crisis makes clear, to understand the geography of agriculture, one needs also to take into account a whole host of related factors besides crops and farming. We begin by looking at traditional agricultural practices and proceed through the three major revolutions of agricultural change. Next we explore the ways geographers have investigated the dramatic transformations in agriculture over the past half century as it has become increasingly industrialized through technological, political, social, and economic forces. Finally, we examine the effects globalization has had on producing, marketing, delivering, and consuming food.

The study of agriculture has a long tradition in geography. Because of geographers' interest in the relationships between people and land, it is hardly surprising that agriculture has been a primary concern. Geography is committed to viewing the physical and human systems as interactively linked. Such an approach combines an understanding of spatial differentiation and the importance of place with the recognition that agricultural practices are affected by local, regional, national, and globally extensive processes. It also provides geographers with a powerful perspective for understanding the dynamics of contemporary agriculture.

One of the most widely recognized and appreciated contributions that geography has made to the study of agriculture is the mapping of the factors that shape it. Geographers map soil, temperature, and terrain, as well as the areal distribution of different types of agriculture and the relationships between agriculture and other practices or variables.

Major changes in agriculture worldwide have occurred in the past five decades. Of these, the decline in the number of people employed in farming in both the core and the periphery is perhaps the most dramatic. In addition, the use of chemical, mechanical, and biotechnological innovations and applications has significantly intensified farming practices **(Figure 8.1)**. Agriculture has also become increasingly integrated into wider regional, national, and global economic systems at the same time that it has become more directly linked to other economic sectors, such as manufacturing and finance. The repercussions from these profound changes range from the structure of global finance to the social relations of individual households.

Agricultural Practices

Geographers examine agricultural practices to understand the myriad ways humans have learned to modify the natural world to sustain themselves. In addition to understanding agricultural systems, geographers are also interested in investigating the lifestyles and cultures of different agricultural communities. They and other social scientists often use the adjective **agrarian** to describe the way of life that is deeply embedded in the demands of agricultural production. *Agrarian* not only defines the culture of distinctive agricultural communities but also refers to the type of tenure (or landholding) system that determines who has access to land and what kind of cultivation practices are employed there.

FIGURE 8.1 Soybean plantation in Brazil Pictured here is a vast field of genetically modified soybeans. Brazil is the second biggest soybean producer in the world after the United States. Two-thirds of Brazilian soybeans are genetically modified.
(*Source:* Paul Springett 05/Alamy)

Agriculture is a science, an art, and a business directed at the cultivation of crops and the raising of livestock for sustenance and profit. The unique and ingenious methods humans have learned to transform the land through agriculture are an important reflection of the two-way relationship between people and their environments **(Figure 8.2)**. Just as geography shapes our choices and behaviours, so we are able to shape the physical landscape.

Before humans discovered the advantages of agriculture, they procured their food through hunting (including fishing) and gathering. **Hunting and gathering** characterizes activities whereby people feed themselves by killing wild animals and gathering fruits, roots, nuts, and other edible plants. Subsistence agriculture replaced hunting and gathering activities in many parts of the globe when people came to understand that the domestication of animals and plants could enable them to settle in one place over time rather than having to go off frequently in search of edible animals and plants **(Figure 8.3)**. **Subsistence agriculture** is a system in which agriculturalists consume most of what they produce.

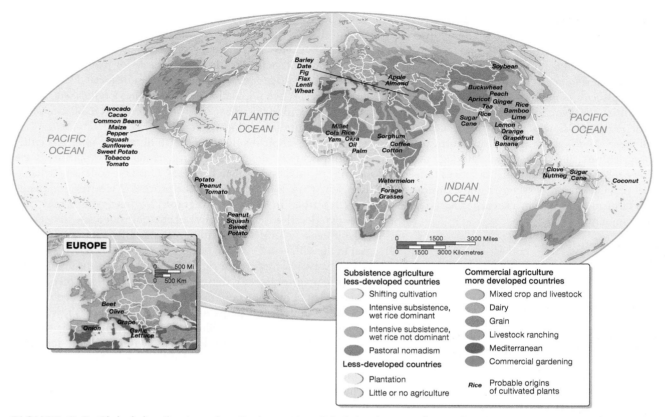

FIGURE 8.2 Global distribution of agriculture The global distribution of agricultural practices is illustrated in this map. Notice the differences between core and periphery with respect to commercial versus subsistence agriculture. The periphery, though it does contain commercial agriculture, contains more subsistence agriculture, while the core countries contain virtually none. Also mapped are the origins of cultivated plants. (*Source:* Adapted from H. Veregin [ed.], *Goode's World Atlas*, 21st ed. Skokie, IL: Rand McNally, 2005, pp. 38–39.)

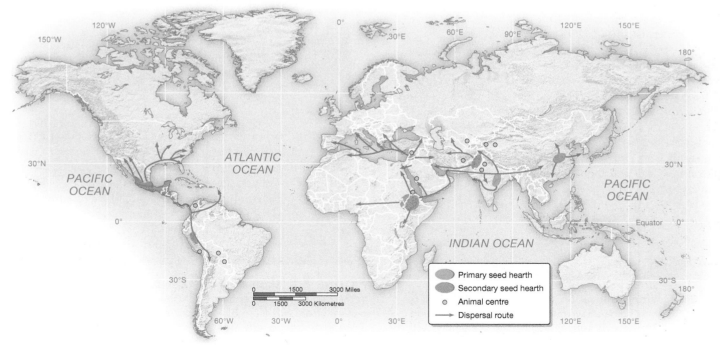

FIGURE 8.3 Areas of plant and animal domestication The origins of plant and animal domestication are not definitively known, and much of what is represented on this map is speculative. Archaeological evidence to date supports the distribution shown here and developed in the mid-twentieth century by Carl Sauer. Primary seed hearths are those places where domestication is believed to have first begun. Secondary seed hearths followed soon after. (*Source:* Adapted from J. M. Rubenstein, *The Cultural Landscape: An Introduction to Human Geography*, 7th ed., Prentice Hall © 2003, p. 319.)

During the twentieth century, the dominant agricultural system in the core countries became **commercial agriculture**, a system in which farmers produce crops and animals primarily for sale rather than for direct consumption by themselves and their families. Worldwide, subsistence agriculture is diminishing as increasing numbers of places are incorporated into a globalized economy with a substantial commercial agricultural sector. Still widely practised in the periphery, however, subsistence activities usually follow one of three dominant forms: shifting cultivation, intensive subsistence agriculture, and pastoralism. Although many people in the periphery rely on these traditional practices to feed themselves, traditional practices are increasingly being abandoned or modified as peasant farmers convert from a subsistence and barter economy to a cash economy.

Shifting Cultivation

In **shifting cultivation**, a form of agriculture usually found in tropical forests, farmers aim to maintain soil fertility by rotating the fields they cultivate. Shifting cultivation (also called land rotation) contrasts with another method of maintaining soil fertility, **crop rotation**, in which the fields under cultivation remain the same, but the crops planted are changed to balance the types of nutrients withdrawn from and delivered to the soil.

Shifting cultivation is globally distributed in the tropics—especially in the rain forests of Central and West Africa; the Amazon in South America; and much of Southeast Asia, including Thailand, Burma, Malaysia, and Indonesia—where climate, rainfall, and vegetation combine to produce soils lacking in nutrients. The practices involved in shifting cultivation have changed very little over thousands of years **(Figure 8.4)**. Shifting cultivation requires less energy than modern forms of farming, though it can successfully support only low population densities.

The typical agrarian system that supports shifting cultivation is one in which small groups of villagers hold land in common tenure. Through collective agreement or a ruling council, sites are distributed among village families and then cleared for planting by family members. As villages grow, tillable sites must be located farther and farther away. When population growth reaches a critical stage, several families within the village normally split off to establish another village at a more remote location.

Because tropical soils are poor in nutrients, repeated cultivation quickly depletes soil fertility, which means that fields are actively planted for less than five years. Once the soil nears exhaustion, a new site is identified, and the process of clearing and planting (described in the next paragraph) begins again. It may take over two decades for a once-cleared and cultivated site to become tillable again, after decomposition returns sufficient organic material to the soil.

The typical method for preparing a new site is through **slash-and-burn** agriculture. Existing plants are cropped close to the ground, left to dry for a period, and then ignited. The burning process adds valuable nutrients to the soil, such as potash, which is about the only readily available fertilizer. Once the land is cleared and ready for cultivation, it is known as **swidden**. While generally an agricultural practice that is workable when undertaken by small populations on limited portions of land, slash-and-burn can also be ecologically destructive when large numbers of farmers participate, especially in areas with vulnerable and endangered species, such as rain forests **(Figure 8.5)**. Slash-and-burn techniques to plant

FIGURE 8.5 Slash-and-burn, Xishuangbanna, China
In the mid-twentieth century, the Xishuangbanna region of China pictured here was a remote tropical rain forest, China's only one. Since then, the government and people of Xishuangbanna have begun to convert the area to rubber tree and sugarcane plantations with slash-and-burn techniques. While the transformations have lifted much of the region out of abject poverty, rapid soil erosion is occurring. Some estimates indicate that Xishuangbanna will be a dust bowl in 30 years. (*Source:* Ryan Pyle/Corbis)

FIGURE 8.4 Shifting cultivation One way to maintain soil fertility is by rotating the fields on which cultivation occurs. Shifting cultivation is pictured here as agriculturalists prepare a new field so that the old fields can "rest" and be regenerated. It is also possible to plant certain crops in order to restore soil fertility. That is, a crop that leaches the soil of one kind of nutrient is followed during the next growing season by a dissimilar crop that returns that nutrient to the soil. (*Source:* Rob Huibers/Hollandse Hoogte/Redux)

marijuana, coca, and opium poppies in Colombia since the late 1990s have led to significant devastation in the country's portion of the Amazon rain forest.

Notwithstanding its impacts on the environment, shifting cultivation can be an elegant response to a fragile landscape. The fallow period, an essential part of the process, is a passive and effective way of restoring plant nutrients to the soil. The burning of stumps and other debris makes the soil more workable, and seeding can proceed with a minimum of effort. Mixing different seeds and seedlings in the same tillage mimics the natural pattern of differing plant heights and types characteristic of the rain forest. It also helps protect the soil from leaching and erosion. Shifting cultivation requires no expensive inputs because no manufactured fertilizers, pesticides, herbicides, or heavy equipment are necessary. Finally, the characteristically staggered sowing allows for food production throughout the year.

Slash-and-burn agriculture relies largely on human labour, as well as extensive acreage for new plantings because old sites are abandoned frequently when soil fertility is diminished. Although a great deal of labour is involved in cutting and clearing vegetation, once the site is planted, there is little tending of crops until harvest time.

From region to region the kinds of crops grown, and their arrangement in the swidden, vary depending upon local taste and plant domestication histories. In the warm, humid tropics, tubers—sweet potatoes and yams—predominate, while grains such as corn or rice are more widely planted in the subtropics. The practice of mixing different seeds and seedlings in the same swidden is called **intertillage (Figure 8.6)**. Not only are different plants cultivated, but their planting is usually staggered so that harvesting can continue throughout the year. Staggered planting and harvesting reduces the risk of disasters from crop failure and increases the nutritional balance of the diet.

Shifting cultivation also frequently involves a gender division of labour that may vary from region to region **(Figure 8.7)**. For the most part, men are largely responsible for the initial tasks of clearing away vegetation, cutting down trees, and burning the

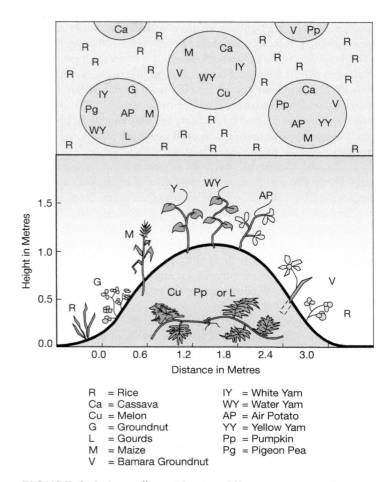

R	= Rice	IY	= White Yam
Ca	= Cassava	WY	= Water Yam
Cu	= Melon	AP	= Air Potato
G	= Groundnut	YY	= Yellow Yam
L	= Gourds	Pp	= Pumpkin
M	= Maize	Pg	= Pigeon Pea
V	= Bamara Groundnut		

FIGURE 8.6 Intertillage Planting different crops together in the same field has many benefits, including the spreading out of food production over the farming season, reduction of loss from disease and pests, greater protection from loss of soil moisture, and control of soil erosion. This diagram illustrates what an intertilled site might contain and how the planting is arranged. Hill-planted seeds have tall stalks and a deeper root system; those planted on flat earth tend to be spreading plants that produce large leaves for shading.

FIGURE 8.7 Gender division of labour in rice processing in Tamil Nadu, India Rice production is a major source of livelihood for both poor men and women in India. Women in this image are shown threshing the rice while men look on from the rice bales above them. In addition to production activities, to which they contribute more than men, women also process, clean, select, and store the seeds for next year's crop, and are primarily responsible for preparing and cooking rice for household consumption and sometimes for market sale. (*Source:* V. Muthuraman/SuperStock/Alamy)

stumps. Women are typically involved with sowing seeds and harvesting crops. Research on shifting cultivation indicates that the actual division of tasks between men and women (and sometimes children) results from traditional cultural practices, as well as the new demands placed upon households by globalization. (Recall the discussion of Sudanese children in Chapter 6.) For instance, many women have found it necessary to complement their subsistence agricultural activities with craft production for local tourist markets.

Although sometimes portrayed as an ingenious, well-balanced response to the environmental constraints of the tropics and subtropics, shifting cultivation is not without limitations. Its most obvious limitation is that it can be effective only with small populations. Increasing populations cause cultivation sites to be located farther and farther from villages, with the result that cultivators expend as much energy travelling to sites as they garner from the crops they produce. Indeed, it is not unusual for land closest to a village to be entirely fallow or unseeded because the soil is exhausted from previous plantings.

Increasingly, population pressures and ill-considered government policies are undermining the practicality of shifting cultivation, resulting in irreparable damage to the environment in many parts of the world. In Central and South America, for example, national governments have used rural resettlement programs to address urban population pressures. In some cases, relocated individuals not familiar with shifting cultivation techniques have employed them improperly. In others, individuals have been relocated to areas unsuitable for such cultivation practices. In parts of the Brazilian Amazon, for instance, shifting cultivators have acted in concert with cattle grazers, resulting in accelerated environmental degradation.

Although shifting cultivation was likely once practised throughout the world, population growth and the greater need for increased outputs per acre have led to its replacement by more intensive forms of agriculture.

Intensive Subsistence Agriculture

The second dominant form of subsistence activity is **intensive subsistence agriculture**, a practice involving the effective and efficient use of a small parcel of land to maximize crop yield; a considerable expenditure of human labour and application of fertilizer are also usually involved. Unlike shifting cultivation, intensive subsistence cultivation can often support larger populations. Consequently, intensive subsistence usually occurs in Asia, especially in India, China, and Southeast Asia.

Recall that shifting cultivation involves the application of a relatively limited amount of labour and other resources to cultivation. Conversely, intensive subsistence agriculture involves fairly constant human labour in order to achieve high productivity from a small amount of land. In the face of fierce population pressure and limited arable land, intensive subsistence agriculture reflects the inventive ways in which humans confront environmental constraints and reshape the landscape in the process. In fact, the landscape of intensive subsistence agriculture is often a distinctive one, including raised fields and terraced hillside plots **(Figure 8.8)**.

Intensive subsistence agriculture is able to support large rural populations. In contrast to shifting cultivation, fields are planted year after year as fertilizers and other soil enhancers are applied to maintain soil nutrients. For the most part, the limitations on the size of plots have more to do with the size of the population than geography. In Bangladesh and southern China, for example, where a significant proportion of the population is engaged in intensive subsistence agriculture, land is passed down from generation to generation—usually from fathers to sons—so that each successive generation, if there are multiple male offspring, receives a smaller and smaller share of the family holdings. Yet even with shrinking plot size each family must produce enough to sustain itself.

Under conditions of a growing population and a decreasing amount of arable land, it is critical to plant subsistence crops that produce a high yield per hectare. Different crops fulfill this need in

FIGURE 8.8 Intensive subsistence agriculture Where usable agricultural land is at a premium, agriculturalists have developed ingenious methods for taking advantage of every square metre of usable terrain. Landscapes like this one—a terraced rice field in Bali, Indonesia—can be extremely productive when carefully tended and can feed relatively large rural populations. They also require a high level of social organization for the collective effort that goes into their maintenance. (*Source: Visionsi/Fotolia*)

different regional climates. Generally speaking, the crops that dominate intensive subsistence agriculture are rice and other grains.

Rice production predominates in those areas of Asia—South China, Southeast Asia, Bangladesh, and parts of India—where summer rainfall is abundant. In drier climates and places where the winters are too cold for rice production, other sorts of grains—among them wheat, barley, millet, sorghum, corn, and oats—are grown for subsistence. In both situations, the land is intensively used. In fact, it is not uncommon in milder climates for fields to be planted and harvested more than once a year, a practice known as **double cropping**.

Pastoralism

Although not obviously a form of agricultural production, pastoralism is a form of subsistence activity associated with a traditional way of life and agricultural practice. **Pastoralism** involves the breeding and herding of animals to satisfy the human needs for food, shelter, and clothing. Usually practised in the cold and/or dry climates of savannahs (grasslands), deserts, and steppes (lightly wooded, grassy plains), where subsistence agriculture is impracticable, pastoralism can be either sedentary (pastoralists live in settlements and herd animals in nearby pastures) or nomadic (pastoralists travel with their herds over long distances, never settling in any one place for very long). Although forms of commercial pastoralism exist—the regularized herding of animals for profitable meat production, as among Basque Americans in Nevada and among the gauchos of the Argentine grasslands—we are concerned here with pastoralism as a subsistence activity.

Pastoralism is largely confined to parts of North Africa and the savannahs of central and southern Africa, the Middle East, and central Asia. Pastoralists generally graze cattle, sheep, goats, and camels, although reindeer are herded in parts of Eurasia. The type of animal herded is related to the culture of the pastoralists, as well as the animals' adaptability to the regional topography and foraging conditions **(Figure 8.9)**. Nomadism is a form of pastoralism that involves the systematic and continuous movement of groups of herders, their families, and the herds in search of forage. Most pastoralists practise **transhumance**, the movement of herds according to seasonal rhythms: warmer, lowland areas in the winter, and cooler, highland areas in the summer. The distinguishing characteristic of pastoralists is that they depend on animals, not crops, for their livelihood.

Like shifting cultivation and intensive subsistence cultivation, pastoralism is not simply a subsistence activity but part of a social system as well. Pastoralist family groups are governed by a leader or chieftain. Groups are divided into units that follow different routes with the herds. The routes are well known; group members are intimately conversant with the landscape, watering places, and opportunities for contact with sedentary groups. This continuous movement, and the different attachment to "place" that it implies, challenges more sedentary societies. As a result, nomadic groups are often persecuted and made to settle down. Pastoralists have also been forced off the land by competition from other land uses and the state's need to track citizens for taxation and military reasons.

APPLY YOUR KNOWLEDGE Consult Figure 8.2, showing the distribution of agricultural practices across the globe, and locate two additional world maps that show climate and topography. What relationships can you discern between climate and agricultural practice and between topography and agricultural practice by comparing the three maps? What kind of agriculture happens where and why does it happen there? ■

FIGURE 8.9 Pastoralism, Mongolia In this image, sheep forage near the summer settlement of yurts—circular tents of felt or skins on a collapsible framework—at the base of Tsaast Uul mountain in Mongolia, where pastoralism is the main livelihood. Note the dryness of the landscape; pastoralism usually occurs where agriculture is not feasible. (*Source:* Matthieu Paley/Getty Images)

AGRICULTURAL REVOLUTION AND INDUSTRIALIZATION

For a long time human geography textbooks treated the differences in agricultural practices worldwide as systems to be described and catalogued, as we have just done. New conceptual approaches to the agricultural sector, however, have transformed the ways agriculture is viewed. Agriculture has become less a human activity to be described through classification and more a complex component of the global economic system to be explained. While the importance and persistence of traditional agricultural forms are acknowledged, such description must be balanced with an understanding of the ways new commercial practices undermine and otherwise change older forms.

Increasingly, geographers and others have come to see world agricultural practices as having proceeded through "revolutionary" phases, just as manufacturing did. As in manufacturing, practices have not been transformed everywhere at the same time; consequently, some parts of the world are still largely unaffected by certain aspects of agricultural change. By seeing agriculture in this new light, we can recognize that, as in manufacturing, geography and society have changed as the global community has moved from predominantly subsistence to predominantly capital-intensive, market-oriented practices. This history has proceeded in alternating cycles: long periods of very gradual change punctuated by short, explosive periods of radical change, resulting in three distinct revolutionary periods.

The First Agricultural Revolution

The first agricultural revolution is commonly recognized as having been founded on the development of seed agriculture and the use of the plow and draft animals **(Figure 8.10)**. Aspects of this transformation were discussed in Chapter 2. Seed agriculture, which emerged through the domestication of crops such as wheat and rice and animals such as sheep and goats, replaced hunting and gathering as a way of living and sustaining life. Seed agriculture arose about 10 000 years ago in several regions around the world. The result was a broad belt of cultivated lands across Southwest Asia, from Greece in the west into present-day Turkey and part of Iran in the east, as well as in parts of Central and South America, northern China, northeast India, and East Africa.

The domestication of plants and animals allowed for the rise of settled ways of life. Villages were built, creating types of social, cultural, economic, and political relationships that differed from those that dominated hunter-gatherer societies. On the floodplains along the Tigris, Euphrates, and Nile rivers, important complex civilizations were built upon the fruits of the first agricultural revolution **(Figure 8.11)**. Over time, the knowledge and skill underlying seed agriculture and the domestication of plants diffused outward from these original areas, having a revolutionary impact throughout the globe.

The Second Agricultural Revolution

A great deal of debate exists among historians as to the timing and location of the second agricultural revolution. Though most historians agree that it did not occur everywhere at the same time, they disagree over which elements were essential to the fundamental transformation of subsistence agriculture. Important elements included

- dramatic improvements in outputs, such as crop and livestock yields
- innovations such as the improved yoke for oxen and the replacement of the ox with the horse
- new inputs to agricultural production, such as fertilizers and field drainage systems

The apex of the second agricultural revolution coincided historically and geographically with the Industrial Revolution in England and Western Europe. Although many important changes

FIGURE 8.10 Plowing with yoked oxen and camels In many parts of the world, agriculturalists rely on draft animals to prepare land for cultivation. Animals were an important element in the first agricultural revolution. By expanding the amount of energy applied to production, draft animals enabled humans to increase food supplies. Many contemporary traditional farmers view draft animals as their most valuable possessions. Pictured here are camels and oxen pulling the plows of Sikh farmers in Punjab State, India. (*Source:* James P. Blair/National Geographic/Getty Images)

FIGURE 8.11 Agricultural fields along the Nile River, Luxor, Egypt The lush fertile farmland in the foreground is enabled by the silt deposited by the Nile River. On the higher slopes of the river valley, however, dry land not suitable for farming is clearly visible. (*Source:* RIEGER Bertrand/hemis.fr/Alamy)

in agriculture preceded the Industrial Revolution, none had more of an impact than the rise of an industrialized manufacturing sector.

On the eve of the Industrial Revolution—in the middle of the eighteenth century—in Western Europe and England, subsistence peasant agriculture was predominant, though partial integration into a market economy was underway. Many peasants were using a crop-rotation system that, in addition to the application of natural and semiprocessed fertilizers, improved soil productivity and led to increased crop and livestock yields. Additionally, the feudal land-holding system—a social and economic system based on peasant service to a lord in exchange for access to land—was breaking down and yielding to a new agrarian system based on an emerging system of private-property relations. Communal lands were being replaced by enclosed, individually owned land or land worked independently by tenants or renters.

Such a situation was a logical response to the demands for food production that emerged from the dramatic social and economic changes accompanying the Industrial Revolution. Perhaps most important of all these changes was the emergence—through the creation of an urban industrial workforce—of a commercial market for food. Many innovations of the Industrial Revolution, such as improvements in transportation technology, had substantial impacts on agriculture. Innovations applied directly to agricultural practices, such as the new types of horse-drawn farm machinery, improved control over—as well as the quantity of—yields.

APPLY YOUR KNOWLEDGE Why was the Industrial Revolution so important to the second agricultural revolution? How did manufacturing technologies change agricultural technologies? Research a technology that debuted in the Industrial Revolution that affected both manufacturing and agricultural practices. ■

The Third Agricultural Revolution

The third agricultural revolution is fairly recent: it began in the late nineteenth century and gained momentum throughout the twentieth century, spreading from its origin in North America throughout the world.

The three phases of the third agricultural revolution are mechanization, chemical farming with synthetic fertilizers, and globally widespread food manufacturing. **Mechanization** is the replacement of human farm labour with machines. Tractors, combines, reapers, pickers, and other forms of motorized machines have, since the beginning of the twentieth century, progressively replaced human and animal labour in the agricultural sectors of core states. In Europe, mechanization did not become widespread until after World War II.

Chemical farming is the application of synthetic fertilizers to the soil—and herbicides, fungicides, and pesticides to crops—to enhance yields **(Figure 8.12)**. Becoming common in the 1950s in

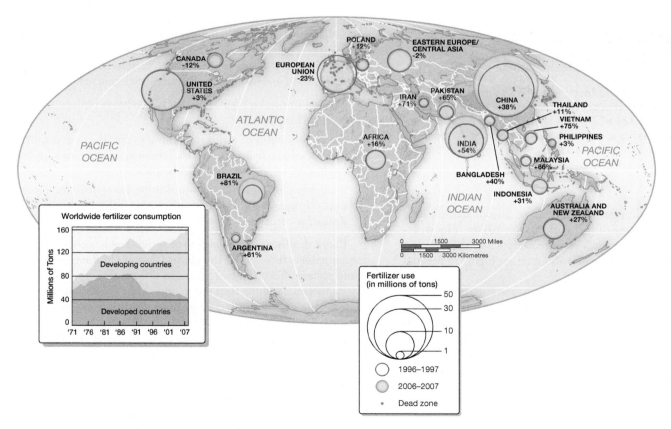

FIGURE 8.12 Worldwide growth in fertilizer use, 1997–2007 As the map indicates, fertilizer use has been growing in peripheral countries faster than in the core, though core countries are still the largest users of fertilizer. One of the biggest problems, and one that is only expected to grow, is increased runoff from fertilizer and resultant dead zones along ocean shores. (*Source:* Adapted from *New York Times,* http://www.nytimes.com/imagepages/2008/04/30/business/20080430_FERTILIZER_GRAPHIC.html. Accessed August 17, 2008.)

FIGURE 8.13 Food manufacturing Pictured here is an automated operation that processes carrots into baby carrots—a food product that fetches a higher retail price than unprocessed carrots. Food processing is one of the ways in which economic value is added to agricultural products before they reach the market. *(Source: Richard Thornton/Shutterstock)*

APPLY YOUR KNOWLEDGE Open a kitchen cupboard and read the labels on four different food products. Identify the various processes involved in making each of the products ready for market. What processing has occurred? Has refining or cooking been involved? What additional ingredients have been added to the product and why (to improve flavour, to extend shelf-life, or for some other reason)? How does the packaging (container, images of the product, colours of the labelling, etc.) enhance the attractiveness of the product? ∎

The Industrialization of Agriculture

Advances in science and technology—including mechanical as well as chemical and biological innovations—have driven the industrialization of agriculture over time. As with industrialization more generally, the industrialization of agriculture unfolded as the capitalist economic system became more advanced and widespread. We regard **agricultural industrialization** as the process whereby the farm has moved from being the centrepiece of agricultural production to being one part of an integrated multilevel (or vertically organized) industrial process that includes production, storage, processing, distribution, marketing, and retailing. Experts in the study of agriculture see it as clearly linked to industry and the service sector, thus constituting a complex agro-commodity production system.

Geographers have helped examine the transformation of an agricultural product into an industrial food product. This transformation has been accomplished not only through the indirect and/or direct altering of agricultural outputs (such as tomatoes or wheat) but also through changes in rural economic activities. Agricultural industrialization involves three important developments:

- changes in rural labour activities as machines replace and/or enhance human labour

- the introduction of innovative inputs—fertilizers and other agrochemicals, hybrid seeds, and biotechnologies—to supplement, alter, or replace biological outputs

- the development of industrial substitutes for agricultural products (Nutrasweet instead of sugar, and artificial thickeners instead of cornstarch or flour, for example)

Recall that the industrialization of agriculture has not occurred simultaneously throughout the globe. Changes in the global economic system affect different places in different ways as different states and social groups respond to and shape these changes. For example, the use of fertilizers and high-yielding seeds occurred much earlier in core-region agriculture than in the periphery, where many people still farm without them. In the late 1960s, however, core countries began exporting fertilizers and high-yielding seeds to regions of the periphery (largely in Asia and Mexico) in an attempt to boost agricultural production. In a development known as the **Green Revolution**, they also sent new machines and institutions, all designed to increase global agricultural productivity, as described in Box 8.1, "Window on the World: The Green Revolution and Its Contemporary Challenges."

Economic crises, a decrease in government programs, and reduced trade barriers have slowed the progress of the Green Revolution in many countries. For example, fertilizer use in

North America, chemical farming diffused to Europe in the 1960s and to peripheral regions of the world in the 1970s. The widespread application of chemicals and their impact on the environment is what Rachel Carson wrote about in her highly influential book *Silent Spring*. (See Chapter 4.)

Food manufacturing also had its origins in late-nineteenth-century North America. **Food manufacturing** adds economic value to agricultural products through a range of treatments—processing, canning, refining, packing, packaging, and so on—occurring off the farm and before the products reach the market **(Figure 8.13)**. The first two phases of the third revolution affect inputs to the agricultural production process, whereas the final phase affects agricultural outputs. While the first two are related to the modernization of farming as an economic practice, the third involves a complication of the relationship of farms to firms in the manufacturing sector, which had increasingly expanded into the area of food early in the 1960s. These three developmental phases of the third agricultural revolution constitute the industrialization of agriculture.

The Green Revolution and Its Contemporary Challenges

The Green Revolution was an attempt to find ways to feed the world's burgeoning population. In 1943, the Rockefeller Foundation provided funds to a group of U.S. agricultural scientists to set up a research project in Mexico aimed at increasing that country's wheat production through expansion of irrigation infrastructure, modernization of management techniques, distribution of hybridized seeds, synthetic fertilizers, and pesticides. Just seven years later, scientists distributed the first Green Revolution wheat seeds to farmers. The project was eventually expanded to include research on maize (corn) as well. By 1967, Green Revolution scientists were exporting their work to other parts of the world and had added rice to their research agenda (**Figure 8.A**). Norman Borlaug, one of the founders of the Green Revolution, went on to win the Nobel Peace Prize in 1970 for promoting world peace through the elimination of hunger.

The initial focus of the Green Revolution was on the development of seed varieties that would produce higher yields than those traditionally used in the target areas. In developing new, higher-yielding varieties, however, agricultural scientists soon discovered that plants were limited in the amount of nitrogen they could absorb and use. The scientists' solution was to increase nitrogen absorption capacity by delivering nitrogen-based fertilizers in water to plants. This required the building of major water and irrigation projects. Then the scientists discovered that the increased nitrogen and water caused the plants to develop taller stalks. With top-heavy seed heads, the tall stalks fell over easily, reducing the amount of seed that could be harvested. The scientists then came up with dwarf varieties of grains that would support the heavy seed heads without falling over. Then another problem arose:

short plants in very moist conditions encouraged the growth of fungi and pests. The scientists responded by developing a range of pesticides.

The Green Revolution thus came to constitute a package of inputs: new "miracle seeds," water, fertilizers, and pesticides. Farmers who use all of the inputs—and use them properly—can achieve the yields that scientists produced in their experimental plots, which are two to five times larger than those of traditional crops. In some countries, the resulting yields are high enough to enable export trade, generating important sources of foreign exchange. In addition, the creation of varieties that produce faster-maturing crops has allowed some farmers to plant two or more crops per year on the same land, increasing their individual production—and wealth—considerably.

Thanks to Green Revolution innovations, rice production in Asia grew 66 percent between 1965 and 1985. India, for example, became largely self-sufficient in rice and wheat. Worldwide, Green Revolution seeds and agricultural techniques accounted for almost 90 percent of the increase in world grain output in the 1960s and about 70 percent in the 1970s. In the late 1980s and 1990s, at least 80 percent of the additional production of grains could be attributed to Green Revolution techniques. Thus, although hunger and famine persist, many argue that they would be much worse if the Green Revolution had never occurred (**Figure 8.B**).

The Green Revolution has not been an unqualified success, however. One important reason is that wheat, rice, and maize are unsuitable crops in many global regions, and research on more suitable crops, such as sorghum and millet, has lagged behind. In Africa, poor soils and lack of water make progress

FIGURE 8.A The CIMMYT headquarters
The Centro International de Mejorimiento de Maiz y Trigo (CIMMYT) (International Maize and Wheat Improvement Center) in Texcoco, Mexico, is involved in plant breeding and research. High-yield-variety seeds were developed here for the Green Revolution. The centre holds the world's premier collection of corn and wheat germplasm—the genetic components of an organism. Modern, refrigerated storage vaults hold many thousands of varieties.
(*Source:* Marco Ugarte/AP Images)

(Continued)

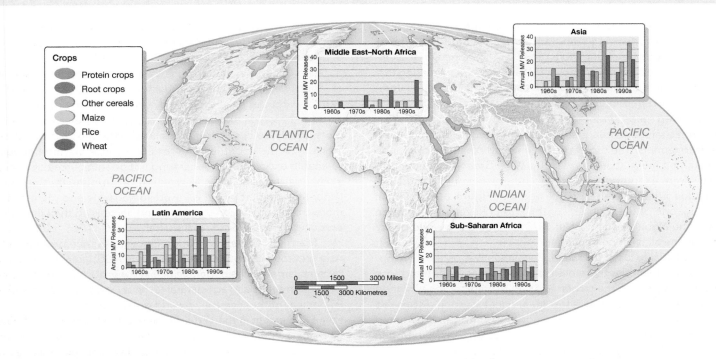

FIGURE 8.B **Effects of the Green Revolution** This map illustrates the increased yields of protein crops (such as beans and peas), root crops, maize, rice, wheat, and other cereals brought about by the Green Revolution in selected countries in Latin America, Asia, sub-Saharan Africa, and the Middle East and North Africa. (*Source:* Data from R. E. Evenson and D. Gollin, "Assessing the Impact of the Green Revolution, 1960–2000," *Science, 300*, May 2, 2005, p. 759.)

more difficult to achieve. Another important factor is the new seed strains' vulnerability to pest and disease infestation, often after only a couple of years of planting. Traditional varieties often have developed resistance to the pests and diseases characteristic of an area, but genetically engineered varieties often lack such resistance.

A social effect of the Green Revolution technology has been a decreased need for human labour. In southeastern Brazil, machines replaced farm workers, creating significant unemployment. Green Revolution technology and training have also tended to exclude women, who play important roles in traditional food production. In addition, the new agricultural chemicals, especially pesticides, have contributed to ecosystem pollution and worker poisonings. Finally, the more intensive use of irrigation has created salt buildup in soils (*salinization*) and water scarcity (**Figure 8.C**).

Critics also argue that the Green Revolution has magnified social inequities by allowing wealth and power to accrue to a small number of agriculturalists while causing greater poverty and landlessness among poorer segments of the population. In Mexico, a black market developed in Green Revolution seeds, fertilizers, and pesticides. Poorer farmers, coerced into using them, accrued high debts that they could not begin to repay. Many lost their lands and

became migrant labourers or moved to the cities and joined the urban poor.

The new seed varieties sometimes produce grains that are less nutritious, less palatable, or less flavourful. The chemical fertilizers and pesticides that must be used are derived from fossil fuels—mainly oil—and are thus subject to the vagaries of world oil prices. Furthermore, the use of these chemicals, as well as monocropping practices, has produced environmental contamination and soil erosion. Water developments have benefited some regions, but less well-endowed areas have experienced an exaggeration of already existing regional inequities. Worse, pressures to build water projects and to acquire foreign exchange to pay for importation of Green Revolution inputs have increased pressure on countries to grow even more crops for export, often at the expense of production for local consumption.

There are two final criticisms that have raised concern about the overall benefits of the Green Revolution. The first is that it has decreased the production of biomass fuels—wood, crop residues, and dung—traditionally used in many peripheral areas of the world. The second is that the Green Revolution has contributed to a worldwide loss of genetic diversity by replacing a wide range of local crops and varieties with a narrow range of high-yielding varieties of a small number of crops. Planting single varieties over large areas (monocultures) has made agriculture more vulnerable to disease and pests. Increasing attention is being paid to these limitations. The International Institute of Tropical Agriculture in Ibadan, Nigeria, focuses on foods for humid and subhumid areas, and the International Crops Research Institute for the Semi-Arid Tropics in Hyderabad, India, focuses on researching staples of the Sahel region, such as sorghum, millet, pigeon pea, and groundnut. In both places, the aim is to produce varieties that produce decent yields over good and bad years. They are also working to develop plants that will increase production of biomass in the form of animal fodder and fuel residues, as well as of food, and that give optimal yields when intertilled—a very common practice in Africa. In the Sahel, scientists are working on crops that mature more quickly to compensate for the serious drop in the average length of the rainy season the region has recently experienced.

Despite criticisms, it is clear that the global agricultural system has grown spectacularly. And yet, as a recent *New York Times* article states, not spectacularly enough. As described in the chapter opener, the rapid growth in agricultural output that was the hallmark of the twentieth century has declined in the twenty-first to the point where demand is quickly outstripping supply, driven not just by population growth but also by changing food preference among developing countries like China. With consumption outstripping supply, stockpiles of wheat, rice, soybeans, and grain are also being diminished,

creating serious concern among policymakers. Climate change has been identified as one of the most harmful and least easily remediable factors behind lessening food supplies. For instance, the 2003 heat wave in Europe, believed to have been worsened by human-induced global warming, slashed agricultural output in some countries by as much as 30 percent. And a long drought in Australia, also possibly linked to climate change, cut its wheat and rice production. Other contributing events include the prolonged 2009–2010 drought in Ukraine and 2011 floods in the midwestern United States and in Colombia, South America, which have undermined the global food system.

Although the Green Revolution has come under much justified attack over the years, its main objective of finding innovative new ways to feed the world's peoples has continued. In the process, the world's agricultural system has been expanded into hitherto very remote regions, and important knowledge has been gained about how to conduct science and how to understand the role that science plays in improving agriculture.

Many of the world's leading agricultural researchers believe that it is possible to continue to develop seeds that will be able to withstand drought, flooding, increasing carbon dioxide, and maybe even increasing temperatures (though there is less optimism about the last problem). The twenty-first century poses unforeseen problems for agricultural science, problems that must be solved in order to feed the world's growing population.

FIGURE 8.C Irrigated Rice Paddy, India The introduction of high-yielding, semi-dwarf types of rice, starting in 1962 with the Green Revolution, emphasized the intensive use of fertilizers and pesticides. Rice production increased substantially. However, this achievement was made at a cost to the environment where semiaquatic organisms, which have always been part of these ecosystems, including wild fish, frogs, shrimps, clams, and snails have disappeared. In addition, to keep soil salinity low, a large quantity of additional water is needed but is seldom available resulting in soil degradation as well as species loss. (*Source:* Tim Gainey/Alamy)

FIGURE 8.14 Commercial flower
production for export markets,
Argentina Pictured here is a field of allium,
flowers that produce a blue, lilac, or purple-
coloured bloom, on a flower plantation near
Mendoza, Argentina. In the background are
vineyards. Once grown only in home gardens, alliums are becoming commercialized
all over the world, from Argentina to New
Zealand. (*Source:* Michael Lewis/Corbis)

countries such as Brazil and Mexico has declined in the face of high
prices, fewer subsidies, and increased competition from imported
corn and wheat, especially from the United States. Many governments have shifted from giving top priority to self-sufficiency in
basic grains to encouraging crops that are more competitive in international trade, such as fruit, vegetables, and flowers **(Figure 8.14)**.
Nontraditional agricultural exports (NTAEs) such as these contrast with traditional exports, such as sugar and coffee. NTAEs have
become increasingly important in areas of Mexico, Central America,
Colombia, and Chile, replacing grain production and traditional
exports, such as coffee and cotton. These new crops obtain high
prices but also require heavy applications of pesticides and water
to meet export-quality standards. They also require fast refrigerated
transport to market and are vulnerable to climatic variation and to
the vagaries of the international market, including changing tastes
for foods and health scares about pesticide or biological contamination. An example of a nontraditional agricultural export is shrimp,
as discussed in Box 8.2, "Geography Matters: The Blue Revolution
and Global Shrimp."

One increasingly significant aspect of industrial agricultural
transformation is contract farming. **Contract farming** is an agreement between farmers and processing and/or marketing firms for
the production, supply, and purchase of agricultural products—
from beef, milk, and poultry to cotton, flowers, and vegetables. The
legal arrangement requires the firm to provide specified support
through, for example, the supply of fertilizer or seeds and the provision of technical advice. The farmer is, in turn, obliged to produce a specific commodity in quantities and at quality standards
determined by the firm. A great deal of agricultural production in
the contemporary global system proceeds according to contracts.
For instance, New Brunswick-based McCain, the world's largest
producer of french fries, obtains 80 percent of its raw product from
contract farmers.

Contract farming has been seen by some as a strategy for maintaining the livelihoods of small farmers marginalized by the growth

of more corporate forms of farming. For farmers, contractual
arrangements can provide access to services and credit as well as
new technology. And the fixed price offered for the product can
help reduce risk and uncertainty. On the other hand, there are
risks associated with the contract. The most worrisome is the
indebtedness that often occurs when farmers are unable to meet
the conditions of the contract or when firms fail to honour their
agreements.

Biotechnology and Agriculture

In addition to the Blue and the Green revolutions, agriculture
has also undergone a **Biorevolution.** The Biorevolution involves
the genetic engineering of plants and animals and has the potential to surpass the productivity increases of the Green Revolution.
Ever since the nineteenth century, when Austrian botanist Gregor
Mendel identified hereditary traits in plants and French chemist
Louis Pasteur explained fermentation, the manipulation and management of biological organisms has been key to the development
of agriculture. The central feature of the Biorevolution is **biotechnology,** which is any technique that uses living organisms (or parts
of organisms) to improve, make, or modify plants and animals or
to develop microorganisms for specific uses. Recombinant DNA
techniques, tissue culture, cell fusion, enzyme and fermentation
technology, and embryo transfer are some of the most talked-about
aspects of biotechnology in agriculture.

A common argument for applying biotechnology to agriculture is the belief that these techniques can help reduce agricultural production costs and serve as a kind of resource management
(where certain natural resources are replaced by manufactured
ones). Biotechnology has been hailed as a way to address growing
concern over the rising costs of cash-crop production, spoilage of
stored surplus, environmental degradation from chemical fertilizers
and overuse, soil depletion, and related challenges now obstructing
profitable agricultural production.

The Blue Revolution and Global Shrimp

by Brian J. Marks

(updated in 2014 by M. Imort)

The coastal deltas of the Mississippi and Mekong rivers are vast estuaries where river and sea water mixes in a complex of marshes, swamps, and natural ridges built by river sediment over millennia. These deltas are major shrimp-producing regions for the United States and Vietnam. The similarities and differences between these two shrimping regions speak to the broad forces shaping contemporary global food systems as well as how such forces act on and are shaped by specific places.

In some ways, the Louisiana and Mekong Delta shrimp industries could not be more dissimilar. While Louisianians catch shrimp from the sea (**Figure 8.D**), Vietnam relies primarily on **aquaculture**, the growing of aquatic creatures in ponds on shore or in pens suspended in water (**Figure 8.E**). Louisiana's industry involves far fewer people and is oriented to the domestic U.S. market; the Mekong Delta's employs many more and is export-oriented. In Louisiana, some 5700 shrimpers netted 63 000 tonnes from the Gulf of Mexico in 2006. This makes up more than a third of U.S. shrimp production but less than 5 percent of U.S. shrimp consumption. By contrast, 300 000 shrimp farmers in the Mekong Delta grew 287 000 tonnes that year, or about 75 percent of Vietnam's shrimp production, the vast majority of which is exported to core countries.

A commercial shrimp fishery first developed in Louisiana in the late nineteenth century to export sun-dried shrimp to Asia. Filipino and Chinese fishermen were central to the establishment of the shrimp-drying industry and taught the practice to others. After World War II, frozen shrimp began to predominate in the market, and shrimp prices rose markedly, tapping into the growing affluence of consumers. Louisiana shrimping developed around family ownership and operation of boats. Siblings, in-laws, children, and spouses participated in catching shrimp and pooled financial resources and experience to build boats and set up relatives in the business. Communities of Cajuns, Native Americans, African Americans, Croatians, Canary Islanders (*Isleños*), and, after 1985, Vietnamese and Cambodians have been prominent in Louisiana shrimping. Shrimpers run everything from 25-foot (7.6-metre) day boats that work in inshore bays, lakes, and bayous to 100-foot (30.5-metre) freezer boats that can operate for a month in the deeper waters of the Gulf of Mexico. In recent decades, the industry has experienced challenges due to changing shrimp prices and costs of production, hurricanes, Mississippi River floods that disrupt the season, and increasing government regulations put in place to protect endangered sea turtles and other "bycatch" species— other species that may be caught inadvertently with the shrimp. Finally, the Deepwater Horizon oil spill in 2010 has added consumer concerns over persistent oil and dispersant contamination and sea life deformities to the industry's worries.

FIGURE 8.D Louisiana shrimpers These fishermen are sorting wild-caught shrimp harvested near Bayou Lafourche, Louisiana. (*Source: Philip Gould/Corbis*)

But all these issues did not do as much to cripple the Louisiana shrimp industry, remarkable for its ability to bounce back from such adversity in the past, as the collapse of shrimp prices following the dramatic expansion of shrimp imports into the U.S. market. Between 2000 and 2003 alone, shrimp imports increased almost 50 percent. During the 2000s, Gulf shrimp prices fell by 39 percent,

FIGURE 8.E Vietnamese shrimp farmer This shrimp farmer is spreading agricultural lime in a shrimp pond in Cà Mau province, the southern tip of the Mekong Delta. Shrimp aquaculturalists use lime as a fertilizer and to regulate acidity in the pond water. Most shrimp farms in Vietnam lack the capital to grow shrimp as intensively as this one, which uses paddlewheel aerators to increase dissolved oxygen in the water, allowing more shrimp to be grown. (*Source: Richard Vogel/AP Images*)

(Continued)

while diesel prices more than doubled (**Figure 8.F**). This created a **cost/price squeeze**, which involves the simultaneous decrease in selling prices and rise in production costs that reduce a business's profit margin. Half of Louisiana shrimpers gave up during that decade. Those remaining lived at a considerably reduced standard of living, intensified their fishing effort, targeted larger, more expensive shrimp to retail to consumers, diversified into other businesses, or replaced hired deckhands with unpaid family members.

The local changes in Louisiana were largely the result of the global proliferation of shrimp aquaculture, which was responsible for just 5 percent of the global shrimp supply in 1980 but had increased to 52 percent in 2008. This increase is the result of a "**Blue Revolution**"—the large-scale expansion of aquaculture in the late twentieth century. Alongside the Green Revolution (discussed in Box 8.1), which transformed agriculture in many parts of the periphery, the Blue Revolution has shifted primary-sector activities toward a greater dependence on capitalized inputs—credit, machinery, fuel, feeds, fertilizers, and pesticides—instead of human labour and natural productivity. On the one hand, the Blue and Green revolutions have greatly increased food production in many places, but on the other hand they have engendered conflict over how the new practices redistribute power and wealth.

For example, advances in fish-farming species like carp and tilapia in countries like China have increased the availability of fish for millions of people, yet to date aquaculture has found its greatest economic success in catering to the demand of affluent consumers in the core for products like shrimp and salmon. The major consumers of farmed shrimp are Japan, the United States, and the European Union, while the largest exporters are Thailand, India, Indonesia, Vietnam, and Mexico. Shrimp is big business—the most consumed seafood in the United States and a source of billions of dollars in exports for peripheral countries.

The global shrimp industry is also a major source of controversy; coastal residents in some exporting nations denounce shrimp farming for destroying wetlands; damaging nearby agriculture with salt water; seizing land, water, and access to the sea from communities; and causing violent conflicts between shrimp farmers and their neighbours. The so-called "Pink Gold Rush" of shrimp exports has come with a high social and ecological cost. Globalizing shrimp has also created new economic hazards for shrimp producers themselves.

In Vietnam, the modern shrimp industry is much younger than Louisiana's. Most Mekong Delta shrimp farmers grew rice before 2000, after decades of hard work converting saline coastal wetlands into freshwater environments where rice, fruit, and fish could be grown for subsistence and domestic markets. By the late 1990s, Vietnam had achieved self-sufficiency in food grains, and the national government pursued an export-oriented economic development strategy, allowing farmers to shift away from rice toward more profitable cash crops. At that time, very low rice prices coincided with exceptionally high shrimp prices (**Figure 8.G**). (Louisiana shrimpers also took on new debt to expand in these years.)

The high prices encouraged farmers to reconvert some 280 000 hectares of coastal rice land to saltwater shrimp ponds in the early 2000s—just as global farmed shrimp production surged and prices began their dramatic downward slide. As in Louisiana, family farmers make up the vast majority of shrimp producers in the Mekong Delta, relying on unpaid household labour and limited credit to operate their small farms. Initially, Vietnamese farmers achieved good incomes from shrimp, but disease problems plagued shrimp farming, harming productivity and pushing some out of business. Even many successful farmers incurred higher debt to finance intensification.

By the late 2000s, as shrimp prices continued to fall, the cost of fertilizers and chemicals rose with the price of oil. Rice prices, on the

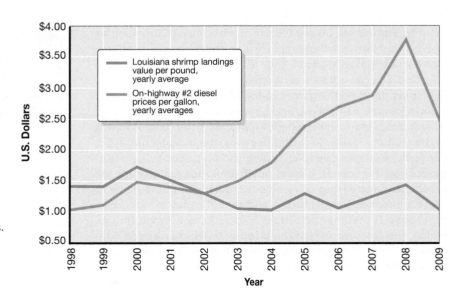

FIGURE 8.F Price trends in Louisiana shrimp and diesel prices, 1998–2009 Shrimp prices fell by more than a third in the 2000s while diesel prices more than doubled, leading to a cost–price squeeze for shrimpers.
(*Source:* U.S. Energy Information Agency Short-Term Outlook Real and Nominal Prices, http://www.eia.gov/emeu/steo/realprices/index.cfm and NOAA Fisheries Annual Commercial Landing Statistics, http://www.st.nmfs.noaa.gov/st1/annual_landings.html.)

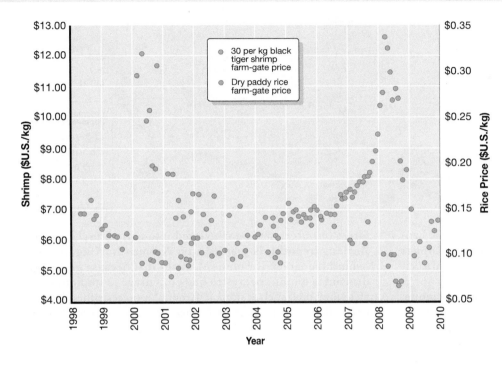

FIGURE 8.G Price trends for shrimp and rice in the Mekong Delta, 1998–2009 When many coastal Mekong Delta farmers abandoned rice for shrimp in 2000, rice was much cheaper and shrimp more expensive than it would be later in the decade. (*Source:* United States Department of Agriculture Vietnam Rice monthly reports, *Báo Sóc Trang* and *Báo Cá Mau* [newspapers] weekly shrimp price reports.)

other hand, skyrocketed, and many producers wanted to go back to rice cultivation. Some areas adopted rice–shrimp farming in rotation, growing shrimp during the saline dry season and rice in the rainy season, but for most farmers in the coastal Mekong Delta the increase of salts in the soil (salinization) and the decay of water control infrastructures meant rice could no longer survive in their fields. Most producers could not reverse course and became effectively "stuck" with growing shrimp for the foreseeable future even though the price trends that pushed them toward aquaculture had reversed.

For both Louisiana and Mekong Delta shrimp producers, the early 2000s have been a time of profound and often difficult change. Small family producers in both regions sell shrimp to a global market characterized by price volatility that has squeezed their margins while expanding the supply of cheap shrimp for consumers and the major corporations that export, import, and wholesale seafood. While they face common challenges due to globalization, shrimpers in the United States and Vietnam have been affected by the challenges in different ways and have pursued varied coping strategies. A policy for their mutual benefit could include higher and more stable international shrimp prices to reconcile the needs of producers with the operations of the global seafood industry.

Indeed, biotechnology has provided impressive responses to these and other challenges. One particularly spectacular aspect of biotechnology is **biopharming,** in which genes from other life forms (plant, animal, fungal, bacterial, or human) are inserted into host plants. In essence, this is bioengineering plants so that they produce pharmaceuticals for treating illnesses ranging from diarrhea to cancer. Quebec-based Medicago, for example, is trying to speed up the production of flu vaccines by using tobacco plants as "breeders" for the required proteins. Pharma crops are still in the experimental stage, and the research is highly confidential. In the U.S., it is estimated that there are over 400 pharma crops currently at the experimental stage, with many of them being anonymously field tested in open-air settings **(Figure 8.15).** One of the expected benefits is lower costs of medication, though it is too soon to tell how this decrease might work in practice. The major disadvantage

seen by farmers is that only a small part of the price of the pharma crops is expected to come to them.

While the pharma sector of biotechnology is still in an experimental stage, other aspects of biotechnological research are already fully developed. "Super plants" produce their own fertilizers and pesticides and can be grown on nutrient-lacking soils. Additionally, biotechnologists have been able to clone plants, taking tissue cells from one plant and using them to grow new plants. A tissue culture no more than 1 cubic cm in size has the potential to produce millions of identical plants. Such a procedure has decreased the time needed to grow mature plants ready for reproduction.

While such technological innovations can seem miraculous, there is a downside to biotechnological solutions to agricultural problems. For example, cloned plants are more susceptible to disease than natural ones, which leads to an increasing need for

FIGURE 8.15 Biopharma map of the United States This map shows the number of plantings of genetically engineered pharmaceutical and industrial (pharma) crops approved by the U.S. Department of Agriculture (USDA) in individual states. Since 1991, the USDA has approved more than 100 and perhaps as many as 200 or more applications to grow pharma crops in the United States. The totals on the map (395) are more than the number of applications (100–200) because a single application may include plantings of pharma crops in more than one state. (*Source:* Pharma crop approvals in the United States map. Copyright © Union of Concerned Scientists, www.ucsusa.org. Reprinted with permission.)

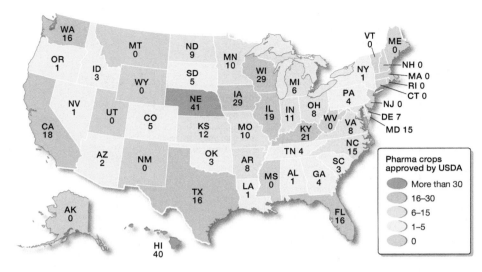

chemical treatment. And while industry may reap economic benefits from the development and wide use of tissue cultures, farmers may suffer because they lack the capital or the knowledge to participate in biotechnological applications.

Biotechnology has truly revolutionized traditional agriculture. Its proponents argue that it provides a new pathway to sustainable production. By streamlining the growth process with such innovations as tissue cultures, disease- and pest-resistant and fertilizer-independent plants, optimists believe that the Biorevolution can maximize global agricultural production to keep up with requirements of population and demand. Moreover, the intensification of agriculture, which the Biorevolution (along with the Green and Blue Revolutions) enables, has reduced the risk that increased

forest resources will be converted into agricultural land. The **Borlaug hypothesis** (named after Norman Borlaug, the force behind the Green Revolution), states that because global food demand is on the rise, restricting crop usage to traditional low-yield methods (such as organic farming) requires either the world population to decrease or the further conversion of forest land into cropland. There is no sign that world population is on the decline, but the hypothesis—which is controversial—proposes that high-yield biotechnologicial techniques will ultimately save forest ecosystems from destruction.

Just as with the Green Revolution, however, biotechnology may have ill effects on peripheral countries (and on poor labourers and small farmers in core countries). **Table 8-1** compares the

TABLE 8-1 Biorevolution Compared with Green Revolution

Characteristics	Green Revolution	Biorevolution
Crops affected	Wheat, rice, maize	Potentially all crops, including vegetables, fruits, agro-export crops, and specialty crops
Other sectors affected	Pesticides, fertilizer, energy, seeds, and irrigation	Pesticides, animal products, pharmaceuticals, processed food products, energy, mining, warfare
Territories affected	Developing countries	All areas, all nations, all locations, including marginal lands
Development of technology and dissemination	Largely public or quasi-public sector, international agricultural research centres (IARCs); R&D millions of dollars	Largely private sector, especially corporations; R&D billions of dollars
Proprietary considerations	Plant breeders' rights and patents generally not relevant	Genes, cells, plants, and animals patentable as well as the techniques used to produce them
Capital costs of research	Relatively low	Relatively high for some techniques; relatively low for others
Access to information	Relatively easy, due to the public funding of research and development	Restricted due to privatization and proprietary considerations
Research skills required	Conventional plant breeding and parallel agricultural sciences	Molecular and cell biology expertise as well as conventional plant-breeding skills
Crop vulnerability	High-yielding varieties relatively uniform; high vulnerability	Tissue-culture crop propagation produces exact genetic copies; even more vulnerability
Side effects	Increased monoculture and use of farm chemicals, marginalization of small farmer, ecological degradation. Increased foreign debt due to decrease in biomass fuels and the increasing reliance on costly, usually imported, petroleum.	Crop substitution replacing periphery exports; herbicide tolerance; increasing use of chemicals; engineered organisms might affect environment; further marginalization of small farmer

(*Source:* Adapted from M. Kenney and F. Buttel, "Biotechnology: Prospects and Dilemmas for Third-World Development," *Development and Change 16*, 1995, p. 70, and H. Hobbelink, *Biotechnology and the Future of World Agriculture: The Fourth Resource.* London: Red Books, 1991.)

In fact, what many of these indebted farmers do out of sheer desperation is commit suicide. In 2009 alone, the most recent year for which official figures are available, 17 638 farmers committed suicide—one farmer every 30 minutes. Over the past 16 years, a quarter of a million Indian farmers have committed suicide, making this the largest wave of recorded suicides in human history. The bottom line is that global agricultural transformations are far from benign and it will require an enormous amount of political co-operation, as underscored in the chapter-opening vignette, to begin to address their profound effect.

> **APPLY YOUR KNOWLEDGE** The industrialization of agriculture has had negative effects on traditional farmers across the globe, including Canada. Read the analysis of the 2011 Census of Agriculture, released online by Statistics Canada, and assess the changes that Canadian family farms have experienced over the past few decades. How do these changes reflect the mechanisms you have just read about? Who ultimately benefits from the changes? ∎

FIGURE 8.16 Workers in a coffee plantation For many peripheral countries, the production of cash crops has been a way to boost exports and bring in needed income for the national economy. But transformations in agriculture are making it possible to grow various crops outside of their normal soil, water, and temperature requirements. This makes it difficult for peripheral countries to maintain a foothold in global cash-crop production. In Kenya, coffee has for decades been a cash crop grown for export. Luxury exports such as coffee generate some of the capital needed to import staple foods such as wheat. (*Source:* WorldFoto/Alamy)

impacts of the Biorevolution and the Green Revolution on various aspects of global agricultural production. For example, biotechnology has enabled the development of plants that can be grown outside of their natural or currently most suitable environment. Yet location-specific cash crops are critical to the economic stability of many peripheral nations—such as cotton in India, bananas in Central America and the Caribbean, sugar in Cuba, and coffee in Kenya, Colombia, and Ethiopia **(Figure 8.16)**. These and other export crops are threatened by the development of alternative sites of production or by multinational agricultural corporations entering foreign markets. Transformations in agriculture have ripple effects throughout the world-system.

A tragic story of the impact of foreign multinationals on domestic cash-crop producers centres around cotton farmers in India. In 2011, the New York University School of Law Human Rights and Global Justice Center released a report called *Every Thirty Minutes: Farmer Suicides, Human Rights and the Agrarian Crisis in India.* The report states

> Economic reforms and the opening of Indian agriculture to the global market over the past two decades have increased costs, while reducing yields and profits for many farmers, to the point of great financial and emotional distress. As a result, smallholder farmers are often trapped in a cycle of debt. During a bad year, money from the sale of the cotton crop might not cover even the initial cost of the inputs, let alone suffice to pay the usurious interest on loans or provide adequate food or necessities for the family. The only way out might be to take on more loans and buy more inputs, which in turn can lead to even greater debt.

GLOBAL CHANGE IN FOOD PRODUCTION AND CONSUMPTION

When geographers talk about the globalization of agriculture, they are referring to the incorporation of agriculture into the world economic system of capitalism. A useful way to think about the term **globalized agriculture** is to recognize that, as both an economic sector and a geographically distributed activity, modern agriculture is increasingly dependent on an economy and set of regulatory practices that are global in scope and organization.

Forces of Globalization

Several forces, institutions, and organizational forms play a role in the globalization of agriculture. Technology, economics, and politics have played a central role in propelling national and regional agricultural systems into becoming global in scope. One important way these forces of change have been harnessed is through new global institutions, especially trade and financial organizations. The result is an integrated, globally organized, agro-production system.

The globalization of agriculture has dramatically changed relationships among and within different agricultural production systems. Important outcomes of these changed relationships have been the elimination of some forms of agriculture and the erosion or alteration of some systems as they become integrated into the global economy. Two examples include the current decline of traditional agricultural practices, such as shifting cultivation in the periphery, and the erosion of national agricultural systems based on family farms in the core. (See Box 8.3, "Geography Matters: The Canadian Farm.")

The Canadian Farm

The European settlement of Canada is intricately connected with the agricultural potential of this country, which in turn is limited by large tracts of mountainous terrain, glacial erosion, and the harsh northern climate. It is therefore not surprising that we find most of Canada's population and most of its productive agricultural land within 200 kilometres of the American border. This thin strip of occupied land, or *ecumene*, represents only 7 percent of the country's total land area. It lies overwhelmingly in the Prairie provinces (Saskatchewan: 39 percent; Alberta: 31 percent; Manitoba: 11 percent), with only 8 percent in Ontario, 5 percent in Quebec, 4 percent in British Columbia, and mere fractions of a percent in the Atlantic provinces (**Figure 8.H**).

The 2011 Census of Agriculture counted a total of 205 730 farms.[2] The largest number is found in Ontario (51 950), followed by Alberta (43 234), Saskatchewan (36 952), and Quebec (29 437). In terms of average farm size, however, the largest farms are located in the Prairies—between 500 and 800 hectares—with farms elsewhere averaging around 150 hectares. Regardless of size, the public perception of farming in Canada is still associated strongly with the family farm (**Figure 8.I**). However, in the course of the third agricultural revolution, the number of family farms in Canada and other core countries has declined dramatically as more corporate forms of farming have emerged. In 1931, about one in three Canadians lived on a farm; today, that number is one in 46 (**Figure 8.J**). And with every year, that decline is accelerating: in the past five years alone, one in ten farmers gave up. Over the same period, the average farm size has gone up; obviously, farming is becoming increasingly consolidated.

Several factors are fuelling this consolidation, some of which are directly connected to the process of globalization:

- *Farm polarization.* In an increasingly global market, many family farms are simply too small to compete because they

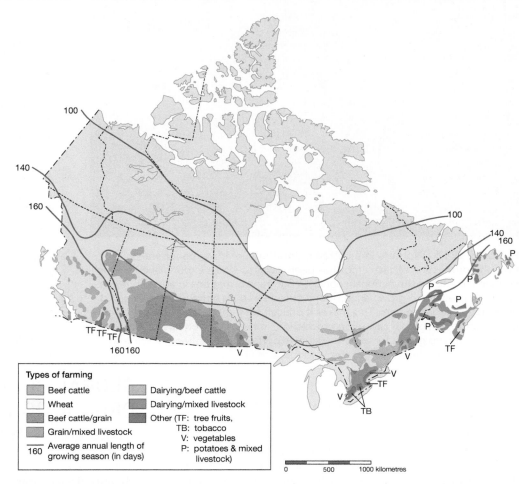

FIGURE 8.H The agricultural regions of Canada This map shows the limited total area of land farmed in Canada, its concentration along the U.S. border, and its division into two major agricultural systems (the Prairies, and Ontario–Quebec). Specialty crops (such as grape vines in British Columbia's Okanagan region and apples in Nova Scotia's Annapolis Valley) can also be seen. (*Source:* Geoffrey J. Matthews and Robert Morrow, *Canada and the World: An Atlas Resource*, 2nd ed. Scarborough: Prentice Hall, 1995, pp. 33–34.)

cannot take advantage of the economies of scale of production. As they give up, they are swallowed by larger farms (**Figure 8.K**). This leads to a polarization of Canadian agriculture in which large farms clearly dominate: a mere 5 percent of Canada's farmers now produce half of the country's total agricultural output. Meanwhile, the only way for smaller farms to survive is to seek out niche markets such as organic foods and specialty crops (**Figure 8.L**), or alternative land uses (**Figure 8.M**).

- *Subsidies.* The increasing liberalization of international trade under such institutions as the World Trade Organization (WTO) and the North American Free Trade Agreement (NAFTA) requires the elimination of domestic subsidies as a way of promoting fairer competition and more open access to the markets of other countries. For Canadian farmers, the

[2]See the 2011 Census of Agriculture on the website of Statistics Canada (www.statcan.gc.ca/ca-ra2011/index-eng.htm). Government policy documents and backgrounders can be found on the website of Agriculture and Agri-Food Canada, the federal government ministry responsible for agriculture, at www.agr.gc.ca.

FIGURE 8.I A "typical" Canadian family farm The drastic decline in the Canadian farm population has caused some commentators to observe that the "typical" family farm is now just a myth because so many of them have been bought out by larger corporations or have become incorporated themselves. The local food movement, however, has begun to reinvigorate small-scale farming near urban centres. (*Source:* M. Imort)

FIGURE 8.J Abandoned farm on Manitoulin Island, Ontario Over the past century, Canadian agriculture has changed dramatically as farms were forced to compete in a globalizing food market. For many farms on marginal soils of the Canadian interior that proved impossible, and they were abandoned. As a consequence, many rural areas now have a lower population density than at the turn of the twentieth century. (*Source:* M. Imort)

loss of subsidies has exacerbated the long-running decline in overall farm income. Twenty-five years ago, more than a third of Canadian farm income came from government subsidies; today, that share is a mere 14 percent.

■ *The "cash squeeze."* On the other side of the ledger, farm inputs (such as fertilizers, pesticides, seed, farm machinery, land, labour, and financing) are continuing to increase in cost. In spite of higher producer prices for agricultural products

(Continued)

FIGURE 8.K Farm consolidation near Redvers, Saskatchewan A frequent sight on the Prairies, but increasingly also in other parts of Canada, is that of abandoned farm buildings surrounded by actively farmed fields: as one farm gives up, its land is bought or leased by a surviving one.

(*Source:* Courtesy of Alan E. Nash)

FIGURE 8.L A field of ginseng near Lillooet, British Columbia One of the new developments in farming is to grow organic or niche-market crops. In this case, the demand for herbal products in Canada and abroad has supported the expansion of ginseng cultivation, a high-value crop that is grown under a protective black net.

(*Source:* Courtesy of Alan E. Nash)

over the past few years, balancing cost and revenue remains a challenge for many small farms. Larger farms, meanwhile, have easier access to the necessary capital: more than one-third of the total farm receipts accrue to only 1.6 percent of all farms.

- *Demographics.* Canada's farming population is aging even faster than the general population: half of all farm operators are older than 55 years of age. Beyond the effects of the aging

baby boom, this also indicates a larger problem with passing farms on to the next generation as fewer young people want (or feel that it is possible) to earn their livelihood by farming. Already half of all farmers have to seek off-farm employment to make ends meet—20 percent even work full-time.

Small or large, all Canadian farms must adapt to the changing market for which they ultimately produce. What follows are just some of the most important changes over the past decade. To

FIGURE 8.M From tobacco farm to wind farm As markets for agricultural products change, so must farmers. This photo was taken in southwestern Ontario's former "Tobacco Belt" and shows the now obsolete tobacco drying sheds once typical for this area. The wind-prone location on the north shore of Lake Erie made it possible for this farmer to lease out her land to renewable energy producers. Tobacco farmers further inland are converting to ginseng and other high-value crops. (*Source:* M. Imort)

begin with, declining consumer demand has caused a 20 percent decline in beef and pork production. Meanwhile, cash crops such as canola and soybeans are expanding: in Prince Edward Island, soybeans and potatoes now cover almost the same acreage. The growing demand for year-round vegetables has expanded the greenhouse area, and certified organic operations have doubled their share to 2 percent of all farms. Most dramatic, however, is the expansion of some so-called "super foods": acreage of blueberries and cranberries has doubled.

Finally, Canadian farming is not just an occupation; it is a way of life. Changes in Canadian agriculture also have effects on a host of other sectors from school enrolment and health care infrastructure to the opportunities for rural residents to age in place. Among the most pressing problems in rural Canada (from a

policy-maker's perspective) are the decline of the socioeconomic infrastructure in these areas and the emigration of the young—both factors that erode an area's ability to sustain itself. The Social Sciences and Humanities Research Council (SSHRC) has funded 15 university researchers to examine how Canada can rebuild capacity in rural areas. Using 32 research sites, the project (known as the New Rural Economy or NRE) explores how we can develop enhanced political institutions, improve service delivery, better manage natural resources, and increase communications in rural centres.[3]

[3]The website for the New Rural Economy (NRE2) project is at http://nre.concordia.ca/nre2.htm.

Agriculture is one part of a complex and interrelated worldwide economic system. Important changes in the wider economy—whether technological, social, political, or otherwise—affect all sectors, including agriculture. National problems in agriculture, such as production surpluses, soil erosion, and food price stability, affect other economic sectors globally, nationally, and locally in different ways. The same is true of global factors—such as the price and availability of oil and other petroleum products critical to commercialized agriculture, the stability of the U.S. dollar in the world currency market, and recessions or inflation.

Because of the systemic impact of many problems, integration and coordination of the global economy is needed to anticipate or respond to them. In the past several decades, global and international coordination efforts among states have occurred. These include policies advanced by the World Trade Organization (WTO), various free trade zones, as well as the formation of supranational economic organizations such as the European Union (EU) and the Association of Southeast Asian Nations (ASEAN).

It is important to point out, however, that these new forms of co-operation have their opponents. African activists have been involved in frequent and sustained protests against the involvement of European Union companies in biofuel farming there (which we describe in more detail in the material that follows). Similarly, Indian tribal women in the state of Orissa have been involved for several years in a campaign to prevent foreign and national companies from planting genetically modified (GM) crops. Exhibiting 500 indigenous rice varieties, women argued before the state assembly that the government would put at risk this rich array of rice species if genetically modified organisms entered the region. These and many other protests across the globe demonstrate that the global transformation of agriculture faces resistance.

At the same time that supranational organizations and coordination efforts have been addressing global food problems, states continue to be essential in mediating crises at national levels. By

changing public policy, states attempt to regulate agro-industries in order to maintain production, consumption, and corporate profits. One way that governments try to maintain the profitability of the agricultural sector while keeping food prices affordable is through direct and indirect subsidies to agricultural producers. For example, governments subsidize agriculture by paying farmers not to grow certain crops that are expected to be in excess supply, or by buying up surplus supplies and guaranteeing a fixed price for them. Billions of dollars are paid out each year in agricultural subsidies, the effects of which are complex and global in impact. Government efforts, while perhaps stabilizing agricultural production in the short term, can lead to problems within the larger national and international agricultural system. For instance, guaranteeing a fixed price for surplus food rarely prompts producers to lower their production, so the problem of overproduction continues. Once in possession of the surplus, governments must then destroy it, or sell it, or donate it to foreign countries, where the "dumping" of cheap foodstuffs may undermine the ability of local producers to compete.

Many states in the less-developed world also subsidize the price of food in the marketplace. Such policies are meant to keep the workforce well fed and healthy, as well as to avoid problems of civil unrest should food prices exceed the general population's ability to pay. Nineteenth-century bread riots—a response to the high cost of flour and bread—were a common occurrence in Europe. More recently, the toppling of Haiti's government in 2009 followed extensive protests by the population over high food prices.

For years, bread subsidies were the norm across the Middle East, used as a way of placating the population. But in 2011 in Tunisia, civil unrest was predicated in part on the high cost of food because national grain subsidies had not kept pace with soaring prices. It is important to keep in mind that the revolution in Tunisia was about more than just bread. Basic human rights are the most pressing demands across the Middle East from Tunisia to Yemen. When a government fails to provide those rights for the majority of

FIGURE 8.17 Demonstrators in Yemen holding up bread
In the spring of 2011 the protesters in Sanaa, Yemen, used bread
as a way to express their discontent with their government. On
the bread is written the word "Leave" in Arabic demanding the
resignation of Yemeni President Ali Abdullah Saleh. The example
reminds us that food has a political dimension, too. (Source: Muhammed
Muheisen/AP Images)

its citizens, instead using handouts or subsidies as a substitute for
democratic or economic reforms, bread becomes a powerful symbol of all these citizens lack. In Yemen, demonstrators baked loaves
of bread that spelled out the command "leave" in Arabic. The message they were sending is that the very commodity that the regime
has used to ensure obedience has now become a symbol and source
of defiance **(Figure 8.17)**.[4]

> **APPLY YOUR KNOWLEDGE** Research agricultural
> subsidies in Canada. Which producers (grain, dairy,
> etc.) receive the most subsidies? How are they jus-
> tified in the documents you read? Compare the
> Canadian data with that of two other countries—one
> from the periphery and one from the core. What
> impacts might these government subsidies have on
> the agriculture sector of peripheral nations? ▪

The Organization of the Agro-Food System

Although the changes that have occurred in agriculture worldwide
are complex, certain elements that serve as important indicators of
change can help us understand them. Geographers and other scholars interested in contemporary agriculture have noted three prominent and interconnected forces that signal a dramatic departure

from previous forms of agricultural practice: agribusiness, food
chains, and integration of agriculture with the manufacturing, service, finance, and trade sectors.

The concept of agribusiness has received a good deal of attention in the past three decades, and in the popular mind it has come
to be associated with large corporations, such as ConAgra or
DelMonte. Our definition of agribusiness departs from this conceptualization. Although multi- and transnational corporations
(TNCs) are certainly involved in agribusiness, **agribusiness** is a
system rather than a kind of corporate entity. It is a set of economic
and political relationships that organizes food production from the
development of seeds to the retailing and consumption of the agricultural product. Defining agribusiness as a system does not mean
that corporations are not critically important to the food production
process. In the core economies, the transnational corporation is the
dominant player, operating at numerous strategically important
stages of the food production process. TNCs have become dominant for a number of reasons, but mostly because of their ability to
negotiate the complexities of production and distribution in many
geographical locations. That capability requires special knowledge
of national, regional, and local regulations and pricing factors.

The concept of a food supply chain (a special type of commodity chain; see Chapter 2) is a way to understand the organizational
structure of agribusiness as a complex political and economic system of inputs, processing and manufacturing, and outputs. A **food
supply chain** is composed of five central and connected sectors
(inputs, production, processing, distribution, and consumption)
with four contextual elements acting as external mediating forces
(the state, international trade, the physical environment, and credit
and finance). **Figure 8.18** illustrates these linkages and relationships, including how state farm policies shape inputs, prices, farm
structure, and even the physical environment.

The food supply chain concept illustrates the network of connections among producers and consumers and regions and places.
Consider for example, the linkages that connect cattle production
in the Amazon and Mexico, the processing of canned beef along the
United States–Mexico border, the availability of frozen hamburger
patties in core grocery stores, and the construction of McDonald's
restaurants in Moscow **(Figure 8.19)**. Because of complex food
chains such as this, it is now common to find that traditional agricultural practices in peripheral regions have been displaced by
expensive, capital-intensive practices.

That agriculture is not an independent or unique economic
activity is not a particularly new realization. Beginning with the
second agricultural revolution, agriculture began slowly but inex-
orably to be transformed by industrial practices. What is different
about the current state of the food system is the way in which farming has become just one stage of a complex and multidimensional
economic process. This process is as much about distribution and
marketing—key elements of the service sector—as it is about growing and processing agricultural products.

Food Regimes and Alternative Food Movements

A **food regime** is a specific set of links that exist between food production and consumption. Like the agricultural revolutions already
described, food regimes emerge during key historical periods, when

[4]Annia Ciezaldo, "Let Them Eat Bread: How Food Subsidies Prevent (and
Provoke) Revolutions in the Middle East," *Foreign Affairs* (online), March 23, 2011,
http://www.foreignaffairs.com/articles/67672/annia-ciezadlo/let-them-eat-bread.

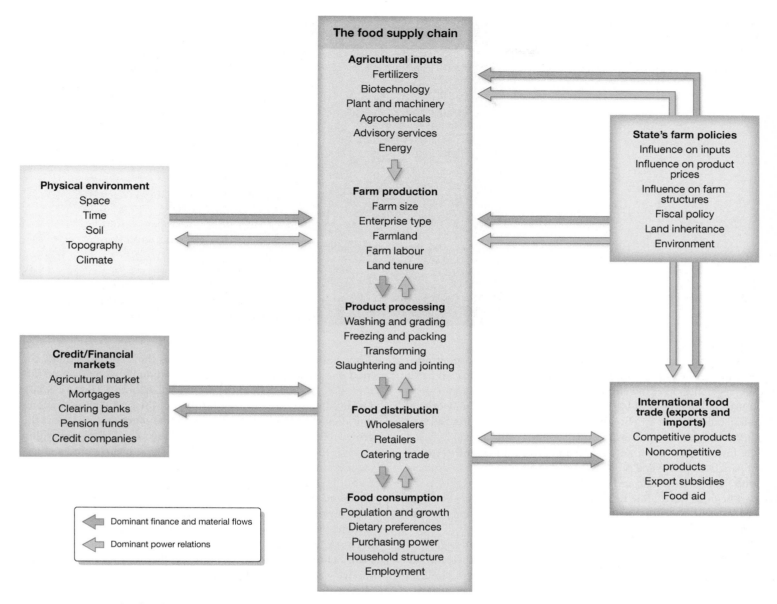

FIGURE 8.18 The food supply chain The production of food has been transformed by industrialization into a complex system that comprises distinctly separate and hierarchically organized sectors. Mediating forces (the state, the structure and processes of international trade, credit and finance arrangements, and the physical environment) influence how the system operates at all scales of social and geographical resolution. (*Source:* After I. Bowler [ed.], *The Geography of Agriculture in Developed Market Economies.* New York: J. Wiley & Sons, 1992, p. 12.)

different cultural, political, and economic forces are in operation. In contrast to a food chain, which describes the network within which specific food items are produced, manufactured, and marketed, a food regime indicates the ways a particular type of food item is dominant during a specific time period. Although hundreds of food chains may be in operation at any one time, agricultural researchers believe that only one food regime dominates each particular period.

During the decades surrounding the turn of the nineteenth century, an independent system of nation-states emerged and colonization expanded. (See Chapters 2 and 9.) At the same time, the industrialization of agriculture began. These two forces of political and economic change were critical to the fostering of the first food regime, in which colonies became important sources of exportable foodstuffs by supplying the industrializing European states with

cheap food in the form of wheat and meat. The expansion of the colonial agriculture sectors, however, created a crisis in production back in Europe. The crisis stemmed from the higher cost efficiency of colonial food production, which undercut the prices of European-produced food, put domestic agricultural workers out of work, and forced members of the agricultural sector in Europe to improve cost efficiency. The development of industrialized agriculture in Europe helped drive down operating costs and restabilized the sector (reducing even more the need for farm workers). This movement toward the integration of agriculture and industry is also referred to as agro-industrialization.

A wheat and livestock food regime characterized global agriculture until the 1960s; researchers believe that a fresh fruit and vegetable regime is currently dominant. This new pattern of food

FIGURE 8.19 World's largest cattle feedlot This feedlot near Greeley, Colorado, is a subsidiary of the food giant ConAgra. It holds 120 000 head of cattle.

(*Source:* Collection10/GlowImages/Alamy)

consumption and production has been called the "postmodern diet." The more perishable agro-commodities of fresh fruits and vegetables have become central to diets of people in the core. Integrated networks of food chains, using integrated networks of refrigeration systems, deliver fresh fruits and vegetables from all over the world to Western Europe, North America, and Japan. Echoing the former food networks that characterized nineteenth-century imperialism, peripheral production systems supply core consumers with fresh, often exotic and off-season, produce. Consumers in the core regions have come to expect the full range of fruits and vegetables to be available year-round, and unusual and exotic produce has become increasingly popular.

Alongside the emergence of a core-oriented food regime of fresh fruits and vegetables, it is important to note an additional aspect of food production practices that has been taking hold in core regions over the past 25 years and accelerating especially over the past decade. One goal of sustainability in agriculture has been increased commitment to organic crops—both proteins (such as beef, eggs, soy) and produce (fruits and vegetables). **Organic farming** describes farming or animal husbandry that occurs without the use of commercial fertilizers, synthetic pesticides, or growth hormones. It is important to point out that organic food production is not the primary mode of practice, but rather that it has become a growing force alongside the dominant **conventional farming** (an approach that uses chemicals in the form of plant protectants and fertilizers and intensive, hormone-based practices to breed and raise animals) **(Table 8-2)**. We discuss issues of food safety in more detail later in the chapter, but safety issues as well as overall health concerns and an evolving commitment to food as a gastronomic experience, among mostly white, middle-class households, is at the centre of a number of alternative movements that are driving organically produced food as well as the local food and slow food movements.

Local food is often also organically grown, and its designation as local means that it is produced within a fairly limited distance from where it is consumed—usually 100 miles (160 kilometres).

Thus, if one is a "locavore" or follows the "100-mile diet," the food one consumes should be produced on farms that are no further than 100 miles from the point of distribution **(Figure 8.20)**. Local food movements have resulted in the proliferation of communities of individuals who have joined together to support the growth of new farms within the local "food shed" (the area within the 100-mile radius). These individuals have been behind a movement known as Community Supported Agriculture. **Community Supported Agriculture (CSA)** operates by collecting subscriptions and then paying a farmer up front to grow food locally for CSA members for a season or a specified time frame. The farmer is then able to purchase seeds, hire workers, cultivate produce and livestock, and deliver the harvest without relying on interest-bearing loans. The CSA members, in return for their investment in the farm, receive weekly shares of produce (and sometimes meats, eggs and cheese, flowers, and milk) that reflect the season and local growing conditions.

CSA farmers are expected to grow their food organically, and members accept what the farmers grow at the same time that they assume the financial risks that are part of the vagaries of any agricultural enterprise. CSA farms are usually small, independent, and labour-intensive. The CSA movement is seen to be helping to restore family farms to the national landscapes from which they have been disappearing for 40 years as more corporate forms of farming have taken hold. The CSA movement originated in Japan but has spread to other core regions, including North America and Europe. In addition to the emergence of CSA, it is important to note that urban agriculture is also on the rise. (See Box 8.4 "Visualizing Geography: The Growth of Urban Agriculture.")

Europe has contributed its own focus to alternative food production and consumption through the slow food movement. **Slow food** (see Chapter 6), as the name suggests, is an attempt to resist fast food by preserving the cultural cuisine and the associated food and farming of an ecoregion. The movement was started in Italy in the mid-1980s and there are now over 85 000 chapters (known as *convivia*) worldwide.

TABLE 8-2 Conventional vs. Alternative Food

Conventional	Alternative
Cheap food to most of the Western world, where the amount of money spent on food in the household budget has steadily decreased	Logic of sustainable development, not mass production
Quantity over quality where agriculture is part of consumption; food is a commodity like any other.	The idea of (real or idealized) "quality" predominates—expressed in such parameters as farmers' markets, CSA, free-range, organic, not genetically modified, integrated pest-management schemes, authenticity, traceability.
Fast, convenient foods: for nutritionists, the year 2000 was significant since it was the first time the number of overweight people matched the number of undernourished people—at 1.1 billion.	Slow, pleasurable food and consumers with an ethical consciousness; a new moral economy surfaces where issues of provenance take a central role and consumers demand knowledge of where their food comes from, whether it contains additives, and whether pesticides were used in production.
"Hard Power"—retailer-led supply chains, emasculation of primary producers as supermarkets drive down costs to below that of even production.	"Soft Power"—food sells itself through ethical persuasion and the new "moral economy."
Corporate capital, combined with science and technology enable large-scale food processing and a reliance on large retailers—at the expense of small, independent farms.	Social, as opposed to corporate capital; direct farmer-to-consumer interaction, relational, trust-based, sense of "community," and attempts to restore small farm enterprises
Food is "liberated" from nature; technological fixes predominate.	Food is relocated in specific ecological niches and the externalized costs of the conventional system—such as soil degradation, water pollution, animal welfare issues, and health care costs—are addressed.
Logic of deterritorialization—where geographies are a result of the intensification and stretching of the links and networks between production and consumption	Logic of reterritorialization—where geographies are shaped by the resurgence of local and regional practices as central forces in new articulations of production and consumption
Geographic specialization, monoculture, and spatial homogenization in North America and Europe produce a large quantity of standardized products.	The "local" as a set of social networks and cultural contexts that are harnessed in place—which provide the foundation for development, innovation, and economic relations
Placeless landscape of food production (U.K., U.S.) versus place-based landscapes (France, Italy)—where region-specific foods are much more prevalent and provenance is understood as a selling point	Transparent food chain, traceable, where producers attempt to regain power against the conventional price-driven "race to the bottom" and consumers' knowledge of provenance helps produce local networks and promotion of social capital

FIGURE 8.20 Local food advertisement Large chain grocery stores in core countries are becoming increasingly involved in marketing produce, and even processed foods, generated in the local area. Much of this increase is the result of consumer demand. (*Source:* Toby Talbot/AP Images)

Although most people think of agriculture as a rural activity, urban agriculture made possible the emergence of the world's first cities. Until recently, however, urban agriculture was largely ignored in the development of urban economic policies, apparently because produce generated from it was seen as belonging to the informal sector of the local economy and not significant in terms of income-generating potential. Most definitions of **urban agriculture** focus on the establishment or performance of agricultural practices in or near an urban or city-like setting. On the urban fringes, it is known as **peri-urban agriculture**. In countries like China, official policies have long recognized, and even fostered, urban and peri-urban agricultural practices. In many core countries, however, particularly since the Industrial Revolution, urban agriculture has been officially discouraged or made difficult as arable land has been used for real estate development or seriously degraded through industrial processes.

Whether encouraged or discouraged by official policy, urban residents across the globe are increasing their participation in growing crops and raising livestock, for reasons as diverse as food security, income production, taste, and health concerns. A recent publication by the Food and Agricultural Organization of the United Nations has estimated that 800 million people are actively engaged in urban agriculture around the world. And 200 million of these produce goods for market sale. One-half of the vegetables consumed in Havana, Cuba, are grown in the city's farms and gardens. Singapore has 10 000 urban farmers who produce 80 percent of the city's poultry and 25 percent of its vegetables. Currently, 14 percent of Londoners and 44 percent of Vancouver's residents grow some food in their gardens. Most official discussions of urban agriculture indicate that it is primarily engaged in by poor households where people often go hungry for days, although not necessarily the poorest of people participate since those individuals often lack access to land (**Figure 8.N**).

Throughout the core, urban agriculture is often seen as a leisure activity that helps supplement the routine purchase of commercial foodstuffs. Increasingly, however, urban agriculture, in the form of community and school gardens has become a way to improve the diets of low-income adults and children by enabling them to have easy access to fresh, healthy fruits and vegetables and, in some cases, poultry and even beef, pork, and fish (through aquaculture). Detroit, for instance, has experienced a dramatic growth in urban agriculture and provides an interesting case of how poverty in rich countries like the United States is being partly addressed by providing low-income individuals with the skills and the resources they need to grow, and sometimes sell, their own fresh produce (**Figure 8.O**).

Urban Farming is a not-for-profit organization that emerged in Detroit and has gone on to develop community gardens in most major cities in the United States as well as some areas abroad. Starting with three gardens in 2005, Urban Farming now has over 50 000 community, residential, and partner gardens that provide free food for the community. The mission of Urban Farming is "to create an abundance of food for people in need by planting, supporting and encouraging the establishment of gardens on unused land and space while increasing diversity, raising awareness for health and wellness, inspiring and educating youth, adults and seniors to create an economically sustainable system to uplift communities around the globe."[5]

There are many local organizations in most major North American cities and large towns that are involved in reclaiming unused land for urban food production. Within Detroit the Garden Resource Program, a consortium of organizations that began in 2003, helps support 875 urban gardens and farms in the metropolitan area (**Figure 8.P**). In New York City, where open space is at a premium, organizations such as schools and co-operatives have even transformed their rooftops into gardens. Teachers use the gardens not only to inform their students about soil quality, crop production, irrigation systems, and other aspects of successful gardening, they also use the gardens to teach about food security, food cultures, the importance of co-operation, and the satisfaction of seeing a challenging goal come to fruition. And gardening has also been taken up on university campuses, where students interested in sustainable practices have convinced university officials to give over land to university community gardens.

Although urban agriculture is a growing movement in core countries, it is in the periphery where it more often is an important means of economic and personal survival. As wage cuts, inflation, job loss, civil strife, and natural disasters become more frequent, urban agriculture in the periphery has become a way to address

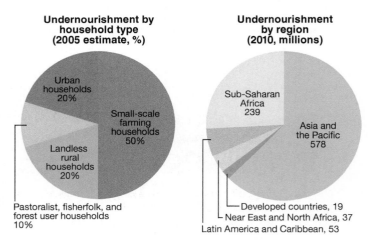

Undernourishment by household type (2005 estimate, %)

- Urban households 20%
- Small-scale farming households 50%
- Landless rural households 20%
- Pastoralist, fisherfolk, and forest user households 10%

Undernourishment by region (2010, millions)

- Sub-Saharan Africa 239
- Asia and the Pacific 578
- Developed countries, 19
- Near East and North Africa, 37
- Latin America and Caribbean, 53

FIGURE 8.N Where the hungry people are Most of the hungry people are in rural areas in developing countries. But as this graph also makes clear, one-fifth of households that contain undernourished individuals are located in cities. Urban hunger is as real as rural hunger, despite the availability of food in urban markets. (*Source:* The material on page 32 , from Figure 17: Where are the hungry people?, In Growing a Better Future: Food justice in a resource-constrained world, Robert Bailey (2011) is reproduced with the permission of Oxfam GB, Oxfam House, John Smith Drive, Cowley, Oxford OX4 2JY, UK www.oxfam.org.uk. Oxfam GB does not necessarily endorse any text or activities that accompany the materials.)

[5]Web site: http://www.urbanfarming.org/, accessed June 6, 2011.

FIGURE 8.O Urban gardening movement in Detroit, Michigan Pictured at the left are members of a Detroit neighbourhood who have converted land close to their homes into a community garden. Pictured below is an Urban Farming community garden. (*Source:* Jim West / Alamy [left] Courtesy ROAR [right])

FIGURE 8.P Detroit is growing greener This oblique aerial image shows metropolitan Detroit to the north of the Detroit River and Windsor, Ontario, to the south. (In this view, north is up.) In this shortwave infrared image, barren or built-up areas appear red to pink, vegetation appears green, and water is dark blue. (*Source:* NASA)

FIGURE 8.Q Urban rooftop gardens in China The green rooftop of a residential building in Chongqing, southwest China, is shown here. Many apartment dwellers here in Chongqing make full use of the space on the rooftops, where gardens include green plants, flowers, and vegetables. With inflation squeezing the income of Chinese people, many residents grow vegetables to combat rising commodity prices. (*Source:* Redux Pictures)

food insecurity (Figure 8.Q). This can occur in a number of ways. At the household level, urban agriculture can provide income through the sale of produce at markets. It also provides family members with more nutritionally rich foods and a more diverse diet. Further, urban agriculture can help stabilize household food consumption against temporary shortages due to layoffs or loss of family member's income due to illness.

(Continued)

As we will discuss in Chapter 10, urban populations throughout the world are growing more than twice as fast as rural populations. According to the UN Centre for Human Settlements, half of the world's population now lives in cities. And as development experts seek ways of maintaining economic growth without destroying the environment, urban agriculture has increasingly drawn their attention as a way of making cities sustainable. Proponents of urban agriculture contend that it should not be understood as an alternative to conventional agriculture but rather as a supplementary branch of modern agricultural systems. For most development experts, an ideal urban agricultural system would incorporate various elements of modern, sustainable agriculture based on reusable, self-contained waste and nutrient cycles through resource conservation and management based on nonchemical fertilizers and pest-management techniques.

It is important to recognize that urban agriculture cannot solve the world's food-security problems. For example, small urban gardens will not replace agribusiness as the primary players in the global food system. Moreover, there are legitimate health concerns surrounding urban agriculture, particularly in terms of recycling urban waste water into agricultural inputs. While health concerns about urban agricultural practices should not be taken lightly, there is evidence that they are far outweighed by the current and potential benefits of urban agriculture. Particularly in developing countries and poorer inner-city neighbourhoods throughout the world, urban agriculture can be crucial to a family's survival and is certainly a boost to its overall health.

Although slow food, local food and CSAs, and organic and ecologically sustainable agricultural practices are movements that signal a shift in food production and consumption, they in no way are challenging the dominance of more conventionally produced, distributed, marketed, and consumed food. Moreover, as a number of critics of the movements have pointed out, these alternative practices are largely organized and promoted by white, middle-class members of core regions and exclude, often simply through cost and associated accessibility, poor people. The latter are denied these purportedly healthier eating opportunities because they lack the information, income, and proximity to access them. The result is that poor people turn to cheap, easily accessible food, also known as fast food.

APPLY YOUR KNOWLEDGE Identify the sites in your region where locally produced food is available, including grocery stores as well as farmers' markets. Create a map of where these sources are located. Are they accessible by public transit? What kinds of neighbourhoods are well-served? What kinds are underserved? ■

Fast Food

Fast food was born in the United States as a product of the post–World War II economic boom and the social, political, and cultural transformations that occurred in its wake. The concept of **fast food**—edibles that can be prepared and served very quickly in packaged form in a restaurant—actually preceded the name for it. What made fast food *fast* was the adoption of industrial organizational principles applied to food preparation in the form of the Speedee Service System. The system, invented by Richard and Maurice McDonald in their San Bernardino, California, McDonald Brothers Burger Bar Drive-In in 1948, revolutionized the restaurant business. To preclude the labour and material costs of standard restaurant food preparation, each Burger Bar worker was assigned one task in an assembly-line operation—cooking the burger, placing it on the bun, or packaging it for take-away, for instance—and the product was standardized so that the same condiments—ketchup, onions, mustard, and two pickles—were added to each patty. As Eric Schlosser writes in his *New York Times* best-selling book *Fast Food Nation*, once Raymond Kroc came along in 1954 and convinced the McDonald brothers to agree to franchise (licensing of trademarks—the golden arches—and methods of doing business), the fast-food concept began to expand all over the United States, so that by 1951 *Merriam-Webster's Dictionary* included it as a new word; and by 1964, there were 657 McDonald franchises. Quickly, other enterprising individuals seized the idea and started numerous fast-food franchises.

Today, fast food is so ubiquitous in North America—and increasingly so throughout the world—that it is taken for granted by many consumers. To appreciate just how omnipresent fast food is, consider the following statistics published by the National Restaurant Association in the United States. In 2010 there were 50 000 fast-food locations nationwide. Serving over 70 billion meals or snacks, their annual sales totalled US$558 billion. Over 13 million Americans are employed in the fast-food industry, making it one of the largest private-sector employers in the country. Every day, 1 in 3.5 Americans visits a fast-food establishment. French fries are the most eaten vegetable in the country, and McDonald's feeds more than 47 million people a day—many more than the entire population of Canada.

While it may be tempting to disparage fast food as a "typical" American affliction, we should take care to acknowledge that Canadians are only marginally less inclined to indulge in fast-food consumption. For example, 1 in 4 Canadians visits a fast-food outlet every day, and 1 in 5 meals is eaten away from home. Hence, the observations made in this section, while relating to the U.S. in numerical terms, in principle also apply to the situation in Canada—and other core countries, for that matter.

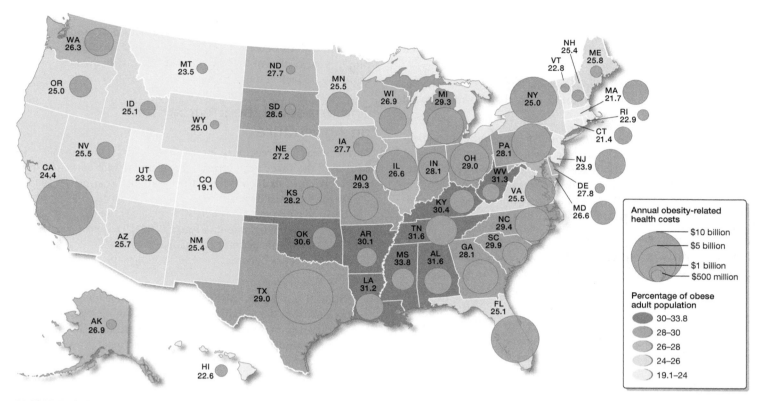

FIGURE 8.21 Economic costs of obesity in the United States, 2009 This map shows the percentage, by state, of individuals whose Body Mass Index (BMI) is 30 or higher. (BMI measures percentage of body fat based on weight and height; a BMI of 30 or above indicates obesity.) It also provides economic impact data expressed in health costs. (Not reflected here are other cost factors such as absenteeism, lost employment opportunities, or the higher cost of gasoline that airlines expend transporting obese people.) Note that, due to the private structure of the health care system in the U.S., health costs depicted here are higher in the wealthier states, where more residents can afford medical care. By contrast, the relatively poor southern states with high incidences of obesity show relatively low health costs. (*Source:* Data from ODC Behavioral Risk Factor Surveillance System; US Census Bureau, Population Division, December 2009.)

Health practitioners, alternative food activists, journalists, and others have turned a critical eye on fast food in order to expose some of its dietary, labour-related, and ecological shortcomings **(Figure 8.21)**. Worries focus on the doubling of obesity and diabetes rates among children since the late 1970s. Researchers found that children who consumed fast food two or more times a week gained approximately 10 more pounds over a 15-year period and had twice as great an increase in insulin resistance than subjects who consumed fast food less than once per week.

Diseases related to the increased consumption of fast food and many prepared, processed foods—energy-dense, nutrient-poor foods with high levels of sugar and saturated fats—as well as reduced physical activity, have also led to adult obesity rates that have risen threefold or more since 1980 across North America, the United Kingdom, Eastern Europe, the Middle East, the Pacific Islands, Australasia, and China. Moreover, the obesity epidemic is often increasing faster in rapidly developing peripheral countries than in the core. The explanation for this epidemic reflects the impacts of economic growth, modernization, and globalization on daily nutritional practices. The World Health Organization explains

As incomes rise and populations become more urban, diets high in complex carbohydrates give way to more varied diets with a higher proportion of fats, saturated fats, and sugars. At the same time, large shifts towards less physically demanding work have been observed worldwide. Moves towards less physical activity are also found in the increasing use of automated transport, technology in the home, and more passive leisure pursuits.[6]

In addition to its negative impact on human health, the rapacious growth of fast food production and distribution processes is dramatically affecting Earth's resources, especially forests and farmland. The Beyond Beef Campaign, an international coalition of environment, food safety, and health activist organizations, lists the following facts about beef production and its environmental impacts:

■ One hamburger patty imported from Latin America requires the clearing of 5 square metres of rain forest and the destruction of 75 kilograms of living matter, including 20 to 30 different plant species, 100 insect species, and dozens of bird, mammal, and reptile species.

■ Cattle degrade the land by stripping vegetation and compacting the earth. Each kilogram of feedlot steak costs about 30 kilograms of eroded topsoil.

[6]World Health Organization, http://www.who.int/dietphysicalactivity/publications/facts/obesity/en, accessed June 9, 2011.

- Nearly half of the total amount of water used annually in the United States goes to grow feed and provide drinking water for cattle and other livestock. Producing a kilogram of grain-fed steak requires more than 10 000 litres of water.

- Cattle produce nearly 1 billion tonnes of organic waste each year. The average feedlot steer produces more than 20 kilograms of manure every day.[7]

The impacts of fast food production and consumption on people and places are complex, from the convenience for busy consumers and the provision of play spaces for children to the elimination of forests and the debilitating health effects of overconsumption. How we manage these effects and address the causes has wide-ranging implications for people and the planet.

APPLY YOUR KNOWLEDGE How many fast food restaurants are in your town? Pick three and research their menus and the nutritional value of several popular items. This information is usually available on the Internet. Note the prices for these items. What can you conclude about the nutritional value of each item and its price? ∎

THE ENVIRONMENT AND AGRICULTURAL INDUSTRIALIZATION

Agriculture always involves the interaction of biophysical as well as human systems. This relationship makes agriculture distinct from other forms of economic activity that do not depend so directly on the environment. This relationship also necessitates that communities determine how best to manage the environment in order to facilitate the continued production of food. Because the relationships between the human system of agriculture and the biophysical system of the environment are highly interactive, it is important to look at the ways they shape each other.

The Impact of the Environment on Agriculture

Farmers have increasingly managed the environment over the course of the three agricultural revolutions. The current widespread use of fertilizers, irrigation systems, pesticides, herbicides, and industrial greenhouses even suggests that agriculture has become an economic practice that can ignore the limitations of the physical environment **(Figure 8.22)**. Yet because agriculture is an economic activity, its management of the environment in which it occurs becomes critical. As geographer Martin Parry writes

> Soil, terrain, water, weather, and pests can be modified and many of the activities through the farming year, such as tillage and spraying, are directed toward this. But these activities must be cost-effective; the benefits of growing a particular crop, or increasing its yield by fertilizing, must exceed the costs of doing so. Often such practices are simply not economic, with the result that factors such as soil quality, terrain, and climate continue to affect agriculture by limiting the range of crops and animals that can profitably be farmed. In this way the physical environment still effectively limits the range of agricultural activities open to the farmer at each location.[8]

Though the impact of the environment on industrialized agricultural practices may not at first seem obvious, it does occur.

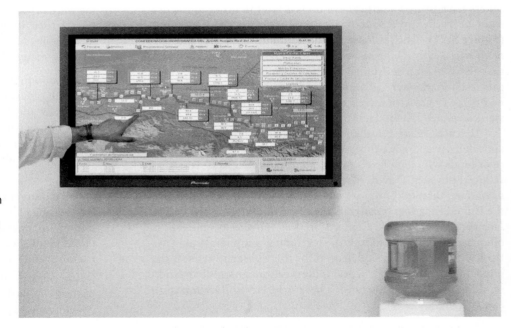

FIGURE 8.22 Modern irrigation system Modern irrigation systems are electronically programmed to deliver different amounts of water at different times of the day or days of the week. This figure shows a computer screen with a program that allows farmers to calculate the quantity of water used to irrigate the lands on the outskirts of Valencia, Spain. (*Source:* Bernat Armangue/AP Images)

[7]Beyond Beef, http://www.mcspotlight.org/media/reports/beyond.html, accessed June 6. 2011.

[8]M. Parry, "Agriculture as a Resource System," in I. Bowler (ed.), *The Geography of Agriculture in Development Market Economics*. Harlow, England: Longman Scientific and Technical, 1992, p. 208.

FIGURE 8.23 Impact of pesticides on pollinators Pollination is the transfer of pollen from one flower to another and is critical to agricultural production. Pollination is frequently provided by insects seeking nectar, pollen, or other floral rewards. Since 2010, many countries have warned of an impending pollination crisis as both wild and managed pollinators are disappearing at alarming rates as a result of pesticide poisoning, as well as habitat loss, diseases, and pests. (*Source:* ArtMediaPix/Alamy)

Examples include the availability of water, the quality of soil, air temperature, and length of the growing season, among other factors. Of course, on the other hand, there are also many readily observable contemporary and historical examples of the ways that agriculture destroys, depletes, or degrades the environmental resources on which its existence and profitability depend, as we discuss in the material that follows.

The Impact of Agriculture on the Environment

As discussed in Chapter 4, one of the earliest treatises on the impact of chemical pesticides on the environment was Rachel Carson's *Silent Spring,* which identified the detrimental impacts of synthetic chemical pesticides—especially DDT—on the health

of human and animal populations **(Figure 8.23)**. Although the publication of the book, and the environmental awareness that it generated, led to a ban on the use of many pesticides in most industrialized nations, chemical companies continued to produce and market these types of products in peripheral countries. Some of these pesticides, aimed at combating malaria and other insect-borne diseases, are applied to crops such as coffee and bananas that are sold in the markets of developed countries. Thus, a kind of "circle of poison" has been set into motion, encompassing the entire global agricultural system.

Among the most pressing issues facing agricultural producers today are soil degradation and denudation, which are occurring at rates more than a thousand times the natural rates. Most forms of agriculture tend to increase soil degradation, and the effects on worldwide soil resources and populations are dramatic, as **Table 8-3** illustrates. For comparison, the total area affected is three times the size of Canada.

The problem of soil degradation and loss is particularly critical in the humid tropical areas of the globe—especially in South America and Asia. Arguably the most critical hotspot with respect to soil and related environmental impacts is the moist Brazilian *cerrado,* or grassland, which is being converted to soybean production in order to feed the growing biofuels industry (which we discuss in more detail in the next section). In addition to soil erosion and degradation, the conversion of the *cerrado* is also threatening the species richness of birds, fishes, reptiles, amphibians, and insects. Some local animal and plant species face extinction.

The quantity and quality of soil worldwide are important determining factors for the quantity and quality of food that can be produced **(Figure 8.24)**. The loss of topsoil worldwide is a critical problem because topsoil is a fixed resource that cannot be readily replaced. It takes between 100 and 500 years to generate 10 millimetres of topsoil—but the world is losing topsoil

TABLE 8-3 Global Soil Degradation

Region	Degrading Area (km²)	Affected People
Asia	9 128 498	1 070 737 071
Africa	6 596 641	230 604 253
Europe	656 007	48 457 913
South America	4 719 162	149 905 245
Oceania	2 364 959	5 494 554
North America	3 968 971	36 654 152
World Total	35 058 104	1 537 679 148

(*Source:* Adapted from Z. G. Bai, D. L. Dent, L. Olsson, and M. E. Schaepman, *Global Assessment of Land Degradation and Improvement 1: Identification by Remote Sensing.* Report 2008/01, FAO/ISRIC, Rome and Wageningen, 2008, p. 24, Table 1.)

FIGURE 8.24 Desertification, Gansu, China A woman walks along the leading edge of the Kumtag Desert as it threatens to engulf her onion farm. The sand is advancing at the rate of up to 4 metres a year. (*Source:* Peter Parks/AFP/Getty Images)

through erosion at rates that are 10 to 100 times faster than the replenishing rate.

The nature–society relationship previously discussed in Chapter 4 is very much at the heart of agricultural practices. Yet as agriculture has industrialized, its impacts on the environment have multiplied and in some parts of the globe are at crisis stage. In some regions the agricultural system leads to overproduction of foodstuffs, but in others the quantity and quality of water and soil severely limit the ability of a region's people to feed themselves.

APPLY YOUR KNOWLEDGE Choose three common commercial crops (such as wheat, apples, or potatoes) that are grown in Canada. Identify the areas in the country where these three crops are grown, and consult soil, temperature, and rainfall maps to learn what local environmental conditions enable these crops to be grown in those areas. Next, identify what effect crop cultivation has on that same environment. Which crop has the most negative impact on the local environment? Which has the least? ■

EMERGING PROBLEMS AND OPPORTUNITIES IN THE GLOBAL FOOD SYSTEM

In this final section, we examine two problematic issues in the world food system, as well as an encouraging new prospect. These cases certainly do not illuminate the myriad challenges and possibilities facing food producers and policymakers today, but they do provide a sense of the broad range of issues.

Food and Health

We have spent most of this chapter describing the ways food is cultivated, processed, engineered, marketed, financed, and consumed throughout the world. What we have yet to do is talk about access to this most essential of resources. Although there is more than enough food to feed all the people who inhabit

Earth, access to food is uneven, and many millions of individuals in both the core and the periphery have had their lives shortened or harmed because war, poverty, or natural disaster has prevented them from securing adequate nutrition. In fact, hunger is very likely the most pressing problem facing the world today **(Figure 8.25)**.

Hunger can be chronic or acute. Chronic hunger is nutritional deprivation that occurs over a sustained period of time: months or even years. Acute hunger is short-term and is often related to catastrophic events—personal or systemic. Chronic hunger, also known as **undernutrition**, is the inadequate intake of one or more nutrients and/or of calories. Undernutrition can occur in individuals of all ages, but its effects on children are dramatic, leading to stunted growth, inadequate brain development, and a host of other serious physical ailments.

Globally, 24 000 people die each day from the complications brought about by undernutrition. Children are the most frequent victims. Children who are poorly nourished suffer up to 160 days of illness each year, and poor nutrition plays a role in at least half of the 10.9 million child deaths each year. Moreover, undernutrition magnifies the effect of every disease, including measles and malaria. Malnutrition can also be caused by diseases (such as diarrhea) that reduce the body's ability to convert food into usable nutrients. **Malnutrition** is the condition that develops when the body does not get the right amount of the vitamins, minerals, and other nutrients it needs to maintain healthy tissues and organ function. A person with malnutrition can be either under- or overnourished.

Perhaps the most widely publicized examples of acute hunger are famines, especially those that have occurred in parts of the periphery over the last few decades. **Famine** is acute starvation associated with a sharp increase in mortality. The most widely publicized famines of the late twentieth century occurred in Bangladesh in 1974 and Ethiopia in 1984–1985. The causes of these two famines (and other twentieth-century famines that preceded them) were complex. The crisis of starving people so often publicized by the news media is usually just the final stage of a process that has been unfolding for a far longer period, sometimes years or even decades. Experts who study famine argue that there are at least two critical factors behind long-standing vulnerability to famine. The first has to do with a population's command over food resources in terms of their livelihood. The second has to do with a trigger

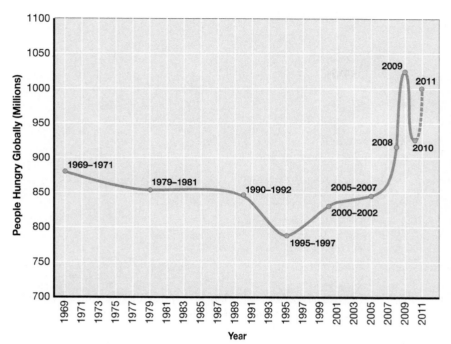

FIGURE 8.25 Number of hungry people worldwide
Almost one in eight people worldwide is chronically
undernourished. After steadily declining, global hunger
began to rise again in the 1990s. The number of hungry
people peaked in 2009 at 1 billion and has dropped to
roughly 850 million since then, mainly because of progress made in Asia and Latin America. In Africa, however,
the number of hungry people has been growing: one
in four Africans is hungry. Most hungry people live in
rural areas and are small-scale producers. (*Source:* The material
on page 31, from Figure 16: The number of hungry people worldwide, In Growing
a Better Future: Food justice in a resource-constrained world, Robert Bailey (2011)
is reproduced with the permission of Oxfam GB, Oxfam House, John Smith Drive,
Cowley, Oxford OX4 2JY, UK www.oxfam.org.uk. Oxfam GB does not necessarily
endorse any text or activities that accompany the materials.')

11 000 people depend for their livelihoods to the U.K.
firm Sun Biofuels PLC for a jatropha (a shrubby plant
that produces seeds that are 40 percent oil) plantation
(**Figure 8.26**). A recent report by the World Bank states
that biofuels production has forced global food prices
up by 75 percent. The price of food is a complex variable affected by causes that include the emergence and
growth of biofuels production but is also related to rising demand among increasingly more affluent populations, commodities speculation, rapidly escalating energy prices,
and poor harvests.

While it is important to understand the complex causes and
repercussions of hunger and undernutrition, perhaps the most relevant point to take away from this discussion is that it is a problem
that can be solved. Neither short-term nor long-term hunger is due
to inadequate supply, so the solution must lie in improving access
to supplies. This could occur, under a radical scenario, through a
massive redistribution that would give all the world's people access
to the same amount of food resources. Barring such a dramatic
restructuring of the current economic system, the solution to the
problem of hunger lies in improving access to livelihoods that pay
well enough that adequate nutrition becomes a human right and not
dependent upon the vagaries of economic or natural systems.

For both core and peripheral populations, issues of food
safety have also grown in significance. Over the past several years,
"food scares" caused by tainted foodstuffs have been routinely
in the headlines: California spinach and German bean sprouts
tainted with *E. coli* bacteria, *salmonella* in canned tomatoes from
Mexico and in hummus in the United Kingdom, toxic chemicals
routinely added to pickled vegetables in China, and potentially
cancer-causing dioxins (which entered grazing pastures through
illegally dumped toxic waste) in buffalo milk used in the production of Italian mozzarella.

The impact of food scares is widespread, affecting not only
those who have become ill or died but also farmers and grocers
along with the credibility of government agencies meant to protect
consumers from tainted and toxic foods. Mostly, the recent apparent escalation in food scares reminds consumers of the vulnerability
of the global food system.

Genetically Modified Organisms

A **genetically modified organism,** or **GMO** as it is commonly
known, is any organism that has had its DNA modified in a

mechanism, which may be a natural phenomenon like drought or a
human-made situation such as civil war.

People who study famine and other forms of hunger have come
to conceptualize nutritional vulnerability in terms of the notion of
food security. **Food security,** for a person, a household, or a country, is assured access to enough food at all times to ensure active
and healthy lives. And while famine is a dramatic reminder of the
precarious nature of food security, it is important to appreciate that
chronic hunger resulting from food insecurity is a far more widespread and devastating problem than famine, which tends to be
shorter in duration and more contained geographically. Related
to food security is the concept of **food sovereignty,** the right of
peoples, communities, and countries to define their own agricultural, labour, fishing, food, and land policies that are ecologically,
socially, economically, and culturally appropriate to their unique
circumstances.

Even in Canada, where food is abundant and overeating is a
national problem, 5 percent of the population is undernourished
or experiences food-security problems at one time or another each
year. In the periphery, where food availability is more limited than in
core countries, undernutrition is far more pervasive. Furthermore,
in some parts of the world, among some social classes, there are
higher levels of undernutrition among women and girls than among
men and boys. This is largely because different cultural and social
norms favour men and boys, who eat first, leaving the leftovers for
females, or who eat certain high-status foods, such as proteins like
meat or fish, that women are not allowed to eat.

As mentioned in the chapter-opening vignette, one of the factors thought to be adding to the most recent food emergency is
the increasing amount of cropland around the globe now being
redirected to raising biofuels. Land grabs for biofuels are happening across Asia, Latin America, and Africa and often involve violence. Some 150 000 families in Argentina and 90 000 families in
Paraguay have been displaced by soy production. In Tanzania, the
government has handed over 9000 hectares of land on which over

FIGURE 8.26 Jatropha plantation
Workers are shown here in a field of jatropha
plants, a source of bio-diesel, at the International
Crops Research Institute for the Semi-Arid Tropics,
in Hyderabad, India. Bio-diesel contains no petroleum, but it can be blended with petroleum diesel
to create a bio-diesel blend or can be used in its
pure form for fuel. (*Source:* Mahesh Kumar A/AP Images)

laboratory rather than through cross-pollination
or other forms of evolution. Examples of GMOs
include a bell pepper with DNA from a fish
added to make it more drought-tolerant, a potato
that releases its own pesticide, and a soybean that
has been genetically engineered to resist fungus.

Genetic modification has both critics and
supporters. Proponents argue that it allows great
advances in agriculture (for instance, plants that
are more resistant to certain diseases or water
shortages), as well as other beneficial creations,
such as petroleum-eating bacteria that can help
clean up oil spills. But opponents worry that genetically modified
organisms may have unexpected and irreversible effects on human
health and the environment and may result in maturation problems
in children or in mutant plant and animal species (**Figure 8.27**).

Government regulations on GMOs vary widely from country to country. In Canada, all GMOs are required to pass a safety
assessment, but there is no requirement to label GMO foods for
the consumer's information. Among other crops, Canada produces substantial amounts of genetically modified canola, corn,
soybean, and sugarbeet. In the United States genetic modification
is permitted on the principle that there is no evidence yet that it
is dangerous—consequently, there is also no labelling requirement.
GMO foods are fairly common in the United States, with some estimates saying that 50 percent of all processed foods (including those
imported to Canada) contain genetically modified ingredients.
This would hardly be surprising, given that 90 percent of all corn
and soybeans grown in the U.S. are genetically
modified. While the U.S. food-safety establishment maintains that GMOs are safe until proved
otherwise, the EU has taken the opposite position: genetic modification has not been proved
safe, so they will not accept GMOs from Canada,
the United States, or any other country until they
pass an in-depth scientific evaluation in the EU.
To date, only a handful of GMOs have cleared
this hurdle.

GMOs represent perhaps the most highly
technological way to date in which nature and

FIGURE 8.27 Protest over GMOs, Paris,
France Jose Bove (centre), food activist and
leader of the *Conféderation paysanne*, a
French agricultural union that supports sustainable agriculture, leads thousands of anti-GMO
activists in protest in the streets of Paris close
to where the National Assembly was voting on
GMO laws in spring 2008.

(Pierre Merimee\Corbis)

society come together in the global food system. At present, so little
is known about the impacts of GMOs on human health, the environment, or even the wider global economic system that it is difficult
to sort the costs from the benefits of their increasing incorporation
into global food production. What is clear is that genetic modification is not just a passing fad and the debate cannot be reduced to
a simple question of "good" vs. "bad." GMOs are neither entirely
evil nor entirely good; certain applications may be widely beneficial,
while others may not. Regulatory structures are crucial to protecting human health and the environment, as well as spreading whatever benefits may accrue from GMOs beyond the core and into the
periphery. But regulatory structures are not easily implemented.

Global debate and activism—both popular and governmental—
over GMOs are still in the early stages. Some of the most vocal
opponents of GMOs are concerned that engineered food is

destined for consumption by poor people in the periphery, while "real" food, produced by artisans and organic growers, will be available only to rich people in the core and little attention will be paid to the importance of reducing world hunger or access to a safe diet as a global human right.

> **APPLY YOUR KNOWLEDGE** Search the Internet for news stories on recent protests against genetically modified food. What are the protesters' concerns, and how do they go about pressing their demands? ■

Future Geographies

We began this chapter with a story about the impending global food crisis that is predicted to be full-blown by the year 2030. Not surprisingly, the crisis is expected to affect poor people in developing countries where food resources are already scarce for political, climatic, and financial reasons. There is very little disagreement among policymakers and scholars that this food crisis will occur unless the world's governments take a different attitude and approach to food production (**Figure 8.28**). An effective approach requires global co-operation, increased support for small farmers across the globe, an appreciation for how sustainable agricultural practices are, and a recognition of the impacts of climate change on growing seasons and farmlands. There is reason to be optimistic, as policymakers are already responding to the anticipated problem and small farmers are beginning to receive resources and financial support from governments and nonprofit organizations. But whether these efforts will be adequate is still unclear.

Other trends that are currently unfolding suggest that issues like obesity in the core regions may begin to decline as more and more core consumers express their desire for the increased

availability of healthy foods. There are signs for optimism in the growing alternative food movements that exist not only in wealthy countries but also in India and South America, where food is becoming so expensive as to be beyond the reach of millions. Sustainable, community gardening will not be able to feed the world, but it may be able to provide healthy produce to those who cannot afford to buy their food on the open market—as long as they have access to land.

The global production systems seem poised to continue to produce vast quantities of grain, enough to feed the world. But feeding the world will also require the recognition that not all people have the resources to afford the increasing cost of food on the world market. Issues of redistribution of food also need to be confronted. Food revolutions such as biotechnology are likely to continue to expand, but the results of new approaches are not likely to be equally affordable for all people.

The future of the global food system is being shaped at this very moment in food science laboratories, in corporate boardrooms, on the street in organized protests, and in settlements throughout the world. The biggest issues that food-policy experts, national governments, consumers, and agriculturalists face concern the availability and quality of food in a world where access to safe, healthy, and nutritious foodstuffs is unevenly distributed. For the periphery, the most pressing concern is adequate food supplies to feed growing populations. For the core, concerns about food quality abound in a system that is increasingly industrialized and biologically engineered.

$3.5 billion
Contributions to WFP (World Food Program)

$9.8 billion
ODA (official development assistance) for agriculture

$20 billion
Biofuels subsidies

$57 billion
Worldwide subsidies for renewable energy

$252 billion
Industrialized countries' agricultural support

$312 billion
Worldwide subsidies for fossil fuels (consumption only)

FIGURE 8.28 Where governments are investing As this graphic shows, investment in food is one of the smallest expenditures that governments make. Fossil-fuel consumption subsidies are the greatest expenditure. There needs to be a reversal with respect to these choices or we face a future where billions of people will go hungry. (All figures in US$.)

(*Sources:* The material on page 60, from Figure 24: Governments are good at investing in public bads In Growing a Better Future: Food justice in a resource-constrained world, Robert Bailey (2011) is reproduced with the permission of Oxfam GB, Oxfam House, John Smith Drive, Cowley, Oxford OX4 2JY, UK www.oxfam.org.uk. Oxfam GB does not necessarily endorse any text or activities that accompany the materials.')

CONCLUSION

Agriculture has become a highly complex, globally integrated system. While traditional forms of agricultural practices, such as subsistence farming, continue to exist, they are overshadowed by the global industrialization of agriculture. This industrialization includes not only mechanization and chemical applications but also the linking of the agricultural sector to the manufacturing, service, and finance sectors of the economy. In addition, states have become important players in the regulation and support of agriculture at all levels, from the local to the global.

The dramatic changes that have occurred in agriculture affect different places and different social groups. Households in both the core and the periphery have strained to adjust to these changes, often disrupting existing patterns of authority and access to resources. Just as people have been affected by the transformations in global agriculture, so have the land, air, and water.

The geography of agriculture today is a far cry from what it was 100 or even 50 years ago. As the globalization of the economy has accelerated in the past few decades, so has the globalization of agriculture. The changes in global agriculture do not necessarily mean increased prosperity in the core, nor are the implications of these changes simple. For example, the production of oranges in Florida is directly influenced by the newer Brazilian orange industry. Both industries affect the prices of oranges in the marketplaces of Europe and Asia. Additionally, other forces, such as social reactions to genetically engineered foods, agricultural research, trade concerns, and a host of other factors, have repercussions throughout the world food system.

Learning Outcomes Revisited

- Compare and contrast traditional agriculture practices across the globe.

  Although traditional agricultural practices, including subsistence farming, shifting cultivation, and pastoralism, no longer dominate agricultural practices on a global scale, they are still engaged in throughout the world, in some cases alongside more mechanized forms. Globalization, in addition to restructuring entire national farming systems, has also transformed farming households in the core, periphery, and semiperiphery. Thus, traditional forms of agriculture are waning as more and more places are drawn into a globalized economy supported by a strong commercial agricultural sector.

- Describe the three revolutionary phases of agricultural development, from the domestication of plants and animals to the latest developments in biotechnology and industrial innovation.

  The three revolutionary phases have not occurred simultaneously throughout the globe, but have been adopted and adapted to differing degrees, based on levels of development, culture, and physical geography. The first phase involved the domestication of seeds and animals. The second revolved around the improvement of outputs and innovations for making farming more efficient, such as organic fertilizers and field drainage systems. The third is based on the industrialization of agriculture through mechanization, chemicals, and food manufacturing.

- Analyze the ways that the forces, institutions, and organizational forms of globalization have transformed agriculture.

  Two of the most important forces behind agricultural transformation are multinational and transnational corporations and states. Institutions like the World Trade Organization as well as regional associations like the European Union have also been important influences. And the organization of agriculture itself has experienced significant changes as it has moved from a family-oriented business model to a corporate undertaking that stretches across national boundaries.

- Examine the organization of the agro-commodity system from the farm to the retail outlet, including the different economic sectors and corporate forms.

  The farm is no longer the central piece in the chain of agricultural organization, but one of several important components that include seed and fertilizer manufacturers, food processors, food distributors, and consumers. The organizational structure of agriculture is composed of five central and connected sectors (inputs, production, processing, distribution, and consumption) with four contextual elements acting as external mediating forces (the state, international trade, the physical environment, and credit and finance).

- Scrutinize the ways that agriculture has transformed the environment, including soil erosion, desertification, deforestation, soil and water pollution, and plant and animal species degradation.

  While most of the core countries have instituted legislation to address some of the environmental problems associated with agriculture, these problems exist throughout the global system to greater and lesser degrees. As agriculture has industrialized, its impacts on the environment have multiplied and spread so that some parts of the globe are at crisis stage. In some regions, the agricultural system has led to overproduction of foodstuffs, but in others the quantity and quality of food production is severely limited by physical constraints and environmental degradation. The challenge of the twenty-first century is to work toward a more sustainable relationship between humans and the environment, especially with respect to food production.

■ Probe the current issues that food-policy experts, national governments, consumers, and agriculturalists face with respect to the availability and quality of food, as well as the alternative practices that are emerging to address some of these issues in a world where access to safe, healthy, and nutritious foodstuffs is unevenly distributed.

Genetic modification is one way of improving productivity, though it does not address issues of access to food. Opportunities for the world's poor—who are increasingly residing in urban settings—to grow their own food is another way. Another way to improve food availability and quality is to recognize access to food as a human right and work toward more even distribution. Other responses include promoting more sustainable farming practices and supporting small farmers' efforts to produce efficiently and effectively.

KEY TERMS

agrarian *(p. 278)*
agribusiness *(p. 300)*
agricultural industrialization
   (p. 286)
agriculture *(p. 278)*
aquaculture *(p. 291)*
biofuel *(p. 276)*
biopharming *(p. 293)*
Biorevolution *(p. 290)*
biotechnology *(p. 290)*
Blue Revolution *(p. 292)*
Borlaug hypothesis *(p. 294)*
chemical farming *(p. 285)*
commercial agriculture *(p. 280)*

Community Supported
   Agriculture (CSA) *(p. 302)*
contract farming *(p. 290)*
conventional farming *(p. 302)*
cost/price squeeze *(p. 292)*
crop rotation *(p. 280)*
double cropping *(p. 283)*
famine *(p. 310)*
fast food *(p. 306)*
food manufacturing *(p. 286)*
food regime *(p. 300)*
food security *(p. 311)*
food sovereignty *(p. 311)*

food supply chain *(p. 300)*
genetically modified organism
   (GMO) *(p. 311)*
globalized agriculture *(p. 295)*
Green Revolution *(p. 286)*
hunting and gathering *(p. 278)*
intensive subsistence agriculture
   (p. 282)
intertillage *(p. 281)*
local food *(p. 302)*
malnutrition *(p. 310)*
mechanization *(p. 285)*
nontraditional agricultural export
   (NTAE) *(p. 290)*

organic farming *(p. 302)*
pastoralism *(p. 283)*
peri-urban agriculture *(p. 304)*
shifting cultivation *(p. 280)*
slash-and-burn *(p. 280)*
slow food *(p. 302)*
subsistence agriculture *(p. 278)*
swidden *(p. 280)*
transhumance *(p. 283)*
undernutrition *(p. 310)*
urban agriculture *(p. 304)*

REVIEW AND DISCUSSION

1. Visit your local supermarket and identify seven different types of produce. Determine what company produced them and where and how they were grown. You may need to ask the produce manager where they come from, but the tiny labels (with the PLU codes) will tell you whether they are commercially grown, organic, or GMO crops. Once you have determined the source of the produce, calculate how far it travelled (food miles) to reach your town.

2. Explore further the impact of the environment on agriculture by researching the projections that are being made about climate change and agricultural change. How will climate change affect the traditional areas of the globe where staples (such as rice, wheat, and potatoes) are grown? How will it affect the areas where more popular fruits (such as oranges, apples, and wine grapes) are grown? Speculate on what you think the political and economic effects of the changing geography of global agriculture will be.

3. Building on the previous exercise, what do you think will be the consequences of climate change for Canada in particular? Will this country increase its ability to grow agricultural crops? What factors other than climate might influence what can be grown?

4. Odds are, your breakfast is the result of the activities of a whole chain of producers, processors, distributors, and retailers whose interactions provide insights into both the globalization of food production and the industrialization of agriculture. Consider the various foods you consume in your typical breakfast and describe not only where (and by whom) they were produced—grown and processed—and how they were transported (by whom) from the processing site, but also where and by whom they were retailed. Summarize how the various components of your meal illustrate both the globalization and the industrialization of agriculture.

Mastering GEOGRAPHY™

Log in to www.masteringgeography.com for MapMaster™ interactive maps, geography videos, RSS feeds, flashcards, weblinks, an eText version of *Human Geography: Places and Regions in Global Context*, and self-study quizzes to enhance your study of food and agriculture.

MapMaster™ presents 13 Place Name and 13 Layered Thematic interactive maps to help students practise and master their geographic literacy, spatial reasoning, and critical thinking skills.

9

POLITICAL GEOGRAPHIES

Learning Outcomes

- Express the geopolitical model of the state and explain how it links geography and state practices with respect to the key issues of power and territory.

- Compare and contrast the ways that different contemporary theorists—from Deleuze to Althusser—approach the state as a political and geographical entity.

- Interpret how imperialism, colonialism, heartland theory, domino theory, the end of the Cold War, and the emergence of the new world order are key examples of ways geography has influenced politics and politics has influenced geography.

- Demonstrate how the growth and proliferation of international and supranational organizations created the foundation for the emergence of global forms of governance.

- Recognize how events of international political significance are usually the result of East/West and North/South divisions, whereas national and local political issues emerge out of tensions related to regionalism and sectionalism.

- Describe the difference between the politics of geography and the geography of politics as manifestations of the two-way relationship between politics and geography.

In January 2011, the people of Sudan voted on whether ten states of the southern part of the country would separate from the northern states and become an independent country. The referendum was the result of the longest civil war in African history. Flaring first from 1955 until 1972, the war was reignited in 1983 and ended in 2005 when the Comprehensive Peace Agreement gave a degree of autonomy to the southern states. Roughly 2 million people died as a result of the war; another 4 million were displaced.

Sudan's boundaries were determined by the British, who ruled (in an awkward partnership with Egypt) from 1899 until 1955. The North, where the capital, Khartoum, is located, is populated by some 22 million people, most of them Arabic-speaking Muslims. It is more economically developed and contains most of the country's urban centres. The South, which contains about 6 million people, is largely rural with a subsistence-based economy. Southern Sudanese people practise indigenous religions, though some of them are Christians. The South is home to many more tribal groups, and many more distinct languages are spoken there. The North is largely a desert region, whereas the South contains both deserts and tropical areas.

The animosity between North and South has been characterized in several different ways: as a racial conflict between Arabs and Africans and as a religious conflict among Muslims and Christians and animists. But it is also the case that the kingdoms and powerful rulers of the North have exploited the southern peoples for centuries. Britain added to this tension by

Citizens of the new state of South Sudan cheer as Sudan's flag is replaced by that of the Republic of South Sudan during an independence day celebration on July 9, 2011. (*Source:* Audra El Vilaly)

treating the two parts of the country separately during the colonial period and continuing to exploit the underdeveloped South to the advantage of the North.

The January 2011 referendum, in which nearly 98 percent of eligible voters participated, provided a landslide of support for secession. Africa's newest nation—called South Sudan—gained formal independence on July 9, 2011. Unfortunately, the path to full sovereignty continues to be difficult because of many unresolved issues. Among these are a North–South border that has never been clearly defined. The border region dissects water basins and differing tribal areas, creating an arbitrary divide that may separate people and their livelihoods. Some areas of the border remain contested by the two governments as well as local communities and tribes who refuse to recognize any demarcations whatsoever. Northern air and ground attacks upon Abeyi, the border state that contains rich oil reserves, also continue, as no agreement has been made on how to share the oil, Sudan's most valuable natural resource.

What has proved most destabilizing for the nascent state, however, is the continuing tension within the ethnically and linguistically diverse population of South Sudan. In late 2013, a civil war erupted between two of the larger groups, the Dinka and the Nuer. Within weeks, fighting had killed 10 000 and displaced more than a million. By spring 2014, a famine was looming and the UN warned of the threat of a genocide. High hopes for the peaceful birth of a new state were dashed by its own citizens. What does it take for a state to form, survive, and succeed? ▪

THE DEVELOPMENT OF POLITICAL GEOGRAPHY

This chapter explores how new boundaries and geopolitical arrangements continue to emerge around the globe at the same time that established boundaries persist. Exploration, imperialism, colonization, decolonization, and the Cold War between East and West are powerful forces that have created and transformed national boundaries. Much of the political strife that currently grips the globe involves local or regional responses to the impacts of globalization of the economy. The complex relationships between politics and geography are two-way. In addition, political geography is not just about global or international relationships. It is also about the many other geographic and political divisions that stretch from the globe to the neighbourhood and to the individual body.

Political geography is a long-established subfield in the wider discipline of geography. The ancient Greek philosopher Aristotle is often considered the first political geographer. His model of the state is based upon factors such as climate, terrain, and the relationship between population and territory. Other important political geographers have promoted theories of the state that incorporate elements of the landscape and the physical environment as well as the population characteristics of regions. From about the fourteenth through the nineteenth centuries, scholars interested in political geography theorized that the state operated cyclically and organically. They believed that states consolidated and fragmented based on complex relationships among and between factors such as population size and composition, agricultural productivity, land area, and the role of the city.

Political geography in the late nineteenth century was influenced by two important traditions within the wider discipline of geography: the people–land tradition and environmental determinism. Different theorists placed more or less emphasis on each of these traditions in their own political geographic formulations. The traditions' effects are evident in the factors deemed important to state growth and change. Why these factors were identified as central undoubtedly had much to do with the widespread influence of Charles Darwin on intellectual and social life. His theory of competition inspired political geographers to conceptualize the state as a kind of biological organism that grew and contracted in response to external factors and forces. It was also during the late nineteenth century that foreign policy as a focus of state activity began to be studied. This new field came to be called *geopolitics*.

The Geopolitical Model of the State

Geopolitics is the state's power to control space or territory and shape international political relations. Geopolitical theory originated with Friedrich Ratzel (1844–1904), a German geographer and biologist who was greatly influenced by the idea that Charles Darwin's theories could also be applied to the social realm. His model portrays the state as behaving like a biological organism, with its growth and change seen as "natural" and inevitable.

Although it has evolved since Ratzel first introduced the concept, geopolitical theory has become one of the cornerstones of contemporary political geography and state foreign policy more generally. And, although the organic view of the state has been abandoned, the twin features of power and territory still lie at the heart of political geography. In fact, the changes that have occurred in Africa, Europe, and particularly the former Soviet Union over the past 25 years suggest that Ratzel's most important insights about geopolitics are still valid.

Figure 9.1 illustrates Ratzel's conceptualization of the interaction of power and territory through the changing face of Europe from the end of World War I to the present. The fluidity of the maps reflects the unstable relationship between power and territory, especially some states' failure to achieve stability. The most recent map of Europe portrays the precarious nation-state boundaries in the post–Cold War period. Germany has reunited. Estonia, Latvia, and Lithuania have reappeared after decades of forced integration into the Soviet Union, which has dissolved. Czechoslovakia has split peacefully into the Czech Republic and Slovakia. Yugoslavia has disintegrated into seven successor states, but not without much civil strife and loss of life. And the map continues to change, as the 2014 annexation of the Crimean Peninsula by Russia exemplifies. At the time of writing, it was not certain whether eastern and southern parts of Ukraine will experience the same fate.

Tensions in Eastern Europe have intensified as former members of the Soviet Union such as Georgia and Ukraine move politically closer to Europe and further away from Russia. These emerging Western allegiances of Russia's direct neighbours have brought the European Union (EU) and North Atlantic Treaty Organization (NATO) to Russia's doorstep, undermining its position as the dominant power in Eastern Europe. Russia has begun to push back by taking an increasingly aggressive stance and sometimes using military force against its neighbours (for example, Georgia, Ukraine, and Moldova), ostensibly to protect Russian minorities in those countries. The result of these conflicts has either been outright annexation of territory by Russia (the Crimean Peninsula in 2014) or the creation of so-called breakaway republics with Russian military presence (Transnistria 1992, Abkhazia 1994, and South Ossetia 2008). At the time of writing, a similar scenario with uncertain outcome was unfolding in eastern and southern Ukraine and tensions were escalating between Russia and the West, with talk of a new Cold War issuing from both sides. In fact, NATO was considering the permanent deployment of troops in Eastern Europe. All of these developments powerfully illustrate the centrality of territorial boundaries to the operations of the state.

Boundaries and Frontiers

Boundaries enable territoriality to be defined and enforced, and allow conflict and competition to be managed and channelled. The creation of boundaries is, therefore, an important element in making territories. It follows from the concept of territoriality that boundaries are normally *inclusionary*; that is, they are constructed to regulate and control specific sets of people and resources *within* those boundaries (**Figure 9.2**). Encompassed within a clearly defined territory, all sorts of activity can be controlled and regulated. The delimited area over which a state exercises control and which is recognized by other states is **territory**. Such an area may include both land and water, and even airspace.

Boundaries can also be *exclusionary* when they are designed to control the flow of people and resources *across* those boundaries. National boundaries, for example, can control the flow of immigrants or imported goods. Municipal boundaries may separate different tax

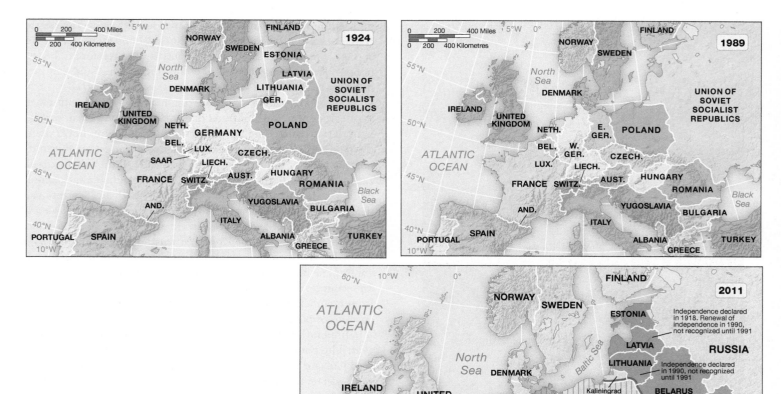

FIGURE 9.1 The changing map of Europe: 1924, 1989, 2011 The boundaries of the European states have undergone dramatic changes since World War I. The changing map of Europe illustrates the instability of international politics and the dynamism in the geography of political boundaries.

structures or access to certain services; land-use zoning boundaries can regulate access to upscale neighbourhoods; field boundaries can regulate access to pasture, and so on (**Figure 9.3**).

One aspect of boundaries that is of increasing interest to geographers is how they are organized and policed. Since 9/11, for example, the relevance of policing borders with respect to international travel has grown dramatically. States across the world, led by Israel, the United Kingdom, and the United States, have been instituting a wide range of practices to secure borders by electronic screening. By way of passports that contain RFID (radio frequency

identification) chips, as well as retinal scanning and related biometrics (electronic technologies for recognizing an individual based on one or more physical or behavioural elements), state agencies are increasingly able to know more and more personal information about travellers. These practices have the effect of creating virtual (technologically generated) boundaries that fortify the territorial ones.

Once established, boundaries tend to reinforce spatial exclusion as well as differentiation. The outcomes result partly because different sets of rules, both formal and informal, apply within

FIGURE 9.2 Boundary between Canada and the United States Most boundaries are established to regulate and control specific sets of people and resources within a given territory—they are *inclusionary*. Such boundaries need to be clearly identified but do not necessarily need to be fortified. This photograph shows part of the Canada–United States border, a good example of an inclusionary boundary. To an extent, heightened border controls since the attacks of September 11, 2001, have made the Canada–United States border more like an exclusionary border. *(Source: Reproduced with the permission of Natural Resources Canada 2011, courtesy of the Geological Survey of Canada (Photo 2001-063B by Gustafson, Carl))*

different territories, and partly because boundaries often restrict contact between people and foster the development of stereotypes about "others." This restricted contact, in turn, reinforces the role of boundaries in regulating and controlling conflict and competition between territorial groups.

Boundaries can be established in many ways and with differing degrees of permeability. At one extreme are informal, implied boundaries that are set by markers and symbols but never delineated on maps or in legal documents. Good examples are the "turf" of a city gang or the range of a pastoral tribe. At the other extreme are formal boundaries established in international law, delimited on maps, demarcated on the ground, fortified, and aggressively defended against the movement not only of people but also of goods, money, and even ideas. An example of this sort of boundary is the one between the United States and Mexico (**Figure 9.4**). There are also formal boundaries that have some degree of permeability. The boundaries between the states of the European Union, for example, have become quite permeable, and people and goods from member states can now move freely between them with no customs or passport controls.

Impermeability does not necessarily mean immutability, however. The boundary between East and West Germany, part of the Iron Curtain for more than 40 years, was aggressively defended, yet it was removed in 1989 when Germany reunified (**Figure 9.5**). Similarly, as mentioned previously, the boundaries of the former Soviet Union have been dramatically redrawn since 1989, allowing states like Lithuania, Latvia, and Estonia to reappear. Boundaries are important elements of geopolitics and of the geography of domestic politics.

APPLY YOUR KNOWLEDGE Using Google Earth, compare and contrast the international boundaries between the United States and Canada, and between the United States and Mexico. How do they differ? How are they similar? Speculate as to why these differences and similarities exist. ∎

FIGURE 9.3 Boundary between rural and urban places Some boundaries signal differences in settlement activities that may actually be governed by land-use regulations. The division between agricultural activities and suburban living is clearly shown in this image. *(Source: Image Source/Alamy)*

FIGURE 9.4 Boundary between the United States and Mexico The U.S.–Mexico border is *exclusionary*. It is heavily patrolled and lined with barbed-wire chain-link fences along the highly urbanized parts. Aerial surveillance is also extensive along the border. In an effort to stem the flow of illegal immigration and narcotics from Mexico, the U.S. government has quadrupled the number of border patrol officers over the past two decades. (*Source:* Ted Wood/Aurora Photos/Alamy)

FIGURE 9.5 Berlin Wall The boundary between East and West Germany was virtually impermeable for more than 40 years. This photograph is of the scene on November 12, 1989, when Berliners tore the wall down in celebration of the reunification of Germany. (*Source:* AP Photo/FILE/Lionel Cironneau)

Frontier Regions

Frontier regions occur where boundaries are very weakly developed. They involve zones of underdeveloped territoriality: areas that are distinctive for their marginality rather than for their belonging. In the nineteenth century, vast frontier regions still existed—major geographic realms that had not yet been conquered, explored, and settled (such as the Canadian North, the American West, the Australian interior, and sub-Saharan Africa). All of these are now largely settled, with boundaries set at a range of jurisdictional levels from individual land ownership to local and national governmental borders. Only Antarctica, virtually unsettled, exists today as a frontier region in this strict sense of the term—although some geographers now regard the deep ocean floors, outer space, and cyberspace as frontier regions.

There remain, nevertheless, many regions that are still somewhat marginal in that they have not been fully settled or do not have a recognized economic potential, even though their national political boundaries and sovereignty are clear-cut. Such regions—the Sahara Desert, for example—often span international boundaries simply because they are inhospitable, inaccessible, and (at the moment) economically unimportant. Political boundaries are often drawn through them because they represent the line of least territorial controversy.

> **APPLY YOUR KNOWLEDGE** Examine a map of the Gobi Desert. Identify which countries are part of it. How might this frontier region have strategic political significance for those countries? How does the desert terrain contribute to that strategic significance? ■

Boundary Formation

Generally speaking, formal boundaries tend first to follow natural barriers, such as rivers, mountain ranges, and oceans. For example, important mountain-range boundaries include the Pyrenees between France and Spain; the Alps between Italy and France, Switzerland, and Austria; and the Himalayas between India and Nepal and China. Chile, though, provides the ultimate example: a cartographic freak, restricted by the Andes to a very long and relatively thin strip along the Pacific coast. Examples of countries with boundaries formed by rivers include China and North Korea (the Yalu Tumen), Laos and Thailand (the Mekong), and Zambia and Zimbabwe (the Zambezi). Similarly, major lakes divide Canada and the United States (the Great Lakes), France and Switzerland (Lake Geneva), and Kenya and Uganda (Lake Victoria).

Where no natural features occur, formal boundaries tend to be fixed along the easiest and most practical cartographic device: a straight line. Examples include the boundaries between Egypt and Sudan and Libya (**Figure 9.6**), between Syria and Iraq, and between Canada and the United States west of the Great Lakes. Straight-line boundaries are often established through colonization, which is the outcome of a particular form of territoriality. The reason, once again, is practicality. Straight lines are easy to survey and even easier to delimit on maps of territory that remains to be fully charted, claimed, and settled. Straight-line boundaries were established, for example, in many parts of Africa during European colonization in the nineteenth century.

In detail, however, formal boundaries often detour from straight lines and natural barriers in order to accommodate special needs

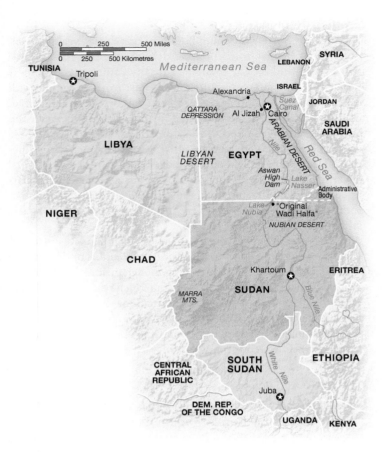

FIGURE 9.6 Borders between Egypt and Libya and Sudan The boundaries shown on this map illustrate several aspects of boundary formation. For example, the straight-line boundary between Egypt and Sudan was drawn in 1899 by the British colonial power for administrative simplicity and without much regard for ethnic diversity or physical geography. An exception is the tiny detour around the settlement of Wadi Halfa, which originally was accessible only from the south and was thus added to Sudan. Meanwhile, the zig-zagging part of the boundary between Sudan and Chad mostly follows the natural line of meandering riverbeds. The triangular area along the Red Sea on the eastern end of the border of Sudan and Egypt, called "Administrative Body," is the result of a 1922 boundary adjustment by the British, the legitimacy of which is interpreted differently by Egypt and Sudan. It is a point of recurring controversy and sometimes outright conflict between the two countries.

and claims. Colombia's border, for instance, was established to contain the source of the Orinoco River; the Democratic Republic of Congo's border was established to provide a corridor of access to the Atlantic Ocean; and Sudan's north central border detoured to include the settlement Wadi Halfa. (See Figure 9.6.)

After primary divisions have been established, internal boundaries tend to evolve as smaller, secondary territories are demarcated. In general, the higher the population density, the smaller these secondary units tend to be. Their configuration is generally similar to that of larger units, following physical features, accommodating special needs, and assuming straight lines where there are no appropriate natural features or where colonization has made straight boundaries

expedient. This last reason explains the rectilinear pattern of administrative boundaries in Canada west of the Great Lakes.

Territories delimited by formal boundaries—national states, provinces, counties, townships, municipalities, and so on—are known as *de jure* spaces or regions. *De jure* means "legally recognized." The term is most frequently used to describe nested hierarchies (**Figure 9.7**) and overlapping systems of legally recognized territories.

These *de jure* territories are often used as the basic units of analysis in human geography, largely because they are both convenient and significant units of analysis. They are often, in fact, the only areal units for which reliable data are available. They are also important in their own right because of their status as units of governance or administration. Much regional analysis and nearly all attempts at regionalization, therefore, are based on a framework of *de jure* spaces.

GEOPOLITICS AND THE WORLD ORDER

There is, arguably, no other concept to which political geographers devote more attention than the state. The state is one of the most powerful institutions—if not the most powerful—implicated in the process of globalization. The state effectively regulates, supports, and legitimates the globalization of the economy.

States and Nations

The **state** is an independent political unit with recognized boundaries, although some of these boundaries may be in dispute. In contrast to a state, a **nation** is a group of people sharing certain elements of culture, such as religion, language, history, or political identity. Members of a nation recognize a common identity, but they need not reside within a common geographical area. For example, the Jewish nation includes members of the Jewish culture and faith throughout the world, regardless of their place of origin or residence. The term **nation-state** refers to an ideal form consisting of a homogeneous group of people governed by their own state. Thus, in a true nation-state, all people residing in the state belong to the same nation. **Sovereignty** is the exercise of state power over people and territory; that power is recognized by other states and codified by international law.

Citizenship is a category of belonging to a nation-state that includes civil, political, and social rights as well as obligations. Before the concept of citizenship arose in the eighteenth century, an individual owed loyalty to a ruler rather than to a state. Power was vested in that ruler—the sovereign—and was passed on through family lines. Power—or sovereignty—thus became embedded in a few aristocratic families (the monarchs), not in space/territory and certainly not in the people over whom they ruled.

The American Declaration of Independence (1776) and the French Revolution (1789) both took power from the ruler and transferred it to the people. Once power was decoupled from the ruler and vested in the people, a link was soon forged between the area that those people inhabited and the space in which they exercised their sovereign power. In this way, the two concepts of space (state) and people (nation) began to fuse, and the *nation-state* became the most important model for state formation.

Modern citizenship as a political category was thus a product of the popular revolutions—from the English Civil War to the

FIGURE 9.7 Nested hierarchy of *de jure* territories *De jure* territories are constructed at various spatial scales. Administrative and governmental territories are often "nested," with one set of territories fitting within the larger framework of another, as in this example of region, department, arrondissement, canton, and commune in France.

French Revolution—that transformed monarchies into republics. In the process, these revolutions produced the need to reimagine the socially and culturally diverse populations occupying the territory of the state as a nation. Where once people were considered subjects of a ruler with no need for a unified identity, nationhood required of these same people a sense of an "imagined community," one that rose above divisions of class, culture, and ethnicity. This new identity was called *citizen*, and citizenship came to be based on a framework of civil, political, and social rights and responsibilities.

Given that nations were created out of very diverse populations, it is not surprising that multinational states—states composed of more than one regional or ethnic group—are the norm. Spain is such a multinational state (composed of Catalans, Basques, Gallegos, and Castilians), as are Bolivia, Canada, France, Kenya, and the United States. Indeed, a very limited number of nation-states are uni-national; Iceland and Japan are among them. Since World War I, it has become increasingly common for groups of people sharing an identity different from the majority, yet living within the same political unit with the majority, to agitate to form their own state. This has been the case with the Québecois in Canada and the Basques in Spain. It is out of this desire for autonomy that the term *nationalism* emerges.

Nationalism is the feeling of belonging to a nation, as well as the belief that a nation has a natural right to determine its own affairs. Nationalism can accommodate itself to very different social and cultural movements, such as the white supremacy movements in the United States and Europe (**Figure 9.8**), the movements for independence in Estonia, Latvia, and Lithuania during the Soviet era, and Quebec separatism. The impact of minority nationalism on the world map was especially pronounced during the twentieth century.

APPLY YOUR KNOWLEDGE Nationalism as a political movement is on the rise around the globe. Identify two national movements—one that is left-wing (politically progressive) and one that is right-wing (politically conservative)—and trace their origins and current missions. How do these two movements differ? In what ways are they the same? ■

Russia's State and National Transformation

The history and the present status of the former Soviet Union clearly illustrates the tensions among and between states, nations, and nationalism. Both enduring nationalism and the desire for sovereignty are evident in the history of the Russian Empire. Russia's strategies to bind the 100-plus nationalities (non-Russian ethnic peoples) into a unified Russian state were often punitive and not at all successful. Non-Russian nations were simply expected to conform to Russian cultural norms. Those that did not were more or less persecuted. The result was opposition and, among many if not most of the nationalities, sometimes rebellion and refusal to bow to Russian cultural dominance.

Such was the legacy that Vladimir Lenin and the Bolsheviks inherited from the Russian Empire following the overthrow of the czar in 1917. The solution orchestrated by Lenin was *recognition* of the many nationalities through the newly formed Union of Soviet Socialist Republics (U.S.S.R.). Lenin believed that a *federal system*, with *federal units* that each contained a homogenous national population, would ensure political equality among at least the major nations in the new state. This political arrangement recognized the different nationalities and provided them a measure of independence. Federation was also a way of bringing reluctant areas of the former Russian Empire into the Soviet fold. A **federal state** allocates some power to units of local government within the country. Canada and the United States are examples of federal states with their systems of province/state, county, and municipal government. A federal state can be contrasted with a **unitary state**, in which power is concentrated in the central government. Russia under the czar was a unitary state.

Although the Soviet Union officially was still a federal system when Mikhail Gorbachev came to power in 1985, the U.S.S.R. actually operated as a unitary state with power concentrated in Moscow. Gorbachev's goal was a massive restructuring of the faltering Soviet economy through radical economic and governmental reforms (*perestroika*) and the direct democratic participation of the republics in shaping those reforms through open discussions, freer dissemination of information, and independent elections (*glasnost*). Effectively, Gorbachev lifted the restrictions that had been placed on the legal formation of national identity.

By 1988, grassroots national movements were emerging, first in the Baltic republics and later in Transcaucasia, Ukraine, and

FIGURE 9.8 English Defence League, 2011 Pictured are members of the right-wing English Defence League in a march in the city of Luton. The movement blends ardent support for English nationalism with xenophobic activities directed mainly at Islamic immigrants. (*Source:* Leon Neal/afp/Getty Images/Newscom)

FIGURE 9.9 Successor states of the former Soviet Union This map shows the various independent countries that emerged from the breakup of the Soviet Union in 1991. Not identified on the map are the 22 member republics of the Russian Federation (shown in uniform green on this map), some of which continue to experience nationalist insurgencies that fight for secession from Russia. One example is Chechnya, outlined in white on the map in the area just northeast of Georgia. (*Source:* Reprinted with permission from Prentice Hall, from J. M. Rubenstein, The Cultural Landscape: An Introduction to Human Geography, 5th ed. © 1996, p. 318.)

Central Asia. By 1991, the relatively peaceful breakup of the Soviet Union was under way, and new states had emerged to claim their independence, a process facilitated by the federated structure of the U.S.S.R. (**Figure 9.9**). Russia (the core of the former Soviet Union) became a federal state with 22 federal republics and entered into the Commonwealth of Independent States (CIS) with some of the newly independent states. The CIS is a **confederation**, a group of sovereign states united for a common purpose. The newly independent states that chose confederation in the CIS did so mostly for economic (and to a lesser extent, for military) purposes. Notably, the Baltic states of Estonia, Latvia, and Lithuania chose to become members of the EU and NATO instead. (Note that the popular Canadian use of the term confederation differs from this definition, which can make things confusing: when Canadians speak of *confederation*, they usually refer to the process of forming the Canadian dominion in 1867. As we said already, Canada is actually a federal state.)

With the end of Soviet domination in Eastern Europe in 1991, regions such as the Balkans (the mountainous isthmus of land between the Danube River and the plains of northern Greece that includes Albania, Bulgaria, continental Greece, southeast Romania,

European Turkey, and most of the former Yugoslavia) also experienced national movements resulting in the redrawing of political boundaries. Yet while the breakup of the former U.S.S.R. had been primarily peaceful (with significant exceptions such as Georgia and Chechnya), the redrawing of national boundaries in the Balkans has resulted in bitter and widespread ethnic conflict.

The region is situated at a geopolitical crossroads where East meets West, Islam meets Christendom, the Ottoman Empire met the Austro-Hungarian Empire, and communism once confronted capitalist democracy. Conflict has been characteristic of the region for centuries. It was in the Balkans, for instance, where ethnic tensions triggered a fateful political assassination in 1914 that eventually pulled all of Europe and North America into World War I.

In the late twentieth century, conflict in the Balkans surrounded the breakup of Yugoslavia, a multinational state that had been created by the victors of World War I without much regard for the existing mosaic of ethnicities and religions. In the wake of the fall of communism, the various nationalities grew restive and grasped the chance to form their own nation-states. Through the 1990s, they fought several wars among themselves that led to the creation of the

FIGURE 9.10 Kosovo, 1999 Children run through a NATO bomb-damaged street in Pristina, the capital and largest city of the now independent Republic of Kosovo. (*Source:* Boitano Photography/Alamy)

seven independent states of Bosnia-Herzegovina, Croatia, Kosovo, Macedonia, Montenegro, Serbia, and Slovenia.

The war in Kosovo in the late 1990s was a particularly horrifying one. Kosovo was a multi-ethnic region within Serbia that lost its autonomy in 1989 when Serbian nationalist leader Slobodan Milosevic placed it under military occupation (**Figure 9.10**). A year later Kosovo's Parliament was abolished and its political leaders fled. Milosevic orchestrated numerous attempts to rid the region of ethnic Albanians, who formed the majority in Kosovo region. Fuelled by the racist rhetoric and military support of Milosevic, a civil war between Serbs and ethnic Albanians eventually erupted. By late 1999, tens of thousands of ethnic Albanians had been massacred and eight hundred thousand had fled Kosovo. A controversial 11-week air war by NATO helped bring the conflict to a halt, although atrocities continued as ethnic Albanians retaliated against Serbs. An international war tribunal was set up in The Hague to try Milosevic and others on human rights violations, including the possible charge of genocide. Milosevic was found in his cell in 2006, dead of apparent heart failure, before a verdict was reached.

Theories and Practices of States

The definition of the state provided in the previous section is a static one. The state, through its institutions—such as the military or the educational system—can act to protect national territory and harmonize the interests of its people. Therefore, the state is also a *set of institutions* for the protection and maintenance of society. A state is not only a place, a bounded territory, it is also an active entity that operates through the rules and regulations of its various institutions, from social-service agencies to governing bodies and the courts, in order to shape national populations.

An especially influential state theorist whose work has inspired a large number of political geographers is Louis Althusser (1918–1990). Althusser developed an approach that identifies the operations of the state in two ways. The first is to view the state as an ideological force operating through the institutions of the schools, the media, the family, and religion to produce citizens who conform to state expectations. The second, and complementary, way is to view the state as repressive. It uses force, through different institutions like the courts, army, and the police, to compel citizens to comply with its rules. These two related aspects of a model for understanding the state have been employed by political geographers in a number of ways, but perhaps the most common is to explore how the spaces of these various institutions, such as the school or the family, are produced and operate to do the work of shaping citizens. For instance, in the case of the Kosovo war, political geographers could use Althusser's theory to examine how state-controlled media whipped up Serbian nationalist feelings to create support for the state policy of ethnic cleansing.

A theorist who has also been a significant influence on political geography is Michel Foucault (1926–1984). Foucault pushed Althusser's ideas further by formulating a way for understanding just *how* the various institutions of the state operate to do the work of shaping citizens. Foucault explored the way that power, knowledge, and discourse operate in concert to produce particular kinds of subjects: citizens, women, soldiers, criminals, terrorists. For Foucault, **discourse** is an institutionalized way of thinking. For example, an army turns civilians into soldiers through the conjunction of power (in the form of both force and co-operation) and knowledge (accumulated insights about training, discipline, warfare) that come together as military discourse. This discourse or institutionalized way of thinking produces rules, identities, practices, exclusions, and a range of other elements that make large numbers of individuals function as an effective collective, rather than as individuals. In the case of the Kosovo war, the collective soldier identity produced by the military discourse could enable Serbian soldiers to ignore their individual morality and hurt or kill other human beings in the service of a "higher objective" such as the creation of a Greater Serbia.

A third state theorist important to geographers is Gilles Deleuze (1925–1995), who sees the state not as a set of institutions—the courts, the legislature, the military, etc.—but as a force. This force is greater than formal institutions at the same time that it works through them. For Deleuze, the state is not a thing but a principle that operates through power and authority. Rather than seeing the state as having been created during a particular period of human history and then expanding its power over time, he sees the state as having always existed in different forms, even before the emergence of the institutions by which we most clearly recognize it now. Deleuze believes that the state is best thought of as a *machine*, with its purpose being to regulate and dominate. This machine of the state operates through mundane practices that produce a population willing to submit to political sovereignty. In short, the state is a force that produces a population willing to submit to the power of a ruler, whether that ruler be a police officer, a forest ranger, a professor, or a queen.

Geographers have incorporated these and other theories and models of the state to explain the unfolding and impact of different kinds of political spaces, from the organization and influence of the classroom to the development and effects of international laws. For political geographers, theories and models of geopolitics have been their most prominent contributions to understanding the role and behaviour of the state. The Arab Spring of 2011 offers an illustration of geopolitics and the relationship of a national population to its state. (See Box 9.1, "Window on the World: The Arab Spring.")

The Arab Spring

The Arab Spring—that period of revolutionary fervour across the Middle East and North Africa in Spring 2011—is generally seen to have started in Tunisia. Some, however, would say that the inspiration came from the "Green Revolution" (also known as the "Persian Awakening") that had occurred two years earlier in Iran, a non-Arab country. In June 2009, millions of protestors took to the streets of Iran, charging that the election was rigged, keeping President Mahmoud Ahmadinejad illegally in power. Police and the *Basij*, a paramilitary group, used batons, pepper spray, and, in some cases, firearms against both peaceful demonstrators and rioters. The government of Iran reports that 36 people died as a result of the police response to the protests; supporters of opposition candidate, Mir-Hossein Mousavi, allege that there were 72 deaths. The most high-profile killing was of a young Iranian woman, Neda Agha-Soltan, a bystander who was shot in the chest by the *Basij*. Amateur videos of the killing spread virally across the Internet after being posted on Facebook and YouTube, and incited further protests. In response, Iranian authorities closed universities in Tehran, blocked websites, jammed cell phone transmissions and text messaging, and banned all rallies.

Tunisia's was the next uprising to occur in the region, and there is no doubt that its "Jasmine Revolution" served to embolden other national protests in the spring of 2011. Sustained public anger there, which forced President Zine al-Abidine Ben Ali out of office after nearly a quarter century, was ignited by the suicide of a young, unemployed man, Mohamed Bouazizi, who set fire to himself on December 17 after corrupt officials prevented him from selling fruits and vegetables on the street. The United Nations estimates that 219 people died in the Tunisian protests. A key reform enacted in response to the protests was the dismantling of the political police as well as the state security force, which appeared to have been responsible for extensive human rights abuses.

From Tunisia, the desire for accountability in government; the end of corruption, police brutality, restrictions on free speech, poverty, and rising food prices; as well as anger about the personal enrichment of the political elite spread to fuel protests in Morocco, Algeria, Jordan, Saudi Arabia, Bahrain, Oman, Egypt, Libya, Yemen, and Syria (**Figure 9.A[a]–[j]**). In all of these places the protests were largely and deliberately peaceful as individuals attempted to move their leaders by a firm commitment to nonviolence and open dialogue. In Egypt, the video blogging of 26-year-old Asmaa Mahfouz was instrumental in sparking the protests. She urged the Egyptian people to join her on January 25 in Tahrir Square to bring down Mubarak's regime. Her posts went viral and the event attracted 80 000 attendees. After weeks of protests and violent clashes with hundreds of people killed and thousands injured, the world watched in awe as President Hosni Mubarak, in power for three decades, resigned in response to the demands of millions of protestors as well as pressure from the international community.

FIGURE 9.A(a) Benghazi, Libya Shown here are local residents of Benghazi who joined a protest against dictator Muammar Gaddafi. The protests turned into civil war and violent regime change there. (*Source:* Gambarini Maurizio/dpa/abaca/Newscom)

FIGURE 9.A(b) Casablanca, Morocco In the city of Casablanca, the economic centre of the country, demonstrators assembled through much of the summer, calling for reforms in the Arab world's oldest reigning monarchy. (*Source:* Abdelhak Senna/afp/ Getty Images/Newscom)

Egyptians elected Mohamed Morsi, a leading figure in the Islamist Muslim Brotherhood, to the presidency. Soon thereafter, members of the Mubarak regime were put on trial and sentenced to prison. In 2013, however, a stunning reversal happened when, following widespread protests against Morsi's attempt to push through an Islamist constitution, the military staged a counter-coup, arrested President Morsi, and outlawed the Muslim Brotherhood as a terrorist organization. It

(Continued)

FIGURE 9.A(c) Qatif, Saudi Arabia Shiite protestors wearing masks chant slogans demanding democratic reforms. (*Source*: STR/AP Images)

appears that a majority of the population supports this reversal because the upheavals of the post-revolutionary period (with violent clashes among different religions, ethnicities, and ideologies) have decimated the all-important tourism industry, leading many Egyptians to favour a return to "strong-man government." Consequently, in July 2014, the army's commander-in-chief, Abdel Fatah al-Sisi, was elected president—continuing a pattern that has prevailed in Egypt since the withdrawal of the British in 1954.

In response to thousands of protestors gathering across Morocco's cities in February 2010, King Mohammed VI, a member of the dynasty that has been ruling Morocco for some 350 years, promised "comprehensive constitutional reform."

FIGURE 9.A(d) Amman, Jordan While strict controls on protesting have been exercised here, some risked arrest in order to broadcast their demands for more democratic government.
(*Source*: Mohammad Abu Ghosh/Xinhua/Photoshot/Newscom)

In Morocco—rather different from its neighbours in that the country has a successful economy, an elected parliament, and a reformist monarchy—the protestors pushed for reform to "restore dignity and end graft." Some observers believe that Morocco may yet experience the more massive protests besetting other North African states if real reforms are not enacted. Behind the facade of a relatively prosperous and democratic country is a brewing problem of a growing impoverished youthful population with little chance of employment and a government elite living obscenely lavish lives.

Like Morocco, Algeria is a country that on the surface seems generally prosperous, based on its sizable oil and gas reserves.

FIGURE 9.A(e) Algiers, Algeria Physicians were part of the protests that spread in Algeria against the government, arguing for improvements to working conditions and access to health care.
(*Source*: Mohamed Kadri/Xinhua News Agency/Newscom)

FIGURE 9.A(f) Manama, Bahrain Protestors here formed a seven kilometre human chain to register their anti-government sentiments. (*Source*: Newscom)

FIGURE 9.A(g) Hurghada, Egypt Protests occurred throughout Egypt and eventually ousted the president. (*Source:* Paul Vinten/Shutterstock.Com)

FIGURE 9.A(h) Sana'a, Yemen At a Friday prayer ceremony, people also staged anti-government protests, as shown here. (*Source:* Sinan Yiter/aa/abacapress/Newscom)

But the wealth is not spread equitably, and the protests appear to have been triggered by high food prices in particular. Protests here did not reach the levels of indignation, nor the overall numbers, of neighbouring countries' unrest, presumably because Algerians are afraid of slipping back into the chaos of civil war they experienced during the "Black Decade" of the 1990s, when more than 200 000 were killed by violence between Muslim extremists and the army. In response to the protests, President Bouteflika lifted the country's 19-year state of emergency, promised to create a constitutional commission that would strengthen democracy, and permitted private radio and TV stations for the first time. He also launched new social and economic programs to address poverty. In 2014, the 76-year-old was re-elected to his fourth term as president.

Saudi Arabia experienced no significant protests, probably for several reasons. First, opposition movements are banned there; second, the country's vast oil reserves make it one of the wealthiest of the Arab states (at the first sign of dissent, the government showered US$127 billion of additional benefits on its citizens to placate them); third, the country is deeply conservative, with a population that supports King Abdullah. Protests in Saudi Arabia were small and involved minority Shia Muslims who gathered in support of Shia Muslim protestors in Bahrain. In Bahrain, 30 people died in protests demanding that King Hamad take action to increase political freedoms and eliminate job discrimination that favours the governing Sunni Muslim minority. As small groups of demonstrators gathered in the centre of the capital

FIGURE 9.A(i) Muscat, Oman While anti-government activists were protesting the lack of a constitution in this monarchical state, pro-government demonstrators, pictured here, were defending their leader, Sultan Qaboos.

(*Source:* Sultan Al Hasani/AP Images)

FIGURE 9.A(j) Syrian refugees in Hatay, Turkey As the Syrian government began to use violence against protestors, many Syrians began leaving the country. Here Syrians who found refuge in Turkey are protesting against Syrian President Bashar al-Assad. (*Source:* Mustafa Ozer/afp/ Getty Images/Newscom)

(*Continued*)

city, Manama, King Hamad swiftly imposed a state of emergency and cleared the protestors' camps in a brutal show of force aided by Saudi and United Arab Emirates soldiers. International condemnation forced the king to open a national dialogue, but the process appears to be stalled and protests continue to simmer, sometimes turning into deadly clashes between Shia youth and security forces.

In both Jordan and Oman, protests were relatively limited in 2011 but flared up in 2012 over public discontent with the slow pace of promised reform. The demands of the protestors are similar to those of all of the other countries involved in the Arab Spring movement: job creation, controls on food prices, an end to government corruption, and more democratic government. Youthful populations across the Middle East and North Africa are usually the key foundational elements of the protests.

We have saved Libya, Yemen, and Syria for last because it is in these three countries where revolutions have turned into armed insurrection. This turn to aggression is uncharacteristic of the larger movement in the region, where nonviolent protest was the explicit objective. Why protests in these three have become violent has much to do with the entrenched intransigence of the leaders and the deep frustration and righteous anger of the protestors.

In Libya, Colonel Muammar Gaddafi, one of the most autocratic and longest-ruling dictators in the Middle East and North Africa, was overthrown in an armed uprising. The protests began peacefully on February 15, 2011, in Benghazi, the second-largest city in Libya. The protests were immediately met with violence as Gaddafi ordered the police to open fire, killing 500–700 protestors. In response, the protests grew into an armed uprising that spread across the country, pitting government forces against civilians. As the fighting escalated, the rebels received international support from a NATO-led coalition, including air strikes on Gaddafi's forces. After six months of fighting, rebels captured the capital, Tripoli, and killed the dictator. In 2012, Libya was declared a pluralist, democratic state, and elections created an interim parliament dominated by liberal and secular forces. Since then, the new government has been unable to disarm the several hundred militias that formed during the conflict, and factional fighting has led to increased instability.

The situations in Syria and Yemen also turned violent. Yemen is the Arab world's poorest nation. Almost half of its 23 million people live on US$2 a day or less and one-third suffer from chronic hunger. Government corruption is rampant, unemployment is high, and the country's median age, at 17.9 years, is the youngest in the region. In addition, the presence of al-Qaeda in Yemen as well as separatist challenges to government authority have made the country an increasingly unstable place. Protests against the rule of President Ali Abdullah Saleh began on February 11, 2011. Security forces used harsh violence against unarmed protestors wearing pink ties and scarves as a sign of solidarity with the peaceful Jasmine Revolution in Tunisia. The killing of up to 2000 protestors prompted the international community to push both sides into a National Dialogue Conference to chart a new course for the country. A civil war was averted, and Yemen appears on track for a new constitution and national elections—a rare success story.

The situation could not be any more different in Syria, where the spark of the Arab Spring has led to an all-out conflagration that has consumed the entire country. In early 2011, protestors were emboldened by the success of the Arab Spring in other countries to demand an end to government human rights abuses. The protests were galvanized by images of the mutilated body of Hamza al-Khatib, a 13-year-old boy tortured to death after being arrested at an anti-government demonstration. Government forces responded to the spreading protests with tanks, artillery, and snipers. The use of heavy weapons against its own population caused massive defections from the army, and by mid-2011 a civil war had erupted between forces loyal to President Bashar al-Assad and defectors forming the Free Syrian Army. The conflict has been intensifying since then and outside involvement has been increasing: Sunni Gulf states (Saudi Arabia and Quatar) are arming the rebel forces, while Shia fighters from Iran and Lebanon's Hezbollah militia are fighting alongside government forces armed by Russia. The result is a proxy war between Shia and Sunni regional powers that has been devastating the country, killing more than 100 000 people, with every tenth being a child. Millions of internally displaced persons (IDPs) and refugees have lost their homes and livelihoods, and a resolution is nowhere in sight. To make matters worse, the sectarian violence is re-entering neighbouring Iraq, leading to new record levels of violence there. Three years after the Arab Spring's beginnings, the region was still in a state of flux, with unexpected fallout occurring throughout. Countries that were once thought to be firmly in the hands of ruthless dictators have experienced regime change (Libya) or continued civil war (Syria). Monarchies (Morocco, Jordan) have proven more resilient than thought, while some democratic developments have reversed (Egypt) or gone into unexpected directions (Yemen).

Geopolitically, the conflict between Sunni and Shia Islam has moved to the fore across the region, increasingly blurring the "traditional" conflict lines between the West and Israel on one side and the Muslim Arabs with their Russian ally on the other. Contrary to all expectations, Shia Iran has been able to increase its influence in the region, prompting aggressive countermeasures by Sunni Saudi Arabia and Quatar. Meanwhile, the West and the U.S. in particular are seeing their influence wane.

Source: Adapted from Arab Uprising: Country by Country, BBC World News, http://www.bbc.com/news/world-12482315; Stephen Blight and Sheil Pulham, The Path of Protest, guardian.co.uk, http://www.guardian.co.uk/world/interactive/2011/mar/22/middle-east-protest-interactive-timeline; Kevin Conolly, Arab Spring: 10 Unpredicted Outcomes, http://www.bbc.com/news/world-middle-east-25212247.

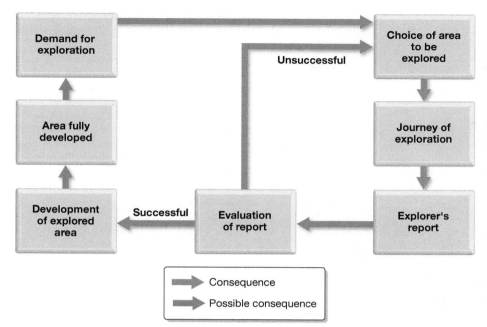

FIGURE 9.11 Principal steps in the process of exploration This diagram illustrates the main elements in the process of exploration, beginning with a need in the home country. Geographers have figured prominently in the process of exploration by identifying areas to be explored as well as actually travelling to those places and cataloguing resources and people. In fact, organizations like the Royal Geographical Societies in England and France were explicitly formed to aid in the expansionary efforts of their home countries. Nineteenth-century geography textbooks are records of these explorations and the ways geographers conceptualized the worlds they encountered. Exploration is one step in the process of imperialism; colonization is another. (*Source:* Adapted from J. D. Overton, "A Theory of Exploration," *Journal of Historical Geography, 7,* 1981, p. 57.)

APPLY YOUR KNOWLEDGE Using Althusser's ideas, reflect on how your school has "operated to make you Canadian." What sort of rituals did you follow? How did the school routines instill ideas in you about what it means to be Canadian? ▪

Imperialism and Colonialism

Geopolitics may involve the extension of power by one group over another. Two ways this may occur are through the related processes of imperialism and colonialism. Recall from Chapter 2 that imperialism is the extension of state authority over the political and economic life of other territories. Over the past 500 years, imperialism has resulted in the political or economic domination of strong core states over the weaker states of the periphery. Imperialism always involves some form of *authoritative control* of one state by another, but it does not necessarily imply formal governmental control over the dominated area; it may also involve a process by which some countries pressure the governments of other independent countries to behave in certain ways. This pressure can take many forms, such as military threat, economic sanctions, or cultural domination.

As discussed in Chapter 2, the process of imperialism begins with exploration (**Figure 9.11**), often prompted by the state's perception that there is a scarcity or lack of a critical natural resource. It culminates in development via colonization or the exploitation of indigenous people and resources, or both. In the first phases of imperialism, the core exploits the periphery for raw materials. As the periphery becomes developed, colonization may occur and economies based on money transactions—or "cash economies"—may be introduced where none previously existed. The periphery may also become a market for the manufactured goods of the core. Eventually, though not always, the periphery—because of the availability of cheap labour, land, and other inputs to production—can become a new arena for large-scale capital investment. (See Chapter 7.) Some peripheral countries improve their status and become

semiperipheral or even core countries. **Figure 9.12** is a map of the colonies created by European imperialism in Africa.

Colonialism is a form of imperialism. It involves the formal establishment and maintenance of rule by a sovereign power over a foreign population through the establishment of settlements. The colony does not have any independent standing within the world system and instead is considered an adjunct of the colonizing power. From the fifteenth to the early twentieth centuries, colonialism constituted an important component of core expansion. Between 1500 and 1900, the primary colonizing states were Britain, Portugal, Spain, the Netherlands, and France. **Figure 9.13** illustrates the colonization of South America, largely by Spain and Portugal.

Important states more recently involved in colonization and imperialist wars include the United States in the late nineteenth century (in the Philippines, Hawaii, and Cuba) and Japan in the twentieth century (in Korea and Taiwan). Although colonial penetration often results in political dominance by the colonizer, such is not always the case. For example, Britain may have succeeded in setting up British colonial communities in China, but it never succeeded in imposing British administrative or legal structures in any widespread way. And at the end of the colonial era a few former colonies, such as Canada, Australia, and the United States, became core states themselves. Others, such as Rwanda, Bolivia, and Cambodia, remain firmly within the periphery. Some former colonies, such as Mexico and Brazil, have come close to the core but have not fully attained core status and are categorized within the semiperiphery.

The Effects of Colonialism

Since the beginning of the twentieth century, the effects of colonialism have continued to be felt as peoples all over the globe struggle for political and economic independence. An example is the extension of British rule in India, which began with the establishment of the East India Trading Company in the mid-eighteenth century. The British government gave the company the power to establish forts and settlements, as well as to maintain an army. The company

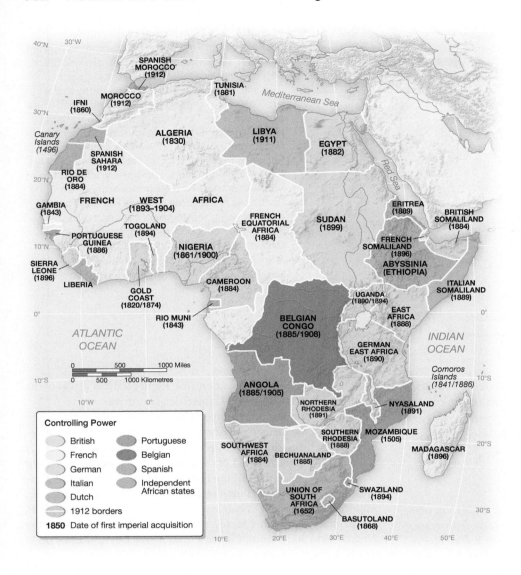

FIGURE 9.12 European colonies in Africa, 1496–1912 Lying within easy reach of Europe, Africa was the most likely continent for early European expansion. The Belgian, British, Dutch, French, German, Italian, Portuguese, and Spanish states all laid claim to various parts of Africa and in some cases went to war to protect those claims. The partitioning of the African continent by the imperial powers created a crazy quilt that cross-cut pre-existing affiliations and alliances among the African peoples.

(*Source:* Adapted from *Harper Atlas of World History.* New York: HarperCollins, 1992, p. 139.)

soon established settlements—including factories—in Mumbai (formerly Bombay), Chennai (formerly Madras), and Calcutta. What began as a small trading and manufacturing operation burgeoned over time into a major military, administrative, and economic presence by the British government and did not end until Indian independence in 1947. During that 200-year period, Indians were brutalized and killed and their society transformed by British influence. That influence permeated nearly every institution and practice of daily life—from language and judicial procedure to railroad construction and cultural identity (**Figure 9.14**).

The reasons Britain was able to be so callous in its colonial practices are complex. Theorist Edward Said has proposed the concept of Orientalism to explain them, at least in part. For Said, **Orientalism** is a discourse (as described earlier in the chapter) that positions the West as culturally superior to the East. Said developed the concept to describe the way the West has both historically and contemporarily treated Arabs. This same argument can be applied to the British in India or to other Western powers with respect to their colonies: the colonizers represent themselves as superior and enlightened and regard the colonized as inferior and in need of

disciplining. According to this logic, the colonizer has a moral obligation to colonize and "improve" the "natives"—a notion exemplified by the phrase "the white man's burden."

The postcolonial history of the Indian subcontinent has included partition and repartition, as well as the eruption of regional and ethnic conflicts. In 1947, Pakistan split off from India and became a separate Muslim state. In 1971, Bangladesh, previously part of Pakistan, declared its independence. Regional conflicts include radical Sikh movements for independence in the states of Kashmir and Punjab. Ethnic conflicts include decades of physical violence between Muslims and Hindus over religious beliefs and the privileging of Hindus over Muslims in the national culture and economy. It would be misleading, however, to attribute all of India's current strife to colonialism. The Hindu caste system, which distinguishes social classes based on heredity and plays a significant role in political conflict, preceded British colonization and persists to this day.

The 1994 civil war in Rwanda is another example of the lingering ill effects of colonialism. As in India, where an estimated 1 million Hindus and Muslims died in a civil war when the British pulled out,

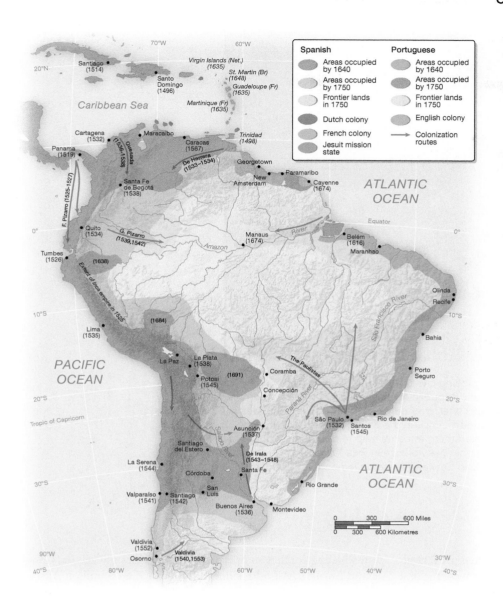

FIGURE 9.13 Colonization in South America and the Caribbean, 1496–1667 The Spanish and Portuguese dominated the colonization and settlement of South America. The Dutch, French, and English were a minor and largely tentative presence. African colonization focused upon gaining new subjects and the acquisition of additional territories; South American colonization yielded rich commodity and mineral returns. (*Source: Adapted from Rand McNally Atlas of World History. Skokie, IL: Rand McNally, 1992, p. 85.*)

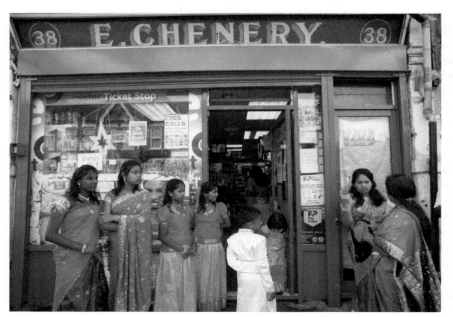

FIGURE 9.14 Indians in the United Kingdom The British presence in India affected culture, politics, the economy, and the layout of cities, as well as numerous other aspects of everyday life. Indian society absorbed and remoulded many British political and cultural practices so that contemporary Indian government, for example, embodies both British and Indian ideals and practices. Importantly, Indian culture has come to influence British culture even more directly through immigrants who have migrated to the United Kingdom. (*Source: Alamy*)

FIGURE 9.15 Refugees returning to Rwanda Fleeing civil unrest in their own country, Rwandans from the Hutu tribe increasingly sought refuge in the Democratic Republic of Congo (formerly Zaire) when the Tutsi-led government assumed power in 1994. Two-and-a-half years later, over half a million Rwandan refugees in the Democratic Republic of Congo occupied some of the largest refugee camps in the world. In late 1996, they began streaming back into Rwanda when the Tutsi-led government urged them to come help rebuild the country. Faced with two difficult alternatives—dire conditions in the camps or possible violence in Rwanda—many refugees chose to go home. Tens of thousands of Rwandans jammed the road between eastern Democratic Republic of Congo and Rwanda for over three days. *(Source: Jenny Matthews/Alamy)*

the exit of Belgium from Rwanda left colonially created tribal rivalries unresolved and seething. Although the Germans were the first to colonize Rwanda, the Belgians, who took over after World War I, granted political dominance to the Tutsi by allowing them special access to education and the bureaucracy.

Previously, a complementary relationship had existed between the Tutsi, who were cattle herders, and the more numerous Hutu, who were agriculturists. In effect, colonialism introduced difference into an existing political and social structure that had operated more or less peacefully for centuries. In 1959, the Hutus rebelled and the Belgians abandoned their Tutsi favourites to side with the Hutus. In 1962, the Belgians ceded independence to Rwanda, leaving behind a volatile political situation that has erupted periodically ever since, most tragically in the 1994 civil war. After a year of violence in which over half a million Tutsis were killed, the Hutus were driven across the border to the Democratic Republic of Congo (DRC) and a new Tutsi-led Rwandan government was formed. The Hutu refugees gathered in UN camps that gradually came to be controlled by armed extremists, who transformed them into virtual military bases and used them to attack the Tutsis in Rwanda (**Figure 9.15**). When Rwanda's Tutsi-led military, with Uganda's support, invaded the DRC to break up the camps, over a million refugees were released. At the same time, many of the extremists fanned out across Central Africa,

instigating conflict and perpetrating atrocities in Uganda, Congo, and Burundi. All told, since 1994, more than 5 million Africans have lost their lives in the so-called Congo Wars—the bloodiest conflict since World War II.

To help address the culture of impunity that angered so many Rwandans, the UN established a truth commission, known as the "Gacaca Court System," based on Rwandan traditional justice. Although its work has had some important moral impacts, the commission's aim—enabling Tutsis and Hutus to work together to rebuild their society and economy—has not been realized. Hundreds of thousands of children have become orphans as their parents either died in the atrocities or their mothers were infected with HIV/AIDS through rape and have since died. The country spends more on debt repayments to international banks than it does on education and health. Seventy percent of all households in Rwanda live below the national poverty line. Half the adult population can neither read nor write, and one in three children does not attend school. In short, the economic situation in Rwanda is worse than it was before the 1994 ethnic cleansing, which doesn't bode well for the country's long-term political stability. As in the case of India, colonialism is not the only cause of Rwanda's continuing troubles, but it plays a considerable role. Rwanda indeed presents a sobering example of how colonial policies can continue to thwart peripheral countries and even lead to war decades after decolonization.

Find three different recent news articles from reputable sources about a political issue in the Middle East. Consider the articles from the perspective of Orientalism. How do the articles depict the West and the Middle East? Is the West depicted as being culturally superior to the Middle East? If so, show how that is accomplished. If not, explain how the journalists avoid adopting an Orientalist explanation. ∎

The North/South Divide and Decolonization

The colonization of Africa, South America, parts of the Pacific, Asia, and smaller territories scattered throughout the Southern Hemisphere resulted in a political geographic division of the world into North and South, known as the **North/South divide**. In the North are the imperialist states of Europe, the United States, Russia, and Japan. In the South are colonized states. (When the North/South divide is used in an economic sense, Australia and New Zealand are seen as part of the North.)

The crucial point is that a relation of dependence was set up between countries in the South (the periphery) and those in the

North (the core) that began with colonialism and persists even today. Only a few peripheral countries have become prosperous and economically competitive since achieving political autonomy, though that is beginning to change, as we saw in Chapter 7. Political independence is markedly different from economic independence, however, and the South remains very much oriented to the economic demands of the North.

The reacquisition by colonized peoples of control over their own territory is known as **decolonization**. In many cases, sovereign statehood has been achievable only through armed conflict. From the American Revolutionary War to the twentieth-century decolonization of Africa, the world map created by the colonizing powers has repeatedly been redrawn. Many former colonies achieved independence after World War I under the auspices of the newly formed League of Nations. One of the first international organizations ever formed, the League of Nations had a goal of international peace and security. An **international organization** is one that includes two or more states seeking political and/or economic co-operation with each other. **Figure 9.16** shows the member countries of the League.

Within the League, a system was designed to assess the possibilities for independence of colonies and to ensure that the process occurred in an orderly fashion. Known as the *colonial mandate*

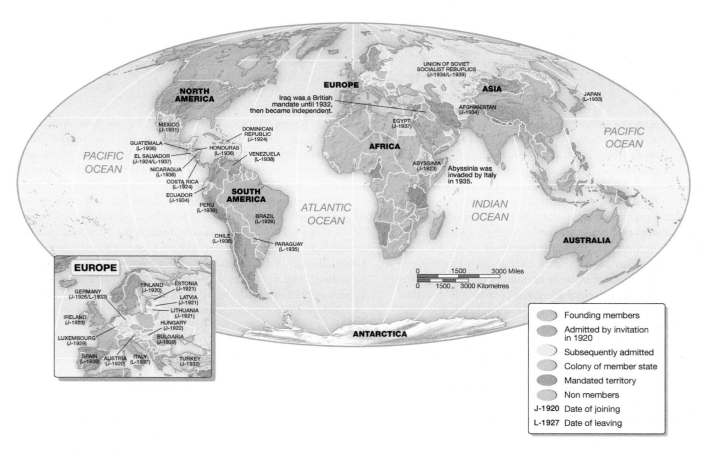

FIGURE 9.16 Countries participating in the League of Nations U.S. president Woodrow Wilson was a central figure in the creation of the League of Nations, but he was unable to convince his own country to join as the U.S. public favoured isolationism. The absence of the U.S. greatly reduced the effectiveness of this, the first international organization of the twentieth century. Britain and France played important roles in the League but were never able to secure arms limitations and security agreements among the membership. Perhaps the League's greatest success, before it was dissolved in 1946, was pressing for the decolonization of Africa.

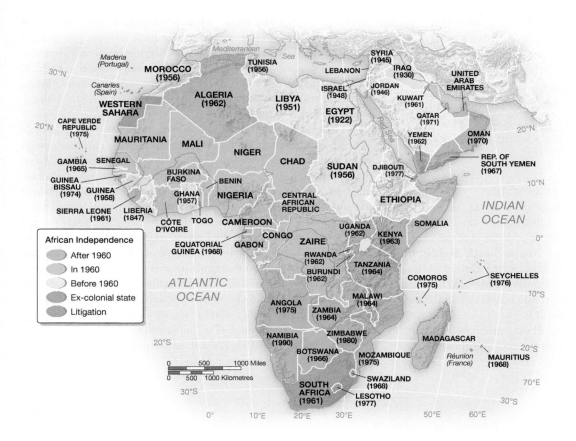

FIGURE 9.17
Decolonization of Africa, before and after 1960 Britain, France, and Belgium—the dominant European presences in African colonization—were also the first to divest themselves of their colonies. Britain was the first colonial power to grant independence. France granted independence to its African colonies soon after. In the French-speaking former colonies, the transition to independence occurred largely without civil strife (with the notable exception of Algeria). Belgium's withdrawal as well as the withdrawal of Britain from the remainder of its colonial holdings did not go at all smoothly, with civil wars breaking out. Portugal did not relinquish its possession of Guinea Bissau, Mozambique, or Angola until 1974. (*Source:* Adapted from *The Harper Atlas of World History, Revised Edition,* Librairie Hachette, p. 285. Copyright © 1992 by HarperCollins Publishers, Inc.)

system, it had some success in overseeing the dismantling of numerous colonial administrations. **Figures 9.17**, **9.18**, and **9.19** illustrate decolonization during the twentieth century in Africa, Asia, and the South Pacific, and during the nineteenth century in South and Central America. Although the League of Nations proved effective in settling minor international disputes, it was unable to prevent aggression by major powers and was dissolved in 1946. It did, however, serve as the model for the United Nations.

Decolonization does not necessarily constitute an end to domination within the world system, however. Even though a former colony may exhibit all the manifestations of independence, including its own national flag, governmental structure, currency, educational system, and so on, its economy and social structures may continue to be dramatically shaped in a variety of ways by core states. Participation in foreign aid, trade, and investments from core countries subjects the periphery to relations that are little different from those they experienced as colonial subjects. In the former British colony Kenya, for example, core countries' provision of foreign aid monies, development expertise, and educational opportunities to selected individuals has created a class of native civil servants that is in many ways more strongly connected to core processes and networks than those operating within Kenya. This relatively small group of men and women, often foreign educated, emerged as the first capitalist middle class in Kenyan history, and their children routinely enter middle-class occupations as well.

Commercial relations also enable core countries to exert important influence over peripheral, formerly colonized,

countries. For example, as discussed in Chapter 8, *contract farming* has become a central mechanism around which agricultural production in the periphery is organized for core consumption. Conditions of production of specified agricultural commodities are dictated by core countries to growers in the periphery. For example, Japanese and EU firms issue contracts that set the conditions of production for the Thai broiler (chicken) industry; Chiquita Brands, Inc., a U.S. firm, issues contracts for Honduran banana production. In this way, a core country can invoke a new form of colonialism in places it never formally colonized. As explained in Chapter 2, this new form, known as *neocolonialism,* is the domination of peripheral states by core states not by direct political intervention (as in colonialism), but by economic and cultural influence and control.

Exploration and, to a lesser extent, colonization are still occurring in Antarctica (**Figure 9.20**). This ice-covered landmass provides an unusual example of twentieth-century imperialism in which strong states exerted power in an area where no people and, therefore, no indigenous state power existed. At present, while no one country exclusively "owns" the continent, 15 countries lay claim to territory and/or have established research stations there: Argentina, Australia, Belgium, Brazil, Chile, China, France, Germany, India, Japan, New Zealand, Norway, the United Kingdom, the United States, and Uruguay. Argentina and Chile have even established small permanent villages with populations between 50 and 80 people to mark their claim to permanent settlement on the continent. The ultimate reason for all countries'

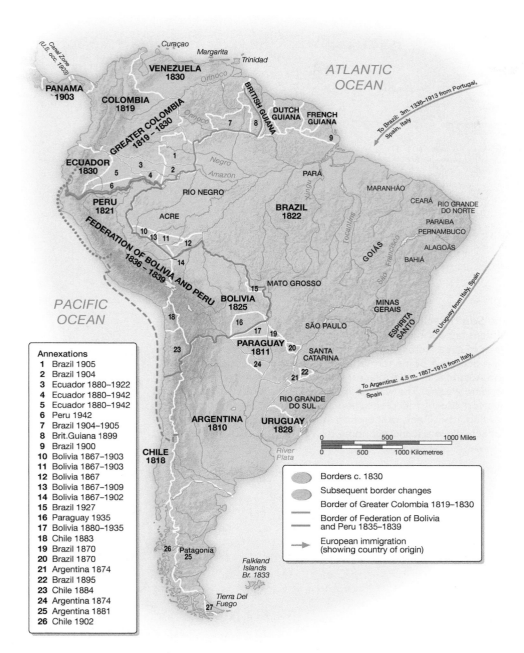

FIGURE 9.18 Independent South America, nineteenth century
Independence came much earlier to South America than to Africa. (It had also been colonized much earlier than Africa.) What was most influential in the independence movements there was the presence of local Spanish and Portuguese elites. This colonial ruling class became frustrated with edicts and tax demands from the home country and eventually waged wars—not unlike the U.S. Revolutionary War—against Spain and Portugal for independence. (*Source:* Adapted from *Rand McNally Atlas of World History.* Skokie, IL: Rand McNally, 1992, p. 113.)

interest in establishing a claim in Antarctica may be the presence of mineral resources ranging from gold and silver to cobalt, chromium, molybdenum, and titanium. The unclaimed sector contains no known mineral reserves.

Heartland Theory

Because imperialism and colonialism have shaped the world political map, it is helpful to understand one of the theories that drove them. By the end of the nineteenth century, numerous formal empires were well established, and imperialist ideologies were dominant. To justify the strategic value of colonialism and explain the dynamic processes and possibilities behind the new world map created by imperialism, Halford Mackinder (1861–1947)

developed a theory. Mackinder was the first professor of geography at Oxford University and director of the London School of Economics. He later went on to serve as a member of Parliament from 1910 to 1922 and as chairman of the Imperial Shipping Committee from 1920 to 1945. Given his background in geography, economics, and government, it is not surprising that his theory highlighted the importance of geography to world political and economic stability and conflict.

Mackinder believed that Eurasia was the most likely base from which a successful campaign for world conquest could be launched. He considered its closed heartland, with its great landmass and considerable resources, to be the "geographical pivot," the location central to establishing global control. Mackinder premised his model on the conviction that the age of maritime exploration was

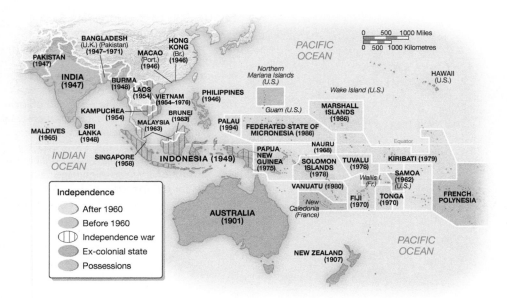

FIGURE 9.19 Independence in Asia and the South Pacific, before and after 1960 Decolonization and independence are not uniform phenomena. Different factors influence the shape that independence takes. The form of colonial domination that was imposed is as much a factor as the composition and level of political organization that existed in an area before colonization occurred. Some former colonies gain independence without wars of liberation; in Asia, these include India and Australia. In other places, the colonizers were prepared to surrender their colonies only after wars of liberation were waged. The war for independence in Vietnam lasted from 1954 until 1976, exacting huge costs from all involved. Mostly, decolonization and political independence forced societies into a nation-state mould for which they had little, if any, preparation. It is little wonder, then, that few former colonies have succeeded in competing effectively in a world economy. (*Source:* Adapted from *The Harper Atlas of World History, Revised Edition*, Librairie Hachette, p. 283. Copyright © 1992 by HarperCollins Publishers, Inc.)

FIGURE 9.20 Territorial divisions of Antarctica Even the uninhabitable terrain of Antarctica has become a site for competition among states. The radial lines delineating the various claims bear no relationship to the physical geography of Antarctica; rather, they are cartographic devices designed to formalize and legitimate colonial designs on the region. (*Source:* Reprinted with permission from Prentice Hall, from J. M. Rubenstein, The Cultural Landscape: An Introduction to Human Geography, 5th ed., 1996, p. 294; and http://www.coolantarctica.com/Antarctica%20 fact%20file/science/threats_mining_oil.htm).

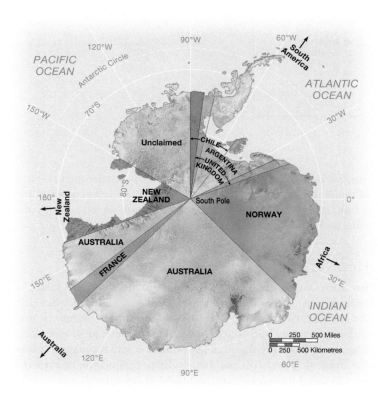

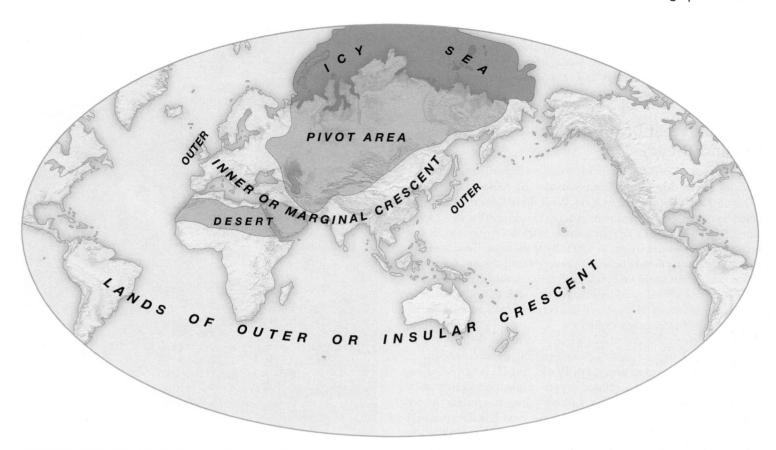

FIGURE 9.21 Mackinder's map of the heartland theory A quintessential geographical conceptualization of world politics, Mackinder's heartland theory has formed the basis for important geopolitical strategies throughout the decades. While the pivot area (the heartland) of Eurasia is wholly continental, the outer crescent is mostly oceanic and the inner crescent part continental and part oceanic. This seemingly clear distinction is partly achieved through cartographic means: Mackinder used the spatial distortions inherent in the Mercator projection (see Chapter 1) to overemphasize the importance of the northern landmass of Eurasia and the size of the southern oceans. He also split North and South America so that they appear on both sides of the map, literally putting them on the margins of global affairs. Mackinder's worldview map provides a good example of how cartographic representations can be employed to support ideological arguments. (*Source:* Adapted from M. I. Glassner and H. DeBlij, *Systematic Political Geography,* 3rd ed. New York: J. Wiley & Sons, 1980, p. 291.)

drawing to a close. He theorized that land transportation technology, especially railways, would reinstate land-based power, and sea prowess would no longer be as essential to political dominance. Eurasia, which had been politically powerful in earlier centuries, would rise again because it was adjacent to the borders of so many important countries and it was strategically buttressed by an inner and outer crescent of landmasses. In addition, by its sheer size, it contained many resources and was not vulnerable to invasion (**Figure 9.21**).

When Mackinder presented his geostrategic theory in 1904, Russia controlled a large portion of the Eurasian landmass protected from challenge by British sea power. In an address to the British Royal Geographical Society, Mackinder suggested that the "empire of the world" would be in sight if one power, or combination of powers, came to control the heartland. He believed that Germany allied with Russia, and China organized by Japan were alliances to be feared. Mackinder's theory was a product of the age of imperialism. To understand why British foreign policy adopted

this theory, it is important to remember that antagonism was increasing among the core European states, leading to World War I a decade later.

As it turned out, Mackinder had underestimated the importance of future technologies in his geopolitical assessment, especially the importance of aircraft, which completely altered the vulnerability of places to attack by distant aggressors. Nevertheless, by pointing to the important general observation that "space is power" (or more precisely, that "location confers a strategic advantage dependent on the available technology"), Mackinder's approach paved the way for later geopolitical theories such as the *domino theory* and modern efforts to achieve a *balance of power* between geopolitical power blocs.

The general idea of equating space with power that underlies Mackinder's geopolitical theory continues to have resonance today. An example is the aggressive Russian nationalism of president Vladimir Putin. Putin's harsh response to the Western leanings of the Baltic states and Ukraine, and Russia's invasion of Georgia, Chechnya (a renegade member of the Russian Federation), and more recently the Crimean Peninsula have some observers suggesting that a new round of Russian empire-building is underway and that Mackinder's theories are anything but outdated.

The East/West Divide and the Domino Theory

In addition to a North/South divide based on imperialism and colonialism, the world order of states can also be viewed as dividing along an East/West split. The **East/West divide** refers to the gulf between communist and noncommunist countries that developed after 1945 and played a significant role in global politics until the breakup of the Soviet Union in 1991. By the second decade of the twentieth century, the major world powers were backing away from colonization. Still, many were reluctant to accelerate decolonization for fear that newly independent countries in Africa and elsewhere would choose communist political and economic systems instead of some form of Western-style capitalism.

Propelled by the enormous expansion of the American war economy, the United States had assumed the dominant position among core countries at the end of World War II. When tensions between East and West escalated into the Cold War shortly after 1945, it became the goal of U.S. foreign policy to contain Soviet influence, and Western geopolitics for the next few decades followed an approach that came to be known as the domino theory. The **domino theory** held that if one country in a region chose, or was forced to accept, a communist political and economic system, neighbouring countries would fall to communism as well, just as one falling domino in a line of dominoes causes all the others to fall. To prevent the spread of communism, the United States and the West in general adopted economic, political, and military measures that included outright military intervention.

Domino theory first took root in 1947, when the post-war United States feared communism would spread from Greece to Turkey to Western Europe. It culminated in U.S. wars in Korea, Vietnam, Nicaragua, and El Salvador, as well as indirect involvement in the Middle East and elsewhere. However, preventing the domino effect was based not just on military aggression. Co-operation was also emphasized. For example, the international military alliance NATO was established in 1949 with the stated purpose of safeguarding the West against Soviet aggression. After World War II, the core countries set up a variety of foreign aid, trade, and banking organizations such as the World Bank and the International Monetary Fund (IMF) to open foreign markets and bring peripheral countries into the global capitalist economic system. The strategy not only improved productivity in the core countries but also was seen as a way of strengthening the position of the West in its confrontation with the East.

The Vietnam War and its aftermath was probably the most serious global manifestation of the logic of the domino theory and wrought terrible social and environmental damage on Southeast Asia as well as serious impacts on U.S. domestic and international politics. More than a million Vietnamese died, along with 58 000 Americans. The U.S. forces sprayed 2 million hectares of Vietnam with defoliants, such as Agent Orange, that poisoned ecosystems

FIGURE 9.22 Agent Orange in the Vietnam War
Approximately 80 million litres of herbicides, given the code name Agent Orange, were used in Vietnam between 1962 and 1971 to defoliate the jungle in order to deny cover to communist forces. The toxins contained in Agent Orange resulted in serious health problems for anyone who came into contact with it. They include diabetes, chloracne, Hodgkin's disease, multiple myeloma, non-Hodgkin's lymphoma, prostate cancer, respiratory cancer, soft tissue sarcoma, and neuropathic problems as well as birth defects in the children of those exposed. (*Source:* Everett Collection Inc/Alamy)

and caused irreparable damage to human health (**Figure 9.22**). Neighbouring Cambodia and Laos were also bombed with napalm and defoliated to disrupt communist supply lines and camps. Incredibly, the total tonnage of bombs dropped by the U.S. Air Force in the Vietnam was four times larger than that dropped by all sides in the entire World War II. The media images of destruction and loss of lives sparked protest marches worldwide and, ironically, turned large segments of the populations in the West against American foreign policy. Notwithstanding the increasing internal opposition, the domino theory essentially guided Western foreign policy toward the communist bloc until the dissolution of the Soviet Union in 1991.

The New World Order and Terrorism

With the fall of the Berlin Wall in 1989 and the opening up of former socialist and communist countries, such as China and Russia, to Western-style capitalist economic development, the Cold War was widely regarded as over—until Russia's increasingly aggressive stance in the Ukraine crisis in 2014 made many observers wonder whether we are entering a new Cold War period. Looking back now, the peace dividend of the "new world order" that many in the West had hoped for following the collapse of the Soviet Union did not quite materialize. The **new world order** assumes that with the triumph of capitalism over communism, the United States is the world's only superpower and therefore its policing force. With the political, economic, and cultural dominance of the United States comes the worldwide promotion of liberal democracy and of a global economy predicated on transnational corporate growth through organizations like the World Bank and the World Trade Organization.

However, the move toward liberal, Western-style democracies and the capitalist consumption practices necessary to the success of the new global economy have created considerable opposition and instability in some parts of the world. This instability is especially problematic where the Cold War struggle between the United States and the Soviet Union was once waged, in countries that once appeared ripe for succumbing to communism. The recent history of Afghanistan provides a telling illustration of this instability and its geopolitical implications. (See Box 9.2, "Geography Matters: From the Cold War to the New World Order and the War on Terror.")

With the emergence of a new world order, radical forms of warfare and political practices replaced more conventional ones. The attacks of September 11, 2001, and the resulting war on terrorism make clear that terrorism now is seen as the pivotal factor in current global geopolitics.

Terrorism is a complicated concept whose definition very much depends on social and historical context. A very simple definition is that **terrorism** is the threat or use of force to bring about political change. It is most commonly understood as actions by individuals or groups of individuals against civilian populations to undermine state practices or institutions. But the state can also be an agent of terrorism. Terrorism involves violent acts directed against society—whether by anti-government actors, governments themselves, angry mobs or militants, or even psychotic individuals—and it will always mean different things to different people.

The term *terrorism* was first used during the French Revolution (1789–1795) to describe the new revolutionary government's repression of its people during the "Reign of Terror." Fifty years later, the term was used to describe revolutionaries who violently opposed existing governments. As the nineteenth century came to a close, the definition of "terrorism" was expanded to apply to militant worker and nationalist political organizations. By the mid-twentieth century, the term was used to describe many left-wing groups, as well as subnationalists (minority groups within the nation-state), or radical ethnic groups. In the 1980s, terrorism was identified as a brand of ethnic or subnational warfare sponsored by rogue regimes. Ethnic and subnational terrorism affects many countries today, including China, India, Israel, the Philippines, Russia, and Uzbekistan.

Faith-based Terrorism

While subnational resistance organizations using terrorist tactics continue to operate throughout the world, the most widely recognized terrorism of the new century has religious roots. The

September 11 attacks have helped bring the realities of religious terrorism sharply into public focus. The connection between religion and terrorism is nothing new as terrorism has been perpetrated by religious fanatics for more than 2000 years. Indeed, words like *zealot*, *assassin*, and *thug* all stem from the names of fundamentalist religious movements of previous eras. And while the links between Muslims and terrorism in the world today are especially strong and geographically widespread, it is critical to understand that Muslim terrorism is not the only form of terrorism. For instance, domestic terrorism sparked by fundamentalist Christian organizations in the United States has taken the lives of hundreds of innocent people and continues to be a threat there and elsewhere. A chilling example of domestic terrorism in the United States is the bombing of the Alfred P. Murrah Federal Office Building in Oklahoma City in April 1995, when 168 people were killed (**Figure 9.23**).

FIGURE 9.23 The Oklahoma City Bombing Memorial In 1995, two white supremacists exploded a van filled with explosives in front of a federal office building in Oklahoma City. Both were connected to the Christian Identity movement through a paramilitary survivalist organization known as the Michigan Militia Corps. The Christian Identity movement is based on a belief in the superiority of whiteness as ordained by God. It is just one of several religious extremist groups in the United States, including other forms of white supremacy movements, apocalyptic cults, and Black Hebrew Israelism. (*Source:* MWaits/Shutterstock)

From the Cold War to the New World Order and the War on Terror

Afghanistan, known in ancient times as Gandhar, was once famous for its wealth, art, and culture (**Figure 9.B**). Its trading centres were important links on ancient trading routes between Central Asia and South Asia, and their wealth soon attracted invaders. Alexander the Great swept into Afghanistan—then a part of the Persian Empire—in 329 B.C.E. This invasion paved the way for a cultural awakening and the emergence of the Gandhar school of art, known for its amalgamation of Indian and Greek styles.

But invading Afghanistan is easier than maintaining control of it. The problem, put simply, is physical geography. Afghanistan is dominated by the rugged Hindu Kush Mountains, which sweep from the east to the west, sinking into the desert near the north-western city of Herat. Tens of thousands of square kilometres of the Hindu Kush form an intricate and seemingly endless maze of valleys and ravines. Jagged scree-strewn mountains and rugged valleys and caves provide ideal territory in which to fight a guer-rilla war against occupying forces. The problems of topography are compounded by the weather. By late October swirling snow descends on the mountains, sealing off many of the passes, val-leys, and high plateaus and making troop movement almost impossible until late spring.

Despite the inhospitable terrain and weather, Afghanistan has attracted one invader after another, from the Arabs and the Persians to the Turkic Ghaznavids and the Mongol invasion led by Genghis Khan. Late in the eighteenth century, Afghanistan's geopolitical significance increased still more. For the eastward-expanding Russian Empire, Afghanistan represented the last bar-rier to a thrust toward the rich plains of India. For the British, who were establishing a hold on India, Afghanistan represented a bas-tion against Russian expansion. Both the Russians and the British desperately wanted to control Afghanistan, and so began the Great Game—as the struggle between the two imperial powers for control of Afghanistan was called. The British were able to block the Russians but were not able to establish territorial control. After three wars with the stubborn Afghans, the British finally granted Afghanistan independence in 1921. A brief period of Afghan inde-pendence followed, during which Mohammad Zahir Shah, who reigned from 1933 to 1973, established a relatively liberal constitu-tion. Five years later, a bloody coup imposed a Marxist-style reform program that ran counter to deeply rooted Islamic traditions in the country. As a result, Afghan opposition to the Marxist government emerged almost immediately.

FIGURE 9.B Afghanistan and Pakistan As this map illustrates, Afghanistan is a landlocked, mountainous country sharing borders with six other countries. When war occurred here in the twentieth century, many of the people fled to these neighbouring countries for safety, including Pakistan, where al-Qaeda and the Taliban have subsequently established strongholds.

The Soviet Union, trying to pull Afghanistan into the com-munist bloc, assisted the Marxist government with military aid. Before long, the Soviets had sent more than 120 000 ground troops to suppress the Islamic freedom fighters (*mujahideen*) that were leading the Afghan fight against the communist govern-ment. Poorly armed at first, the *mujahideen* began receiving sub-stantial assistance in the form of weapons and training from the United States, Pakistan, and Saudi Arabia in 1984. The *mujahideen* exploited Afghanistan's terrain expertly: when a convoy passed through a narrow valley, they fired from surrounding ridges to disable the first and last vehicles in the Soviet columns and then slowly picked off the soldiers trapped in the middle. After suffering 15 000 dead and 50 000 wounded, the Soviet Union withdrew its troops in 1989, but peace remained elusive: with the demise of their common enemy, the militias' ethnic, clan, religious, and personality differences surfaced, and civil war ensued. Fighting in Kabul and in northern provinces caused thousands of civilian deaths and created new waves of internally displaced persons (IDPs) and refugees, hundreds of thousands of whom trekked across the mountains to Pakistan for sanctuary. Eventually, the hard line Islamist faction of the *mujahideen*—the Taliban—gained control of Kabul and most of Afghanistan.

The new Taliban regime not only imposed harsh religious laws and barbaric social practices on the Afghan population but also harboured an entirely new geopolitical force with worldwide implications: Osama bin Laden and his al-Qaeda terrorist network, who were responsible for numerous attacks on the West, including the attacks of September 11, 2001. The United States, with support from Canada, Australia, the United Kingdom, and others bombed and invaded Afghanistan in October 2001 as part of its war on terrorism. The aims of the military campaign were to capture Osama

bin Laden, destroy the al-Qaeda network, and overcome the Taliban's hold on the country. Osama bin Laden was assassinated on May 1, 2011, in neighbouring Pakistan, but the other aims essentially remained elusive despite considerable effort and sacrifice: more Canadians died in Afghanistan than in any other mission since the Korean War. After more than a decade of increasingly bloody, costly, and unpopular fighting, all Western combat troops will leave the country by the end of 2014.

Meanwhile, with U.S. and Canadian troops on the ground in Afghanistan, al-Qaeda had moved part of its operations to neighbouring Pakistan. In the remote and semiautonomous tribal areas in the northwestern part of the country, the Federally Administered Tribal Areas (FATA), al-Qaeda was able to regroup, recruit, and train without noteworthy government interference (**Figure 9.C**).

The United States, while not sending troops to Pakistan, has been deploying drones in Pakistan's tribal areas against suspected al-Qaeda and Taliban targets since 2004. Currently, the U.S. military continuously flies 65 combat-air patrols over Iraq and Afghanistan, with each patrol consisting of up to four drones. The Pakistani government simultaneously privately supports and publicly condemns the drone attacks. A highly regarded

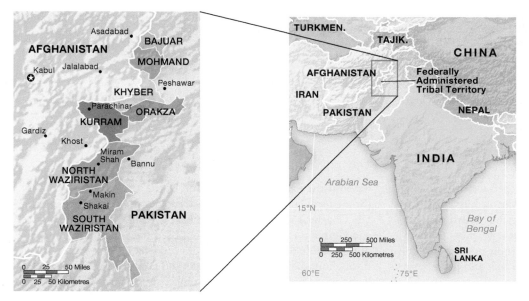

FIGURE 9.C Federally Administered Tribal Areas, Pakistan FATA is a tribal region in northwestern Pakistan. Jurisdictionally, the region consists of tribal areas and frontier regions. Historically, FATA acted as the "Great Game" buffer zone between Russia and British-controlled India. (*Source*: Source for Pakistan internal boundaries, Geocart; source for Federally Administered Tribal Areas, CIA.)

(*Continued*)

study by the New America Foundation has shown that there were 257 reported U.S. drone strikes in Pakistan between 2004 and 2011. These strikes were implicated in the deaths of up to 2486 individuals (**Figure 9.D**). Tense relations now exist between Pakistan and the United States following the killing of bin Laden. The U.S. covert assassination operation humiliated the Pakistani government—who many regional specialists believe knew where bin Laden was all along—and it has retaliated by cutting back on counterterrorism co-operation with the United States.

Source: New America Foundation, "The Year of the Drone," 2011, available at www.Newamerica.net, accessed June 30, 2011.

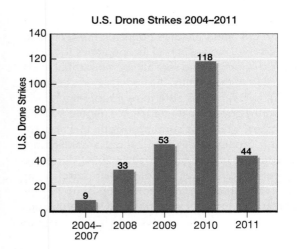

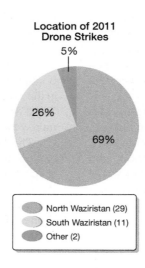

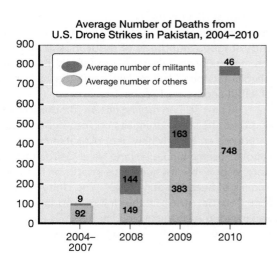

FIGURE 9.D U.S. drone strikes, 2004–2011 The New America Foundation study shows that the 257 reported drone strikes in northwest Pakistan between 2004 and 2011 have killed approximately 1575 to 2486 individuals, of whom 1282 to 2015 were described as militants in reliable press accounts. The report estimates that the true nonmilitant fatality rate since 2004 is approximately 20 percent. Between 2011 and 2013, another 98 strikes were executed. (*Source:* Reprinted by permission of New American Foundation: National Security Studies Program.)

Another, more recent example of faith-based terrorism is the bombing and shooting that occurred in Norway on July 24, 2011. In this case, a young Christian man, fearing that Muslims were polluting the Norwegian nation, killed 77 people, most of them young people (**Figure 9.24**). Terrorism with roots in religious fervour is widespread and has occurred in both rich and poor parts of the globe.

The War on Terror in Iraq

The United States responded to the terrorist attacks of September 11, 2001, by declaring a global war against terrorism and identifying first Afghanistan and then Iraq as the greatest threats to U.S. security. Although the evidence of involvement in the 9/11 attacks by Iraq and its leader, Saddam Hussein, was highly questionable, the United States bombed and invaded Iraq on March 19, 2003, without the explicit authorization of the UN Security Council. (Some legal authorities take the view that the action violated the UN Charter.) Some of the staunchest U.S. allies (Canada, France, and Germany) as well as Russia opposed the attack, and hundreds of thousands of antiwar protestors repeatedly took to the streets throughout the world for the weeks and months preceding and following the onset of war launched by coalition forces of the United Kingdom and the United States.

The motivation for the war, as expressed by British Prime Minister Tony Blair and George W. Bush, was that Iraq had stockpiled "weapons of mass destruction"—chemical and biological weapons capable of massive human destruction. In the days leading up to the war, UN weapons inspector Hans Blix and his team were unable to locate any weapons despite an intensive search of the country. President Bush, however, proceeded to justify a

FIGURE 9.24 Oslo, Norway, terrorist bombing An Oslo facade destroyed by a bomb set off by Anders Behring Breivik in the summer of 2011. (*Source:* Jeff Gilbert/Alamy)

dramatically stepped-up "war on terrorism" (following the invasion in Afghanistan) on the grounds that "neutralizing" Iraq's leader, Saddam Hussein, was necessary for global security.

Figure 9.25 shows the 4459 American and approximately 150 000 Iraqi casualties up to the summer of 2011. An especially distressing and long-term aspect of the Iraq war, as well as other recent wars, is the impact on returning veterans' mental health:

the U.S. Department of Veteran Affairs has stated that there are about 1000 suicide attempts per month among U.S. veterans. Besides the mental health impacts, there are, of course, also very significant physical ones, including lost limbs and serious brain and organ injuries.

In early 2004, the 9/11 Commission (more formally known as the National Commission on Terrorist Attacks Upon the United

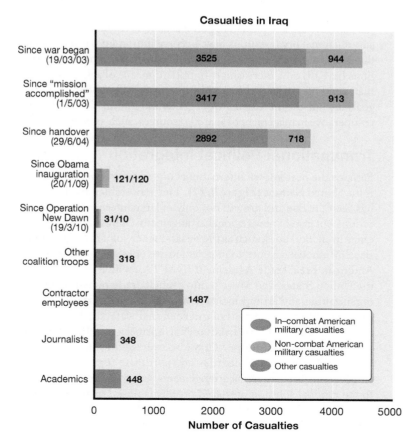

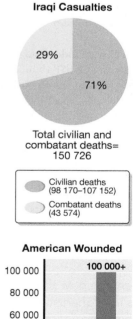

FIGURE 9.25 Casualties from the war in Iraq as of 2011 This graphic includes both the wounded and dead among military and civilian personnel participating in the U.S. war effort in Iraq. More than half of those who died were younger than 24 years of age. (*Source:* http://antiwar.com/casualities)

States) concluded that there was no credible evidence that Saddam Hussein, the captured and executed former president of Iraq, had assisted al-Qaeda to prepare for or carry out the 9/11 attacks. There is also general agreement among U.S. intelligence and military personnel that Iraq had most likely destroyed its programs for biological and chemical weapons production before the UN team began its inspection.

Despite the fact that coalition troops have now left the country, peace has not returned to Iraq, as sectarian violence still occurs on a regular basis throughout much of the country, especially in Baghdad. Tactics in use include mortars, suicide bombers, roadside bombs, small-arms fire, and rocket-propelled grenades, as well as sabotage against the oil infrastructure of the country. Moreover, the civilian humanitarian situation is among the most critical in the world. Millions of Iraqis have insufficient access to clean water, sanitation, and health care.

Although the war in Afghanistan and its implications for Pakistan are addressed in Box 9.2, Geography Matters, it is also important to point out the implications of the assassination of Osama bin Laden that occurred on May 1, 2011, in Abbottabad, Pakistan, which was seen by many as a symbolic end to the war on terror. Bin Laden, the founder of al-Qaeda, the jihadist organization responsible for the attacks of September 11, 2001, had been in hiding for a decade before he was killed in a covert operation. Bin Laden believed that the United States and its political, economic, and cultural values persecuted and oppressed Muslims around the world and the only way to end this violence was with violence. Bin Laden's fundamental approach was to provoke leading economic powers into endless war in Muslim countries. At the same time, al-Qaeda continued to recruit new jihadists to the organization's cause, perpetuating an asymmetric but highly costly conflict. Bin Laden believed that endless war would lead to the economic collapse of the West and its values.

For the United States, the costs of the war were indeed staggering. The U.S. Treasury estimates the direct cost at US$845 billion. Nobel-prize winning economist Joseph Stiglitz and his co-author Linda Bilmes argue that the true cost of the war is closer to US$3 trillion when the indirect costs are also accounted for, including interest on the debt raised to fund the war, the rising cost of oil, health care costs for returning veterans, and the cost of replacing destroyed military hardware and degraded operational capacity.[1]

With Osama bin Laden dead, the war on terror has not actually ceased. In fact, the war still goes on in Afghanistan and, more covertly, in Pakistan. Even more worrisome, the war on terror, with its many civilian casualties, may actually have produced more recruits willing to fight against a West increasingly perceived as neocolonial.

APPLY YOUR KNOWLEDGE Research how the deployment of Canadian soldiers in Afghanistan was reported in the media. What type of information was most prominent? How much was reported about the actual situation in Afghanistan? ∎

[1] J. Stiglitz and L. Bilmes, *The Three Trillion Dollar War*. New York: W.W. Norton, 2008.

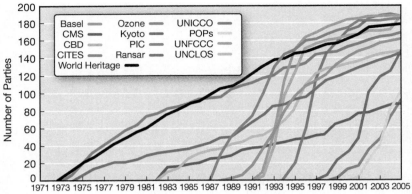

FIGURE 9.26 Growth of states, intergovernmental organizations, and nongovernmental organizations in the twentieth century The number of states has grown steadily over the twentieth century, but intergovernmental organizations (IGOs) and international nongovernmental organizations (INGOs) have experienced dramatic growth, particularly since the 1960s. Although states remain the main forms of national government, they have turned over many of their governing responsibilities to international governing organizations and nongovernmental organizations. (*Source:* Yearbook of International Organizations 1985-1986, 1992-1993, 1998-1999, 2003-2004. Union of International Associations, Brussels)

INTERNATIONAL AND SUPRANATIONAL ORGANIZATIONS AND NEW REGIMES OF GLOBAL GOVERNANCE

Just as states are key players in political geography, international and supranational organizations have become important participants in the world-system in the past century (**Figure 9.26**). These organizations have become increasingly important means of achieving goals that could otherwise be blocked by international boundaries. These goals include the increased flow of goods and information, and more co-operative management of shared resources, such as water.

Transnational Political Integration

Perhaps the best-known international organization operating today is the United Nations (**Figure 9.27**). The period since World War II has seen the rise and growth not only of large international organizations but also of new regional arrangements. These arrangements range from local ones, such as the Swiss–French joint management of Basel-Mulhouse airport, to more extensive ones, such as the North American Free Trade Agreement (NAFTA), which joins Canada, the United States, and Mexico into a single trade region. Regional organizations and arrangements now address a wide array of issues, including the management of international watersheds and river basins, such as the Great Lakes of North America and the Danube and Rhine rivers in Europe. They also oversee the maintenance of health and sanitation standards and coordinate regional planning and tourism. Such regional arrangements seek to overcome barriers to the rational solution of shared problems posed by international boundaries. They also provide larger arenas for the pursuit of political, economic, social, and cultural objectives.

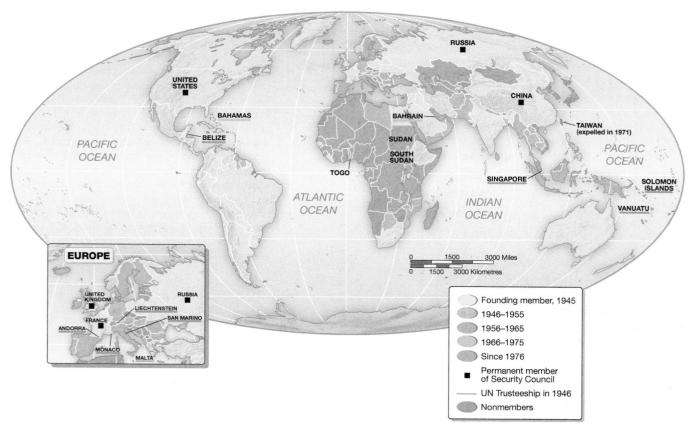

FIGURE 9.27 UN member countries Following World War II and the demise of the League of Nations, a renewed effort was made to establish an international organization aimed at instituting a system of international peace and security. Headquartered in New York City, the United Nations is composed of a Security Council, which includes permanent members (Britain, China, France, Russia, and the United States), and a General Assembly, which includes all those countries identified on the map. At the same time that the United Nations was set up, the United States lobbied for the creation of the International Monetary Fund (IMF) and the World Bank. The U.S. government had believed that World War II resulted from the collapse of world trade and financial dislocation caused by the Great Depression. The task of the IMF and the World Bank is to provide loans to stabilize currencies and enhance economic growth and trade.

A **supranational organization** is a collection of individual states with a common goal that may be economic and/or political in nature. By organizing and regulating designated operations of the individual member states, these organizations diminish, to some extent, individual state sovereignty in favour of the collective interests of the entire membership. The European Union (EU) is perhaps the best example of a supranational organization.

At the end of World War II, European leaders realized that Europe's fragmented state system was no match for the demands and levels of competition arising within the world political and economic system. They responded by creating an entity that would preserve important features of state sovereignty and identity. They also intended to create a more efficient intra-European marketing system and an entity more competitive in global transactions. **Figure 9.28** shows the original member countries of the European Economic Community, which evolved into the EU in 1992, the existing members of the EU, and those countries that are currently candidates for admission. The EU holds elections, has its own parliament and court system, and decides whether and when to allow new members to join. Generally speaking, the EU aims to create a common geographical space within Europe in which goods, services, people, and information move freely and in which a single monetary currency prevails. Whether an EU foreign policy will ever be accomplished remains to be seen, but a common European currency, the euro, has been in circulation since 2002.

Importantly, the most recent global recession has wreaked havoc on the euro and EU monetary stability. Ireland, Portugal, and Greece have huge budget deficits that have put their own economies as well as the monetary union at great risk. Spain has also shown signs of insolvency, and some EU finance personnel anticipate that France or Italy may soon follow. Indeed, the single currency adopted by most European nations is now in danger of looking more like a trap for individual countries that, by giving up their own currency, also give up economic flexibility.

Globalization, Transnational Governance, and the State

As we have already noted, globalization has been as much about restructuring geoeconomics as it has been about reshaping

FIGURE 9.28 Membership in the European Union The goal of the European Union is to increase economic integration and co-operation among the member states. The EU was established in 1992, when the Maastricht Treaty was ratified by the 12 members of the European Economic Community (EEC: Belgium, Denmark, France, Germany, Greece, Ireland, Italy, Luxembourg, Netherlands, Portugal, Spain, and the United Kingdom), which was created in 1967. Upon ratification of the treaty, the countries of the EEC became members of the EU. The treaty established European citizenship for citizens of each member state, enhanced customs and immigration agreements, and allowed for the establishment of a common currency, the euro.

(*Source:* Updated per Europa: Gateway to the European Union, http://europa.eu/abc/european_countries/index_en.htm.)

geopolitics. In fact, some globalization scholars believe that the impact of globalization on politics has been so profound that globalization is leading to the diminution of the powers of the modern state, if not its ultimate disappearance. These scholars believe that because the modern state is organized around a bounded territory and because globalization is creating a new economic space that is transnational, the state is increasingly incapable of responding to the needs of the new transnational economy. Although we do not subscribe to this position, we do recognize that the state is undergoing dramatic changes that are restructuring its role with respect to both local, domestic concerns as well as global, transnational ones.

From the end of World War II until 1989, when the Berlin Wall was dismantled, world politics was organized around two superpowers. The capitalist West rallied around the United States, and the communist East around the Soviet Union. But with the fall of the Berlin Wall signalling the end of communism, the bipolar world order came to an end. The concept of the new world order, organized around global capitalism, emerged and has increasingly solidified around a new set of political powers and institutions, which have recast the role of the state.

The increasing importance of trade-facilitating organizations such as the EU, NAFTA, the Association of Southeast Asian Nations (ASEAN), the Organization of Petroleum Exporting Countries (OPEC), and the World Trade Organization (WTO) is the most telling indicator that the world, besides being transformed into one global economic space, is also experiencing global geopolitical transformations. These organizations are unique in modern history, as they aim to treat the world and different regional clusters as seamless trading areas free of the rules that ordinarily regulate national economies.

The state must now contend with a whole new set of processes and other important political actors on the international stage as well as within its own territory. For instance, the transnational financial network that was established in the 1980s is far beyond the control of any one state to regulate effectively. In fact, what the increasing importance of transnational flows and connections—from flows of capital to flows of migrants—indicates is that the state is less a container of political or economic power and more a site of flows and connections.

The increasing importance of flows and connections means that contemporary globalization has made possible a steadily shrinking world. In short, politics can move beyond the confines of the state into the global political arena, where rapid communications enable complex supporting networks to be developed and deployed, facilitating interaction and decision making. One indication of the increasingly global nature of politics outside of formal political institutions is the rise in environmental organizations whose purview and membership are global, as discussed in Chapter 4.

What is interesting about the institutionalization of global politics is that it has been less involved with the traditional preoccupations of relations between states and military security issues and more involved with issues of economic, ecological, and social security. The massive growth in flows of trade, foreign direct investment, financial commodities, tourism, migration, crime, drugs, cultural products, and ideas has been accompanied by the emergence and expansion of global and regional institutions to manage and regulate these flows. The modern state has been drawn increasingly into this complex of global, regional, and multilateral systems of governance. And as the state has been drawn into these new activities, it has shed or de-emphasized some of its previous responsibilities, such as maintenance of social welfare.

The involvement of the state in new global activities, the growth of supranational and regional institutions and organizations, the critical significance of transnational corporations to global capital, and the proliferation of transnational social movements and professional organizations are captured by the term **international regime**. The term reflects the fact that the arena of contemporary politics is now international, so much so that even city governments and local interest groups—from sister-city organizations to car clubs—are making connections and conducting their activities both within and beyond the boundaries of their own states. An example of this is the human rights movement that has gained ascendancy over the past four to five decades.

Human Rights

Human rights, including the rights to justice, freedom, and equality, are considered by most societies to belong automatically to all people. Until World War II, safeguarding human rights was the provenance of states, whose rules and regulations legislated the proper treatment of its citizens, from prisoners to schoolchildren. Since the late 1940s and 1950s, nearly all states have come to accept the importance of a comprehensive political and legal framework that focuses on human rights and that allows an international organization to intervene in the operations of a sovereign state that is in violation of human rights. The International Bill of Human Rights was adopted by the United Nations in 1948.

In 1998, the United Nations realized another step in the protection of human rights by adopting a treaty to establish a permanent International Criminal Court (ICC). By forming the treaty, the United Nations aimed to create a permanent mechanism to bring to justice the perpetrators of such crimes as genocide, ethnic cleansing, and sexual slavery and put an end to the impunity so often enjoyed by those in positions of power. The court has the mandate to try individuals, not states, for crimes committed after July 2002. What makes the ICC unique is the principle of complementarity, which means that the court can exercise its jurisdiction only when a national court is unable or unwilling to genuinely do so itself. Thus, the importance of the international scale has increased over the past 60 years. It is important to note, however, that not all states support the ICC. Seven UN members voted against the treaty to establish the ICC: China, Iraq, Israel, Libya, Qatar, the United States, and Yemen.

An example of global human rights legislation is the UN Declaration on Rights of Indigenous People, approved in 2007, when 143 countries voted for it; 11 countries abstained; and 4—Australia, Canada, New Zealand, and the United States, all countries with very significant numbers of indigenous people—voted against it. The declaration emphasizes the rights of indigenous peoples to maintain and strengthen their own institutions, cultures, and traditions and development in keeping with their own needs and aspirations. It also prohibits discrimination against them and promotes their full and effective participation in all matters that concern them. The four "no" voting countries expressed concern about the vague language of the declaration and the impact this might have on existing, already-settled treaties.

The emergence of human rights as a globally relevant issue has occurred as groups and organizations, both governmental and nongovernmental, have been able to debate and discuss issues that concern all people everywhere and can do so at the international level through conferences, social media, email listservs, and direct action at international events. The phenomenon of different people and groups across the world in common cause is known as global civil society. **Global civil society** is composed of the broad range of institutions that operate between the private market and the state.

In the next section, we move from the international level to national, regional, and local levels in an effort to show that political geography occurs at all levels of political organization and that each facilitates significant insights about the politics of geography and the geography of politics.

APPLY YOUR KNOWLEDGE Research the arguments made by Canada about why it has not voted in favour of the UN Declaration on Rights of Indigenous People. Do you find the arguments compelling? ∎

THE TWO-WAY STREET OF POLITICS AND GEOGRAPHY

Political geography can be viewed according to two contrasting orientations. The first orientation sees it as the *politics of geography*. This perspective emphasizes that *geography*—the areal distribution/differentiation of people and objects in space—has a very real and measurable impact on politics. Regionalism and sectionalism, discussed later in this section, illustrate how geography shapes politics. This politics-of-geography orientation is also a reminder that politics occurs at all levels of the human experience, from the international order down to the neighbourhood, household, and individual body.

The second orientation sees political geography as the *geography of politics*. This approach analyzes how *politics*—the tactics or operations of the state—shapes geography. Mackinder's heartland theory and the domino theory, discussed earlier in this chapter, attempt to explain how the geography of politics works at the international level. In the heartland theory, the state expands into new territory in order to relieve population pressures. In the domino theory, as communism seeks new members, it expands geographically to incorporate new territories. As an example of the geography-of-politics orientation, consider Palestine and Israel. An examination of a series of maps of Palestine/Israel since 1923 reveals how the changing geography of this area is a response to changing international, national, regional, and local politics. (See Box 9.3, "Visualizing Geography: The Palestinian-Israeli Conflict.")

As alluded to earlier, the conflict between Palestinians and Israelis is rooted at least partly in the failure of the victors of World War I, Britain in particular, to provide the Palestinians with a state of their own when they redrew the boundaries of the region. Almost a century later, the conflict continues to be complex and highly volatile despite persistent regional and international efforts to bring peace to the region. The renewed violence that erupted in the fall of 2000 (and has persisted), just as the peace process seemed to be most promising, underscores the complexity of the problem and the difficulty of resolution. **Figure 9.E** provides a detailed timeline

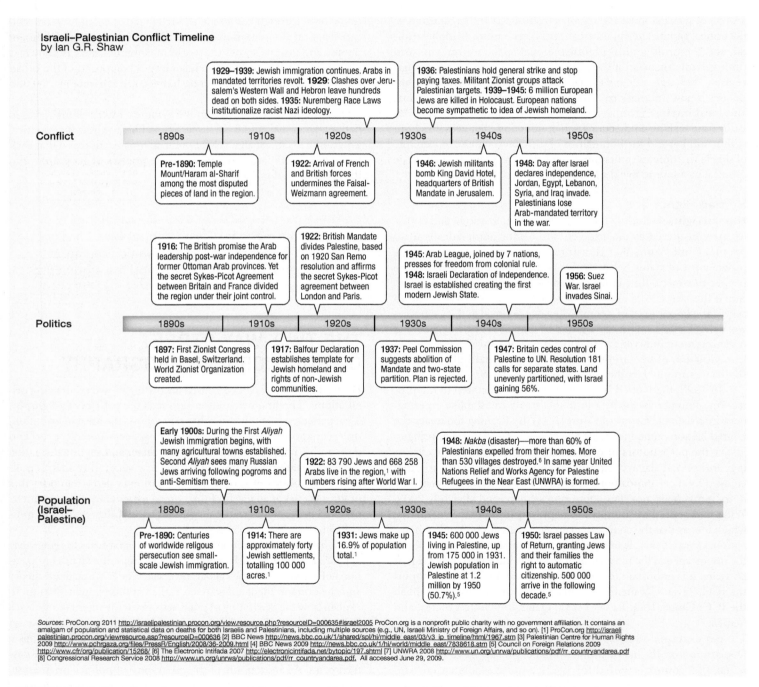

Israeli–Palestinian Conflict Timeline
by Ian G.R. Shaw

Conflict

1929–1939: Jewish immigration continues. Arabs in mandated territories revolt. **1929:** Clashes over Jerusalem's Western Wall and Hebron leave hundreds dead on both sides. **1935:** Nuremberg Race Laws institutionalize racist Nazi ideology.

1936: Palestinians hold general strike and stop paying taxes. Militant Zionist groups attack Palestinian targets. **1939–1945:** 6 million European Jews are killed in Holocaust. European nations become sympathetic to idea of Jewish homeland.

Pre-1890: Temple Mount/Haram al-Sharif among the most disputed pieces of land in the region.

1922: Arrival of French and British forces undermines the Faisal-Weizmann agreement.

1946: Jewish militants bomb King David Hotel, headquarters of British Mandate in Jerusalem.

1948: Day after Israel declares independence, Jordan, Egypt, Lebanon, Syria, and Iraq invade. Palestinians lose Arab-mandated territory in the war.

Politics

1916: The British promise the Arab leadership post-war independence for former Ottoman Arab provinces. Yet the secret Sykes-Picot Agreement between Britain and France divided the region under their joint control.

1922: British Mandate divides Palestine, based on 1920 San Remo resolution and affirms the secret Sykes-Picot agreement between London and Paris.

1945: Arab League, joined by 7 nations, presses for freedom from colonial rule. **1948:** Israeli Declaration of Independence. Israel is established creating the first modern Jewish State.

1956: Suez War. Israel invades Sinai.

1897: First Zionist Congress held in Basel, Switzerland. World Zionist Organization created.

1917: Balfour Declaration establishes template for Jewish homeland and rights of non-Jewish communities.

1937: Peel Commission suggests abolition of Mandate and two-state partition. Plan is rejected.

1947: Britain cedes control of Palestine to UN. Resolution 181 calls for separate states. Land unevenly partitioned, with Israel gaining 56%.

Population (Israel–Palestine)

Early 1900s: During the First *Aliyah* Jewish immigration begins, with many agricultural towns established. Second *Aliyah* sees many Russian Jews arriving following pogroms and anti-Semitism there.

1922: 83 790 Jews and 668 258 Arabs live in the region,[1] with numbers rising after World War I.

1948: *Nakba* (disaster)—more than 60% of Palestinians expelled from their homes. More than 530 villages destroyed.[6] In same year United Nations Relief and Works Agency for Palestine Refugees in the Near East (UNWRA) is formed.

Pre-1890: Centuries of worldwide religous persecution see small-scale Jewish immigration.

1914: There are approximately forty Jewish settlements, totalling 100 000 acres.[1]

1931: Jews make up 16.9% of population total.[1]

1945: 600 000 Jews living in Palestine, up from 175 000 in 1931. Jewish population in Palestine at 1.2 million by 1950 (50.7%).[5]

1950: Israel passes Law of Return, granting Jews and their families the right to automatic citizenship. 500 000 arrive in the following decade.[5]

Sources: ProCon.org 2011 http://israelipalestinian.procon.org/view.resource.php?resourceID=000635#israel2005 ProCon.org is a nonprofit public charity with no government affiliation. It contains an amalgam of population and statistical data on deaths for both Israelis and Palestinians, including multiple sources (e.g., UN, Israeli Ministry of Foreign Affairs, and so on). [1] ProCon.org http://israeli palestinian.procon.org/viewresource.asp?resourceID=000636 [2] BBC News http://news.bbc.co.uk/1/shared/spl/hi/middle_east/03/v3_ip_timeline/html/1967.stm [3] Palestinian Centre for Human Rights 2009 http://www.pchrgaza.org/files/PressR/English/2008/36-2009.html [4] BBC News 2009 http://news.bbc.co.uk/1/hi/world/middle_east/7838618.stm [5] Council on Foreign Relations 2009 http://www.cfr.org/publication/15268/ [6] The Electronic Intifada 2007 http://electronicintifada.net/bytopic/197.shtml [7] UNWRA 2008 http://www.un.org/unrwa/publications/pdf/rr_countryandarea.pdf [8] Congressional Research Service 2008 http://www.un.org/unrwa/publications/pdf/rr_countryandarea.pdf. All accessed June 29, 2009.

FIGURE 9.E Timeline of events surrounding the conflict between Israelis and Palestinians This timeline, prepared by geographer Ian Shaw for use in this textbook, shows the different conflicts as well as the larger political and population issues around which these conflicts have been played out. (*Source:* Ian Shaw)

of events in Israel and Palestine that helps in understanding the complex situation.

The state of Israel is a mid-twentieth-century construction that has its roots in the emergence of **Zionism**, a late-nineteenth-century European movement to establish a legally recognized home in Palestine for the Jewish people. Thousands of European Jews, inspired by the early Zionist movement, began migrating to Palestine around 1900. When the Ottoman Empire was defeated in 1917, the British gained control over Palestine and the neighbouring Transjordan area. In the so-called Balfour Declaration,

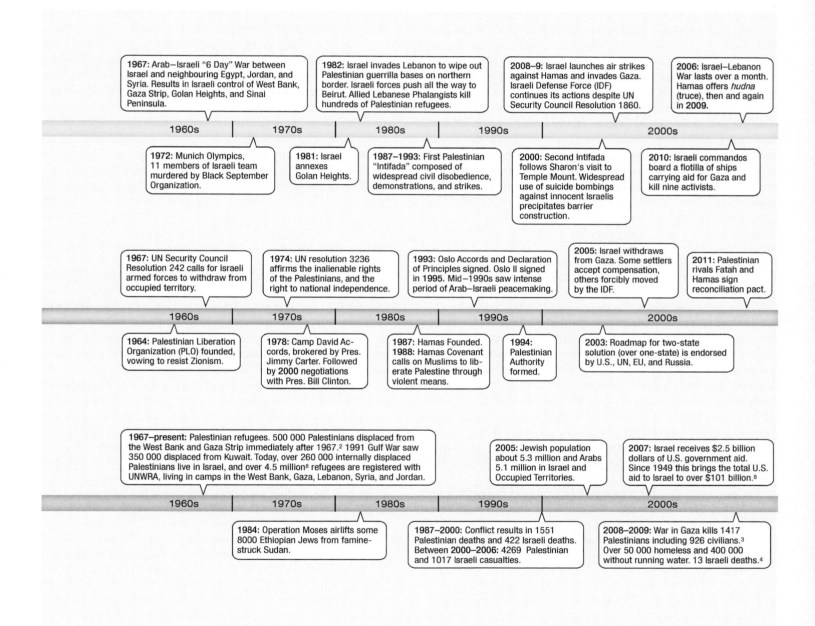

1967: Arab–Israeli "6 Day" War between Israel and neighbouring Egypt, Jordan, and Syria. Results in Israeli control of West Bank, Gaza Strip, Golan Heights, and Sinai Peninsula.

1982: Israel invades Lebanon to wipe out Palestinian guerrilla bases on northern border. Israeli forces push all the way to Beirut. Allied Lebanese Phalangists kill hundreds of Palestinian refugees.

2008–9: Israel launches air strikes against Hamas and invades Gaza. Israeli Defense Force (IDF) continues its actions despite UN Security Council Resolution 1860.

2006: Israel–Lebanon War lasts over a month. Hamas offers *hudna* (truce), then and again in 2009.

| 1960s | 1970s | 1980s | 1990s | 2000s |

1972: Munich Olympics, 11 members of Israeli team murdered by Black September Organization.

1981: Israel annexes Golan Heights.

1987–1993: First Palestinian "Intifada" composed of widespread civil disobedience, demonstrations, and strikes.

2000: Second Intifada follows Sharon's visit to Temple Mount. Widespread use of suicide bombings against innocent Israelis precipitates barrier construction.

2010: Israeli commandos board a flotilla of ships carrying aid for Gaza and kill nine activists.

1967: UN Security Council Resolution 242 calls for Israeli armed forces to withdraw from occupied territory.

1974: UN resolution 3236 affirms the inalienable rights of the Palestinians, and the right to national independence.

1993: Oslo Accords and Declaration of Principles signed. Oslo II signed in 1995. Mid–1990s saw intense period of Arab–Israeli peacemaking.

2005: Israel withdraws from Gaza. Some settlers accept compensation, others forcibly moved by the IDF.

2011: Palestinian rivals Fatah and Hamas sign reconciliation pact.

| 1960s | 1970s | 1980s | 1990s | 2000s |

1964: Palestinian Liberation Organization (PLO) founded, vowing to resist Zionism.

1978: Camp David Accords, brokered by Pres. Jimmy Carter. Followed by 2000 negotiations with Pres. Bill Clinton.

1987: Hamas Founded. **1988:** Hamas Covenant calls on Muslims to liberate Palestine through violent means.

1994: Palestinian Authority formed.

2003: Roadmap for two-state solution (over one-state) is endorsed by U.S., UN, EU, and Russia.

1967–present: Palestinian refugees. 500 000 Palestinians displaced from the West Bank and Gaza Strip immediately after 1967.[2] 1991 Gulf War saw 350 000 displaced from Kuwait. Today, over 260 000 internally displaced Palestinians live in Israel, and over 4.5 million[8] refugees are registered with UNWRA, living in camps in the West Bank, Gaza, Lebanon, Syria, and Jordan.

2005: Jewish population about 5.3 million and Arabs 5.1 million in Israel and Occupied Territories.

2007: Israel receives $2.5 billion dollars of U.S. government aid. Since 1949 this brings the total U.S. aid to Israel to over $101 billion.[8]

| 1960s | 1970s | 1980s | 1990s | 2000s |

1984: Operation Moses airlifts some 8000 Ethiopian Jews from famine-struck Sudan.

1987–2000: Conflict results in 1551 Palestinian deaths and 422 Israeli deaths. Between **2000–2006:** 4269 Palestinian and 1017 Israeli casualties.

2008–2009: War in Gaza kills 1417 Palestinians including 926 civilians.[3] Over 50 000 homeless and 400 000 without running water. 13 Israeli deaths.[4]

(Continued)

they signalled to the Jewish Diaspora that they would "view with favour the establishment in Palestine of a national home for the Jewish people." This was a problematic promise, however, because the Palestinian people already occupied the area and because Arabs in general viewed the arrival of increasing numbers of Jews as an incursion into the sacred lands of Islam. In response to increasing Palestinian–Jewish tensions in the area, the British limited Jewish immigration to Palestine from the late 1930s through the end of World War II—just as Jewish refugees from Europe were desperately looking for a safe haven from murderous Nazi persecution.

In 1947, Britain announced that it would withdraw from Palestine in 1948, turning it over to the newly founded United Nations. The UN, under heavy pressure from the United States, responded by voting to partition Palestine into Arab and Jewish states and designated Jerusalem as an international city, preventing either group from having exclusive control. The Jewish state was to have 56 percent of the mandate of Palestine; an Arab state was to have 43 percent; and Jerusalem, a city sacred to Jews, Muslims, and Christians, was to be administered by the United Nations. The proposed UN plan was accepted by the Jews but angrily rejected by the Arabs, who argued that a mandated territory could not legally be taken from an indigenous population.

The very day Britain withdrew in 1948, war broke out. Combined forces from Egypt, Jordan, and Lebanon, as well as smaller units from Syria, Iraq, and Saudi Arabia, confronted the Israelis. Their goal was not only to prevent the Jewish forces from gaining control over additional Palestinian territory but also to wipe out the newly formed Jewish state altogether. This war, which became known as the first Arab–Israeli war, resulted in the defeat of the Arab forces in 1949, and later armistice agreements enabled Israel to expand beyond the UN plan by gaining the western sector of Jerusalem, including parts of the Old City. In 1950, Israel declared Jerusalem its national capital, though very few countries have recognized this.

Israel maintained the new borders gained during the first Arab–Israeli war for another 18 years until the Six-Day War in 1967, which resulted in further gains for Israel, including the Sinai Peninsula along the Suez Canal and the strategically important Golan Heights in the southwestern corner of Syria. The eastern sector of Jerusalem, previously held by Jordan, was also annexed during the Six-Day War. **Figure 9.F** shows the territorial changes brought about by both wars and peace treaties. (Israel returned all of Sinai to Egyptian control by 1988.)

The territorial expansion of Israel dramatically transformed the landscape of Palestine and created 700 000 Palestinians refugees. Today, five million of their descendants live as refugees either in other Arab countries in the region, abroad, under Israeli occupation in the West Bank (also known as the "Occupied Territory"), or in the Gaza Strip. By the late 1980s, Palestinians in the West Bank and Gaza Strip had become so angered by Israeli territorial policies, particularly the spreading Israeli settlements, that they rose up in rebellion, known as the *intifada* ("uprising"). In addition to the intifada, other Palestinian groups have coalesced in opposition to the Israeli occupation. The Palestinian Liberation Organization (PLO) was formed in 1964 as an organization devoted to returning Palestine to the Palestinians. Since its official recognition, the PLO has become the Palestinian Authority and is seen as the legitimate representative of the Palestinian people. Another, less conciliatory, group representing the Palestinian cause is Hamas (Islamic Resistance Movement), whose activities are largely centred in the Gaza Strip.

Since the mid-1990s, hopes for peace in the region have risen and fallen repeatedly. Multiple rounds of peace talks, often mediated by the United States, did not produce an agreement. In the meantime, Israel is continuing to build settlements on Palestinian territory while at the same time relinquishing direct control of selected territory to Palestinians (for example, by withdrawing from the Gaza Strip in 2005).

In an effort to create a physical separation between Israelis and Palestinians, Israel has been constructing security barriers around Palestinian territory. Since 1994, the Gaza Strip is separated from Israel by a barrier consisting of barbed-wire fencing with sensors and adjoining buffer zones. Since Israel's withdrawal from the Gaza Strip in 2005, Egypt has erected a similar barrier along its border with the Gaza Strip. Both Israel and Egypt argue that the barrier is essential to prevent the infiltration of terrorists. Even more controversial is the security barrier currently being constructed around the West Bank. Once completed, it will consist of about 600 kilometres of wire fences and about 100 kilometres (mainly in urban areas) of a concrete wall that is

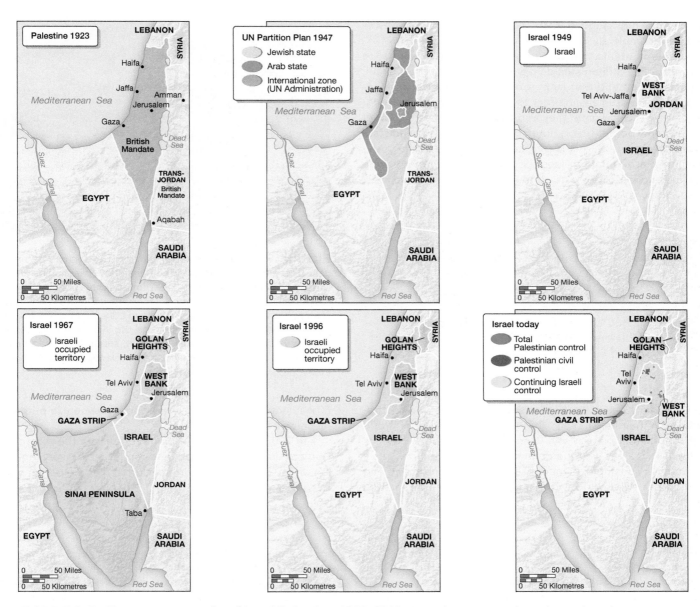

FIGURE 9.F Changing geography of Israel/Palestine, 1923–2011 Since the creation of Israel out of much of what had been Palestine in 1947, the geography of the region has undergone significant transformation. A series of wars between Israelis and Arabs and a number of political decisions by Israel have produced the changing geographies we see here. (*Source:* Adapted with permission from Prentice Hall, from J. M. Rubenstein, *The Cultural Landscape: An Introduction to Human Geography,* 5th ed., 1996, p. 233)

(Continued)

eight metres high (**Figure 9.G**). Together, they will seal off the West Bank completely.

Israel maintains that building the barrier is essential to preventing Palestinian suicide bombers from entering Israel. Palestinians contend that its purpose is geographical containment of the Palestinians in order to pave the way for an expansion of Israeli sovereignty. They also fear that the security barrier creates a new border that is not negotiable if a Palestinian state were to be created. This is particularly objectionable to the Palestinians as the barrier does not always follow the 1949 armistice line and effectively cuts off roughly 10 percent of the West Bank territory.

VIRTUAL GEOGRAPHIES

To learn about the geography of the wall and the small scale of the area under dispute, you can take a helicopter ride with a BBC correspondent at **www.bbc.co.uk/news/world-middle-east-11139865.**

FIGURE 9.G Israeli security barrier The security barrier, called "the wall" or the "apartheid wall" by Palestinians and other opponents, is a physical barrier consisting of a network of fences, trenches, and, as in this section, a concrete wall eight metres high. Israel's stated purpose in constructing it is to create a zone of security between itself and the West Bank. Palestinians charge that it cuts through lived space, separating villagers from their orchards and labourers from their places of work. (*Source:* Joel Carillet/Getty Images)

On a daily basis, the barrier separates Palestinian settlements from their fields, orchards, jobs, and markets. The World Bank reports that poverty and unemployment in the West Bank are highest in areas with the greatest mobility restrictions. As a consequence, unemployment rates in the West Bank are among the highest in the world, with youth unemployment reaching 50 percent. Real wages have dropped between 25 percent and 45 percent since 1999.

In 2003, the United Nations requested the International Court of Justice in The Hague to render an advisory legal opinion on the barrier. The court concluded that the barrier violated international law.

The Politics of Geography

Territory is often regarded as a space to which a particular group attaches its identity. Related to this concept of territory is the notion of **self-determination**, which refers to the right of a group with a distinctive politico-territorial identity to determine its own destiny, at least in part, through the control of its own territory.

Regionalism and Sectionalism

Different groups with different identities—religious or ethnic—sometimes coexist within the same state boundaries. At times, discordance between legal and political boundaries and the distribution of populations with distinct identities leads to movements to claim or reclaim particular territories. These movements, whether conflictual or peaceful, are known as *regional movements*. **Regionalism** is a feeling of collective identity based on a population's politico-territorial identification within a state or across state boundaries. If such feelings develop into an extreme devotion to regional interests and customs, the condition is known as **sectionalism.**

Regionalism often involves ethnic groups who seek autonomy from an interventionist state and the development of political power. The Basque provinces of northern Spain and southern France have sought autonomy from those states for most of the twentieth century (**Figure 9.29**). The Basque people are one of the oldest European peoples, with a distinctive culture and

FIGURE 9.29 Basque independence poster This independence poster is plastered over the door of a shop in Donostia (San Sebastian) in one of the Basque provinces of Spain. The poster is a sign of the passionate opposition the Basques have adopted toward the central government in Madrid. What is most interesting about the sign is that it is written in neither Castilian Spanish (the national language) nor Euskadi (the Basque language), but in English. It appears as though this and declarations like it are directed at international tourists in an attempt to gain the attention of the *global civil society* we discussed earlier. (*Source:* Courtesy of Sallie A. Marston)

FIGURE 9.30 Kurdish independence protest Kurdish protestors take part in a demonstration as they march on a bridge, in 2011 in Istanbul after Turkey's electoral board barred prominent Kurdish candidates from standing in upcoming elections. The Peace and Democracy Party (BDP), Turkey's main Kurdish political movement, urged an extraordinary parliamentary session to resolve the problem. (*Source:* Mustafa Ozer/afp/Getty Images/Newscom)

language. Since the 1950s, agitation for political independence has included—especially for the Basques in Spain—terrorist acts. The Spanish move to parliamentary democracy and the granting of autonomy to the Basque provinces did not squelch the Basque thirst for self-determination. On the French side, the Basque separatist movement is neither as violent nor as active as the movement in Spain.

Another separatist movement is the EZLN (Ejército Zapatista de Liberación Nacional), the Zapatista Army of Liberation, which practises a different type of revolutionary autonomy. Composed largely of indigenous peasants from Chiapas, one of the poorest states in Mexico, the EZLN opposes the Mexican federal state and its embrace of corporate globalization, arguing that it oppresses them by denying the peasant way of life. A key element of the Zapatista ideology is their aspiration to practise politics in a truly participatory way, from the "bottom-up," by guaranteeing the right of indigenous peoples to form and govern traditionally their own municipalities. In doing so, the Zapatistas reject official authorities and elect their own at the same time that they refuse federal government involvement and control. The Zapatistas have been building this autonomous form of governing since 1994 with dramatically beneficial results for community health, education, housing, and general welfare.

We need only look at the long list of territorially based conflicts that have emerged in the post–Cold War world to realize the extent to which territorially based ethnicity remains a potent force in the politics of geography. For example, the Kurds continue to fight for their own state separate from Turkey and Iraq (**Figure 9.30**).

Consider also the former Yugoslavia, whose geography has fractured along ethnic and religious lines (**Figure 9.31**). Regionalism also underlay efforts to peacefully sever Scotland from the United Kingdom, which were rejected in a referendum in 2014.

Of course, the ongoing project of Quebec separation is another example. In describing the Québécois as a nation that has inhabited the land of Quebec since the beginning of the seventeenth century, the separatist movement uses all of the place-making and cultural devices at its disposal—Québécois folk music, architecture, and heritage have all been vigorously promoted, as has the use of the Quebec flag, the *fleur-de-lys* (**Figure 9.32**). But of all the means by which the nationalist project is advanced in Quebec, none has been more successful (or disliked by its detractors) than the insistence that French is the official language of the province. French is the language of the schools, of government, and of road and store signs. English-language store signs are the targets of graffiti artists and the *Office québécois de la langue française* (see Chapter 5). Increasingly, in fact, the attempt to create a nation has overtly shifted from an exclusionary ethnic focus on those descended from the original French settlers of the province to a more broadly based "cultural nationalism" that is based on the French language and embraces anyone sympathetic to its aims.

Finally, we should note that the politics of geography, in terms of sectionalism, also finds strong focus today in rural versus urban politics. In France, for example, attitudes about birth control (and birth rates themselves) are significantly different between the urbanized north of the country and the more rural south. Throughout the EU, farmers have fought the removal of farm subsidies and tariff arrangements advocated by urban-based policymakers because the existing arrangements have long protected agricultural livelihoods. The dispute pits the politics of local farmers against an international organization. In England and Wales, a rural-versus-urban conflict over foxhunting persists. In the countryside, foxhunting is largely

FIGURE 9.31 Map of the former Yugoslavia The former Yugoslavia now consists of seven states: Slovenia, Croatia, Bosnia and Herzegovina, Serbia, Montenegro, Kosovo, and Macedonia. For the most part, the boundaries of Yugoslavia were laid out only in the twentieth century, across segments of the Austro-Hungarian and Ottoman empires that had acquired a complex mixture of ethnic groups. The history of these boundaries has also been the history of ethnic conflict revolving around claims to territory, as well as religious intolerance. As this map shows, with the exception of Slovenia, the new states are home to a mix of nationalities. (*Source*: Redrawn with permission from Prentice Hall, from J. M. Rubenstein, *The Cultural Landscape: An Introduction to Human Geography*, 6th ed., © 1999, p. 260.)

seen as a ritual of rural life, but the Hunting Act of 2004 made it illegal to hunt a mammal using a dog. The act pitted a group called the Countryside Alliance, which continues to seek repeal of the act, against animal rights activists, mostly headquartered in large British cities, and the London-based Parliament.

Competition also exists among cities, as well as among states. The most ubiquitous form of this competition revolves around the desire by local and state authorities to attract corporate investment (as discussed in Chapter 7). Often corporations play the jurisdictions against each other in attempts to obtain the most attractive investment packages. At other times, cities and states compete to induce the government to locate government facilities within their jurisdictions.

APPLY YOUR KNOWLEDGE Research a self-determination movement somewhere in the world. Describe the roles that territory and power play in the aims of the group. ■

FIGURE 9.32 The St. Jean Baptiste parade, Montreal The feast day of Saint Jean the Baptist on June 24 is celebrated as the Quebec National Holiday. Revellers wear white-and-blue clothing and carry the *fleur-de-lys* flag as a sign of national sentiment. (*Source*: Courtesy of Alan E. Nash)

The Geography of Politics and Geographical Systems of Representation

An obvious way to show how politics shapes geography is to demonstrate how systems of political representation are geographically anchored. For instance, Canada has a political system in which democratic rule and territorial organization are linked by the concept of territorial representation.

Democratic rule describes a system in which public policies and officials are directly chosen by popular vote. **Territorial representation** is a system of government formally structured by area, not by social groups. Thus, voters vote for officials and policies that will represent them and affect them *where they live*. In this way, geography and politics—space and power—are intimately connected. Canada has inherited this system from Britain and shares this approach to voting and elections with many other countries.

But unlike Britain (which is a unitary state), Canada is a federal state in which powers are divided between the federal government and the provinces. (Municipal government is under provincial jurisdiction, and the territories are ultimately a federal responsibility.) The bottom line is that in Canada—as in many other representative democracies—politics is geography. People and their interests gain representation in government through the location of their interests in particular places and through their relative ability to capture political control of *geographically based* political units.

In Canada these units form a nested hierarchy of jurisdictions (municipal, provincial and territorial, and federal), each represented by its own spatial unit of representation (*boroughs* or *wards* at the city level, *ridings* at the provincial or territorial and federal level) and its own elected representatives (such as councillors, members of the legislative or national assembly [MPPs, MLAs, or MNAs], and, at the federal level, members of Parliament [MPs]).

At Confederation in 1867, the British North America Act established that the four provinces (Ontario, Quebec, New Brunswick, and Nova Scotia) that composed Canada at the time should have a Parliament comprising two houses. The upper house, the Senate, was to consist of non-elected members appointed to represent their regions. The lower house, the House of Commons, was to be elected by the people. For the purposes of electing the members of the House of Commons (the MPs), the general principle of representation by population was adopted, and the provinces were to be divided into ridings (or seats).

From the very start, the historical compromises at the root of Canadian confederation meant that this general principle has been subject to the need to recognize Canada's diversity, Quebec's status, and the position of the smaller provinces and territories as Canada grew in population size and geographical extent (**Figure 9.33**). The process of changing the allocation of seats according to changes in the census figures is called **reapportionment**. The

FIGURE 9.33 Canada's political geography: provinces and territories For more than 150 years, Canada has been a "work in progress" with provinces and territories emerging at various times. (*Source:* Geoffrey J. Matthews and Robert Morrow, *Canada and the World: An Atlas Resource,* 2nd ed. Scarborough, ON: Prentice Hall, 1995, pp. 5–6; see also the National Atlas of Canada's website at http://atlas.gc.ca/, where a sequence of maps on the territorial evolution of Canada can be found.)

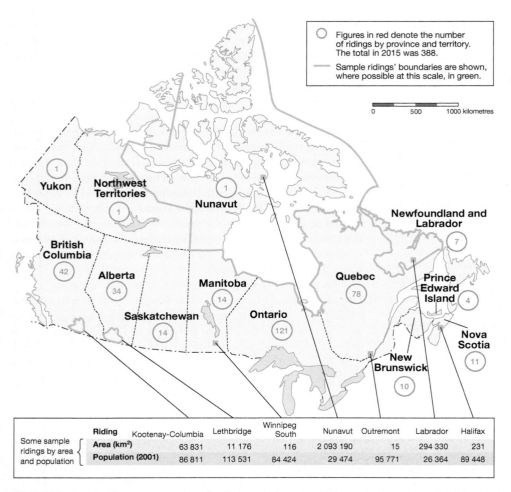

Some sample ridings by area and population	Riding	Kootenay-Columbia	Lethbridge	Winnipeg South	Nunavut	Outremont	Labrador	Halifax
	Area (km²)	63 831	11 176	116	2 093 190	15	294 330	231
	Population (2001)	86 811	113 531	84 424	29 474	95 771	26 364	89 448

FIGURE 9.34 The geography of a federal election This map shows the distribution of federal *ridings* (election districts), by province and territory. Canada's vast territorial expanse and very uneven population distribution pose difficulties for the creation of ridings that are equal in terms of population. Low population densities in rural and northern areas make it very difficult for ridings to reach national averages for population before they become physically too large for one person (the MP) to represent adequately. For example, the entire territory of Nunavut comprises only one federal riding. It is more than 2 million square kilometres but has a population of only 29 474. The much higher population densities of urban and southern regions mean that there are more ridings in these areas and, all other things being equal, that their interests predominate in the House of Commons. Of the examples shown on the map, the small inner Montreal district of Outremont is the smallest, with an area of only 15 square kilometres, but with a population of 95 771. The challenges of balancing competing spatial interests lie at the heart of electoral geography. (*Source:* Number of electoral districts and district boundaries are taken from the Elections Canada website at www.elections.ca.)

Fair Representation Act of 2011 increased the total number of seats from 308 to 388 to account for population growth in British Columbia, Alberta, Ontario, and Quebec (**Figure 9.34**). Other systems of representation exist throughout the world. For example, many electoral systems are based on representing special constituencies in the legislative branch of government. In Pakistan, for example, there are four seats for Christians; four seats for Hindus and people belonging to the scheduled castes; and one seat each for the Sikh, Buddhist, and Parsi communities. The point is that systems of representation are very much tied to the history of a country, with some very sensitive to the way that history and geography (who lives where) come together. These systems are both a product of and an important influence on the political culture of a country.

APPLY YOUR KNOWLEDGE What are the challenges that the Canadian system of representation is facing *in terms of geography*? Do you think all areas/populations are fairly represented? ■

future Geographies

The end of the Cold War, the widespread availability of telecommunications, the transnational reorganization of industry and finance, and the liberalization of trade all suggest that a new global political and economic order is already underway. With the rapid growth of India and China and the growing prominence of the European Union, it would seem that a multipolar world is emerging, one that includes the United States but is no longer dominated by the United States. This new, multipolar world might come close to that elusive "new world order" that seemed within reach after the collapse of communism. On the other hand, some observers expect a reinvigorated Russia under Vladimir Putin to assert itself as a new alternative to the West. If that happens, it will likely cause renewed tension, possibly even a new Cold War. Overall, even under such a scenario of tension, the prospects for political stability and national integrity in the global core are much better than in the global periphery.

In the periphery, the chances for increasing ethnic rivalry and conflict are high. For instance, despite the recent popular vote for the creation of Southern Sudan, conflict there between the Muslim majority and Christian and animist minorities is still ongoing. In addition, rivalries of ethnic groups are simmering, erupting into violence at the slightest provocation. Internal conflicts such as this risk escalation into regional conflicts and possibly even the failure of states. Weak states can become hosts to violent drug cartels (as in Mexico) and terrorist groups (as in Syria and Iraq, where the Islamic State (IS) militants are establishing a territorial base), serving as launching pads for taking the disturbances back to the core. In the extreme, states can fail altogether and disintegrate into wild zones (as in Somalia).

Both core and periphery are increasingly affected by terrorism, the unexpected scourge of the twenty-first century. Terrorism is unpredictable; the threat is always and everywhere. Even worse, it cannot be conquered with the traditional methods of diplomacy, statecraft, or military intervention. The amorphous character of the threat of terrorism has led the democratic core states to embark on a dangerous course: the more they try to reduce the possibility of attack by constantly surveilling their own citizens, the more they risk losing their greatest achievement: human rights, civil rights, and the rule of law.

CONCLUSION

The globalization of the economy has been largely facilitated by states extending their spheres of influence and paving the way for the smooth functioning of markets and industries. Political geography is as much about what happens at the global level as it is about what happens at other levels of spatial resolution, from the region and the neighbourhood to the household and the individual.

Theories of the state have been one of geography's most important contributions to understanding politics. Ratzel's emphasis on the relationship between power and territory and Mackinder's model of the geographical pivot remind us that space and territory shape the actions of states in both dramatic and mundane ways. Time and space shape politics, and events distant in time and space—such as colonialism—continue to have impacts long afterward. For example, the civil war in Northern Ireland, instigated by English colonial practices now centuries old, has only recently shown signs of ceasing. The impacts of English colonization have also been felt in countries throughout the Northern Hemisphere, as well as by neighbours living unhappily side by side for several generations in cities like Belfast and Boston.

Continuing strife also characterizes the enduring North/South divide that pits core countries against peripheral, mostly formerly colonial, countries.

Perhaps the most surprising political/geographical transformation of this century has been the near dissolution of the East/West divide. Although it is too soon to tell whether communism has truly been superseded by capitalism, the distinctions between them are certainly more blurred than they once were.

Perhaps the most significant aspect of contemporary globalization is the emergence of a new world order and a resulting focus on terrorism as well as the growth of transnational institutions of governance. Both forces are reshaping not only governing structures and economic processes (creating new layers of rules, regulations, and policies, as well as new ways of political interaction among and between nation-states) but also the practices of everyday life (as citizens deal with increased personal security measures and the transformation of human rights).

The pairing of the terms *politics* and *geography* serves to remind us that politics is clearly geographical at the same time that geography is unavoidably political. The divisions of area into states, provinces, counties, cities, and towns mean that where we live shapes our politics, and vice versa. Geography is politics, just as politics is geography. And geographical systems of representation, as well as identity politics based on regional histories, confirm this interactive relationship.

Learning Outcomes Revisited

■ Express the geopolitical model of the state and explain how it links geography and state practices with respect to the key issues of power and territory.

The ancient Greek philosopher Aristotle is often considered the first political geographer because his model of the state is based upon factors such as climate, terrain, and the relationship between population and territory. Other important political geographers have promoted theories of the state that incorporated elements of the landscape and the physical environment, as well as population characteristics of regions. Later scholars theorized that the state operated cyclically and organically. Twentieth-century theorists such as Foucault, Althusser, and Deleuze have shifted focus away from viewing the state as a set of institutions; they are more concerned with how state power is assembled and deployed.

- Compare and contrast the ways that different contemporary theorists—from Deleuze to Althusser—approach the state as a political and geographical entity.

  The state is also a set of institutions for the protection and maintenance of society. A state is not only a place, a bounded territory, it is also an active entity that operates through the rules and regulations of its various institutions. State theorist Louis Althusser views the state as both ideological and repressive. Michel Foucault, another state theorist, has explored the ways that power, knowledge, and discourse operate to produce particular kinds of state subjects. Gilles Deleuze sees the state as a force that is greater than the formal institutions that constitute it. Deleuze believes that the state is best thought of as a *machine* whose purpose is to regulate and dominate.

- Interpret how imperialism, colonialism, heartland theory, domino theory, the end of the Cold War, and the emergence of the new world order are key examples of ways geography has influenced politics and politics has influenced geography.

  Geopolitics may involve the extension of power by one group over another. There are many different manifestations of this phenomenon. Imperialism and colonialism involve occupation and control by one state over another. Heartland theory recognizes that a central location is pivotal to political and geographical control, whereas domino theory reflects the significance of proximity in the extension of power and control. During the Cold War blocks of the global political system—capitalist versus communist—were in direct and indirect conflict. The current new world order is a manifestation of the decline of those old conflicts and the emergence of new ones.

- Demonstrate how the growth and proliferation of international and supranational organizations created the foundation for the emergence of global forms of governance.

  Just as states are key players in political geography, so too have international and supranational organizations become important participants in the world-system in the past century. These organizations have become increasingly important means of achieving goals such as the increased flow of goods and information and more co-operative management of shared resources, such as water.

- Recognize how events of international political significance are usually the result of East/West and North/South divisions, whereas national and local political issues emerge out of tensions related to regionalism and sectionalism.

  Capitalist colonialism and imperialism were key factors in producing global state divisions around capitalism versus communism (East/West) and rich versus poor (North/South). More recently, local divisions have emerged that reflect differences in ethnicity, political orientations, and economic commitments, among others. These are expressed through regionalism and sectionalism.

- Describe the difference between the politics of geography and the geography of politics as manifestations of the two-way relationship between politics and geography.

  Political geography can be viewed through two contrasting lenses. The first orientation sees it as the *politics of geography*. This perspective emphasizes that *geography*—the areal distribution/differentiation of people and objects in space—has a very real and measurable impact on politics. The second orientation sees political geography as the *geography of politics*. This approach analyzes how *politics*—the tactics or operations of the state—shapes geography.

KEY TERMS

citizenship *(p. 322)*
confederation *(p. 325)*
decolonization *(p. 335)*
democratic rule *(p. 357)*
discourse *(p. 326)*
domino theory *(p. 340)*
East/West divide *(p. 340)*
federal state *(p. 324)*
geopolitics *(p. 318)*

global civil society *(p. 349)*
human rights *(p. 349)*
international organization *(p. 335)*
international regime *(p. 349)*
nation *(p. 322)*
nation-state *(p. 322)*
nationalism *(p. 324)*

new world order *(p. 341)*
North/South divide *(p. 335)*
Orientalism *(p. 332)*
reapportionment *(p. 357)*
regionalism *(p. 354)*
sectionalism *(p. 354)*
self-determination *(p. 354)*
sovereignty *(p. 322)*

state *(p. 322)*
supranational organization *(p. 347)*
territorial representation *(p. 357)*
territory *(p. 318)*
terrorism *(p. 341)*
unitary state *(p. 324)*
Zionism *(p. 351)*

REVIEW AND DISCUSSION

1. Compare two maps of Europe (not including Russia and the former Soviet Union), one from 1930 and one from the present. How do issues of ethnicity, religion, and political-economic system (communist, capitalist) help explain the changes in boundaries that have occurred? Identify any areas on the map that you feel may be the sites of future border changes and explain why.

2. Research the current sovereignty debate over the Arctic Ocean. Examine the debate in light of the concepts you just read about. Is Canada justified in claiming the Northwest Passage as territorial waters? What sort of arguments are being made for and against?

3. Should Canada adopt a voting system that is not based on territorial representation? What would be the (dis)advantages of changing to another system?

4. Using the state theorists' ideas, discuss how you have been "made" into a Canadian by the institutions you have gone through in your life so far (school, church, cadets, hockey teams, etc.).

5. Research current events for evidence of an "international regime" (e.g., the International Criminal Court). How has the existence of this international regime changed the interaction between states?

Log in to www.masteringgeography.com for MapMaster™ interactive maps, geography videos, RSS feeds, flashcards, weblinks, an eText version of *Human Geography: Places and Regions in Global Context*, and self-study quizzes to enhance your study of political geographies.

MapMaster™ presents 13 Place Name and 13 Layered Thematic interactive maps to help students practise and master their geographic literacy, spatial reasoning, and critical thinking skills.

10 URBANIZATION

Mostly off the world's radar, on a dusty plain in West Africa, is a city of 1.8 million people. Bisected by the Niger River, its two halves—with about 900 000 inhabitants each—are linked by only two bridges. The pressure of movement is so strong that every morning one of these bridges is dedicated exclusively to incoming traffic: minibuses, bicycles, motorbikes, pedestrians, and occasionally private cars. In the evenings, leaving the centre involves joining an exodus of people toward the minibus depots as the process reverses. Green vans loaded with passengers file out to residential neighbourhoods as far as 20 kilometres away.

This is Bamako, Mali. It contracts into its centre every morning and breathes out again in the evening. With each breath Bamako grows bigger. It happens to be one of the fastest-growing cities in the world. Natural population growth is supplemented by migration from the countryside and other Malian cities. Its population in 2008 was 50 percent larger than in 1998, resulting in a city that is now roughly the same size as Budapest, Dubai, or Warsaw. It has 10 times more inhabitants than the next biggest Malian city and accommodates 70 percent of the country's industrial establishments. New neighbourhoods—*quartiers*—formerly villages, become consolidated with the rest of the city, as it grows to the south, east, and west. Some people are now moving out of Bamako into surrounding neighbourhoods in search of cheaper land and some tranquility, but they remain within reach of the city because it provides their

Cars, motorcycles, and pedestrians crowd the busy streets of Bamako, Mali, West Africa. *(Source: Jake Lyell/Alamy)*

livelihoods. Despite its industriousness, Bamako is one of the sleepier cities in West Africa. Many of the manufactured staples travel 1200 kilometres by road from one of the region's metropolises, Abidjan in Côte d'Ivoire, which has more than twice Bamako's population. And Abidjan in turn seems small beside Lagos, Nigeria, with an estimated population of 20 million—whose residents speak of living in a pressure cooker.

In Lagos, some families rent rooms to sleep for six hours and then turn them over to another family that takes their place. Shopping does not necessarily require travel: goods are brought on foot and cart to drivers stuck in Lagos's interminable traffic jams. To some, like the authors of Lagos's 1980 master plan, written when the city had just 2.5 million residents, the continuing growth of the city is "undisciplined."

What can possibly be so attractive about living in Lagos that, despite its congestion and crime, it continues to draw migrants? The short answer: economic density. Lagos is not the most economically dense city in the world, nor even the most densely populated. Those distinctions belong to central London and Mumbai, respectively. Even so, Nigeria's economic future and Lagos's growth are as inextricably tied as Britain's economy is to London's growth. No country has developed without the growth of its cities. As countries become richer, economic activity becomes more densely packed into towns, cities, and metropolises. ∎

URBAN GEOGRAPHY AND URBANIZATION

Urbanization is one of the most important geographic phenomena in today's world. The United Nations Centre for Human Settlements (UNCHS) notes that the growth of cities and the urbanization of rural areas are now irreversible because of the global shift to technological-, industrial-, and service-based economies. The proportion of the world's population living in urban settlements is growing at a rapid rate, and the world's economic, social, cultural, and political processes are increasingly being played out within and between the world's systems of towns and cities. In this chapter we describe the extent and pattern of urbanization across the world, explaining its causes and the resultant changes wrought in people and places.

Urbanization and Changing Human Geographies

From small market towns and fishing ports to megacities of millions of people, the urban areas of the world are the linchpins of human geographies. They have always been a crucial element in spatial organization and the evolution of societies, but today they are more important than ever. Between 1980 and 2010, the number of city dwellers worldwide rose by 1.7 billion. Cities now account for over half the world's population. Much of the developed world has become almost completely urbanized (**Figure 10.1**), and in many peripheral and semiperipheral regions the current rate of urbanization is without precedent (**Figure 10.2**).

Many of the largest cities in the periphery are growing at annual rates of between 4 and 7 percent. At the higher rate, their populations will double in 10 years; at the lower rate, they will double in 17 years. The *doubling time* of a city's population is the time needed for it to double in size, at current growth rates. To put the situation in numerical terms, metropolitan areas like Mexico City and São Paulo are adding half a million persons to their populations each year, nearly 10 000 every week, even taking into account losses from deaths and out-migration. It took London 190 years to grow from half a million to 10 million. It took New York 140 years. By contrast, Mexico City, São Paulo, Buenos Aires, Kolkata (Calcutta), Rio de Janeiro, Seoul, and Mumbai (Bombay) all took less than 75 years to grow from half a million to 10 million inhabitants. Urbanization on this scale is a remarkable geographical phenomenon—one of the most important processes shaping the world's landscapes.

Towns and cities are centres of cultural innovation, social transformation, and political change. They can also be engines of economic development. The gross domestic product of large cities like London, Los Angeles, Mexico City, and Paris is roughly equivalent to that of entire countries like Australia and Sweden. Although they often pose social and environmental problems, towns and cities are essential elements in human economic and social organization.

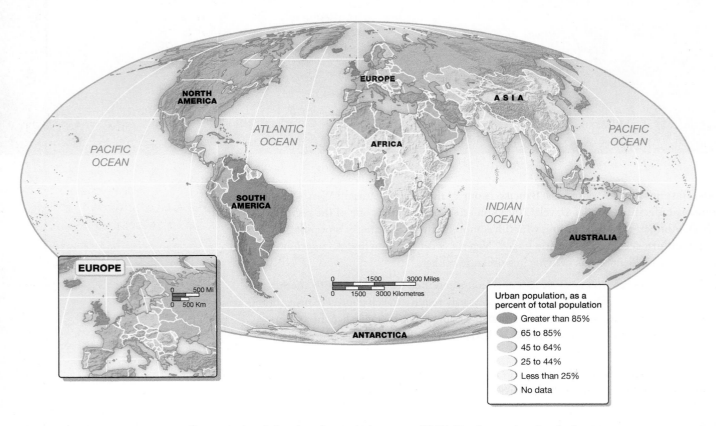

FIGURE 10.1 Percentage of population living in urban settlements, 2009 The lowest levels of urbanization—less than 25 percent—are found in Central Africa and South and Southeast Asia. Most of the core countries are highly urbanized, with between 65 and 95 percent of their populations living in urban settlements. (*Source:* Data from the World Bank: http://data.worldbank.org/indicator/SP.URB.TOTL.IN.ZS.)

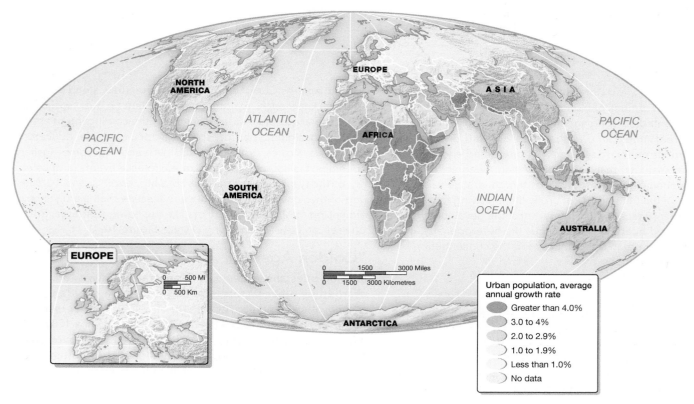

FIGURE 10.2 Rates of growth in urbanization, 2000–2010 This map shows the annual average growth rate between 2000 and 2010 in the proportion of people in each country living in urban settlements. Core countries, already highly urbanized, grew quite slowly. The urban populations of peripheral countries such as Afghanistan, Angola, Burundi, Liberia, Rwanda, and Somalia, on the other hand, grew by more than 5 percent each year, creating tremendous pressure on their cities' capacity to provide jobs, housing, and public services. At a growth rate of 5 percent per year, a city's population will double in less than 15 years. (*Source:* Data from United Nations Human Settlements Programme, *Planning Sustainable Cities.* Global Report on Human Settlements 2009, pp. 238–241; updated data from World Bank 2009 data, http://data.worldbank.org/indicator/SP.URB.TOTL.IN.ZS.)

Experts on urbanization point to four fundamental aspects of the role of towns and cities in human economic and social organization:

- ***The mobilizing function of urban settlement.*** Urban settings, with their physical infrastructure and their large and diverse populations, are places where entrepreneurs can get things done. Cities provide efficient and effective environments for organizing labour, capital, and raw materials and for distributing finished products. In developing countries, urban areas produce as much as two-thirds of total gross domestic product with just one-third of the population.

- ***The decision-making capacity of urban settlement.*** Because urban settings bring together the decision-making machinery of public and private institutions and organizations, political and economic power resides in cities and towns.

- ***The generative functions of urban settlement.*** The concentration of people in urban settings makes for much greater interaction and competition, which facilitates the generation of innovation, knowledge, and information. (See Box 10.1, "Geography Matters: Cities and Civilization.")

- ***The transformative capacity of urban settlement.*** The size, density, and variety of urban populations tend to have a liberating effect on people, allowing them to escape the rigidities of

traditional, rural society and to participate in a variety of lifestyles and behaviours.

APPLY YOUR KNOWLEDGE Provide two examples of how the transformative capacity of urban settlements can be liberating for some people. ■

Studying Urbanization

Urban geography is concerned with the development of towns and cities around the world, with particular reference to the similarities and differences both *within and among* urban places. For urban geographers, some of the most important questions include: what attributes make towns and cities distinctive? How did these distinctive identities evolve? What are the relationships and interdependencies among particular sets of towns and cities? What are the relationships between cities and their surrounding territories? Do significant regularities exist in the spatial organization of land use within cities, in the patterning of neighbourhood populations, or in the layout and landscapes of particular kinds of cities?

Urban geographers also want to know about the causes of the patterns and regularities they find. How, for example, do specialized

Cities and Civilization

Cities are important arenas of cultural production, seedbeds of cultural innovation, centres of fashion and the creation of taste. As Jane Jacobs pointed out long ago in her famous book *The Death and Life of Great American Cities*[1], the density and diversity of urban populations generate serendipity, unexpected encounters, and "new combinations" that lead to innovation. Geographers Ash Amin and Stephen Graham suggest that the generative capacity of cities rests on the multiplexity of urban life, involving four main dimensions: intense face-to-face interactions; the development of dense, specialized quarters and districts; the heterogeneity and cultural hybridity of urban populations; and the concentration of institutional assets in cities.[2]

The Buzz Factor

Personal communications devices and social media have enhanced the generative capacity of contemporary cities, but density, diversity, and face-to-face interactions are still key. They are especially important in facilitating the "creative buzz" associated with the most vibrant and creative city districts. Planning professor Elizabeth Currid has likened it to the dynamics of Andy Warhol's famous "Factory" in Manhattan, a centre of social interaction among artists, photographers, actors, and others, as well as a workplace. As Currid notes, job opportunities, along with professional knowledge, are often heavily reliant on buzz, social contacts, and acquaintances. In Manhattan, the comingling of artists, artisans, designers, photographers, actors, students, educators, and writers in cafés, restaurants, and clubs and—for some—gallery openings, fashion after-parties, music release events, and celebrity birthday parties contributes to a hip, cool "scene," a blurring of the social worlds of work and lifestyle that is a distinctive dimension of Manhattan districts like the Lower East Side, SoHo, Chelsea, and the Meatpacking District (**Figure 10.A**).

"Golden Ages"

In some cities, these elements of generative capacity are supercharged by other factors, creating distinctive "golden ages" of innovation and creativity: Athens 500–400 B.C.E., for example; Rome 50 B.C.E. to 100 C.E.; Florence 1400–1500, Vienna 1780–1910 (**Figure 10.B**), London 1825–1900, Paris 1870–1910 (**Figure 10.C**), and Berlin 1918–1933. Geographer Peter Hall[3] has written about these and other cities, noting that all of them led their respective states or empires, which made them magnets for the immigration of talent. As they drew talent from the far corners of the empires they controlled, it made them cosmopolitan. They were all also

FIGURE 10.A The buzz factor Evening crowds in the Meatpacking District of Manhattan, New York City.
(*Source:* Russell Kord/Alamy)

[1] J. Jacobs, *The Death and Life of Great American Cities*. New York: Random House, 1961.
[2] A. Amin and S. Graham, "The Ordinary City," *Transactions of the Institute of British Geographers, New Series*, 22.4, 1997, pp. 411–429.
[3] P. Hall, *Cities in Civilization*. London: Weidenfeld and Nicolson, 1998.

FIGURE 10.B Vienna The coffee house was the classic setting for meetings of the artists and intelligentsia of Vienna's golden age. Shown here is the Café Landtmann, where people continue to gather. (*Source:* CoverSpot Photography/Alamy)

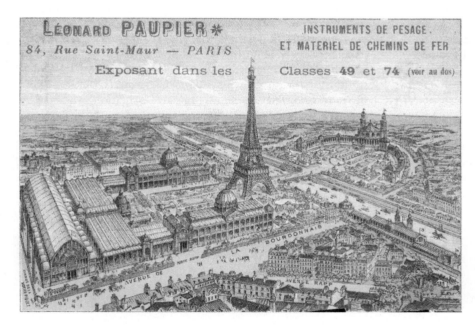

FIGURE 10.C Paris The golden age of Paris was celebrated in a series of World Expositions. This retail advertisement shows a bird's-eye view of the Paris Exposition of 1889. (*Source:* Alamy)

wealthy trading cities. Out of trade came new ways of economic organization, and out of those came new forms of production. Perhaps the most important factor, though, was that all were in the process of rapid economic and social transformation. As a result, they were in a state of uneasy tension between conservative forces and values—aristocratic, hierarchical, religious, conformist—and radical values that were the exact opposite: open, rational, skeptical. These radical values were articulated more often than not by creative people who felt themselves outsiders because they were young or provincial or even foreign, or because they did not belong to the established order of power and prestige. In such circumstances, the ferment of new movements in the arts, new philosophies, new political ideals, and new cultural practices lead to "golden ages," with wealthy individuals and well-funded institutions providing patronage for the avant-garde.

urban districts evolve? Why does urban growth occur in a particular region at a particular time? And why does urban growth exhibit a distinctive physical form during a certain period? In pursuing such questions, urban geographers have learned that the answers are ultimately to be found in the wider context of economic, social, cultural, and political life. Towns and cities must be viewed as part of the economies and societies that maintain them.

Urbanization, therefore, is not simply the population growth of towns and cities. It also involves many other changes, both quantitative and qualitative. Geographers conceptualize these changes in several ways. One of the most important of these is examining the attributes and dynamics of urban systems. An **urban system**, or city system, is any interdependent set of urban settlements within a given region. For example, we can speak of the French urban system, the African urban system, or even the global urban system. As urbanization takes place, urban systems reflect the increasing numbers of people living in ever-larger towns and cities. They also reflect other important changes, such as changes in the relative size of cities, changes in their functional relationships with one another, and changes in their employment base and population composition.

Another important aspect of change associated with urbanization processes concerns urban form. **Urban form** refers to the physical structure and organization of cities in their land use, layout, and built environment. As urbanization takes place, not only do towns and cities grow bigger physically, extending upward and outward, but they also become reorganized, redeveloped, and redesigned in response to changing circumstances.

These changes, in turn, are closely related to a third aspect of change: transformations in patterns of urban ecology. **Urban ecology** is the social and demographic composition of city districts and neighbourhoods. Urbanization not only brings more people to cities, it also brings a greater variety of people. As different social, economic, demographic, and ethnic subgroups become sorted into different territories, distinctive urban ecologies emerge. As new subgroups arrive or old ones leave, these ecologies change.

A fourth aspect of change associated with urbanization concerns people's attitudes and behaviour. New forms of social interaction and new ways of life are brought about by the liberating and transformative effects of urban environments. These changes have given rise to the concept of urbanism, which refers to the distinctive nature of social and cultural organization in particular urban settings. **Urbanism** describes the way of life fostered by urban settings, in which the number, physical density, and variety of people often result in distinctive attitudes, values, and patterns of behaviour. Geographers are interested in urbanism because of the ways in which it varies both within and between cities.

URBAN ORIGINS

It is important to put the geographic study of towns and cities in historical context. After all, many of the world's cities are the product of long periods of development. We can understand a city, old or young, only if we know something about the reasons behind its growth, its rate of growth, and the processes that have contributed to this growth.

In broad terms, the earliest urbanization developed independently in the various hearth areas of the first agricultural revolution. (See Chapter 2.) The very first region of independent urbanism (from around 3500 B.C.E.—see Chapter 4) was in the intensively cultivated river valleys of the Fertile Crescent of the Middle East: the valleys of the Tigris and Euphrates (in Mesopotamia) and the Nile Valley. In Mesopotamia, the rich alluvial soils of the river floodplains fostered the growth of the large rival city-states of the Sumerian empire, including Ur and Erbil (Ancient Arbela—**Figure 10.3**) in present-day Iraq. These fortified city-states contained tens of thousands of inhabitants; social stratification, with religious, political, and military classes; innovative technologies, including massive irrigation projects; and extensive trade connections.

In Egypt, which became a unified state as early as 3100 B.C.E., large irrigation projects controlled the Nile's waters for agricultural and other uses, supporting a series of capital cities that included Thebes, Akhetaten (Tell el-Amarna), and Tanis. Internal peace

FIGURE 10.3 Erbil, Iraq Erbil (Ancient Arbela) in northeast Iraq is located atop a *tell*, a mound representing the remains of generations of sun-dried mud-brick buildings, visible as a hill rising high above the surrounding plain. The 30-metre-high Erbil tell is believed to represent 6000 years of continuous occupation. (*Source:* Sadık Gulec/iStock/Getty Images Plus/Getty Images)

FIGURE 10.4 Ancient Troy This photo shows part of the legendary walls of the ancient city of Troy (situated in Turkey), the site of the Trojan War described by Homer in his *Iliad*. New excavations suggest that the city's origins date back to almost 3000 B.C.E.
(*Source:* Courtesy of Alan E. Nash)

in Egypt meant that there was no need for massive investments in these cities' defensive fortifications. Also, each pharaoh was free to locate a new capital at any site he selected for his tomb, and after his death the city was usually abandoned to the priests.

By 2500 B.C.E. cities had appeared in the Indus Valley, and by 1800 B.C.E. they were established in northern China. Other areas of independent urbanism include Mesoamerica (from around 100 B.C.E.) and Andean America (from around 800 C.E.). Meanwhile, the original Middle Eastern urban hearth continued to produce successive generations of urbanized world-empires, including those of Greece, Rome, and Byzantium. (See Chapter 2.)

Explanations of these first transitions from subsistence minisystems to city-based world-empires differ. The classical archaeological interpretation emphasizes the availability of an agricultural surplus large enough to allow the emergence of specialized, nonagricultural workers. Some urbanization, however, may have resulted from the pressure of population growth. This pressure, it is thought, disturbed the balance between population and resources, causing some people to move to marginal areas. Finding themselves in a region where agricultural conditions were unfavourable, these people either had to devise new techniques of food production and storage or establish a new form of economy based on services such as trade, religion, or defence. Any such economy would have required concentrations of people in urban settlements.

Most experts agree that changes in social organization were an important precondition for urbanization. Specifically, urbanization required the emergence of groups who were able to exact tributes, impose taxes, and control labour power, usually through some form of religious persuasion or military coercion. Once established, this elite group provided the stimulus for urban development by using its wealth to build palaces, arenas, and monuments to display its power and status. This activity not only created the basis for the physical core of ancient cities **(Figure 10.4)** but also required an increased degree of specialization in nonagricultural activities—construction, crafts, administration, the priesthood, soldiery, and so on—which could be organized effectively only in an urban setting.

By 1000 C.E., city-based world-empires had emerged in Europe, the Middle East, and China, including a dozen major cities with populations of 100 000 or more **(Figure 10.5)**.

The urbanized economies of world-empires were a precarious phenomenon, however, and many of them lapsed into ruralism before being revived or recolonized. In a number of cases, the decline of world-empires was a result of demographic setbacks associated with wars or epidemics. Such disasters left too few people to maintain the social and economic infrastructure necessary for urbanization. This lack of labour power seems to have been a major contributing factor to the eventual collapse of the Mesopotamian empire. Similarly, the population of the Roman empire began to decline in the second century C.E., giving rise to labour shortages, abandoned fields, and depopulated towns, and allowing the infiltration of "barbarian" settlers and tribes from east-central Europe. On the other hand, the abandonment of much of the Maya Empire more than 500 years before the arrival of the Spanish may be due to environmental change and social upheaval.

The Roots of European Urban Expansion

In Europe the urban system introduced by the Greeks and re-established by the Romans almost collapsed during the Dark Ages of the early medieval period (476–1000 C.E.). During this time, feudalism gave rise to a fragmented landscape of inflexible and inward-looking world-empires. Feudalism was a rigid, rurally oriented form of economic and social organization based on the communal chiefdoms of Germanic tribes that had invaded the disintegrating Roman empire. Essentially, these rulers held all the land in a chiefdom but allowed it to be farmed by the local population of peasants in return for rents, taxes, and military services. From this unlikely beginning an elaborate urban system developed, its largest centres eventually growing into what would become the nodal centres of a global world-system.

Early medieval Europe, divided into a patchwork of feudal kingdoms and estates, was mostly rural. Each feudal estate was

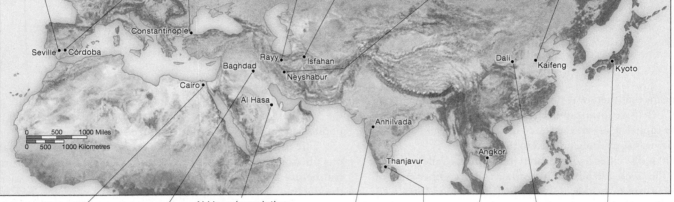

Córdoba (population 450 000):
The largest and most prosperous city of the time, Córdoba was at the cultural forefront in 1000 C.E., renowned for its architecture, craftwork, and dedication to learning.

Seville (population 90 000):
One of the wealthiest and most cultured cities in the Muslim state of Andalusia, Seville excelled in science and the arts.

Constantinople (population 300 000):
Located at a strategic crossroads between Europe and Asia, Constantinople was the centre of the Byzantine Empire and a major trading hub.

Rayy (population 100 000):
Known for its superior silks and ceramics, the city was described at the time as stunningly beautiful.

Isfahan (population 100 000):
Located high atop a fertile plain, Isfahan was a producer of grains and silk and was well-known for its metalwork and rugs.

Neyshabur (population 125 000):
One of Persia's most progressive cities, Neyshabur also served as a major source of turquoise.

Kaifeng (population 400 000):
Situated near the Yellow River, this Song dynasty capital benefited from its proximity to the empire's industrial centre and canal network.

Cairo (population 135 000):
Capital of the Fatimid dynasty, Cairo was known for its many libraries and colleges.

Baghdad (population 125 000):
The capital of the Abassid caliphate, Baghdad was known in 1000 C.E. as the intellectual centre of the world. Persian influence pervaded the city's architecture, literature, and court life.

Al Hasa (population 110 000):
Al Hasa was the centre of the Qarmatian movement, a radical arm of the Shiite Muslim sect that advocated widespread social equality.

Anhilvada (population 100 000):
The size and location of Anhilvada, like many Indian cities, were subject to changes in the path and flow of nearby rivers.

Angkor (population 200 000):
This Khmer capital was the political centre of Southeast Asia and the main market for rice produced by the Khmer empire's high-yield irrigation system.

Thanjavur (population 90 000):
Thanjavur was the capital of India's Chola dynasty. There, King Rajaraja built a massive stone temple dedicated to the god Shiva.

Dali (population 90 000):
Dali peaked in 986 C.E., but the fine marble that was widely sought for buildings and sculptures is still quarried there today.

Kyoto (population 175 000):
Japan's capital since the late eighth century, Kyoto was a religious and cultural centre. It was also renowned for its silk works.

FIGURE 10.5 Major cities in 1000 C.E. The most important cities in 1000 C.E. were the seats of world-empires—the Islamic caliphates, the Byzantine empire, the Chinese empire, and Indian kingdoms—that had developed well-established civilizations with urban systems based on regional trade and protected by strong military rule. (*Source:* Data from T. Chandler, *Four Thousand Years of Urban Growth: A Historical Census.* Washington, D.C.: Worldwatch Institute, 1987; "The Year 1000," *U.S. News & World Report,* August 16, 1999, pp. 66–70.)

more or less self-sufficient regarding foodstuffs, and each kingdom or principality was more or less self-sufficient regarding the raw materials needed to craft simple products. Most regions, however, did support at least a few small towns. The existence of these towns depended mainly on their role:

■ *Ecclesiastical or academic centres*—Examples include St. Andrews in Scotland; Canterbury, Cambridge, and Coventry in England; Rheims and Chartres in France (**Figure 10.6**); Liège in Belgium; Bremen in Germany; Trondheim in Norway; and Lund in Sweden.

FIGURE 10.6 Chartres, France Chartres was an important ecclesiastical centre. The cathedral, built in the thirteenth century, is widely considered to be the finest Gothic cathedral in France.
(*Source:* Philippehalle/Dreamstime)

FIGURE 10.7 Urbino, Italy An important strategic centre in the thirteenth century, with a classic hilltop defensive site, Urbino became an important artistic centre during the Renaissance. (*Source:* Piero20051/Dreamstime)

- *Defensive strongholds*—Examples include the hilltop towns of central Italy, such as Foligno, Montecompatri, and Urbino (**Figure 10.7**); the bastide, or fortress, towns of southwestern France, such as Montauban and Aigues-Mortes (**Figure 10.8**); and gateway towns such as Bellinzona, Switzerland.
- *Administrative centres (for the upper tiers of the feudal hierarchy)*—Examples include Cologne (**Figure 10.9**), Mainz, and Magdeburg in Germany; Falkland in Scotland; Winchester in England; and Toulouse in France.

FIGURE 10.8 Aigues-Mortes, France The walled medieval town of Aigues-Mortes in southern France is one of the best-preserved examples of thirteenth-century military architecture. The town of rectilinear streets is surrounded by a wall with five towers and ten fortified gates. Aigues-Mortes was originally built as a port, with access to the sea via a canal dug through the ponds and marshes of the Camargue. (*Source:* Dea Picture Library/Getty Images)

FIGURE 10.9 Cologne In the late 1400s, when this woodcut was made, Cologne had a population of less than 25 000 but was already a vital commercial and manufacturing centre, with an important cathedral and a university that was already more than 100 years old. The city was founded as the Roman settlement of Colonia—an early example of a world-empire colonizing external territory. (See Chapter 2.) (*Source:* Historical Picture Archive/CORBIS)

From the eleventh century onward, however, the feudal system faltered and disintegrated in the face of successive demographic, economic, and political crises. These crises arose from steady population growth in conjunction with only modest technological improvements and limited amounts of cultivable land. To bolster their incomes and raise armies against one another, the feudal nobility began to levy increasingly higher taxes. Peasants were consequently obliged to sell more of their produce for cash on the market. As a result, a more extensive money economy developed, along with the beginnings of a pattern of trade in basic agricultural produce and craft manufactures. Some long-distance trade even began in luxury goods, such as spices, furs, silks, fruit, and wine. Towns began to increase in size and vitality on the basis of this trade. Indeed, the role of such trade in rejuvenating Europe's cities cannot be overemphasized.

The regional specializations and trading patterns that emerged provided the foundations for a new phase of urbanization based on merchant capitalism (**Figure 10.10**). Beginning with networks established by the merchants of Venice, Pisa, Genoa, and Florence (in northern Italy) and the trading partners of the Hanseatic League (a federation of city-states around the North Sea and Baltic coasts), a trading system of immense complexity soon spanned Europe from Bergen to Athens and from Lisbon to Vienna. By 1400, long-distance trading was well established, based not on the luxury goods of the pioneer merchants, but on bulky staples such as grains, wine, salt, wool, cloth, and metals. Milan, Genoa, Venice, and Bruges had all grown to populations of 100 000 or more. Paris was the dominant European city, with a population of about 275 000. Europe stood poised to extend its grasp on a global scale.

Between the fifteenth and seventeenth centuries, a series of changes occurred that transformed not only the cities and city systems of Europe but the entire world economy. Merchant capitalism increased in scale and sophistication; economic and social reorganization was stimulated by the Protestant Reformation and the scientific revolution. Meanwhile, aggressive overseas colonization made Europeans the leaders, persuaders, and shapers of the rest of the world's economies and societies.

Spanish and Portuguese colonists were the first to extend the European urban system into the world's peripheral regions. They established the basis of a Latin American urban system in just 60 years, between 1520 and 1580. Spanish colonists founded their cities on the sites of Indian cities (in Oaxaca and Mexico City, Mexico; Cajamarca and Cuzco, Peru; and Quito, Ecuador) or in regions of dense indigenous populations (in Puebla and Guadalajara, Mexico; and Arequipa and Lima, Peru). These colonial towns were established mainly as administrative and military centres from which the Spanish Crown could occupy and exploit the New World. Portuguese colonists, in contrast, situated their cities—Recife, Salvador, São Paulo, and Rio de Janeiro—with commercial rather than administrative considerations in mind. They, too, were motivated by exploitation, but their strategy was to establish colonial towns in locations best suited to organizing the collection and export of the products of their mines and plantations.

In Europe, reorganization during the Renaissance saw the centralization of political power and the formation of national states, the beginnings of industrialization, and the funnelling of plunder and produce from distant colonies. In this new context, the port cities of the North Sea and Atlantic coasts enjoyed a decisive locational advantage. By 1700, London had grown to 500 000 people, while Lisbon and Amsterdam had each grown to about 175 000. The cities of continental and Mediterranean Europe expanded at a much more modest rate. By 1700, Venice had added only 30 000 to its 1400 population of 110 000, and Milan's population did not grow at all between 1400 and 1700.

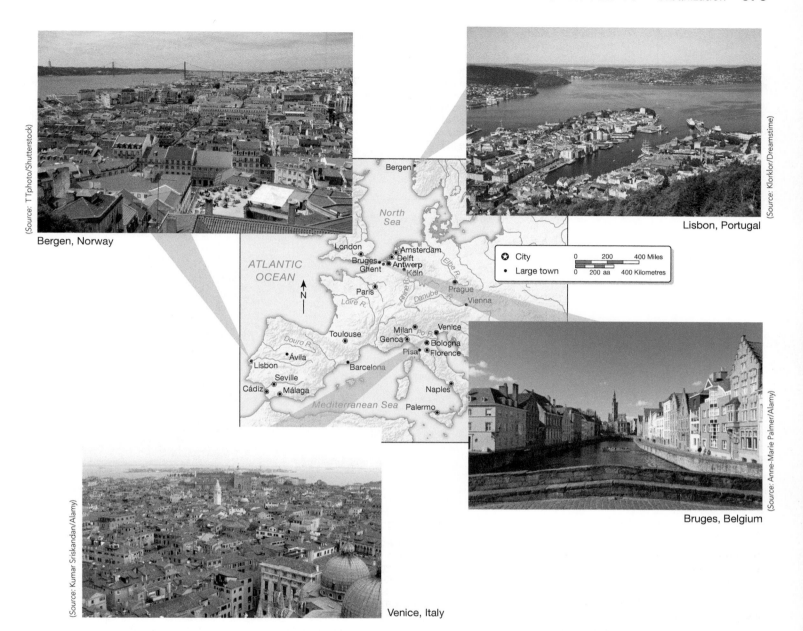

FIGURE 10.10 **The towns and cities of Europe, ca. 1350** Cities with more than 10 000 residents were uncommon in medieval Europe except in northern Italy and Flanders. In the cities of Florence and Delft, the spread of cloth production and the growth of trade permitted relatively intense urbanization. Elsewhere, large size was associated with administrative, religious, educational, and economic functions. By 1350, many of the bigger towns (for example, Barcelona, Cologne, Prague) supported universities as well as a variety of religious institutions. Most urban systems, reflecting the economic and political realities of the time, were relatively small.

(*Source:* Map adapted from P. M. Hohenberg and L. H. Lees, *The Making of Urban Europe 1000–1950*. Cambridge, MA: Harvard University Press, 1995.)

The most important aspect of urbanization during this period, however, was the establishment of gateway cities around the rest of the world (**Figure 10.11**). **Gateway cities** serve as a link between one country or region and others because of their physical situation. These control centres command entrance to, and exit from, their particular country or region. European powers founded or developed thousands of towns in other parts of the world as they extended their trading networks and established their colonies. The great majority of these urban enclaves were ports. Protected by fortifications and European naval power, they

began as trading posts and colonial administrative centres. Before long, they developed manufacturing of their own to supply the pioneers' needs, along with more extensive commercial and financial services.

As colonies were developed and trading networks expanded, some of these ports grew rapidly, acting as gateways for colonial expansion into continental interiors. Into their harbours came waves of European settlers; through their docks were funnelled the produce of continental interiors. Rio de Janeiro (Brazil) grew on the basis of gold mining; Accra (Ghana) on cocoa; Buenos Aires

New York, at first a modest Dutch fur-trading port, became the gateway for millions of European immigrants and for a large volume of U.S. agricultural and manufacturing exports.

Boston first flourished as the principal colony of the Massachusetts Bay Company, exporting furs and fish and importing slaves from West Africa, hardwoods from central America, molasses from the Caribbean, manufactured goods from Europe, and tea (via Europe) from South Asia.

Salvador, Brazil, was the landfall of the Portuguese in 1500. They established plantations that were worked by slave labour from West Africa. Salvador became the gateway for most of the 3.5 million slaves who were shipped to Brazil between 1526 and 1870.

Guangzhou was the first Chinese port to be in regular contact with European traders—first Portuguese in the sixteenth century and then British in the seventeenth century.

Nagasaki was the only port that feudal Japanese leaders allowed open to European traders, and for more than 200 years Dutch merchants held a monopoly of the import–export business through the city.

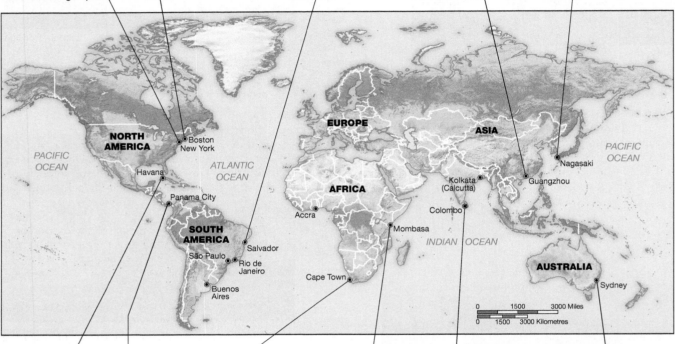

Havana was founded and developed by the Spanish in 1515 because of its excellent harbour. It was used as the assembly point for annual convoys returning to Spain.

Panama City, founded by the Spanish in 1519, became the gateway for gold and silver on its way by galleon to Spain.

Cape Town was founded in 1652 as a provisioning station for ships of the Dutch East India Company. Later, under British rule, it developed into an import–export gateway for South Africa.

Mombasa (in present-day Kenya) was already a significant Arab trading port when Vasco da Gama visited it in 1498 on his first voyage to India. The Portuguese used it as a trading station until it was recaptured by the Arabs in 1698. It did not become an important gateway port until it fell under British imperial rule in the nineteenth century, when railroad development opened up the interior of Kenya, along with Rwanda, Uganda, and northern Tanzania.

Colombo's strategic situation on trade routes saw it occupied successively by the Portuguese, the Dutch, and the British. It became an important gateway after the British constructed an artificial harbour to handle the exports from tea plantations in Ceylon (now Sri Lanka).

Sydney, Australia, was not settled until the late eighteenth century, and even then many of the settlers were convicts who had been forcibly transported from Britain. It soon became the gateway for agricultural and mineral exports (mostly to Britain) and for imports of manufactured goods and European immigrants.

FIGURE 10.11 Gateway cities in the evolving world-system periphery Many of the world's most important cities grew to prominence as gateway cities because they commanded routes into and out of developing colonies.

(Argentina) on mutton, wool, and cereals; Kolkata (India, formerly Calcutta) on jute and cotton textiles; São Paulo (Brazil) on coffee; and so on. As these cities grew into major population centres, they became important markets for imported European manufactures, adding even more to their functions as gateways for international transport and trade.

APPLY YOUR KNOWLEDGE Create a list of probable gateway cities along the Atlantic seaboard of North America. Find out the early histories of these cities: why they were founded, what their principal imports and exports were, how far their reach extended into the interior of North America. ■

Industrialization and Urbanization

In the late eighteenth century, urbanization began to become an important dimension of the world-system in its own right. In 1800, less than 5 percent of the world's 980 million people lived in towns and cities. By 1950, however, 16 percent of the world's population was urban, and more than 900 cities of 100 000 or more existed around the world. The Industrial Revolution and European imperialism had created unprecedented concentrations of humanity that were intimately linked in networks and hierarchies of interdependence.

Cities were synonymous with industrialization. Industrial economies could be organized only through the large pools of labour; the transportation networks; the physical infrastructure of factories, warehouses, stores, and offices; and the consumer markets provided by cities. As industrialization spread throughout Europe in the first half of the nineteenth century and then to other parts of the world, urbanization increased at a faster pace. The higher wages and greater variety of opportunities in urban labour markets attracted migrants from surrounding areas. The countryside began to empty. In Europe the *demographic transition* caused a rapid growth in population as death rates dropped dramatically (see Chapter 3). This growth in population provided a massive increase in the labour supply throughout the nineteenth century, further boosting the rate of urbanization, not only within Europe itself but also in Australia, Canada, New Zealand, South Africa, and the United States as emigration spread industrialization and urbanization to the frontiers of the world-system.

Transport Networks and Urban Systems

Within the world's core regions, the transformation of urban systems hinged on successive innovations in transport technology that opened up agrarian interiors and intensified intercity and interregional trading networks. The first phase of this transformation was based on an old technology: the canal. Merchant trade and the beginnings of industrialization in both Britain and France were underpinned by extensive navigation systems that joined one river system to another. By 1790 France had just over 1000 kilometres of canals and canalized rivers; Britain had nearly 3600 kilometres. The Industrial Revolution provided both the need and the capital for a spate of additional canal building that began to integrate emerging industrial towns. Market towns and hill towns that were not connected to canal systems were isolated from commerce and immediately fell behind.

In the United States, the opening of the Erie Canal in 1825 connected New York, a colonial gateway port, to the Great Lakes and so enabled it to reorient itself toward the continent's growing interior. The Erie Canal was so profitable that it set off a "canal fever" that resulted in the construction of some 2000 kilometres of navigable waterways in the next 25 years. But the scale of the United States was so great that a network of canals was a viable proposition only in more densely settled regions of the East. The same applies to Canada: while several canals were built in the early to mid-nineteenth century, their purpose was to improve transport along the already settled St. Lawrence–Great Lakes corridor, rather than to extend European settlement (**Figure 10.12**).

The effective colonization of the North American interior and the growth of cities did not take place until the development of steam-powered transportation—first riverboats and then railroads. The first steamboats, developed in the early 1800s, offered the

FIGURE 10.12 The Trent–Severn Waterway's lift lock at Peterborough, Ontario The Trent–Severn Waterway connects Trenton (on Lake Ontario) with Port Severn (on Georgian Bay, Lake Huron). Over a distance of 386 kilometres, 44 locks connect a series of lakes and rivers. Two of the locks, at Peterborough (illustrated here) and at Kirkfield, are hydraulic lift locks, which are unique in North America. Based on a design developed in Belgium and England, these were among the first structures built entirely of concrete in Canada. The waterway was built sporadically between 1833 and 1920 and was never a commercial success because of the low population density of its hinterland. It is now used exclusively by recreational boaters. (*Source*: Courtesy of Alan E. Nash)

possibility of opening up the vast interior by way of the Mississippi and its tributaries. The heyday of the river steamboat was between 1830 and 1850 (considerably longer in western Canada). During this period, river ports such as New Orleans, St. Louis, Cincinnati, and Louisville grew rapidly, extending the frontier of industrialization and modernization.

By 1860, the railroads had taken over as the dominant mode of transportation, further extending the frontier of settlement and industrialization and intensifying the growth of existing cities. The railroad originated in Britain, where George Stephenson engineered the world's first commercial railroad in 1825. The economic success of the new transport technology sparked two railroad-building booms that eventually created a highly integrated urban system and allowed Britain's manufacturing industry to flourish.

In other core countries, where sufficient capital existed to license (or copy) the locomotive technology and install the track, railroad systems led to the first full stage of urban system integration. While the railroads integrated the economies of entire countries and allowed vast territories to be colonized, they also brought some important regional and local restructuring and differentiation. In particular, they triggered unprecedented growth in population and importance for cities situated at the focal point of the railroad networks. In the United States, Chicago mushroomed (see below). In Canada, Winnipeg arose as the leading commercial centre on the Prairies. At the same time, the railroad also extended the dominance of the industrialized Ontario–Quebec region over the more agricultural regions further west: Montreal stood unchallenged at the centre of Canada's rail and sea connections (**Figure 10.13**).

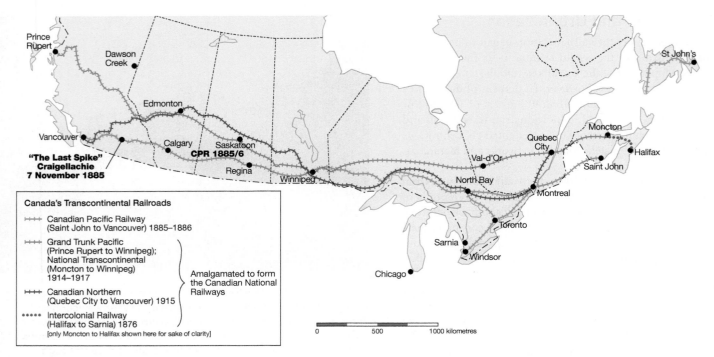

FIGURE 10.13 Canada's transcontinental railroads The construction of Canada's transcontinental railroads between 1885 and 1917 opened up large parts of this country for settlement and economic development. Cities such as Montreal and Winnipeg, where several railroad networks intersected, assumed unprecedented importance. (*Source: Based on John Warkentin, A Regional Geography of Canada: Life and Space, 2nd ed. Scarborough: Prentice Hall, 2000, p. 108, map 4–5.*)

In the twentieth century, the internal combustion engine powered further rounds of urban system development and integration. The development of trucks in the 1910s and 1920s suddenly released factories from the need to locate near railroads, canals, and waterfronts. Trucking allowed goods to be moved farther, faster, and cheaper than before. As a result, trucking made it feasible to locate factories on inexpensive land on city fringes and in smaller towns and peripheral regions where labour was cheaper. It also increased the market area of individual factories and reduced the need for large product inventories. Together, all of these development encouraged urban sprawl.

> **APPLY YOUR KNOWLEDGE** How have changing transportation technologies affected the history of the town or city in which you live? ■

Industrial Cities

The shock city of nineteenth-century European industrialization was Manchester, England, which grew from a small town of 15 000 in 1750 to a city of 70 000 in 1801, a metropolis of 500 000 in 1861, and a world city of 2.3 million by 1911. A **shock city** is seen at the time as the embodiment of surprising and disturbing changes in economic, social, and cultural life. Manchester's phenomenal growth was based on new textile manufacturing technologies. The city's first cotton mill was built in the early 1780s; by the middle of the nineteenth century, Manchester was the world's biggest producer of cotton textiles, with over 100 cotton-spinning mills (**Figure 10.14**).

When industrialization took hold in North America, the shock city was Chicago, which grew from under 30 000 in 1850 to 500 000 in 1880, 1.7 million in 1900, and 3.3 million in 1930 (**Figure 10.15**). When Chicago was first incorporated as a city in 1837, its population was only 4200. Its growth followed the arrival of the railroads, which made the city a major transportation hub. By the 1860s, lake vessels were carrying iron ore from the Upper Michigan ranges to Chicago's blast furnaces, and railroads were hauling cattle, hogs, and sheep to the city for slaughtering and packing. The city's prime geographic situation also made it a major lumber-distributing centre by the 1880s.

Manchester and Chicago were archetypal forms of an entirely new kind of city—the *industrial city*—whose fundamental reason for existence was not, as it was for earlier generations of cities, to fulfill military, political, ecclesiastical, or trading functions. Rather, it existed simply to assemble raw materials and to fabricate, assemble, and distribute manufactured goods. Both Manchester and Chicago had to cope with unprecedented rates of growth and the unprecedented economic, social, and political problems that were a consequence of their growth. Both were also world cities, cities in which a disproportionate part of the world's most important business—economic, political, and cultural—was conducted. Such cities experience growth largely as a result of their role as key nodes in the world economy.

During the Industrial Revolution and for much of the twentieth century, a close and positive relationship existed between rural and urban development in the core regions of the world (**Figure 10.16**). The appropriation of new land for agriculture, together with mechanization and the innovative techniques that urbanization allowed, resulted in increased agricultural productivity. This extra productivity released rural labour to work in the growing manufacturing sector in towns and cities. At the same time, it provided the additional

(a) As the city grew, it spilled out into the surrounding country-side, bringing its characteristic landscape of red-brick terrace housing and "Dark Satanic Mills" with their tall brick chimneys. (*Source:* Paul L. Knox)

b) Railway viaducts, like this one in Stockport, just outside Manchester, brought rail transportation to Manchester early in the nineteenth century and helped make the city a major transportation hub. (*Source:* The Print Collector/Alamy)

(c) Canals were at the heart of the development of industrial Manchester. They enabled coal and raw materials to be carried right to the heart of the city and finished goods to be transported away easily. The Bridgewater Canal, one of the earliest modern canals, ran into Manchester from the Duke of Bridgewater's coal mine at Worsley, about 16 kilometres away. Later, other canals radiated outward from the area and the Ship Canal brought sea-going vessels close to the city centre. (*Source:* Paul L. Knox)

FIGURE 10.14 Manchester, England The "shock city" of the nineteenth century.

FIGURE 10.15 Growth of Chicago In 1870, when Manchester was already a thriving metropolis, Chicago was at the beginning of a period of explosive growth. A year later 9 square kilometres of the city, including the business district, were destroyed by fire. Chicago was rebuilt rapidly, with prosperous industrialists taking the opportunity to build impressive new structures in the downtown area. The city's economic and social elite colonized the Lake Michigan shore. Heavy industry, warehouses, and rail yards crowded the banks of the Chicago River, stretching northwestward from the city centre. To the south of the city were the Union Stockyards and a pocket of heavy industry where the Calumet River met Lake Michigan. The surrounding neighbourhoods of working families' homes spread rapidly outward as wave after wave of immigrants arrived in the city. Chicago's immigrant and African-American neighbourhoods were an entirely new urban phenomenon—highly segregated and with very distinctive social and cultural attributes. The 1880 and 1890 censuses showed that more than three-quarters of Chicago's population was made up of foreign-born immigrants and their children.

FIGURE 10.16 The urbanization process in the world's core regions Urbanization was stimulated by advances in farm productivity that (1) provided the extra food to support the increased numbers of townspeople and (2) made many farmers and farm labourers redundant, prompting them to migrate to cities. Labour displaced in this way ended up consuming food rather than producing it, but this was more than compensated for by increased agricultural productivity and increased capacity of enlarged urban labour forces to produce agricultural tools, machinery, fertilizers, and so on that contributed further to agricultural productivity.

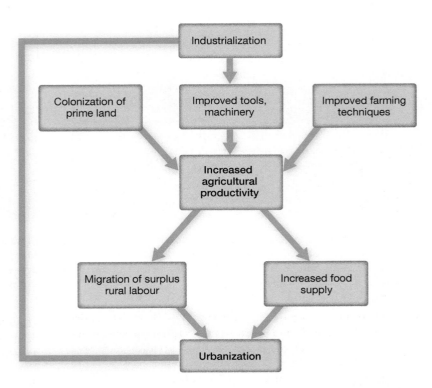

produce needed to feed growing urban populations. The whole process was further reinforced by the capacity of urban labour forces to produce agricultural tools, machinery, fertilizer, and other products that made for still greater increases in agricultural productivity. This kind of urbanization is a special case of *cumulative causation* (Chapter 7), in which a spiral buildup of advantages is enjoyed by particular places as a result of the development of external economies, agglomeration effects, and localization economies.

APPLY YOUR KNOWLEDGE What would be a current example of a shock city? What are the surprising/disturbing changes in the economic, social, and cultural life of the city that make it shocking? (*Hint:* you might want to consider cities in the Middle East.) ■

Imperialism and Peripheral Urbanization

The industrialization of the core economies was highly dependent on the exploitation of peripheral regions. Inevitably, the new international division of labour that resulted from this relationship also had a significant impact on patterns and processes of urbanization in the periphery. European imperialism led to the creation of new gateway cities in peripheral countries and, as Europeans raced to establish economic and political control over continental interiors, these colonial cities were established as centres of administration, political control, and commerce.

Colonial cities are those that were deliberately established or developed by colonial or imperial powers as administrative or commercial centres. Geographers often distinguish between two types of colonial city. The pure colonial city was usually established, or "planted," by colonial administrations in a location where no significant urban settlement had previously existed. Such cities were laid out expressly to fulfill colonial functions, with ceremonial spaces, offices, and depots for colonial traders, plantation representatives, and government officials; barracks for soldiers; and housing for colonists. Subsequently, as these cities grew, they added housing and commercial space for local people drawn by the opportunity to obtain jobs as servants, clerks, or porters. Examples of pure colonial cities are the original settlements of Mumbai (Bombay), Kolkata (Calcutta), Ho Chi Minh City (Saigon), Hong Kong, Jakarta, Manila, and Nairobi.

In the other type of colonial city, colonial functions were grafted onto an existing settlement, taking advantage of a good site

and a ready supply of labour. Examples include Delhi, Mexico City, Shanghai, and Tunis. In these cities the colonial imprint is most visible in and around the city centre in the formal squares and public spaces, the layout of avenues, and the presence of colonial architecture and monuments. This architecture includes churches, city halls, and railway stations (**Figure 10.17**); the palaces of governors and archbishops; and the houses of wealthy traders, colonial administrators, and landowners.

FIGURE 10.17 Colonial architecture and urban design Cities in the periphery of the world-system have grown very rapidly since the colonial era, but the legacy of the era can still be seen in the architecture, monuments, and urban design of the period. This photograph shows part of the High Court building in Mumbai. Note the cricket game played in front of the building: another colonial British legacy. (*Source:* Jeremy Richards/Dreamstime)

The colonial legacy can also be read in the building and planning regulations of many colonial cities. Often, colonial planning regulations were copied from those that had been established in the colonizing country. Because these regulations were based on Western concepts, many turned out to be inappropriate for colonial settings. Most colonial building codes, for example, are based on Western models of family and work, with a small family living in a residential area that is some distance from the male adult's place of work. This is at odds with the needs of large, extended families whose members are involved with a busy domestic economy and with family businesses that are traditionally integrated with the residential setting. Colonial planning, with its gridiron street layouts, zoning regulations that do not allow for a mixture of land uses, and building codes designed for European climates, ignored the specific needs of local communities and misunderstood their cultural preferences.

URBAN SYSTEMS

Every town and city is part of the interlocking urban systems that link regional-, national-, and international-scale human geographies in a complex web of interdependence. These urban systems organize space through hierarchies of cities of different sizes and functions. Many of these hierarchical urban systems exhibit common attributes and features, particularly in the relative size and spacing of individual towns and cities.

In the 1930s, German geographer Walter Christaller recognized that towns and cities function as market centres and that this results in a hierarchical system of central places. A **central place** is a settlement where certain types of products and services are available to consumers. **Central place theory** seeks to explain the tendency for central places to be organized in hierarchical systems, analyzing the relative size and geographic spacing of towns and cities as a function of consumer behaviour. A fundamental tenet of central place theory is that the smallest settlements in an urban system provide only those goods and services that meet everyday needs (bakery and dairy products and groceries, for example) and that these small settlements are situated relatively close to one another because consumers, assumed to be spread throughout the countryside, are not prepared to travel far for such items. On the other hand, people are willing to travel farther for more expensive, less frequently purchased items. This means that the larger the settlement, with a broader variety of more specialized goods and services, the farther it will be from others of a similar size.

Although consumer behaviour certainly helps explain some aspects of urban systems, there are relatively few regions today where the functions of towns and cities are dominated by local markets and shopping. Nevertheless, the urban systems of most regions do exhibit a clear hierarchical structure. This is partly a legacy of past eras, when towns and cities did function mainly as market centres for surrounding agricultural areas. **Figure 10.18** shows a typical example: the Spanish urban system, with smaller towns and cities functioning interdependently with successively larger ones. Note that the whole system is dominated by one or two metropolitan areas whose linkages are national in scope.

Canada's urban system provides an excellent example of the development of such a hierarchy (**Figure 10.19**). The top tier of cities consists of Toronto, Montreal, and Vancouver—cities that provide high-order functions to the national marketplace. Historically, Montreal was Canada's principal city, in terms of population size and economic importance, and served as the control point for European and U.S. investment in Canada. Over the past four decades, however, Toronto has eclipsed Montreal—not least because of investors' concerns about a possible separation of Quebec from Canada. Vancouver is the most recent addition to the first tier of Canadian cities and has benefited from considerable immigration and investment from Hong Kong.

The second tier of Canadian cities consists of Halifax, Quebec City, Ottawa-Hull, London, Winnipeg, Calgary, and Edmonton. These can be

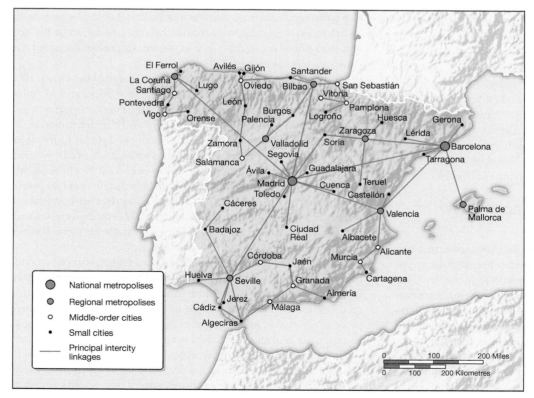

FIGURE 10.18 **The Spanish urban system** Note how the smaller cities tend to be linked to middle-order cities, while these in turn are linked to regional metropolises, which are linked to the national metropolises, Madrid and Barcelona. These linkages represent the major flows of capital, information, and goods within the Spanish urban system. (*Source:* Adapted from L. Bourne, R. Sinclair, M. Ferrer, and A. d'Entremont [eds.], *The Changing Geography of Urban Systems.* Navarra, Spain: Department of Human Geography, Universidad de Navarra, 1989, fig. 2, p. 46.)

FIGURE 10.19 Canada's urban hierarchy This illustration shows the structure and composition of the top levels of Canada's urban system.

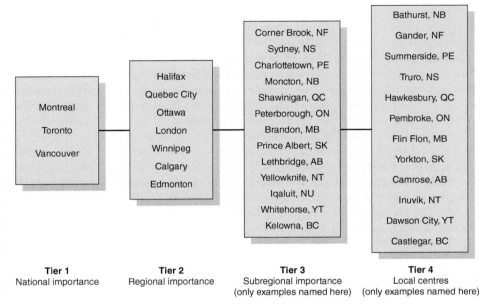

| **Tier 1**
National importance | **Tier 2**
Regional importance | **Tier 3**
Subregional importance
(only examples named here) | **Tier 4**
Local centres
(only examples named here) |

described as general-purpose cities with diverse functions but only regional importance.

The third tier is made up of more specialized centres of subregional importance. Smaller provincial capitals, such as Regina or Charlottetown; northern cities, such as Yellowknife, Whitehorse, and Iqaluit; important centres, such as the rapidly growing city of Kelowna, British Columbia; the university and agricultural service cities of Brandon, Manitoba, and Lethbridge, Alberta; and industrial centres such as Corner Brook, Newfoundland, all provide examples of third-order functions.

The fourth functional tier in the Canadian urban hierarchy comprises those centres that have only local importance—such towns as Castlegar, British Columbia, or Bathurst, New Brunswick, for example, which can provide their populations with little more than a basic range of shopping and services.

In total, the Canadian urban system consists of only approximately 750 communities, of which approximately 140 are cities with more than 10 000 people. As a number of Canadian geographers have observed, this urban system, for most practical purposes, *is* Canada. The relationships between the cities of this system define the major geographical regions of our country. Certainly, the present urban hierarchy, dominated by the cities of the Quebec City–Windsor corridor, embodies the dichotomy between core and periphery, heartland and hinterland, that lies at the root of so much of our country's geographical patterns.

Finally, we must note that urban systems also exhibit clear *functional* differences within such hierarchies. This is yet another reflection of the interdependence of places. The geographical division of labour resulting from such processes of economic development (Chapter 7) means that many medium- and larger-size cities perform specialized economic functions and so acquire distinctive characters. Thus the industrial era produced steel towns (for example, Hamilton, Ontario; Sheffield, England), textile towns (for example, Lowell, Massachusetts; Manchester, England), and auto-manufacturing towns (for example, Windsor and Oshawa, Ontario; Detroit, Michigan; Turin, Italy; Toyota City, Japan).

City-Size Distributions, Primacy, and Centrality

The functional interdependency between places within urban systems tends to result in a distinctive relationship between the population size of cities and their rank within the overall hierarchy. This relationship is known as the **rank-size rule**, which describes a certain statistical regularity in the city-size distributions of countries and regions. The relationship is such that the nth largest city in a country or region is $1/n$ the size of the largest city in that country or region. Thus, if the largest city in a particular system has a population of 1 million, the fifth-largest city should have a population one-fifth as big (that is, 200 000); the hundredth-ranked city should have

a population one-hundredth as big (that is, 10 000), and so on. The actual rank-size relationships for urban systems at all levels of economic development come fairly close to this.

In some urban systems, the rank-size distribution is distorted as a result of the disproportionate size of the largest (and sometimes also the second-largest) city. According to the rank-size rule, the largest city should be just twice the size of the second-largest city. In the United Kingdom, London is more than nine times the size of Birmingham, the second-largest city. In France, Paris is more than eight times the size of Marseilles, France's second-largest city. In Brazil, both Rio de Janeiro and São Paulo are five times the size of Belo Horizonte, the third-largest city. Geographers call this condition **primacy**, occurring when the population of the largest city in an urban system is disproportionately large in relation to the second- and third-largest cities in that system. Cities like Paris and São Paulo are termed *primate* cities.

Primacy is not simply a matter of size. Some of the largest metropolitan areas in the world—Karachi, New York, and Mumbai (Bombay), for example—are not primate. Further, primacy is a condition that is found in both the core and the periphery of the world-system. This suggests that primacy is a result of the roles played by particular cities within their own national urban systems. A relationship does exist between primacy and the world economy, however. Primacy in peripheral countries is usually a consequence of primate cities' early roles as gateway cities. In core countries, it is usually a consequence of primate cities' roles as imperial capitals and centres of administration, politics, and trade for a much wider urban system than their own domestic system.

When a city's economic, political, and cultural function is disproportionate to its population, the condition is known as **centrality**. Centrality refers to the functional dominance of cities within an urban system. Cities that account for a disproportionately high share of economic, political, and cultural activity have a high degree of centrality within their urban system. Very often primate cities exhibit this characteristic, but cities do not necessarily have to be primate in order to be functionally dominant within their urban system. **Figure 10.20** shows some examples of centrality, revealing

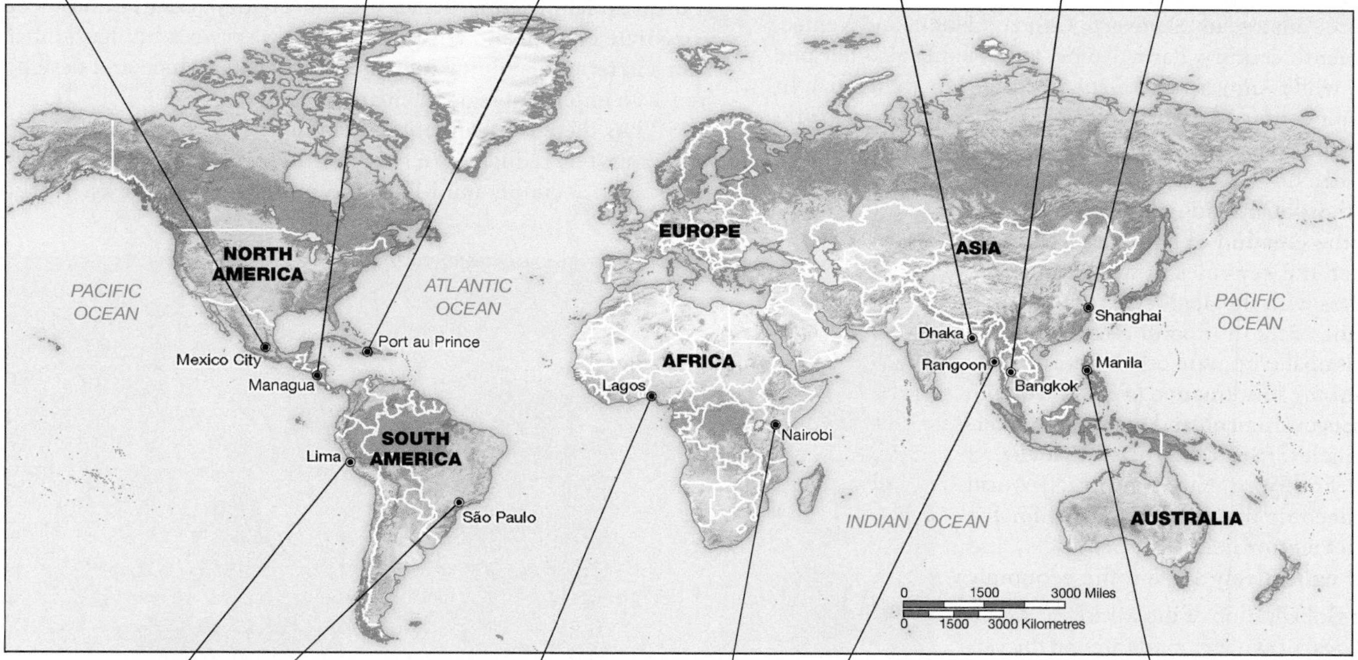
Mexico City, with 18 percent of Mexico's population, accounts for over one-third of its employment in commerce and services, almost two-thirds of its financial assets, two-thirds of its investments in higher education, and over three-fourths of its research and development expenditures.
Managua, with about 28 percent of Nicaragua's population, accounts for about 40 percent of the country's GDP.
Port au Prince, with about 23 percent of Haiti's population, accounts for approximately 40 percent of its GDP.
Dhaka, the capital of Bangladesh, holds 9 percent of the country's population but accounts for nearly 50 percent of its manufacturing employment.
Bangkok, with 12 percent of Thailand's population, accounts for more than 38 percent of its overall GDP, more than 75 percent of its income from manufacturing, and more than 85 percent of its income from banking and financial services.
Shanghai, with less than 2 percent of the Chinese population, accounts for almost 14 percent of China's GDP.
NORTH AMERICA
PACIFIC OCEAN
ATLANTIC OCEAN
EUROPE
ASIA
AFRICA
SOUTH AMERICA
AUSTRALIA
INDIAN OCEAN
PACIFIC OCEAN
Mexico City
Managua
Port au Prince
Lima
São Paulo
Lagos
Nairobi
Dhaka
Rangoon
Bangkok
Shanghai
Manila
0 1500 3000 Miles
0 1500 3000 Kilometres
Lima, with 29 percent of Peru's population, accounts for almost half of its GDP, 80 percent of its consumer goods production, and 90 percent of its banking facilities.
Lagos, with about 10 percent of Nigeria's population, accounts for approximately 25 percent of Nigeria's retailing, 40 percent of its wholesaling, 40 percent of its external trade, and 70 percent of its industrial capacity.
Rangoon, with less than 10 percent of Myanmar's (Burma's) population, accounts for more than 50 percent of its manufacturing industry, over 80 percent of its service industries, and almost all of its government, higher education, and international trade.
Manila, with about 15 percent of the Philippine population, accounts for over 30 percent of the country's GDP and 60 percent of its manufacturing output.
Nairobi, with 8 percent of Kenya's population, accounts for more than 50 percent of its manufacturing employment.
São Paulo, with about 10 percent of the Brazilian population, generates about 25 percent of the country's GDP and accounts for over 40 percent of its manufacturing industry.

FIGURE 10.20 Examples of urban centrality The economic, political, and cultural importance of some cities is disproportionate to their population size. This is a reflection of core–periphery differentials within countries and often becomes a political issue because of the economic disparities. The centrality of these cities also leads to localized problems of congestion, land price inflation, and pollution.

the overwhelming dominance of some cities within the world-system periphery. Bangkok, for instance, with around 12 percent of the Thai population, accounts for approximately 38 percent of the country's overall gross domestic product (GDP); over 85 percent of the country's GDP in banking, insurance, and real estate; and 75 percent of its manufacturing.

World Cities and the Global Urban System

Recall from Chapter 7 that ever since the evolution of a world-system in the sixteenth century, certain cities known as world cities (sometimes referred to as *global cities*) have played key roles in organizing space beyond their own national boundaries. In the first stages of world-system growth, these key roles involved the organization of trade and the execution of colonial, imperial, and geopolitical strategies. The world cities of the seventeenth century were London, Amsterdam, Antwerp, Genoa, Lisbon, and Venice. In the eighteenth century, Paris, Rome, and Vienna also became world cities, while Antwerp and Genoa became less influential. In the nineteenth century, Berlin, Chicago, Manchester, New York, and St. Petersburg became world cities, while Venice became less influential.

Today, the globalization of the economy has resulted in the creation of a global urban system, in which the key roles of world cities are concerned less with the deployment of imperial power and the orchestration of trade and more with transnational corporate organization, international banking and finance (**Figure 10.21**), supranational government, and the work of international agencies. (See Box 10.2, "Visualizing Geography: The World City Network.") World cities have become the control centres for the flows of information, cultural products, and finance that collectively sustain the economic and cultural globalization of the world.

A great deal of synergy exists among the various functional dimensions of world cities. A city like New York, for example, attracts transnational corporations because it is a centre of culture and communications. It attracts specialized business services because it is a centre of corporate headquarters and of global markets, and so on. These interdependencies represent a special case of the geographical *agglomeration effects* that we discussed in Chapter 7. In the case of New York City, corporate headquarters and specialized legal, financial, and business services cluster together because of the mutual cost savings and advantages of being close to one another.

At the same time, different world cities fulfill different roles within the world-system, making for different emphases and combinations (that is, differences in the nature of their world-city functions) as well as for differences in the absolute and relative localization of particular world-city functions (that is, differences in their degree of importance as world cities). For example, Brussels is relatively unimportant as a corporate headquarters location but qualifies as a world city because it is the administrative centre of the European Union and has attracted a large number of nongovernmental organizations and advanced business services that are transnational in scope. Milan is relatively dependent in terms of corporate control and advanced business services but has global status in terms of cultural influence (especially fashion and design) and is an important regional financial centre.

Thus there is a geographical complexity to world cities' roles that cannot be reduced to a simple "hierarchy" or ranking. World cities are not simply mini-Londons and little New Yorks. World

FIGURE 10.21 **Advanced business services** The "square mile" of the City of London is the cornerstone of London as a world city. The district contains the London Stock Exchange, Lloyd's of London, and the Bank of England. There are about 500 banks with offices in the City, many of them specializing in areas such as foreign exchange markets, Eurobonds, and energy futures. The City also accounts for a quarter of the world market for marine insurance and over a third of the market in aviation risks. (*Source:* Mark Beton/Metro/Alamy)

World cities also provide an interface between the global and the local. They contain the economic, cultural, and institutional apparatus that channels national and provincial resources into the global economy and transmits the impulses of globalization back to national and provincial centres. As such, world cities possess several functional characteristics **(Figure 10.D)**. They are the sites of the following:

■ Most of the leading global markets for commodities, commodity futures, investment capital, foreign exchange, equities, and bonds

■ Clusters of specialized, advanced business services, especially those that are international in scope and that are attached to finance, accounting, insurance, advertising, property development, and law

■ Concentrations of corporate headquarters—not just of transnational corporations but also of major national firms and large foreign firms

■ Concentrations of national and international headquarters of trade and professional associations

■ Most of the leading nongovernmental organizations (NGOs) and intergovernmental organizations (IGOs) that are international in scope (for example, the World Health Organization; United Nations Educational, Scientific, and Cultural Organization [UNESCO]; the International Labor Organization; and the International Federation of Agricultural Producers)

■ The most powerful and internationally influential media organizations (including newspapers, magazines, book publishing, and satellite television); news and information services (including news wires and online information services); and culture industries (including art and design, fashion, film, and television)

■ Many terrorist acts because of their importance and visibility

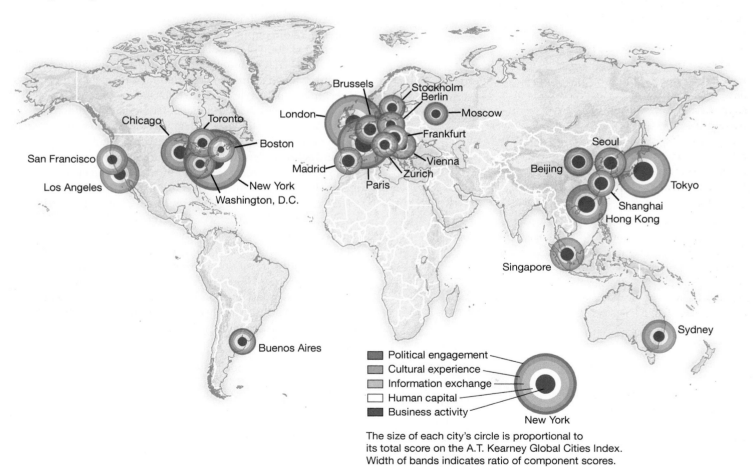

The size of each city's circle is proportional to its total score on the A.T. Kearney Global Cities Index. Width of bands indicates ratio of component scores.

FIGURE 10.D Top 25 cities in the Global Cities Index 2010 Toronto is the lone Canadian city in this categorization. *(Source: A.T. Kearney, The Urban Elite: The A.T. Kearney Global Cities Index 2010. Chicago, Illinois, 2010, p. 3.)*

cities exist in networks of flows among firms and institutions, networks that are complex and multilayered. As a result world cities are connected in different ways and integrated to different degrees in the global urban system. Quantifying these flows and connectivities is difficult, but geographers at the Globalization and World Cities (GaWC) research network have been able to identify breakpoints in cities' aggregate levels of integration within the world city network, resulting in a classification of alpha-, beta- and gamma-level world cities (**Table 10-1**). London and New York are tightly interrelated with one another (so much so that they are sometimes jointly referred to as "NYLON") and are both significantly more integrated into the overall world city network than any other city. Hong Kong is the third most highly integrated city.

Overall, the level of connectivity in the world city network rose steadily between 2000 and 2008, largely as a result of the increased global connectivity of South Asian, Chinese, and Eastern European cities (Shanghai, Beijing, and Moscow, in particular). This reflects the importance of "emerging markets" in globalization. Cities in the United States and sub-Saharan Africa, however, experienced a decline in global connectivity in the period (Los Angeles, San Francisco, and Miami, in particular). U.S. cities have always exhibited lower levels of integration than might be expected because foreign firms find it hard to penetrate the U.S. market while U.S. firms, with a big domestic market, have less reason to gamble on global expansion.

APPLY YOUR KNOWLEDGE Choose two world cities and provide two examples each of how these cities serve to connect global and local regions. Be specific in your answers. For example, you might want to consider how certain cities are centres of transnational corporations or the different ways cities culturally connect different places. ■

WORLD URBANIZATION TODAY

It is difficult to say just how urbanized the world has become. In many areas, urban growth is taking place at such a pace and under such chaotic conditions that experts can provide only informed estimates. The most comprehensive source of statistics is the United Nations, whose data suggest that half of the world's population is now urban. These data incorporate the very different definitions of *urban* used by different countries. Some countries (Canada and Australia, for example) count any settlement of 1000 people or more as urban; others (including Italy and Jordan) use 10 000 as the minimum for an urban settlement, and Japan uses 50 000 as the cut-off. This, by the way, tells us something about the nature of urbanization itself: it is a relative phenomenon. In countries like Peru, where the population is thinly distributed and scattered, a settlement of 2000 represents a significant centre. In countries like Japan, however, with more residents, higher population densities, and a tradition of centralized agricultural settlement, a much larger concentration of people is required to count as "urban."

To get around these national differences in definitions of what counts as "urban," the World Bank has developed a uniform definition of what constitutes an urban area based on an "agglomeration index" that identifies an area of 1 square kilometre as urban if its population density exceeds 150 and it has access to a settlement of more than 50 000 inhabitants within 60 minutes by road. According to this measure, the overall level of urbanization in the world in 2010 was 51 percent. As **Table 10-2** shows, North America is the most urbanized continent in the world, with 82 percent of its population living in urban areas. In contrast, Africa is less than 40 percent urban. To put these figures in perspective, only 29.7 percent of the world's population was urbanized in 1950. **Table 10-3** illustrates the rapid increase in urbanization since then. Today, 1 in 20 people worldwide lives in a megacity of 10 million or more; by 2025, that number will rise to 1 in 10.

TABLE 10-1 Alpha-Level World Cities in 2008

Alpha ++	Alpha +	Alpha	Alpha −
London	Hong Kong	Milan	Warsaw
New York	Paris	Madrid	Jakarta
	Singapore	Seoul	Sao Paulo
	Sydney	Moscow	Zurich
	Tokyo	Brussels	Mexico City
	Shanghai	Toronto	Dublin
	Beijing	Mumbai	Amsterdam
		Buenos Aires	Bangkok
		Kuala Lumpur	Taipei
			Rome
			Istanbul
			Lisbon
			Chicago
			Frankfurt
			Stockholm
			Vienna
			Budapest
			Athens
			Prague
			Caracas
			Auckland
			Santiago

(*Source:* From Taylor et al. (2009b), "Measuring the World City Network: New Developments and Results," *GaWC Research Bulletin 300*; http://www.lboro.ac.uk/gawc/rb/rb300.html.)

TABLE 10-2 Urbanization by Major World Regions, 2009

Continent	Percent of Total Population in Urban Areas
Africa	39.6
Asia	41.7
Latin America	79.3
North America	81.9
Europe	72.5
Oceania	70.2
World	50.2

(*Source:* Data from United Nations, *World Urbanization Prospects: The 2009 Revision.*)

TABLE 10-3   Percentage of Urbanized Population and Number of Large Cities, 1950, 2009, and 2025

	1950	2009	2025 (est.)
Urbanized population in percent	29.7	50.2	52
Number of cities over 1 million	83	374	475
Number of cities over 5 million	8	32	46
Number of cities over 10 million	2	21	29

(*Source:* Data from United Nations, *World Urbanization Prospects: The 2009 Revision.*)

The World Bank's analyses clearly show how levels of urbanization change with a country's level of economic development. There is a strong positive relationship between levels of urbanization and levels of economic development until a GDP per capita of around US$10 000. The early stages of urbanization are associated with a rapid shift in the number of people moving from rural to urban areas. Subsequently, the pace of urbanization slows and density levels off as the proportion of the country's population living in cities surpasses 60 percent and the level of GDP per capita surpasses US$10 000.

The Periphery and Semiperiphery: Overurbanization and Megacities

Few peripheral countries are able to handle the urban population crush, which is causing problems on an unprecedented scale with everything from clean water to disease prevention. Ten million people are dying annually in densely populated urban areas from conditions produced by substandard housing and poor sanitation. In 2005, there were 1.6 billion inadequately housed people across the world and an estimated 100 million homeless. According to the World Bank, 2.6 billion people worldwide do not have access to sanitation. About 1.7 million deaths a year—90 percent of which are children—are attributed to unsafe drinking water and poor sanitation and hygiene, mainly through infectious diarrhea.

In contrast to the world's core regions, where urbanization has largely resulted from economic growth, the urbanization of peripheral regions has been a consequence of demographic growth that preceded economic development. Although demographic transition is a fairly recent phenomenon in the peripheral regions of the world (see Chapter 3), it has generated large increases in population well in advance of any significant levels of industrialization or rural economic development.

The result, for the mainly rural populations of peripheral countries, has been more and more of a bad thing. Problems with agricultural development (see Chapter 8) mean an apparently hopeless future of drudgery and poverty for fast-growing rural populations. Emigration has provided one potential safety valve, but as the frontiers of the world-system closed, the more affluent core countries have put up barriers to immigration. The only option for the growing numbers of impoverished rural residents is to move to the larger towns and cities, where at least there is the hope of employment and the prospect of access to schools, health clinics, piped water, and the kinds of public facilities and services that are often unavailable in rural regions. Cities also have the lure of modernization and the

appeal of consumer goods. Overall, the metropolises of the periphery have absorbed 4 out of 5 of the 1.2 billion city dwellers added to the world's population since 1970.

When natural disasters, environmental degradation, or civil war impacts highly populated rural regions in the periphery, rates of rural–urban migration increase dramatically:

> For several years now, relentless cycles of drought and flooding have wreaked havoc on the tiny country of Malawi, in the heart of southern Africa. In 2002 and 2003, torrential rains caused massive mudslides, washing away bridges and homes and devastating harvests of maize, the main food staple. Unable to eke a living from the ravaged countryside, rural residents have flocked in droves to the country's bourgeoning cities—giving Malawi the dubious distinction of being the world's fastest-urbanizing nation today.[4]

Rural migrants have poured into cities out of desperation and hope rather than being drawn by jobs and opportunities. Because these migration streams have been composed disproportionately of teenagers and young adults, an important additional component of urban growth has followed—exceptionally high rates of natural population increase. On average, about 60 percent of urban population growth in peripheral countries is attributable to natural increase.

The consequence of all this urban population growth is **overurbanization**, which occurs when cities grow more rapidly than they can sustain jobs and housing. In such circumstances, urban growth produces instant slums—shacks set on unpaved streets, often with open sewers and no basic utilities. In general, it is the rate, not simply the level, of urbanization that produces slums; higher levels of urbanization tend to be associated with relatively fewer slums. Shacks are constructed out of any material that comes to hand, such as planks, cardboard, tar paper, thatch, mud, and corrugated iron. Many of these instant slums are squatter settlements, built illegally by families who are desperate for shelter. **Squatter settlements** are residential developments on land that is neither owned nor rented by its occupants. Squatter settlements are often, but not always, slums. In Chile, squatter settlements are called *callampas*, "mushroom cities"; in Turkey, they are called *gecekondu*, meaning that they were built overnight. In Brazil, they are called *favelas*; and in Argentina, simply *villas miserias*. These settlements typically account for well over one-third and sometimes up to three-quarters of the population of major cities (**Figure 10.22**). The most extensive slums, according to United Nations statistics, are in the cities of sub-Saharan Africa, where over 70 percent of the population lives in unfit accommodations.

The United Nations International Children's Fund (UNICEF) has blamed "uncontrollable urbanization" in less-developed countries for the widespread creation of "danger zones" in which increasing numbers of children become beggars, prostitutes, and labourers before reaching their teens.[5] Pointing out that urban populations are growing at twice the general population rate, UNICEF has concluded that too many people are being squeezed into cities that do not have enough jobs, shelter, or schools to accommodate them. As a consequence, the family and community structures that support

[4]State of the World 2005. New York: W. W. Norton & Company, 2005, p. 29.

[5]*The State of the World's Children 2011*. New York: United Nations International Children's Fund (UNICEF), 2011.

FIGURE 10.22 Slum housing in peripheral cities Throughout much of the world, the scale and speed of urbanization, combined with the scarcity of formal employment, have resulted in very high proportions of slum housing, much of it erected by squatters. This photograph shows part of the huge slum district of Mathare in Nairobi, Kenya, which is home to half a million people. (*Source: Jeremy Graham/dbimages/Alamy*)

children are being destroyed, with the result that increasing numbers of children have to work (**Figure 10.23**). For hundreds of thousands of street kids in less-developed countries, "work" means anything that contributes to survival: shining shoes, guiding cars into parking spaces, chasing other street kids away from patrons at an outdoor café, working as domestic help, making fireworks, selling drugs. In Abidjan, in Côte d'Ivoire, 15-year-old Jean-Pierre Godia, who cannot read or write, spends about 6 hours every day trying to sell 10-roll packets of toilet paper to motorists at a busy intersection. He buys the packets for about US$1.20 and sells them for US$2. Some days he doesn't sell any. In the same city, 7-year-old Giulio guides cars into parking spaces outside a chic pastry shop. He has been doing this since he was 5, to help his mother and four siblings, who beg on a nearby corner.

Megacities are very large cities characterized by both primacy and a high degree of centrality within their national economy. Their most important common denominator is their sheer size—most of them number 10 million or more in population. This, together with their functional centrality, means that in many ways they have more in common with one another than with the smaller metropolitan areas and cities within their own countries. Megacities include Mexico City (**Figure 10.24**), Dhaka, Jakarta, Lagos, Manila, Mumbai (**Figure 10.25**), New Delhi, São Paulo, and Teheran. Each has more inhabitants than 100 of the member countries of the United Nations. While most of them do not function as world cities, they do serve important intermediate roles between the upper tiers of the system of world cities and the provincial towns and villages of large regions of the world. They not only link local and provincial economies with the global economy but also provide a point of

contact between the traditional and the modern, and between formal and informal economic sectors. (See Box 10.3, "Window on the World: The Pearl River Delta: An Extended Metropolis.")

The **informal sector** of an economy involves a wide variety of economic activities whose common feature is that they take place beyond official record and are not subject to formalized systems of regulation or remuneration. As we shall see in the next chapter, the slums and squatter settlements in megacities are often associated with severe problems of social disorganization and environmental degradation. Nevertheless, many neighbourhoods are able to develop self-help networks and organizations that form the basis of community in dauntingly poor and crowded cities.

APPLY YOUR KNOWLEDGE Identify two megacities. List two ways they differ from a world city. ∎

The Core: Mature Metropolises

The high levels of urbanization and relatively slow rates of urban growth within the world's core regions are reflected in relatively stable urban systems. There is constant change, nevertheless, in patterns and processes of urbanization as the metropolises, cities, and towns adjust to the opportunities of new technologies and new industries and to the constraints of obsolescent urban infrastructure and land-use conflicts. New rounds of urbanization are initiated in the places most suited to new technologies and new industries. Those places least suited are likely to suffer spirals of deindustrialization and urban decline.

FIGURE 10.24 Mexico City Every year another half million or more people are added to the city. In 2013, the population of the agglomeration had reached 21 million. (*Source:* Aerial Archives/Alamy)

FIGURE 10.23 Child labour A 13-year-old girl makes fireworks at a factory in Sivakasi, India. One in 12 of the world's children (180 million young people aged 5 to 17) are involved in the worst forms of child labour—hazardous work, slavery, forced labour, the military, commercial sexual exploitation, and illicit activities. Of these children, 97 percent are in peripheral and semiperipheral countries. Globally, an estimated 114 million children of primary school age are not enrolled in school, depriving one in 5 children of an education. They are exposed to exploitation and abuse and miss out on developing the knowledge and employable skills that could lift them and their own children out of the poverty cycle.

(*Source:* Tom Stoddart/Getty Images)

Deindustrialization and Agglomeration Diseconomies

Deindustrialization involves a decline in industrial employment in core regions as firms scale back their activities in response to lower levels of profitability (Chapter 7). Such adversity has particularly affected cities like Sydney (Nova Scotia), Hamilton (Ontario), Pittsburgh and Cleveland (United States), Sheffield and Liverpool (United Kingdom), Lille (France), and Liège (Belgium)—places where heavy manufacturing constituted a key economic sector. Cities like these have suffered substantial reductions in employment since the 1970s and 1980s when better and more flexible transport and communications networks allowed many industries to choose from a broader range of potential locations.

In many instances, deindustrialization has been intensified by the dampening effects of *agglomeration diseconomies* (Chapter 7) on the growth of larger metropolitan areas. Agglomeration diseconomies, the negative effects of increasing urban size and density,

FIGURE 10.25 Mumbai With more than 20 million people, Mumbai is India's most populous city. (*Source:* Theowl84/Dreamstime)

include noise, air pollution, increased crime, high commuting costs, inflated land and housing prices, traffic congestion, and crowded port and railroad facilities. They also include higher taxes levied to rebuild decaying infrastructure and to support services and amenities previously considered unnecessary—traffic police, city planners, and homeless shelters, for example.

The result of deindustrialization has been a *decentralization* of jobs and people from larger to smaller cities within the urban

The Pearl River Delta: An Extended Metropolis

The Pearl River Delta (**Figure 10.E**) is one of the fastest-growing urban regions in the world. Anchored by the major metropolitan centres of Guangzhou, Hong Kong, Macau, Shenzhen, and Zhuhai, it is an extended metropolitan region of nearly 50 million people. It is one of three extended metropolitan regions—Beijing-Tianjin and Shanghai are the others—that have been fostered by the Chinese government to be engines of capitalist growth since liberal economic reforms were introduced in the late 1970s.

Hong Kong (**Figure 10.F**) was a British colony until 1997. It is now a metropolis of 7.4 million with a thriving industrial and commercial base that is recognized as a capitalist economic dynamo by the Chinese government, which has created a Special Administrative District for the metropolis. As a result, Hong Kong's citizens have retained their British-based legal system and its guaranteed rights of property ownership and democracy. Hong Kong is the world's largest container port, the third-largest centre for foreign exchange trade, the seventh-largest stock market, and the tenth-largest trading economy.

Hong Kong's financial success encouraged the Chinese government to establish two of its first Special Economic Zones (SEZs) in nearby Shenzhen and Zhuhai. Designed to attract foreign capital, technology, and management practices, these SEZs were established as export-processing zones that offered cheap labour and land, along with tax breaks, to transnational corporations (Chapter 7). Meanwhile, the Chinese government designated the entire delta region an Open Economic Region, where local

FIGURE 10.E Pearl River Delta One of the fastest-growing regions of the world, the Pearl River Delta is an extended metropolitan region of more than 50 million people.

FIGURE 10.F City of Hong Kong Although most of its manufacturing has been transferred to neighbouring Guangdong Province, where wages are much lower, thousands of companies are located in Hong Kong simply for the purpose of doing business with China. As a result, Hong Kong remains a major world city—a major financial hub with a thriving commercial sector and a population of 7.4 million. (*Source:* Bjanka Kadic/Alamy)

governments, individual enterprises, and farm households enjoy a high degree of autonomy in economic decision making.

The relaxation of state control over the regional economy allowed the region's dense and growing rural population to migrate to urban areas in search of assembly-line jobs or to stay in rural areas and diversify agricultural production from paddy-rice cultivation to more profitable activities such as market-farming activities, livestock husbandry, and fishery. Economic freedom also facilitated rural industrialization—mostly low-tech, small-scale, labour-intensive, and widely scattered across the countryside. The triangular area between Guangzhou, Hong Kong, and Macau has quickly emerged as an especially important zone because of its relatively cheap land and labour and because of significant levels of investment by regional and local governments in the transport and communications infrastructure. The result is a distinctive "extended metropolis" in which numerous small towns play an increasingly important role in fostering the process of urbanization, with an intense mixture of agricultural and nonagricultural activities and an intimate interaction between urban and rural areas.

The metropolitan cores of the region, aiming to increase their competitiveness and prominence in the globalizing world economy, have invested heavily in infrastructure improvements. The Guangzhou municipal government, for example, invested more than US$10 billion between 1998 and 2004 in infrastructure construction—including a metro system and an elevated railway network to link the city's new international airport, railway stations, and port. Throughout the region, enormous investments have been made in showpiece infrastructure projects geared to the needs of local and international capital. These include major airports, high-speed toll highways, satellite ground stations, port installations, metro and light-rail networks, and new water-management systems. In turn, these projects have attracted business and technology parks, financial centres, and resort complexes in a loose-knit sprawl of urban development.

Today, the Pearl River Delta provides a thriving export-processing platform that has driven double-digit annual economic growth for much of the past two decades. The region's GDP grew from just over US$8 billion in 1980 to nearly US$270 billion in 2010. During that period, the average real rate of GDP growth in the Pearl River Delta Economic Zone exceeded 16 percent, well above the People's Republic of China national figure of 9.8 percent. By 2010, and with only 3.5 percent of the country's population, the region was contributing 10 percent of the country's GDP and 29 percent of its total trade.

Guangzhou is a megacity with a 2010 population of around 10 million (**Figure 10.G**). Shenzhen has grown from a population of just 19 000 in 1975 to 8.1 million in 2010, with an additional 2 million in the surrounding municipalities. The southern border of the Shenzhen Special Economic Zone adjoins Hong Kong, but the northern border is walled off from the rest of China by an electrified fence to prevent smuggling and to keep back the mass of people trying to migrate illegally into Shenzhen and Hong Kong.

FIGURE 10.G Guangzhou, China An ancient Chinese city that became known as Canton by European traders, Guangzhou has grown rapidly in recent decades, its modern architecture almost completely replacing the old city. (*Source:* Alamy)

systems of core countries, and from metropolitan cores to suburban and ex-urban fringes. In some cases, routine production activities were relocated to smaller metropolitan areas or to rural areas with lower labour costs and more hospitable business climates. In other cases, these activities moved overseas—as part of the new international division of labour (Chapter 2)—or were eliminated entirely.

Counterurbanization and Reurbanization
The combination of deindustrialization in core manufacturing regions, agglomeration diseconomies in major metropolitan areas, and the improved accessibility of smaller towns and rural areas can give rise to the phenomenon of counterurbanization. **Counterurbanization** occurs when cities experience a net loss of population to smaller towns and rural areas. This process results in the deconcentration of population within an urban system. This is what happened in the United States, Britain, Japan, and many other developed countries in the 1970s and 1980s. Metropolitan growth slowed dramatically, while the growth rates of small and medium-size towns and of some rural areas increased. In these countries, counties that for decades had recorded stable populations grew by 15 or 20 percent. Some of the strongest gains were registered in counties that were within commuting range of metropolitan areas, but some remote counties also registered big population increases.

Counterurbanization was a major reversal of long-standing trends, but it seems to have been a temporary adjustment rather than a permanent change. The globalization of the economy and the growth of post-industrial activities in revamped and expanded metropolitan settings have restored the trend toward the concentration of population within urban systems. Most of the cities that were declining fast in the 1970s and 1980s are now either recovering (New York, London) or bottoming out (Paris, Chicago), while most of those that were growing only slowly (Tokyo, Barcelona) are now expanding more quickly. This trend of **reurbanization** involves the growth of population in metropolitan central cores following a period of absolute or relative decline in population.

In Canada, two principal migration streams are driving reurbanization. One consists of immigrants, who disproportionately settle in major metropolitan areas, especially Toronto and Vancouver, as well as some medium-size metropolitan areas such as Kitchener-Waterloo, London, or Windsor. A second migration stream consists of retiring baby boomers and young professionals moving to new condo developments in the central districts of metropolitan areas to live close to restaurants, theatres, and other cultural amenities.

APPLY YOUR KNOWLEDGE   Identify a town or city near you that has experienced counterurbanization or reurbanization over the past 10 years. Provide two reasons for this occurrence. ▪

Future Geographies

The United Nations Human Settlements Program (UN-Habitat) estimates that by 2030, more than 65 percent of the world's population will be living in urban areas, and there will be about 575 cities with a population of a million or more, including about 50 cities of 5 million or more. The number of megacities—those with a population of 10 million or more—will increase, and the populations of most of them will swell significantly (**Table 10-4**). The single most important aspect of future patterns of world urbanization is the striking difference in trends and projections between the core regions and the semiperipheral and peripheral regions. In 1950, two-thirds of the world's urban population was concentrated in the more-developed countries of the core economies. Since then, the world's urban population has increased fourfold, the bulk of the growth having taken place in the less-developed countries of the periphery (**Figure 10.26**). By 2030, around 80 percent of all city dwellers will be in peripheral and semiperipheral countries. By 2030, all but two or three of the 30 largest metropolitan areas are expected to be located in peripheral and semiperipheral regions.

Asia provides some of the most dramatic examples of this trend. From a region of villages, Asia is fast becoming a region of cities and towns. Between 1950 and 2005, for example, Asia's urban population rose more than 10-fold, to over 1.5 billion people. By 2020, about two-thirds of its population will be living in urban areas. Nowhere is the trend toward rapid urbanization more pronounced than in China, where for decades the communist government imposed strict controls on where people were allowed to live, fearing the transformative and liberating effects of cities. By tying people's jobs, school admission, and even the right to buy food to the places where people were registered to live, the government made it almost impossible for rural residents to migrate to towns or cities. As a result, more than 70 percent of China's 1 billion people still lived in the countryside in 1985. Now, however, China is rapidly making up for lost time. The Chinese government, having decided that towns and cities can be engines of economic development, has not only relaxed residency laws but has also drawn up plans to move up to 400 million people to over 430 newly constructed cities over the next decade. Currently, one-quarter of the world's 1000 largest cities are located in China, and the growth seems far from over: according to the United Nations, the number of Chinese cities over 500 000 is set to rise to more than 350 within the next 25 years.

Whatever the current level of urbanization in peripheral countries, almost all are forecast to experience high rates of urbanization, with growth forecasts of unprecedented speed and unmatched size. Karachi, Pakistan, a metropolis of 1 million in 1950, reached 8.5 million in 1995 and is expected to reach 16 million by 2015. Likewise, Cairo, Egypt, grew from 2.4 million to 9.7 million between 1950 and 1995 and is expected to reach 13 million by 2015. Mumbai (India, formerly Bombay), Delhi (India), Mexico City (Mexico), Dhaka (Bangladesh), Jakarta (Indonesia), Lagos (Nigeria), São Paulo (Brazil), and Shanghai (China) are all projected to have populations in excess of 17 million by 2015. For the most

TABLE 10-4 Growth and More Urban Growth

The World's Megacities, 2007 and 2025

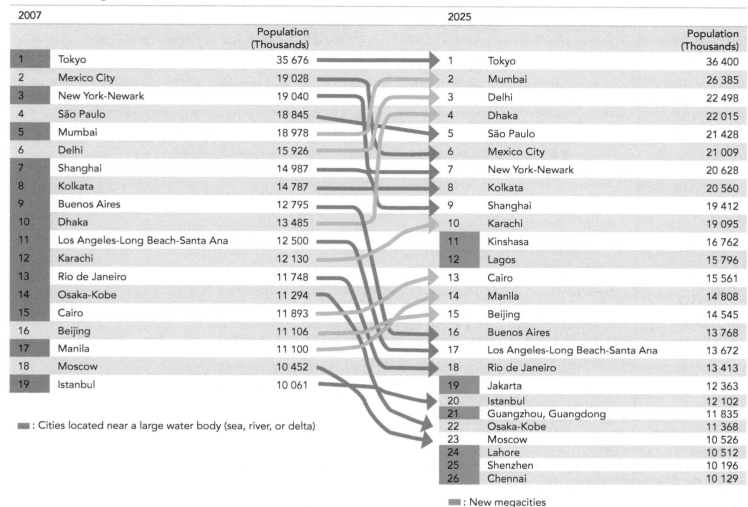

2007		Population (Thousands)		2025		Population (Thousands)
1	Tokyo	35 676		1	Tokyo	36 400
2	Mexico City	19 028		2	Mumbai	26 385
3	New York-Newark	19 040		3	Delhi	22 498
4	São Paulo	18 845		4	Dhaka	22 015
5	Mumbai	18 978		5	São Paulo	21 428
6	Delhi	15 926		6	Mexico City	21 009
7	Shanghai	14 987		7	New York-Newark	20 628
8	Kolkata	14 787		8	Kolkata	20 560
9	Buenos Aires	12 795		9	Shanghai	19 412
10	Dhaka	13 485		10	Karachi	19 095
11	Los Angeles-Long Beach-Santa Ana	12 500		11	Kinshasa	16 762
12	Karachi	12 130		12	Lagos	15 796
13	Rio de Janeiro	11 748		13	Cairo	15 561
14	Osaka-Kobe	11 294		14	Manila	14 808
15	Cairo	11 893		15	Beijing	14 545
16	Beijing	11 106		16	Buenos Aires	13 768
17	Manila	11 100		17	Los Angeles-Long Beach-Santa Ana	13 672
18	Moscow	10 452		18	Rio de Janeiro	13 413
19	Istanbul	10 061		19	Jakarta	12 363
				20	Istanbul	12 102
				21	Guangzhou, Guangdong	11 835
				22	Osaka-Kobe	11 368
				23	Moscow	10 526
				24	Lahore	10 512
				25	Shenzhen	10 196
				26	Chennai	10 129

■ : Cities located near a large water body (sea, river, or delta)

■ : New megacities

Note: Population figures are for urban agglomeration, not city proper. Megacities are cities with populations of more than 10 million.
(*Source: UN Habitat: State of the World's Cities 2008/2009. Harmonious Cities.* Copyright © United Nations Human Settlement Programme, 2008.)

part, this growth will be a consequence of the onset of the demographic transition (Chapter 3), which has produced fast-growing rural populations in regions that face increasing problems with agricultural development (Chapter 8). As a response, many people in these regions will continue to migrate to urban areas seeking a better life.

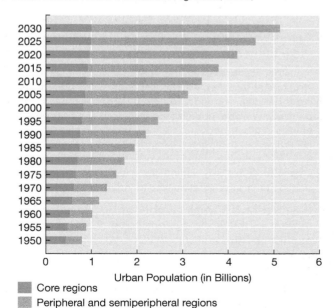

FIGURE 10.26 Urban population growth, 1950–2030
Although the metropolitan areas of the world's core countries have continued to grow, most of them have been overtaken by the startling growth of the "unintended" metropolises of peripheral and semiperipheral countries. (*Source:* Data from United Nations, *World Urbanization Prospects.* New York: UN Department of Economic and Social Affairs.)

CONCLUSION

Urbanization is one of the most important geographic phenomena. Cities can be seedbeds of economic development and cultural innovation. Cities and groups of cities also organize space—not just the territory immediately around them, but in some cases national and even international space. The causes and consequences of urbanization, however, are very different in different parts of the world. The urban experience of the world's peripheral regions stands in sharp contrast to that of the developed core regions, for example. This contrast is a reflection of some of the demographic, economic, and political factors that we have explored in previous chapters.

Much of the developed world has become almost completely urbanized, with highly organized systems of cities. Today, levels of urbanization are high throughout the world's core countries, while rates of urbanization are relatively low. At the top of the urban hierarchies of the world's core regions are world cities such as London, New York, Tokyo, Paris, and Zürich, which have become control centres for the flows of information,

cultural products, and finance that collectively sustain the economic and cultural globalization of the world. In doing so, they help consolidate the hegemony of the world's core regions.

Few of the metropolises of the periphery, on the other hand, are world cities occupying key roles in the organization of global economics and culture. Rather, they operate as connecting links between provincial towns and villages and the world economy. They have innumerable economic, social, and cultural linkages to their provinces on one side and to major world cities on the other. Almost all peripheral countries, meanwhile, are experiencing high rates of urbanization, with forecasted growth of unprecedented speed and unmatched size. In many peripheral and semiperipheral regions, current rates of urbanization have given rise to unintended metropolises and fears of "uncontrollable urbanization," with urban "danger zones" where "work" means anything that contributes to survival. The result, as we shall see in Chapter 11, is that these unintended metropolises are quite different from the cities of the core as places in which to live and work.

Learning Outcomes Revisited

- Describe how the earliest towns and cities developed independently in the various hearth areas of the first agricultural revolution.

  The very first region of independent urbanism, in the Middle East, produced successive generations of urbanized world-empires, including those of Greece, Rome, and Byzantium. By 2500 B.C.E., cities had appeared in the Indus Valley, and by 1800 B.C.E., urban areas were established in northern China. Other areas of independent urbanism include Mesoamerica (from around 100 B.C.E.) and Andean America (from around 800 C.E.). The classical archaeological interpretation emphasizes the availability of an agricultural surplus large enough to allow the emergence of specialized, nonagricultural workers. Some urbanization, however, may have resulted from the pressure of population growth.

- Scrutinize how the expansion of trade around the world, associated with colonialism and imperialism, established numerous gateway cities.

  European powers founded or developed literally thousands of towns as they extended their trading networks and established their colonies. The great majority of the towns were ports that served as control centres commanding entrance to, and exit from, their particular country or region. Protected by fortifications and European naval power, the port cities began as trading posts and colonial administrative centres. Before long, they developed manufacturing of their own to supply the pioneers' needs, along with more extensive commercial and financial services. As colonies developed and trading networks expanded, some of these ports grew rapidly, acting as gateways for colonial expansion into continental interiors.

- Assess why and how the Industrial Revolution generated new kinds of cities—and many more of them.

  Industrial economies required the large pools of labour; the transportation networks; the physical infrastructure of factories, warehouses, stores, and offices; and the consumer markets provided by cities. As industrialization spread throughout Europe in the first half of the nineteenth century and then to other parts of the world, urbanization increased at a faster pace. The higher wages and greater variety of opportunities in urban labour markets attracted migrants from surrounding areas. The countryside began to empty. In Europe, the *demographic transition* caused a rapid growth in population as death rates dropped dramatically. This growth in population provided a massive increase in the labour supply, further boosting the rate of urbanization, not only within Europe itself but also in Australia, Canada, New Zealand, South Africa, and the United States as emigration spread industrialization and urbanization to the frontiers of the world-system.

- Interpret how a small number of "world cities," most of them located within the core regions of the world-system, have come to occupy key roles in the organization of global economics and culture.

  At the top of a global urban system, these cities experience growth largely as a result of their role as key nodes in the world economy. World cities are the control centres for the flows of information, cultural products, and finance that collectively sustain the economic and cultural globalization of the world. The globalization of the economy has resulted in a global urban system in which the key roles of world cities are concerned with transnational corporate organization, international banking and finance, supranational government, and the work of international agencies. World cities also provide an interface between the global and the local. They contain the economic, cultural, and institutional apparatus that channels national and provincial resources into the global economy and transmits the impulses of globalization back to national and provincial centres.

- Compare and contrast the differences in trends and projections between the world's core regions and peripheral regions.

In 1950, two-thirds of the world's urban population was concentrated in the more-developed countries of the core economies. Since then, the world's urban population has increased fourfold, the bulk of the growth having taken place in the less-developed countries of the periphery. The world's core regions are highly urbanized, with slow rates of urban growth. Peripheral regions, although less highly urbanized, have been experiencing exceptionally high rates of urban growth, partly due to rural–urban migration and partly due to natural population increase. Much of the resulting urbanization has taken the form of megacities of 10 million people or more. Overurbanization has occurred where cities have grown more rapidly than they have been able to generate jobs or housing.

KEY TERMS

central place *(p. 379)*
central place theory *(p. 379)*
centrality *(p. 380)*
colonial city *(p. 378)*
counterurbanization *(p. 390)*

gateway city *(p. 373)*
informal sector *(p. 386)*
megacity *(p. 386)*
overurbanization *(p. 385)*
primacy *(p. 380)*

rank-size rule *(p. 380)*
reurbanization *(p. 390)*
shock city *(p. 376)*
squatter settlement *(p. 385)*

urban ecology *(p. 368)*
urban form *(p. 368)*
urban system *(p. 368)*
urbanism *(p. 368)*

REVIEW AND DISCUSSION

1. Search for pictures of what your campus looked like 5, 10, and 30 years ago. How have the urban forms changed? Note five examples of how the campus has changed between then and now. How have the physical structures changed? How is the land used differently? Is the university organized differently? If so, why do you think this is the case? If not, explain why things are the same.

2. Consider the term *world cities*. Choose two cities that you consider to be world cities. Now read over the functional characteristics of world cities that are bulleted on page 383. Pick two bullet points and describe the characteristics in terms of the cities you have chosen. For example, the second bullet point notes how world cities have "clusters of specialized, advanced business services." Do an Internet search and identify the clusters of specialized business services in the cities you have chosen.

3. *Counterurbanization* refers to the process of cities losing population to smaller towns or rural areas. Determine if any Canadian cities have experienced recent counterurbanization. List three reasons for the counterurbanization. Consider whether some cities are currently experiencing reurbanization. List three reasons for this type of population movement.

4. Canada, like most core countries, is already highly urbanized and has a relatively low rate of urbanization. Nevertheless, some Canadian

cities have been growing much faster than others. Which have been the fastest-growing Canadian cities in recent times, and what reasons can you find for their relatively rapid growth? (*Hint:* Statistics Canada publishes data on population change by urban area.)

5. The following cities all have populations in excess of 2 million. How many of them could you locate on a world map? Their size reflects a certain degree of importance, at least within their regional economy. What can you find out about each? Compile for each a 50-word description that explains its chief industries and a little of its history.

| Poona | Ibadan | Recife |
| Bangalore | Turin | Ankara |

6. Halifax and St. John's were Canadian gateway cities on the Atlantic coast, and Quebec city was a gateway city on the St. Lawrence. What can you find out about the commodities and manufactures that they imported and exported in pre-Confederation times? Where did their exports go? List three reasons why they went to those places. On the import side, where did imports come from? List three reasons why these cities needed to import these particular goods. Which geographic concepts do you consider to be useful in explaining these facts?

Mastering GEOGRAPHY™

Log in to www.masteringgeography.com for MapMaster™ interactive maps, geography videos, RSS feeds, flashcards, weblinks, an eText version of *Human Geography: Places and Regions in Global Context*, and self-study quizzes to enhance your study of urbanization.

MapMaster™ presents 13 Place Name and 13 Layered Thematic interactive maps to help students practise and master their geographic literacy, spatial reasoning, and critical thinking skills.

11 CITY SPACES: URBAN STRUCTURE

Learning Outcomes

- Assess how the internal structure of cities is shaped by competition for territory and location.

- Appraise the ways in which social patterns in cities are influenced by human territoriality.

- Describe the spatial structure of a typical North American city.

- Compare and contrast urban structures in different regions of the world.

- Explain the nature and causes of the problems associated with urbanization in various world regions.

China seems to have caught onto sprawl. Yet what is perhaps most distinctive about many of China's affluent new suburbs is not the sprawl itself, but the way it looks. Many suburbs are directly modelled on the tract homes that have defined American suburban growth in the past 30 years. Most of them carry few, if any, Asian influences in their design, layout, and ornamentation. The first suburbs were built to house expatriates, such as diplomats or executives in the local offices of multinational companies; now an increasing number of Chinese with money are eager to get out of the crowded milieu of the city.

Wish to live in Australia—without leaving Beijing? Beijing residents can now buy a home in Sydney Coast, a subdivision that offers its residents a "seven-day Australian-style villa life." "Designed by Australian experts, the project presents a kind of simple and fresh lifestyle," says a brochure for the new development. "Taking a walk along the streets in Sydney Coast, you will get a true sense of Australia."

Beijingers who would prefer to live in California can move into the Yosemite subdivision—or wait for the completion of Napa Valley, a new development under construction about 50 kilometres outside Beijing. Napa Valley attempts to capture a Californian/Mediterranean lifestyle of laid-back, al fresco leisure. "Rustic stone is widely used, with rich stucco colors, along with wood shutters and wrought-iron accents, to create an intimate scale and village-like feel," according to the Chinese Napa Valley's architects and planners.

Thames Town, an English-styled development, near Shanghai, China.
(*Source:* Qilal Shen/epa/Corbis Wire/Corbis)

For those craving to recreate life in seventeenth-century France, there is Chateau Regalia, located on Beijing's northern outskirts. In both form and decoration, Chateau Regalia's homes are an eccentric amalgam of French Baroque and neoclassical architecture. And yes, there's Canada, too: Vancouver Forest is a new subdivision of homes that mimics a typical neighbourhood in British Columbia. It was built by Canadian architects, using Canadian materials to create a mini Canada.

The craze has also caught on in Shanghai, where many more tract homes are built in foreign styles. Thames Town, just outside Shanghai, is one of seven satellite towns built by the municipal government to house 500 000 people. (The other six are themed with architectural styles adopted from Italy, Spain, Canada, Sweden, Holland, and Germany.) Thames Town includes a gothic church, village green, and mock-Tudor pub selling real ale. Built from scratch in little over three years, the suburb encapsulates five centuries of British architecture with half-timbered Tudor-style residences at the centre, shops in Victorian redbrick warehouses on the waterfront, and gabled Edwardian houses bordered by privet hedges, manicured lawns, and leafy roads.[1] ∎

[1]Based on D. Elsea, "China's Chichi Suburbs: American-style Sprawl All the Rage in Beijing," *San Francisco Chronicle*, April 24, 2005, p. 23.

URBAN LAND USE AND SPATIAL ORGANIZATION

The internal organization of cities reflects the way cities function, both to bring people and activities together and to sort them out into functional subareas and neighbourhoods. While there are many complex processes at work in cities, some broad tendencies go a long way toward shaping patterns of urban land use and spatial organization. In this first section of the chapter, we consider two of them: people's need for accessibility and their sense of territoriality.

Accessibility and Land Use

Most urban land users want to maximize the *utility* they derive from a particular location. The utility of a specific place or location refers to its usefulness to particular persons or groups. The price people are prepared to pay for different locations—the bid-rent—is a reflection of this utility. In general, utility is a function of *accessibility*. Commercial land users want to be accessible to one another, to markets, and to workers; private residents want to be accessible to jobs, amenities, and friends; public institutions want to be accessible to clients. In an idealized city built on an isotropic surface, the point of maximum accessibility is the city centre. An **isotropic surface** is a hypothetical, uniform plane: flat, and with no variations in its physical attributes. Under these conditions, accessibility decreases steadily with distance from the city centre. Likewise, utility decreases, *but at different rates for different land users*. This idealized pattern of decreasing accessibility and utility is reflected in concentric zones of different mixes of land use (**Figure 11.1**).

One counterintuitive implication of this model is that the poorest households will end up occupying the periphery of the city. Although this is true in some parts of the world, we know that in the core countries this is often not the case. In fact, the farthest suburbs are generally the territory of wealthier households, while the poor usually occupy more accessible locations nearer city centres. To reflect reality, some of the assumptions of this model must be modified. In this case, we must assume that wealthier households trade off the convenience of accessibility for the greater utility of the privacy provided by larger suburban lots. Poorer households, unable to afford the recurrent costs of transportation, trade off living space for accessibility to jobs and end up in high-density areas,

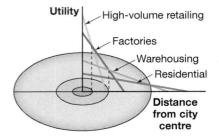

FIGURE 11.1 Accessibility, bid-rent, and urban structure
Competition for accessible sites near the city centre is an important determinant of land-use patterns. Different users are prepared to pay different amounts—the bid-rents—for locations at various distances from the city centre. The result is often a concentric pattern of land uses. (*Source:* Reprinted with permission of Prentice Hall, from P. L. Knox, *Urbanization* © 1994, p. 99.)

at expensive locations, near their low-wage jobs. Because of the presumed trade-off between accessibility and living space, this modified urban land-use model is often referred to as a **trade-off model**.

> **APPLY YOUR KNOWLEDGE** Identify three different trade-offs that you have made in terms of your own living space. List three ways these trade-offs have affected your access to school, transportation, and job. ∎

Territoriality, Congregation, and Segregation

In cities, as at other geographic scales, territoriality provides a means of establishing and preserving group membership and identity. The first step in forming group identity is to define "others" in an exclusionary and stereotypical way. **Congregation**—the territorial and residential clustering of specific groups or subgroups of people—enables group identity to be consolidated in relation to people and places outside the group. Congregation is a place-making activity and an important basis for urban structure and land use. It is particularly important in situations where there are one or more distinctive minority groups. **Minority groups** are population subgroups that are seen—or that see themselves—as somehow different from the general population. The defining characteristics of minority groups can be based on race, language, religion, nationality, caste, sexual orientation, or lifestyle.

For minority groups there are several specific advantages of congregation:

- *Congregation provides a means of cultural preservation. It allows religious and cultural practices to be maintained, and strengthens group identity through daily involvement in particular routines and ways of life.* Particularly important in this regard is the way that clustering fosters within-group marriage and kinship networks.

- *Congregation helps minimize conflict and provides defence against "outsiders."*

- *Congregation provides a place where mutual support can be established through minority institutions, businesses, social networks, and welfare organizations.*

- *Congregation helps establish a power base in relation to the host society.* This power base can be democratic, (e.g., by electing a minority candidate in the local riding), or it can take the form of a territorial heartland for insurrectionary groups.

Congregation is not always voluntary, of course. Host populations are also impelled by territoriality, and they may respond to social and cultural differences by *discrimination* against minority groups. Discrimination can also have a strong territorial basis. It can restrict the territory of minority groups and resist their assimilation into the host society. This resistance can take a variety of forms. Social hostility and the voicing of "keep out" attitudes are probably the most widespread, although other forms of discrimination can have pronounced spatial effects. These forms include exclusion and prejudice in local labour markets, the manipulation of private land and housing markets (for example, when banks reject mortgage applications from certain neighbourhoods), the steering of capital investment away from minority areas, and the institutionalization of discrimination through the practices and spatial policies of public agencies (for example, when transit routes skirt certain areas).

The combined result of congregation and discrimination is **segregation**, the spatial separation of specific subgroups within a wider population. (See Box 11.1, "Visualizing Geography: Racial Segregation in the U.S.") Segregation varies a great deal in both intensity and form, depending on the relative degree and combination of congregation and discrimination. Geographers have identified three principal situations in terms of the spatial form of segregation.

- In *enclaves*, tendencies toward congregation and discrimination are long-standing but dominated by internal cohesion and identity. The Jewish districts of many of today's cities in Europe and the eastern United States are enclaves **(Figure 11.2)**.

- *Ghettos* are also long-standing but are more the product of discrimination than congregation. Examples are the segregation of African Americans and Hispanics in American cities.

FIGURE 11.2 Loyalist neighbourhood in Belfast, Northern Ireland Congregation is an important place-making activity. It enables group identity to be established and preserved in relation to "other" people and places. (*Source:* AP Photo/Peter Morrison/ Canadian Press Images)

- *Colonies* may result from relatively weak and short-lasting congregation, discrimination, or both. The persistence of colonies over time depends on the continuing arrival of new minority-group members. For example, many Canadian cities in the early to mid-twentieth century contained distinctive colonies of German, Portuguese, Irish, and Italian immigrants. These have all but disappeared. More recently, refugees have formed colonies of Vietnamese in Vancouver and Somalis in Toronto, for example.

Economic competition for space and accessibility, along with the tendency toward social and ethnic discrimination, congregation, and segregation, can be traced in many of the world's cities. Patterns are apparent particularly in affluent core regions where economic, social, and cultural forces are broadly similar. Nevertheless, urban structure varies considerably because of the influence of history, culture, and the different roles that cities have played within the world-system. In this chapter, we examine the typical characteristics of North American, European, and Islamic cities, and the unintended metropolises of the periphery.

> **APPLY YOUR KNOWLEDGE** Identify any present or historical enclaves, ghettos, or colonies in your region. List two ways these spatial forms may have resulted from discrimination and two ways that residents potentially benefit from congregation in these communities. ■

SPATIAL PATTERNS AND PROCESSES IN NORTH AMERICAN CITIES

In North American cities the very centres have historically been the principal hubs of shops and offices. They have also featured some of the major institutional land uses such as the city hall, libraries, and museums. A city's centre, known as the **central business district,** or **CBD**, is the nucleus of commercial land uses. It traditionally contains the densest concentration of shops, offices and warehouses, and the tallest nonresidential buildings **(Figure 11.3)**. It usually developed at the nodal point of transportation routes, so it also contains bus stations, railway terminals, and hotels.

The CBD usually is surrounded by a zone of mixed land uses: warehouses, small factories and workshops, specialized stores, apartment buildings, public housing projects, and older residential neighbourhoods. This zone is often referred to as the **zone in transition** because of its mixture of growth, change, and decline **(Figure 11.4)**.

Beyond this zone are residential neighbourhoods, suburbs of various ages and different social and ethnic composition. Just as different categories of land use attract and repel one another, so do different social and ethnic groups. In North America, where urban population growth has been fuelled by streams of migrants and immigrants with very different backgrounds, sociologists have developed an ecological perspective to describe neighbourhoods as being structured by the "invasion" of successive waves of migrants and immigrants.

Among core countries, segregation is particularly common in American cities, where it usually is based on racial and ethnic differences. Usually, maps show ethnic neighbourhoods as sharply bounded blocks at the scale of census tracts that contain hundreds, sometimes thousands, of people. The maps below follow a different approach. Here one dot equals 25 people, and the dots are colour-coded based on the race categories enumerated in the 2000 U.S. census: white is pink, black is blue, Hispanic is orange, and Asian is green. The maps show that just as every city is different, every city is segregated (or integrated) in different ways.

Detroit, for example, is highly segregated, with a highway forming the sharp boundary between blacks in the downtown and whites to the north of it. In Washington, D.C., there is a sharp east-west divide between white and black. In New York, there are areas of extreme racial concentration, but the sheer number of people in those areas means that boundary regions become intensely rich areas of cross-cultural ferment. Long Beach, California, meanwhile, is almost the opposite: because no part of the city is particularly dense, there are a number of blended neighbourhoods, some of which are more extensive than the racially homogeneous ones.

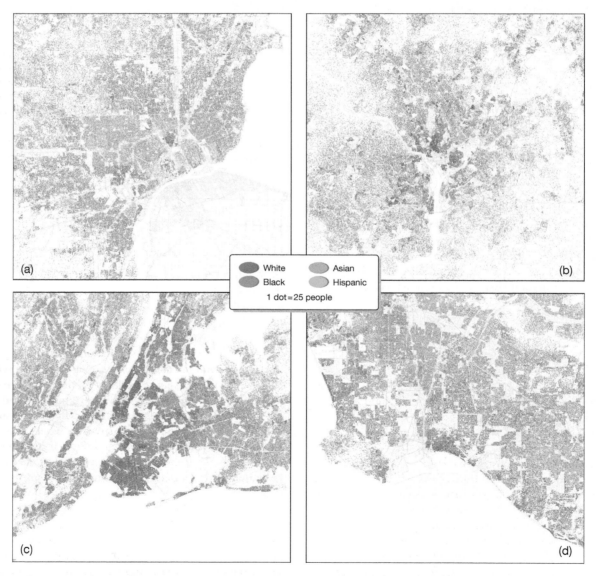

FIGURE 11.A (a) Detroit (b) Washington, D.C. (c) New York City (d) Long Beach (*Source:* Based on infographics by Eric Fischer. See http://www.flickr.com/photos/ walkingsf/sets/72157624812674967/with/4981417821/.)

FIGURE 11.3 The central business district
This photograph of Edmonton shows the concentration of high-rise office buildings that is typical of central business districts (CBDs) in North American metropolitan areas. In Edmonton, as in other major cities, the CBD originally grew around the point of maximum accessibility: near railway stations and the intersection of the city's principal road and water transportation routes. Particularly in the western parts of North America, the location of the city itself is often the result of transportation factors: cities sprang up where the railroad crossed the river. (*Source:* Richard Wear/Design Pics Inc./Alamy)

FIGURE 11.4 The zone in transition This photograph of stores along the western end of Queen Street in Toronto shows part of the zone in transition. In many North American cities, the CBD is surrounded by such a zone, which consists of older neighbourhoods with mixed land uses, some of which are in long-term decline, whereas others are undergoing redevelopment. (*Source:* Alan E. Nash)

Immigration and Neighbourhood Change

When immigrants first arrive in a city looking for work and a place to live, they have little choice but to cluster in the cheapest accommodations, found in the zone in transition around the CBD and typically resulting in enclaves, ghettos, or colonies. Chicago in the 1920s and 1930s provides a classic example of this. Immigrants from Scandinavia, Germany, Italy, Ireland, Poland, Bohemia (now part of the Czech Republic), and Lithuania established themselves in Chicago's low-rent areas, the only places they could afford. By congregating in these areas, immigrants accomplished several things—establish a sense of security; continue speaking their native language; have familiar churches or synagogues, restaurants, bakeries, butcher shops, and taverns; and support their own community newspapers and clubs. African-American migrants from the South joined in the city's zone in transition, establishing their own neighbourhoods and communities. In Chicago, as in other U.S. cities of the period, the various ethnic groups formed a patchwork or mosaic of communities encircling the CBD.

These ethnic communities lasted from one to three generations, after which they started to break up. Many of the younger, city-born individuals did not feel the need for the security and familiarity of ethnic neighbourhoods. Gradually, increasing numbers established themselves in better jobs and moved out into newer, better housing. As the original immigrants and their families left, their place in the transitional zone was taken by a new wave of migrants and immigrants. In this way, Chicago became structured into a series of *concentric zones* of neighbourhoods of different ethnicity and social status (**Figure 11.5**).

Throughout this process of invasion and succession, people of the same background tend to stick together—partly because of the advantages of residential clustering and partly because of discrimination. **Invasion and succession** is a process of neighbourhood change whereby one social or ethnic group succeeds another in a residential area. The displaced group, in turn, invades other areas, creating over time a rippling process of change throughout the city. The result is that within each concentric zone there exists a mosaic of distinctive

FIGURE 11.5 The ecological model of urban land use: Chicago in the 1920s Competition among members of different migrant and immigrant groups for residential space in the city often results in distinctive neighbourhoods that have their own social "ecology." The classic example is Chicago of the 1920s, which had developed a series of concentric zones of distinctive neighbourhoods as successive waves of immigrants established themselves. Over time, most immigrant groups made their way from low-rent, inner-city districts surrounding the CBD (known in Chicago as the Loop) to more attractive and expensive districts farther out. (*Source:* After R. E. Park, E. W. Burgess, and R. D. McKenzie, *The City.* Chicago: University of Chicago Press, 1925, p. 53.)

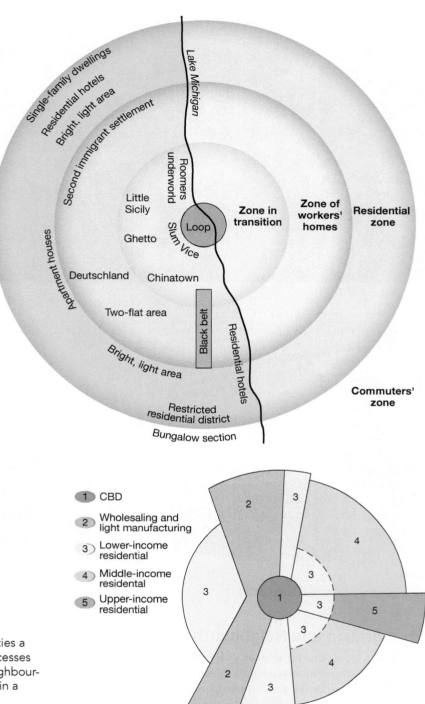

FIGURE 11.6 Chinatown, Montreal In most larger cities a patchwork of distinctive neighbourhoods results from processes of congregation and segregation. Most distinctive are neighbourhoods of ethnic minorities, such as the Chinatowns found in a number of Canadian cities. (*Source:* Courtesy of Alan E. Nash)

FIGURE 11.7 Hoyt's model of urban structure Based on his observations of American cities in the first half of the twentieth century, Hoyt saw the dominant pattern in terms of sectors of industry and the relative arrangement of different classes. (*Source:* Based on C.D. Harris and E.L. Ullman, "The Nature of Cities," *Annals, American Academy of Political and Social Science,* 1945, Figure 5.)

neighbourhoods. Classic examples include the Chinatowns and Little Italys of big Canadian cities, or the Koreatowns and African-American ghettos of big U.S. cities (**Figure 11.6**). Such neighbourhoods can be thought of as *ecological niches* within the overall metropolis—settings where a particular mix of people have come to dominate a particular territory and a particular physical environment, or habitat.

Industry, Class, and Spatial Organization

Households also sort themselves within cities according to differences in class status and affluence and ability to avoid living in or near to industrial districts. The classic study of this tendency resulted in a generalized model of urban land use (**Figure 11.7**). The author of the study, Homer Hoyt, argued that corridors of industry and warehousing will always tend to be surrounded on both sides by sectors of working-class housing, while middle-income housing will always tend to act as a buffer between the industrial/working-class half of the city and the city's main sector of elite neighbourhoods.

The key to the dynamics that produced these patterns was, as Hoyt observed, the behaviour of affluent households. Once the CBD is established and corridors of industrial development laid out, affluent households have first pick of the most desirable sites: away from industry and the press of humanity in the CBD and on high ground free from the risk of flooding. With urban growth, the high-status area expands along the axes of transportation lines. This happens at first in response to the desire among the most affluent to combine accessibility with suburban or exurban living and, subsequently, to a desire among the almost-as-affluent to live in the same neighbourhood as the rich and influential. Middle-class, middle-income housing is established in surrounding sectors by speculative developers, who recognize the desire for "good" addresses among prospective customers. An important consequence of the outward growth of each sector is the banding of the sectors into zones of different age, style, and condition.

Automobiles and Decentralization

The advent of trucks and automobiles allowed both industry and households to become mobile. The tendency for cities to be organized in sectors and zones around a CBD was undermined by this process. In 1945, geographers Chauncy Harris and Edward Ullman described the appearance of new, automobile-based suburban nodes of commercial and industrial activity that were not arranged in any predictable fashion except in relation to surrounding land uses (**Figure 11.8**). In their **multiple-nuclei model**, decentralized nodes of different categories of land use end up in many different configurations, depending on local conditions. These nodes might develop around a government centre, a university, a transit stop, or a highway intersection. If the nodes were office and retailing centres, they would attract middle-income residential development, whereas if they were industrial centres, they would attract working-class residential development. This model quite accurately describes how North American cities began to develop an irregular-shaped patchwork of land uses across which there is a loose functional order.

Looking back, we can see that Harris and Ullman were remarkably prescient: the multiple-nuclei city is a uniquely North American manifestation of contemporary urbanization—ever-increasing metropolitan sprawl with new nodes of economic and residential development. While Canada certainly has its share in this development (for example, in Calgary or in the suburban "doughnut" surrounding Toronto), sprawl has almost become the rule in the United States. (See Box 11.2, "Geography Matters: Smart Growth versus Sprawl in the U.S.")

The Polycentric New Metropolis

In the U.S., continued urban growth has scaled up the irregular-shaped, multiple-nuclei patchwork of land uses into polycentric metropolitan regions. During the middle decades of the twentieth century, American cities in particular were reshaped by the combination of increased automobility, massive highway construction, and mortgage affordability that underpinned the growth of home ownership. In Canada a similar but less pronounced process began with a delay of one or two decades. The resulting spurt of city building produced a dispersed spatial structure and "urban realms," semiautonomous subregions that displaced the traditional core–periphery relationship between city centres and their suburbs. Initially, the shift to an expanded polycentric metropolis was most pronounced in the northeastern United States. Geographer Jean Gottmann captured the moment in 1961 with his conceptualization of "megalopolis"—his term for the highly urbanized region between Boston and Washington, D.C.

In the polycentric new metropolis (**Figure 11.9**), the system of nodes and realms is bound together with ever-expanding multi-lane highways. It is interspersed with smaller clusters of decentralized employment, studded with micropolitan centres, and filled out with

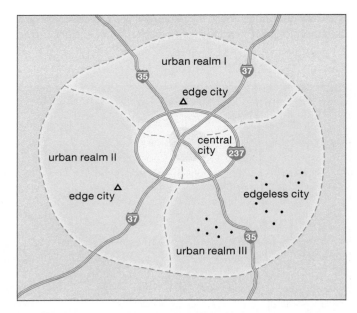

FIGURE 11.9 A typical twentieth-century metropolis It consists of a central city, a ring of suburbs, and a series of far-flung urban realms, studded with edge cities (nodal concentrations of office and retail space) and "edgeless cities" of suburban and exurban office parks and shopping malls. In Canada, only a handful of cities have developed into a polycentric metropolis: Toronto, Montreal, Vancouver, and Ottawa.

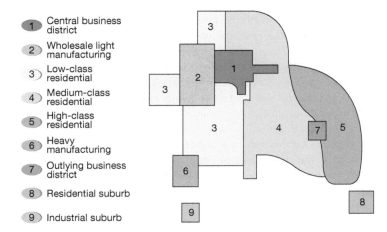

1. Central business district
2. Wholesale light manufacturing
3. Low-class residential
4. Medium-class residential
5. High-class residential
6. Heavy manufacturing
7. Outlying business district
8. Residential suburb
9. Industrial suburb

FIGURE 11.8 Multiple-nuclei model Decentralized nodes of different categories of land use end up in many different configurations, depending on local conditions. (*Source*: Based on C.D. Harris and E.L. Ullman, "The Nature of Cities," *Annals, American Academy of Political and Social Science*, 1945, Figure 5.)

Smart Growth versus Sprawl in the U.S.

Sprawl is endemic to North American urbanization, but it is most pronounced and problematic in the United States. The unplanned, ad hoc nature of most suburban development destroys millions of acres of wildlife habitat and agricultural land every year. Even more troubling, sprawl is often most aggressive in areas that do not have enough water in the first place, such as Arizona, Nevada (**Figure 11.B**), or California (**Figure 11.C**).

Rationalized, standardized, and tightly zoned subdivisions are placeless neighbourhoods that lack visual, demographic, and social diversity. The economics of private subdivision—the "sprawl machine"—lead to a lack of public open space, urban infrastructure, and civic amenities. Increased traffic, punishing commutes, and a chronic dependence on automobiles are the result of low-density, single-family suburban developments. The environmental costs of automobile dependency include air pollution—in particular the generation of millions of tonnes of greenhouse gases from suburban commuters. Run-off from the roads and parking lots pollutes suburban watersheds. The automobile-dependent lifestyles associated with sprawl, meanwhile, leads to increases in rates of asthma, lung cancer, and heart problems. Stress resulting from commuting has adverse effects on marriages and family life. The fragmented and balkanized nature of American local government also intensifies intrametropolitan fiscal disparities: outlying communities have a larger tax base and fewer social service needs to finance in comparison with central cities. This structured inequality exacerbates the exclusionary nature of suburbia and, from a planning perspective, is simply inefficient.

The counterargument is that sprawl is a logical consequence of economic growth and the democratization of society, providing

FIGURE 11.C Sprawl California farmland in the process of being transformed into suburban sprawl. (*Source:* Aerial Archives/Alamy)

FIGURE 11.B Urban sprawl in Las Vegas Until the recession of 2008, Las Vegas was one of the fastest-growing cities in the U.S. The resulting sprawl placed even higher demands on an already strained water supply. (*Source:* M. Imort)

millions of people with the kinds of mobility, privacy, and choice that were once the prerogatives of the rich and powerful. Sprawl reflects market forces and represents the desires and preferences of the broad mass of people. Joel Kotkin, a U.S. blogger and popular speaker on the business circuit, has persistently argued that most people seem to like living in the suburbs: so why all the fuss? Libertarian think tanks like the Reason Foundation and the Heritage Foundation have made efforts to counter antisprawl arguments on the principle of freedom of markets and individual choice. What they overlook, from a geographical perspective, is that the benefits of sprawl—for example, more housing for less cost with higher eventual appreciation—still tend to accrue to Americans individually, while the cost of sprawl in terms of infrastructure building, energy generation, and pollution mitigation tends to be borne by society overall.

The compromise position is "smart growth." Smart growth is pro-growth, but only when it is relatively compact and steered toward strategically designated locales with adequate infrastructure (**Figure 11.D**). Smart growth has been endorsed by the U.S.

FIGURE 11.D Smart growth A Metro Gold Line train passes through Del Mar Station in Pasadena, California. Transit-oriented development there has provided a public plaza, a refurbished train depot, and residential space. (*Source:* Warren Morse)

Environmental Protection Agency (EPA), the Lincoln Institute of Land Policy, and the National Resources Defense Council and has been embraced by an embattled planning profession. A

Smart Growth Network has developed a set of ten basic goals (referred to as "principles") for smart growth: implementing mixed land uses; taking advantage of compact (i.e., higher-density) neighbourhood design; creating housing opportunities and choices; creating walkable communities; fostering distinctive communities with a strong sense of place; preserving open space, farmland, and critical environmental areas; strengthening and directing development toward existing communities; providing a variety of transportation choices; making development decisions predictable, fair, and cost-effective; and encouraging community and stakeholder collaboration in developer decisions.

In practice, however, smart growth has made little headway against the "sprawl machine." In addition to resistance from landowners, developers, and other real estate interests, the most effective challenges to smart-growth policies, to the dismay of planners, have come from citizens. In classic NIMBY (not in my backyard) responses, residential and retail projects around transit stations have been stopped cold or scaled back because of neighbourhood opposition. Even projects in formally designated smart-growth districts have run into local opposition from residents contending that they already face crowded roads and schools and need to preserve the remaining open space in the area.

---

booming stand-alone suburbs. Traditional nodal anchors—downtown commercial centres—remain very important, especially as settings for the advanced business services—advertising, banking, insurance, investment management, and logistics services. But in addition there are other nodes. These vary in character and include

- **edge cities**, decentralized clusters of retailing and office development, often located on an axis with a major airport, sometimes adjacent to a high-speed rail station, and always linked to an urban highway system

- newer business centres, often developing in a prestigious residential quarter and serving as a setting for newer services such as corporate headquarters, the media, advertising, public relations, and design

- outermost complexes of back-office and R&D operations, typically near major transport hubs 30 to 50 kilometres from the main core

- specialized subcentres, usually for education, entertainment, and sporting complexes and exhibition and convention centres[2]

[2]P. Hall, "Global City-Regions in the Twenty-first Century." In A. J. Scott (ed.), *Global City-Regions: Trends, Theory Policy*. New York: Oxford University Press, 2001, pp. 59–77.

Meanwhile, some older inner-urban districts have been redeveloped around mixed-use projects—complexes of shops, offices, and apartments. Some older, centrally located, working-class neighbourhoods have also been invaded by higher-income households seeking the character and convenience of centrally located and (for them) less expensive residences—a process known as **gentrification**. Gentrification results in the physical renovation and upgrading of housing (**Figure 11.10**), but it also displaces existing households, which can no longer afford the increased rents that are a consequence of gentrification.

APPLY YOUR KNOWLEDGE Create a map like the one in Figure 11.9 for the metropolitan area with which you are most familiar. Label urban realms, major highways, edge cities, secondary business centres, and other important features. ■

Canadian Cities

Originally, the patterns and processes outlined in the previous section were believed to apply equally across North America (a region that, in urban geography, traditionally excludes Mexico). Beginning

FIGURE 11.10 Gentrification In this newly renovated row of townhouses in Halifax, Nova Scotia, the process of gentrification has redeveloped an older neighbourhood that had previously been occupied by lower-income households. (*Source:* Dick Hemingway)

with the publication in 1986 of Goldberg and Mercer's *The Myth of the North American City,*[3] however, scholars have highlighted important differences between Canadian and U.S. cities. When compared with the average U.S. city, for example, Canadian cities

- are more compact in size
- have a higher density of population
- have far fewer inner-city zones of poverty ("urban blight") and contain far lower levels of poverty overall
- have greater levels of public transit provision and use
- have greater levels of public investment in infrastructure and facilities
- have more dispersed immigrant populations
- have more powerful and less fragmented municipal governments
- in total, represent an even larger share of the country's population than in the United States

History and politics contribute significantly to these differences. Historically, the Canadian city developed as part of a colonial economy that was import-dependent and export-driven. As a result, Canada required only a handful of administrative and port centres, which continue to predominate in our country and its urban systems. In contrast, the American urban system has many more urban centres of all sizes because it grew from a locally run economy, producing food and manufactured goods for its own needs.

Political differences contribute most significantly to the differences between urban settlements in the two countries. In Canada, the government and public sector have always been deeply involved in urban affairs. In contrast, the United States favours fragmented and less powerful municipal administrations because Americans place a high value on individual rights and freedoms and local autonomy.

Canada's more expansive social welfare net has meant that far fewer people experience poverty and homelessness than in the United States. This is reflected in the relative lack of inner-city "urban blight" areas in this country, an unfortunate hallmark of American cities and one that is partly responsible for what has been called the "white flight" to the suburbs. The existence of fewer and less fragmented municipalities in this country makes local government much more effective, not least because inner cities and suburbs are part of the same tax base. Canada's universal health care system and provincial and territorial commitments to education also result in more equitable distributions of institutions and schools throughout our cities.

The provision of government-subsidized public transit systems, coupled with the more extensive zoning and land-use controls in this country, has meant that Canadian cities are generally more dense and compact than their American counterparts, where controls are seen as restrictions on individual property rights and public spending as inhibiting free competition.

The net result, according to many commentators, is that when compared with the United States, Canada has been able to create far more "liveable" cities. In its approach to urban life, Canada is in many ways much closer to Europe than to the United States, which is why Canadian cities are often described as representing an "intermediate" urban form.

Ironically, just as Canadian urban geographers are beginning to document the distinct qualities of the Canadian city, they are also beginning to see signs of their disappearance—mainly caused by increasing cutbacks in government spending. Troubling trends, such as the increasing incidence of poverty, homelessness, and food bank use across Canadian cities, suggest that in the future, our cities may more closely resemble those of the United States. For the time being, however, we can still find that many of the problems of North American cities we will discuss in the next section are more pronounced in the U.S. than in Canada.

Problems of North American Cities

For all their relative prosperity, the cities of the world's core regions have their share of problems. The most acute problems are localized in central city areas and are interrelated: fiscal problems, infrastructure problems, and localized cycles of poverty and spirals of

[3]M.A. Goldberg and J. Mercer, *The Myth of the North American City: Continentalism Challenged.* Vancouver: University of British Columbia Press, 1986.

neighbourhood decay. **Central cities** are the original, core jurisdictions of metropolitan areas.

Fiscal Problems

The term *fiscal* refers to government revenue or taxes. Economic restructuring and metropolitan decentralization over the past several decades have left central cities with a chronic "fiscal squeeze." A **fiscal squeeze** occurs when increasing limitations on tax revenues combine with increasing demands for expenditures on urban infrastructure and city services. The revenue-generating potential of most central cities has steadily fallen as metropolitan areas have lost both residential and commercial taxpayers to suburban jurisdictions. Growth industries, white-collar jobs, retailing, and more affluent households have moved out to suburban and exurban jurisdictions, taking their local tax dollars with them.

At the same time, growth in property-tax revenues from older, decaying neighbourhoods has slowed as the growth of property values has slowed. Simultaneously, these older, decaying neighbourhoods cost more to maintain and service. The residual populations of these neighbourhoods, with high proportions of elderly and poor households, are increasingly in need of municipal welfare services. Large numbers of low-income migrants and immigrants also bring increased demands for municipal services. Added to all this, central city governments are still responsible for services and amenities used by the entire metropolitan population: municipal galleries and museums, sports facilities, parks, traffic police, and public transport, for example. The net result is that many central city jurisdictions are in a precarious financial position. In a constant drive to develop revenue-generating projects, cities compete fiercely with one another to finance and attract tourism developments, museums, sports franchises, and business and conference centres.

In Canada, these problems are far less acute than in many U.S. cities. This is because our central cities have lost far less revenues, our cities are more compact, and our municipal governments cover much wider areas than do cities in the United States. The recent administrative mergers of large cities (Toronto, Montreal, Ottawa, Hamilton, Winnipeg, Quebec City, and Halifax) with their respective suburbs into "Greater" municipalities are as much an attempt by the provinces to win greater efficiencies from local government as they are responses to the growing status of Canadian suburbs.

Nonetheless, these mergers have also sparked passionate debate. Critics mourn the loss of local identity and control over their own affairs. Proponents argue that the advantages of merger include a greater municipal tax base and the end to fragmented local planning jurisdictions that make integrated city planning impossible.

Infrastructure Problems

As fiscal problems have intensified, public spending on the urban infrastructure has declined. As a result, many roads, bridges, power lines, water mains, sewers, and drains have greatly deteriorated and urgently need upgrading or replacing. The City of Toronto, for example, has almost 6000 kilometres of water mains that are, on average, 55 years old (17 percent are over 80 years old, and 6.5 percent are even more than 100 years old). Every day, three or four water mains break and need to be dug up for repair. Despite

spending between $120 and $160 million a year on its water mains, the city can replace only 100 kilometres of pipes annually.[4]

Apart from the leakage, an even greater concern is for the safety of the drinking water: old water systems are unable to cope with the leaching of pollutants into city water. Common pollutants include chlorides, oil, phosphates, and nondegradable toxic chemicals from industrial wastewater; dissolved salts and chemicals from highway de-icing; nitrates and ammonia from fertilizers and sewage; and coliform bacteria from septic tanks and sewage. Finally, many cities still use water-cleaning technology dating from World War I, and a number of coastal cities in Canada still discharge untreated sewage into the sea and therefore need to invest in expensive treatment systems.

Poverty and Neighbourhood Decay

In U.S. cities, inner-city poverty and neighbourhood decay have become increasingly pronounced in the past several decades as manufacturing, warehousing, and retailing jobs have moved out to suburban and edge-city locations and as many of the more prosperous households have moved out to be near these jobs. The spiral of neighbourhood decay typically begins with substandard housing occupied by low-income households that can afford to rent only a minimal amount of space. The consequent overcrowding not only causes greater wear and tear on the housing itself but also puts pressure on the neighbourhood infrastructure of streets, parks, schools, and playgrounds. The need for maintenance and repair increases quickly and is rarely met. Individual households cannot afford it, and landlords have no incentive, because they have a captive market. Public authorities face a fiscal squeeze and are in any case often indifferent to the needs of such neighbourhoods because of their relative lack of political power.

Shops and privately run services such as restaurants and hair salons are afflicted with the same syndrome of decay. With a low-income clientele, profit margins must be kept low, leaving little to spare for upkeep or improvement. Many small businesses fail, or relocate to more favourable settings, leaving commercial property vacant for long periods. In extreme cases, property is abandoned when the owners are unable to find renters or buyers. Residential buildings may also be left derelict.

Meanwhile, a dismal cycle of poverty intersects with these localized spirals of decay. The **cycle of poverty** involves the transmission of poverty and deprivation from one generation to another through a combination of domestic circumstances and local conditions. This cycle begins with an absence of employment opportunities and, therefore, a concentration of low incomes, poor housing, and overcrowded conditions. Such conditions are unhealthy. Overcrowding makes people vulnerable to poor health, which is compounded by poor diets. This contributes to absenteeism from work, which results in decreased income. Similarly, absenteeism from school because of illness contributes to the cycle of poverty by constraining educational achievement, limiting occupational skills, and leading to low wages. Crowding also produces psychological stress, which contributes to social disorganization and a variety of pathological behaviours, including crime and vandalism. Such conditions not only affect people's educational achievement and employment opportunities but also lead to *labelling* of the

[4]The *Toronto Water* website of the City of Toronto: www.toronto.ca/water/index.htm.

FIGURE 11.11 Poverty areas Concentrations of poverty are found not only in decaying inner-city areas but also in newer public housing projects and in older suburbs that have filtered down the housing scale, as in this example in Washington D.C., a short distance from the U.S. Capitol. (*Source: Christopher Pillitz/Getty Images*)

neighbourhood, whereby all residents may find their employment opportunities affected by the poor image of their community.

One of the most important elements in the cycle of neighbourhood poverty is the educational setting. Schools, obsolete and physically deteriorated like their surroundings, are unattractive to teachers—partly because of the physical environment and partly because of the social and disciplinary environment. Fiscal squeeze leaves schools resource-poor, with relatively small budgets for staff, equipment, and materials. Over the long term, poor educational resources translate into poor education, however positive the values of students and their parents. Poor education limits occupational choice and, ultimately, results in lower incomes. Students, faced with evidence all around them of unemployment or low-wage jobs at the end of school careers, find it difficult to be positive about school. The result becomes a self-fulfilling prophecy of failure, and people become trapped in areas of concentrated poverty (**Figure 11.11**).

Many areas of concentrated poverty are also racial ghettos, although not all ghettos are poverty areas. Recall that ethnic and racial congregation can mitigate the effects of poverty. Nevertheless, discrimination is usually the main cause of ghettoization. In the United States, discrimination in housing markets is illegal, but it nevertheless takes place in a variety of ways. One example of housing-market discrimination by banks and other lending institutions is the practice of redlining. **Redlining** involves marking off bad-risk neighbourhoods on a city map and then using the map to determine lending policy. This practice results in a bias against minorities, female-headed households, and other vulnerable groups who tend to be localized in low-income neighbourhoods. Redlining tends to become another self-fulfilling prophecy, since neighbourhoods starved of property loans become progressively more run-down and therefore increasingly unattractive to lenders. Discrimination affects education and labour markets as well as housing markets. In the case of ghetto poverty, all three types of discrimination come together, reinforcing the cycle of poverty and intensifying the disadvantages of the minority poor.

APPLY YOUR KNOWLEDGE Does your university town have a "student ghetto"? Is it due to congregation, segregation, or both? What are the fiscal, business, or neighbourhood problems that are created by its existence? List and explain any discriminations or other patterns you can identify. ∎

EUROPEAN CITIES

European cities, like North American cities, reflect the operation of competitive land markets and social congregation along ethnic lines. They also suffer from similar problems of urban management, infrastructure maintenance, and poverty. What makes most European cities distinctive in comparison with North American cities is that they are much older and thus represent the product of several major epochs of urban development.

Features of European Cities

As we saw in Chapter 2, many of today's most important European cities were founded in the Roman period, and it is not uncommon for the outlines of Roman and medieval urban development to be preserved in their street plans. Many distinctive features of European cities derive from their long history. In the historic cores of some older cities, the layout of streets reflects ancient patterns of rural settlement and field boundaries. Beyond these historic cores, narrow, complex streets are the product of the long, slow growth of European cities in the pre-automobile era, when hand-pushed and horse-drawn carts were the principal means of transportation, and urban development was piecemeal and small-scale. At the same time, the constraints of peripheral defensive walls made urban land expensive and encouraged a tradition of high-density living in tenements and apartment houses (**Figure 11.12**).

FIGURE 11.12 Distinctive historical characteristics of European cities This photograph of Florence, Italy, shows the city's narrow and complex streets, compact form, and high density, which are a legacy of pre-automobile urban development. (*Source:* Paul L. Knox)

Plazas and squares are another important historical legacy in many European cities. Greek, Roman, and medieval cities were all characterized by plazas, central squares, and marketplaces, and those elements are still important nodes of urban activity (**Figure 11.13**). European history also means that its cities bear the accessories and scars of war. The legacy of defensive hilltop and clifftop sites and city walls has limited and shaped the growth of modern European cities, while in more recent times the bombings and shellings of World War II destroyed many city buildings (**Figure 11.14**).

The legacy of a long and varied history includes a rich variety of symbolism. Europeans are reminded of their past not only by large numbers of statues and memorials but also by cathedrals, churches, and monasteries; by guildhalls and city walls; by the palaces of royalty and the mansions of aristocracy; and by city halls and the libraries, museums, sports stadiums, and galleries that are monuments to civic achievement. European cities are also typically compact in form, resulting in high densities of population.

FIGURE 11.13 Vigevano, Italy Widely considered to be one of the finest piazzas in Italy, the Piazza Ducale in Vigevano dates from 1492 and is a product of early Renaissance town planning. Unified by the arcades that completely surround the square, the piazza provides an important social space for the citizens of the town. (*Source:* Paul L. Knox)

FIGURE 11.14 Cologne, Germany, 1945 About 90 percent of Cologne's central area was destroyed or severely damaged by Allied bombing during World War II. One of the few structures to survive almost intact was the Gothic cathedral with its vast stained glass windows. The windows shattered, allowing the shock waves to blow right through the building without doing too much structural damage. (*Source:* Bettmann/Corbis)

Other distinctive features of European cities include

- *Low skylines*—Although the larger European cities have a fair number of high-rise apartment buildings and a sprinkling of office skyscrapers, they all offer a predominantly low skyline. This is partly because much of their growth came before the invention of the elevator and the development of steel-reinforced, concrete building techniques and partly because of master plans and building codes (some written as long ago as the sixteenth century) seeking to preserve the dominance of monumental buildings like palaces and cathedrals. (Kingston, Ontario, is one of the rare cities in Canada to have such controls.)

- *Lively downtowns*—The CBDs of European cities have retained their focal position in residents' shopping and social lives because of the relatively late arrival of the suburbanizing influence of the automobile and strong planning controls directed against urban sprawl.

- *Neighbourhood stability*—On average, Europeans change residence every 10 years, about half as often as Canadians. In addition, the physical life cycle of city neighbourhoods tends to be longer because of the past use of durable construction materials, such as brick and stone. As a result, European cities provide relatively stable socioeconomic environments.

- *Municipal socialism*—For decades, European welfare states have provided a broad range of municipal services and amenities, from clinics to public transit systems. Perhaps the most important to urban structure is social housing (public housing), which accounts for 20 to 40 percent of all housing in most larger English, French, and German cities. In recent years, neoliberal policies have resulted in a reduction in public services in many European countries (remember the privatization of the municipal water supply from Chapter 4).

The richness of European history and the diversity of Europe's geography mean that there are important regional variations: the industrial cities of northern England, northeastern France, and the Ruhr district of Germany, for example, are quite different in character from the cities of Mediterranean Europe. One of the most interesting regional variations is in Eastern Europe, where the legacy of an interlude of 44 years of socialism (1945–1989) was grafted onto cities that had already developed mature patterns of land use and social differentiation. Major examples include Belgrade, Budapest, Katowice, Kraków, Leipzig, Prague, and Warsaw. Public ownership of land meant that the economics of land-use competition (see Figure 11.1) could be ignored, resulting in huge public housing estates both in outlying districts and in bombed-out city centres **(Figure 11.15)**. The structure of the inner cities was little altered, however, apart from the addition of socialist monuments and the renaming of streets. In fact, inner cities were often purposefully neglected because of their "bourgeois" legacy.

Urban Design and Planning

European city planning and design have a long history. Most Greek and Roman settlements were laid out on grid systems, within which the siting of key buildings and the relationship of neighbourhoods to one another were carefully considered.

The roots of modern Western urban planning and design can be traced to the Renaissance and Baroque periods (between the

FIGURE 11.15 Socialist architecture in former East Berlin This modernist public housing complex sits right in the centre of East Berlin and is typical of the Socialist architecture of Eastern Europe. (*Source:* M. Imort)

fifteenth and seventeenth centuries) in Europe. Artists and intellectuals dreamed of ideal cities, and rich and powerful regimes used urban design to produce extravagant symbolizations of wealth, power, and destiny. Inspired by the classical art forms of ancient Greece and Rome, Renaissance urban design sought to recast cities to show off the power and the glory of the state and the Church. Spreading slowly from its origins in Italy at the beginning of the fifteenth century, Renaissance design had diffused to most of the larger cities of Europe by the end of the eighteenth century.

At the same time, the development of artillery technology changed the way cities needed to protect themselves from attack: a surge of planned redevelopment brought massive fortifications; geometric-shaped redoubts, or strongholds; and an extensive *glacis militaire*—a sloping, clear zone of fire for the defenders just outside the new city walls. Inside the walls, cities were recast according to a new aesthetic of grand design **(Figure 11.16)**—fancy palaces and geometrical plans, streetscapes, and gardens that emphasized views of dramatic perspectives. These developments were often of such a scale that they effectively fixed the layout of cities well into the eighteenth and even into the nineteenth century, when walls and/or glacis eventually made way for urban redevelopment in the form of parks, railway lines, or ringroads.

As societies and economies became more complex with the transition to industrial capitalism, national rulers and city leaders in Europe looked to urban design to impose order, safety, and efficiency, as well as to symbolize the new seats of power and authority. An important early precedent was set in Paris by Napoleon III, who presided over a comprehensive program of urban redevelopment and monumental urban design. The work was carried out by Baron Georges Haussmann between 1853 and 1870. Haussmann demolished large sections of old Paris to make way for broad, new, tree-lined avenues and numerous public open spaces and monuments. In doing so, he made the city not only more efficient (wide boulevards meant better flows of traffic) and a better place to live (parks and gardens allowed more fresh air and sunlight into a crowded city and were held to be a "civilizing" influence) but

FIGURE 11.16 Sabbioneta, Italy Sabbioneta was built by nobleman Vespasiano Gonzaga in the mid-sixteenth century as an ideal town, with a central piazza, a ducal palace (shown here), churches, gardens, theatre, and residences all encompassed within a star-shaped plan, bounded by thick walls bearing the Gonzaga family crest. (*Source: sfm Italy/Alamy*)

also safer from revolutionary politics (wide boulevards were hard to barricade but easy to use artillery on; monuments and statues instilled a sense of pride and civic identity). At the same time, planning restrictions ensured that the new buildings along the avenues presented a unified front, giving Paris its unmistakable architectural "face" (**Figure 11.17**).

The preferred architectural style for these new designs was the **Beaux Arts** style, which takes its name from L'École des Beaux Arts in Paris. In this school, architects were trained to draw on Classical, Renaissance, and Baroque styles to synthesize new designs for the Industrial Age. The idea was that the new buildings would blend artfully with the older palaces, cathedrals, and civic buildings that dominated European city centres. Haussmann's ideas were widely influential and extensively copied.

Early in the twentieth century there emerged a different intellectual and artistic reaction to the pressures of industrialization and

urbanization. The **modern movement** was based on the idea that buildings and cities should be designed and run like machines. (See Chapter 6.) Equally important to the modernists was the idea that urban design should not simply reflect dominant social and cultural values, but, rather, help create a new moral and social order. The movement's best-known advocate was Le Corbusier, a Swiss architect who provided the inspiration for technocratic urban design. Modernist buildings sought to dramatize technology, exploit industrial production techniques, and use modern materials and unembellished, functional design. Le Corbusier's ideal city (*La Ville Radieuse*) featured linear clusters of high-density, medium-rise apartment blocks, elevated on stilts and segregated from industrial districts; high-rise tower office blocks; and transportation routes—all separated by broad expanses of public open space.

After World War II, modernist architecture and urban planning became globally pervasive in the form of the so-called International

FIGURE 11.17 Boulevard des Italiens, Paris Central Paris owes much of its character to the *grands boulevards* that were key to the urban renewal schemes of Baron Georges-Eugène Haussmann. (*Source: Lebrecht Music and Arts Photo Library/Alamy*)

FIGURE 11.18 Brasilia
The Brazilian National Congress
buildings, Brasilia, offer an
example of International Style.
(*Source:* StockBrazil/Alamy)

Style. Its boxlike steel-frame buildings with concrete and glass façades were avant-garde yet respectable and, above all, comparatively inexpensive to build. This tradition of urban design, more than anything else, has imposed a measure of unprecedented uniformity on cities around the world. Due to globalization, International Style buildings have appeared in big cities in every part of the world. In fact, we could say that the International Style has been one of the first visible instances of globalization. Furthermore, the International Style has often been the preferred style for large-scale urban design projects around the world. One of the best examples is Brasilia (**Figure 11.18**), the capital of Brazil, founded in 1956 in an attempt to shift the country's political, economic, and psychological focus away from the past, differentiate it from the former colonial cities on the coast, and orient the country toward the future and the interior (see Chapter 6).

Modern urban design has had many critics, mainly on the grounds that it tends to take away the natural life and vitality of cities, replacing varied and human-scale environments with monotonous and austere settings. In response, historic preservation has become an important element of urban planning in every city that can afford it. In addition, postmodern urban design has brought a return to traditional and decorative motifs and introduced a variety of deliberately "playful" and "interesting" architectural styles in place of the functional designs of modernism. (See Box 6.4.) It is no coincidence that postmodern design has flourished in the most recent phase of globalization. Having emerged as a deliberate reaction to the perceived shortcomings of modern design, its emphasis on decoration and self-conscious stylishness has made it a very convenient form of packaging for the new global consumer culture. It is geared to a cosmopolitan market, and it draws quite deliberately on a mixture of elements from different places and times. In many ways, it has become the new transnational style for the more affluent communities of the world's cities.

APPLY YOUR KNOWLEDGE Search the Internet to find six images that best capture the typical features of European cities, such as narrow, complex streets, plazas and market squares, symbolism, low skylines, lively downtowns, neighbourhood stability, and municipal socialism. ∎

ISLAMIC CITIES

Islamic cities provide good examples of how social and cultural values and people's responses to their environment are translated into spatial terms through the built environment. Because of similarities in cityscapes, layout, and design, geographers are able to talk about the Islamic city as a meaningful category. It is a category that includes thousands of towns and cities, not only in the Arabian Peninsula and the Middle East—the heart of the Islamic Empire under the prophet Muhammad (570–632 C.E.)—but also in regions into which Islam spread later: North Africa, coastal East Africa, South-Central Asia, and Indonesia. Most cities in North Africa and South-Central Asia are Islamic, and many elements of the classic Islamic city can be found in towns and cities as far away as Seville, Granada, and Córdoba in southern Spain (the western extent of Islam), Kano in northern Nigeria and Dar es Salaam in Tanzania (the southern extent), and Davao in the Philippines (the eastern extent).

The fundamentals of the layout and design of the traditional Islamic city are so closely attached to Islamic cultural values that they are referenced in the Qur'an, the holy book of Islam. Although urban growth in the Islamic world does not have to conform to any overall master plan or layout, certain basic regulations and principles are intended to support Islam's emphasis on personal privacy

FIGURE 11.19 Mosque The dominant feature of traditional Islamic cities is the *Jami*, or main mosque. This photograph shows the main prayer hall and court of Badshahi Mosque, Lahore, Pakistan. (*Source:* Lichtmeister/Shutterstock)

and virtue, on communal well-being, and on the inner essence of things rather than on their outward appearance.

The most dominant feature of the traditional Islamic city is the *Jami*—the principal mosque (**Figure 11.19**). Located centrally, the mosque complex is a centre not only of worship but also of education and a broad range of welfare functions. As cities grow, new, smaller mosques are built toward the edge of the city, each out of earshot of the call to prayer from the Jami and from one another. The traditional Islamic city was walled for defence, with several lookout towers and a *Kasbah,* or citadel (fortress), containing palace buildings, baths, barracks, and its own small mosque and shops.

Traditionally, gates controlled access to the city, allowing careful scrutiny of strangers and permitting the imposition of taxes on merchants. The major streets led from these gates to the main covered bazaars or street markets (*suqs,* **Figure 11.20**). The suqs nearest the Jami typically specialize in the cleanest and most prestigious goods, such as books, perfumes, prayer mats, and modern consumer goods. Those nearer the gates feature bulkier and less valuable goods such as basic foodstuffs, building materials, textiles, leather goods, and pots and pans. Within the suqs, every profession and line of business has its own alley, and the residential districts around the suqs are organized into distinctive quarters, or *ahya',* according to occupation (or sometimes ethnicity, tribal affiliation, or religious sect).

Privacy is central to the construction of the Islamic city. Above all, women must be protected, according to Islamic values, from the gaze of unrelated men. Traditionally, doors must not face each other across a minor street, and windows must be small, narrow, and above eye level. Cul-de-sacs (dead-end streets) are used where

FIGURE 11.20 The *suq* The *suq,* a covered bazaar or open street market, is one of the most important distinguishing features of a traditional Islamic city. Typically, a suq consists of small stalls located in numerous passageways. Many important suqs are covered with vaults or domes. This photograph is of the Bazaar-i Vakil suq in Shiraz, Iran. (*Source:* Robert Preston Photography/Alamy)

FIGURE 11.21 Housing in Kalaa Sghira, Tunisia Seen from above, the traditional Islamic city is a compact mass of residences with walled courtyards. (*Source: Roger Wood/CORBIS*)

possible to restrict the number of persons approaching the home. Angled entrances prevent intrusive glances. Larger homes are built around courtyards, which provide an interior and private focus for domestic life.

The rights of others are also emphasized in Islamic urban design. The Qur'an specifies an obligation to neighbourly co-operation and consideration—traditionally this consideration is interpreted as applying to a minimum radius of 40 houses. Roofs, in traditional designs, are surrounded by parapets to preclude views of neighbours' homes, and drainage channels are steered away from neighbours' houses. Refuse and wastewater are carefully recycled. Public thoroughfares were originally designed to be wide enough to allow two fully laden camels to pass each other and high enough to accommodate a camel and rider. The overall result is a compact, cellular urban structure within which it is possible to maintain a high degree of privacy (**Figure 11.21**).

Because most Islamic cities are located in hot, dry climates, these basic principles of urban design have evolved in conjunction with certain practical solutions to intense heat and sunlight. Twisting streets, as narrow as permissible, help maximize shade, as does latticework on windows and cellular residential courtyard design. In some regions, local architectural styles include air ducts and roof funnels with adjustable shutters that can be used to create dust-free drafts (**Figure 11.22**).

While all these features are still characteristic of Islamic cities, they are most evident in the old cores, or *medinas*. Like cities everywhere, however, Islamic cities also bear the imprint of globalization. Although Islamic culture is self-consciously opposed to many aspects of globalization, it has been unable to resist altogether the penetration of the world economy and the infusion of the Western-based culture of global metropolitanism. The result can be seen in international hotels, skyscrapers and office blocks, modern factories, highways, airports, and stores. Indeed, the leading cities of some oil-rich states have become the "shock cities" of the early twenty-first century, with phenomenal rates of growth characterized by breathtakingly ambitious architectural and urban design projects. (See Box 11.3, "Window on the World: Shock City of the 21st Century: Dubai, United Arab Emirates.") Meanwhile, Islamic culture and urban design principles have not always been able to cope with the pressures of contemporary rates of urbanization, so the larger Islamic cities in less-affluent states—cities such as Algiers, Cairo, Karachi, and Teheran—now share with other peripheral cities the common denominators of unmanageable size, shanty and squatter development, and low-income mass housing. In the next section, we examine the problems of large and rapidly growing metropolises throughout the periphery.

FIGURE 11.22 Islamic architecture In Islamic societies elaborate precautions are taken through architecture and urban design to ensure the privacy of individuals, especially women. Entrances are L-shaped and staggered across the street from one another. Windows are often placed above pedestrian eye level. Architectural details also reflect climatic influences: window screens and narrow, twisting streets maximize shade, while air ducts and roof funnels create dust-free drafts, as in this photograph of traditional wind towers in the city of Yazd, Iran. (*Source: Terry Bruce/Alamy*)

Shock City of the 21ˢᵗ Century: Dubai, United Arab Emirates

Dubai is one of seven territories that constitute the United Arab Emirates (UAE). Since the discovery of oil in the UAE in the 1950s, the country has undergone a profound transformation, from an impoverished region of small desert principalities to a modern state with a high standard of living. Before the discovery of oil in the 1950s, the UAE's economic base was mainly fishing and pearling. Because oil reserves will last only another 20 years, the government has been pursuing a major diversification program with investment in national infrastructure, health care, education, and tourism **(Figure 11.E)**. As a result, Dubai has become a major financial and trading centre and an important tourist destination for the wealthy: only 5 percent of its revenues still come from oil and gas.

The city of Dubai has grown exponentially: the first census in 1968 (three years before independence from Great Britain) counted barely 60 000 residents. By 1995, that number had increased tenfold to more than 600 000, and it more than tripled again by 2014. Dubai's population of 2.1 million is dominated by migrant workers from Asia and the Middle East, who account for almost 80 percent of the city's residents. Dubai's construction boom is sustained by more than 500 000 low-skilled, poorly paid South Asian migrant workers who live in substandard conditions with few rights. Because they are mostly male, the ratio between males and females in Dubai is 3:1, which brings its own suite of social problems. The UAE has a minimum legal wage, but it is rarely enforced, so that migrant construction workers receive, on average, the equivalent of US$175 a month.

Dubai's "shock city" status derives as much from spectacular affluence as its phenomenal rate of growth. It has established a reputation for luxury shopping, with the duty-free

FIGURE 11.F Dubai luxury shopping The main foyer in the Mall of the Emirates in Dubai. (*Source:* David Pearson/Alamy)

stores at Dubai airport exploiting the city's role as a stopping-off point between Europe and Asia. The over-the-top Mall of the Emirates **(Figure 11.F)** includes Ski Dubai, an enormous indoor complex that provides five different runs with fresh snow for skiing, snowboarding, and tobogganing. Two artificial islands built in the shape of date palm trees extend from the Dubai City waterfront and support more than 60 luxury hotels and 10 000 exclusive residences, as well as marinas, water theme

FIGURE 11.E Dubai skyline Awash—for a while—with petrodollars, Dubai was able to offer generous tax breaks to companies willing to relocate their activities to the city. The city did so in an effort to create a major business hub to provide an economic base when the oil and gas run out. The city's skyline quickly came to reflect its emerging role as a globally important business hub, with scores of towers, many of them designed by famed architects from around the world. The Burj Khalifa tower, at 818 metres, now claims the title of the tallest building in the world—nearly 25 percent taller than the second-highest building in the world (Shanghai Tower in Shanghai, China). (*Source:* Philip Lange/Shutterstock)

(Continued)

FIGURE 11.G Dubai luxury development Aerial view of villas on the Palm Jumeirah, an artificial island in Dubai. (*Source:* David Pearson /Alamy)

parks, restaurants, shopping malls, sports facilities, health spas, cinemas, etc. **(Figure 11.G)**.

In the wake of the financial meltdown of 2008, Dubai's real estate boom came to an abrupt halt, and most of the immigrant workforce was immediately sent home **(Figure 11.H)**. Thousands of skilled white-collar workers from Europe, the United States, and other parts of the Arab world also began to leave. Many of them, having lived the high life during the boom, found themselves unable to meet the payments for expensive real estate or luxury cars. In the months following October 2008, more than 3000 cars were abandoned outside the city's international airport, most of them with keys left in the ignition. Some also had used-to-the-limit credit cards in the glove compartment. Others had notes of apology attached to the windshield:

their owners had fled rather than risk jail for defaulting on loans.[5] A year after it was inaugurated with a massive water-and-fireworks display, more than 800 of the Burj Khalifa tower's 900 ultraluxury apartments remained unoccupied, while scores of other towers remained completely unoccupied. Some areas, such as Business Bay, were left as entire districts of unfinished buildings. Since 2011, Dubai's economy and real estate market have made a healthy recovery, partly fuelled by individuals and capital fleeing instability in the neighbouring countries affected by the Arab Spring.

[5]S. Verman "Driven Down by Debt, Dubai Expats Give New Meaning to Long-stay Car Park," *The Times*, February 5, 2009, http://business.timesonline.co.uk/tol/business/markets/the_gulf/article5663618.ece.

FIGURE 11.H Dubai real estate bust Development stalled in Dubai between 2009 and 2011 as a result of the global financial meltdown of October 2008 that caused real estate values to drop by 50 percent.

(*Source:* Yvette Cardozo/Alamy)

FIGURE 11.23 Lagos, Nigeria Lagos, like most metropolises in the world's periphery, grew relatively slowly until the late twentieth century. The combination of the demographic transition, political independence, and an economic boom stimulated by the discovery of oil reserves in southeastern Nigeria triggered an explosive growth in population. Because of its difficult site on sand spits and lagoons, this growth has resulted in an irregular sprawl and, in the central area, a density of population higher than that of Manhattan Island in New York. (*Source:* Pius Utomi Ekpei/ AFP/Getty Images/Newscom)

APPLY YOUR KNOWLEDGE Research an Islamic city that is similar in size to the community in which you live, and list two similarities and two differences between your own town or city and the Islamic city you have researched. ■

CITIES OF THE PERIPHERY: UNINTENDED METROPOLISES

The cities of the world-system periphery, often still referred to as Third World cities, are numerous and varied. What they have in common is the experience of unprecedented rates of growth driven by rural "push"—overpopulation and the lack of employment opportunities in rural areas—rather than the "pull" of prospective jobs in towns and cities. Faced with poverty in overpopulated rural areas, many people regard moving to a city much like playing a lottery: you buy a ticket (in other words, go to the city) in the hope of hitting the jackpot (landing a good job). As with all lotteries, most people lose, and the net result is widespread underemployment. **Underemployment** occurs when people work less than full-time even though they would prefer to work more hours,

or when they work in a position for which they are overqualified. Underemployment is difficult to measure with any degree of accuracy, but estimates commonly range from 30 to 50 percent of the employed workforce in peripheral cities.

Because of their rapid growth and high underemployment, the peripheral metropolises of the world, the shock cities of the late twentieth century—Mexico City (Mexico), São Paulo (Brazil), Lagos (Nigeria, **Figure 11.23**), Mumbai (formerly Bombay, India), Dhaka (Pakistan), Jakarta (Indonesia), Karachi (Pakistan), and Manila (the Philippines)—embodied the most remarkable and unprecedented changes in economic, social, and cultural life. Socioeconomic conditions in these cities are still shocking, in the sense of being deplorably bad, but they are no longer shocking in the sense of being unprecedented. Rather, they have become all too familiar.

Recall from Chapter 10 that peripheral metropolises play a key role in international economic flows, linking provincial regions with the hierarchy of world cities and, thus, with the global economy. Within peripheral metropolises, this role results in a pronounced **dualism**, or juxtaposition in geographic space of the formal and informal sectors of the economy. This dualism is evidenced by the contrast between high-rise modern office and apartment towers and luxurious homes and the slums and shantytowns (**Figure 11.24**).

FIGURE 11.24 Rio de Janeiro This photograph, looking toward the buildings of wealthier Rio on the horizon, shows very clearly the dualism of peripheral metropolises, with a *favela* in the foreground. (*Source:* Paul Springett 05/Alamy)

FIGURE 11.25 Garbage picking Scavengers pick out recyclable garbage at the Nong Khaem dump, Bangkok, Thailand. (*Source:* Caroline Penn/Alamy)

The Informal Economy

In many peripheral cities, more than one-third of the population is engaged in the informal sector of the urban economy, and in some—for example Chennai, India; Colombo, Sri Lanka; Delhi, India; Guyaquil, Ecuador; and Lahore, Pakistan—the figure is more than one-half. People who cannot find regularly paid work must resort to various ways of gleaning a living. Some of these ways are imaginative, some desperate, some pathetic. Examples range from street vending, shoe shining, craft work, and street-corner repairs to scavenging in garbage dumps (**Figure 11.25**). The informal sector consists of a broad range of activities that represent an important coping mechanism (**Figure 11.26**). For too many, however, coping means resorting to begging, crime, or prostitution. Occupations such as selling souvenirs, driving pedicabs, making home-brewed beer, writing letters for others, and dressmaking may seem marginal from the point of view of the global economy, but more than a billion people around the world must feed, clothe, and house themselves entirely from such occupations. Across Africa, the International Labor Office (ILO) estimates, informal-sector employment is growing 10 times faster than formal-sector employment.

In most peripheral countries, the informal labour force includes children. In environments of extreme poverty, every family member must contribute something, and so children are expected to do their share. Industries in the formal sector often take advantage of this situation. In the Philippines, for example, batches of rural children are ferried by syndicates to work in garment-manufacturing sweatshops in urban areas. Other firms farm out their production under subcontracting schemes that are based not in factories but in home settings that use child workers. In these settings, labour standards are nearly impossible to enforce.

Despite this side of the picture, the informal sector has a few positive aspects. Pedicabs, for example, provide an affordable, non-polluting means of transportation in crowded metropolitan settings. Garbage picking provides an important means of recycling paper, steel, glass, and plastic products. One study of Mexico City estimated that as much as 25 percent of the municipal waste ends up being recycled by the 15 000 or so scavengers who work over the city's official dump sites. This positive contribution to the economy, though, scarcely justifies the lives of poverty and degradation experienced by the scavengers.

FIGURE 11.26 Informal economic activities In cities where jobs are scarce, people cope through the informal sector of the economy, which includes a very broad variety of activities, including agriculture (for example, backyard hens), manufacturing (craft work), and retailing (street vending). This photograph shows the floating market in Bangkok, Thailand. (*Source:* Shutterstock)

Urban geographers also recognize that the informal sector represents an important resource to the formal sector of peripheral economies. The informal sector provides a vast range of cheap goods and services that reduce the cost of living for employees in the formal sector, thus enabling employers to keep wages low. Although this network does not contribute to urban economic growth or help alleviate poverty, it does keep companies competitive within the context of the global economic system. For export-oriented companies, in particular, the informal sector provides a considerable indirect subsidy to production. This subsidy is often passed on to consumers in the core regions in the form of lower prices for goods and consumer products made in the periphery.

Consider, for example, the paper industry in Cali, Colombia. This industry is dominated by one company, Cartón de Colombia, which was established in 1944 with North American capital and subsequently acquired by the Mobil Oil Company. Most of the company's lower-quality paper products are made from recycled waste paper. Sixty percent of this waste paper is gathered by the 1200 to 1500 garbage pickers in Cali. Some work the city's municipal waste dump; some work the alleys and yards of shopping and industrial areas; and some work the routes of municipal garbage trucks, intercepting trash cans before the truck arrives. They are part of Cali's informal economy, for they are not employed by Cartón de Colombia; nor do they have any sort of contract with the company or its representatives. They simply show up each day to sell their pickings. In this way the company avoids paying both wages and benefits and is able to dictate the price it will pay for various grades of waste paper. The company can operate profitably while keeping the price of its products down—the arrangement is a microcosm of core–periphery relationships.

APPLY YOUR KNOWLEDGE Identify an informal economic function in your town or city. List three positive and three negative effects of the activities involved in this type of economy. ∎

Slums of Hope, Slums of Despair

The informal labour market is directly paralleled in informal shanty-towns and squatter housing: because so few jobs with regular wages exist in the cities of the periphery, few families can afford rent or house payments for sound housing. Unemployment, underemployment, and poverty mean overcrowding. In situations where urban growth has swamped the available stock of cheap housing and outstripped the capacity of builders to create affordable new housing, the inevitable outcome is makeshift shanty housing. Such housing has to be constructed on the cheapest and least desirable sites. Often this means building on bare rock, over ravines, on derelict land, on swamps, or on steep slopes. Nearly always it means building without any basic infrastructure of streets or utilities. Sometimes it means adapting to the most extreme ecological niches, as in Lima, Peru, where garbage pickers actually live on the waste dumps, or in Cairo, Egypt, where for generations the poor have adapted catacombs and cemeteries into living spaces. In many cities, more than half of the housing is substandard. The United Nations estimated in 2010 that more than 1.75 billion people worldwide live in inadequate housing in urban areas.

Globalization and the accompanying trend toward neoliberal economic policies have intensified problems of poverty and slum housing in many cities. The United Nations Human Settlement Programme reported in 2004 that

the reduction of fiscal deficits has partly entailed reduction of public expenditure through downsizing of the civil service and privatization of state enterprises, resulting in the laying-off of large numbers of public-sector employees in many countries. Trade liberalization has often resulted in the closure of some industries that have been unable to compete against cheap imports, again leading to massive retrenchment and higher unemployment levels. Rising urban unemployment and increasing poverty have forced large numbers of the urban poor into the informal sector. Underpaid formal-sector employees have also entered the informal sector as a survival strategy. This, in turn, leads to the erosion of the tax base and decreasing ability of national and local governments to assist the poor through social and basic services. The removal of price controls on subsistence goods, and increased utility charges through privatization . . . have resulted in rising inequalities and increasing poverty. . . . As a result, cities end up with their prime resources largely appropriated by the affluent.[6]

Faced with the growth of slums, the first response of many governments has been to eradicate them. Encouraged by Western development economists and housing experts, many cities sought to stamp out unintended urbanization through large-scale eviction and clearance programs. In Caracas (Venezuela), Lagos (Nigeria), Bangkok (Thailand), Kolkata (formerly Calcutta, India), Manila (the Philippines), and scores of other cities in the periphery, hundreds of thousands of shanty dwellers were ordered out on short notice, and their homes bulldozed to make way for public works, land speculation, luxury housing, and urban renewal and, on occasion, to improve the appearance of cities for special visitors. Seoul, South Korea, has probably had the most forced evictions of any city in the world. Since 1966, as part of sustained government clean-up campaigns, millions of people in Seoul have been forced out of accommodations that they owned or rented. The Beijing Olympics in 2008 displaced 1.5 million people, according to the Geneva-based Centre on Housing Rights and Evictions (COHRE). Its report[7] blames the Chinese government for widespread forced evictions along with other human rights violations during preparations for the Olympics. Demolitions and evictions were often undertaken without due process, without the provision of adequate compensation sufficient to attain alternative accommodation, and without access to legal recourse. In some cases, tenants were given little or no notice of their eviction and did not receive the promised compensation. The city also subjected alleged unlicensed taxi operators, street vendors, vagrants, and beggars to

[6]United Nations Human Settlement Programme, *The State of the World's Cities 2004/2005. Globalization and Urban Culture.* Sterling, VA: Earthscan, 2004, p. 102.

[7]Centre on Housing Rights and Evictions (COHRE), 2008, "One World, Whose Dream?: Housing Rights Violations and the Beijing Olympic Games," http://www.cohre.org/store/attachments/One_World_Whose_Dream_July08.pdf.

FIGURE 11.27 Self-help as a solution to housing problems Self-help is often the only solution to housing problems because wages are so low and so scarce that builders cannot construct even the most inexpensive new housing and make a profit, and because municipalities cannot afford to build sufficient quantities of subsidized housing. One of the most successful ways of encouraging self-help housing is for municipal authorities to create the preconditions by clearing sites, putting in the footings for small dwellings, and installing a basic framework of water and sewage utilities. The future residents then build the rest of the house themselves. This "sites-and-services" approach has become the mainstay of urban housing policies in many peripheral countries. This photograph shows self-help housing in Ndola, Zambia. (Source: The World Bank)

"Re-education through Labour" (a form of imprisonment without charge) to "clean up" the city for the Olympics.

Yet Seoul and Beijing, more than most other cities, could afford to build new low-income housing to replace the demolished neighbourhoods. Most peripheral cities cannot do so, which means that displaced slum dwellers have no option but to create new squatter and shanty settlements elsewhere in the city. Most cities, in fact, cannot evict and demolish fast enough to keep pace with the growth of slums caused by in-migration. The futility of slum clearance has led to a widespread re-evaluation of the wisdom of such policies. The thinking now is that informal-sector housing should be seen as a rational response to poverty. Shanty and squatter neighbourhoods not only provide affordable shelter but also function as important reception areas for migrants to the city, with supportive communal organizations and informal employment opportunities that help them to adjust city life. They can, in other words, be "slums of hope." City authorities, recognizing the positive functions of informal housing, are now increasingly disposed to be tolerant and even helpful to squatters rather than sending in police and municipal workers with bulldozers.

In fact, many informal settlements are the product of careful planning. In parts of Latin America, for example, it is common for community activists to draw up plans for invading unused land and then quickly build shanty housing before landowners can react. The activists' strategy is to organize a critical mass of people large enough to be able to negotiate with the authorities to resist eviction. It is also common for activists to plan their invasions for public holidays so that the risk of early detection is minimized. As the risk of eviction diminishes over time, some residents of informal housing are able to gradually improve their dwellings through self-help (**Figure 11.27**).

Nevertheless, there are many shanty and squatter neighbourhoods where self-help and community organization do not emerge. Instead, grim and desperately miserable conditions prevail. These are "slums of despair," where overcrowding, lack of adequate sanitation, and lack of maintenance lead to shockingly high levels of ill health and infant mortality and where social pathologies are at their worst. Consider, for example, the squatter settlement of Dharavi, a "mega-slum" in Mumbai, India.[8] Dharavi is about 2.5 square kilometres in size and population estimates vary between 500 000 and 1 million people. (See Chapter 3 on the difficulties of census enumeration.) This means that as many as 2000 people crowd into the area equivalent to a football field. In a city where house rents are among the highest in the world, Dharavi provides a cheap and affordable option to those who move to Mumbai to earn their living. Rents can be as low as 185 rupees ($4) per month. Recycling is one of the slum's biggest industries. In Dharavi nothing is considered garbage. Thousands of tonnes of scrap plastic, metals, paper, cotton, soap, and glass revolve through Dharavi each day. Ruined plastic toys are tossed into massive grinders, chopped into tiny pieces, and melted down into multicoloured pellets, ready to be refashioned into knockoff Barbie dolls. Dharavi also houses about 15 000 hutment factories, each typically stuffed with children as well as adults sewing cotton, melting plastic, hammering iron, moulding clay, or producing embroidered garments, export-quality leather goods, pottery, and plastic.

The aggregate annual turnover of these businesses is estimated to be more than US$650 million a year, yet conditions for residents are miserable. In Dharavi, there is only one toilet per 1440 people—and during the monsoon rains, flooded lanes run with human excrement. Most people have food intakes of fewer than the recommended minimum of 1500 calories a day; 90 percent of all infants and children under the age of 4 have fewer than the minimum calories needed for a healthy diet. More than half of the children and almost half the adults have intestinal worm infections. Infant and child mortality is high—though nobody knows just how high—with

[8]See *The Economist*, 2007, "A Flourishing Slum," http://www.economist.com/world/asia/displaystory.cfm?story_id=10311293; M. Jacobson, "Mumbai Slum," *National Geographic, 2007*, http://ngm.nationalgeographic.com/ngm/0705/feature3/index.html; C. W. Dugger, "Toilets Underused to Fight Disease, U.N. Study Finds," *New York Times*, 2006, http://www.nytimes.com/2006/11/10/world/10toilet.html?_r=1&ex=1189828800&en=905358c57769b677&ei=5070&oref=slogin.

malaria, tetanus, diarrhea, dysentery, and cholera as the principal causes of death among under-fives.

Transport and Infrastructure Problems

The informal labour market is also reflected in cities' inability to provide a basic infrastructure of highways, transportation, schools, utilities, and emergency services. Because the informal sector yields no tax revenues, municipal funds are insufficient to provide an adequate infrastructure or to maintain a safe and sanitary environment. Even though the governments of peripheral cities typically spend nearly all of their budgets on transport and infrastructure in an effort to keep up with population growth, conditions are bad and getting rapidly worse. Peripheral cities have always been congested, but in recent years the modernizing influence of formal-sector activities has turned the congestion into near gridlock. Sharp increases have occurred in the availability and use of automobiles. India has become one of the world's fastest-growing automobile markets. More than 2.5 million cars were sold there in 2010. Yet India's transportation infrastructure has not caught up with this sudden growth, nor have its drivers. The auto accident rate is the highest in the world. India has about 1 percent of the world's cars but 10 percent of the entire world's traffic fatalities.

Not only are there more people and more traffic but the changing spatial organization of peripheral cities has increased the need for transportation. Traditional patterns of land use have been superseded by the agglomerating tendencies inherent in modern industry and the segregating tendencies inherent in modernizing societies. The greatest single change, however, has been the separation of home from work, which has meant a significant increase in commuting.

In spite of innovative responses to urban transportation needs, road transportation in many cities is breaking down, with poorly maintained roads, traffic jams, long delays at intersections, and frequent accidents. Governments have invested in expensive new freeways and street-widening schemes, but because they tend to focus on city centres (which are still the settings for most jobs and most services and amenities), they ultimately fail. New freeways disgorge vehicles into a congested and chaotic mixture of motorized traffic, bicycles, animal-drawn vehicles, and hand-drawn carts. Some of the worst traffic tales come from Mexico City—where traffic backups total more than 90 kilometres each day, on average—and Bangkok, where the 24-kilometre trip into town from Don Muang Airport can take 3 hours. In São Paulo, Brazil, gridlock can span 160 kilometres, rush-hour traffic jams average 85 kilometres in length, and 15-hour traffic jams are not unusual. The costs of these traffic backups are enormous. The annual costs of traffic delays in Singapore have been estimated at US$305 million; in Bangkok, Thailand, they have been estimated at US$272 million—the equivalent of around 1 percent of Thailand's gross national product.

Water supplies and sewerage also present acute problems for many cities (**Figure 11.28**). Definitions of what constitutes an adequate amount of safe drinking water and sanitation vary from country to country. Although many governments classify the existence of a water tap within 100 metres of a house as "adequate," such a tap does not guarantee that the household will be able to secure

FIGURE 11.28 Infrastructure problems When city governments are unable to raise sufficient revenues through local taxes, infrastructure is neglected. Putting water and sewage lines into neighbourhoods that were built without these basic utilities is arduous and expensive, yet without them, public health is seriously threatened. This photograph shows water lines being installed in a low-income neighbourhood of Cartagena, Colombia. (*Source:* The World Bank)

enough water for good health. Communal taps often function only a few hours each day, so residents must wait in long lines to fill even one bucket. In Rajkot, India, a city of 600 000 people, piped water routinely runs for only 20 minutes each day.

The World Bank estimates that worldwide around 65 percent of urban residents in less-developed countries have access to a satisfactory water source, and only about 40 percent are connected to sewers (90 percent of which discharge their waste untreated into a river, a lake, or the sea). Hundreds of millions of urban dwellers have no alternative but to use contaminated water or water whose quality is not guaranteed. A small minority, usually the residents of the most affluent neighbourhoods, have water piped into their homes, while the majority have piped water nearby. Those not served are obliged to carry water in small quantities over long distances or to use water from streams or other surface sources (**Figure 11.29**). In Colombo, Sri Lanka, about one-third of all houses have indoor piped water, and another one-fourth have piped water outside. In Dar es Salaam (Tanzania), Kinshasa (Democratic Republic of the Congo), and many other peripheral cities, almost half the population has no access to piped water, either indoors or outdoors.

FIGURE 11.29 Water-supply problems
Many peripheral cities have grown so quickly
and under such difficult conditions that large
sections of the population do not have access
to supplies of clean water, even in new housing developments, as in this slum-clearance
project in a suburb of Bangalore, India.
(*Source:* S. Forster/Alamy)

In many cities, including Bangkok, Bogotá, Dar es Salaam, Jakarta, Karachi, and São Paulo, only one-fourth to one-third of all garbage and solid waste is collected and removed—the rest is partially recycled informally, tipped into gullies, canals, or rivers, or simply left to rot. Sewage services are just as bad. In Latin America, for example, only about 2 percent of collected sewage receives any treatment. In Mexico, more than 90 percent of wastewater treatment plants are nonfunctional, and in cities like Bogotá, Buenos Aires, Mexico City, and Santiago, some 50 to 60 million cubic metres of mostly untreated sewage is discharged every day into nearby bodies of water. São Paulo has over 1600 kilometres of open sewers, and raw sewage from the city's slums drains into the Billings reservoir, a major source of the city's drinking water. In Bangkok, less than 5 percent of the population is connected to a sewer system. Jakarta has no waterborne sewage system at all. Septic tanks serve about one-quarter of the city's population; others must use pit latrines, cesspools, and ditches along the roadside. A survey of over 3000 towns and cities in India found that only 8 had full sewage-treatment facilities, and another 209 had partial treatment facilities. Along the Ganges, 114 towns and cities dump untreated sewage into the river every day, along with waste from DDT factories, tanneries, paper and pulp mills, petrochemical and fertilizer complexes, and other industrial pollutants. Each day the Yamuna River picks up 200 million litres of untreated sewage and 20 million litres of industrial effluents as it passes through Delhi. In China, inadequate sewerage and meagre municipal wastewater plants have resulted in widespread water-quality deterioration. Shanghai has had to move its water-supply intake 40 kilometres upstream at a cost of US$300 million because of degradation of river water quality around the city.

These problems can provide opportunities for the informal sector, however. Street vendors, who get their water from private tanker and borehole operators, sell water from 10- or 20-litre canisters. Vendors typically charge 5 to 10 times the local rate set by public water utilities; in some cities, they charge 60 to 100 times as much. Similarly, many cities have evolved informal-sector mechanisms for sewage disposal. In many Asian cities, for example, human waste is removed overnight by handcart operators. Unfortunately, it is rarely disposed of properly and often ends up polluting the rivers or lakes from which the urban poor draw their water.

Environmental Degradation

With pressing problems of poverty, slum housing, and inadequate infrastructure, it is not surprising that peripheral cities are unable to devote many resources to environmental problems. Because of the speed of population growth, these problems are escalating rapidly. Industrial and human wastes pile up in lakes and lagoons and pollute long stretches of rivers, estuaries, and coastal zones. Groundwater is polluted through the leaching of chemicals from uncontrolled dump sites, and the forests around many cities are denuded by the demand of cities for timber and domestic fuels. This environmental degradation is, of course, directly linked to human health. People living in such environments have much higher rates of respiratory infections, tuberculosis, and diarrhea, and much shorter life expectancies than people living in surrounding rural communities. Children in squatter settlements may be 50 times as likely to die before the age of 5 as those born in affluent core countries.

Air pollution has escalated to very harmful levels in many cities. With the development of a modern industrial sector and the growth of automobile ownership, but without enforceable regulations on pollution and vehicle emissions, tonnes of lead, sulphur oxides, fluorides, carbon monoxide, nitrogen oxides, petrochemical oxidants, and other toxic chemicals are pumped into the atmosphere every day in large cities. The burning of charcoal, wood, and kerosene for fuel and cooking in low-income neighbourhoods also contributes significantly to dirty air. In cities where sewerage systems are deficient, the problem is compounded by the presence of airborne dried fecal matter. Worldwide, according to UN data, more than 1.1 billion people live in urban areas where air pollution exceeds healthful levels.

A UN study of 20 megacities found that every one of them had at least one major pollutant at levels exceeding World Health

Organization (WHO) guidelines. Fourteen of the 20 had *two* major pollutants exceeding WHO guidelines, and 7 had *three*. Such pollution is not only unpleasant but dangerous. The World Bank has cited China as having 16 of the 20 most air-polluted cities on Earth. China's spectacular economic growth has brought with it air pollution levels that are blamed for more than 400 000 premature deaths a year.

The European Space Agency, utilizing satellite imagery, determined that Beijing and its surrounding areas have the world's highest levels of nitrogen dioxide, a substance poisonous to the lungs. In Manila, the Philippines, the Asian Development Bank found levels of suspended particulate matter in the air to be 200–400 percent above guideline levels. In Mexico City, where sulphur dioxide and lead concentrations are 2 to 4 times higher than the WHO guidelines, 7 in 10 newborns have dangerously high levels of lead in their bloodstream.

WHO studies demonstrate that it is unhealthy for human beings to breathe air with more than 100 to 120 parts per billion (ppb) of ozone contaminants for more than one day a year. Yet Mexico City residents breathe this level, or more, for over 300 days a year. In Bangkok, Thailand, where air pollution is almost as severe as in Mexico City, research has shown that lead-bearing air pollutants reduce children's IQ by an average of 3.5 points per year until they are 7 years old. It has also been estimated that Bangkok's pall of dust and smoke causes more than 1400 deaths annually and costs US$3.1 billion each year in lost productivity resulting from traffic- and pollution-linked illnesses. Proximity to industrial facilities, often the result of the need and desire of the poor to live near places of employment, poses another set of risks. A notorious accident at the Union Carbide factory in Bhopal, India, in 1984 caused 2988 deaths and more than 100 000 injuries, mostly among residents of the shantytowns near the chemical factory.

APPLY YOUR KNOWLEDGE Research a specific megacity (as categorized by the United Nations) and examine it in terms of the presence of slum housing, environmental degradation, and infrastructure concerns. List and explain three causes of any one of these problems. ∎

Future Geographies

The future of urban structure in 10 to 20 years seems relatively easy to predict. In spite of many ideas about urban planning and the prospect of new and improved transportation, the patterns and problems described in this chapter seem set to continue. The reasons are straightforward. Demographic trends are established and accessibility, agglomeration, territoriality, congregation, segregation, and sprawl will continue to shape people's behaviour. In North American cities, continuing fiscal constraints dictate that infrastructure problems will continue and likely intensify. The political and financial interests behind the "sprawl machine" ensure a continuation of polycentric, metroburban development. The past 200 years of economic, social, and urban history provide no reason at all to expect any mitigation of urban poverty or neighbourhood decay. Similarly, the basic templates of urban structure are well established in both European and Islamic cities. Change will likely be marginal, even as economic and demographic modifications take place and as the impact of new technologies—electric cars, perhaps—alter the locational behaviour of people and businesses.

We can apply a similar logic to the unintended metropolises of the periphery. Faced with continuing streams of migration as well as high rates of natural increase among their relatively youthful populations, the megacities of the periphery will continue to expand, virtually unchecked. Informal economic activities will continue to have an important role, and cityscapes will continue to be dominated by stark contrasts between the towers of international business and elite residences and slums and informal housing (**Figure 11.30**). Sheer pressure of numbers will ensure continuing problems of congestion, water supply, sanitation, and

FIGURE 11.30 The future is already here Demographic trends mean that the megacities of the periphery will continue to expand, virtually unchecked, for the foreseeable future. As a result, cityscapes in much of the world will continue to be dominated by stark contrasts between rich and poor, as in this image of Worli village, Mumbai, India. (*Source:* India Images/Dinodia Photos/Alamy)

environmental degradation. What is less predictable is how individual cities might change as a result of the introduction of progressive planning policies or new transportation systems or—from a more pessimistic perspective—as a result of localized economic problems, political unrest, or environmental disasters.

CONCLUSION

Patterns of land use and the functional organization of economic and social subareas in cities are partly a product of economic, political, and technological conditions at the time of the city's growth, partly a product of regional cultural values, and partly a product of processes of globalization. Geographers can draw on several perspectives in looking at patterns of land use within cities, including an economic perspective that emphasizes competition for space and a sociocultural perspective that emphasizes ethnic congregation and segregation. Nevertheless, urban structure varies considerably because of the influence of history, culture, and the different roles that different cities have played within the world-system.

The evolution of the unintended metropolis of the periphery has been very different from the evolution of metropolitan areas in the world's core regions. Similarly, the problems they have faced are very different. In the core regions, the consequences of an economic transformation to a postindustrial economy have dominated urban change. Traditional manufacturing and related activities have been moved out of central cities, leaving decaying neighbourhoods and a residual population of elderly and marginalized people. New, postindustrial activities have begun to cluster in redeveloped CBDs and in edge cities around metropolitan fringes.

In other parts of the world, traditional patterns of land use and the functional organization of economic and social subareas have been quite different, reflecting different historical legacies and different environmental and cultural influences. A basic trend affecting the cities of the world's periphery is demographic—the phenomenal rates of natural increase and in-migration. An ever-growing informal sector of the economy, in which people seek economic survival, is reflected in extensive areas of shanty housing. High rates of unemployment, underemployment, and poverty generate acute social problems, which are overwhelming for city governments that are understaffed and underfunded. If present trends continue, such problems are likely to characterize increasing numbers of the world's largest settlements. Meanwhile, globalization processes are recasting metropolitan structure and intensifying social and economic inequalities.

Learning Outcomes Revisited

■ Assess how the internal structure of cities is shaped by competition for territory and location.

In general, all categories of land users—commercial and industrial, as well as residential—compete for the most convenient and accessible locations within the city. An important exception is that wealthier households tend to trade off the convenience of accessibility for the greater utility of the privacy provided by larger suburban lots. Poorer households, unable to afford the recurrent costs of transportation, trade off living space for accessibility to jobs.

■ Appraise the ways in which social patterns in cities are influenced by human territoriality.

Territoriality provides a means of establishing and preserving group membership and identity. Processes of congregation and discrimination often result in segregation, the spatial separation of specific subgroups within a wider population. Segregation varies a great deal in both intensity and form.

■ Describe the spatial structure of a typical North American city.

Most larger cities are structured around a central business district (CBD); a transitional zone; suburbs; secondary business districts and commercial strips; and industrial districts. In larger metropolitan areas, a polycentric structure is typical, with "edge cities," new business centres, and specialized subcentres. The internal organization of cities reflects the way that they function, both to bring certain people and activities together and to sort them out into neighbourhoods and functional subareas. During the middle decades of the twentieth century, North American cities were reshaped by the combination of increased automobility, massive highway construction, and mortgage affordability that underpinned the growth of home ownership. The resulting spurt of city building produced a dispersed spatial structure and the emergence of a polycentric metropolitan structure.

■ Compare and contrast urban structures in different regions of the world.

Urban structure varies considerably because of the influence of history, culture, and the different roles that cities have played within the world-system. European cities have evolved under circumstances very different from those in North American cities and consequently exhibit some distinctive characteristics that reflect their history. Islamic cities provide examples of how social and cultural values and people's responses to their environment are translated into spatial terms through urban form and the design of the built environment. The new cities of the world's peripheral regions are characterized and shaped by explosive growth.

■ Explain the nature and causes of the problems associated with urbanization in various world regions.

The most acute problems of the cities of the world's core regions are localized in the central city areas that have borne the brunt of restructuring from an industrial to a postindustrial economy, while the problems of the cities of the periphery stem from the way in which their demographic growth has outstripped their economic growth. The central city districts of cities in the world's core regions typically experience several interrelated problems: fiscal problems, infrastructure problems, and localized spirals of neighbourhood decay and cycles of poverty. In peripheral cities high rates of long-term unemployment and underemployment, low and unreliable wages of informal-sector jobs, chronic poverty, and slum housing are common.

KEY TERMS

Beaux Arts *(p. 409)*

central business district (CBD) *(p. 397)*

central city *(p. 405)*

colony *(p. 397)*

congregation *(p. 396)*

cycle of poverty *(p. 405)*

dualism *(p. 415)*

edge city *(p. 403)*

enclave *(p. 397)*

fiscal squeeze *(p. 405)*

gentrification *(p. 403)*

ghetto *(p. 397)*

invasion and succession *(p. 399)*

isotropic surface *(p. 396)*

minority group *(p. 396)*

modern movement *(p. 409)*

multiple-nuclei model *(p. 401)*

redlining *(p. 406)*

segregation *(p. 397)*

trade-off model *(p. 396)*

underemployment *(p. 415)*

zone in transition *(p. 397)*

REVIEW AND DISCUSSION

1. Research the ethnic, class, and gender makeup of your city or town. Examine the data through the lens of congregation and the territorial and residential clustering of specific groups or subgroups of people. Identify where these different groups congregated. Does a pattern of discrimination or segregation emerge? Explain your observations.

2. Conduct research on the different ethnic groups in your city over the past 20 years. Map out and list three ways the congregation of these groups changed. Would you identify the change as "invasion and succession?" Has the infrastructure around these groups changed? Explain your observations.

3. Create a list of the various modes of transportation that are commonly available in your community. List three ways in which the transportation shapes your city or town. Identify two major problems with the current transportation configuration of your city (*Hint:* compare how long it takes a person to get from point A to B using various modes of transportation.) On a piece of paper map out how these problems could be corrected.

4. Collect a week's worth of local newspapers and review the coverage of urban problems. What kinds of problems in what kinds of communities are covered? Compile a list of the different categories of problems, and then carefully analyze the content of the week's coverage, calculating the number of column inches devoted to each category. What kinds of urban phenomena are behind the problems?

5. Most cities consist of "ordinary" cityscapes that are strongly evocative because they are widely understood as being a particular kind of place. Write a brief essay (500 words, or two double-spaced, typed pages) describing an "ordinary" cityscape with which you are familiar. What are its principal features, and how might it be considered typical of a particular kind of place?

Mastering**GEOGRAPHY**™

Log in to www.masteringgeography.com for MapMaster™ interactive maps, geography videos, RSS feeds, flashcards, weblinks, an eText version of *Human Geography: Places and Regions in Global Context,* and self-study quizzes to enhance your study of city spaces and urban structure.

MapMaster™ presents 13 Place Name and 13 Layered Thematic interactive maps to help students practise and master their geographic literacy, spatial reasoning, and critical thinking skills.

GLOSSARY

A

accessibility: the opportunity for contact or interaction from a given point or location in relation to other locations.

acid rain: the wet deposition of acids on Earth created by the natural cleansing properties of the atmosphere.

actor-network theory (ANT): a theory that views the world as composed of "heterogeneous things," including humans and nonhumans and objects.

adaptability: a broad-based term which encompasses all actions taken to address the changes that climate change produces.

aesthetic: culturally determined standard of beauty and good taste.

affect: emotions that are embodied reactions to the social and physical environment and that also have the power to result in or enable action.

age–sex pyramid: a representation of the population based on its composition according to age and sex.

agglomeration diseconomies: the negative economic effects of urbanization and the local concentration of industry.

agglomeration effects: cost advantages that accrue to individual firms because of their location among functionally related activities.

aging: a term used to describe the effects of an increasing proportion of older age groups on the population.

agrarian: referring to the culture of agricultural communities and the type of tenure system that determines access to land and the kind of cultivation practices employed there.

agribusiness: a set of economic and political relationships that organizes agro-food production from the development of seeds to the retailing and consumption of the agricultural product.

agricultural industrialization: the process whereby the farm has moved from being the centrepiece of agricultural production to becoming one part of an integrated string of vertically organized industrial processes including production, storage, processing, distribution, marketing, and retailing.

agriculture: a science, an art, and a business directed at the cultivation of crops and the raising of livestock for sustenance and profit.

allophone: a person whose mother tongue is neither English nor French.

ancillary activities: such activities as maintenance, repair, security, and haulage services that serve a variety of industries.

anglophone: a person whose mother tongue is English.

animistic perspective on nature: the view that natural phenomena—both animate and inanimate—possess an indwelling spirit or consciousness.

anthropocene: the modern geological era during which humans have dramatically affected the global environment.

aquaculture: the growing of aquatic creatures in ponds on shore or in pens suspended in water.

areal units: spatial units of measurement, such as a city block or province, used for recording statistics.

autarky: self-sufficiency of a state that does not contribute significantly to the flows of imports and exports that constitute the geography of trade.

B

baby boom: the increased number of births in the two decades following World War II.

backwash effects: the negative impacts on a region of the economic growth of some other region.

Beaux Arts: a style of urban design that sought to combine the best elements of all of the classic architectural styles.

biofuels: renewable fuels derived from biological materials that can be regenerated, including corn, soy, and sugar cane.

biometric census: a census in which individuals are photographed and fingerprinted to create a national database.

biopharming: a process in which genes from other life forms (plant, animal, fungal, bacterial, or human) are inserted into host plants.

bioprospecting: the scientific or commercial practice of searching for a useful application, process, or product in nature.

biorevolution: the genetic engineering of plants and animals.

biotechnology: any technique that uses living organisms (or parts of organisms) to improve, make, or modify plants and animals or to develop microorganisms for specific uses.

Blue Revolution: the large-scale expansion of aquaculture in the late twentieth century.

Borlaug hypothesis (named after Norman Borlaug, the force behind the Green Revolution): states that because global food demand is on the rise, restricting crop usage to traditional lowyield methods (such as organic farming) requires either the world population to decrease or the further conversion of forest land into cropland.

brownfield site: abandoned, idle, or underused industrial and commercial land on which redevelopment is hindered by the effects of contamination.

C

capitalism: a form of economic and social organization characterized by the profit motive and the control of the means of production, distribution, and exchange of goods by private ownership.

carbon tax: a tax on emissions of CO_2 and other greenhouse gases.

carrying capacity: the maximum population that can be maintained in a place at rates of resource use and waste production that are sustainable in the long term without damaging the overall productivity of that or other places.

cartography: the art and sicence of making maps.

census: the count of the number of people in a country, region, or city.

central business district (CBD): the central nucleus of commercial land uses in a city.

central city: the original, core jurisdiction of a metropolitan area.

central place theory: a theory that seeks to explain the relative size and spacing of towns and cities as a function of consumer behaviour.

central places: settlements in which certain products and services are available to consumers.

centrality: the functional dominance of cities within an urban system.

centrifugal forces: forces that can lead to the disintegration of the state.

centripetal forces: forces that integrate the state.

chemical farming: the application of synthetic fertilizers to the soil, and of herbicides, fungicides, and pesticides to crops to enhance yields.

citizenship: a category of belonging to a nation-state that includes civil, political, and social rights as well as obligations.

climate change: is defined by the Intergovernmental Panel on Climate Change (IPCC) as "a change in the state of the climate that can be identified (e.g., using statistical tests) by changes in the mean and/ or the variability of its properties, and that persists for an extended period, typically decades or longer. It refers to any change in climate over time, whether due to natural variability or as a result of human activity."

cognitive distance: the distance that people perceive to exist in a given situation.

cognitive images (mental maps): psychological representations of locations that are created from people's individual ideas and impressions of these locations.

cognitive space: space defined and measured in terms of people's values, feelings, beliefs, and perceptions about places and regions.

cohort: a group of individuals who share a common temporal demographic experience.

colonial cities: cities that were deliberately established or developed as administrative or commercial centres by colonial or imperial powers.

colonialism: the establishment and maintenance of political and legal domination by a state over a separate society.

colonization: the physical settlement in a new territory of people from a colonizing state.

colony: in urban geography, a colony describes a form of spatial segregation that results from relatively weak and short-lasting congregation, discrimination, or both.

Columbian Exchange: the interaction between the Old World (Europe) and the New World (the Americas) initiated by the voyages of Columbus.

commercial agriculture: farming primarily for sale, not for direct consumption.

commodity chains: networks of labour and production processes beginning with the extraction or production of raw materials and ending with the delivery of a finished commodity.

Community Supported Agriculture (CSA): a cooperative that collects subscriptions and then pays a farmer up front to grow food locally for CSA members for a season or a specified time frame.

comparative advantage: the specialization of a country in an economic activity that does not duplicate or compete with the domestic suppliers within core countries.

confederation: a group of sovereign states united for a common purpose.

conformal projections: map projections on which compass bearings are rendered accurately.

conglomerate corporations: corporations that consist of several divisions engaged in quite different activities.

congregation: the territorial and residential clustering of specific groups or subgroups of people.

conservation: the notion that natural resources should be used thoughtfully and that humans should serve as stewards, not exploiters, of the natural world.

contract farming: an agreement between farmers and processing and/or marketing firms for the production, supply, and purchase of agricultural products.

conventional farming: an approach to agriculture that uses chemicals in the form of plant protectants and fertilizers and intensive, hormone-based practices to breed and raise animals.

core regions: regions that dominate trade, control the most advanced technologies, and have high levels of productivity within diversified economies.

cosmopolitanism: an intellectual and aesthetic openness toward divergent experiences, images, and products from different cultures.

cost/price squeeze: a situation in which a business's profit margin is reduced by the simultaneous decrease in selling prices and rise in production costs.

counterurbanization: the net loss of population from cities to smaller towns and rural areas.

creative destruction: the withdrawal of investments from activities (and regions) that yield low rates of profit to reinvest in new activities (and new places).

crop rotation: a form of agriculture in which the fields under cultivation remain the same, but the crops planted are changed to balance the types of nutrients withdrawn from and delivered to the soil.

crude birth rate (CBR): the ratio of the number of live births in a single year for every thousand people in the population.

crude death rate (CDR): the number of deaths in a single year for every thousand people in the population.

crude density (arithmetic density): the total number of people divided by the total land area.

cultural adaptation: the use of complex strategies by human groups to live successfully as part of a natural system.

cultural complex: the combination of traits characteristic of a particular group.

cultural ecology: the study of the relationship between a cultural group and its natural environment.

cultural geography: study of the ways in which space, place, and landscape shape culture at the same time that culture shapes space, place, and landscape.

cultural hearth: the geographical origin or source of innovations, ideas, or ideologies (term coined by geographer Carl Sauer).

cultural landscape: a characteristic and tangible outcome of the complex interactions between a human group and a natural environment.

cultural nationalism: an effort to protect regional and national cultures from the homogenizing impacts of globalization.

cultural region: the area where certain cultural practices, beliefs, or values are practised by more or less the majority of the inhabitants.

cultural system: a collection of interacting elements that, taken together, shape a group's collective identity.

cultural trait: a single aspect of the complex of routine practices that constitute a particular cultural group.

culture: a shared set of meanings that are lived through the material and symbolic practices of everyday life.

cumulative causation: a spiral buildup of advantages that occurs in specific geographical settings as a result of the development of external economies, agglomeration effects, and localization economies.

cycle of poverty: transmission of poverty and deprivation from one generation to another through a combination of domestic circumstances and local neighbourhood conditions.

D

decolonization: the re-acquisition of control by colonized peoples over their own territory.

deep ecology: an approach to nature revolving around two key ideas: self-realization and biospherical egalitarianism.

deforestation: the permanent clearing and destruction of forests.

deindustrialization: a relative decline in industrial employment in core regions.

democratic rule: a system in which public policies and officials are directly chosen by popular vote.

demographic collapse: phenomenon of near genocide of indigenous populations.

demographic transition: a model of population change in which high birth and death rates are replaced by low birth and death rates.

demographics: the characteristics of a human population including elements such as gender, race, age, income, disabilities, educational attainment, and migration patterns among different groups and death rates among others.

demography: the study of the characteristics of human populations.

density: a numerical measure of the relationship between the number of people and some other unit of interest expressed as a ratio.

dependency ratio: the measure of the economic impact of the young and old on the more economically productive members of the population.

dependency: describes a high level of reliance by a country on foreign enterprises, investment, or technology.

derelict landscapes: landscapes that have experienced abandonment, misuse, disinvestment, or vandalism.

desertification: the spread of desert conditions resulting from deforestation, overgrazing, and poor agricultural practices, as well as reduced rainfall associated with climatic change.

dialects: regional variations from standard language, in terms of accent, vocabulary, and grammar.

diaspora: a spatial dispersion of a previously homogeneous group.

digital divide: inequality of access to telecommunications and information technology, particularly the Internet.

discourse: an institutionalized way of thinking.

distance-decay function: the rate at which a particular activity or process diminishes with increasing distance.

division of labour: the specialization of different people, regions, or countries in particular kinds of economic activities.

domino theory: the belief that if one country in a region chose or was forced to accept a communist political and economic system, then neighbouring countries would fall to communism as well.

double cropping: a practice in which fields are planted and harvested more than once a year (usually restricted to milder climates).

doubling time: the measure of how long it will take the population of an area to grow to twice its current size.

dualism: the juxtaposition in geographical space of the formal and informal sectors of the economy.

E

East/West divide: the gulf between communist and noncommunist countries that developed after 1945.

ecofeminism: the view that patriarchal ideology is at the centre of our present environmental malaise.

ecological footprint: a measure of the biologically productive land area needed to support a population by providing for its needs and absorbing its wastes.

ecological imperialism: introduction of exotic plants and animals into new ecosystems.

eco-migration: a population movement caused by the degradation of land and essential natural resources.

economic base: set of manufacturing, processing, trading, or service activities that serve markets beyond the city.

economies of scale: cost advantages to manufacturers that accrue from high-volume production, since the average cost of production falls with increasing output.

ecosystem: a community of different species interacting with one another and with the larger physical environment that surrounds them.

ecotheology: a movement that calls for a re-evaluation of the Western relationship to nature.

ecotourism: an activity which, in addition to following the goals of "sustainable tourism," also (1) contributes to the conservation of an area's natural and cultural heritage, (2) includes local indigenous communities in its planning, (3) interprets the natural and cultural heritage of the destination to the visitor, and (4) is aimed at small groups.

ecumene: the total habitable area of a country. Because it depends on the prevailing technology, the available ecumene varies over time. It is an important concept in Canada's case, because the ecumene is so much smaller than the country's total area.

edge cities: nodal concentrations of shopping and office space that are situated on the outer fringes of metropolitan areas, typically near major highway intersections.

emigration: a movement in which a person *leaves* a country.

enclave: a form of spatial segregation dominated by internal cohesion and identity.

Enlightenment: an eighteenth-century European movement that sought to replace ideas of authority or explanation drawn from God with those that individual humans could establish through their own reason.

environmental determinism: a doctrine holding that human activities are shaped and constrained by the environment.

environmental ethics: a philosophical perspective that prescribes moral principles as guidance for our treatment of nature.

environmental justice: the view that the pollution of poor neighbourhoods by, for example, factories and hazardous-waste dumps, is the result of a structured and institutionalized inequality that is pervasive in both the capitalist core and the periphery.

environmental refugees: people who have been physically displaced from their homes and livelihoods by the deterioration of the local environment.

environmental scarcity: a scarcity of renewable natural resources that, if not addressed by technological, social, or economic means, may cause social disruption or violent conflict.

epidemiological transition: a theory stating that the prevailing forms of illness changed from infectious to degenerative types as the demographic transition occurred.

equal-area (equivalent) projections: map projections that portray areas on Earth's surface in their true proportions.

equidistant projections: map projections that represent distance accurately in only one direction (usually north-south), although they usually provide accurate scale in the perpendicular direction (which in most cases is the equator).

ethnicity: a socially created system of rules about who belongs and who does not belong to a particular group, based on actual or perceived commonality.

ethnocentrism: the attitude that a person's own race and culture are superior to those of others.

ethology: the scientific study of the formation and evolution of human customs and beliefs.

export-processing zones (EPZs): small areas within which especially favourable investment and trading conditions are created by governments to attract export-oriented industries.

external arenas: regions of the world not yet absorbed into the modern world-system.

external economies: cost savings that result from circumstances beyond a firm's own organization and methods of production.

F

famine: acute starvation associated with a sharp increase in mortality.

fast food: edibles that can be prepared and served very quickly in packaged form in a restaurant.

fast world: people, places, and regions directly involved, as producers and consumers, in transnational industry, modern telecommunications, materialistic consumption, and international news and entertainment.

federal state: a.form of government in which powers are divided between the federal government and smaller units of government (such as provinces) within the country.

female infanticide: the practice of aborting, killing, or abandoning female babies by their own parents.

feminist geography: a field that examines the extent to which women and men experience spaces and places differently and how these differences themselves are part of the social construction of gender as well as that of place.

fertility: the childbearing performance of individuals, couples, groups, or populations.

fiscal squeeze: a financially difficult situation for cities that arises when increasing limitations on tax revenues combine with increasing demands for expenditures on urban infrastructure and city services.

flexible production systems: a production system in which manufacturers can quickly respond to changing market conditions by changing between different levels of output or product configurations.

folk culture: the traditional practices of small groups, especially rural people with a simple lifestyle (compared with modern, urban people), who are seen as homogeneous in their belief systems and practices.

food chain: five central and connected sectors (inputs, production, product processing, distribution, and consumption) with four contextual elements acting as external mediating forces (the state, international trade, the physical environment, and credit and finance).

food manufacturing: adding value to agricultural products through a range of treatments—such as processing, canning, refining, packing, and packaging—that occur off the farm and before they reach the market.

food regime: the specific set of links that exist between food production and consumption, as well as capital investment and accumulation opportunities.

food security: the assured access to enough food at all times to ensure active and healthy lives for a person, a household, or a country.

food sovereignty: the right of peoples, communities, and countries to define their own agricultural, labour, fishing, food, and land policies that are ecologically, socially, economically, and culturally appropriate to their unique circumstances.

food supply chain: a special type of commodity chain that is composed of five central and connected sectors (inputs, production, processing, distribution, and consumption) with four contextual elements acting as external mediating forces (the state, international trade, the physical environment, and credit and finance).

forced migration: the movement by an individual against his or her will.

Fordism: an economy based on mass production and mass consumption, based on higher wages and sophisticated advertising techniques.

foreign direct investment: overseas business investments made by private companies.

francophone: a person whose mother tongue is French.

friction of distance: the deterrent or inhibiting effect of distance on human activity.

functional regions (nodal regions): regions that, while they may exhibit some variability in certain attributes, share an overall coherence in structure and economic, political, and social organization.

G

gateway city: a city that serves as a link between one country or region and others because of its physical situation.

gender: category reflecting the social differences between men and women rather than the anatomical differences that are related to sex.

genetically modified organism (GMO): any organism that has had its DNA modified in a laboratory rather than through cross-pollination or other forms of evolution.

genre de vie: a functionally organized way of life that is characteristic of a particular cultural group.

genres de vie **(or "ways of living"):** a functionally organized way of life characteristic of a particular culture group.

gentrification: the movement into older, centrally located working-class neighbourhoods by higher-income households seeking the character and convenience of less-expensive and well-located residences.

geodemographic analysis: the practice of assessing the location and composition of particular populations.

geodemographic research: investigation using census data and commercial data (such as sales data and property records) about the populations of small districts to create profiles of those populations for market research.

geographic information system (GIS): an organized set of computer hardware, software, and spatially coded data that is designed to capture, store, update, manipulate, and display spatially referenced information.

geographical imagination: a capacity that allows us to understand changing patterns, processes, and relationships among people, places, and regions.

geographical path dependence: the historical relationship between the present activities associated with a place and the past experiences of that place.

geopolitics: the state's power to control space or territory and shape international political relations.

ghetto: a form of spatial segregation that is the product of discrimination rather than congregation.

global change: combination of political, economic, social, historical, and environmental problems at the world scale.

global civil society: a collective term for the broad range of institutions that operate between the private market and the state.

Global Positioning System (GPS): a system of satellites that orbit Earth on precisely predictable paths, broadcasting highly accurate time and locational information.

globalization: the increasing interconnectedness of different parts of the world through common processes of economic, environmental, political, and cultural change.

globalized agriculture: a system of food production increasingly dependent on an economy and a set of regulatory practices that are global in scope and organization.

Green Revolution: the export of a technological package of fertilizers and high-yielding seeds, from the core to the periphery, to increase global agricultural productivity.

greenhouse gases (GHGs): any gas that absorbs infrared radiation in the atmosphere, including, but not limited to, water vapour, carbon dioxide (CO_2), methane (CH_4), and nitrous oxide (N_2O).

greening: the adding of biomass (including grasses as well as trees) to a formerly dry area due to increasing rainfall.

gross domestic product (GDP): an estimate of the total value of all materials, foodstuffs, goods, and services produced by a country in a particular year.

gross migration: the total number of migrants moving into and out of a place, region, or country.

gross national income (GNI): a measure of the income that flows to a country from production, no matter where in the world that production occurs.

growth poles: economic activities that are deliberately organized around one or more high-growth industries.

guest workers: individuals who migrate temporarily to take jobs in other countries.

H

hajj: the obligatory once-in-a-lifetime journey of Muslims to Mecca.

health care density: the ratio between the total population and the number of physicians.

hearth areas: geographic settings where new practices have developed and from which they have spread.

heartland theory: a geopolitical view that considered Asia, with its great landmass and considerable resources, as the "geographical pivot," the location central to establishing global control.

hegemony: domination over the world economy exercised by one national state in a particular historical epoch through a combination of economic, military, financial, and cultural means.

hinterland: the sphere of economic influence of a town or city.

historical geography: the study of the geography of the past.

human geography: the study of the spatial organization of human activity and of people's relationships with their environments.

human rights: the rights to justice, freedom, and equality, which are considered by most societies to belong automatically to all people.

human security: a concept that includes environmental sustainability and population-carrying capacity in the measure of a country's ability to promote and defend its citizens' interests.

humanistic approach: places the individual—especially individual values, meaning systems, intentions, and conscious acts—at the centre of analysis.

hunting and gathering: activities whereby people feed themselves through killing wild animals and fish and gathering fruits, roots, nuts, and other edible plants.

hybridity: a term expressing the possibility that identities are not fixed, but are flexible and often dependent on the context.

hydraulic empire: a state in which despotic rulers organized labour-intensive irrigation and drainage schemes that allowed for significant increases in agricultural productivity.

hydraulic fracturing (fracking): the injection of a highly pressurized mixture of water, sand, and chemicals into bedrock layers to create artificial fractures that allow oil and gas to flow to the borehole and be extracted.

I

identity: the sense a person makes of himself or herself through their subjective feelings based on their everyday experiences and social relations.

imagined community: a group of people who believe that they share a common bond and thus are part of the same nation.

immigration: a movement in which a person *arrives in* another country.

imperialism: the deliberate exercise of military power and economic influence by powerful states in order to advance and secure their national interests.

import substitution: copying and making goods previously available only by trading.

infant mortality rate: the annual number of deaths of infants under one year of age compared with the total number of live births for that same year.

informal sector: economic activities that take place beyond official record and are not subject to formalized systems of regulation and remuneration.

infrastructure (fixed social capital): the underlying framework of services and amenities needed to facilitate productive activity (e.g., canals, railways, harbour installations, roads, and bridges).

initial advantage: the critical importance of an early start in economic development; a special case of external economies.

intensive subsistence agriculture: practice that involves the effective and efficient use—usually through a considerable expenditure of human labour and application of fertilizer—of a small parcel of land to maximize crop yield.

internal migration: a move within a particular country or region.

internally displaced persons (IDPs): individuals who were uprooted within their own countries due to civil conflict or human rights violations, sometimes by their own governments.

international division of labour: the specialization, by countries, in particular products for export.

international migration: a move from one country to another.

international organization: a group that includes two or more states seeking political or economic co-operation with each other.

international regime: the involvement of the state in new global activities, the growth of supranational and regional institutions and organizations, the critical significance of transnational corporations to global capital, and the proliferation of transnational social movements and professional organizations.

intersubjectivity: shared meanings that are derived from everyday practice.

intertillage: the practice of mixing different seeds and seedlings in the same swidden.

invasion and succession: a process of neighbourhood change whereby one social or ethnic group succeeds another.

irredentism: the assertion by the government of a country that a minority living outside its formal borders belongs to it historically and culturally.

Islam: an Arabic term that means "submission," specifically submission to God's will.

Islamism: an anticolonial, anti-imperial political movement that resists core, especially Western, forces of globalization—namely modernization and secularization.

isolate: a language that has no known relationship with any other and cannot be assigned to a language family.

isotropic surface: a hypothetical, uniform plane—flat and with no variations in its physical attributes.

J

Judeo-Christian perspective on nature: the view that nature was created by God and is subject to God in the same way that a child is subject to parents.

just-in-time production: a production system in which manufacturers no longer maintain inventories of supplies but rely on frequent deliveries by subcontractors.

L

landscape as text: the idea that landscapes can be read and written by groups and individuals.

landscape: a comprehensive product of human action such that every landscape is a complex repository of society

language branch: a collection of languages that possess a definite common origin but has split into individual languages.

language family: a collection of individual languages believed to be related in their prehistoric origin.

language group: a collection of several individual languages that are part of a language branch, share a common origin, and have similar grammar and vocabulary.

language shift: an indicator of the number of people who adopt a new language, usually measured by the difference between mother tongue and home language populations.

language: a means of communicating ideas or feelings by means of a conventionalized system of signs, gestures, marks, or articulate vocal sounds.

latitude: the angular distance of a point on Earth's surface, measured in degrees, minutes, and seconds north or south of the equator, which is assigned a value of 0°.

law of diminishing returns: the tendency for productivity to decline with the continued application of capital and/or labour to a given resource base.

leadership cycles: periods of international power established by individual states through economic, political, and military competition.

life expectancy: the average number of years an newborn infant can expect to live.

lifeworld: the taken-for granted pattern and context for everyday living through which people conduct their day-to-day lives without conscious attention.

local food: food that it is produced within a fairly limited distance from where it is consumed—usually 100 miles (160 kilometres). It is often also organically grown.

localization economies: cost savings that accrue to particular industries as a result of clustering together at a specific location.

logistics: the movement and storage of goods and the management of the entire supply chain, from purchase of raw materials through sale of the final product.

longitude: the angular distance of a point on Earth's surface, measured in degrees, minutes, and seconds east or west from the prime meridian (the line that passes through both poles and through Greenwich, England, which is assigned a value of 0°).

M

malnutrition: the condition that develops when the body does not get the right amount of the vitamins, minerals, and other nutrients it needs to maintain healthy tissues and organ function.

map projection: a systematic rendering on a flat surface of the geographic coordinates of the features found on Earth's surface.

masculinism: the assumption that the world is, and should be, shaped mainly by men for men.

materialism: a school of thought that emphasizes that the material world—its objects and nonhuman entities—is at least partly separate from humans and possesses the power to affect humans.

mechanization: the replacement of human farm labour with machines.

medical geography: a subdiscipline that specializes in understanding the spatial aspects of health and illness.

megacity: a very large city characterized by both primacy and a high degree of centrality within its national economy.

metropolitanism: the process by which the economic growth of a city enables it to attain a position of national dominance and, in so doing, creates the geographical structure of a metropolis and hinterland.

middle cohort: members of the population 15 to 64 years of age who are considered economically active and productive.

migration: a long-distance move to a new location.

minisystem: a society with a single cultural base and a reciprocal social economy.

minority groups: population subgroups that are seen—or that see themselves—as somehow different from the general population.

mobility: the ability to move, either permanently or temporarily.

model: often described as a theory or concept, a model is best thought of as "a simplification of reality" designed to help generalize our understanding of a particular process or set of phenomena; it can take the form of a diagram, equation, or simple verbal statement (such as a law) and may be used as a summary of past and present behaviour or to predict future events.

modern movement: the idea that buildings and cities should be designed and run like machines.

modernism: a forward-looking view of the world that emphasizes reason, scientific rationality, creativity, novelty, and progress.

modernity: a forward-looking view of the world that emphasizes reason, scientific rationality, creativity, novelty, and progress.

mother tongue: the first language learned at home in childhood and still understood by the individual at the time of the census (as defined by Statistics Canada).

multiple-nuclei model: a model of urban structure with decentralized nodes of different categories of land use. Configurations may differ, depending on local conditions.

Muslim: a member of the Islamic community of believers, whose duty is obedience and submission to the will of God.

N

nation: a group of people often sharing common elements of culture, such as religion or language, or a history or political identity.

nationalism: the feeling of belonging to a nation as well as the belief that a nation has a natural right to determine its own affairs.

nation-state: an ideal form consisting of a homogeneous group of people governed by their own state.

natural decrease: the deficit of births relative to deaths.

natural increase: the surplus of births over deaths.

nature: a social creation as well as the physical universe that includes human beings.

neo-colonialism: economic and political strategies by which powerful states in core economies indirectly maintain or extend their influence over other areas or people.

neo-Fordism: an economy in which the logic of mass production coupled with mass consumption has been modified by the addition of more flexible production, distribution, and marketing systems.

neoliberal policies: economic policies that are predicated on a minimalist role for the state that assume the desirability of free markets not only for economic organization but also for political and social life.

neoliberalism: a school of economic thought that pursues a reduction in the role and budgets of governments, including reduced subsidies and the privatization of formerly publicly owned and operated concerns such as utilities.

neo-Malthusians: people who believe that growing human populations the world over, with their potential to exhaust Earth's resources, pose the most dangerous threat to the environment.

net migration: the gain or loss in the total population of a particular area as a result of migration.

new world order: an assumption (during the 1990s) that with the triumph of capitalism over communism, the United States would be the world's only superpower and therefore its policing force.

newly industrializing countries (NICs): countries, formerly peripheral within the world-system, that have acquired a significant industrial sector.

non-representational theory (NRT): a theory that understands human life as a process that is always unfolding, always becoming something different, even if only slightly so.

nontraditional agricultural exports (NTAEs): crops such as fruit, vegetables, and flowers that are more competitive in international trade than traditional exports.

North–South divide: the differentiation made between the colonizing states of the Northern Hemisphere and the formerly colonized states of the Southern Hemisphere.

nutritional density: the ratio between the total population and the amount of land under cultivation.

O

official languages: languages (in Canada, English and French) in which the government has a legal obligation to conduct its affairs, and in which the public has the right to receive federal services.

offshore financial centres: islands or microstates that have become specialized nodes in the geography of worldwide financial flows.

oil sands: a mixture of bitumen (a type of oil), sand, clay, and water.

old-age cohort: members of the population 65 years of age and older who consumer behaviour are considered beyond their economically active and productive years.

ordinary landscapes (vernacular landscapes): the everyday landscapes that people create in the course of their lives.

organic farming: farming or animal husbandry that occurs without the use of commercial fertilizers, synthetic pesticides, or growth hormones.

Orientalism: a discourse that positions the West as culturally superior to the East.

overurbanization: a condition in which cities grow more rapidly than the jobs and housing they can sustain.

P

Paleolithic period: the period when chipped-stone tools first began to be used.

pandemic: an epidemic that spreads rapidly around the world with high rates of illness and death.

pastoralism: subsistence activity that involves the breeding and herding of animals to satisfy the human needs of food, shelter, and clothing.

peripheral regions: regions with dependent and disadvantageous trading relationships, obsolete technologies, and undeveloped or narrowly specialized economies with low levels of productivity.

peri-urban agriculture: the establishment or performance of agricultural practices on the urban fringes.

physical geography: a branch of geography dealing with Earth's natural processes and their outcomes.

picturesque: a landscape design inspired by eighteenth-century landscape painters in the Romantic tradition.

place making: any activity, deliberate or unintentional, that enables space to acquire meaning.

place: a specific geographic setting with distinctive physical, social, and cultural attributes.

plantations: large landholdings that usually specialize in the production of one particular crop for market.

political ecology: an approach to cultural geography that studies human–environment relationships through the relationships of patterns of resource use to political and economic forces.

popular culture: the practices and meaning systems produced by large groups of people whose norms and tastes are often heterogeneous and change frequently, often in response to commercial products.

population policy: an official government strategy designed to affect any or all of several objectives, including the size, composition, and distribution of population.

postmodern urban design: a style characterized by a diversity of architectural styles and elements, often combined in the same building or project.

postmodernity: a view of the world that emphasizes an openness to a range of perspectives in social inquiry, artistic expression, and political empowerment.

preservation: an approach to nature advocating that certain habitats, species, and resources should remain off-limits to human use, regardless of whether the use maintains or depletes the resource in question.

price elasticity of demand: the degree to which levels of demand for a product or service change in response to changes in its price.

primacy: a condition in which the population of the largest city in an urban system is disproportionately large in relation to the second- and third-largest cities in that system.

primary activities: economic activities that are concerned directly with natural resources of any kind.

producer services: services that enhance the productivity or efficiency of other firms' activities or that enable them to maintain specialized roles.

proxemics: the study of the social and cultural meanings that people give to personal space.

pull factors: forces of attraction that influence migrants to move to a particular location.

purchasing power parity (PPP): measures how much of a common "market basket" of goods and services a currency can purchase locally.

push factors: events and conditions that impel an individual to move away from a location.

Q

quaternary activities: economic activities that deal with the handling and processing of knowledge and information.

R

race: a problematic classification of human beings based on skin colour and other physical characteristics.

racialization: the practice of creating unequal castes based on the norm of whiteness.

range: the maximum distance that consumers will normally travel to obtain a particular product or service.

rank-size rule: a statistical regularity in city-size distributions of countries and regions.

reapportionment: the process of changing the allocation of seats in the legislature according to changes in the census figures.

redlining: a discriminatory practice that involves marking off bad-risk neighbourhoods on a city map and then using the map to determine lending policy.

refugees: individuals who cross national boundaries to seek safety and asylum.

region: a territory that encompasses many places, all or most of which share similar attributes that are distinct from the attributes of places elsewhere.

regional geography: the study of the ways in which unique combinations of environmental and human factors produce territories with distinctive landscapes and cultural attributes.

regionalism: the coexistence of different religious or ethnic groups with distinctive identities within the same state boundaries, often concentrated within a particular region and sharing strong feelings of collective identity.

regionalization: the geographer's equivalent of scientific classification, with individual places or areal units being the objects of classification.

religion: belief system and a set of practices that recognize the existence of a power higher than humans.

remote sensing: the collection of information about parts of Earth's surface by means of aerial photography or satellite imagery designed to record data on visible, infrared, and microwave sensor systems.

resiliency: a measure of how damaging an event will be and how quickly and efficiently an area or group of vulnerable people within an area will recover from such an event.

reurbanization: involves the growth of population in metropolitan central cores following a period of absolute or relative decline in population.

risk society: notion of a society in which the significance of wealth distribution is being eclipsed by the distribution of risk and in which politics—both domestic and international—is increasingly about avoiding hazards.

rites of passage: the acts, customs, practices, or procedures that recognize key transitions in human life.

romanticism: the philosophy that emphasizes interdependence and relatedness between humans and nature.

S

sacred space: an area recognized by individuals or groups as worthy of special attention as a site of special religious experiences or events.

scale: the general concept that there are various scales or levels of analysis (local, regional, national, global), that they are linked, and that processes operating at one scale can have significance at other.

secondary activities: economic activities that process, transform, fabricate, or assemble the raw materials derived from primary activities, or that reassemble, refinish, or package manufactured goods.

sectionalism: an extreme devotion to regional interests and customs.

segregation: the spatial separation of specific population subgroups within a wider population.

self-determination: the right of a group with a distinctive politico-territorial identity to determine its own destiny, at least in part, through the control of its own territory.

semiotics: the practice of writing and reading signs.

semiperipheral regions: regions that are able to exploit peripheral regions but are themselves exploited and dominated by core regions.

sense of place: feelings evoked among people as a result of the experiences and memories that they associate with a place and the symbolism they attach to it.

sexuality: a set of practices and identities that a given culture considers related to each other and to those things it considers sexual acts and desires.

shifting cultivation: a system in which farmers aim to maintain soil fertility by rotating the fields within which cultivation occurs.

shock city: a city that is seen as the embodiment of surprising and disturbing changes in economic, social, and cultural lives.

siltation: the buildup of sand and clay in a natural or artificial waterway.

site: the physical attributes of a location—its terrain, soil, vegetation, and water sources, for example.

situation: the location of a place relative to other places and human activities.

slash-and-burn agriculture: a method for preparing new fields in which existing plants are cropped close to the ground, left to dry for a period, and then ignited.

slow food: an attempt to resist fast food by preserving the cultural cuisine and the associated food and farming of an ecoregion.

slow world: people, places, and regions whose participation in transnational industry, modern telecommunications, materialistic consumption, and international news and entertainment is limited.

society: sum of the inventions, institutions, and relationships created and reproduced by human beings across particular places and times.

sovereignty: the exercise of state power over people and territory, recognized by other states and codified by international law.

spatial analysis: the study of many geographic phenomena in terms of their arrangement as points, lines, areas, or surfaces on a map.

spatial diffusion: the way in which things spread through space and over time.

spatial interaction: a collective term for all kinds of movements and flows involving human activity.

spatial justice: the fairness of the distribution of society's burdens and benefits, taking into account spatial variations in people's needs and in their contributions to the production of wealth and social well-being.

spread effects: the positive impacts on a region of the economic growth of some other region.

squatter settlements: residential developments on land that is neither owned nor rented by its occupants.

staples thesis: a proposition arguing that the export of Canada's natural resources, or staples, locked this country into dependency as a resource hinterland for more advanced economies and so delayed the maturing of its own economy.

staples trap: an over-reliance on the export of staples, which makes an economy (national or regional) vulnerable to fluctuations in world prices and without alternatives when resource depletion occurs.

state: an independent political unit with recognized boundaries, although some of these boundaries may be in dispute.

strategic alliances: commercial agreements between transnational corporations, usually involving shared technologies, marketing networks, market research, or product development.

sublime: a landscape so impressive that it inspires awe or wonder.

subsistence agriculture: farming for direct consumption by the producers, not for sale.

supranational organizations: collections of individual states with a common goal that may be economic and/or political in nature; such organizations diminish, to some extent, individual state sovereignty in favour of the group interests of the membership.

sustainability: the interdependence of the economy, the environment, and social well-being.

sustainable development: a balance among economic growth, the environmental impacts of that growth, and the fairness, or social equity, of the distribution of the costs and benefits of that growth.

swidden: land that is cleared using the slash-and-burn process and is ready for cultivation.

symbolic landscapes: representations of particular values or aspirations that the builders and financiers of those landscapes want to impart to a larger public.

T

technology systems: clusters of interrelated energy, transportation, and production technologies that dominate economic activity for several decades at a time.

technology: physical objects or artifacts, activities or processes, and knowledge or know-how.

terms of trade: the ratio of the prices at which exports and imports are exchanged.

territorial representation: a system of government formally structured by area, not by social groups.

territoriality: the persistent attachment of individuals or peoples to a specific location or territory.

territory: the delimited area over which a state exercises control and that is recognized by other states.

terrorism: the threat or use of force to bring about political change.

tertiary activities: economic activities involving the sale and exchange of goods and services.

threshold: the minimum market size required to make the sale of a particular product or service profitable.

time–space convergence: the rate at which places move closer together in travel or communication time or costs.

topological space: the connections between, or connectivity of, particular points in space.

topophilia: the emotions and meanings associated with particular places that have become significant to individuals.

total fertility rate (TFR): the average number of children a woman will have throughout the years that demographers have identified as her childbearing years, approximately ages 15 through 49.

trade-off model: a modified urban land use model that assumes that households seek a trade off between accessibility, affordability, and privacy when they make decisions where to reside.

trading blocs: groups of countries with formalized systems of trading agreements.

transhumance: the movement of herds according to seasonal rhythms: warmer, lowland areas in the winter and cooler, highland areas in the summer.

transnational corporations: companies with investments and activities that span international boundaries and with subsidiary companies, factories, offices, or facilities in several countries.

transnationalism: the multitude of processes between people and organizations that extend beyond national boundaries.

U

underclass: a subset of the poor, isolated from mainstream values and the formal labour market.

underemployment: when people work less than full-time even though they would prefer to work more hours, or when they work in a position for which they are overqualified.

undernutrition: the inadequate intake of one or more nutrients and/or of calories.

undocumented workers: individuals who arrive in the country without official entry visas and are considered by the government to be in the country illegally.

unitary state: a form of government in which power is concentrated in the central government.

urban agriculture: the establishment or performance of agricultural practices in or near an urban or city-like setting.

urban ecology: the social and demographic composition of city districts and neighbourhoods.

urban form: the physical structure and organization of cities in their land use, layout, and built environment.

urban system: an interdependent set of urban settlements within a specified region.

urbanism: the way of life fostered by urban settings, in which the number, physical density, and variety of people often result in distinctive attitudes, values, and patterns of behaviour.

urbanization economies: external economies that accrue to producers because of the package of infrastructure, ancillary activities, labour, and markets typically associated with urban settings.

utility: the usefulness of a specific place or location to a particular person or group.

V

vertical disintegration: the evolution from large, functionally integrated firms within a given industry toward networks of specialized firms, subcontractors, and suppliers.

virgin soil epidemics: the outbreak of a disease to which the population at risk has no natural immunity or previous exposure within the lifetime of the oldest member of the group.

virtual water: the water embedded in the production of the food or other things we consume.

visualization: a computer-assisted representation of spatial data, often involving three-dimensional images and innovative perspectives, that reveals spatial patterns and relationships more effectively.

vital records: information about births, deaths, marriages, divorces, and the incidences of certain infectious diseases.

voluntary migration: the movement by an individual based on choice.

vulnerability: a concept relating to the total exposure to risk.

vulnerable populations: populations that include common characteristics making them more susceptible to "fall through the cracks," including the very young, the old, and those with existing health conditions.

W

world cities: places that, in the globalized world economy, are able not only to generate powerful spirals of local economic development but also to act as pivotal points in the reorganization of global space.

world music: the musical genre defined largely by the surge of non–English-language recordings released in the United Kingdom and the United States during the 1980s.

world-empire: mini-systems that have been absorbed into a common political system while retaining their fundamental cultural differences.

world-system: an interdependent system of countries linked by economic and political competition.

Y

youth cohort: members of the population who are less than 15 years of age and generally considered too young to be fully active in the labour force.

Z

Zionism: a late nineteenth-century European movement to establish a legally recognized homeland in Palestine for the Jewish people.

zone in transition: area of mixed commercial and residential land uses surrounding the CBD.

INDEX

Q